WHITE SLAVE CHILDREN
of Charles County, Maryland:
The Search for Survivors

WHITE SLAVE CHILDREN
of Charles County, Maryland:
The Search for Survivors

Richard Hayes Phillips, Ph.D.

Many will say to me in that day, Lord, Lord, have we not
prophesied in thy name? and in thy name have cast out devils?
and in thy name done many wonderful works?
And then I will profess unto them, I never knew you:
depart from me, ye that work iniquity. -- Matthew 7:22-23

Inasmuch as ye have done it unto one of the least of these
my brethren, ye have done it unto me. -- Matthew 25:40

And whosoever shall offend one of these little ones that
believe in me, it is better for him that a millstone were hanged
about his neck, and he were cast into the sea. -- Luke 9:42

For we wrestle not against flesh and blood,
but against principalities, against powers,
against the rulers of the darkness of this world,
against spiritual wickedness in high places. -- Ephesians 6:12

For there is nothing covered, that shall not be revealed;
neither hid, that shall not be known. Therefore whatsoever
ye have spoken in darkness shall be heard in the light;
and that which ye have spoken in the ear of closets shall be
proclaimed upon the house tops. -- Luke 12:2-3

Copyright © 2015 by Richard Hayes Phillips
All rights reserved

For hardcover copies of this book. contact the author:
Richard Hayes Phillips, 4 Fisher Street, Canton, New York, 13617

Paperback edition published by
Genealogical Publishing Company
Baltimore, Maryland, 2015

LIBRARY OF CONGRESS CATALOGING-IN-PUBLICATION DATA
Phillips, Richard Hayes, 1951-
White Slave Children of Charles County, Maryland: The Search for Survivors
ISBN paperback edition: 978-0-8063-2031-1
1. History -- 17th century   2. Slavery -- Maryland
3. Kidnapping -- Ireland -- Scotland -- England -- New England   I. Title

TABLE OF CONTENTS

PREFACE	vii
GUIDE TO THE RECORDS	xii
GUIDE TO THE INDEXES	xiii
PHILIP LYNES	1
HENRY HARDY	8
JOHN BAYNE	13
DISHONORABLE MENTIONS	25
HOW THE SYSTEM WORKED	30
HOW THE RESISTANCE WORKED	46
CHARLES COUNTY MASTER INDEX	61
ENCYCLOPEDIA OF SURVIVORS	87
WITHOUT INDENTURES, NOT YET FREE	161
RECAPTURED RUNAWAYS	166
PETITIONS FOR FREEDOM	202
ABUSE AND NEGLECT	240
VITAL RECORDS	251
WITNESSES WHO STATED THEIR AGES	278
GRANTEE INDEX TO DEEDS	289
GIFTS OF LIVESTOCK	324
INDEX TO DEATHS AND ESTATES	334
INDEX TO ORPHANS	351
SURVIVORS FROM ELSEWHERE	392
SURNAME INDEX	396

Everyone I ever heard, and everything I ever read, told me that all the slaves were black, and all the whites subjected to forced labor were indentured servants, or convict laborers, or impressed sailors. Everyone was wrong. Nobody told me about white slavery in colonial America. If I had trusted the experts, the authorities, I would have missed this story altogether.

PREFACE

"Ye poore petitioner came in a servant in ye yeare 1668 & was ... adjudged to be fourteene yeares of age, & soe ordered to serve eight yeares, ... and ye poore petitioner was by ye said Francis Kilbourne very hardly used, who being carried up upon a frontier plantation above Piscataway, was there like to be starved for want of victualls & cloathing, & there left alone in a strange place at a great distance from any neighbours to ye mercy of ye Indians" [1]

So begins the petition of John Greene, kidnapped from parts unknown, shanghaied aboard a ship, transported to the Chesapeake Bay and up the Potomac River, and brought before the Justices of the Charles County Court, known officially as the "Worshippfull Commissioners," or "your Worships," for short. They examined him, adjudged him to be fourteen years of age, and sentenced him to eight years of slavery. It was all according to law.

The kidnapping was according to English law dated 1659:

> it "may be lawful for ... two or more justices of the peace within any county, citty or towne corporate belonging to this commonwealth to from tyme to tyme by warrant ... cause to be apprehended, seized on and detained all and every person or persons that shall be found begging and vagrant ... in any towne, parish or place to be conveyed into the port of London, or unto any other port ... from where such person or persons may be shipped ... into any forraign collonie or plantation ..." [2]

The slavery was according to Maryland law dating to 1654, amended 1671:

> "whosoever shall Transport any Servant into this Province without Indenture and such Servant being above the Age of Twenty Two yeares shall be obleiged to serve the full Space and Tearme of Five yeares if between eighteen and twenty two without indenture six yeares if betweene fivetene and eightene without Indenture Seaven years if under fiftene and coming in without Indenture as aforesaid Such Servant shall serve till he or she arrive to the full age of Two and Twenty Yeares" [3]

John Greene was one of 5327 white slave children found in the surviving court records of colonial Maryland and Virginia. [4] The history books like to deny the existence of white slavery. All the slaves were black, they say, and all the whites were "indentured servants" or "convict laborers." But this is not true. These children committed no crime, and they had no indentures.

An indenture is, by definition, a written contract. We were taught in school about indentured servants, impoverished young workers from England or Germany who wanted to come to America. They contracted, in writing, by indenture, to work without wages for a number of years to pay off the cost of their passage and lodging, after which time they were free.

John Greene, according to his own testimony, arrived in America in May 1668, at which time ships carrying white slave children are known to have sailed from London, Bristol, and Boston. [5] He was first sold to Benjamin Rozer, "high Sherrife" of Charles County, [6] who brought him to Charles County Court to have his age adjudged on 8 September 1668 [7]. He was then sold by Benjamin Rozer to Daniell Johnson, and after his decease "became servant to Francis Kilbourne, who married ye administratrix of ye said Daniell Johnson," his widow, Elizabeth Johnson, in the spring of 1671, [8] and took John Greene to the "frontier plantation above Piscataway."

There, "left alone in a strange place," cold, hungry, and at "ye mercy of ye Indians," John Greene was a voice in the wilderness. "Being reduced to these extremities," he "was constrained to engage himselfe to serve Philip Lines above two years longer than the time your Worshipfull Court did adjudge him to serve." [9] It was not lawful for any master to make any bargain with any servant for any time longer, "not untill his first time of servitude be fully expired," [10] for the obvious reason that any such bargain is made under duress. And "neverthelesse, ye poore petitioner is still kept a servant by ye said Philip Lines who intends to make him serve two yeares longer." It was now 14 November 1676. John Greene had already served eight and one half years. It was ordered by the Court "that ye said John Greene be free according to ye time of his first servitude." [11]

John Greene did get free. He did outlive his servitude. But he never again appears in the records. No one knows what happened to him.

Some critics object to my use of the word "slavery" to describe what happened to these children, because they were in bondage for a term of years, and not for life. These children were transported without indentures, without their consent, against their will, which is why they were brought to court in the first place. Many of them survived their ordeal, but this does not negate their previous condition of involuntary servitude. Some Negro slaves were freed by manumission, and many were freed due to the Civil War, but no one would claim that they were never slaves. No one race has a monopoly on victimhood.

NOTES

[1] Charles County Court Records [07.pdf #129].

[2] Egerton Mss. 2395, folios 227-229, BL. Dr. Justin Clegg at the British Museum has confirmed its authenticity, and he dates it to 1659.

[3] "Proceedings and Acts of the General Assembly, April 1666-June 1676," Volume 2, Page 335, October 1671.
http://aomol.msa.maryland.gov/000001/000002/html/am2--335.html
See also Perpetual Laws of Maryland, 1685 [12.pdf #171, Folio 92].

[4] Phillips, Richard Hayes, Ph.D., *"Without Indentures: Index to White Slave Children in Colonial Court Records,"* Genealogical Publishing Company, Baltimore, Maryland, 2014. In which 5290 white servants without indentures are identified. Another 37 children have been found subsequently. Not all of the servants without indentures were children, but most of them were. (See next page in this volume, and *"Without Indentures,"* page xviii).

[5] Children transported on the *Duke of Yorke*, a London ship, appeared in Court at York County, Virginia, on 24 June 1668. Children transported on the *Elizabeth*, a Boston ship, appeared in Court at York County, Virginia on 10 April 1668. Children transported on the *Happy Entrance*, a Bristol ship, appeared in Court at York County, Virginia on 10 April 1668.

[6] Archives of Maryland Online [Volume 60 Page 106].

[7] Archives of Maryland Online [Volume 60 Page 142].

[8] Elizabeth Johnson, administratrix of Daniell Johnson deceased, 10 March 1671 [08.pdf #39]. John & Elizabeth Kilbourne, administrators of Daniell Johnson deceased, 13 June 1671 [08.pdf #46]. See Index to Deaths and Estates.

[9] Charles County Court Records [07.pdf #129].

[10] Charles County Court Records. Margarett Atkinson, petition for freedom, 13 January 1680 [09.pdf #152]; also Grace Holmes, 13 March 1694 [18.pdf #145]; George Carter, 9 March 1708 [23.pdf #237]; Francis Ross, 13 June 1710 [23.pdf #402]; William Hilton, 10 August 1714 [25.pdf #243]; and Joan Ruby, 14 March 1721 [27.pdf 45].

[11] Charles County Court Records [07.pdf #129].

STATEMENT OF PURPOSE

It is the purpose of this book to find out what became of the white slave children of Charles County, Maryland, or as many of them as possible.

It is important to limit the scope and purpose of one's research in order that the goal be attainable. Therefore I chose to search the records of one county only. It was important that there be no gaps in the records, or nearly so, lest the lack of appearance be misinterpreted as nonexistence. It was important to choose a county where many children without indentures were brought to Court, so that a larger number of names could be tracked with the same amount of effort. And it was so much the better to choose a county where the records had never been transcribed, because I could make numerous indexes to handwritten records available for the first time. Not being one to shrink from a Herculean task, I chose Charles County, Maryland.

Moreover, the Charles County Court Records (1658-1733) are beautifully microfilmed, scanned, and posted on the Archives of Maryland website. I could, with brief citations, steer my readers to online images of actual handwritten records. This would be slow old-fashioned archival research, allowing others to take full advantage of access in the digital age.

And it did not hurt that 333 (38%) of the 872 white slave children without indentures brought before the Charles County Court were owned by men who served, at one time or another, as Worshippfull Commissioners on that very Court. This was bound to make the work more interesting.

Not all of the servants without indentures were children, but most of them were. Specific ages were adjudged by the Charles County Court for 800 individuals. Of these, 493 were adjudged to be under eighteen, and 706 were adjudged to be under twenty-one. Most of them were teenagers. The median age was sixteen. For Maryland and Virginia as a whole, the ages were lower. (See *"Without Indentures,"* op. cit., p. xviii). Of those over twenty-one, 94 of 124 were brought to Charles County. Of those under ten, 173 of 187 were brought elsewhere.

age 3	0	age 9	4	age 15	73	age 21	58
age 4	1	age 10	14	age 16	78	age 22	27
age 5	1	age 11	24	age 17	87	age 23	2
age 6	3	age 12	55	age 18	67	age 24	6
age 7	3	age 13	64	age 19	54	age 25	1
age 8	2	age 14	84	age 20	92	age 26	0

METHODOLOGY

The first thing to do was to search the Court Records for servants only. Here I would find their stories, their accounts of life in bondage. Three important categories quickly became apparent: recaptured runaways, complaints of abuse or neglect, and petitions for freedom. Names, dates, and citations would not be enough. I wrote detailed abstracts for these entries, distilling their stories into three comprehensive indexes.

The next thing to do was to search the Court Records for standard genealogical information, compiling countywide indexes that could be cross-checked with my master index of white slave children without indentures. Six important categories quickly became apparent: vital records, witnesses who stated their ages, land records, livestock records, deaths and estates, and orphan children. I compiled basic indexes for the first five (names, dates, citations), and I wrote detailed abstracts for the orphans. I searched all the Court Records two or three times, compiling several indexes at once.

Some of the land records were not online, and I needed any Last Will and Testament left by any of the survivors, so I revisited the Hall of Records, Maryland State Archives, Annapolis, Maryland, photographed or abstracted the necessary documents, and completed my indexes.

The end product would be an Encyclopedia of Survivors. The master index of white slave children without indentures brought to Charles County Court to have their ages adjudged, now 872 names, would be cross-checked with the nine new indexes. All the survivors found would be listed. The entries from the nine new indexes would be collated beneath their names, with other information from the court records, thus creating basic biographies.

During this research, thirty-nine individuals came to my attention as being worthy of reproach: for complicity with kidnappings at Gravesend; for running a house of ill repute; for sexually abusing their servants; for beating and wounding their servants; for suspicion of murdering a servant; for leaving their servants without food or clothing; for enslaving an innocent traveling man; for embezzling the estates of orphans; for forcing orphan apprentices to labor in the fields; for imposing severe penalties upon recaptured runaway servants; for refusing to set free servants whose time had expired; or simply because so many of their servants ran away on so many occasions. The narrative of this book begins with full-fledged biographies of three of the worst monsters, followed by thirty-six dishonorable mentions.

GUIDE TO THE RECORDS

Almost all the information in the following indexes is taken directly from the County Court Records of Charles County, Maryland (1658-1733), all of which are online at the Archives of Maryland website. All the rest is taken from the Land Records (Liber Q1, Z1, C2, F2, H2, L2 & M2), the Registers of Wills (Liber A2, AB3, AD5, AC4, AE6), and Inventories & Accounts (Liber 22, 24). They are the original handwritten books, available for public inspection at the Hall of Records, Maryland State Archives, Annapolis, Maryland. These are indexes to primary records. The citations refer to the online images, or else to the pages in the original handwritten books.

The online images are in thirty-two Adobe (.pdf) files which can be downloaded in their entirety. These are scans of microfilms of the original handwritten records. The citations give the .pdf file number and the image number, for example: [10.pdf #55] To find these:

Go to: http://guide.mdsa.net
Click: "View by Agency"
Enter – Jurisdiction: Charles County
    Agency: Court
Click: Filter
Scroll down to Charles County Court (Court Record) [Microfilm], click
Select desired volume, click Additional Links, then click PDF File

Note that some citations, primarily between 1668 and 1670, refer to typewritten transcriptions, for example: [Vol. 60:230] To find these, click Additional Links for Volume 5 [CM376-5], then click on Volume 60, then enter the desired page number and click "go."

Other citations refer to original handwritten books that are not online. The citation gives the Liber and Folio, that is, the Book and Page, for example: [Liber G Page 48] or Liber C:126 or [Liber AB No. 3 Folio 72]. The books are available for inspection at the Hall of Records.

A few citations refer to Liber G or Liber T. These books no longer exist. But their indexes were transcribed by hand before the original books were lost, and an index is better than nothing. Twelve more white slave children having their ages adjudged were located by searching these indexes.

GUIDE TO THE INDEXES

CHARLES COUNTY: This is the same index found in my previous book, *"Without Indentures: Index to White Slave Children in Colonial Court Records,"* with additions and corrections found by subsequent searching of records in Charles County, and citations added after each of the entries. Thirty-six additions bring the total of white slave children without indentures to 872.

ENCYCLOPEDIA OF SURVIVORS: This is the heart of the book. It was compiled from the indexes described below, buttressed with lawsuits, and completed with children and others named in the Last Will and Testament, if any. Altogether, of the 872 white slave children without indentures, 189 who outlived their servitude were found in the Charles County records, and another eight in the Town Records of Massachusetts.

INDEXES TO SERVANTS, WITH OR WITHOUT INDENTURES

RECAPTURED RUNAWAYS: In Maryland, a recaptured runaway servant could be, and usually was, sentenced to an additional ten days of servitude for each day of "runaway time." The judges, at their discretion, could add months or even years to the sentence as compensation to the master for the cost of "taking him up." Altogether, 300 recaptured runaways were found in the Charles County Court Records, and of these, 17 were without indentures.

PETITIONS FOR FREEDOM: With or without indentures, servants were not always freed by their masters when their terms of servitude had expired. Others, although free, had to go to court to get their "corn & clothes," that is, the freedom dues required by Act of Assembly to "every man servant" and to "all woman servants" at the expiration of servitude, to wit: "a good cloth sute either of kirsey or broad cloth, a shift of white lineing to bee new, one new paire of shoes, and stockings, two hoes, one axe, and three barrells of corn." [12] Altogether, 179 petitions for freedom were found in the Charles County Court Records, and of these, 32 were from servants without indentures.

ABUSE AND NEGLECT: Forty-two servants and one hireling found the courage to testify against their masters or overseers for severe usage and cruel treatment. Others, no doubt, never made it to Court. Eleven were beaten. Thirteen were without food, clothing, or shelter. One was murdered. Two committed suicide. Six were in need of medical attention. Read this index in its entirety. Read it and weep.

---

[12] Perpetual Laws of Maryland [12.pdf #170, Folio 91].

GUIDE TO THE INDEXES

GENERAL COUNTYWIDE INDEXES

VITAL RECORDS: These consist of births or baptisms, marriages, and deaths or burials. Many of these vital records are culled from three lengthy listings in the Court Records and Land Records. The rest are scattered about the Court Records as stand alone entries, or are found when a mother states the birth date of a child she is putting up for adoption. For the first time, these vital records for Charles County are collected and collated by family.

WITNESSES WHO STATED THEIR AGES: Witnesses who swore to a deposition outside of Court were often asked to state their ages. This was especially true at proceedings of a Land Commission which met from time to time beginning in 1719. Witnesses were asked to verify that certain trees were the same ones declared to mark the boundaries when the lands were first surveyed long ago. From these records we have close estimates of the birth years of the adult witnesses, and these can be matched up with birth records, or with white slave children whose ages were adjudged by the Court.

GRANTEE INDEX TO DEEDS: These land records are indexed roughly alphabetically (with variant spellings of the same name grouped together), according to the grantee, that is, the recipient of the land. Most of them are deeds or assignments, and a few are surveys. Land records were included with the Court Records until 1695 (and again from 1712-1713); these are microfilmed, scanned, and online. The index was completed through 1722 by searching the handwritten books at the Hall of Records.

GIFTS OF LIVESTOCK: Often a child received a gift of livestock, or registered his or her mark of hogs and cattle. These transactions are included in the index if a family relationship is identified. On occasion these are gifts of real estate, and are identified as such in the index. Livestock records were included with the Court Records until 1695 (and again from 1712-1713); these are microfilmed, scanned, and online. The index was completed through 1733 by searching the handwritten books at the Hall of Records.

INDEX TO DEATHS AND ESTATES: The purpose of this index is to identify the earliest date on which a person was referred to as deceased, that is, a date before which the person died. Some of the references are in probate cases, in which the estate was settled in court. If the deceased left a Last Will and Testament, there is an executor and/or executrix of the estate.

GUIDE TO THE INDEXES

If the deceased left no will, there is an administrator of the estate. Other references are in deeds of real estate, in which cases the heir or heirs are identified. On occasion the only reference is to the burial, in which case the person seeking compensation is identified, who may or may not be an heir or administrator. The index was completed through 1722 by searching the handwritten books at the Hall of Records.

INDEX TO ORPHANS: Children of single mothers, widowed or otherwise, were considered orphans, and if their mother could not support them on her own, she put them up for adoption through the Court. Unless otherwise stated in the father's will or by the Court, girls were to serve their guardians until the age of sixteen, boys until the age of twenty-one. There were requirements that generally applied to the guardian: to "provide sufficient and necessary meat drink washing lodging & apparel both linen & woolen," to bring them up "in ye Religion established by the Laws of England," to teach them "to read distinctly in ye Bible," and at the end of their terms of servitude to give them "a decent suit of apparel," of "either broad cloth or kersey," that is, "coat jacket & breeches" with "hat shoes stockings & shirt." These common provisions are not repeated in the index.

Some orphans received six months or a year or two of schooling, and were taught "to write a legible hand." Sometimes the boys were apprentices, their masters agreeing to teach them a trade. Examples include that of a shipwright, cooper, tailor, shoemaker, cordwainer, carpenter, joiner, tanner, and blacksmith. Some were given a set of tools when free. Others were given "a horse, bridle & saddle," or "a cow with a calf by her side." These and other unusual provisions do appear in the index. The index was completed through 1722 by searching the handwritten books at the Hall of Records.

SURNAME INDEX: This is the index to the book. It tells all the page numbers in this volume on which persons with a given surname, by any spelling, may be found. It is especially useful when searching for grantors of real estate, or for heirs, executors and administrators of estates, which are not alphabetized anywhere else in this volume. Please note that the surname you are searching may appear numerous times on the same page.

SURVIVORS FROM ELSEWHERE: Vital records from seven other counties in Maryland, available online, provide proof of thirty-two more survivors of white child slavery. This list is included near the end of this book.

PHILIP LYNES

There are 179 petitions for freedom in the Charles County Court Records. Nineteen of them were from servants to Philip Lynes (Lines, Linos). There are 42 complaints of abuse or neglect. Nine of them were from servants of Philip Lynes. There are 300 recaptured runaways. Twelve of them were servants of Philip Lynes. There is a pattern here.

Among the recaptured runaways, five of the fifteen with the longest sentences were servants of Philip Lynes:

RECAPTURED RUNAWAYS, FIFTEEN LONGEST SENTENCES

Servant	Absence	Sentence	Master
Rosamond Law	338 days	3380 days	Alexander Wilson
Mollatto Will	180 days	3260 days	Capt. Benoni Thomas
Thomas Fountain	300 days	3000 days	Capt. Joseph Douglass
John Bacon	235 days	2850 days	Henry Hawkins
Silent Ball	264 days	2640 days	several *
Thomas Robinson	2 years	7 years	Philip Lynes
Daniel Taylor	13 months	6 years	Philip Lynes
TeagueTurlayes	240 days	2000 days	Philip Lynes
(name omitted)	200 days	2000 days	William Smallwood
Anthony Bunn	108 days	1851 days	Thomas Matthews
William Babberry	1213 days	5 years	William Hall, Surgeon
John Lauler	1730 days	5 years	Henry Buttridge
Catherine Fletcher	176 days	1760 days	Philip Lynes
John Hawkins	164 days	1730 days	Philip Lynes
Hugh Williams	164 days	1730 days	Robert Henly

* William Thompson, Benjamin Posey, Thomas Davis, John Ward

Two of these cases were commuted sentences. The runaways could have been sentenced to ten days of servitude for each day of "runaway time." Philip Lynes allowed Thomas Robinson to serve seven years instead of twenty years, and Daniel Taylor to serve six years instead of almost eleven.

Among the petitions for freedom, there were twenty-seven servants with valid indentures, whose time had expired, and still their masters would not let them go. Nine of them were servants of Philip Lynes, at least six of whom served extra time before being freed by the Court. Anne Powell "served ye said Lynes one year wanting two days above ye time of her Indenture" [11.pdf #135]. Thomas Bennett was detained "as his servant for near these two yeares for what reason your petitioner knoweth not" [17.pdf #138]. Because "James Adams had served ye said Philip Lynes two months over & above ye four yeares hee was sold for," he was awarded "ye sume of two hundred pounds of tobacco" [17.pdf #18]. On the other nine occasions on which Lynes extracted forced labor, (one being a white slave child without indentures), he was not fined at all.

PETITIONS FOR FREEDOM FROM PHILIP LYNES

Servant	Indenture	Extra time	Penalty
James Adams	4 years	2 months	200 pounds of tobacco
David Ambros	2 years	16 days	none
Sarah Bald	4 years	not stated	none
Thomas Bennett	not stated	nearly 2 years	none
Mary Bowles	4 years	not stated	none
James Burchner	4 years	35 days	none
John Greene	* 8 years	6 months	none
James Lyle	not stated	6 months	none
Thomas Patrick	not stated	not stated	none
Anne Powell	4 years	nearly 1 year	none

* a white slave child without indentures

Six servants to Philip Lynes had to go to Court to get their "freedom corne & clothes." One of these, Mary Bowles, had to go to Court twice: once on 10 November 1691 to win her freedom [17.pdf #157]; and again on 8 November 1692 for her "one good cloth suite of clothes either of kersey or broad cloth a shift of white linen to be new one pair of shoes & stockins and three barrells of Indian corne which hee oweth her and unjustly detaineth" [17.pdf #280]. Three times the Court ordered Philip Lynes to pay Owen Doyne his "freedom corne & clothes," including "two hoes, one axe" [17.pdf #102, 115, 245]. It is not certain that he ever received them.

One petitioner for freedom from Philip Lynes, named James Thornebrooke or Thornborrow, was a special case. A young white man without indentures, James was brought to Court by Philip Lynes on 11 August 1686, adjudged to be 21 years of age, and ordered to serve six years [13.pdf #120]. On 12 January 1692 he was "free & discharged from ye service of ye said Philip

Lynes" for having kept him "from January until August Court following before he brought him to Court to be adjudged which was above six months, contrary to ye Act of Assembly" [17.pdf #190]. Philip Lynes then alleged that James Thornborrow owed service "for runaway time," [17.pdf #277] "for severall dayes" absence "at severall times," but "ye said Philip Lynes not proveing any thing against ye said James Thornburrough that hee had at any time absented himselfe" out of his service, it was ordered by the Court "that ye said James Thornburrough is free & discharged from ye service of ye said Lynes," "and ought to be free by reason of his hard useage that hee ye said James Thornburrough did undergoe in ye time of his servitude with ye said Philip Lynes" [18.pdf #25]. James Thornborough had been in Court before.

Which brings us to the complaints of abuse and neglect.

Catherine Jones, a white slave child without indentures, was brought to Court by Philip Lynes on 8 June 1686, adjudged to be 16 years of age, and sentenced to seven years of servitude. On 11 August 1691 she came to Court complaining "of her hard useage by Henry Thompson one of ye overseers of ye said Lynes," who was ordered to remove her from her overseer Henry Thompson to another plantation and to cloth her well" [17.pdf #139]. On 8 November 1691, James Thornborough, Edward Darnall and Catherine Jones, all three of them without indentures, [13] "came here into Court naked & made complaint that for want of clothes they were allmost starved, and ye said Philip Lynes being absent," it was "ordered that Major James Smallwood lett them have necessary clothes to preserve them from perishing with cold," the cost to be deducted "out of what tobaccoe shall be allowed to ye said Lynes in ye County levy this yeare" [17.pdf #157]. One year later, on 10 November 1692, Catherine Jones, servant to Philip Lynes "gentleman," was back in Court, "a poor distressed & almost naked servant," "haveing endured a long & hard servitude under severall overseers of ye said Lynes and being kept soe bare of clothes that shee was allmost perrished with cold and constantly compelled to doe her labour allmost naked." She had gotten from ye said Lynes "one shift & one linen petticoate with which shee endured all last winter," and "she is in apparent danger of perishing this winter with cold if not releived by your worshipps." Philip Lynes was ordered to give her "good woollen clothes shoes & stockings" within twenty days, or else "to discharge her & sett her free" [17.pdf #276]. He was not fined or punished.

---

[13] Edward Darnell was brought to Court by Philip Lynes on 13 March 1688, adjudged to be 17 years of age, and ordered to serve six years [14.pdf #176]. He lived to be 84 years old (see Encyclopedia of Survivors).

There are other such examples. On 9 December 1685, Adam Wharton, servant to Philip Lynes, in Court, "exhibited his greivous complaint," "being lately found in Capt. Warren's quarter naked of all cloaths & in a perishing condition." It was ordered that Capt. Warren should "in charity provide things necessary for ye said servant till ye said Lynes shall give good security" [13.pdf #47]. Eight months later, on 10 August 1686, "as to ye servant Adam Horton," Philip Lynes was to receive 400 pounds of tobacco from Capt. Warren, presumably as compensation for loss of service, & then ye said Philip to have ye said servant" [13.pdf #119]. As it happens, Adam Horton was an orphan, son of Joseph Horton, age not stated, bound to Philip Lines on 8 June 1675 [07.pdf #63] [14]

On 9 March 1697, James Line and Teague Turlayes, servants to Philip Lynes, "did make their complaint against ye said Philip Lynes their master for want of clothing & lodgeing." It was ordered by the Court "that ye said Philip Lynes forthwith cloth his said two servants with necessary & convenient clothing, and to provide them a bed to lie on" [19.pdf #111]. Three months later, on 8 June 1697, James Line and Teague Turlayes, servants to Philip Lynes, made "further complaint against ye said Philip Lynes their master for not complyeing with a former order of this Court upon their former complaint made." The case was continued until "ye next Court," "for that ye said Philip Lynes is not here" [19.pdf #131].

Some servants to Philip Lynes were beaten and abused. On 14 September 1686, the Court "ordered that a sumons issue to Henrie Goodrick Overseer to Mr. Lynes to appear next Court to answer ye complaint of John Lew servant to ye said Lynes and moreover that there be an express order of this Court delivered to ye said Goodrick forbidding him at his perill to offer anie abuse to ye said Lew or soe much as to give him any correction till further order from this Court" [13.pdf #120].

On 13 January 1691, Henry Shalter, servant to Philip Lynes, complained that he "was ordered by ye said Lynes to live with John Bould who doth very much beate & abuse your Petitioner," and prayed "that hee may serve ye remaineing part of his time with some other person in ye said Lynes his employ." It was ordered by the Court that Henry Shalter be placed elsewhere "by Mr. James Mackewen who doth now looke after ye businesse & concernes of ye said Philip Lynes" [17.pdf #89].

-- --

[14] The only other orphans bound to Philip Lines (or Lynes) by the court were unnamed "orphans of Robert Downes" deceased, ages not stated. It was ordered that Philip Lines take them "into his custody," 14 August 1678 [09.pdf #39]

On 14 January 1690, James Lewis was "presented," that is, indicted, by the Grand Jury "upon suspicion of murdering one Owen Carr servant to Mr. Philip Lynes." James Lewis "was comitted to ye custody of ye Sherife of this County." Ten months later, on 11 November 1690 "ye said James Lewis remaineing still in custody of ye said Sherife and being allmost naked & ready to perish for want of clothing," it was ordered by the Court "that ye Sherife discharge ye said James Lewis hee takeing his own bond for his good behavior & appearance at ye next Provintiall Court" [17.pdf #83].

The irony is inescapable. Six servants to Philip Lynes went to Court to complain of being naked, or nearly so, and likely to perish from the cold; and when a servant to Philip Lynes is actually murdered, the accused is freed from custody for "being allmost naked & ready to perish for want of clothing."

And now, "the humble petition of Thomas Smith." On 8 March 1680, Thomas Smith, a hired hand to Philip Lines, working for wages, was on his way to Court to give evidence before Justice Robert Henley against "Thomas Powell & John Dyall two servants belonging to Philip Lines," and "ye said Lines overtakeing ye petitioner on ye roade this day Comeinge to Court" "did beate him with a great cane many blowes soe that ye said cane with beateinge him hee ye said Lines broke to your petitioners great damadge." The very next day, on 9 March 1680, the Grand Jury presented "Philip Lines of this County planter, for that this day hee did sett upon, beate & sorely abuse Thomas Smith his hirelinge, comeinge on his way to this present Court." Philip Lines appearing in Court "in his proper person" openly admitted that "hee did strike him two or three blowes with his caine, & ye head of ye Cane came off." Lines explained that he did overtake him coming to Court, and asked him where he was going, and he said he was going to Court, but would not tell him "what he was goeing about." The Court accepted his excuse. The Court ordered "that Philip Lines bee not fined for beateing of Thomas Smith, because hee did it ignorantly not knoweinge what hee was comeinge to Court about." [09.pdf #154]

And who is this monster, who beats a witness so hard that he breaks his own cane? Whose overseers, at least four of them, do beat, abuse, or murder the "servants" in their custody? Who leaves a child alone in the wilderness, cold and hungry, at the mercy of the Indians? Who will not clothe his "servants," even in the winter, either during their slavery or after they are free?

Phillipe Lynes, son of Henry and Mary Lynes, Baptized 17 November 1646,
    Saint Andrew, Holborn, London, England

This is the best match found in the International Genealogical Index.

Philip Lynes (Lines, Linos) first appears in the records of Charles County, Maryland on 9 January 1674, when he purchases 150 acres on the west side of Piscataway River [06.pdf #146]. Together with another 82 acres purchased in March 1674, [06.pdf #150] this was the plantation in the wilderness where John Greene was left to fend for himself.

Philip Lynes quickly became one of the largest landowners in Charles County (and vicinity). There are no fewer than 34 deeds (or surveys) to Philip Lynes (or Lines) on the record. Within three years he owned nearly three thousand acres; by 1680 he owned nearly four thousand acres; and by 1690 he owned nearly seven thousand acres; (see Grantee Index To Deeds).

On 13 June 1676, Philip Lines "Gentleman," probably twenty-nine years old, was sworn as an attorney of the Charles County Court [07.pdf #111].

On 11 March 1690, Philip Lynes recorded "his marke of geese ducks turkeyes hens cocks & capons (viz:) a piece taken out of the right webb of ye right foot" [16.pdf #109]. This was an extremely rare if not unprecedented occurrence. These registered marks were almost always for cattle and hogs. To register marks for fowl was a sure sign of an established aristocrat.

On 12 January 1692, Philip Lynes being absent, Justice Henry Hawkins won a judgment against the estate of Philip Lynes "in ye hands of Henry Thompson, William Hawling, Richard Leman, William Frost, Thomas Austin, John Barrett & John Fearnley" [17.pdf #205].

On 14 August 1694, the Grand Jurors presented "Philip Lynes late of Charles County for forgery." Named as Witnesses were Henry Hardy, Thomas Baker & James Cotterell [18.pdf #317]. The case never went to trial.

On 8 June 1703, Mr. Philip Lynes was appointed "Chiefe Ranger of this County [22.pdf #107]. Four years later he was reappointed. On 14 January 1707, "Mr. Philip Lynes's Commission for Cheife Ranger" was "read and ordered to be recorded" [23.pdf #161].

On 13 August 1706, John Seymour, Governor of Maryland, authorized Philip Lynes "to keep a Publique Ferry over Potomock River," "at ye landing at Pickawaxon," being "very convenient for a ferry." He would be "appointed with a good sufficient boate," and his rights were exclusive; "none other person whatsoever" was "to keep such ferry over said River on any pretense whatsoever as they will answer ye contrary at their perrill" [Liber Z Page 271]. On the same day, 13 August 1706, Mr. Philip Lynes obtained another servant. He brought to Court one Elizabeth Oliver, a white woman without indentures, "late servant" to Ubgatt Reeves, and set her free in open Court, whereupon she bound herself "to the said Philip Lynes for the full terme of three yeares and a halfe" in exchange for the said Lynes paying her fine and fees concerning her "haveing a bastard child." Mr. Lynes promised "in open Court not to put her under an Overseer," and "to pay her corne and cloaths at the expiration of her time" [23.pdf #139]. [15]

On 14 March 1709, as the capstone of his career, "The Honorable Philip Lynes Esquire" sat as presiding Justice on the Charles County Court. It was his only such appearance. He died five months later. His Last Will and Testament, dated 6 August 1709, was probated 15 August 1709 [Liber AB No. 3 Folio 28]. Philip Lynes, in his will, left, as Item number one, "to Madam Jean Seymour, Mrs. Mary Contee, my brother Capt. Thomas Seymour and my friend William Bladen each ten pounds sterling" to buy mourning rings. While this might seem rather presumptuous, that he would pay for the accoutrements to prove he would be missed, the important thing about this provision is the family relationships it reveals. Capt. Thomas Seymour was the brother of John Seymour, Royal Governor of Maryland, the same governor who had granted to ye said Philip Lynes the exclusive right to operate a ferry across the Potomac River. Mrs. Mary Contee, "a favorite cousin" of the Governor, was the former Mary Townley who married Col. John Contee of Charles County, Maryland, [16] a wealthy landowner (see Grantee Index to Deeds) and one of "your Worshipps," who owned three white slave children (see *Without Indentures*, page 109). William Bladen was the Naval Officer at Port Annapolis who collected import duties on 363 white "servants, which he reported to the House of Delegates on 1 November 1698. [17] Think of the forty servants to Philip Lynes who were abused in one way or another, and their master so well connected. To whom should they petition for redress of grievances?

Philip Lynes was survived by his wife Anne. Her will, dated 20 November 1711, was probated 17 December 1711 [Liber AB No. 3 Folio 41]. Her executors were Walter Story and Michael Martin. There were no children.

---

[15] Elizabeth Oliver, servant to Ubgatt Reeves, was brought to Court on 1 April 1701, adjudged to be 20 years of age, ordered to serve six years [21.pdf #108].

[16] http://boards.ancestry.com/surnames.seymour/740/mb.ashx

[17] See "Duties Paid for Imported White Servants," in *"White Slave Children of Colonial Maryland and Virginia: Birth and Shipping Records,"* in preparation.

HENRY HARDY

Henry Hardy was stigmatized at birth. He was baptized 5 April 1646 at Saint Peter, Burnley, Lancashire, England, and is identified as the "base child of Henry Howard & Issabell Hardy." That is to say, a bastard. [18]

At the age of eighteen, Henry Hardy was transported to America as a white slave without indentures. He was sold to Thomas Percei, brought to Court on 12 July 1664, adjudged to be twenty years of age, and ordered to serve six years [02.pdf #377].

On 4 June 1665, Thomas Percy purchased from Richard Watson 150 acres "on the north side of Potomack River" [02.pdf #564]. On 5 November 1666, Thomas Percey died [03.pdf #597]. He left no will. We do not know with whom Henry Hardy completed his six years of servitude.

Henry Hardy does not appear in the Court Records as a recaptured runaway, or complaining of abuse or neglect, or petitioning for freedom. It may be presumed that he gained his freedom in 1670, at the age of twenty-four.

Henry Hardy reappears in the Court Records on 11 April 1676 in a lawsuit for an unpaid debt, [07.pdf #108] and on 27 March 1677 in a probate case as an appraiser of the estate [08.pdf #31]. On 14 August 1677, Thomas Discorah, son of Martin & Dorothy Discorah, age not stated, was bound to Henry Hardy [09.pdf #79]. On 10 June 1679, Henry Hardy presented to the Court two white slaves without indentures. John Lenham was adjudged to be nineteen years of age, and Mary Bennett was adjudged to be twenty-two years of age. Both were ordered to serve six years [09.pdf #84]. [19] Henry Hardy was doing unto others what was done unto him.

---

[18] A variety of notations were used to identify bastard children in the baptismal records of Lancashire, England. Some were identified as a "baster" or "bastard," some as the "supposed" son or daughter of a named father, some as "illegitmus" (the Church of England was still using Latin in many of its records), some as a "base child" or "base born child," and others as "b: s." or "b: d."

[19] John Lenham did survive his servitude. His name appears in the Court Records four more times, under various spellings. "The marke of John Lennam for livestock" was recorded in 1683 [11.pdf #149]. John Lannum was a witness on 11 November 1690 [17.pdf #170]. John Lannam was a plaintiff on 9 August 1692 [17.pdf #250] and again on 10 June 1707 [23.pdf #189]. (See Encyclopedia of Survivors). What became of Mary Bennett is not known.

On 8 June 1686, the terms of servitude of his two white slaves being expired, Henry Hardy secured two orphans to be his servants, Richard Fowke, age 18, and Hallilujah Fowke, age 15, orphans of Richard Fowke deceased [13.pdf #117]. On 13 March 1688, Richard Fowke, being 21 years old, was freed "from ye service of Henry Hardy" [14.pdf #175]. [20]

On 10 November 1691, "Henry Hardy Gentleman" was sworn and admitted an attorney of the Charles County Court [17.pdf #157]. He was forty-five years old.

On 21 August 1694, Henry Hardy of Pyckyawaxon married Elinor Cumpton, "ye daughter of John Cumpton of St. Maryes County" [Liber Q Page 23].

Around this time, one John Dawson received a gift of a yearling heifer from his master Henry Hardy, recorded 24 April 1693 [18.pdf #18]; and two runaway servants to Henry Hardy were recaptured and brought to Court: John Goles in 1694, and William Crocker in 1695 [Liber T Page 290]. [21]

On 25 July 1696, "Capt. Henry Hardy" and nine others were "ordained and appointed" Worshippfull Commissioners for Charles County Court [19.pdf #39]. Thirty-two years earlier, Henry Hardy stood before this Court and was sentenced to six years of servitude. Now he would sit on the Court.

On 10 August 1697, John Knowlwater, age not stated, whose father John Knowlwater had run away to Virginia, was bound to Capt. Henry Hardy, and if the father "shall at any time hereafter come & desire to have his son hee is willing to restore & returne him to him again" [19.pdf #135]

On 4 April 1699, Thomas Jackson, servant to Henry Hardy, an indentured servant whose "father paid his passage," "haveing served him full four yeares," and "ye said Hardy claimes three yeares service more," petitioned "to be sett free to worke for himselfe" and "to have satisfaction for his clothes." Thomas Jackson, "being under age," was allowed to make "choice of John Cumpton ye Elder to be his guardian" [20.pdf #29]. The said "John Cumpton of St. Maryes County" was the father of Henry Hardy's first wife, the former Elinor Cumpton [Liber Q Page 23].

---

[20] Hallalujah Fowke sued Henry Hardy in 1694 [Liber T Page 62] but the Court Record has been lost, and all we have is a transcription of its index.

[21] The Court Record has been lost, and all we have is a transcription of its index.

Henry Hardy was now married to Anne Hardy, widow of Richard Ashman deceased and administrator of his estate. His probate case first appears in the Court Records on 4 October 1698. "Henry Hardy & Anne his wife" are named as the administrators of the estate of Richard Ashman [19.pdf #256].

From the vital records of Charles County [16.pdf #121] [22.pdf #129] we know that Richard and Ann Ashman "of Wiccocomicoe" had six children:

>Elizabeth, daughter, born 29 June 1680
>Richard, son, born 4 February 1682
>Mary, daughter, born 3 August 1685
>Standidge, son, born 1 October 1687
>Allward Hardy, son, born 12 June 1691
>John, son, born 4 February 1694

Around this time, on 12 March 1700, William Crocker, servant to Henry Hardy, petitioned the Court "alleadging that he was free." Henry Hardy "proveing in Court that he had unlawfully absented himselfe nineteen days," William Crocker was sentenced to 190 days of servitude [20.pdf #177].

And then, on 10 March 1702, "Anne Hardy the wife of Capt. Henry Hardy" came to Charles County Court, suing for a legal separation. "Upon a differrence beteene her & her husband," she "petitions that shee with her children may be permitted to live upon her owne land and to be allowd a sufficient maintenance to subsist upon" [22.pdf #4]. She bravely stood before nine Worshippfull Commissioners of the Charles County Court, including her own estranged husband, Capt. Henry Hardy [22.pdf #2].

The Court appointed two of their brethren to work out the difference between them, [22.pdf #4] to no avail. On 10 August 1703, "Anne ye wife of Capt. Henry Hardy" came back to Court, with her estranged husband sitting on the bench [22.pdf #124]. To begin with, the Court ordered that "Richard Ashman bee discharged from ye said Capt. Henry Hardyes service" [22.pdf #125]. He had turned twenty-one on 4 February 1703 [16.pdf #121]. His freedom was six months and six days overdue. And then Anne Hardy "complaines against her said husbands harsh & ill usage of her children & desires that they may be taken away from him and that they may all be bound out to trades" [22.pdf #125]. She was referring to her three minor children, all boys: Standidge, age 15; Allward, age 12; and John, age 9 [16.pdf #121] [22.pdf #129]. She was asking the Court to take her own children away from her to spare them from the abuse of their stepfather.

The Court appointed two of its brethren to investigate the matter [22.pdf #125]. On 14 September 1703, "upon a difference betweene Capt. Henry Hardy & Anne his wife about her children ye orphants of Richard Ashman deceased her former husband," the brethren "returned ye ensueing paper or agreement." "Standidge Ashman & Allward Hardy Ashman & John Ashman" "by & with ye consent of their said mother" do "acknowledge & obleidge themselves to live with & serve ye said Henry Hardy & Anne his wife & ye survivour of them" until "the age of twenty yeares" and "in case of both their decease" then "to be sett free," Henry Hardy agreeing "at the end of their respective termes to give every one of them a new suite" "with the rest of freedom dues" [22.pdf #129].

Three years later, on 13 August 1706, Anne Hardy won a legal separation with alimony for life: "Anne Hardy the wife of Capt. Henry Hardy comes into Court and complaines against her said husband and saith that through his harsh usage shee is not able to live and cohabbitt with him and therefore desires with the approbation of the Court shee may live (away) from him," and "Capt. Hardy being present in Court in his propper person consents thereto and propounds to allow her fifteen hundred pounds of tobacco yearely and every yeare dureing her naturall life" [23.pdf #138].

Immediately upon which the following deposition was entered upon the record:

July ye 13th 1706
"Mary Symmons aged about nineteen yeares deposeth that Capt. Henry Hardy hath often and violently endeavoured to committ a rape on her and threatned to kill her if she did not yield to his lustfull desires and often used most filthy wayes as shee (her) selfe words it by takeing out his nakedness and forceing it in her hand and otherwise
    Sworn before me   John Contee

Whereupon the matter "being fully heard seen understood and maturely deliberated" by the Court, it was ordered that "Capt. Hardy be acquitted and discharged" [23.pdf #138].

The Court moved on to other matters. Another white slave without indentures was brought before them. Margarett Macclannen, servant to John Speake, was adjudged to be twenty years of age, and ordered to serve six years [23.pdf #138].

At the very next Court, on 10 September 1706, Capt. Henry Hardy, lately acquitted of charges of sexual assault and attempted rape graphically described in a sworn deposition, had the temerity to bring his accuser, the said Mary Symmons, to court, "to be adjudged for runaway time." [22] "Whereupon the matter in controversy was heard, and the Court ordered that Mary Symmons be free from Capt. Henry Hardys service" [23.pdf #141].

This is the last we hear of Capt. Henry Hardy in the Court Records, except as a party to lawsuits. He had stepped down from the bench the year before, in 1705, at the age of fifty-nine, and he was no longer practicing law. He had served on the Charles County Court for nine years, from 11 August 1696 [19.pdf #39] until 12 June 1705, [23.pdf #76] and during this time he sat on the bench at all sessions except four: 19 April 1698, 10 January 1699, 3 December 1700 and 10 November 1702. He sat on the bench while one hundred and thirty five white "servants" without indentures were brought before the Court to have their ages adjudged and be sentenced to slavery.

Born in Lancashire, stigmatized as a bastard, kidnapped, transported, and sold into slavery, Henry Hardy, an abused child if ever there was one, became a child abuser. He outlived his servitude, bought white slaves of his own, became an attorney, became a Worshippfull Commissioner, and sentenced one hundred and thirty five "servants" without indentures, mostly children, to slavery. He abused his own wife and her children, forcing her to leave him. He sexually assaulted an indentured servant, repeatedly, and tried to have her punished for running away from him. He was a monster.

The Last Will and Testament of Henry Hardy was dated 21 December 1705, before the legal separation from his estranged wife Anne Hardy. He lived another nine years, or nearly so, and he never updated his will. His age at death was 68. Named in his will were his wife Ann, his daughter Ann, and his "kinsmen" George and Henry Hardy the sons of George Hardy. "Mr. Philip Briscoe & his son John Briscoe" were named in the will as executors. [Liber AB No. 3 Folio 75]. When the will was probated on 20 September 1714, Walter Story, former High Sheriffe of Charles County, was named as executor [Register of Wills, Page 189]. When his probate case first came to Court on 14 June 1715, Anne Hardy was named as administrator [25.pdf #276]. Four years later, on 9 June 1719, Richard Ashman, the eldest son of Anne Hardy, was administrator [26.pdf #112].

---

[22] From this we learn that Mary Symmons was an indentured servant. There is no record of her as a white slave child without indentures having her age adjudged.

JOHN BAYNE

The first time John Bayne appeared in Court was when he bought a twelve year old boy. He was really fourteen, but he looked like he was twelve. John Waterworth, son of William Waterworth, was baptized 2 February 1668 at Saint Mary the Virgin, Blackburn, Lancashire. John Bayne brought him to Court on 8 August 1682 at the age of fourteen. He was adjudged to be twelve years old, which cost him an extra two years of servitude. He would, according to law, serve ten years [10.pdf #117].

I don't know where John Bayne was born, but he came from "old money."

John Bayne was the son of Walter Bayne (or Beane), of Charles County, Maryland. He was a minor when his father died, and afterward he lived with his mother. The Last Will and Testament of Walter Bayne was dated 12 April 1670, and probated 28 May 1670 [Liber A No. 2 Folio 9]. In his will, he left to his "sonne John Beane" one thousand acres "in St. Maries County, the said John "to have the full possession of it when he shall arrive at the full age of one and twenty years." He also gave unto his "said sonne John "that which is now my dwelling plantation" being 450 acres of land, "provided that my loving wife Ellenor for the term of her natural life shall possess and enjoy the same to her proper beneffit and use." Also named in his will were his "eldest daughter Judith the present wife of Mr. Matthew Hill," [23] and his "second daughter Elizabeth" (to each of them he left three hundred acres of land), and his "third and youngest daughter Ellaner" (to whom he left fifty acres of land). His wife Ellenor was appointed "sole executrix" of his estate, amounting to 2100 acres, together with Negroes, horses, and cattle, to be divided amongst his children. [24]

On 8 June 1676, Elinor Bayne, "widdow," purchased from William Russell another 75 acres, with houses, edifices, orchards and gardens, contiguous to land "now in ye possession of ye above said Elinor" [07.pdf #128]. Elinor Beane hired Morris Miles "to come & live on her plantation & there as an Overseer to take charge & looke after her servants that did worke in ye ground." On 11 June 1679, she was still executrix of the estate [09.pdf #93].

---

[23] Matthew Hill died before 9 March 1680, on which date his probate case first came to Court. Elinor Bayne was administrator of his estate. [09.pdf #150]

[24] The probate case of Walter Bayne first appears in the Court Records on 12 September 1671. Elinor Bayne is administratrix. [06.pdf #49]

Shortly thereafter, John Bayne bought the aforesaid John Waterworth, whom he brought to Court on 8 August 1682. He had the boy for ten years.

On 18 March 1688, William Hutchison, Deputy Surveyor, sold 150 acres of land in Charles County to John Bayne [18.pdf #52]. His residence was not stated. This brought his total holdings to 1600 acres.

In 1690, John Waterworth was 22 years old, with only two years of servitude ahead of him. So John Bayne bought two new boys: Daniell Linghams for himself, and Samuell Burgesse for his mother. This way he would have a boy in both places. He brought them to Court on 11 March 1690. He presented to the Court indentures for both of them. Both were rejected with the same words: "ye said Indentures being not under ye seale of any office," and the servant "not being bound before any of his majestys justices of ye peace, nor could prove ye same." Daniell Linghams and Samuell Burgesse were ordered to serve "according to ye custome of ye countrey," [16.pdf #114] that is, as servants without indentures. [25]

Within the month, Samuell Burgesse ran away from Elinor Bayne. She brought him to the very next Court, on 10 June 1690, to be adjudged for sixty days runaway time, for which he was sentenced to 600 days servitude [17.pdf #18]. That would be sixty days absence out of ninety. [26]

On the same day, 10 June 1690, John Bayne asked to be "lycensed to keepe and ordinary or house of entertainment at Chandler Town at ye head of Portobaccoe Creeke" in Charles County. The license was granted, "John Bayne yearely paying a fine" (that is, a fee) "of twelve hundred pounds of tobaccoe" and "provideing sufficient accomodations for horse & man," and "not sufferreing any evill rule or order in his said house" [17.pdf #18].

---

[25] Their ages were not adjudged, an oversight that often occurred when indentures were presented and rejected. This left the boys without a date certain on which to expect their freedom. Not knowing their ages at the time of their court appearance makes it impossible to match them up with their birth or baptismal records.

[26] Samuell Burgesse did outlive his servitude. He turns up in the Court Records being sued by John Ratclife on 10 November 1696, [19.pdf #84] and by Thomas Whichaley on 13 February 1700 [20.pdf #153]. He died before 13 January 1702, at the house of Arthur Elie, who "nursed tended and cherished him" [21.pdf #164]. (See Encyclopedia of Survivors)

A scant nine months later, John Bayne was indicted. On 10 March 1691, the Grand Jury presented John Bayne "for that hee," "at Portobaccoe in Charles County," on 14 December 1690, "being ye Sabbath day," "did sell strong liquors contrary to ye Act of Assembly" [17.pdf #99]. On 11 August 1691, five months later, the case went to trial. John Bayne pleaded not guilty, a jury was empanelled, and John Bayne was acquitted [17.pdf #138].

In the meantime, on 10 July 1691, "John Bayne of St. Maryes County, gentleman," bought one thousand and sixty acres of land known as "Locust Thickett" in "ye upper part of Charles County" [17.pdf #234]. This brought his holdings to 2660 acres. Note that his stated residence was Saint Mary's County, where he owned one thousand acres inherited from his father.

Four months later, on 9 November 1691, "John Bayne of St. Maryes County" gave to his daughter Anne Bayne "halfe of a parcell of land which lyeth on ye south side of Kiscompkum Runn called by ye name of Locust Thickett," "being by estimation five hundred acres," or not quite half [17.pdf #160]. This left his holdings at 2160 acres.

On 8 November 1692, John Bayne was again indicted. The Grand Jurors, "by ye Information of Capt. Philip Hoskins one of their Majestyes Justices of this Court," presented John Bayne, "for that hee," "at Chandler Towne," in Charles County, "at severall dayes & times" (to wit) 20 September 1692, 28 September 1692, 29 September 1692, 5 October 1692, and 5 November 1692, "obstinately" "and without any lycense or admittance of ye Justices" "did undertake upon himselfe to keep & hath kept an ordinary or publick house of entertainement and there" "comonly & publickly did sell & retayle wyne, cyder & other liquors to severall" people. Two or three witnesses are named for each of the five occasions [17.pdf #275, 276]. John Bayne was now, officially, on the record, running a house of ill repute. [27]

The Court was not done with him yet. There was a second count. The Grand Jury also presented John Bayne "for that hee ye said John Bayne" on 25 September 1692 "being ye Sabbath day" "with his cart & horses did bring severall liquors to his ordinary at Chandler Towne" "and there did unloade & deliver ye said liquors and ye same day with ye cart & horses aforesaid returned back again." Three witnesses are named [17.pdf #276]. [28]

---

[27] Among the informants against John Bayne, on 20 September 1692, was John Wilkinson, formerly a white slave child without indentures. Brought to Court on 10 June 1674, he was adjudged to be eighteen years of age and ordered to serve six years [06.pdf #158]. He was still alive in 1722 (see Encyclopedia of Survivors).

On 31 January 1693, John Bayne's attorney asked for a continuance, which was not granted, the Court demanding "that ye said John Bayne should immediately answer unto ye aforesaid presentments." His attorney then had the two presentments "removed by writt of certiorari," which is an order from a higher court ordering a lower court to turn over transcripts and related documents for judicial review. The Charles County Court would turn over the papers, and the case would be tried at "ye next Provintiall Court to be held at ye City of St. Maryes on ye first Tuesday in May next comeing" [18.pdf #24]. This was a most unusual procedure, to demand an appeal before the trial ever happened in the first place.

And then came into Court "Capt. Philip Hoskins, Robert Thompson Junr., Moses Jones, [28] Lawrence Rochforth, Ignatius Wheeler, Robert Taylor & Morris Lloyd" "in their proper persons" and acknowledged themselves indebted "in ye sume of five pounds apiece" upon condition that they shall "personally appeare before ye Justices" "at ye next Provintiall Court" "to give evidence against John Bayne [18.pdf #24].

There is no further record of the case. We do not know the outcome.

A scant six months after his narrow escape from justice at Charles County Court, John Bayne bought "two Irish servants," both of them boys. He brought them to Court in Saint Mary's County, "att a Court holden in Newtowne," on 1 August 1693, with Mr. John Bayne himself sitting on the bench as one of the "Gentleman Justices," passing judgment upon his own "servants." Patrick Morand was adjudged to be thirteen years of age and ordered to serve nine years. Patrick Cusack was adjudged to be seventeen years of age and ordered to serve seven years [21.pdf #92] [29]

---

[28] Among the witnesses against John Bayne on 25 September 1692, being ye Sabbath day, was Moses Jones, formerly treated as a white slave child without indentures. Brought to Court on 8 June 1675, he was adjudged to be seventeen years of age and ordered to serve seven years [07.pdf #63]. Four years later, on 10 June 1679, he produced his Indentures in Court, "his time of servitude was fully expired," and he was ordered to "be free" [09.pdf #84]. (See Encyclopedia of Survivors).

[29] All Judgment Records for Saint Mary's County Court prior to 1807 have been lost. This record exists only because it was transcribed into the Charles County Court Record on 11 March 1701.

On 29 October 1696, John Bayne "of Charles County" purchased from Gilbert Clarke 428 acres of land "called Aberdeen," lying "on ye south side of the main fresh that falleth into Mattawoman Creek" in Charles County [24.pdf #199]. This brought his total holdings to 2588 acres.

Around this time, Mary Jenckins, an orphan, was "bound out by this Court" to Capt. John Bayne, "with whome and Mrs. Anne Bayne and also with Mr. Walter Bayne" she would serve [23.pdf #201]. [30]

On 9 June 1696, Capt. John Bayne showed up at Charles County Court with "a Comission from his Excellency ye Governour for ye sherifes place of this County." The Court had no choice. He was sworn as sheriff, and as recognizance acknowledged himself indebted "in ye full & just sume of two hundred thousand pounds of good sound merchantable leaf tobaccoe" [19.pdf #38]. On 9 November 1697 he hand picked his deputy, "Thomas Whichaley by Capt. John Bayne sherife being appointed by him to be one of his undersherifes" [19.pdf #169]. These are impressive problem solving skills. Capt. John Bayne would now be able to operate his house of ill repute with impunity.

Almost immediately, Capt. John Bayne began purchasing twelve year old boys and bringing them to Court: Alexander Mills on 1 February 1698 [19.pdf #186]; John Morrough, John Bryan and Anthony Coney on 19 April 1698 [19.pdf #206]. All were white slave children without indentures. All were adjudged to be twelve years of age and ordered to serve ten years. All were owned by Capt. John Bayne. It is all on the record. You can look it up. It was his interest in twelve year old boys that brought him to my attention.

Capt. John Bayne did lose an indentured servant around this time. William Rawlins, servant to Capt. John Bayne, petitioned for freedom, "alledging here in Court that by his Indenture ye time that he came in for is expired." At two Court appearances, on 9 November 1697 [19.pdf #169] and again on 11 January 1698, [19.pdf #180] his case was continued, he "not haveing

--   --

[30] On 12 August 1707, having been bound "about tenn yeares since" and the time of her service having "expired & ended," Mary Jenckins petitioned the Court for "a yeare or more schooleing which the said Capt. Bayne always neglected to give your petitioner in his lifetime & also since his death by ye said Mrs. Anne and Mr. Walter Bayne." The Court ordered "that itt was the petitioners owne neglect therefore the said petition is rejected" [23.pdf #201]. The original record does not appear in Liber V No. 1, which commences on 9 June 1696. The preceding Court Record, Liber T No. 1, has been lost. Only a transcription of its index survives.

his Indenture here;" but on 1 February 1698 "his Indenture was produced here in Court by Edward Rookwood" who had "assigned him to ye said John Bayne." William Rawlins was "discharged from ye service of his said master," and Capt. John Bayne was ordered by the Court to pay him "one hundred pounds of tobacco" for the three months he had served "since ye expiration of ye time of his servitude" [19.pdf #186].

Capt. John Bayne and Thomas Whichaley were recommissioned as Charles County sheriff and under sheriff on 9 August 1698 [19.pdf #234]. Within eight months, Capt. John Bayne obtained six more servants, all of them boys:

On 29 November 1698, Capt. John Bayne produced in Court an Indenture "under ye hand & seale of ye said John Elliott" his servant, which "was adjudged to be good & valid." John Elliott was ordered to serve Capt. John Bayne for "three whole yeares and six moneths," commencing 21 March 1696, according to Indenture [19.pdf #261]. He had one year left to serve.

On the same day, 29 November 1698, "Benjamin & Charles Warren two of the orphan sons of Coll. Humphrey Warren," were bound until the age of twenty-one to "live with & serve Capt. John Bayne," "hee findeing & alloweing them sufficient meate drinke washing & lodgeing and clothing both linen & woollen," and also "to learne them to reade & write" [19.pdf #261]. Notley Warren, son of Coll. Humphrey Warren, was executor of his father's estate [19.pdf #38].

Here is the family chart, drawn from the vital records [16.pdf #122].

Warren, Humphrey & Elizabeth, of Wikocomico
    Notley, son, born 16 December 1675
Warren, Humphrey & Margery, of Wiccocomico
    Benjamin, son, born 23 January 1682
    Charles, son, born 10 November 1684
    John, son, born 18 June 1687
    Humphrey, son, born 15 November 1691

On 4 April 1699, Capt. John Bayne brought three more white slave children without indentures to Charles County Court to have their ages adjudged. Alexander Faulkner was adjudged to be fourteen years of age and ordered to serve eight years. Charles Daniellson was adjudged to be fifteen years of age and ordered to serve seven years. Alexander Ross was adjudged to be eighteen years of age and ordered to serve seven years. [20.pdf #27]

On 13 June 1699, his three year commission as Sheriff "being now expired," and "noe comission sent" from the Governor "to any other person to officiate in ye said place & office of sherife," Capt. John Bayne asked the Court what he should do. It was the Court's opinion "that ye said John Bayne may proceede in ye sherifes place" untill "some other" person is commissioned, "soe that ye Countyes busines may not be deferred" [20.pdf #69]

Two months later, on 8 August 1699, Mr. Gerrard Fowke was sworn as sheriff, and John Stone as under sheriff [20.pdf #79]. The same day, Capt. John Bayne brought to Court another white slave child without indentures, by the name of John Rye, adjudged to be twelve years of age and ordered to serve ten years [20.pdf #79].

On 12 September 1699, John Bayne, former High Sheriff of Charles County, was "constituted ordained & appointed" a Worshippfull Commissioner of the Charles County Court [20.pdf #88]. On 14 November 1699, Thomas Wichaley, former under sheriff of Charles County, was "sworne & admitted an Attorney to this Court" [20.pdf #99]. The same day, Capt. John Bayne brought to Court another white slave child without indentures, the youngest one yet, by the name of John Cameright, adjudged to be eight years of age and ordered to serve fourteen years [20.pdf #99].

This was the last child John Bayne would ever purchase.

On 12 March 1700, "Capt. John Bayn" brought to Court "a runaway servant named Patrick Casey." He swore to 23 days absence, for which "the said Patrick" was sentenced to 230 days servitude [20.pdf #177]. Capt. John Bayne was not present on 3 December 1700, when "a man servant belonging to Capt. John Bayne," his name spelled as "Patrick Cusy," was presented by Thomas Whichaley for 47 days runaway time, "proved by the oathe of James Lattimar" [21.pdf #57]. Capt. John Bayne was not present on 11 March 1701 when the same servant, his name spelled as "Patrick Cusack," petitioned the Court. Whereas he had been "adjudged here in this Court last December" for 47 days runaway time, the 23 dayes "proved by the said Capt. Bayne in March court last is disallowed" being part of the 47 days. Patrick Cusack was ordered to serve "till the tenth day of May next and from thence one hundred and five days and after that to be discharged" [21.pdf #92].

Capt. John Bayne sat on the bench as a "Worshippfull Commissioner" at three sessions of Charles County Court, commencing 12 March 1700, 13 August 1700, and 10 September 1700 [21.pdf #2, #17, #40]. He never again sat on the bench, or appeared before the Court "in his proper person."

As administrator of the estate of Notley Warren on 14 January 1701, [21.pdf #81] and of the estates of Notley Warren and his father Humphrey Warren who predeceased him on 1 April 1701 [21.pdf #118] & [21.pdf #119], John Bayne was represented in Court by his attorneys William Stone and Thomas Whichaley. He was absent, but referred to in the present tense.

The Last Will and Testament of John Bayne [Liber TB No. 11 Page 243] was dated 5 October 1700, after which time John Bayne was supposed to have gone to England. But the uncertainty is palpable, twice expressed in the Last Will and Testament of his mother, Ellinor Bayne, [Liber A No. 2 Page 232] dated six weeks later, on 21 November 1700. She left "all my negroes" to Walter Bayne and Ebsworth Bayne, to be divided between the two "by Coll. John Courts in case my son John Bayne doth not return from England." And she named "my well beloved son John Bayne" as sole executor "in case he return safe out of England but otherwise I do appoint constitute & ordaine my grandson Walter Bayne."

On 11 June 1701, "Mr. Wichaley" agreed "to bring an account of the amerciaments out of Capt. Baynes bookes," meaning the fines he imposed during his term as sheriff [21.pdf #126]. "Mr. Thomas Wichaley" returned the account to the next Court on 13 August 1701 [21.pdf #138]. It seems rather obvious that the whereabouts of Capt. John Bayne were unknown.

The Last Will and Testament of John Bayne was proved on 25 October 1701, five witnesses attesting under oath "that they did each of them see the said deceased Bayne in his life time signe seale and deliver" the same. [31] But this only proved that the will was genuine. It did not prove he was dead.

Consider the Deposition of Thomas Whichaley, [Liber TB No. 11 Page 248] taken 5 December 1701, six weeks after the will was proved. It "being demanded how it comes to be soe much blotted and interlined," the deponent swore that all the changes to the will were made and approved by John Bayne himself, and that the deponent "offered to write it over" "saying it should all be of one hand writing," "but Mr. Bayne answered him passionately that if he staid soe long he should not be able to goe at all he being just then goeing down to St. Georges to take shipping for England and his horses then up and himselfe then ready to goe." This from a man who, just moments earlier, had declared himself "sick and weak in body but in sound and perfect minde and memory" [Liber TB No. 11 Page 243].

---

[31] John Bayne's will was witnessed by Elinor Bayne his mother, Elinor Beale his sister, Thomas Whichaley his attorney, and by William Holt and Joseph Coneper.

From these accounts of Ellinor Bayne and Thomas Whichaley derive the family legends: that Capt. John Bayne died on 10 July 1701 in Liverpool, England, and is buried at Saint Nicholas Church. But there is no record of it.

On 11 November 1701, Coll. John Courts petitioned that he and his wife were "God Father and God Mother for a sonne of Coll. Humphrey Warren named John Warren who is now fatherlesse and motherlesse and was formerly under the tuition of Notley Warren and afterwards under the tuition of Capt. John Bayne who was Executor of Notley Warren and is att present under the care of Mrs. Ann Bayne" and so "is brought up to nothing but idlenesse swearing and all other ill vices," "likewise the said Capt. John Bayne hath leased the said Warren's plantation to William Hawton Junior who hath five servants and himselfe who clears and destroyes the land." "I will keepe him close to schoole untill I have learned him to read and write a legible hand," "and as to his plantation," "I will take care that there shall be an orchard of an hundred winter trees planted" "within a twelve month after I have it in possession and to have it carefully looked after as an orchard ought to bee." "I see that the lad is going totally to ruine." "The petition being read Madam Ann Bayne being present," the Court ordered "that the said orphan and lands bee delivered to the said Coll. John Courts " [21.pdf #160].

Not until 10 March 1702 do these words appear in the Court Records: "Anne Bayne Executrix of the Last Will and Testament of John Bayne Deceased" [22.pdf #9] [22.pdf#10]. Three weeks later, this explanation is given: "and the said John Bayne is since dead as by the insinuation of Anne Bayne."

What an interesting word choice. My Funk & Wagnalls dictionary defines the verb to "insinuate" as "to indicate indirectly, as if by devious, artful, and questionable means." By "insinuation," she gains control of the estate.

John Bayne died possessed of all his real estate. He never sold any of it, although he did give half of Locust Thickett to his daughter [17.pdf #160]. In his will, [Liber TB No. 11 Page 243] he divided 3550 acres of land, and twelve negroes, among his three children, Ebsworth, Anne, and Walter. He left to Thomas Whichaley "a Servant four years to serve at least and the horse called Cropp and five pounds sterling to be paid out in a mourning suit and not otherwise." The rest of his personal estate was "to be delivered" by five Trustees, namely Coll. John Courts, Major James Smallwood, Coll. John Addison, Major William Dent, and Major Benjamin Hall, all of whom served, at one time or another, as "Worshippfull Commissioners." Three of the five Trustees owned white slave children without indentures. Coll. John Courts owned seventeen, Major James Smallwood owned ten, and Major William Dent owned seven (*Without Indentures*, pp. 108-112, plus Hogg).

The personal estate of Capt. John Bayne (in the summer of 1701) included eleven white slave children without indentures, all of them boys or very young men; and four orphans, three of them brothers, the other a girl.

Morand (Moreland), Patrick, 1 August 1693, age 13, nine years [21.pdf #92]
Cusack (Casey), Patrick, 1 August 1693, age 17, seven years [21.pdf #92]
Jenckins, Mary, before 9 June 1696, age not stated, orphan [23.pdf #201]
Mills, Alexander, 1 February 1698, age 12, ten years [19.pdf #186]
Morrough, John, 19 April 1698, age 12, ten years [19.pdf #206]
Bryan, John, 19 April 1698, age 12, ten years [19.pdf #206]
Coney, Anthony, 19 April 1698, age 12, ten years [19.pdf #206]
Warren, Benjamin, 29 November 1698, age 16, orphan [19.pdf #261]
Warren, Charles, 29 November 1698, age 14, orphan [19.pdf #261]
Faulkner, Alexander, 4 April 1699, age 14, eight years [20.pdf #27]
Daniellson, Charles, 4 April 1699, age 15, seven years [20.pdf #27]
Ross, Alexander, 4 April 1699, age 18, seven years [20.pdf #27]
Rye, John, 8 August 1699, age 12, ten years [20.pdf #79]
Cameright, John, 14 November 1699, age 8, fourteen years [20.pdf #99]
Warren, John, before 11 November 1701, age 14, orphan [21.pdf #160]

Note: Patrick Casey was sentenced to 470 days runaway time.

Five of the boys, the white slave children adjudged to be twelve, are listed as property in "An Inventory of the Estate of Capt. John Bayne Deceased," appraised "by Capt. Phillip Briscoe and Capt. Henry Hardy," 10 July 1702:

"John Bryon a servant boy neare 5 years to serve"
"a servant boy Anthony Cony ye same time" (5 years)
"a servant boy John Mograugh ye same time" (5 years)
"a servant boy named J(?) Rye neare 6 years to serve"
"Alexander Mills a servant boy 3 years & 8 months to serve"

[Inventories & Accounts, Vol. 22, Folios 34 & 36]

These boys were in a secure location. They did not run away. They were still on the premises in July 1702, a year and nine months after Capt. John Bayne went missing. They were the boys of the brothel, the house of ill repute. Five boys, five Trustees. You do the math.

Conspicuously absent from the Inventory are five Scottish and Irish lads:

Morand (Moreland), Patrick, 1 August 1693, age 13, now 21
Cusack (Casey), Patrick, 1 August 1693, age 17, now 25
Faulkner, Alexander, 4 April 1699, age 14, now 16
Daniellson, Charles, 4 April 1699, age 15, now 17
Ross, Alexander, 4 April 1699, age 18, now 20

They were the five servants who, with William Hawton Junior, were clearing and destroying the land on the orphan John Warren's plantation under lease from Capt. John Bayne [21.pdf #160]. It looks like they did run away.

Also absent from the Inventory are the orphans of Coll. Humphrey Warren, who were already bound to other guardians before the will was probated.

Other servants listed, between the Negroes and the cows, are "Joseph Cooper a Taylor," "an orphan girle called Mary," [32] "Hugh Dowen 9 months to serve," and "a servant called Sawny Rose a year & ½ to serve" [Folio 34]; and these, listed between the bulls and the horses, "William Owen 9 months to serve," "John Boin a boy nere 5 years to serve," "Robert Manhaine a boy 3 years & ½ to serve," "a boy called Charles ye same time" (3½ years), "Thomas Day 2 years and 7 months to serve," and "a servant named Sarah a runaway and hath a bastard child and 4 months to serve," [Folios 35 & 36].

Five servants of Capt. John Bayne, with and without indentures, if still alive, were already free during his lifetime: John Waterworth, Daniell Linghams, Samuell Burgesse, William Rawlins, and John Elliott.

This leaves only John Cameright, the littlest boy, unaccounted for. He had "four years to serve at least." He may have gone to Thomas Whichaley.

The Inventory of the Goods and Chattles of Madam Anne Bayne, dated 15 July 1703, named, among others, the following servants: [33]

"J(?) Rye haveing to serve 4 years next March"
"Alex Mills 2 yeares next May"
"Anthony Cony to serve 3 years next March"
"John Bryan to serve 3 years next March"
"John Magrah to serve 3 years next March"

[Inventories & Accounts, Vol. 24, Folio 134 et seq., at 138, 139, 140]

These are the same five boys. They were still on the premises in July 1703, thirty-three months after Capt. John Bayne went missing.

---

[32] Mary Jenckins, who later served "Mrs. Anne and Mr. Walter Bayne." She was free before 12 August 1707 [23.pdf #201].

[33] Also named in the Inventory of Madam Anne Bayne are "Joseph Cooper Taylor to serve about 8 or 9 months," "John Cage 12 months ye 22 of next March," "Charles Dicoson and Robert Mahawn next November 2 years & 9 months," "John Dean next February 1 year," "John Boyne next month 4 years," and "Sarah Orway till the full"

There is another family legend about an ancestor named John Bryan coming on a ship to America and losing his parents at sea, and a wealthy captain who was also on the ship took him to Maryland and raised him. [34] This touching story is not how it happened. On 19 April 1698, Capt. John Bayne brought to Court not one twelve year old boy, but three: John Bryan, Anthony Coney, and John Morrough (Mograugh, Magrah). They weren't all three of them sailing happily across the Atlantic when they lost their parents all six of them. This was not a kindly sea captain. This was not the good ship Lollipop. Capt. John Bayne was a monster.

In the year 1698, at least twelve white slave ships sailed the Irish Sea, in search of human cargo for the plantations of Maryland and Virginia. Import duties were paid for 390 "white servants" carried on nine of these ships; the shipping records for the other three ships list "European goods and servants" as "cargo." In the same year, at least thirty white slave ships sailed from London, their captains paying import duties for at least 559 "white servants." [35] In the year 1698, in the surviving Court Order Books of colonial Maryland and Virginia, 235 white servants without indentures had their ages adjudged and were sentenced to slavery [36]. John Bryan was one of them.

John Bryan did not get free until 9 March 1708, when Patrick Moreland was summoned "to give evidence between John Bryan and Mr. Walter Bayne" [23.pdf #236]. This was the same Patrick "Morand" whom Capt. John Bayne had brought to Court in Saint Mary's County on 1 August 1693, [21.pdf #92] at which time he was adjudged to be thirteen years old and sentenced to serve nine years. John Bryan had served ten years, or nearly so. He was now twenty-two years old, or nearly so. And still he needed help to get free from Walter Bayne, who was administrator of the estate of Anne Bayne deceased [23.pdf #90]. The Court heard Patrick Moreland, and ordered that John Bryan be free from the service of Walter Bayne," "John Bryan quitting his freedom dues which he is willing to do" [23.pdf #236].

John Bryan was a survivor. So was Patrick Moreland, who freed John Bryan. So was John Magrah, who was administrator for Patrick Moreland [26.pdf #112]. Their records are few, but they are proof of freedom.

---

[34] http://boards.ancestry.com/thread.aspx?mv=flat&m=247&p=surnames.obryan

[35] See "Kids as Cargo" and "Shipping Records," in *"White Slave Children of Colonial Maryland and Virginia: Birth and Shipping Records,"* in preparation.

[36] In 1698 there were 235. In 1699 there were 677. In 1700 there were 204.

DISHONORABLE MENTIONS

Beale, John, and Elinor his wife, sister of Capt. John Bayne, four of their servants being runaway and recaptured on multiple occasions: Jane Bushell twice, 54 days in all [23.pdf #206]; Grace Evans twice, 53 days in all [24.pdf #59] & [25.pdf #120]; Alice Magrah three times, 62 days in all; Jeremiah Todd twice, 45 days in all [22.pdf #80], [22.pdf #130] & [23.pdf #115].

Bould, John, Overseer to Philip Lynes, "who doth very much beate & abuse" Henry Shalter, servant to Philip Lynes, 13 January 1691 [17.pdf #89].

Bowman, John, for transporting "into this Countrey" at least seven servants, and by his Oath "hee had ye counterparts of their Indentures & did reade them aboard of his ship at Gravesend, and they were kidnappers Indentures," 10 June 1690 [17.pdf #18].

Browne, William, "administrator for imbezzelling the Estate of Capt. John and Frances Wilder deceased to the great prejudice of the orphants," 11 March 1707 [23.pdf #169].

Causeen, Ignatius, for "beating threatening" and "soe unreasonably" using his servant Ann Chandler that she "is not able to serve" him, 13 March 1711 [24.pdf #60].

Coody, William, "who has most barbarously and inhumanely treated his hired servant" Thomas Ingram, 8 November 1726 [30.pdf #175].

Douglass, Joseph, Captain, for imposing upon Thomas Fountain "a Mallatto servant" the third longest sentence ever handed down in Charles County Court for a recaptured runaway, 300 days absence, 3000 days servitude, 11 March 1729 [31.pdf #118], two months before his expected date of freedom at age thirty-one [22.pdf #163].

Emanson, Mrs., wife of Nicholas Emanson, for beating Elizabeth Hasell their servant; six witnesses testified, including two sons of Mrs. Emanson, saying: his mother "beat her & putt her in irons," & "another time his mother whipt her & severall times she hath been beaten for running away," & "her mistris tyed her to a bed post & whipped her," & "her mistris tooke her & whipt her & goeing in afterwards to sweep the roome there was a puddle of blood in the room & great wounds in her back," 11 January 1670 [Vol. 60:233].

DISHONORABLE MENTIONS

Goodrick, Henrie, Overseer to Philip Lynes, for abuse of John Lew, servant to Philip Lynes, "there be an express order of this Court delivered to ye said Goodrick forbidding him at his perill to offer anie abuse to ye said Lew" 14 September 1686 [13.pdf #120].

Green Thomas, for "barbarous usage & treatment" of his servant William McMillian, "notwithstanding ye admonition given his master by some of the Justices of the Court" "he still continues to abuse the said William by beating," 8 June 1725 [30.pdf #4].

Hawkins, Henry, Junr., "Worshippfull Commissioner," for purchasing two Jacobite rebels "taken in ye Rebellion at Preston and Transported into this Province without Indenture," and, while sitting on the bench, ordering them to return to his service, 13 March 1722 [27.pdf #126].

Hawkins, Henry, Senr., "Worshippfull Commissioner," for twice, while sitting on the bench, ordering four of his own servants to serve acording to "Act of Assembly" or "ye Custome of ye Countrey," their Indentures being adjudged "kidnappers Indentures," 12 January 1686 [13.pdf #47] & 10 June 1690 [17.pdf #18].

Hawkins, Henry, Senr., "Worshippfull Commissioner," and Elizabeth his wife, five of their servants being runaway and recaptured on six separate occasions: John Bacon, 235 days [14.pdf #49]; Anne Capper 75 days [12.pdf #23] and 47 days [12.pdf #97]; Jeremiah Ellison, 149 days [11.pdf #187]; John Newton, 10 days [14.pdf #142]; and David Southerly, 7 days [23.pdf #88].

Hodgson, Richard, for "unlawfully & unreasonable beateing & woundeinge" of his servant Edward Webster, 13 January 1680 [09.pdf #143].

Jameson, Thomas, for abusing his servant Daniel Kelly, who "upon hard usage did runn away eight days" and "has been lasht, and beate for the same," 11 August 1702 [22.pdf #38].

Jenkins, Thomas, joyner, "for not keeping Thomas Wharton his apprentice to his trade as he was bound to by this Court butt has hired him to James Mancaster to work in the ground this yeare," he being "an orphan child" aged thirteen years, 12 June 1711 [24.pdf #94].

DISHONORABLE MENTIONS

Kilbourne, Francis, for leaving John Green his servant on "a frontier plantation above Piscataway," wanting food & clothing, "alone in a strange place at a great distance from any neighbours to ye mercy of ye Indians," 14 November 1676 [07.pdf #129].

Lewis, James, Overseer to Philip Lynes, "upon suspicion of murdering one Owen Carr servant to Mr. Philip Lynes," 14 January 1690 [17.pdf #83].

Loftee or Lofton, John, for causing the orphans of George and Susannah Scroggin, both deceased, to "demand an account and security from John Lofton their father in law that their Estates bee not by him imbezzelled," 13 August 1700 [21.pdf #19] et seq.

Loftley or Lofton, John, for causing Hugh Davies, "a cripple," to go to Court at least three times for his freedom corn and clothes, two hoes, one axe, and one gun, 13 January 1702 [21.pdf #181], 10 November 1702 [22.pdf #78] & 8 June 1703 [22.pdf #117].

Luckett, Samuell, "for unreasonably beateing and abuseing" his servant Mary Cammell, 11 March 1707 [23.pdf #169].

Lyndsey, Thomas, & "Jane his wife ye relict & executor of Richard Jones deceased," who "had embezled & waisted ye cheife part of ye estate belonging to" Anne Jones & Richard Jones, his orphans, 11 March 1690 & 10 June 1690 [Liber Q Page 9].

Maddock, Cornelius, who demanded of his former servant punishment for runaway time, "Whereupon ye said Abigail Clampett in Open Court in ye presence of ye said Cornelius Maddock did stripp herselfe naked from ye Waist upwards and Exposed to ye Justices view both on her Back, Belly, Armes & Wrists many Markes of Seveare & Cruel Whippings & Tyings whilest shee was ye said Maddocks servant," 9 November 1703 [22.pdf #144].

Shaw, Ralph, for promising to "to bee in the stead of a father" to John Clarke, son of Coniers Clarke widow, "and to keep him at schoole," "but soe it is" that he "doth not use him as a son but" "rather a white Negro" and "puting him under an over seer to make tobacco and corne instead of goeing to schoole," 2 March 1700 [20.pdf #194].

DISHONORABLE MENTIONS

Smallwood, James, "Worshippfull Commissioner," seven of his servants being runaway and recaptured on at least nine separate occasions: John Bennett, 20 days [19.pdf #180]; Patrick Coherin, 31 days [23.pdf #152]; Richard Corder, 60 days in all [17.pdf #69]; Archilaus Gill, 100 days [25.pdf #266]; Mary Smith, 60 days [14.pdf #8, 9]; James Welch, 85 days in all [20.pdf #4]; and Henry Williams, 180 days [23.pdf #235].

Story, Walter, Capt., High Sheriff of Charles County, for enslaving James Lee, an innocent man committed into his custody upon suspicion of being a runaway, and no master being found, Capt. Story demanded satisfaction for his fees, and obtained a Court order "that the said James Lee doe remaine with the said Capt. Walter Story two yeares fully" "to commence from the last of October next for his fees aforesaid" and then to be free, 11 June 1706 [23.pdf #123]

Thomas, Benoni, Capt., for imposing upon Mollatto Will his servant the second longest sentence ever handed down in Charles County Court for a recaptured runaway, 180 days absence, 3260 days servitude, 11 June 1706 [23.pdf #123].

Thompson, Henry, Overseer to Philip Lynes, for "hard usage" of Catherine Jones, servant to Philip Lynes, ordered by Court to "remove her from her overseer Henry Thompson to another plantation and to cloth her well," 11 August 1691 [17.pdf #139]. Henry Thompson was himself a white slave child without indentures, brought to Court on 11 March 1679, adjudged to be sixteen years of age, and ordered to serve seven years. (See Encyclopedia of Survivors).

Turner, Arthur, for abuse and neglect of John Ward an orphan bound to him, who "hath bin so ill treated" "with a most rotten filthy stincking lodge that even loathed all the beholders thearof his apparrell beeing all ragged and torne and his haer seemed to bee raked of with ashes," 3 November 1663 [02.pdf #255, 256, 257].

Ward, Joseph, for abusing Richard Ward an orphan bound to him, leaving him "naked without a shirt and never a bed to lie on," 10 January 1699 [20.pdf #4], and because Hesther Allin, orphan daughter of Philip Allin deceased, "in ye possession of one Joseph Ward," "by ye said Ward & wife is greiveously abused," 4 October 1698 [19.pdf #241].

DISHONORABLE MENTIONS

Warren, Humphrey, "Worshippfull Commissioner," for altering the Indenture of his servant Thomas Damer or Damour who did "covenant & agree to serve the term of fower yeares," "yet nevertheless Humphrey Warren blotted out your petitioners name and put in the name of another servant," thus placing him "in danger of serveing seven yeares," 11 March 1673 [06.pdf #135, 136].

Wathen, John, for "harsh usage" of Thomas Benjer his servant, before 8 August 1704 [23.pdf #20, #21].

Wheeler, Thomas, "for unlawfully beating his servant Margaret Evans after due admonishment given him to the contrary by one of the Justices of this Court," and blaming his actions on "the ill language of the said servant," 13 November 1705 [23.pdf #104].

Whitter, William, for detaining Mary Fitzgerald "as a servant notwithstanding she is country born, now nineteen years of age & never bound or contracted to him," 13 August 1723 [28.pdf #76].

Willson, William, Overseer to William Dent, for "abuseing" Turlough Bryan, servant to William Dent, "hee had unreasonably beaten & wounded him," 13 June 1699 [20.pdf #68] & 12 September 1699 [20.pdf #90].

Wilson, Alexander, for imposing upon Rosamond Law his servant the longest sentence ever handed down in Charles County Court for a recaptured runaway, 338 days absence, 3380 days servitude, 14 June 1715 [25.pdf #271].

HOW THE SYSTEM WORKED

PETITIONS FOR FREEDOM

The Court Records, especially the Petitions for Freedom, reveal how the system worked for servants with and without indentures.

My Funk & Wagnalls dictionary defines the noun "indenture" as

1. *Law.* An instrument of contract under seal; an instrument in duplicate between parties, each party keeping a counterpart. 2. A legal instrument for binding an apprentice or a servant to his master; often used in plural.

The parties to a contract are bound thereby. A valid indenture, a written contract under seal, would be approved by the Court if presented by either party at any time during or after the term of servitude. There was no need to have the Indenture copied into the Court Record, although sometimes this was done. Examples include:

John Harrison & Mary his wife, four years, 26 August 1680 [12.pdf #21]
Peter Evans aged twenty five yeares from the County of Denby, 4 June 1680 [12.pdf #21]
John Watson a tanner from York Shire last from ye Citty of London aged eight & twentie years, to serve four years, 9 May 1683 [14.pdf #162]
Mary Power, Spinster, five years, 20 November 1684 [13.pdf #18]
John Maning, son of Edmond Maning, being tenn years of age, to serve untill the full age of twenty one years, 3 April 1713 [24.pdf #177]

Twenty-seven indentured servants produced their Indentures, or proof of them, in Court when petitioning for freedom after their terms of servitude had expired. As noted above, nine of them were servants to Philip Lynes. All twenty-seven were freed by the Court. (See Petitions for Freedom).

Five produced their indentures. [37] One indenture was produced by the mistress. [38] Six who could not produce their indentures brought witnesses to Court. [39] Two produced their indentures and brought witnesses. [40] One produced his indenture and a witness with corroboration. [41] Two produced depositions from the men who sold them. [42] In one case, the man who sold him produced the indenture. [43] One produced a certificate from the owner of the ship. [44] Two produced testimony from commanders of the ship. [45] One who lost her indentures produced a witness. [46] Two whose indentures were stolen produced three witnesses. [47] One, being a pauper, was assigned an attorney. [48] Two were freed, having served their full time, but the manner of proof was not written into the Court Record. [49]

Ten indentured servants produced their Indentures in Court when petitioning for freedom, but their terms of servitude had not yet expired, and they were ordered to serve out the remainder of their time according to Indenture. [50]

---

[37] Mary Bowles, James Burchner, Francis Crandall, Edward Hammon, Rodricke Lloyd.

[38] "Mrs. Anne Burford produceing here in Court Elizabeth Evens her Indenture"

[39] Sarah Bald, Thomas Bennett, Patrick Benson, Anne Butler, Abigail Hamond, Thomas Patrick.

[40] Richard Capner and Richard Conyers.

[41] John Deane, "produceing an Indenture in Court" and "ye oath of Mr. Walter Story" and "a letter from under ye hand of his uncle Samuell Story"

[42] James Adams and George Riscorla.

[43] "William Rawlins his Indenture was produced here in Court by Edward Rookwood" "who assigned him to ye said John Bayne"

[44] David Ambrose, servant to Philip Lynes, "came in a vessell belonging to me, one Kelley Inerehaut" (?)

[45] Captain Edward Blagg Junior made oath "that one Sarah Burroughes now a servant with Robert Downes was a passenger in ye ship Industry whereof he was Comander in November 1670;" and Richard Walsh, servant to Matthew Barnes, citing "Nathaniell Milles marriner of our ship"

[46] Anne Powell, servant to Philip Lynes.

[47] Abram Parker and Robert Smallpage, servants to Benjamin Rozer.

[48] ordered by Court "that ye said James Lyle be admitted to prosecute ye said Philip Lynes in forma pauperis, and Mr. William Shaw one of ye atturneys of this Court is assigned to him for his Councell here in Court"

[49] Owen Murphy and Thomas Thornely.

[50] Paul Burroughs, John Clifford, Anne Davison, Morris Fitzgerrald, John Miller, John Monroe, John Neale, William Newman Junr., Daniel Ross, Thomas Warner.

Some were brought to Court as servants without indentures, had their ages adjudged, and were sentenced accordingly; and then, at a later Court appearance, were able to produce their indentures. Examples include:

Champ, Stephen, servant to William Marshall, 12 January 1669 [Vol. 60:180]
Gray, Ruth, servant to Henry Bonner, 10 March 1680 [09.pdf #156]
Jones, Moses, servant to Zachary Wade deceased, 10 June 1679 [09.pdf #84]
Patterson, William, servant to William Dent, 29 November 1698
    [19.pdf #261]

Compare these with the dates of their first Court appearances:

Champe, Steephen, 8 March 1664, age 14, William Marshall [02.pdf #322]
Gray, Ruth, 13 June 1676, age 21, Richard Edelen [07.pdf #111]
Jones, Moses, 8 June 1675, age 17, Zachary Wade [07.pdf #63]
Patterson, William, 14 June 1698, age 16, William Dent [19.pdf #217]

Stephen Champ(e) had served five years, Ruth Gray had served four years, and Moses Jones had served four years. All three were freed by the Court. William Patterson had served five and a half months when he brought his Indenture to Court. He was ordered to "serve ye tearme of foure yeares and noe longer" according to his Indenture.

The Court ruled many indentures invalid. Three had their Indentures rejected at their first Court appearance and were treated always as servants without indentures. [51] Two served out their time, only to have their Indentures ruled invalid when petitioning for freedom, and were treated thereafter as servants without indentures. [52] These were rejected for not being under seal of any office, or sworn to before a justice of the peace, the servant not being able to prove the Indenture was signed sealed & delivered.

Three Indentures were alleged to be counterfeit, the culprits being the servants. Two "had counterfeited a Justice of the peace his hand & seale," [53] the other had his Indenture altered from five years to four years. [54]

---

[51] John Bass, servant to Robert Thompson Junr.; Samuell Burgesse, servant to Mrs. Elinor Bayne; Daniel Linghams, servant to John Bayne.

[52] Catherine French, servant to Thomas Cooke; and Christopher Whittimore, servant to Henry Hawkins.

[53] William Fraizer and Robert Gluffur.

[54] John Handerkin.

Some indentures were ruled invalid on petition of the servant. One was freed because his Indenture was entered into "in time of his minority and without the consent of either parent or guardian." [55] Seven were freed because their Indentures were entered into while still a servant, [56] which was contrary to Act of Assembly providing that "noe indenture made by any servant dureing the tyme of service" "shall any wayes oblidge any servant for longer time then by his first Indenture or determination of the Court" [57]

Seven indentures were ruled invalid because they were "kidnappers indentures." Those words are on the record. On 10 June 1690, seven man servants [58] petitioned the Charles County Court "about their freedom & whether their Indentures were valid & good. And it appeareing by ye Oath of Mr. John Bowman who transported them into this Countrey that hee had ye counterparts of their Indentures & did reade them aboard of his ship at Gravesend, and they were kidnappers Indentures but whether they were good or not hee could not tell, and noe proofe appearing here in Court that ye said Indentures were signed sealed & delivered by ye said John Williams with whom they did indent, & ye same not being under ye seale of an Office, or under ye hand of any Justice of ye peace," they were ordered by the Court to "returne to their severall masters service & serve acording to ye Custome of ye Countrey, their Indentures being adjudged invalide by ye Courte" [17.pdf #18]. Think about what this means. If these young men had agreed to and sworn to those indentures before a justice of the peace they would be free. Because they had been kidnapped and transported, an act of piracy, and were given fake indentures, they would return to the service of their masters.

Five of these seven young men appeared in the Court records more than four years previously, in the winter of 1686. Two of them, on two different days, produced an Indenture which the court found invalid, without explanation.

Spurling, Jeremiah, 12 January 1686, age 18, Henry Hawkins [13.pdf #47]
Yappe, Roger, 12 January 1686, age 21, Henry Hawkins [13.pdf #47]
Archiball, John, 9 February 1686, age 22, Alexander Smith [13.pdf #48]
Lees, Thomas, 9 March 1686, age 22, John Court Jun., "produced an indenture
    which is found invalid" [13.pdf #49]
Smith, James, 9 February 1686, age 21, Samuell Luckett, "ye servant produced
    an Indenture ye Court adjudgeth ye same Invalid" [13.pdf #48]

John Hall and Christopher Whittimore, listed in 1690, were not found in 1686.

These "kidnappers indentures" had already expired or were about to, which is why these young men were in Court trying to get free. But they didn't stand much of a chance. Five of the seven were owned by "Worshippfull

Commissioners" sitting on the Court. [59] John Archibald, Thomas Lees, James Smith, and Roger Yappe would serve six years. [60] Jeremiah Spurling would serve seven years. We don't know the ages of the other two, John Hall and Christopher Whittimore. They never had their ages adjudged. We don't know, and they didn't know, when they would be free.

John Hall and Christopher Whittimore should have been free after five years, by law, by rights, because they were not brought to Court to have their ages adjudged within six months after their arrival in America. A longer delay could be advantageous only to the owner, and was contrary to Act of Assembly, unless the owners "clayme but five years service of such servant" [61] Two white slaves without indentures, Mary Davis and James Thornborrow, gained their freedom on this basis. [62]

Three servants petitioned for freedom successfully by proving their time had expired, one "being now at age of two & twenty yeares," [63] one "hath served his full time of servitude according to the judgment of St. Maryes County Court," [64] and one "hath served five years and upwards coming in without Indenturs beeing then 18 years of age" [65] in 1661, when five years was the term of service for those 18 to 22. [66]

Four servants petitioned for freedom unsucessfully because their time had not expired. [67] Two of them, Edward Typton and John Wilkinson, are in the Encyclopedia of Survivors.

And four Jacobite Rebels, "taken in ye Rebellion at Preston and Transported into this Province without Indenture," having "served the full Term of five years" being "past the age of twenty two years at the Time of (their) Transportacion" petitioned for freedom but were denied, on 13 March 1722, without explanation [27.pdf #126]. Their names were Malcolm McCollum, Daniel Stewart, John Cameron, and James McIntosh. [68] The Battle of Preston took place in November 1715. The rebels had been in America six years already. They should have been free in five years. But they never had their ages adjudged. We don't know, and they didn't know, when they would be free. Daniel Stewart is in the Encyclopedia of Survivors.

There were five persons sold into slavery without legal basis. [69] By far the most interesting case is that of Edmond Brunon, who was rescued "by ye personal attestation of Richard Land of this Countie that ye said Brunon was brought into these parts as a cabbin boy by a master of a ship who had noe disposing power of him otherwise than by his primary contract as a cabbin boy." The Court ordered "that ye said Edmond Brunon be free to all intents & purposes," [14.pdf #10] even from his contract as a cabin boy.

Two servants were freed by their masters. Samuel Fendall freed John Owen "Taylor" on 8 March 1670, saying he "is now his own man, and noe way is farther obliged to me" [06.pdf #29]. John Meekes freed Thomas Hogin on 13 October 1663, "the said Meekes in open Court declared him to bee a free man" "by vertue of an Act of Assembly prohibiting masters to covenant with their servants for any longer time" of service than the "custom of the country," his Indenture being "no valid" [02.pdf #242]. It was the first successful petition for freedom in the history of Charles County, Maryland.

---

[55] Francis Arrington, servant to Thomas Thompson.

[56] Margaret Attkinson, George Carter, John Greene, William Hilton, Grace Holmes, Francis Ross, Joan Ruby.

[57] Perpetual Laws of Maryland [12.pdf #171, Folio 93]

[58] John Hall, Christopher Whittimore, Jeremiah Spurling & Roger Yappe, servants to Mr. Henry Hawkins Senior; John Archbald servant to Henry Hawkins Junior; Thomas Lees servant to John Courte; and James Smith servant to Samuell Luckett.

[59] Henry Hawkins Senr. owned four, John Courte owned one.

[60] Thomas Lees, Christopher Whittimore, and Roger Yappe are in the Encyclopedia of Survivors.

[61] Perpetual Laws of Maryland [12.pdf #171, Folios 92, 93]

[62] Mary Davis, servant to Mr. Robert Doyne, [14.pdf #158] "Sherife of this Countie," [14.pdf #158] "was by him kept nine or ten months before shee was brought to Court to be adjudged" [18.pdf #195]. And "Philip Lynes kept ye said James Thorneborrow from January until August Court following before he brought him to Court to be adjudged" [17.pdf #190]. (See Encyclopedia of Survivors).

[63] Dorothy Frawner, late servsnt to Robert Doyne deceased.

[64] Henry Moore, servant to John Beale.

[65] Michaell Pickering, servant to Robert Hendly.

[66] "Proceedings and Acts of the General Assembly," Volume 1, Pages 409, 453.

[67] John Butterfield, Hannah Knightsmith, Edward Typton, John Wilkinson.

[68] See *Without Indentures*, Appendix, pp. 275-283.

[69] Edmond Brunon, Mary Fitzgerald, Lomax Macknew, Margaret Macmillian, Abraham Perrey.

One East Indian, one American Indian, seven Mulattos, and three Negroes also petitioned for freedom.

Negroes were slaves for life. The legal phrase was "durante vita," or, in translation, "during life." [70] The only possible exceptions would be a Negro with valid Indentures; or a Negro freed by his master, the legal term being "manumission." Mulattos born of a Negro and a free born white woman were slaves until the age of thirty-one, [71] unless they were bound as orphans, by Indenture, in which case, the girls might be free at the age of sixteen, the boys at the age of twenty-one. The law required that free born white women who married Negro slaves "shall serve the master of such slave dureing the life of her husband," [72] therefore they would never lawfully marry, and the Mullatto children brought to Court were always bastards.

There were seven Petitions for Freedom from Mulattos, and all, except John Glover, were ultimately successful.

Birke, John, "a Mollatto," servant to Mrs. Elizabeth Hawkins, ordered by Court "that the said Mollatto is free att twenty one yeares of age" [23.pdf #181]

Gamon, Charles, servant to Philip Lynes deceased, 9 March 1725, "born of a free white woman & a Mullatto" "is above thirty one years," "was not bound by any Indenture," whereupon it is judged "that the same Charles be free" [29.pdf #26]

Glover, John, "a Mollatto," servant to Samuell Luckett, "borne in ye month of February" 1680, by oath of his mother Sarah Smith [22.pdf #125]; ordered by Court that the said John Glover shall "remaine a servant until the age of thirty and one yeares," 9 March 1703 [22.pdf #90]; John Glover, "Mollatto servant" to John Hanson, 9 March 1708 [23.pdf #237] & 8 June 1708 [23.pdf #253]

Pratt, Elizabeth, "a malloto girle," 12 August 1712, "detayned as a servant by ye widdow & relict of John Southeron,""arrived to ye age of eighteen years," ordered by Court to "be discharged according to pettition" [25.pdf #91]

Russell, James, "a Mallatto," servant to Notley Rozier, 13 March 1722, "is thirty one years of age" [27.pdf #127]

Russell, Thomas, "a Mallatto servant of Mr. Notley Rozier," 14 August 1722, " he is past ye age of thirty one years," ordered by Court "that the said Thomas be free & discharged" [27.pdf #178]

Sarah "a Molattoe girl belonging to ye Estate of William Smith deceased," 4 April 1699, "sixteene yeares of age," ordered by Court "that Sarah a Molattoe bee discharged" [20.pdf #29]

John William, "an East Indian," slave to Richard Hodgson and formerly to Mrs, Johannah Hodgson his mother, "purchased "about fifteen or sixteen yeares since," [23.pdf # 153] though claimed as "a servant dureing life," was freed by the Court on 14 January 1707 [23.pdf #161].

"Nicholas Clash an Indian", or Nicholas Cloyce, servant to Coll. Edward Pye, was declared "to be free" "to all intents & purposes" on 9 August 1687 [16.pdf #22]. He then agreed to a one year Indenture, on 13 June 1688 [16.pdf #22] with Coll. Edward Pye, and had to go to Court again to be freed a second time, on 11 March 1690, "haveing served several yeares longer than his just time" [16.pdf #114]. He appears as a father in the Vital Records: "John Clash ye son of Nicholas & Mary Clash of Portobaccoe was borne" 20 September 1693 [Liber Q Page 21].

Mingoe, "a Negro man belonging to Mr. William Stone," claimed a verbal agreement from "Mr. Joshua Doyne late of this County Gent. deceased" that he "should serve his sonn Dennis Doyne" for seven years. Mingo claimed that after Dennis Doyne died, he was sold to Mr. William Stone by "William Doyne brother to the aforesaid Dennis Doyne." The story does not bear scrutiny. Joshua Doyne was still alive on 17 January 1698, when he sold, or rather gifted, a tract of land to his son Dennis Doyne [Liber C Page 239]. Mingoe came to court less than five years later, on 10 November 1702. The Court ordered that "he be continued as a servant dureing life" [22.pdf #64].

---

[70] "all negroes and other slaves allready within this province and all negroes and other slaves to bee hereafter Imported into this province shall serve durante vita and all children born of any negro or other slave shall bee slaves as theire fathers ware, for the terme of their lives," An Act Concerning Negroes and other Slaves made Anno 1664 [12.pdf #140, Folio 24]

[71] The Court considered the age of freedom for Mulattoes to be thirty-one, but the law actually stated the age of thirty. The text is as follows:

"whatsoever free born woman shall intermarrage with any slave from and after the last day of this present General Assembly shall serve the master of such slave dureing the life of her husband and yet all the Issue of such free borne weoman soe married, shall bee slaves as theire fathers where and bee it enacted that all the Issues of English or other free born woeman that have already Married negroes, shall serve the masters if theire parence till they bee thirty yeares of age and noe longer," An Act Concerning Negroes and other Slaves made Anno 1664 [12.pdf #140, Folio 24]

[72] Ibid. [12.pdf #140, Folio 24]

John Hayes, "a Negro," claimed that "he came in a servant to Capt. Crabb with indenture out of England for seven years & that giving his Indenture to his master to keep could never get again, supposing he has destroyed it to keep him a slave and has kept him almost sixteen years and do intend to keep him all the days of his life." John Hayes tried and failed to obtain his freedom on 14 June 1720, when the Court ordered that "ye above named John Hayes be a slave during life" [26.pdf #173]; and on 13 August 1728, when he was again "adjudged a slave" [31.pdf #177].

There was one other Petition for Freedom from a Negro. He was already free and he wanted his clothes. Here is the court record, in its entirety:

> "Negro Jupitter Petitions the Court Concerning Cloaths, Mr. Contee being then in Court says he Never Denyed to pay his just Debts, Ordered that the Petitioner Pay all the Charge, Mr. Contee to pay him his Due According to his Indenture"
>
> 4 April 1704 [22.pdf #194]

He had Indentures! There are seventy-five years of Charles County Court Records online, and this is the only black indentured servant, and the only successful petition for freedom, or corn, or clothes, from a black man, that I ever saw. This was an extraordinary man.

Negro Jupiter appears again in the Court Records.

> Memorandum: Whereas Jupiter a free Negro being by the Sherriff Brought here into Court, which said Negro was Comitted to his Custody on Suspicion of Hogg Stealing which said matter being herd before the Grand Jury which said Jury were not Induced by the Evidence produced to them to find any presentment against the said Negro.
>
> Whereupon the said Negro prays that he may be cleared by Proclimacon
>
> The said Negro acquitted.
>
> 13 March 1711 [24.pdf #60].

He was taken into custody by the Sheriff on suspicion of hog stealing, brought before the Grand Jury, and acquitted without indictment.

HOW THE SYSTEM WORKED

RECAPTURED RUNAWAYS

There wasn't much point in bringing a recaptured runaway Negro slave to Court. Negroes were slaves for life, and could not be sentenced to additional time of servitude. [73] The only punishment, or "correction," was whipping, which masters and their overseers were allowed to do. [74]

Three recaptured Mulatto servants, and one recaptured Indian servant, were brought to Charles County Court. On 11 August 1691, James Boareman, "an Indian servant to Capt. John Dent of St. Maryes County," was ordered to be taken into custody and "be delivered to his said master" [17.pdf #138].

On 13 November 1711, John Glover, "a mollato," servant to John Hanson Junr., confessed to 80 days absence, was sentenced to 800 days of servitude, and four months "for four hundred pounds of tobacco expended for takeing him up" [25.pdf #16]. This was the same John Glover who was adjudged to be free at the "age of thirty and one yeares," 9 March 1703 [22.pdf #90]; which would be February 1711, as John Glover was "borne in ye month of February" 1680, by oath of his mother Sarah Smith [22.pdf #125]. Nine months after his thirty first birthday, his date of freedom, he was brought to Court for 80 days absence and given the maximum sentence. Now his expected date of freedom would be May 1714.

On 11 June 1706, Mollatto Will, servant to Capt. Benoni Thomas, confessed to 180 days absence, was sentenced to 1800 days servitude, and "four yeares more for eighteen hundred pounds of tobacco and two pounds and sixpence sterling paid for takeing him up" [23.pdf #123]. This was 3260 days of

---

[73] Virginia law phrased it this way: "negroes who are incapable of makeing satisfaction by addition of time" ["Statutes at Large; Being a collection of All the Laws of Virginia from the First Session of the Legislature in the Year 1619," William Waller Hening, editor, March 1660/61, Act XXII].

[74] In Virginia it was legal to murder your own slave. "if any slave resist his master (or other by his masters order correcting him) and by the extremity of the correction should chance to die, that his death shall not be accompted ffelony, but the master (or that other person appointed by the master to punish him) be acquit from molestation, since it cannot be presumed that prepensed malice (which alone makes murther ffelony) should induce any man to destroy his owne estate." ["Statutes at Large," William Waller Hening, editor, ibid., October 1669, Act I].

servitude, nearly nine years, the second longest sentence ever handed down in Charles County Court for a recaptured runaway. He would not be free until the age of forty.

On 11 March 1729, Thomas Fountain, "a Mallatto servant" to Captain Joseph Douglass, for 30 days absence "whilst John Snoggen was his overseer," and nine months from "the said Douglass," ten months in all, and "four hundred and fifty pounds of tobacco" expended "in takeing him up," ordered to serve "ten dayes for one of his runaway time" (one hundred months servitude) "in full for that and the expences aforesaid" [31.pdf #118]. This was eight years and four months, the third longest sentence ever handed down in Charles County Court for a recaptured runaway. Thomas Fountain is one of four Mullatos in the Index to Orphans. [75] He was "bought of William and Mary Vestry by Mrs. Land and given to her daughter Pennellope Douglass," and was bound to Joseph Douglass on 14 March 1704, "he being six yeares old in May next" [22.pdf #163]. Now he was two months shy of his thirty-first birthday. He would not be free until the age of thirty-nine.

Recaptured runaway white servants, with or without indentures, did not always fare much better. The Perpetual Laws of Maryland were harsh.

> any servant or servants whatsoever unlawfully absenting him her or themselves from his her or their said master, mistris, dame, or overseer shall serve <u>tenn days for every one dayes</u> absence (emphasis in original) [12.pdf #170, Folio 90]

> noe servant or servants whatsoever within this province shall travell by land or watter tenn miles from the house of his her or theire master mistris, or dame, without a noat under theire handes or under the hand of his her or their overseers (if any bee), under the penalty of being taken for a runaway [12.pdf #169, #170, Folios 89, 90]

---

[75] Kate or Katherine, daughter of Elizabeth Edelin spinster, bound to "John Nicholls of Charles County and Batheshebah his wife," he a former white slave child without indentures, 26 February 1708 [23.pdf #236]. Alice Macdonald, daughter of Grace Macdonald now dead or removed out of this County," bound to Thomas & Elizabeth Howard, 14 June 1720 [26.pdf #172]. Ann Willis, "a mallato basterd" "brought here into Court" by Kenett Mackenzey, "left at his house," and "it being afecnate child," bound to Kenett Mackenzey, 10 November 1713 [25.pdf #182]

such person or persons if apprehended not being sufficiently knowen, or able to give a good account of himselfe, to be left to the discresition of judgment of such magistrate before whom such persons as aforesaid shall bee brought to judge thereof (emphasis in original) [12.pdf #170, Folio 90]

and every person or persons apprehending seizing and takeing up such runawayes and persons travelling without passes ... shall have and receive two hundred pounds of tobacco to bee paid by the owner of such runaway so apprehended and taken up if a servant, and if a freeman and refuseing to pay the same then to make sattisfacione by servitude or otherwise as the Justices of the provinciall or County Court where such persons shall bee soe apprehended and taken up shall thinck fit" (emphasis in original) [12.pdf #170, Folio 90]

These last provisions are most pernicious. Traveling strangers beware. Anyone "not sufficiently known," or not "able to give a good account of himself," could be "taken for a runaway," and if innocent, if a free man, and refusing to pay "two hundred pounds of tobacco" to the persons "apprehending seizing" and taking him up, could be sentenced to servitude at the discretion of the Court. And this actually happened, at least twice.

On 10 August 1697, James Fuller was "seized & taken up as a Runnaway" and "comitted into ye Custody of ye Sherife," but "nothing appeareing to ye Court here that hee is a runaway servant," it was "Ordered that ye said James Fuller be discharged hee makeing satisfaction to ye persons seizeing & taking up as a Runaway ye sum of two hundred pounds of tobaccoe" [19.pdf #136]. It was lucky for him he could pay the fine. The sheriff at the time was Capt. John Bayne [19.pdf #38] & [19.pdf #234].

On 21 March 1706, "by vertue of a warrant from under the hand and seale of Mr. Joseph Manning one of the Justices of this Court," James Lee was committed into the custody of "Capt. Walter Story high sherriff of this County" "upon suspition of being a runaway and no master being found for the said James Lee," he was ordered by the Court on 11 June 1706 to "remaine with the said Capt. Walter Story two yeares fully" "to commence from the last of October next" as "sattisfaction for his fees" [23.pdf #123].

Seventy-two years later, on 1 July 1778, the delegates to the Continental Congress signed the Articles of Confederation. The very first right of the people enshrined therein is the right to travel freely [Article IV].

Recaptured runaways faced a two-part sentence. They could be sentenced for the "runaway time," and for the cost of "taking them up."

The ratio of "tenn days for every one dayes absence" provided by law was treated as a maximum, and was applied eight times out of ten. There are 293 judgments in which the ratio for "runaway time" is specified:

ten to one	231	seven to one	6	four to one	5
nine to one	1	six to one	6	three to one	4
eight to one	21	five to one	17	two to one	2

There are 300 recaptured runaways in seventy-five years of Charles County Court Records. Only once did the judges state their formula for "taking them up." Angus Ross, servant to Thomas Coombs, on 9 November 1731, was sentenced "two days for each one of his runaway time," and "one month for each hundred pounds of tobacco" expended in taking him up [32.pdf #15].

The ratio for "taking them up" was treated as a sentencing guideline. There are 83 judgments with separate penalties for tobacco expended:

> 37 received one month for each hundred pounds of tobacco
> 25 received longer sentences   21 received shorter sentences

That is how the system worked. The judges could be quite arbitrary.

Some recaptured runaways with very long absences received no leniency for their "runaway time." The three Mulattos (see above), absent 80 days, 180 days, and ten months, all received the maximum sentences of ten days for one. So did 34 others who were absent 80 days or longer, including 23 who were absent 100 days or longer, 18 who were absent 140 days or longer, and five who were absent 200 days or longer. One of these, a servant to William Smallwood, absent 200 days, is not named in the record. Another, the aforesaid Teague Turlayes, servant to ye said Philip Lynes, without necessary clothing or a bed to lie on, [19.pdf #111] was absent 240 days in all, but forty days were deducted because Teague Turlayes "went severall times to complaine" to the Court [19.pdf #73]. (See Abuse and Neglect).

Rosomon or Rosamond Law was absent twice: 148 days from Robert Hagar, 1480 days servitude, 12 November 1706 [23.pdf #152]; and 338 days from Alexander Wilson, 3380 days servitude, 14 June 1715 [25.pdf #271]. The second sentence was the longest ever handed down in Charles County Court for a recaptured runaway. She would not be free until September 1724.

Silent Ball ran away five times, from three different masters: 132 days from William Thompson, 11 November 1690 [17.pdf #69]; 11 days from William Thompson and 30 days from Benjamin Posey, 11 September 1694 [18.pdf #194]; 41 days from Benjamin Posey, 11 August 1696 [19.pdf #41]; and 50 days from Thomas Davis, 8 June 1697 [19.pdf #130]. Each time, Silent Ball was given the maximum sentence of ten days for one. It adds up. On 10 January 1699, she petitioned the Court "to gett Copyes of ye severall Judgments entered against her for her Runaway time" [20.pdf #4].

John Bacon, servant to Mr. Henry Hawkins, was absent "ye space of 235 days," for which he was sentenced to "seaven years nine months three weekes & five dayes," which works out to 2850 days, not 2350 [14.pdf #9]. I don't know who did the math, but Mr. Henry Hawkins was sitting on the bench that day as one of the "Worshippfull Commissioners" [14.pdf #7].

The penalty for "taking them up" was rarely more than two months longer or shorter than one month for each hundred pounds of tobacco. The most lenient sentence went to James Hollywood. For "ye sum of six hundred pounds of tobaccoe disburst & expended for ye takeing up & bringing home him twice out of ye Colony of Virginia," he was to serve three months [18.pdf #144]. But some sentences were extraordinarily harsh.

Bunn, Anthony, for "two thousand one hundred and twenty pounds of
    tobacco," three years [31.pdf #118]
Careless, Mary, for fifty-two days absence and "three hundred pounds of
    tobacco, two years & a half," i.e., nineteen months for the tobacco
    [27.pdf #108]
Crouch, Edmund, "two whole years" for "tymes and expenses"
    [25.pdf #181]
Gains, Grizzle, "three years" "for three pounds current money & eleven
    hundred & fifty pounds of tobacco expended about her"
    [26.pdf #96]
Todd, Jeremiah, for one thousand two hundred and tenne pounds of tobacco,
    "one whole yeare and a halfe" [23.pdf #115]
Wild, Catherine, for "six hundred & twenty pounds of tobacco," "ten months
    for the tobacco" and "six weeks for ten shillings" [29.pdf #25]
Wormely, Mary, for "six hundred pounds of tobacco," one year
    [28.pdf #53]

And the aforesaid James Lee, an innocent man taken into custody "upon suspition of being a runnaway," to pay the reward of "two hundred pounds of tobacco" to "every person or persons apprehending seizing and takeing up such runawayes and persons travelling without passes," two years of slavery.

These formulas, inconsistently applied, often resulted in longer sentences for the tobacco expended than for the runaway time itself. This happened on thirty-two occasions. Here is the most egregious example:

Coody, Charron, servant to John Allen, 8 March 1715, 6 days absence, ordered "that he serve according to law" (60 days servitude), and "eighteen months in consideration of" "sixteen hundred pounds of tobacco which the said John had paid" [25.pdf #265]

It is hard to imagine how so much tobacco was expended in six days, unless eight different people were claiming the reward. The Court Record states that John Allen did produce accounts of his fees, which were not transcribed. But the effect upon Charron Coody was devastating. For six days absence he was sentenced to twenty months of servitude, a ratio of a hundred to one.

John Butterfeild, for 3 days absence, was sentenced to 30 days for the "runaway time" and four months "for the charges." That is 150 days for 3, a ratio of 50 to 1 [28.pdf #185]. The aforesaid Edmund Crouch, for 19 days absence, was sentenced to 190 days for the "runaway time" and "two whole years" for "tymes and expenses." That is 920 days for 19, a ratio of 48 to 1 [25.pdf #181]. Christopher Collins and Edward Edge, for 7 days absence, were sentenced to 70 days for the "runaway time" and eight months for "forty shillings" expended. That is 310 days for 7, a ratio of 44 to 1 [31.pdf #118]. Alexander Ware, for 7 days absence, was sentenced to 70 days for the "runaway time" and six months for the expenses." That is 250 days for 7, a ratio of 35 to 1 [23.pdf #372]. Within eight months he was brought back to Court, having run away for a longer time [24.pdf #29].

There were 300 recaptured runaways brought to Charles County Court. Seventy-four of them had multiple absences: forty-two from one master, and thirty-two from multiple masters. The aforesaid Silent Ball was absent five times from three masters, a total of 264 days. Thomas Burdett was absent three times from three masters, for 23 days [22.pdf #22] & [23.pdf #46].

James Drunckore did "runaway at severall times" from Mrs. Anne Burford, 112 days in all, 13 September 1692 [17.pdf #255]. He ran away from William Forester, 33 days; and from "his wife Dorothy Forster before marryage," 8 days, 13 March 1694 [18.pdf #144]. For these he was given the maximum sentence of ten days for one, 1120 days and 410 days. He appears one more time in the surviving index to a lost Court Order Book for "judgment of his runaway time" [Liber T Page 110]. And never again after that. We don't know if he ever got free.

Bryan Harrison was absent "severall times" from Robert Thompson, 98 days in all, for which he was sentenced to 980 days for the "runaway time" and four months "for four hundred pounds of tobaccoe expended," 9 September 1690 [17.pdf #37]. He was absent "severall times" from Jefferry Cole, 10 days in all, for which he was sentenced to 100 days servitude and three months "for four hundred pounds of tobaccoe," 9 June 1691 [17.pdf #114]. He ran away again from Jefferry Cole. He appears twice in the index for the lost book, "for runaway time & order for sattisfaction for his taking him up in Virginia," 1694 [Liber T Page 30] and for "his judgment for runaway time," 1695 [Liber T Page 290]; and one more time in a surviving book, 45 days absence, 450 days servitude, 10 November 1696 [19.pdf #73]. And never again after that. We don't know if he ever got free.

These vindictive sentences created an incentive to run away again. Of the 300 recaptured runaways in the Charles County Court Records, forty were without indentures. Of these, seventeen appear in the records later on as free persons, and are listed in the Encyclopedia of Survivors. Twenty-three are listed as "Without Indentures, Elsewhere in Record, Not Yet Free." They never again appear in the records. We don't know what became of them.

That is the problem with an Index to Recaptured Runaways. We do not know the names of the runaways who succeeded. Well, except when we do.

Bradey, Joseph, servant to Capt. Randolph Brandt Senior, 26 January 1692, absent seven times, 26 days in all, account filed, servant not appearing, no order or judgment by Court [17.pdf #254]

Obviously, Joseph Bradey had run away again. He was not recaptured.

Four servants are actually identified as successful runaways. John Parnham Senr. entrusted four of his servants, "namely Joakin Jones, Daniel Russell, Isaac Jones and John Miller," with a "Craft," a boat, "to fetch in Tobacco." And guess what. He never got the tobacco so he couldn't pay his taxes, and he never got his boat back either. And "the said Servants are all runaway," and so, being "deprived of their service," he humbly prays that "they may be struck out of the List of Taxables" 8 August 1732 [32.pdf #100].

Equipped with a boat so large it took four strong young men to row it, carrying a load of tobacco which was the currency of the day, all they had to do to get free was to head north and keep on rowing, to the head of the Chesapeake Bay, to Pennsylvania, to Quaker country.

HOW THE RESISTANCE WORKED

The Quakers of Germantown, Pennsylvania were the first religious body in the English colonies to publicly protest against slavery. The "Germantown Protest" was drafted on 18 February 1688 by Francis Daniell Pastorius and signed by him and three other Germantown Quakers -- Garret Hendericks, Derick up de Graeff, and Abraham up den Graef. It begins as follows:

> These are the reasons why we are against the traffik of men-body, as followeth. Is there any that would be done or handled at this manner? viz., to be sold or made a slave for all the time of his life? How fearful and faint-hearted are many on sea when they see a strange vessel — being afraid it should be a Turk, and they should be taken, and sold for slaves into Turkey. Now what is this better done, as Turks doe? Yea, rather is it worse for them which say they are Christians, for we hear that ye most part of such negers are brought hitherto against their will and consent and that many of them are stolen. Now tho they are black we cannot conceive there is more liberty to have them slaves, as it is to have other white ones. There is a saying that we shall doe to all men like as we will be done ourselves; making no difference of what generation, descent or colour they are. And those who steal or rob men, and those who buy or purchase them, are they not alike? Here is liberty of conscience wch is right and reasonable; here ought to be likewise liberty of ye body, except of evil-doers, wch is an other case. But to bring men hither, or to rob and sell them against their will, we stand against. [76]

We do not know what became of Joakin Jones, Daniel Russell, Isaac Jones and John Miller. Our best evidence is geography. White slaves who escaped by boat would not have gone onto the open ocean. Nor would they have ventured into the inlets of the Chesapeake Bay, where they might be recaptured and returned to their owners. They would have headed north to Pennsylvania, seeking refuge with the Quakers.

That is what runaway Negro slaves did in North Carolina in the early days of the republic. In the 1790 census for Randolph County, three Quaker men had free colored persons living in their houses. William Newby had one, Jonathan Phelps had three, and William Hill had five. In the 1800 census for Randolph County, there were ten Quaker households that housed more than

---

[76] "The Germantown Protest," http://www.yale.edu/glc/aces/germantown.htm

sixty free colored persons altogether. Two of them, Henry Yount and Jesse Henley, had twenty-one each. It was no secret. They told the census taker straight out. They were members of Back Creek Monthly Meeting. [77]

White slaves who escaped on foot could not have traveled northward, for the inlets of the Chesapeake Bay would have prevented them from passing from one peninsula to the next. If they were of English descent they might have been able to blend into a community in some county far away, but not if they had a Scottish or Irish accent. Their only hope of safety would have been in the mountains, beyond the long arm of the law. Of the 300 recaptured runaways found in the Charles County Court Records, fifteen who were enslaved in Maryland were recaptured elsewhere, always in Virginia. Of these, five ran away from Philip Lines and were all brought back to Court on 10 January 1682. [78] Nine of the other ten runaways recaptured in Virginia were brought back to Court between 1690 and 1706. [79] This is a strong indication as to where these runaways were heading. They must have crossed the Potomac River somewhere above the Fall Line (the site of present-day Washington, D.C.), possibly as far upstream as its confluence with the Shenandoah River (the site of present-day Harpers Ferry). If they could cross the rivers here, they were free. The Shenandoah Valley was unsettled territory, beyond the long arm of the law.

> "Extending north and south through the valley was a relatively good Indian path, called by various names including the Appalachian Warriors' Path and the Shenandoah Hunting Path. By the mid-eighteenth century, it had been developed into the Great Wagon Road, which eventually led from Pennsylvania southward through the valley and on to Georgia." [80]

---

[77] The others were Pharaoh Fentress, John Henley, Benjamin Hill, William Hill, William Newby, Phinehas Nixon, John Smith, and Thomas Winslow.

[78] James Gilbard (1682), John Hawkins (1682), Elizabeth Powell (1682), Thomas Powell (1682), Hugh Williams (1682). See "Recaptured Runaways."

[79] John Cooke (1699), Mary Dallyson (1680), John Edgerley (1703), Henry Evers (1698), Bryan Harrison (twice, 1690, 1694), James Hollywood (twice, 1694), James Kenneday (1706), Joseph Leman (1704), William Sumerton (1697), John Thompson (1690). See "Recaptured Runaways."

[80] ."A History of Roads in Virginia," Produced by the Virginia Department of Transportation Office of Public Affairs," 2002.
http://www.loudounhistory.org/history/virginia-transportation.htm

This Indian path led all the way to the Cumberland Gap, near the boundaries of present-day Kentucky, Tennessee, and Virginia. It is the only pass in the otherwise continuous Cumberland Mountain ridge line. It was not unknown to the white man. The earliest written account of Cumberland Gap was written by Abraham Wood of Virginia in the 1670s. [81]

Some of the runaways, or their descendants, may have made it this far. The evidence is circumstantial, based upon the surnames. The last runaways listed in this book were recaptured in 1732. The earliest surviving records for the State of Kentucky are the 1800 tax list, the 1810 census, and the early marriages dating to 1796. Thus the families, if any, of these recaptured runaways cannot be traced forward. But some of the surnames can be.

Of the 300 recaptured runaways found in the Charles County Court Records, only twenty-seven appear in the Court Records later on as free persons. Of these, seventeen were without indentures and appear in the Encyclopedia of Survivors, [82] and the other ten are listed as Recaptured Runaways, Elsewhere in the Record. [83]

That leaves 273 recaptured runaways unaccounted for. Of these, seventy were female, and their married names will never be known. This leaves 203 recaptured runaways, all of them male. Some of them died during servitude. Some of them survived, but kept a low profile, and never again appeared in the Court Records. Some of them served their sentences, and moved to another county or another colony to start a new life. But some of them ran away again, this time successfully. After all, tacking on additional months or years to their original sentences as punishment for running away created even more incentive to run away again. Many of these runaways had common surnames found in many places in the early records. But some had distinctive surnames which appear primarily in the records of Kentucky.

---

[81] https://en.wikipedia.org/wiki/Cumberland_Gap

[82] Robert Barton, Samuell Burgesse, Hugh Davies, Argalus Gill, William Gray, Thomas Hill, James Holliewood, Grace Holmes, Robert Jones, James Low, Margaret Macclannen, Daniell Mahoni, Ellis Morris, William Roberts, Walter Toy, Edward Waters, James Welch

[83] Silent Ball, Thomas Barker, Joseph Cheatham, Taddy Ganer, John Hawkins, William Hoskins, Edward Lewis, Wiliam Moody, Thomas Ruth, John Thompson.

EARLY KENTUCKY RECORDS

Surname	Counties
Atterberry	Barren, Hardin, Grayson, Ohio
Caddock	Barren
Cavenaugh	Christian, Clark, Hopkins, Madison
Ellison	Montgomery, Warren
Farrell	Clark, Cumberland, Livingston
Goddard	Bourbon, Fleming, Scott
Groves	Caldwell, Fleming, Hopkins, Montgomery, Muhlenberg
Hagan	Barren, Clark, Nelson, Washington
Herald	Floyd, Garrard, Livingston, Warren, Washington
Lackey	Clark, Garrard, Madison
Lawler	Franklin, Jefferson, Mercer, Shelby
Leach, Leech	Barren, Mason, Scott
McDonnall	Clark, Hardin, Mason, Nelson
McNew	Hardin, Henry, Muhlenberg, Shelby
Pell	Bracken, Lewis
Rouse	Boone, Mason
Todd	Bourbon, Fayette, Madison, Shelby
Turley	Bourbon, Madison, Montgomery, Pulaski
Ware	Campbell, Clark, Franklin, Shelby

Three of the recaptured runaways with these surnames are among the white slave children without indentures who have been matched up with their baptismal records in a companion volume, *"White Slave Children of Colonial Maryland and Virginia: Birth and Shipping Records,"* in preparation.

James Lackey was the son of Henry and Mary Lackey, Baptized 22 April 1690, Crediton, Devon, England.

James Leach was the illegitimate child of Alexander Roads and Susan Leach, Baptized 19 July 1663, Saint Mary, Oldham, Lancashire, England.

Jeremiah Tod was the son of Jeremiah and Anne Tod, Baptized 14 December 1684, Epping, Essex, England.

Running away was, of course, the most direct form of resistance to slavery. But aiding and abetting the resistance, in any way, was a crime. Consider the following excerpts from "An Act Relating to Servants and Slaves." [84]

"noe Servant or Servants whatsoever within this province whither by Indenture or according to the Custome of the Countrey or hired for wages shall travell by Land or water tenn miles from the house of his her or their Master or mistrisse or dame without a noate under their hands or under the hand of his her or their Overseer (if any be) under the Penalty of being taken for a Runnaway & to Suffer Such penaltyes as are hereafter provided against Runnawayes."

"any Such Servant or Servants as aforesaid unlawfully absenting him her or themselves from his her or their said master mistrisse Dame or Overseer Shall Serve tenn dayes for every one dayes absence"

"any person or persons whatsoever within this Province that shall wittingly or willingly deteyne any such Servant or Servants unlawfully absenting him her or themselves as aforesaid shall be fined five hundred pounds of Tobacco for every night or four & twenty houres that such person or persons shall give Entertainment to such servant or servants one halfe to the Lord Proprietary & the other halfe to the Informer"

Some people, at great risk to themselves, did "entertain" runaway slaves. On 11 June 1706, Edward Darnall was indicted for "entertaining" William Mackeboy, "a servant man belonging to Mr. John Smith" "for the space of one night or twenty four hours without the leave or lycence of him the said John Smith." Cornelius White was assigned to defend him, a jury was "impannelled," and the said Edward Darnall was "acquitted and discharged." [23.pdf #122, #142]. (See Encyclopedia of Survivors) Edward Darnall had reason to be sympathetic. A former white slave child without indentures, he was one of the three servants to Philip Lynes who, on 8 November 1691, "came here into Court naked & made complaint that for want of clothes they were allmost starved" [17.pdf #157]. (See Encyclopedia of Survivors).

---

[84] "Proceedings and Acts of the General Assembly," May-June 1676, Liber W H & L, pp. 102-107, Archives of Maryland Online, Volume 2, Pages 523-528. http://msa.maryland.gov/megafile/msa/speccol/sc2900/sc2908/000001/000002/html/am2--523.html See also Perpetual Laws of Maryland [19.pdf #169 et seq.]

There was no way to protest the laws of Maryland, or the acts of those charged with enforcing those laws. Such criticism was likewise illegal. This was the very first provision of the laws enacted in 1658. [85]

> "1st That all ministers of Justice & Officers military with all other persons whatsoever be & remaine indemnified on both sides & freed from any Charge or questioninge for any Act or passage made or done in ye transactions of ye affaires of this Province"

There appears to have been no formal protest against slavery in Maryland until after the onset of the American Revolution. "In 1780 the National Methodist Conference in Baltimore officially condemned slavery, and in 1784 the church went further, threatening Methodist preachers with suspension if they owned slaves." "In the mid-1790s the Methodists and Quakers drew together to form the Maryland Society for the Abolition of Slavery." [86]

During the colonial period, opposition to slavery in Maryland was entirely underground. What the record shows, therefore, is not formal protestations, but acts of kindness -- a willingness by others to help the survivors make a new life for themselves, and by the survivors, when well established on their own, to make a better life for those less fortunate. The evidence is scattered throughout the Encyclopedia of Survivors, and is highlighted here.

Mathew Saunders was the first of the survivors to own land. He was not able to do it alone. He became a free man c. 8 July 1669, and within two years time, on 14 March 1671, at age twenty-four, he and William Boyden purchased 80 acres from John Boyden. [87] Five years later, on 9 March 1676, he and Thomas Bryant purchased 150 acres from Garrett Sinnett. Not until 8 June 1683, at age thirty-five, was Mathew Saunders able to purchase land on his own, 200 acres from none other than Philip Lynes.

---

[85] "Acts made at a generall Assembly held at St. Leonards Begining ye 16th of Aprill Anno Domini 1658 by Capt. Josias Fendall Esqre" [19.pdf #135]

[86] https://en.wikipedia.org/wiki/History_of_slavery_in_Maryland See also "A Guide to the History of Slavery in Maryland," The Maryland State Archives, Annapolis, Maryland, and the University of Maryland College Park, Maryland," page 9. http://msa.maryland.gov/msa/intromsa/pdf/slavery_pamphlet.pdf

[87] John Boyden was the father of William Boyden (see "Gifts of Livestock"). Both were large landowners (see "Grantee Index to Deeds").

The second survivor to own land was John Hammond. He was not able to buy it all at once. He became a free man c. 7 April 1675. Within one year, at age twenty-one, William and Ruth Loveday sold him "one & Equall halfe of eighty five acres," on 14 March 1676, and a year and a half later they sold him the other half, on 13 November 1677. [88]

The third survivors to own land were Rice Waedman (Wayman, Waynman, Wainman), who became free c. 14 March 1671 at age twenty-seven, and Joseph Wolfe (Wolph), who became free c. 8 March 1673 at age twenty-one. [89] They bought 200 acres together, at the ages of thirty-four and twenty-seven, from John and Margarett Cassock, on 12 October 1678. [90]

Two other survivors needed partners with whom to purchase land. Thomas Phillips, who became a free man c. 13 March 1684, bought 234 acres, at age twenty-seven, with William Griffine, from Joseph and Margrett Cornall, on 2 June 1687. Francis Marbury (Marberry, Malberry), who became a free man c. 13 November 1684, bought 200 acres, at age thirty-one, with Morris Loyde, from Edward and Mary Scott, on 28 November 1690. [91]

Altogether, of the 194 persons listed in the "Encyclopedia of Survivors," only 33 became landowners in Charles County, Maryland, unless there were others whose deeds were never recorded. All these land acquisitions were by purchase. None were by land patents from the Province of Maryland. [92]

---

[88] William Loveday died shortly thereafter, before 9 September 1679 (see "Index to Deaths and Estates").

[89] Rice Waynman and Joseph Wolph were lifelong friends (see "Index to Deaths and Estates").

[90] John and Margaret Cassock, and their children, Benjamin and Sarah, appear elsewhere in the record (see "Grantee Index to Deeds," "Gifts of Livestock," and "Index to Deaths and Estates").

[91] Morris Loyd later bought land on his own, on 29 December 1694 (see "Grantee Index to Deeds"). He died before 9 June 1696 (see "Index to Deaths and Estates").

[92] In 1663, Maryland repealed "that Clause Injoyning fifty Acres of Land to be allowed to Servants att the end of his or their Service," and "for the future there shall be nothing allowed to any Servant att the end or Expiracon of his or their Service more then their Clothes, Howes, Axe & Corne" See "Proceedings and Acts of the General Assembly, January 1637/8-September 1664," Volume 1, Page 496, Sept.-Oct. 1663. http://aomol.net/000001/000001/html/am1--496.html

Gifts of livestock were usually from parent to child, or otherwise within the family. But sometimes these gifts were acts of generosity between friends.

Sometimes these gifts of livestock were from one survivor to the child of another. Joseph Gray, a survivor, who became a free man c. 10 June 1673, together with Richard Newton, [93] "for the Intire Love and Affection that wee beare unto John Jones Sonn unto Moses Jones," gave him "two yearling Heiffers" on 10 September 1689. Moses Jones was a survivor who became a free man on 10 June 1679, at age twenty-one, when he produced his indenture in Court after four years of servitude, three years before his otherwise expected date of freedom. Mary Wolph, "ye daughter of Joseph Wolph," a survivor (see above), registered her "marke of a cow calfe given her by Richard Wayman," a survivor (see above), on 8 August 1682.

Sometimes these gifts of livestock were to the child of a survivor from a friend who had not been a slave. Mary Wilkinson, "ye daughter of Lancelott & Mary Wilkinson," registered "her marke of a cow given her by Magdalen Tayler ye wife of William Tayler" on 14 November 1693. [94] Lancelot Wilkinson, a survivor, had become a free man c. 9 January 1678.

Sometimes these gifts of livestock were from a survivor to the child of a friend who had not been a slave. Peter Farnadis (Pedro Fernandez), "cooper," a survivor, who became a free man c. 13 April 1676, gave "unto Edward Branner Sonne of Henry Branner," planter, "one Mare yearlen" on 14 September 1686. [95] Henry Thompson, "planter," a survivor, who became a free man c. 11 March 1686, [96] gave "unto Margarett Mankin ye daughter of Stephen & Mary Mankin one dark bay filly with a small blaze in its face & one white foote ye said filly being a yeare old next March," on 10 January 1693. [97]

---

[93] Richard Newton was the son of "old" John Newton (see "Gifts of Livestock"). He had a wife named Jane and a son named Richard (see "Vital Records").

[94] William Taylor died before 14 September 1697. Magdalen Taylor, his wife, was adminstrator of his estate (see "Index to Deaths and Estates").

[95] Henry Branner became a landowner, purchasing 100 acres "on ye South Side of Mattawoman Creeke," on 1 March 1688 (see "Grantee Index to Deeds"). Henry Brawner, "of Mattawoman," had a wife named Mary and a son named John (see "Vital Records").

Four survivors of child slavery who died young, as free men, in their thirties, had their estates administered by fellow survivors. Rice Waynman (see above), at age forty-one, was administrator of the estate of Joseph Wolph (see above), who died before 9 September 1685 at age thirty-four, [98] and was executor of the estate of Mary Wolfe, his widow, who died before 12 January 1686. Robert Benson, at age forty-three, was administrator of the estate of John Francis, who died before 9 September 1690 at age thirty. [99] Marke Lampton, at age forty-two, was the executor of the estate of Joshuah Hingle, who died before 10 March 1691 at age thirty-four. [100] John Magrah, at age thirty-three, was administrator of the estate of Patrick Moreland (or Morand), who died before 9 June 1719 at age thirty-nine. [101]

Four persons are on the record as having tended to survivors of child slavery in their dying days. Doctor William Hall "did attend upon Mr. William Barrett in his sicknes & administred medicines to him." William Barrett

---

[96] Henry Thompson was an abused child who became a child abuser. He was adjudged to be sixteen on 11 March 1679 and ordered to serve seven years. He became an Overseer to Philip Lynes, and was brought to Court on 11 August 1691 for "hard usage" of Catherine Jones, servant to Philip Lynes (see "Dishonorable Mentions"). Henry Thompson died before 8 August 1699. Isabella Thompson was administrator of his estate (see "Index to Deaths and Estates").

[97] Stephen and Mary Mankin had three sons named John, Josiah, Stephen (see "Gifts of Livestock"), James, and Tubman (see "Vital Records" and "Index to Orphans"), and two daughters, Margarett (see "Gifts of Livestock") and Hope (see "Vital Records" and "Index to Orphans"). Stephen Mankin died before 4 April 1699 (see "Index to Deaths and Estates"). His wife, the former Mary Stigaleer, survived him, but gave up three minor children for adoption (see "Index to Orphans").

[98] Joseph Wolph had no land, but he did have "hogges & cattle" (see "Encyclopedia of Survivors").

[99] John Francis had no land, but he did have "hogges & cattle" (see "Encyclopedia of Survivors").

[100] Joshua Hingle had no land, and no recorded mark for livestock. The only evidence that he survived his servitude is his probate case.

[101] Patrick Moreland had no land, but he did have "cattle and hoggs" (see "Encyclopedia of Survivors"). Both he and John Magrah had been "servants" to Capt. John Bayne -- Moreland in the field, Magrah in the house of ill repute.

died before 9 June 1691 at age twenty-nine. [102] Mary Brawner, widow, petitioned the Court "for an alloweance for her trouble in lookeing after and takeing care of one Joseph Voux and his wife in ye time of their sicknes ye one being eight dayes ye other sixteene dayes sick and for her trouble in burying of them." Joseph Vaux died before 19 April 1698 at age thirty. [103] Arthur Elie (or Etie) petitioned the Court that Samuell Burgess "lay very sick at your petitioners house who in the time of his sicknesse your petitioner nursed tended and cherished him to the utmost of his ability and soone after dyed." Samuell Burgesse died before 13 January 1702. Because his age was not adjudged when he was sentenced to serve "according to ye custome of ye country" on 11 March 1690, his "Indenture not being under ye seale of any Office," we do not know his age when he died. [104] Johanna Bawdry petitioned the Court "for an allowance in ye next County Levy for burying Jonathan Wood," who died before 8 March 1720 at age thirty-three. [105]

Twenty-one survivors of child slavery adopted orphans or bastards. Their actions display an empathy that was utterly lacking in the men who captured them, transported them, sold them, and enslaved them.

---

[102] William Barrett had no land, and no recorded mark of livestock, and was apparently indigent. Doctor William Hall was granted "four hundred pounds of tobaccoe" by the Court for his medical services. William Hall had a wife named Mary and a son named John (see "Vital Records").

[103] Joseph Vaux had no land, and no recorded mark of livestock. Mary Brawner was allowed "eight hundred pounds of tobaccoe" by the Court for her care giving. She was the widow of Henry Branner or Brawner, "of Mattawoman," who purchased 100 acres "on ye South Side of Mattawoman Creeke," on 1 March 1688 (see "Grantee Index to Deeds"). His son Edward was given one mare yearling by Pedro Fernandez, a survivor, on 14 September 1686 (see "Gifts of Livestock"). His son John was born 2 April 1693 (see "Vital Records").

[104] Samuell Burgess was a servant to Mrs. Elinor Bayne, mother of Capt. John Bayne. On 13 February 1700, two years before his death, he was sued by Thomas Whichaley, formerly an "undersherife" to John Bayne. Arthur Elie, or Etie, was probably Arthur Effye Jr., son of Arthur Effye Sr., born c. 1665, who was aged 26 on 11 August 1691 (see "Vital Records").

[105] Jonathan Wood had no land, and no recorded mark for livestock. The only evidence that he survived his servitude is his burial. The petition of Johanna Bawdry was "adjudged frivilous & therefore rejected."

In three cases, a survivor adopted the child of a fellow survivor. John Hammond adopted Onsley Hill, born 5 May 1677, the orphan child of Thomas Hill, who died before 13 January 1680 at the age of twenty-five, and his wife Mary, both of them former "servants" to Benjamin Rozer. [106] The adoption was finalized on 8 January 1684, after John Hammond had cared for the child for four years. [107] Thomas Hill (not the same person), on 9 June 1713, adopted Benjamin Nicholls, "an infant child of a certayne John Nicholls deceased," who "contracted with the said Nicholls in his life tyme that for keeping & maintayneing the said child for one yeare he was to have an receive a cow & calfe & five hundred pounds of tobacco." Edward Milstead, on 8 March 1692, adopted John Hanby, thirteen months old, bastard child of Francis Hanby, "which he had by Elizabeth Hazleton." [108]

Some of these orphans were so fortunate as to be bound to a survivor who had become a skilled craftsman, as his apprentice, to learn a trade. John Chandler, on 11 November 1707, adopted Edward Kite, "being two yeares old," the son of Anne Kite, he "to learne him the trade of a shoe maker" and "at the expiration of his time to sett him out with a sett of shoe makers tooles." Nine months later, on 10 August 1708, John Chandler adopted Thomas Douglass, age not stated, by his own consent, he "to learne the trade of a tanner and shoomaker." John King, on 8 March 1720, adopted Thomas Barron, "a minor orphan of about fifteen years of age," he "to learn ye said Thomas ye art and (mastery) of a shipwright & to give him six months schooling." Edward Williams, on 8 June 1708, adopted Charles Regon, orphan, parents not named, age not stated, he "to learn him the said Charles Regon the trade of a cooper (viz.) to make tobacco hogs heads," "and at the expiration" of his time "to give him a sett of coopers tooles and a new suit of cloaths either of broad cloth or of kersey with hat shoes and stockings."

---

[106] The wife of John Hammond was the former Abigail Yates. She was also a former servant to Benjamin Rozer, coming from London "in ye good ship called ye Pelican of London Captn. John Bowman Comander," arriving on 2 June 1674 with indentures for four years (see "Encyclopedia of Survivors").

[107] John Hammond received from the Court eight hundred pounds of tobacco per year for "keepeing and mainyaineing Onsley Hill" during this time (see "Encyclopedia of Survivors").

[108] Edward Milstead had himself "begotten on ye bodie of Susan Clarke" a bastard child named William Milstead, who was given up for adoption to Thomas Craxton "of Nangemie in Charles Countie," on 9 November 1686 (see "Encyclopedia of Survivors"). This was his chance to make amends.

Other orphans were simply rescued. Thomas Dickison, on 10 January 1699, adopted Richard Ward, age not stated, after he complained to the Court "against Joseph Ward his master for abusing of him and not allowing him sufficient & necessary clothing & bedding." The Court, stating "that ye said Richard Ward" was "naked without a shirt and never a bed to lie on," ordered him "removed out of ye said Joseph Wards custody" and bound to Thomas Dickson (sic), he "findeing & allowing him sufficient meate drinke washing lodgeing & clothing." Rice Wayman (see above), on 11 January 1676, adopted Beteres Clarke, three years old, an abandoned child, the daughter of Robert Clarke "who is runaway" and Mary Clarke deceased.

SURVIVORS WHO ADOPTED ORPHANS AND BASTARDS

Name of survivor	Age	Date of Adoption	Name and age of child
Benson, Robert	age 40	8 Mar 1687	Bartlett, Thomas
Benson, Robert	age 46	8 Aug 1693	Herrickson, Hans (4)
Chandler, John	age 29	11 Nov 1707	Kite, Edward (2)
Chandler, John	age 30	10 Aug 1708	Douglass, Thomas
Compton, William	age 52	11 Mar 1712	Penny, James (14)
Cooper, John	age 49	11 Aug 1713	Sharman, Elizabeth (7)
Cooper, John	age 49	11 Aug 1713	Sharman, Bead (4)
Dickison, Thomas	age 40/41	10 Jan 1699	Ward, Richard
Glasson, John	age 33	Mar 1716	Haream., Eleanor
Glasson, John	age 33	Mar 1716	Haream., Thomas
Hamond, John	age 25	13 Jan 1680	Hill, Onsley (2)
Hill, Thomas	age 59	9 Jun 1713	Nicholls, Benjamin *
Jones, Moses	age 33	11 Aug 1691	Bartlett, Mary (9)
King, John	age 31	8 Mar 1720	Barron, Thomas (15)
Macdonald, Daniel	age 29	9 Jun 1713	Jackson, William (2)
Millsteade, Edward	age 36	8 Mar 1692	Hanby, John (1)
Milstead, Edward	age 64	14 Jun 1720	Ward, James (15)
Nicholls, John	age not judged	26 Feb 1708	Kate or Katherine (2)
Richardson, William	age 34	12 Aug 1707	Thompson, Charity
Sanders, Matthew	age 72	9 Jun 1719	Robertson, Robert
Sanders, Matthew	age 72	9 Jun 1719	Robertson, William
Thompson, James	age 33	8 Sep 1696	Gillroy, Catherine
Tymothy, William	age 29	8 Mar 1681	"a bastard child"
Wayman, Rice	age 32	11 Jan 1676	Clarke, Beteres (3)
Wilder, Robert	age 29	10 Jan 1682	"an orphan child"
Williams, Edward	age 51	8 Jun 1708	Regon, Charles
Williams, John	age 45	11 Nov 1701	Smoote, John

* Benjamin Nicholls, son of John and Bethsheba Nicholls deceased, was born 8 March 1713, and was three months old when adopted.

Finally, there were nine survivors who purchased servants without indentures on the auction block. This was the most direct method of rescue available. There was no formal protest. The purchasers were not breaking any laws. They would not be charged with any crime, so long as they brought the purchased children to court to have their ages adjudged and be sentenced to serve according to law. It was not a crime to be merciful.

The nine who were rescued were aged 14 to 22. None of the nine appear in the record as recaptured runaways, or complaining of abuse or neglect, or petitioning for freedom. [109] There is no evidence of mistreatment.

The nine purchasers were established middle-aged men, aged 39 to 54. The purchases took place between 1688 and 1710. [110]

The first survivor to rescue a child from the auction block was Marke Lampton, on 12 June 1688. [111] He was 39 years old, with a wife and five children, aged eight months to ten years. Three more children were born later. He owned hogs and cattle, and at least 353 acres of land.

The second survivor to rescue a child from the auction block was Robert Benson, on 8 August 1693. He was 46 years old, and probably not married. He owned 113 acres of land, and at least "one bay mare." He had adopted one boy, Thomas Bartlett, age not known, six years earlier.

In 1699 the market was flooded with white slave children. This was one year after the Royal African Company lost its monopoly on the African slave trade, and the handwriting was on the wall. Unlimited numbers of Negroes, much the more valuable as slaves for life, would soon knock the bottom out of the market for white children with limited terms of servitude.

---

[109] Of the nine who were rescued, John Cole is the only one who appears in the "Encyclopedia of Survivors." His will was dated 28 May 1724. Age at death 49. He was survived by his "loving wife" and six children.

[110] There was a tenth survivor who purchased kidnapped children, namely, Henry Hardy, on 10 June 1679. He was an abused child who became a child abuser. A full biography of Henry Hardy appears earlier in this book.

[111] These are the dates on which the nine children were brought to Court, not the dates on which they were purchased.

Thirty-one white servants without indentures were brought to Charles County Court in 1698, sixty-seven in 1699, twenty-one in 1700, and seventeen in 1701. Five survivors rescued one each from the auction block in 1699, and another did so in 1700. They were:

Thomas Dickison, on 14 March 1699. He was 40 or 41 years old, with a wife named Anne, and a daughter named Mary. He had adopted one girl, Elizabeth Vinton, age not stated, in 1688, and one abused boy, Richard Ward, age not stated, two months earlier, on 10 January 1699.

William Tymothy, on 14 March 1699. He was 47 years old. He had adopted a bastard child in 1680. He had purchased an indentured servant, Stephen Bridges, whom he brought to Court in 1690 for being absent "severall times." He had a wife, and a daughter born 12 October 1693, both named Mabella. He died less than a year later, before 13 February 1700.

James Cotterell, on 4 April 1699. He was 42 years old, with a wife, the former Elizabeth Burford, and three children, aged five to ten. He had previously owned 100 acres of land, which he sold in 1690.

John Booker, on 13 June 1699. He was 43 years old, with a wife Anne, the widow of Richard Price deceased, whom he married in 1689, and one stepson, age eleven. He owned livestock, and was Constable "for ye Lower parts of Nanjemy Parish."

John Williams, on 13 June 1699. He was 43 years old, with a wife and two children, aged fourteen and eleven. He owned 250 acres of land, and he owned hogs and cattle. He was a convicted felon, having marked a heifer not belonging to him.

Mathew Sanders, on 13 February 1700. He was 52 years old, with wife and five children. He owned 200 acres of land, and he owned hogs and cattle. He had owned an indentured servant, Richard Capner, who successfully petitioned the Court for his freedom in 1683.

The last survivor to rescue a servant without indentures from the auction block was Edward Milstead, on 14 November 1710. He was 54 years old, with a wife and three children: a lawfully begotten daughter, an illegitimate son, and an adopted son. He later adopted "an orphan lad" fifteen years old.

SURVIVORS WHO RESCUED SERVANTS WITHOUT INDENTURES

Name of survivor	Age	Date	Name and age of servant
Benson, Robert	age 46	8 Aug 1693	Cole, John (18)
Booker, John	age 43	13 Jun 1699	Browne, Andrew (21)
Cotterell, James	age 42	4 Apr 1699	Lawrence, James (17)
Dickison, Thomas	age 40/41	14 Mar 1699	Doane, Charles (14)
Lampton, Mark	age 39	12 Jun 1688	Kenes, Mary (22)
Millstead, Edward	age 54	14 Nov 1710	Smith, Margrett (20)
Sanders, Mathew	age 52	13 Feb 1700	Currs, Edward (17)
Tymothy, William	age 47	14 Mar 1699	Morris, James (15)
Williams, John	age 43	13 Jun 1699	Fordice, Alexander (19)

After 1710, only forty-seven white servants without indentures were brought to Charles County Court. In 1729 alone, twenty-four imported Negro children were brought to Charles County Court. And this number does not include adults imported from Africa, or Negro children born in America. The complexion of slavery in Maryland (and Virginia) had changed. There may have been underground resistance to Negro slavery. But there would be no formal protest against slavery in Maryland for another seventy years.

Still, the actions of these nine survivors of white child slavery should stand as a testament to the highest aspirations of humanity. None of them were wealthy. Some of them were flawed. But all of them knew from first-hand experience what the loss of liberty feels like, and they did what was in their power to do. They could not stop the enslavement of all, but each of them could, and did, rescue one. They exemplified a variant of the golden rule:

Do unto others as you wish someone had done unto you.

CHARLES COUNTY

Abbott, Susanna, 8 March 1681, age 20, Philip Lines, by his wife Margarett Lines [10.pdf #55]
Acres, John, 10 June 1673, age 13, Jeremiah Dikeson [Vol. 60:498]
Adames, Edward, 8 August 1682, age 17, Jacob Morris [10.pdf #177]
Ailer, Elizabeth, 9 March 1680, age 20, Francis Wyne [09.pdf #153]
Ailer, Mary, 9 March 1680, age 14, Francis Wyne [09.pdf #153]
Aldis, William, 8 June 1675, age 10, Owen Jones [07.pdf #63]
Aldon, Mary, 12 March 1678, age 21, John Dent [08.pdf #73]
Allinson, Annabella, 12 June 1677, age 17, Philip Lines [08.pdf #32]
Anderson, John, March 1716, servant to Raphael Neale [Liber G Page 48]
Anderson, Lawrence, 9 January 1672, age 20, Capt. William Boreman, by Richard Edelen [06.pdf #56]
Anderson, Margaret, 8 June 1714, age 20, Mr. Justice Harrison [25.pdf #219]
Anderson, Railph, 10 November 1674, age 20, Railph Shaw [07.pdf #19]
Anglish, John, 13 March 1677, age 16, Arthur Turner, by William Jenkinson [08.pdf #22]
Archiball, John, 9 February 1686, age 22, Alexander Smith [13.pdf #48]
Armstrong, Richard, 11 January 1670, age 19, William Barton [Vol. 60:230]
Arnley, Jane, 11 March 1679, age 13, Thomas Speeke, "of St. Maries County" [09.pdf #81]
Astere, George, 3 February 1664, age 14-15, Alexander Simpson [02.pdf #307]
Attchison, George, 12 January 1669, age 16, John Paine [Vol. 60:179]
Attkins, William, 12 January 1675, age 17, Robert Henley, by William Potter [07.pdf #33]
Atwick, Joseph, 8 November 1687, age not judged, John Court, produced Indentures "for four yeares," upon inspection, ordered to serve "according to ye Custom of ye Country" [14.pdf #160]
Austrich, William, 13 June 1676, age 13, James Tyre, by William Tymothy [07.pdf #111]
Avis, Matthew, 11 March 1679, age 18, William Smith [09.pdf #82]
Baen (?), Thomas, 13 June 1699, age 11, Thomas Harguesse [20.pdf #68]
Bailey, Grace, 11 June 1678, age 20, Thomas Baker, by Henry Trewne [08.pdf #92]
Baily, William, 11 April 1676, age 14, Robert Middleton [07.pdf #101]
Baiteman, Patrick, 10 June 1679, age 17, William Chandler [09.pdf #84]
Baker, Hamlet, 12 July 1664, age 14, George Newman [02.pdf #377]
Ball, Thomas, 12 January 1669, age 17, Ignatius Causine [Vol. 60:179]
Baraclow, Tobie, 8 November 1664, age 18, William Perfect [02.pdf #458]
Barker, Robert, 11 January 1670, age 21-22, Daniell Johnson [Vol. 60:230]
Barker, William, 8 March 1664, age 20, Richard Stone [02.pdf #320]
Barlow, Joel, 8 August 1671, age 12, James Neale Junior [06.pdf #46]

CHARLES COUNTY

Baron, Richard, 12 March 1667, age 15, Humphrey Warren Junior
    [03.pdf #174], "Died on ye 27th of July 166(7)" [03.pdf #297]
Barret, Joseph, 12 July 1664, age 19, John Morris [02.pdf #377]
Barrett, John, 13 March 1677, age 15, William Smith [08.pdf #22]
Barrett, John, 11 March 1679, age 14, Michael Minock [09.pdf #82]
Barrett, William, 10 January 1682, age 20, Captn. Ignatius Causin
    [10.pdf #130]
Barrow, John, 10 June 1679, age 15, William Hatch [09.pdf #84]
Barton, George, 10 March 1674, age 21-22, Zachary Wade [06.pdf #149]
Barton, Robert, 13 June 1682, age 21, Major William Boardman, by
    Edmond Dennis [10.pdf #165]
Bass, John, 11 November 1690, age not judged, Robert Thompson Junr.,
    "Indenture being reade here in Court and noe sufficient" [17.pdf #69]
Battle, Anthony, 8 March 1670, age 16, John Okeane [Vol. 60:242]
Bawlding, Robert, 13 April 1669, age 21, Robert Henly [Vol. 60:188]
Baylie, John, 12 July 1664, age 15-16, Richard Smith, by Mr. Francis Pope,
    "as Administrator" [02.pdf #404]
Bayly, Nicholas, 12 August 1673, age 16, Ignatius Causine [06.pdf #140]
Beaton, Murdoe (?), 13 August 1728, age 12, Captain Matthew Barnes
    [31,pdf #77]
Bee, Thomas, 8 November 1664, age 20, James Bowlin [02.pdf #449]
Bell, Bridgett, 10 June 1679, age 16, Major John Wheeler [09.pdf #84]
Bell, Elizabeth, 11 June 1678, age 21, Robert Henley [08.pdf #92]
Bellingham, Alice, 12 January 1675, age 16, Robert Henley [07.pdf #33]
Bellingham, Mary, 12 January 1675, age 12, Matthew Hill [07.pdf #33]
Benathon, Christian, male, 10 February 1663, age 19, Richard Foxton (?)
    [02.pdf #125]
Bene, Thomas, 8 March 1681, age 17, Thomas Gerrard [10.pdf #55]
Bennett, John, 9 March 1675, age 20, Hugh French, by Job Corner [07.pdf #47]
Bennett, John, 9 June 1702, age 17, Samuell Luckett [22.pdf #31]
Bennett, Mary, 10 March 1674, age 20-21, Edward Price [06.pdf #150]
Bennett, Mary, 10 June 1679, age 22, Henry Hardy [09.pdf #84]
Benson, John, 14 June 1670, age 11, Mr. Prouce, by Thomas Allanson
    [Vol. 60:256]
Benson, Robert, 8 August 1665, age 18-19, Edward Richardson [02.pdf #547]
Berry, Elizabeth, 14 March 1682, age 14, Thomas Baker [10.pdf #148]
Berry, John, 11 August 1685, age 17, Ralph Shaw [12.pdf #96]
Bigs, Ambros, 8 March 1664, age 19, Thomas Baker [02.pdf #322]
Binns, James, 13 January 1680, age 17, Thomas Gerrard [09.pdf #139]
Bird, Mary, 14 November 1710, age 19, John Speake [24.pdf #29]
Birtch, Robert, 22 April 1662, age 14-16, Henry Addames [01.pdf #211]

CHARLES COUNTY

Bishop, Archibald, 12 September 1699, age not judged, Richard Harrison, "now being sick and not capable of being brought to Court to be adjudged of his age" [20.pdf #101]
Bishop, Will, 12 March 1672, age 15, James Walker [06.pdf #59]
Bitton, Margarett, 8 June 1708, age 20, Richard Villson [23.pdf #253]
Blaack, William, 14 January 1701, age 15, William Hungerford [21.pdf #68]
Blackbeard, Peeter, 8 November 1664, age 17, James Bowlin [02.pdf #449]
Blanch, John, 8 March 1664, age 14, William Barton Junior [02.pdf #321]
Board, Jane, 11 March 1679, age 17, John Wood [09.pdf #82]
Bone, Isabell, 14 March 1665, age 24, Peeter Car [02.pdf #509]
Bone, Teague, 13 June 1699, age 13, Edward Rockwood [20.pdf #68]
Bonner, Elizabeth, 10 August 1675, age 19, Richard Harrison [07.pdf #74]
Booker, John, 11 August 1674, age 18, Alexander White [06.pdf #163]
Booth, John, 8 March 1664, age 13, Thomas Mathews [02.pdf #321]
Boswell, Marmeducke, 8 March 1664, age 12, Richard Fouke [02.pdf #321]
Bowing, William, 10 March 1668, age 16, Archiball Waahob, six years [03.pdf #301]
Bowman, John, 17 March 1663, age 17, Mr. Robert, by John Duglas [02.pdf #164]
Boyde, John, 1694, servant to William Smallwood [Liber T Page 78]
Bradshaw, John, 8 June 1686, age 17-18, Phillip Lynes [13.pdf #118]
Bradshaw, Thomas, 11 January 1670, age 20, John Paine [Vol. 60:230]
Bradstone, Frances, 10 June 1707, age 16, Coll. John Contee [23.pdf #180]
Branor, Edmond, 19 April 1698, age 17, Michaell Martin [19.pdf #207]
Braybanke, Abraham, 10 June 1679, age 15, William Hatch [09.pdf #84]
Brayson, Agnes, 14 November 1710, age 19, Robert Hanson [24.pdf #29]
Breeding, John, 13 March 1711, age 11, John Wilkinson [24.pdf #59]
Brenan, Katherine, 12 September 1699, age 20, Edward Phillpott [20.pdf #101]
Bride, Teague, male, 13 June 1693, age 15, Raiph Smith, by Capt. John Courts [18.pdf #81]
Bridges, Stephen, 9 March 1686, age 25, John Court Jun. [13.pdf #49]
Bright, Edward, 11 June 1678, age 12, James Smallwood [08.pdf #93]
Bright, Thomas, 8 March 1670, age 21, Mr. Young [Vol. 60:243]
Brooke, John, 12 January 1686, age 21, Henry Hawkins [13.pdf #47]
Brooke, Thomas, 10 March 1674, age 11, John Lambert [06.pdf #149]
Brookes, Hen(ry), 10 June 1673, age 19, Mrs. Beane, by Mathew Hill [06.pdf #137]
Brooks, James, 12 March 1700, age 14, Joseph Harrison [20.pdf #177]
Broonely, Thomas, 8 November 1670, age 21, Edmond Lynsy [Vol. 60:262]
Broune, Ales, female, 10 January 1665, age 22, William Smoote [02.pdf #463]
Browne, Andrew, 13 June 1699, age 21, John Booker [20.pdf #69]
Browne, Elisabeth, 10 January 1665, age 20, William Marshall [02.pdf #462]

CHARLES COUNTY

Browne, Gustavus, 8 June 1708, age 20, Jonathan White [23.pdf #254]
Browne, Henry, 14 November 1710, age 18, Capt. William Harbert [24.pdf #30]
Browne, James, 12 January 1686, age 15, Domindigo Agambrah [13.pdf #47]
Browne, Joan, 16 December 1662, age 18, James Nealle Esq., "by his overseer" Thomas Carvell [02.pdf #90]
Browne, John, 8 June 1708, age 16, Francis Goodrich [23.pdf #253]
Browne, Robert, 4 April 1699, age 15, Anthony Neale [20.pdf #26]
Browne, Thomas, 12 July 1664, age 20, Miss Weekes, by Thomas Lomax [02.pdf #377]
Browne, Thomas, 8 June 1675, age 18, John Faning [07.pdf #63]
Browne, Thomas, 10 January 1682, age 16, Peter Car [10.pdf #130]
Bryan, Anne, 13 June 1699, age 21, Thomas Wakefeild [20.pdf #68]
Bryan, John, 19 April 1698, age 12, Capt. John Bayne [19.pdf #206]
Bryan, John, 14 June 1698, age 22, Thomas Jenkins [19.pdf #217]
Bryan, Turlough, 19 April 1698, age 19, Maj. William Dent [19.pdf #206]
Bryan, William, 14 June 1698, age 16, Ralph Smith [19.pdf #217]
Buckham, Isabel, 9 June 1719, age 13, Richard Nevill [26.pdf #112]
Buckler, Benjamin, 10 January 1682, age 9, Thomas Mitchell [10.pdf #130]
Bull, William, 10 June 1679, age 18, John Gooch [09.pdf #84]
Burges, John, 28 January 1662, age not judged, James Waker, sold by Humphrey Warring "of London, Marchant," four years [01.pdf #190]
Burgesse, Samuell, 11 March 1690, age not judged, Mrs. Elinor Bayne, by John Bayne her son, Indenture not "good and authentick," ordered to serve "according to ye Custome of ye Countrey" [16.pdf #114]
Burke, Catherine, 19 April 1698, age 14, John Wilder [19.pdf #206]
Burke, John, 9 March 1675, age 15, Anne Fowke, by James Keech [07.pdf #47]
Burke, Oliver, 4 April 1699, age 13, William Hunt [20.pdf #26]
Burkhaine, John, 10 January 1671, age 15, Jeremiah Dickinson [06.pdf #3]
Burnett, John, 12 March 1700, age 17, Randall Garland [20.pdf #176]
Caddington, Elizabeth, 12 January 1686, age 15, Henry Hawkins [13.pdf #47]
Calvin, William, 9 June 1719, age 16, Doughlass Gifford [26.pdf #112]
Cameright, John, 14 November 1699, age 8, Capt. John Bayne [20.pdf #99]
Cammelle, Mary, 11 June 1706, age 20, Samuell Luckett [23.pdf #123]
Campbell, Daniel, 9 June 1719, age 12, Charles Byrne [26.pdf #112]
Campbell, John, 14 November 1710, age 14, Edward Chapman [24.pdf #30]
Campin, John, 12 November 1706, age 19, Ralphaell Neale [23.pdf #152]
Canland, John, 11 June 1678, age 16, Capt. John Wheeler [08.pdf #93]
Canley, John, 12 August 1690, age 15, Raiph Smith, by John Duglas [17.pdf #30]
Capshaw, Francis, 10 November 1674, age 15, Alexander Smith [07.pdf #19]

CHARLES COUNTY

Careadale, Thomas, 11 January 1670, age 16-17, Capt. Boareman [Vol. 60:230]
Carey, Cornelius, 12 March 1678, age 18, Justinian Dennis [08.pdf #73]
Carey, Hugh, 11 June 1678, age 14, Edward Price [08.pdf #92]
Carnaggey, James, 14 November 1710, age 16, John Manning [24.pdf #29]
Carnee, Thomas, 13 June 1699, age 16, William Hawton Senior [20.pdf #68]
Carpenter, Christopher, 14 March 1682, age 12, James Smallwood
    [10.pdf #148]
Carpenter, Henry, 11 April 1676, age 16, William Perfitt [07.pdf #101]
Carrey, Nicholas, 14 January 1701, age 14, Capt. Thomas Smoot [21.pdf #68]
Cathew, Christopher, 13 June 1682, age 14, Philip Lines [10.pdf #165]
Cayne, James, 10 June 1674, age 12, Richard Beck [06.pdf #158]
Champe, Steephen, 8 March 1664, age 14, William Marshall [02.pdf #322]
Chantler, John, 10 November 1696, age 18, William Wilkison [19.pdf #73]
Chaplin, Thomas, 11 January 1676, age 11, Garratt Sinnett [07.pdf #96]
Chapman, Elizabeth, 13 June 1699, age 16, John Vandry [20.pdf #68]
Chapman, George, 9 January 1672, age 22, Benjamin Rozer [06.pdf #56]
Chesson, John, 12 May 1663, age 14 "and a half," John Meekes [02.pdf #177]
Chew, Aedith, 14 January 1668, age 14, Garret Synnett [03.pdf #296]
Childman, Joane, 8 August 1665, age 20, Edmond Lendsey [02.pdf #547]
Chomley, Francis, 11 January 1670, age 16, Henry Adames [Vol. 60.230]
Christoe, Robert, 4 April 1699, age 16, Thomas Simpson [20.pdf #26]
Clarke, James, 9 January 1672, age 13, Richard Edelen [06.pdf #56]
Clarke, John, 15 November 1665, age 12, Zachery Waed [02.pdf #57]
Clarke, Mary, 28 January 1662, age not judged, Joseph Harrisson, sold by
    Humphery Warrin, four years "from the 29th of September 1661
    until the 29th of September 1665" [01.pdf #190]
Clarke, Nicholaus, 10 January 1665, age 16, Robert Hendley [02.pdf #462]
Clarke, Rebeckah, 13 June 1699, age 16, William Hawton Junr. [20.pdf #68]
Clarke, Thomas, 12 June 1705, age 17, Coll. James Smallwood [23.pdf #79]
Clary, Morris, 10 January 1682, age 18, Owen Newen [10.pdf #130]
Clemence, Nicholaus, 3 February 1664, age 11-12, William Marshall
    [02.pdf #307]
Coates, Henly, 14 March 1699, age 13, John Liverett [20.pdf #24]
Cobb, Samuel, 8 June 1669, age 15, Thomas King [Vol. 60:196]
Cole, John, 8 August 1693, age 18, Robert Benson [18.pdf #87]
Collard, Daniel, March 1716, servant to John Marten [Liber G Page 47]
Collingwood, Robert, 12 March 1672, age 21, Robert Clarke [06.pdf #59]
Collins, Alice, 12 August 1673, age 21-22, Robert Robins [06.pdf #140]
Comely, Anne, 8 June 1708, age 20, Walter Winter [23.pdf #253]
Comorains, John, 13 March 1722, age not judged, Henry Hawkins,
    "taken in ye Rebellion at Preston," "had served the full Term
    of five years" [27.pdf #126]

CHARLES COUNTY

Coney, Anthony, 19 April 1698, age 12, Capt. John Bayne [19.pdf #206]
Cooke, John, 9 February 1686, age 14, Richard Newman [13.pdf #48]
Cooper, John, 14 January 1679, age 15, Capt. William Barton [09.pdf #62]
Cooper, Roger, 11 March 1679, age 16, William Hinsey, by Joseph Bullott
    [09.pdf #81]
Cooper, Thomas, 11 June 1667, age 15, Richard Randall [03.pdf #209]
Cooper, William, 13 November 1705, age 13, Samuell Southeron [23.pdf #104]
Copp (?), John, 11 August 1685, age 17, Richard Wade [12.pdf #96]
Cornute, Hendrick, 14 June 1670, age 20, John Okeane [Vol. 60:256]
Cornwall, Francis, female, 14 March 1682, age 20, Thomas Jenkins
    [10.pdf #148]
Corrandell, Joane, 8 June 1708, age 16, Isabella Orrell [23.pdf #253]
Cottlycott, William, 10 March 1685, age 17, John Court Junior [12.pdf #61]
Cottwell, James, 13 March 1677, age 20, Thomas Gerrard [08.pdf #22]
Court, Cleat, 13 April 1669, age 17, Daniell Johnson [Vol. 60:188]
Crawford, David, 9 June 1719, age 17 "ye first day of next December,"
    John Posey [26.pdf #112]
Crawford, William, March 1716, servant to Thomas Turner [Liber G Page 47]
Crottee (?), Thomas, 19 April 1698, age 12, Mrs. Elinor Bayne, by
    Michaell Browne [19.pdf #206]
Crouch, Anne, 9 February 1686, age 18, Coll. John Court Junr. [13.pdf #48]
Cumber, Catherin, 14 March 1665, age 17, George Newman [02.pdf #509]
Cumberbeech, Edward, 8 June 1697, age 15, Ralph Smith [19.pdf #130]
Cumpton, Christopher, 14 June 1681, age 16, Philip Lines [10.pdf #79]
Cumpton, William, 11 January 1676, age 17, John Hatch [07.pdf #96]
Cunningham, George, 9 January 1672, age 16, Alexander Smith [06.pdf #56]
Currs, Edward, 13 February 1700, age 17, Matthew Sanders [20.pdf #142]
Curtis, John, 10 November 1674, age 16, Francis Wine [07.pdf #19]
Cusack, Patrick, 11 March 1701, John Bayne, "brings here into Court two
    Irish servants," age 17 in original order dated 1 August 1693,
    Saint Mary's County [21.pdf #92]
Dallison, Allen, 4 April 1699, age 13, Thomas Hussey [20.pdf #26]
Damer, Thomas, 12 January 1669, age 17, John Cage [Vol. 60:179]
Damon (?), Daniel, 1695, servant to Peirce Fearson [Liber T Page 177]
Daniellson, Charles, 4 April 1699, age 15, Capt. John Bayne [20.pdf #27]
Darnell, Edw., 13 March 1688, age 17, Phillip Lynes[14.pdf #176]
Daverill, Thomas, 11 January 1670, age 20, Thomas Dent [Vol. 60:230]
Davies, Alice, 8 June 1675, age 19, Thomas Howell [07.pdf #63]
Davies, Griffin, 8 June 1675, age 17, Nicholas Prodday, by Richard Fowke
    [07.pdf #63]
Davies, Hugh, 12 August 1690, age 14, Raiph Smith, by John Duglas
    [17.pdf #30]

CHARLES COUNTY

Davies, James, 8 March 1670, age 16, John Ward [Vol. 60:242]
Davies, William, 12 November 1672, (age 18-22), John Stone, six years [06.pdf #94]
Davis, John, 10 June 1674, age 13, Humphry Warren [06.pdf #158]
Davise, Marie, 13 September 1687, age 17, Mr. Robert Doyne, "Sherife of this Countie" [14.pdf #158]
Deakons, Thomas, 13 April 1669, age 11, Henry Bonard [Vol. 60:188]
Denealey, John, 14 August 1705, age 14, Coll. John Contee [23.pdf #89]
Denison, John, 4 April 1699, age 18, Hugh Teares [20.pdf #27]
Derritt, Edward, 11 April 1676, age 21, Humphrey Warren [07.pdf #101]
Dickison, Thomas, 13 March 1677, age 18-19, James Tyre, by Thomas Harris [08.pdf #22]
Dicksey, John, 10 January 1665, age 15, Edward James [02.pdf #462]
Dickson, Elizabeth, 10 June 1679, age 20, Cleborne Lomax [09.pdf #84]
Dike, Mathew, 12 March 1672, age 20, Mathew Stone [06.pdf #59]
Divell, James, 10 January 1671, age 14, Thomas Stone [06.pdf #3]
Doane, Charles, 14 March 1699, age 14, Thomas Dickson [20.pdf #24]
Dod, John, 14 September 1703, age 16, Maj. William Dent [22.pdf #129]
Dods, Thomas, 12 January 1675, age 12, Robert Henley, by William Potter [07.pdf #33]
Dolton, Richard, 11 March 1679, age 18, Richard Chandler, by Nicholas Cooper [09.pdf #81]
Donah, Daniell, 10 March 1685, age 21, Robert Thompson, "offers an indenture which is adjudged voyd" [12.pdf #61]
Donahan, Fineene, 11 August 1685, age not judged, Thomas Hussey, "brought an Indenture which was judged Invalid" [12.pdf #96]
Donohan, Cornelius, 11 August 1685, age 19, Thomas Hussey [12.pdf #96]
Doughty, Robert, 8 June 1669, age 15, John Ward [Vol. 60:196]
Dover, Christopher, 10 June 1674, age 20, Thomas Mathewes [06.pdf #158]
Downes, William, 9 January 1683, age 13, Major John Wheeler [11.pdf #59]
Doyle, Edmond, 19 April 1698, age 21, Elizabeth Marshall, by Edward Philpott [19.pdf #206]
Doyle, Owen, 14 August 1683, age 20, Phillip Lynes[11.pdf #128]
Doyne, Patrick, 13 June 1699, age 19, William Hawton Senr. [20.pdf #68]
Draper, Raiph, 14 June 1681, age 16, Philip Lines [10.pdf #79]
Dreyden, George, 8 August 1699, age 20, Joseph Harrison, "hee saith that he had an Indenture but it was Lost" [20.pdf #79]
Drishen, Dennis, 14 June 1698, age 12, Capt. Randolph Brandt [19.pdf #217]
Druncore, James, 10 March 1686, age 15, Thomas Burford [13.pdf #49]
Duglasse, John, 12 January 1686, age not judged, Thomas Gerrard, "his Indenture adjudged void" [13.pdf #48]
Dunn, Isaac, 10 March 1674, age 14, John Hatch [06.pdf #149]

CHARLES COUNTY

Dunn, Patrick, 13 June 1699, age 20, Thomas Orrell [20.pdf #68]
Dunnington, Francis, 12 January 1686, age 20, Madam Mary Chandler
    [13.pdf #47]
Duppe, Thomas, 11 June 1667, age 20, Alexander Smyth [03.pdf #209]
Dyal, John, 12 June 1722, age 15, George Elgin [27.pdf #163]
Dyall, James, 13 June 1699, age 11, Thomas Jones [20.pdf #68]
Eady, Elizabeth, 14 November 1710, age 21, John Rogers [24.pdf #30]
Eason, John, 11 March 1679, age 11, Capt. Humphrey Warren [09.pdf #82]
Eaton, Thomas, 10 June 1679, age 18, Thomas Clipsham [09.pdf #84]
Edge, Thomas, 10 March 1674, age 17-18, Zachary Wade [06.pdf #149]
Edwards, John, 13 March 1677, age 12, Margarett MackCormack [08.pdf #22]
Ellis, Hugh, 12 January 1675, age 13, Francis Goodricke [07.pdf #33]
Ellison, John, 11 January 1676, age 16, Samuell Cressey [07.pdf #96]
Ellison, John, 13 June 1699, age 15, John Liverett [20.pdf #68]
Emerson, Anthoni, 10 January 1665, age 17, Thomas Smoote, by
    Thomas Gibson [02.pdf #462]
Eniburson, Christopher, 13 April 1669, age 16, Capt. James Neile [Vol. 60:188]
Eniburson, Derick, 13 April 1669, age 14, Capt. James Neile [Vol. 60:188]
Ennis, David, 11 August 1685, age 16, Thomas Hussey [12.pdf #96]
Eure, Christopher, 12 January 1669, age 19, William Marshall [Vol. 60:179]
Evens, Joan, 19 April 1698, age 17, Thomas Smoote [19.pdf #206]
Faarnandez, Pedro, 13 April 1669, age 17, Capt. James Neile [Vol. 60:188]
Farmer, Richard, 10 June 1673, age 16, John Allen [06.pdf #137]
Farrel, Bryan, 8 November 1687, age 17, John Speake [14.pdf #160]
Farrell, Hugh, 12 August 1701, age 18, William Moss [21.pdf #136]
Farrow, James, 10 June 1674, age 15, John Ward, by Richard Beck
    [06.pdf #158]
Faulkner, Alexander, 4 April 1699, age 14, Capt. John Bayne [20.pdf #27]
Feddiman, Jeoffry, 11 June 1700, age 14, John Douglas [21.pdf #9]
Feild, Charles, 10 August 1680, age 20, Major William Boareman
    [09.pdf #182]
Fencoke, Ane, 10 February 1663, age 18, Richard Dod [02.pdf #125]
Fenner, Thomas, 11 January 1670, age 19, Samuell Eaton [Vol. 60:230]
Fisher, Elizabeth, 12 June 1677, age 16, James Smallwood [08.pdf #32]
Fitzgerald, Morris, 8 March 1726, age 10, John Smoot [30.pdf #64]
Fitz Gerralds, John, 4 April 1699, age 14, James Smallwood [20.pdf #26]
Fitz Gerralds, Peter, 19 April 1698, age 12, Hugh Teares [19.pdf #206]
Fitz Gerreld, Morris, 10 March 1685, age 17, John Wright [12.pdf #61]
Fleman, John, 4 April 1699, age 15, Robert Hagar [20.pdf #26]
Flood, Francis, 8 March 1720, age 24, "as a servant of late Dorothy Parry's,"
    by Daniel Jenifer [26.pdf #160]
Foard, Katherine, 14 August 1683, age 20, Phillip Lynes [11.pdf #128]

CHARLES COUNTY

Forbis, William, 14 August 1694, age 17, William Dent [18.pdf #182]
Ford, Peter, 10 March 1685, age 16, Ralph Smith [12.pdf #61]
Fordice, Alexander, 13 June 1699, age 19, John Williams [20.pdf #69]
Forrest, James, 10 June 1707, age 6, John Allen Senr. [23.pdf #181]
Forrester, Edward, 13 February 1700, age 14, George Newman [20.pdf #142]
Forster, Edward, 14 September 1703, age 13, George Brett [22.pdf #130]
Foster, Leonard, 11 June 1678, age 12, William Smith [08.pdf #92]
Fowler, James, 11 March 1729, age 15, Richard Coombs, Junr. [31.pdf #117]
Fowler, William, 8 January 1678, age 14, William Boardman Junior
    [08.pdf #56]
Fowtrell, George, 13 June 1676, age 22-23, James Bowlinge, by
    Richard Edelen [07.pdf #111]
Francis, John, 14 June 1681, age 21, Alexander Smith [10.pdf #79]
Francisson, Francis, 13 April 1669, age 10, Benjamin Rozer [Vol. 60:188]
Franckum, Francis, 11 April 1676, age 16, William Barton [07.pdf #101]
Franklin, George, 8 June 1731, age 14, Richard Chapman [31.pdf #262]
Freete, Teague, 13 March 1683, age 13, John Courte [11.pdf #83]
French, Ann, 8 November 1670, age 21, Benjamin Rozer [Vol. 60:262]
Furth, Joseph, 8 March 1664, age 17, John Clarke [02.pdf #321]
G(?)dy, James, 10 June 1701, age 13, Francis Goodrick Senr. [21.pdf #126]
Galey, Lorance, 8 June 1675, age 14, Captaine James Neale [07.pdf #63]
Gandi, William, 10 February 1663, age 17, John Cage [02.pdf #124]
Gardiner, Helena, 8 June 1708, age 16, Henry Hawkins [23.pdf #253]
Garnsheer, Joseph, 12 November 1685, age not stated, master not stated,
    "his Indentures Judged to be Invalid" [13.pdf #46]
Gaskoyne, Samuel, 8 June 1669, age 17, John Wheeler [Vol. 60:196]
Gateley, Edward, 11 March 1679, age 13, Thomas Harris, by
    Joseph Bullott [09.pdf #81]
German, George, 11 January 1670, age 21, William Barton [Vol. 60:230]
Gerrard, Joane, 10 June 1701, age 22, Michaell Martin, Gent., by
    Coll. James Smalwood [21.pdf #126]
Ghost, Jane, 11 June 1678, age 20, William Harguess [08.pdf #92]
Gibbons, Thomas, 9 February 1686, age 14, William Barton [13.pdf #48]
Gibbs, John, 13 April 1669, age 19, Peter Carr [Vol. 60:188]
Gibson, William, 13 January 1680, age 11, Henry Adames, by
    Philip Mason [09.pdf #139]
Gilbard, James, 10 June 1679, age 21, Philip Linos [09.pdf #84]
Gilbert, Jane, 9 March 1686, age 20, William Hatch [13.pdf #49]
Gill, Argalus, 8 June 1703, age 10, Coll. James Smallwood [22.pdf #105]
Gillcross, (torn) bert, 4 April 1699, age 13, Elizabeth Hawkins [20.pdf #26]
Ginney, John, 12 March 1672, age 14, John Ward [06.pdf #59]
Glasson, John, 12 September 1699, age 16, Joseph Manning [20.pdf #101]

CHARLES COUNTY

Gleeves, George, 10 August 1680, age 20, Capt. James Neale [09.pdf #182]
Glover, Mary, 10 June 1679, age 20, Thomas Hussy [09.pdf #84]
Gluffur, Robert, 14 January 1690, age not judged, William Marshall, Indenture judged not "good and valid," ordered to serve "according to ye Custome of ye Countrey" [16.pdf #111]
Goddard, George, 13 June 1682, age not judged, Thomas Gibson, Indenture adjudged "to be of noe Effect and invalid" [10.pdf #165]
Goer, James, 12 June 1694, age 12, Captain William Barton [18.pdf #165]
Goffe, William, 11 March 1729, age 14, Robert Maslow [31.pdf #117]
Good, Lucie, 12 July 1664, age 20, Richard Foucke [02.pdf #377]
Gosh, Richard, 8 January 1678, age 15, Peter Car, by Joseph Bullott [08.pdf #56]
Grandsworth, Mary, 16 December 1662, age 22 "and upward," John Courts [02.pdf #90]
Grant, Robert, 14 November 1710, age 19, Francis Serson [24.pdf #31]
Graves, Thomas, 11 March 1679, age 16, John Vandry, "of St. Maries County" [09.pdf #81]
Gray, Jepharie, 12 July 1664, age 13, George Thompson [02.pdf #376]
Gray, Joseph, 8 March 1664, age 13, Garrat Sennet [02.pdf #321]
Gray, Ruth, 13 June 1676, age 21, Richard Edelen [07.pdf #111]
Gray, William, 10 June 1684, age 13, Joseph Manning, by Adam Stone [11.pdf #204]
Green, John, 8 September 1668, age 14, Benjamin Rozer [Vol. 60:142]
Green, Richard, 10 June 1673, age 17, John Allen [06.pdf #137]
Greene, James, 10 June 1674, age 15, Benjamin Rozer [06.pdf #158]
Greyden, Margarett, 8 August 1671, age 21, Henry Bonner [06.pdf #46]
Grosser, Mary, 10 June 1674, age 18-20, Peter Carr [06.pdf #158]
Groule, Richard, 8 March 1681, age 13, Joseph Maninge, by his son in law Mr. Stone [10.pdf #55]
Groves, George, 12 January 1686, age 11, Edward Evans [13.pdf #47]
Gryer, John, 14 November 1682, age 20, Richard Williams [11.pdf #29]
Guesse, Richard, 8 June 1686, age 15, Henry Adams [13.pdf #117]
Guinn, Timothy, 9 January 1700, age 11, John Theobalds [20.pdf #131]
Gunner, Moyses, 10 January 1665, age 19, Thomas Smoot, by Thomas Gibson [02.pdf #462]
Gutridge, James, 14 March 1682, age 15, Philip Linos [10.pdf #148]
Gwin, Richard, 8 March 1664, age 19, Francis Pope [02.pdf #320]
Gwynn, Peter, 13 June 1699, age 18, Robert Yates [20.pdf #69]
Hagar, William, 13 April 1669, age 14, Thomas Baker [Vol. 60:188]
Halerd, William, 11 June 1678, age 18, Edward Price [08.pdf #92]
Halfpin, Thomas, 4 April 1699, age 18, Richard Edelen [20.pdf #27]
Hall, Charles, 8 August 1682, age 22, Edward Mings [10.pdf #177]

CHARLES COUNTY

Hall, Isaack, 13 April 1669, age 13, Henry Bonard [Vol. 60:188]
Hall, John, 10 June 1674, age 18, William Hensly [06.pdf #158]
Hall, John, 10 June 1690, age not judged, Henry Hawkins [17.pdf #18]
Hall, Margrett, 10 June 1673, age 18, Mrs. Young, by Robert Worrell [06.pdf #137]
Hall, William, 11 January 1676, age 17, Thomas Speeke, by Edward Evans [07.pdf #96]
Halliburton, Elizabeth, 12 June 1705, age 19, Capt. William Barton [23.pdf #80]
Hallinak, Michael, 10 June 1701, age 13, Michael Smalwood [21.pdf #126]
Hambye, Francis, 2 January 1686, age 19, Giles Blizard [13.pdf #47]
Hammonde, John, 7 April 1668, age 15, Jeremiah Dickenson [03.pdf #310]
Hardy, Henry, 12 July 1664, age 20, Thomas Percei [02.pdf #377]
Harper, Peter, 8 March 1692, age 13, Robert Thompson Junior [17.pdf #209]
Harrard, William, 14 November 1710, age 15, Joseph Manning [24.pdf #29]
Harris, Jane, 13 June 1676, age 20, Richard Jones [07.pdf #111]
Harris, William, 13 June 1693, age 13, Capt. John Courts [18.pdf #81]
Harrison, Anne, 10 November 1674, age 21, William Barton Junior [07.pdf #19]
Harrison, Robert, 10 November 1674, age 13, Alexander Smith [07.pdf #19]
Hastings, James, 9 June 1719, age 9, John Philbert [26.pdf #112]
Hatherton, John, 10 March 1674, age 12, Edward Price [06.pdf #149]
Hayles, Mary, 10 March 1671, age 20, Zachary Wade [06.pdf #39]
Hays, Isabella, 8 June 1708, age 20, Mullinax Rattclife [23.pdf #253]
Hays, John, 10 June 1701, age 18, Coll. James Smalwood [21.pdf #125]
Haywood, Mary, 10 January 1682, age 12, Thomas Jenkins [10.pdf #130]
Hedge, Thomas, 10 June 1718, age 11, John Speake [26.pdf #38]
Henley, John, 9 September 1701, age 14, William Smalwood [21.pdf #148]
Henry, Ann, 13 February 1700, age 20, James Williams [20.pdf #142]
Hensley, Edward, 10 June 1674, age 17, John Bowles [06.pdf #158]
Herbert, John, 13 March 1677, age 18, Captn. Josias Fendall, by Humphrey Warren [08.pdf #22]
Herbert, William, 11 April 1676, age 17, Robert Rowlants [07.pdf #101]
Herman, Robert, 3 February 1664, age 17-18, Henry Addames [02.pdf #307]
Hernold, John, 14 June 1698, age 14, Randolph Garland [19.pdf #217]
Hey, Charles, 9 June 1668, age 16, Benjamin Rozer [03.pdf #315]
Hicks, Thomas, 8 March 1681, age 15, Robert Robins [10.pdf #55]
Hill, Thomas, 14 June 1670, age 16, Mr. Rozer [Vol. 60:256]
Hill, Thomas, 8 June 1686, age 13, Giles Blizard [13.pdf #117]
Hill, Vall, 12 March 1672, age 12, William Hinsey [06.pdf #59]
Hinch, Matheu, 8 November 1670, age 21, Benjamin Rozer [Vol. 60:262]
Hincks, Dorothy, 12 January 1669, age 19, John Wheeler [Vol. 60:179]

CHARLES COUNTY

Hinde, William, 12 March 1678, age 12, Thomas Clarke [08.pdf #73]
Hindle, Joshua, 11 June 1678, age 21, Francis Goodrich [08.pdf #93]
Hinsey, John, 10 June 1701, age 18, Francis Goodrick Junr., "hee had Indentures in Ireland before hee came aboard the Shipp which are casually or accidentally lost or Imbezzelled" "Capt. William Broadhead Master of the said Shipp, Joseph Howell the Mate, William Beard the Carpenter" [21.pdf #126]
Hinsley, Thomas, 14 March 1682, age 21, Philip Linos [10.pdf #148]
Hire, Railph, 11 March 1679, age 20, Thomas Taylor [09.pdf #82]
Hobkins, Thomas, 28 January 1662, age not stated, Edward Swan, four years [01.pdf #190]
Hobson, John, 12 May 1663, age 13, Robert Hundley [02.pdf #174]
Hodgins, Charles, 10 March 1674, age 14, Archebald Walkup [06.pdf #148]
Hodgly, John, 8 March 1670, age 21, Joseph Harrison [Vol. 60:242]
Hogdin, Jonathan, 9 November 1680, age 18, John Redich, by John Hamilton [10.pdf #33]
Hogg, Frances, 14 January 1701, age 18, Major William Dent [21.pdf #67]
Hoggin, Henry, 11 January 1676, age 21, Philipp Lines [07.pdf #96]
Hoghland, Patrick, 9 January 1700, age 15, Major James Smallwood [20.pdf #131]
Holliewood, James, 12 June 1688, age 18, William Smith [14.pdf #177]
Hollis, Thomas, 4 April 1699, age 15, Thomas Smoote [20.pdf #26]
Holmes, Grace, 14 June 1681, age 22, Philip Linos [10.pdf #79]
Holt, William, 10 June 1684, age 20, Capt. Ignatius Causeene [11.pdf #204]
Holton, Joseph, 14 June 1670, age 22, Mr. Rozer [Vol. 60:256]
Honnker, Elisabeth, 9 August 1664, age 15, James Lee [02.pdf #418]
Hoskings, Thomas, 11 March 1679, age 12, Robert Thompson Junior [09.pdf #82]
Hoskins, Jeremi, 13 April 1669, age 21, John Bowles [Vol. 60:188]
Hoskins, Lauran, 13 April 1669, age 17, John Bowles [Vol. 60:188]
Houghton, James, 8 August 1682, age 14, Capt. Henry Aspenall [10.pdf #177]
Howard, Philise, 8 November 1664, age 20 "according to her owne acknowledgment," William Barton Junior [02.pdf #449]
Howes, Thomas, 12 March 1678, age 16, Capt. Josias Fendall, by Adam Weaver [08.pdf #73]
Hoyle, Samuell, 8 November 1670, age 21-22, Benjamin Rozer [Vol. 60:262]
Hubberton, Mary, 10 March 1671, age 18, Bartholomew Coates [06.pdf #39]
Hudson, Robert, 11 April 1676, age 13, Richard Midgeley [07.pdf #101]
Humble, Barbary, 11 January 1676, age 20, Philipp Lines [07.pdf #96]
Hundly, Henry, 12 July 1664, age 21, Miss Elisabeth Atwicks [02.pdf #377]
Hungerlee, William, 13 June 1693, age 15, Samuell Luckett [18.pdf #81]
Hunt, John, 13 April 1669, age 16, William Barton [Vol. 60:188]

CHARLES COUNTY

Hunter, Richard, 9 January 1672, age 21, Benjamin Rozer [06.pdf #56]
Hunter, William, 11 January 1676, age 14, Thomas Hussey [07.pdf #96]
Huntsman, Samuell, 10 September 1678, age 14, Thomas Allanson
    [09.pdf #40]
Hussey, Gerrard, __ January 1684, age 18, Phillip Lynes [11.pdf #186]
Hutchins, Elianor, 10 June 1674, age 13, Henery Hawkins [06.pdf #158]
Hutchison, Katharine, 14 November 1710, age 22, James Semmes [24.pdf #30]
Ide, Margaret, 19 November 1661, age 18, "who Confessed her Age to bee
    about eighteen," Henry Addames, five years [01.pdf #174]
Ireland, Elisabeth, 22 April 1662, age 17, Edward Swan [01.pdf #211]
Ives, Richard, 12 March 1678, age 19, William Chandler [08.pdf #73]
Ivory, Catherine, 8 August 1693, age 15, Anne Neale, by her son,
    Anthony Neale [18.pdf #87]
Jackson, James, 8 September 1674, age 19, John Wright [Vol. 60:575]
Jackson, Mary, 10 March 1671, age 21, Robert Henley [06.pdf #39]
Jackson, Thomas, 22 April 1662, age 16, Thomas Gerrard Esq., by
    Samuel Dobson [01.pdf #211]
James, Elizabeth, 12 June 1705, age 4, Coll. John Contee [23.pdf #79]
Jeffers, Marie, 8 July 1662, age 14, John Cain [01.pdf #227]
Jeffreyes, Thomas, 8 March 1681, age 18, Joseph Maninge, by his son in law
    Mr. Stone [10.pdf #55]
Jeffs, John, 14 June 1670, age 13, John Courts [Vol. 60:256]
Jennings, John, 9 January 1677, age 17-18, Benjamin Rozer [08.pdf #14]
Joanes, Mary, 28 July 1663, age 20, Walter Beane [02.pdf #195]
Johnson, Jemmima, 9 March 1680, age 13, Coll. Benja. Rozer Esqre.
    [09.pdf #153]
Johnson, John, 12 July 1664, age 12-13, Edmond Lendsey [02.pdf #377]
Johnson, Thomas, 11 April 1676, age 17, Henry Adames [07.pdf #101]
Jones, Edward, 10 March 1674, age 14, John Lambert [06.pdf #149]
Jones, Elleanor, 12 June 1688, age 22, William Smith, indenture judged
    "not to be good without further proofe" [14.pdf #177]
Jones, John, 9 January 1694, age 14, John Wilder [18.pdf #128]
Jones, John, August 1715, servant to George Nailor [Liber G Page 27]
Jones, Katherine, 8 June 1686, age 16, Phillip Lynes [13.pdf #118]
Jones, Mary, 8 August 1682, age 18, John Stone [10.pdf #177]
Jones, Moses, 8 June 1675, age 17, Zachary Wade [07.pdf #63]
Jones, Philip, 13 March 1677, age 21, Robert Henly [08.pdf #22]
Jones, Robert, 12 September 1682, age 21, Thomas Hussey [11.pdf #18]
Jordan, Margeret, 10 January 1665, age 16, Samuell Fendall [02.pdf #463]
Jordan, Mary, 12 June 1683, age 20, John Godson [11.pdf #122]
Keelby, John, 10 June 1674, age 16, Peter Carr [06.pdf #158]
Kelley, Michael, 12 March 1700, age 12, James Hicks [20.pdf #177]

CHARLES COUNTY

Kelly, Margarett, 12 March 1700, age 21, Joseph Manning [20.pdf #177]
Kendall, Francis, 13 June 1676, age 14, John Newton [07.pdf #111]
Keneday, Nicholas, 10 August 1714, age 18, Thomas Plunket [25.pdf #241]
Kenes, Mary, 12 June 1688, age 22, Mark Lampton, indenture judged
 "not to be good without further proofe" [14.pdf #177]
Kenneday, James, 9 January 1700, age 12, Thomas Hussey [20.pdf #131]
Kennyday, Nicholas, 4 April 1699, age 22, Samuel Luckett [20.pdf #26]
Kent, Robert, 13 April 1669, age 12, John Dent [Vol. 60:188]
Kerkley, William, 12 March 1672, age 10, Richard Morris [06.pdf #59]
Killcart, John, 12 January 1686, age 15, William Hatch [13.pdf #47]
Killpatrick, Alexander, 4 April 1699, age 14, George Tubman [20.pdf #26]
King, John, 11 June 1700, age 11, Nicholas Cooper [21.pdf #9]
Kinge, Thomas, 10 March 1685, age 20, Joseph Maning [12.pdf #61]
Kingsbury, George, 12 January 1686, age 19, Henry Hawkins [13.pdf #47]
Kingstone, Thomas, 13 June 1676, age 14, James Tyre, by William Tymothy
 [07.pdf #111]
Kiniken, James, 9 December 1685, age 13, Ralph Smith [13.pdf #47]
Kirby (?), Paul, 8 June 1675, age 16, William Barton [07.pdf #63]
Kirmichael, John, 9 June 1719, age 14 "ye first day of next January,"
 Thomas Wright [26.pdf #112]
Kirten, Zachary, 13 June 1676, age 14, Captn. Josias Fendall, by his brother
 Samuel Fendall [07.pdf #111]
Knightsmith, Hannah, 14 June 1681, age 20, Thomas Taylor [10.pdf #79]
Kue, John, 8 June 1686, age 19, Phillip Lynes [13.pdf #118]
Lackimore, Edward, 12 January 1686, age 14, Henry Hawkins [13.pdf #47]
Lacquey, James, 8 June 1708, age 18, Francis Goodrich [23.pdf #253]
Lallee, Cornelius, 19 April 1698, age 12, Thomas Smoote [19.pdf #206]
Lamber, Ami, 9 August 1664, age 20, John Pain [02.pdf #418]
Lampton, Marke, 10 January 1665, age 16, William Robbison, by
 Daniell Johnson [02.pdf #463]
Lane, Anne, 17 March 1663, age 18, Humphery Warren, by William Heard
 [02.pdf #164]
Lane, William, 7 April 1668, age 14, William Perfect [03.pdf #310]
Laurence, Thomas, 12 March 1672, age 12, Henry Bonner [06.pdf #59]
Lawrence, James, 4 April 1699, age 17, James Cotteroll [20.pdf #26]
Lawson, Thomas, 8 August 1699, age 18, William Newman [20.pdf #79]
Leech, James, 8 June 1675, age 11, Edmund Taylor [07.pdf #63]
Leeds, Robert, 8 August 1665, age 21, Edward Richardson [02.pdf #547]
Lees, Thomas, 9 March 1686, age 22, John Court Jun., "produced an indenture
 which is found invalid" [13.pdf #49]
Lenham, John, 10 June 1679, age 19, Henry Hardy [09.pdf #84]

CHARLES COUNTY

Lewis, Edward, 10 January 1699, age not judged, Thomas Stone, "one of ye Executors of Mr. John Stone deceased," "alledgeing here in Court that hee had an Indenture for four yeares and had lost ye same, but has evidence to prove it" [20.pdf #4]
Linge, Francis, male, 8 March 1664, age 17, Henry Adames [02.pdf #329]
Linghams, Daniell, 11 March 1690, age not judged, John Bayne, Indenture judged not "good and authentick," ordered to serve "according to ye Custome of ye Countrey" [16.pdf #114]
Linsey, Cornelius, 20 January 1680, age 19, William Chandler [09.pdf #144]
Lockraft, John, 1 April 1701, age 13, Francis Green [21.pdf #108]
Loftas, Margarett, 8 September 1674, age 19, Richard Fowke [Vol. 60:575]
Low, James, 8 August 1699, age 14, John Gray [20.pdf #79]
Luces, Thomas, 9 January 1672, age 20, Richard Edelen [06.pdf #56]
Lybscome, Dorothy, 12 August 1673, age 22, Benjamin Rozer [06.pdf #140]
Lyle, John, 8 March 1664, age 17, Mathias Obrian [02.pdf #320]
Macann, Richard, 11 March 1729, age 15, Giles Green [31.pdf #117]
Macclannen, Margarett, 13 August 1706, age 20, John Speake [23.pdf #138]
Macdaniel, James, 11 August 1719, age 21, Thomas Hussey Luckett [26.pdf #123]
Mac Dannell, Danniele, 8 June 1708, age 19, John Manning [23.pdf #253]
Machen, John, 10 June 1679, age 20, Major John Wheeler [09.pdf #84]
Mack Cartie, Dermud, 11 June 1667, age 13-14, Richard Jones [03.pdf #209]
Mackdonal, Daniell, 4 April 1699, age 15, Thomas Hussey [20.pdf #26]
Mackenhine, John, 13 April 1669, age 18, James Macky [Vol. 60:188]
Mackollom, Markam, 13 March 1722, age not judged, John Wilder, stated in petition dated November 1721 that "he was taken in ye Rebellion at Preston and Transported into this Province without Indenture," "had served the full Term of five years," "was past the age of twenty two years at the Time of his Transportacion" [27.pdf #126]
Mackontosh, James, 13 March 1722, age not judged, Henry Hawkins, "taken in ye Rebellion at Preston," "had served the full Term of five years" [27.pdf #126]
Mack William, James, 4 April 1699, age 16, Hugh Teares [20.pdf #27]
Maclaine, Laughlin, 12 June 1705, age 17, Robert Green [23.pdf #79]
Macniel, James, 8 June 1714, age 21, Robert Hanson [25.pdf #219]
Macough, James, 13 June 1699, age 21, Thomas Stone [20.pdf #69]
Macrackin, James, 1694, servant to Samuell Luckett [Liber T Page 78]
Maddock, William, 9 February 1686, age 20, Thomas Gerrard [13.pdf #48]
Magrah, Honour, 13 February 1700, age 18, George Tubman, by Henry Hawkins [20.pdf #142]
Magray, Mary, March 1717, age 15, John Thomas [Liber G Page 177]

75

CHARLES COUNTY

Magregor, Dunkin, 14 November 1710, age 12, Henry Holland Hawkins [24.pdf #30]
Magregor, Margret, 8 August 1710, age 19, Capt. John Gray [23.pdf #409]
Mahawne, Joane, 12 March 1700, age 18, Joseph Manning [20.pdf #177]
Mahawney, Tymothy, 8 August 1693, age 17, Coll. Humphrey Warren [18.pdf #87]
Mahoni, Daniell, 10 March 1685, age 15, Thomas Craxon [12.pdf #61]
Malberry, Francis, 13 November 1677, age 18, Joseph Manninge [08.pdf #48]
Manhew, John, 11 January 1676, age 19, Philipp Lines [07.pdf #96]
Manithurb, Thomas, 10 January 1665, age 16, Robert Hendley [02.pdf #462]
Mannerley, Margarett, 11 March 1679, age 9, Joshuah Doyne "of St. Maries County" [09.pdf #81]
Manwaren, Walter, 11 August 1668, age 20, Richard Smoot [Vol. 60:139]
Marden, John, 11 August 1668, age 13, Alexander Sympson [Vol. 60:139]
Markeat, Anthony, 28 January 1662, age 14, Arthur Turner, seven years [01.pdf #190]
Markfearson, Markham, 4 April 1699, age 16, Alexander Wilson [20.pdf #26]
Marlow, Anthony, 9 January 1672, age 17, Samuel Fendall [06.pdf #56]
Marr, Henry, 10 June 1718, age 14, Francis Oden [26.pdf #38]
Marrome, James, 14 March 1665, age 17, Walter Beane [02.pdf #509]
Marsh, William, 11 August 1674, age 18, Thomas Gerrard [06.pdf #163]
Martiall, Richard, 12 April 1676, age 14, Benjamin Rozer [07.pdf #101]
Mason, John, 9 November 1680, age 21, John Redich, by John Hamilton [10.pdf #33]
Mason, William, 13 March 1677, age 13, Philipp Lines [08.pdf #22]
Massey, John, 9 January 1672, age not judged, Benjamin Rozer, "he is willing to serve five whole years" commencing 2 October 1671 [06.pdf #56]
Mathews, John, 5 January 1664, age 14, John Lewgar [02.pdf #276]
Mattox, David, 12 January 1692, age 15, George Plater, by Michael Martin [17.pdf #189]
Mattox, Thomas, 12 January 1692, age 12, William Dent [17.pdf #189]
Maxfield, Richard, 10 August 1675, age 17, Francis Wine [07.pdf #74]
Maybanck, Elizabeth, 10 June 1674, age 13, John Wood [06.pdf #158]
Medcaph, Robert, 10 January 1665, age 11, John Duglas [02.pdf #462]
Megrough (Magrah), Alice, 19 April 1698, age 19, Hugh Teares [19.pdf #206]
Micaney, Andrew, 10 March 1671, age 21, John Douglas, by Peter Carre [06.pdf #39]
Michell, Marke, 8 March 1664, age 12, Zachery Waed [02.pdf #321]
Miles, Elizabeth, 13 August 1678, age 17, William Wells [09.pdf #16]
Miles, Nathaniell, 9 March 1680, age 14, Archibald Wahob [09.pdf #153]
Mill, Isabella, 14 November 1710, age 21, Barton Hungerford [24.pdf #29]

CHARLES COUNTY

Millborne, Rachell, 8 November 1664, age 18, Richard Smoot [02.pdf #449]
Miller, Andrew, 14 November 1710, age 16, Elizabeth Hawkins [24.pdf #29]
Miller, Daniel, 8 June 1714, age 20, William Stone Senr. [25.pdf #219]
Mills, Alexander, 1 February 1698, age 12, Capt. John Bayne [19.pdf #186]
Milshaw, John, 11 March 1679, age 15, John Ward [09.pdf #81]
Milstead, Edward, 12 January 1675, age 19, William Chandeler [07.pdf #33]
Mires, Christopher, 13 June 1682, age 21, Thomas Craxstone [10.pdf #165]
Mitchell, Anthony, 8 January 1678, age 17-18, Thomas Gerrard [08.pdf #56]
Mitchell, James, 4 April 1699, age 13, Francis Harrison [20.pdf #26]
Mongerrell, Edmond, 10 March 1685, age 13, John Hanson [12.pdf #61]
Monroe, William, 11 August 1719, age 20, Ignatius Luckett [26.pdf #123]
Monteal, Richard, 10 February 1663, age 14, William Perfect [02.pdf #124]
Moore, John, 1694, servant to Anne Neale [Liber T Page 45]
Moore, John, 4 April 1699, age 16, Edward Philpott [20.pdf #26]
Morand (Moreland), Patrick, 11 March 1701, John Bayne, "brings here into Court two Irish servants," age 13 in original order dated 1 August 1693, Saint Mary's County [21.pdf #92]
Morrell, Christopher, 10 June 1673, age 20, Richard Chandler [06.pdf #137]
Morris, Annas, female, 11 April 1676, age 18, Richard Morris [07.pdf #101]
Morris, Edward, 8 August 1699, age 14, Andrew Simpson [20.pdf #79]
Morris, Ellis, 12 September 1682, age 19, James Neale Junior [11.pdf #18]
Morris, James, 14 March 1699, age 15, William Tymothy [20.pdf #24]
Morris, John, 10 June 1674, age 16, Peter Carr [06.pdf #158]
Morris, John, 4 April 1699, age 15, Coll. John Courts [20.pdf #27]
Morrough (Mograugh), John, 19 April 1698, age 12, Capt. John Bayne [19.pdf #206]
Moulton, Margarett, 11 August 1674, age 14, Robert Greene [06.pdf #163]
Mounke, Elisabeth, 10 February 1663, age 18, John Cherman [02.pdf #137]
Mow, Peter, 11 January 1670, age 7, Christopher Brimins [Vol. 60:230]
Murphy, Magloughlin, 9 November 1697, age 18, Capt. John Wilder [19.pdf #169]
Murphy, Mary, 12 March 1700, age 22, Richard Combes [20.pdf #177]
Murphy, Matthew, 19 April 1698, age 14, Jefferry Cole, by John Wilder [19.pdf #206]
Murraine, Nicholas, 12 March 1678, age 17, Mrs. Anne Fowkes [08.pdf #73]
Murrie, Hugh, 11 June 1723, age 16, Richard Speake [28.pdf #53]
Murty, William, 19 April 1698, age 21, Francis Goodrick [19.pdf #206]
Nailee, John, 10 August 1675, age 12, Thomas Matthewes [07.pdf #74]
Nash, Samuell, 14 March 1682, age 20, Philip Linos [10.pdf #148]
Nayler, John, 8 August 1699, age 13, Henry Hawkins [20.pdf #79]
Neale, Henrie, 11 August 1668, age 16, John Courts [Vol. 60:139]
Neale, Robert, 9 February 1686, age 20, Thomas Gerrard [13.pdf #48]

CHARLES COUNTY

Neeves, Mary, 8 January 1678, age 17, Thomas Mudd [08.pdf #56]
Neisbut, Edmond, 10 January 1665, age 18, Richard Stone, by
    Jeromy Dickeson [02.pdf #463]
Nellson, Allexander, 14 November 1699, age 15, William Glover [20.pdf #99]
Nenan, Dennis, 20 January 1680, age 22, William Chandler [09.pdf #144]
Newall, James, 12 July 1664, age 14, George Bradshow [02.pdf #405]
Newman, Ann, 11 January 1670, age 17, William Barton [Vol. 60:230]
Newman, Hannah, 12 January 1686, age 11, Henry Hawkins [13.pdf #47]
Newton, John, 14 June 1681, age 20, Henry Hawkins [10.pdf #79]
Newton, Richard, 9 January 1694, age 14, Capt. Ignatius Causin [18.pdf #128]
Nichols, John, 8 November 1687, age not judged, John Court, produced
    Indentures "for four yeares," upon inspection, ordered to serve
    "according to ye Custom of ye Country" [14.pdf #160]
Nichols, Rachell, 14 March 1682, age 17, Captn. James Neale [10.pdf #148]
Nicholson, Esther, 10 August 1680, age 7, Henry Hawkins [09.pdf #182]
Nicholson, John, 10 August 1680, age 10, Henry Hawkins [09.pdf #182]
Nicholson, Margaret, 9 June 1691, age 22, George Plater [17.pdf #113]
Nicholson, William, 10 August 1680, age 6, John Stone [09.pdf #182]
Nicolls, Christobell, 12 January 1675, age 20, Thomas King [07.pdf #33]
Noland, William, 4 October 1698, age 18, Peter Villett [19.pdf #238]
Nolinn, Patrick, 13 April 1669, age 20, Mr. Dickinson [Vol. 60:188]
Norman, Thomas, 13 April 1669, age 21, Henry Adames [Vol. 60:189]
Normansell, Thomas, 9 March 1686, age 19, Thomas Clarke, "ye servant
    produced an Indenture which ye Court adjudged Invalid" [13.pdf #49]
Northon, John, 4 April 1699, age 10, Coll. John Courts [20.pdf #27]
Norton, Amy, 8 June 1680, age 17, Thomas Mitchell [09.pdf #167]
Nowlan, James, 11 November 1718, age 20, James Semmes [26.pdf #72]
Oakes, Francis, 8 June 1686, age 19, Henry Hawkins [13.pdf #117]
Oard, Peter, 12 March 1672, age 18, Robert Henley [06.pdf #59]
Oliver, Elizabeth, 1 April 1701, age 20, Ubgatt Reeves [21.pdf #108]
Orlock, Turlow, 13 March 1683, age 15, Coll. William Diggs Esqre.
    [11.pdf #83]
Orson, Bearer, 12 January 1669, age 13, Robert Clearke [Vol. 60:179]
Osborne, Thomas, 9 June 1702, age 17, Francis Goodrick Senr. [22.pdf #31]
Oulson, John, 9 January 1672, age 21, Robert Rowland, by Humphry Warren
    [06.pdf #56]
Oxford, William, 11 August 1696, age 11, Capt. Philip Hoskins [19.pdf #41]
Page, Margerie, 5 January 1664, age 19, Walter Beane [02.pdf #276]
Parker, Ann, 8 June 1669, age 19, John Cage [Vol. 60:196]
Parker, Francis, 8 June 1708, age 14, Coll. John Contee [23.pdf #254]
Parker, John, 8 March 1670, age 18, Jeremiah Dickison [Vol. 60:242]
Parker, Jonas, 8 June 1675, age 15, John Courtes, by Cleborne Lomax
    [07.pdf #63]

CHARLES COUNTY

Parkes, Robert, 11 January 1676, age 18, Thomas Dent [07.pdf #96]
Patrige, Mary, 3 February 1664, age 11-12, John Hatch [02.pdf #307]
Patterson, William, 14 June 1698, age 16, William Dent [19.pdf #217]
Pattison, John, 10 June 1673, age 13, Benjamin Rozer [06.pdf #137]
Pauding, William, 13 April 1669, age 16, Henry Adames [Vol. 60:189]
Payne, Thomas, 10 January 1665, age 15, Thomas Stone, by William Boyden
    [02.pdf #462]
Peacocke, William, 13 March 1677, age 14, Philipp Lines [08.pdf #22]
Pearson, John, 11 January 1676, age 17, Railph Shaw [07.pdf #96]
Pearson, Nathaniell, 11 April 1676, age 16, Dennis Huscula (?), by
    Richard Edelen [07.pdf #101]
Peeso, Cornape, 12 January 1669, age 13, William Marshall [Vol. 60:179]
Pembrooke, Mary, 11 June 1678, age 20, Robert Rowlants [08.pdf #92]
Perkins, James, 8 March 1664, age 13, Joseph Harrisson [02.pdf #321]
Perkins, William, 11 August 1702, age 16, Samuell Luckett [22.pdf #39]
Perry, Thomas, 13 June 1699, age 11, Philip Briscoe [20.pdf #68]
Persivall, Charles, 10 June 1673, age 12, Mrs. Coates [06.pdf #137]
Phegg, Charles, 14 March 1682, age 14, Thomas Gerrard [10.pdf #148]
Philips, Edward, 11 January 1676, age 17, Thomas Dent [07.pdf #96]
Philips, John, 12 March 1678, age 16, John Fearson [08.pdf #73]
Philips, Thomas, 13 March 1677, age 17, James Bowling [08.pdf #22]
Phyllips, Hugh, 8 September 1668, age 21, Colonel Gerrard Fowke
    [Vol. 60:142]
Pickard, Robert, 11 March 1679, age 17, John Lambert [09.pdf #82]
Pickering, Michell, c. 13 March 1661, "beeing then" age 18, Robert Hendley,
    freed by court 13 March 1666 [02.pdf #600]
Piper, James, 12 March 1672, age 11, Richard Morris [06.pdf #59]
Pirks, John, 9 June 1702, age 12, Francis Goodrick Junr. [22.pdf #31]
Player, John, 10 January 1665, age 15, John Wright [02.pdf #462]
Poke, Margrett, 14 November 1710, age 19, George Dent [24.pdf #29]
Poore, Peter, 14 November 1682, age 21, William Smith [11.pdf #29]
Potts, John, 8 June 1686, age 24, Capt. Bowling [13.pdf #117]
Potts, Thomas, 9 September 1679, age 20, John Wood, by William Wells
    [09.pdf #112]
Powcher, Thomas, 9 February 1686, age 20, John Court, "his Indenture void"
    [13.pdf #48]
Powell, Robert, 8 March 1670, age 16, Mr. Adams [Vol. 60:242]
Prince, Abigall, 11 January 1670, age 23, Thomas Dent [Vol. 60:230]
Proser, Ann, 14 November 1710, age 24, Robert Price [24.pdf #30]
Purnie, John, 12 Jauary 1686, age 18, Madam Mary Chandler [13.pdf #47]
Ranford, William, 10 June 1673, age 13, John Clarke [06.pdf #137]
Rawfeild, John, 14 November 1710, age 14, Anne Lynes [24.pdf #31]

CHARLES COUNTY

Rawson, Susan, 14 March 1665, age 17, Daniell Johnson [02.pdf #509]
Ray, William, 19 April 1698, age 13, John Frye [19.pdf #206]
Rayley, Edward, 13 March 1677, age 14, James Bowling [08.pdf #22]
Rea, John, 8 March 1670, age 5, Robert Rowland [Vol. 60:242]
Redman, Cornelius, 14 June 1698, age 20, Anne Taylor, "widdow"
 [19.pdf #217]
Reed, Thomas, 10 January 1665, age 18, William Hinshaw, by Robert Hendley
 [02.pdf #462]
Reeding, Isabell, 10 November 1674, age 19, Thomas Hussey [07.pdf #19]
Renes, Elleanor, 12 June 1688, age 22, William Smith, Indenture judged
 not good "without further proof" [14.pdf #177]
Renisson, John, 10 January 1665, age 19, William Robisson, by Daniell Johnson
 [02.pdf #463]
Rennicke, Anne, 10 November 1674, age 16, Elinor Beane, by John Long
 [07.pdf #19]
Rhenick, Owen, 19 April 1698, age 13, Richard Edelen [19.pdf #207]
Rhyne, John, 19 April 1698, age 15, William Hungerford [19.pdf #206]
Richardson, Bernerd, 13 March 1677, age 17, Coll. John Duglas [08.pdf #22]
Richardson, Joseph, 12 January 1675, age 21, John Clarke [07.pdf #33]
Richardson, Thomas, 13 January 1680, age 13, Henry Adames, by Philip Mason
 [09.pdf #139]
Richardson, William, 14 June 1687, age 14, Capt. Randolph Brandt
 [14.pdf #142]
Rilson (?), Henry, March 1717, servant to Thomas Osborne [Liber G Page 177]
Ring, Ralph, 10 March 1671, age 22, Samuel Cressey [06.pdf #39]
Roberts, Richard, 13 June 1682, age 22, Major William Boardman, by
 Edmond Dennis [10.pdf #165]
Roberts, William, 9 January 1677, age 20, Benjamin Rozer [08.pdf #14]
Robertson, Marie, 10 March 1668, age 17, John Coates, "But yet It was
 the request of her Master that she should serve but sixe yeares"
 [03.pdf #300]
Robertson, Peter, 9 June 1719, age 15, Col. Walter Story [26.pdf #112]
Robins, Henry, 12 April 1676, age 17, Benjamin Rozer [07.pdf #101]
Robinson, Anne, 12 January 1675, age 23, John Clarke [07.pdf #33]
Robinson, Samuell, 11 June 1678, age 21, Capt. Humphrey Warren
 [08.pdf #92]
Rogers, Richard, 1694, servant to William Barton [Liber T Page 78]
Rogers, Mary, 14 March 1682, age 20, Philip Linos [10.pdf #148]
Rose, John, 8 March 1670, age 15, Mr. Adams [Vol. 60:242]
Ross, Alexander, 4 April 1699, age 18, Capt. John Bayne [20.pdf #27]
Ross, Francis, 12 September 1699, age 11, Ubgatt Reeves [20.pdf #101]
Rouze, Anne, 11 March 1679, age 19, William Smith [09.pdf #82]

CHARLES COUNTY

Roy, Michal, 9 January 1700, age 14, Francis Green [20.pdf #131]
Rye, John, 8 August 1699, age 12, Capt. John Bayne [20.pdf #79]
Salt, Mary, 11 March 1679, age 20, Thomas Speeke, "of St. Maries County" [09.pdf #81]
Sanders, Elizabeth, 12 November 1700, age 16, Benoni Thomas [21.pdf #51]
Sanders, Mathew, 8 July 1662, age 15, John Cain [01.pdf #227]
Sanders, William, 10 March 1685, age 17, John Hanson [12.pdf #61]
Savage, Catherine, 13 February 1700, age 20, John Gwinn [20.pdf #142]
Scarryott Richard, 9 January 1672, age 12, Archibald Wahab [06.pdf #55]
Scot, Eribecca, 12 July 1664, age 15, James Lensey [02.pdf #377]
Scott, Jennet, 14 November 1710, age 22, Anthony Neale [24.pdf #31]
Scoutch, Alexander, 4 April 1699, age 20, William Herbert [20.pdf #26]
Seawell, Rebeckah, 13 March 1677, age 20, Thomas King [08.pdf #22]
Seer, Thomas, 10 March 1668, age 13, Colon. Gerrard Fowke, by James Macoy [03.pdf #301]
Seney, Daniell, 11 June 1667, age 14-15, Henry Moore [03.pdf #209]
Shanhikin, Derby, 14 March 1699, age 17, Randolph Garland [20.pdf #24]
Shaw, John, 13 June 1682, age 17, Railph Smith [10.pdf #165]
Shaw, Mary, 12 June 1683, age 19, Capt. Casheene [11.pdf #122]
Shaw, Thomas, 11 March 1729, age 12, James Lattimar [31.pdf #117]
Shelton, Mary, 14 March 1682, age 17, Joseph Piles [10.pdf #148]
Shihorr, William, 9 January 1700, age 12, Thomas Hussey [20.pdf #131]
Shiner, Daniell, 17 March 1663, age 15, Mr. Robert, by John Duglas [02.pdf #164]
Short, George, 10 January 1671, age 17-18, Clement Theobalds [06.pdf #3]
Shott, John, 4 April 1699, age 17, James Finley [20.pdf #26]
Sigeley, Samuell, 9 November 1680, age 16, John Mun [10.pdf #33]
Simmes, Francis, 13 January 1686, age 17, Capt. William Barton [13.pdf #48]
Simmons, John, 9 June 1719, age 10, Ignatius Luckett [26.pdf #112]
Simmons, Mary, 17 December 1662, age 14, James Boulin [02.pdf #101]
Simmons, William, 13 February 1700, age 12, Samuel Luckett [20.pdf #142]
Simpson, Alexander, 28 January 1662, age not judged, Edmond Tyler, sold by Humphrey Warrin, six years "from the 29th of September 1661 until the 29th of September 1667" [01.pdf #190]
Simpson, Elizabeth, 13 March 1711, age 22, Robert Sanders [24.pdf #60]
Simpson, Samuell, 12 August 1673, age 15, John Goodge, by Captn. Josias Fendall [06.pdf #140]
Singleton, Richard, 10 June 1674, age 13, Richard Beck [06.pdf #158]
Skinner, Thomas, 11 June 1667, age 15, Robert Hunley [03.pdf #209]
Slater, John, 13 March 1677, age 16, Thomas King [08.pdf #22]
Small, Margaret, 9 June 1719, age 14 "ye Twenty fifth day of next December," William Goody [26.pdf #112]

CHARLES COUNTY

Smith, Benjamin, 4 April 1699, age 19, William Dent [20.pdf #27]
Smith, Elizabeth, 12 March 1678, age 12, Thomas Clarke [08.pdf #73]
Smith, James, 8 January 1678, age 20, Thomas Mudd [08.pdf #56]
Smith, James, 9 February 1686, age 21, Samuell Luckett, "ye servant produced
    an Indenture ye Court adjudgeth ye same Invalid" [13.pdf #48]
Smith, Margrett, 14 November 1710, age 20, Edward Millstead [24.pdf #31]
Smith, Robert, 10 June 1674, age 15, John Munn [06.pdf #158]
Smith, William, 9 January 1677, age 20, John Fanning [08.pdf #14]
Snell, Margaret, 12 March 1672, age 20, Ann Fowkes [06.pdf #59]
Sneton, John, 8 March 1664, age 24, James Mackey [02.pdf #322]
Snosell, Christopher, 8 March 1664, age 20, Richard Stone [02.pdf #320]
Snowden, William, 11 March 1679, age 10, John Vandry, "of St. Maries
    County" [09.pdf #81]
Soot, Banjamin, 8 March 1692, age 12, Robert Thompson Junior [17.pdf #209]
Southerland, Daniel, 9 June 1730, age 13, William Macferson [31.pdf #197]
Spurling, Jeremiah, 12 January 1686, age 18, Henry Hawkins [13.pdf #47]
Standly, Thomas, 8 March 1664, age 14, John Piles, by Humphery Warren
    [02.pdf #321]
Steaphens, William, 10 January 1688, age 21, Joseph Cornell [14.pdf #173]
Stephens, Mary, 10 March 1674, age 19, John Lambert [06.pdf #148]
Stephens, Mary, 13 June 1682, age 19, Thomas Stonestreet [10.pdf #165]
Stephens, Richard, 14 January 1679, age 10, Thomas Gerrard [09.pdf #62]
Steward, George, 14 November 1710, age 13, Walter Winter [24.pdf #31]
Steward, John, 12 June 1705, age 17, John Thompson [23.pdf #79]
Stewart, Daniel, 13 March 1722, age not judged, William Penn, "taken in
    ye Rebellion at Preston," "had served the full Term of five years"
    [27.pdf #126]
Stidman, Edward, 12 June 1677, age 14, Capt. Ignatius Causin [08.pdf #32]
Still, Alexander, 13 March 1711, age 16, John Wilkinson [24.pdf #59]
Stone, Elisabeth, 17 March 1663, age 14, William Heard [02.pdf #164]
Stone, Mathias, 10 March 1674, age 14, Archebald Walkup [06.pdf #148]
Stonehouse, Thomas, 8 June 1675, age 13, Richard Pinner [07.pdf #63]
Storker, Isabella, 10 June 1707, age 11, John Thompson [23.pdf #180]
Stratton, Philise, 14 March 1665, age 19, Henry Warren [02.pdf #509]
Stringer, George, 8 January 1678, age 15, Henry Hawkins [08.pdf #56]
Sudburie, Gregorie, 9 June 1668, age 16, Robert Hunley, by Francis Pope
    [03.pdf #315]
Summer, Jonathan, 17 December 1662, age 12, Capt. Josias Fendall
    [02.pdf #101]
Swaine, George, 13 June 1676, age 14, Captn. Josias Fendall, by his brother
    Samuel Fendall [07.pdf #111]
Sweenehee, Sarah, 12 March 1678, age 20, Francis Goodrich [08.pdf #73]

CHARLES COUNTY

Swillavan, Owen, 4 April 1699, age 14, Thomas Hagan [20.pdf #26]
Symmes, John, 9 June 1691, age 9, George Plater [17.pdf #113]
Sympson, Allexander, 8 August 1699, age 15, William Barton [20.pdf #79]
Sympson, James, 14 November 1699, age 19, Henry More [20.pdf #99]
Taylor, Elizabeth, 11 June 1667, age 19, Alexander Smyth [03.pdf #209]
Taylor, George, 11 April 1676, age 14, William Perfitt [07.pdf #101]
Taylor, Jheromie, 8 March 1664, age 21, John Lumbroso [02.pdf #322]
Taylor, John, 10 January 1665, age 17, Daniell Johnson [02.pdf #463]
Taylor, Richard, 11 January 1676, age 16, John Posie [07.pdf #96]
Taylor, Thomas, 12 June 1677, age 13, George Godfrey [08.pdf #32]
Thatcher, Mary, 11 March 1679, age 19, John Clarke [09.pdf #82]
Thomas, Anne, 11 January 1676, age 22, John Butcher [07.pdf #96]
Thomas, Edward, 11 August 1685, age 12, Capt. Ignatius Causseene
    [12.pdf #96]
Thompson, Henry, 11 March 1679, age 16, Thomas Clipsham [09.pdf #82]
Thompson, James, 12 January 1675, age 12, Francis Goodrich [07.pdf #33]
Thompson, John, 11 June 1678, age 15 "ye first day of next January,"
    Robert Greene [08.pdf #92]
Thompson, John, 12 January 1686, age 17, Henry Hawkins [13.pdf #47]
Thompson, John, 9 June 1719, age 14, William Williams [26.pdf #112]
Thorett, Tymothy, 4 April 1699, age 12, Coll. John Courts [20.pdf #27]
Thornebrooke, James, 11 August 1686, age 21, Phillip Lynes [13.pdf #120]
Tibbitt, John, 10 June 1673, age 17, James Bowleing, by Richard Edelen
    [06.pdf #137]
Tidror, James, 17 March 1663, age 15, John Bouls [02.pdf #164]
Tillee, Thomas, 9 June 1668, age 20, Nathaniel Barton [03.pdf #315]
Tillzey, Mabella, 13 March 1677, age 18, James Tyre, by Thomas Harris
    [08.pdf #22]
Tipton, Edward, 11 August 1668, age 18, Humphrey Warren Junr.
    [Vol. 60:139]
Toby, James, 12 March 1700, age 12, John Decreego [20.pdf #177]
Tod, Thomas, 10 January 1671, age 13, William Love [06.pdf #3]
Todd, Jeremiah, 14 June 1698, age 14, Elinor Stone [19.pdf #217]
Tomkins, Joan, 8 March 1687, age 20, Randolph Hanson [14.pdf #83]
Tomson, Henry, 8 March 1664, age 17, Walter Beane [02.pdf #321]
Towell, Charles, 9 August 1698, age 17, Thomas Hagan [19.pdf #231]
Toy, Walter, 9 June 1702, age 13, Benjamin Smallwood [22.pdf #31]
Toy, William, 9 June 1702, age 14, Ltt. Coll. James Smallwood [22.pdf #31]
Treemairne, John, 9 August 1681, age 17, Captn. Humphrey Warren
    [09.pdf #90]
Tubb, Thomas, 13 April 1669, age 21, Zack Wade [Vol. 60:189]
Tuborne, Katherine, 9 November 1703, age 17, Francis Greene [22.pdf #143]

CHARLES COUNTY

Turner, Walter, __ January 1684, age 18, John Stone [11.pdf #186]
Turner, William, 11 January 1670, age 22, Humphrey Warren Junior
   [Vol. 60:230]
Tusan, Zara, 8 March 1664, age 16, Robert Hundley [02.pdf #320]
Twifer, Anne, 22 April 1662, age 17, William Marshall [01.pdf #211]
Tymothie, William, 11 June 1667, age 15, John Bowles [03.pdf #209]
Uppenbridge, John, 8 June 1680, age 13, John Broade [09.pdf #167]
Vaine, Henrie, 7 April 1668, age 14, George Newman [03.pdf #310]
Vaughan, Richard, 12 November 1715, age 12, Charles Digges [26.pdf #3]
Vaux, Joseph, 8 June 1686, age 19, Phillip Lynes [13.pdf #118]
Verritt, John, 11 April 1676, age 17, John Hatch [07.pdf #101]
Violett, Ambrose, 10 June 1701, age 19, John Beale [21.pdf #126]
W____ , Margrett, 8 November 1670, age 20, Benjamin Rozer [Vol. 60:262]
Waalwort, Isaac, 11 June 1667, age 22, William Marshall [03.pdf #209],
   "Buried his Man Izall (sic) on the last Day of August 1667"
   [03.pdf #297]
Wade (Ware), Allexander, 14 November 1699, age 11, John Godshall
   [20.pdf #99]
Waedman, Rice, 14 March 1665, age 21, Archibell Whahob [02.pdf #509]
Wager, Joseph, 19 April 1698, age 13, John Allen [19.pdf #206]
Walker, George, 14 November 1710, age 17, Patrick Maggelee [24.pdf #29]
Wallen, William, 9 June 1696, age 13, Thomas Mudd [19.pdf #20]
Walsh, Richard, 11 November 1718, age 15, Mary Theobalds [26.pdf #72]
Waltom, Ralph, 14 March 1665, age 14, Peeter Car [02.pdf #509]
Ward, Anne, 12 May 1663, age 16, John Nevill [02.pdf #187]
Ward, Henry, 8 June 1675, age 15, Richard Smoote, by William Barton
   [07.pdf #63]
Ward, Richard, 11 April 1676, age 12, Humphrey Warren [07.pdf #101]
Warner, Christopher, 13 April 1669, age 20, Robert Downes [Vol. 60:188]
Waters, Edward, 9 June 1702, age 15, Richard Wade [22.pdf #31]
Waterworth, Catherine, 8 August 1682, age 14, John Munn [10.pdf #177]
Waterworth, John, 8 August 1682, age 12, John Bayne [10.pdf #177]
Weatherburne, Jane, 11 June 1706, age 18, John Cofer [23.pdf #123]
Webb, Aaron, 12 March 1706, age 6, Maddam Sarah Barton [23.pdf #115]
Webb, Moses, 4 April 1704, age 8, Maj. William Barton [22.pdf #193]
Webb, Rozamon, 4 April 1704, age 11, Maj. William Barton [22.pdf #193]
Webster, Nicholaus, 8 March 1664, age 17, John Piles, by Humphery Warren
   [02.pdf #321]
Welch, James, 13 June 1693, age 15, Major James Smallwood [18.pdf #81]
Welch, Thomas, 14 June 1698, age 16, Philip Briscoe [19.pdf #217]
Welch, William, 4 April 1699, age 15, John Fendall [20.pdf #26]
Westbrooke, William, 14 June 1698, age 17, Richard Harrison [19.pdf #217]

CHARLES COUNTY

Whaland, Dennis, 19 April 1698, age 20, Edward Philpott [19.pdf #206]
Wheeler, David, 10 January 1682, age 18, Thomas Mitchell [10.pdf #130]
Whilden, John, 11 June 1667, age 24, Edward Swanne [03.pdf #209]
White, Matthew, 8 March 1726, age 11, Colo. John Fendall [30.pdf #64]
Whitehead, John, 8 January 1678, age 18, Capt. Humphrey Warren
 [08.pdf #56]
Whitehorne, John, 14 March 1682, age 16, Thomas Mudd [10.pdf #148]
Whitt, Samuell, 14 November 1676, age 11-12, Benjamin Rozer [07.pdf #126]
Whittimore, Christopher, 11 March 1690, age not judged, Henry Hawkins
 [16.pdf #114]
Whorton, John, 14 March 1665, age 17, Thomas Mathews [02.pdf #521]
Wiggs, David, 13 April 1669, age 13, Robert Downes [Vol. 60:188]
Wilder, Robert, 8 August 1671, age 16-17, John Bowles [06.pdf #46]
Wilfray, Lusi, 8 June 1675, age 18, Bennett Marshegay [07.pdf #63]
Wilkinson, John, 10 June 1674, age 18, John Taylor [06.pdf #158]
Wilkinson, Lancelot, 9 January 1672, age 18, Humphry Warren [06.pdf #55]
Wilkison, David, 4 April 1699, age 16, Michaell Martin [20.pdf #26]
Wilkison, John, 14 March 1699, age 17, Francis Goodrich [20.pdf #24]
Willbee, Michael, 11 March 1679, age 12, George Godfrey, by John Wright
 [09.pdf #81]
Williams, Edward, 11 March 1679, age 20, Henry Hawkins [09.pdf #81]
Williams, Jane, 13 March 1677, age 14, Philipp Lines [08.pdf #22]
Williams, Jenkin, 12 January 1675, age 21, Benjamin Rozer [07.pdf #33]
Williams, John, 13 March 1677, age 21, Thomas Gerrard [08.pdf #22]
Williams, John, 14 March 1682, age 10, John Allward [10.pdf #148]
Williams, John, 4 April 1699, age 12, Benjamin Posey [20.pdf #26]
Williams, Katherine, 13 June 1676, age 17-18, Captn. Josias Fendall,
 by his brother Samuel Fendall [07.pdf #111]
Williams, Peter, 12 January 1669, age 13, Thomas Hussy [Vol. 60:179]
Williams, William, 11 March 1679, age 22, Capt. Ignatius Causin [09.pdf #82]
Willman, Henry, 11 June 1678, age 12, William Smith [08.pdf #92]
Willson, Gils, 14 March 1665, age 22-23, Alexander Smith [02.pdf #509]
Willson, John, 10 June 1707, age 10, Thomas Plunkett [23.pdf #180]
Willson, Joseph, 10 June 1707, age 7, Leonard Greene [23.pdf #180]
Wilson, Lawrence, 9 January 1672, age 20, Capt. William Boreman, by
 Richard Edelen [06.pdf #56]
Winter, John, 11 March 1679, age 15, Capt. Ignatius Causin [09.pdf #82]
Wollis, Anne, 17 March 1663, age 18, John Courts [02.pdf #164]
Wood, Jonathan, 14 January 1701, age 14, Capt. William Barton [21.pdf #67]
Woodkeepe, Richard, 9 September 1673, age 12, Cornelius Mackarles
 [06.pdf #141]

CHARLES COUNTY

Woolf, Joseph, 8 March 1664, age 13, Robert Perkins [02.pdf #321]
Woolfe, Robert, 11 June 1678, age 17, Robert Rowlants [08.pdf #92]
Wormely, Thomas, 14 January 1701, age 16, John Payne [21.pdf #67]
Worrell, Mary, 8 January 1706, age 18, Richard Harrison [23.pdf #111]
Worthington, Joseph, 11 August 1685, age 15, Edw. Rookard [12.pdf #96]
Wright, George, 13 June 1676, age 18-19, Benjamin Rozer, by
    Alexander Gallant [07.pdf #111]
Wright, John, March 1717, age 10, Thomas Harris [Liber G Page 178]
Wyott, John, 10 June 1673, age 16, Mrs. Beane, by Mathew Hill [06.pdf #137]
Yappe, Roger, 12 January 1686, age 21, Henry Hawkins [13.pdf #47]
Young, Jane, 11 March 1679, age 20, Elinor Bayne, by Mathew Hill
[09.pdf #82]
Younge, Charles, 12 August 1673, age 10, Samuell Fendall [06.pdf #140]
_____, Ruth, 8 November 1670, age 14, John Stone [Vol. 60:261]
_____, _____, 12 August 1673, age 21, Thomas Harris of Pickoaxon,
    by Thomas Wornell [06.pdf #140]
_____, _____, female, not named, 11 June 1706, age 20, Patrick
    Maggalee [23.pdf #123]

ENCYCLOPEDIA OF SURVIVORS

ARMSTRONG, RICHARD, 11 January 1670, age 19, William Barton [Vol. 60:230]. Expected date of freedom 1676. "It is ordered that Mr. William Barton one of ye administrators of Richard Smoote deceased pay unto Richard Armestrong ye sume of one hundred pounds of tobaccoe out of ye estate of ye said Richard Smoote," 10 January 1677 [08.pdf #18]

ASTERE, GEORGE, 3 February 1664, age 14-15, Alexander Simpson [02.pdf #307]. Expected date of freedom 1672. George Austrey to Thomas Mitchell, 100 acres, 10 March 1689 [17.pdf #190]

BARKER, WILLIAM, 8 March 1664, age 20, Richard Stone [02.pdf #320]. Expected date of freedom 1670. Richard (surname omitted) v. William Barker, agreed, 11 August 1691 [17.pdf #149]. William Barker carpenter v. Thomas Dutton carpenter, dispute concerning "equall partnership," judgment for defendant, 8 November 1692 [17.pdf #280]. Thomas Greenfeild administrator of Richard Charlett deceased v. William Barker, judgment for defendant, 4 October 1698 [19.pdf #246]. "William Barker appointed & sworne Constable in ye roome of Thomas Coleman for Benedict Hundred," 14 November 1699 [20.pdf #99]. Thomas Hussey v. William Barker planter, judgment for plaintiff, 13 February 1700 [20.pdf #156]. Catherine Willson & Joshua Cecill executors of Jonathan Willson deceased v. William Barker planter, judgment for defendant, 13 February 1700 [20.pdf #163]. "JONAS PARKER is appointed Constable in the room of William Barker for Benedict Leonard hundred," 12 November 1700 [21.pdf #51]. Joseph Harrison v. William Barker, judgment for plaintiff, 12 November 1700 [21.pdf #54]. Joseph Harrison v. William Barker, 11 March 1701 [21.pdf #106]. Richard Jenkins v. William Barker, agreed, 13 January 1702 [21.pdf #177]. Barbara Barker, Elizabeth Barker and Sarah Barker, orphan daughters of William Barker deceased, ages not stated, petition for division of father's estate, 14 March 1704 [22.pdf #163]. Age at death 60.

BARRETT, WILLYAM, son of Daniell Barrett, Baptized 4 November 1661, Broad Clyst, Devon, England. Barrett, William, 10 January 1682, age 20, Captn. Ignatius Causin [10.pdf #130]. Expected date of freedom 1688. William Barrett v. John Bracher, taking of "bay colored gelding," judgment for defendant, 11 November 1690 [17.pdf #75]. Petition of Doctor William Hall, that he "did attend upon Mr. William Barrett in his sicknes & administred medicines to him for all which his account amountes & hee doth deserve for ye same four hundred pounds of tobaccoe, and for as much as

ENCYCLOPEDIA OF SURVIVORS

noe administration is yett granted to any person for ye said estate," ordered by Court "that ye said Doctor William Hall have preferrence in point of payment with ye administrator when administration is granted, for ye said four hundred pounds of tobaccoe before any other person," 9 June 1691 [Liber Q Page 31]. William Barrett, probate case, Daniell Hincks executor, 14 March 1693 [18.pdf #71]. Age at death 29.

BARTON, GEORGE, 10 March 1674, age 21-22, Zachary Wade [06.pdf #149]. Expected date of freedom 1680. "George Barton his marke of cattle & hoggs," 1680 [09.pdf #177].

BARTON, ROBERT, son of George Barton, Baptized 22 June 1662, Dalston, Cumberland, England. Barton, Robert, 13 June 1682, age 21, Major William Boardman, by Edmond Dennis [10.pdf #165]. Expected date of freedom 1688. Bartin, Robert, servant to William Keele, 8 January 1684, 28 days absence, ordered to serve "such proportion of time in consideration of his said running away as by act of Assembly in ye case made & provided is required," (280 days servitude) [11.pdf #187] Expected date of freedom 1689. Capt. John Bayne v. Robert Barton planter, agreed, 12 January 1697 [19.pdf #99].

BAYLIE, JOHN, 12 July 1664, age 15-16, Richard Smith, by Mr. Francis Pope, "as Administrator" [02.pdf #404]. Expected date of freedom 1671. John Bayly v. Thomas Helgar, 15 January 1679 [09.pdf #76]. Richard & Anne Ashman to John Bayly, 100 acres, 13 January 1680 [09.pdf #140]. John Bayly, son of John & Mary Bayly, born 20 January 1680 [16.pdf #120]. James Bayly, son of John & Mary Bayly, born 10 January 1683 [16.pdf #120]. William Rosewell v. John Bayley, 10 August 1686 [13.pdf #100]. James Bayly, son of John Bayly, gift of livestock, 1687 [14.pdf #106]. John Bayly, probate case, Joseph & Mary Wilson administrators, 13 January 1691 [17.pdf #92]. Age at death 42.

BAYLY, NICHOLAS, 12 August 1673, age 16, Ignatius Causine [06.pdf #140]. Expected date of freedom 1680. Phillip Lynes v. Nicholas Bayly, "the said action was agreed," 10 March 1685 [12.pdf #60].

BENNETT, JOHN, 9 March 1675, age 20, Hugh French, by Job Corner [07.pdf #47]. Expected date of freedom 1681. John Bennett, former servant to Hugh French, 8 August 1682, whereas in 1682 at Portobacco "ye time of ye service of ye said John with ye said Hugh was expired & ended," ordered by Court "that ye aforesaid John Bennett plaintiff doe recover against ye aforesaid Hugh French defendant one new cloth suite of good kersey or broad cloth, one new shift of white linen, one new pair of shoes & stockins, two hoes, one ax, & three barrells of Indian corne," "and allsoe ye sume of two hundred twenty & one pounds of tobaccoe for his costs & charges of suite" [10.pdf #186].

BENNETT, JOHN, 9 June 1702, age 17, Samuell Luckett, "being proved to be a servant by Charles Moones oath before Coll. Addison," [22.pdf #31]. Expected date of freedom 1709. Francis Searson v. John Bennett, "pretending to hire himselfe to George Godfrey," "continued untill the next Court," "ordered that the said John Bennett remaine with the said Francis Searson and to be here the next Court," 12 January 1703 [22.pdf #81] ordered by Court "that the said John Bennett bee and remaine with the said Francis Searson untill the expiration of his time mentioned in a covenant or agreement between them," 9 March 1703 [22.pdf #89]. John Bennet, former servant to George Godfrey, ordered by Court to recover his freedom dues and 238 pounds of tobacco, 11 March 1712 [25.pdf #35].

BENSON, ROBERT, son of Peter and Elizabeth Benson, Baptized 26 November 1646, Saint Martin in the Fields, Westminster, London, England. Benson, Robert, 8 August 1665, age 18-19, Edward Richardson [02.pdf #547]. Expected date of freedom 1672. Robert Benson v. John Pembrooke, 12 August 1684 [11.pdf #230]. Robert Benson v. Edward Gough, taking of "one bay mare," 8 September 1685 [13.pdf #25] and [13.pdf #52]. Thomas Bartlett, son of Ralph Bartlett deceased, age not stated, bound to Robert Benson, 8 March 1687 [14.pdf #91]. JOHN FRANCIS, probate case, Robert Benson administrator, 9 September 1690 [17.pdf #52]. George & Alice Langham to Robert Benson, 113 acres, 20 October 1690 [17.pdf #299]. John Wood v. Robert Benson, judgment for plaintiff, 11 August 1691 [17.pdf #145]. George Plater v. Robert Benson, agreed, 8 September 1691 [17.pdf #155]. Robert Benson v. John Turnling administrator of John Turling deceased, agreed, 14 March 1693 [18.pdf #65]. Hans Herrickson, son of Hans & Judith Herrickson deceased, "being now about four yeares of age," bound to Robert Benson, 8 August 1693 [18.pdf #87]. COLE, JOHN, without indentures, 8 August 1693, age 18, Robert Benson [18.pdf #87]. Matthew Barnes & Robert Benson, "their presentment," 1695 [Liber T Page 173]. WILLIAM HUNTER to Robert Benson, 200 acres, 8 March 1697 [Liber Q Page 118]. Robert Laftan, probate case, Robert Benson administrator, 8 March 1698 [19.pdf #201].

ENCYCLOPEDIA OF SURVIVORS

Robert Benson planter, presented for "feloniously takeing theiveing pilferrig stealeing & carrying away" "one hilling howe of value of eighteene pounds of tobaccoe" from Carwood Torrey merchant, defendant confessing, "one hundred pounds of tobaccoe for a fine," 4 October 1698 [19.pdf #239].

BIRD, MARY, 14 November 1710, age 19, John Speake [24.pdf #29]. The Grand Jurors "present Mary Bird for having a bastard child by information of John Payne Constable, 10 March 1719 [26.pdf #96], defendant confessing, "twelve lashes so that ye blood appear," 9 June 1719 [26.pdf #113].

BISHOP, WILL, 12 March 1672, age 15, James Walker [06.pdf #59]. Expected date of freedom 1679. "William Bishop his marke of cattel & hoggs," 1688 [16.pdf #30]. William Bishop, "his allowance on ye administration of Smith's estate," 1695 [Liber T Page 140]. John Bayne v. William Bishop administrator of John Smith, 1695 [Liber T Page 198]. "William Glover one of the Constables of Durham Parrish nominates William Bishop to be Constable in his stead," 9 March 1703 [22.pdf #88].

BOOTH, JOHN, 8 March 1664, age 13, Thomas Mathews [02.pdf #321]. Expected date of freedom 1673. "John Booth his marke of hoggs & cattle, 1680 [09.pdf #164]. Henry Henley v. John Booth & Mary his wife, "slaunder & defamacon" for killing a hogge, acquitted, 10 August 1680 [10.pdf #23]. John Booth v. LANCELOTT WILKINSON, agreed before trial, 11 January 1681 [10.pdf #49]. John Booth v. Henry Henley, agreed before trial, 8 August 1682 [10.pdf #181].

BOWMAN, JOHN, 17 March 1663, age 17, Mr. Robert, by John Duglas [02.pdf #164]. Expected date of freedom 1670. John Bowman, probate case, Richard Corks administrator, 14 November 1693 [18.pdf #122]. John Bowman, probate case, Richard Cox administrator, 1694 [Liber T Page 90] and 1695 [Liber T Page 189]. Age at death 47.

BRANOR, EDMOND, 19 April 1698, age 17, Michaell Martin [19.pdf #207]. Expected date of freedom 1705. Edward Brawner, List of Taxable Inhabitants, 56 squirrells heads, 12 November 1717 [26.pdf #18]. The Grand Jurors "do present Edward Braner for breach of Sabbath by information of Andrew Johnson & John Sutton," 14 August 1722 [27.pdf #176].

ENCYCLOPEDIA OF SURVIVORS

BRIGHT, THOMAS, son of Edward and Mary Bright, Baptized 10 June 1651, Great Waltham, Essex, England. Bright, Thomas, 8 March 1670, age 21, Mr. Young [Vol 60:243]. Expected date of freedom 1676. Thomas Tickerell, probate case, Thomas & Jane Bright executors, 23 August 1684 [11.pdf #240].

BROOKE, JOHN, son of Joseph and Mary Brooke, Baptized 22 January 1665, Corse, Gloucester, England. Brooke, John, 12 January 1686, age 21, Henry Hawkins [13.pdf #47]. Expected date of freedom 1692. John Brookes "his mark," 1696 [Liber T Page 366]. Paul Burras, probate case, John & Jane Brooks administrators, 8 June 1708 [23.pdf #263]. John Brookes wico (Wiccomico -- ed.), List of Taxable Inhabitants, 66 squirrells heads, 12 November 1717 [26.pdf #19]. John Brookes wico (Wiccomico -- ed.), List of Taxable Inhabitants, 2 crows heads, 12 November 1717 [26.pdf #19]. Timothy Carrington v. John Brooks, agreed, 13 March 1722, [27.pdf #148]. John Brooks, will dated 30 June 1712, probated 30 March 1714, William Gody executor [Liber AB No. 3 Folio 72]. Named in will: his "eldest sonne" John; his "youngest sonne" Matthew; his daughter Elizabeth "the wife of Abel Wakefield"; his daughter Sarah Brooks; his daughter Mary Tennison; his daughter Jean; his son William Gody or Goody "and Margrett his wife my daughter." Age at death 49.

BROUNE, GUSTAVUS, son of Gustavus Broune and Jean Mitchelson, Baptized 20 April 1689, Dalkeith, Midlothian, Scotland. Browne, Gustavus, 8 June 1708, age 20, Jonathan White [23.pdf #254]. Expected date of freedom 1714. Philemon & Mary Hemsley to Gustavus Brown, 300 acres, 2 November 1714 [Liber F Page 51]. Anne Read, servant to Doctor Gustavus Brown, 8 March 1715, 65 days absence, (650 days servitude), and eight months for "six hundred pounds of tobacco" "expended in regaining her" [25.pdf #265]. Gustavus Brown, "his order about his runaway servant," August 1715 [Liber G Page 32]. Gustavus Brown v. Richard Butts, March 1716 [Liber G Page 84]. Gustavus Brown v. Groves executor, agreed, March 1716 [Liber G Page 91]. Henry Ossley v. Gustavus Brown, judgment confessed, June 1716 [Liber G Page 133]. Gustavus Brown, "complaint of his servant Alice Coleins adjudged no cause," March 1717 [Liber G Page 173]. Samuell Bowman v. Gustavus Brown, agreed, June 1717 [Liber G Page 235]. Thomas Dent to Gustavus Browne, 70 acres, 22 April 1718 [Liber H Page 184]. Thomas Dent to Gustavus Browne, 183 acres, 22 April 1718 [Liber H Page 187]. Charles and Elizabeth Adams to Gustavus Browne, 215 acres, 18 August 1718

ENCYCLOPEDIA OF SURVIVORS

[Liber H Page 191]. Doctor Gustavus Browne, bill of exchange, 19 September 1719 [Liber H Page 346]. Gustavus Browne v. John Morton, assault & battery, agreed, 10 November 1719 [26.pdf #158]. Gustavus Browne v. John Morton, agreed, 8 March 1720 [26.pdf #166]. Gustavus Browne and eight others, ordained and appointed Worshippfull Commissioner for Charles County Court, 14 June 1720 [26.pdf #171]. Gustavus Browne v. Elias Hennington, agreed, 9 August 1720 [27.pdf #25]. Gustavus Brown v. JAMES THOMPSON, agreed, 14 November 1721 [27.pdf #124]. Anne Dent to Gustavus Brown, relinquishments of dower, 6 December 1722 [Liber L Page 61], ref. Thomas Dent to Gustavus Browne, 22 April 1718 [Liber H Page 184] and [Liber H Page 187]. John Palmer, servant to Dr. Gustavus Brown, 10 November 1724, 148 days absence, and "two hundred pounds of tobacco expended in taking him up," ordered to serve "tenn days for one of his runnaway time (1480 days servitude) & tenn weeks for the expences aforesaid [29.pdf # 7]. Mary Johnson, servant to Doctor Gustavus Brown, 14 March 1732, 38 days absence, and "four hundred pounds of tobacco" expended "in takeing her up," ordered to serve "five days for each one of her runaway time" (190 days servitude), and "six months for the expences aforesaid" [32.pdf #51]. Gustavus Brown, Doctor, will dated 4 March 1761, probated 12 May 1762, Richard Brown, John Moncure, Philip Key, Collonel Richard Harrison & Robert Yates, executors [Liber AD, No. 6, Folio 219]. Refers to his "estate in Scotland England Maryland or elsewhere." Named in will: his wife Margrett; his "two children by her" named Gustavus Richard Brown and Margrett Brown; his "eldest son the Rev. Mr. Richard Brown"; his daughter Frances Moncure; his daughter Sarah Scott; his daughter Mary Threlkeld; his daughter Elizabeth Wallace; his daughter Jane Campbell; his daughter Cecilia Key; his daughter Ann Clagget; John Mitchelson "of Middleton in Scotland" and his brother Samuel Mitchelson; refers to his "farm in and about Newstead lying in Scotland"; his "kinsman" Samuel Mitchelson; Philip Key; Collonel Richard Harrison; Robert Yates; his "son" John Moncure. Age at death 73.

BROWNE, JAMES, 12 January 1686, age 15, Domindigo Agambrah [13.pdf #47]. Expected date of freedom 1693. Priscilla Slye administratrix of Robert Slye v. James Browne, "abated by ye death of ye plaintiff," 29 November 1698 [19.pdf #265]. John Sanders v. James Browne, judgment for plaintiff, 11 March 1701 [21.pdf #117]. Richard Nellson v. James Browne, agreed, 10 March 1702 [22.pdf #17].

ENCYCLOPEDIA OF SURVIVORS

BROWNE, THOMAS, 10 January 1682, age 16, Peter Car [10.pdf #130]. Expected date of freedom 1688. "Thomas Browne his marke of cattle & hoggs," 1691 [17.pdf #155]. Thomas Browne married Alice Horton, 26 July 1692 [16.pdf #122]. Thomas Browne, son of Thomas & Alice Browne of Pyckyawaxon Parish, Born 21 December 1693 [Liber Q Page 21]. Thomas Browne v. HENRY HARDY, for "false feigned and scandalous infamous and approbrious words," judgment for defendant, 14 June 1709 [23.pdf #310]. Thomas Browne v. John Yates, judgment for defendant, 14 June 1709 [23.pdf #310].

BRYAN, JOHN, 19 April 1698, age 12, Capt. John Bayne [19.pdf #206]. Expected date of freedom 1708. "John Bryon a servant boy neare 5 years to serve," "An Inventory of the Estate of Capt. John Bayne Deceased," 10 July 1702. Trustees: Coll. John Courts, Major James Smallwood, Coll. John Addison, Major William Dent & Major Benjamin Hall. "John Bryan to serve 3 years next March," The Inventory of the Goods and Chattles of Madam Anne Bayne," 15 July 1703. John Bryan, servant to Walter Bayne, 9 March 1708, "PATRICK MORELAND appeareing here" "to give evidence between John Bryan and Mr. Walter Bayne," ordered by Court "that the said John Bryan be free from the service of the said Walter Bayne," "the said John Bryan quitting his freedom dues which he is willing to do" [23.pdf #236]. Samuel Perrie & Comp. v. John Bryon, judgment for plaintiff, 13 March 1722 [27.pdf #157].

BRYAN, TURLOUGH, 19 April 1698, age 19, Maj. William Dent [19.pdf #206]. Expected date of freedom 1704. Turlough Bryan, servant to William Dent, 13 June 1699, "came here into Court and made complaint against William Wilson late of Charles County planter his overseer for abuseing of him and that hee had unreasonably beaten & wounded him," ordered by Court that "ye sherife take ye said William Wilson and him in safe custody keepe untill hee putt in good & sufficient security for his appearance here att ye next Court [20.pdf #68]. Turlough Brian, servant to William Willson, 12 September 1699, complaint "for unreasonable beateing & wounding him the said Turlough Brian," and "the said William Willson cometh & saith that he is in no wise guilty," whereupon "the wittnesses respectively being produced sworne heard & examined," "the said William Willson by the Court here was adjudged guilty," and fined "two hundred pounds of tobacco" [20.pdf #90]. Turlough Obryan, servant to Major William Dent, "desires with ye approbation of this Court to bargaine with his said master, that in consideration ye his master will give his consent that hee may marry with one FRANCES HOGG a servant woman of ye said Major Dent, they will each of them serve ye said Major Dent two whole years upon which agreement they are both to bee free, ye fourteenth day of November in ye yeare 1705, and Major Dent promises to release ye rest of ye said Frances Hoggs service," 14 September 1703 [22.pdf #129].

BUCKERES, JOHN, son of William Buckeres, Baptized 11 November 1655, West Calder, West Lothian, Scotland. Booker, John, 11 August 1674, age 18, Alexander White [06.pdf #163]. Expected date of freedom 1681. John Booker v. John Clarke, 11 March 1684 [11.pdf #199]. "The marke of John Booker" for livestock, 1685 [13.pdf #19]. John Booker v. Christopher Woolcock, judgment for plaintiff, 12 January 1692 [17.pdf #202]. "John Booker appointed Constable in ye roome of John Gray for ye Lower parts of Nanjemy Parish," 10 November 1696 [19.pdf #72] [19.pdf #111]. BROWNE, ANDREW, without indentures, 13 June 1699, age 21, John Booker [20.pdf #69]. Richard Jones, probate case, John Booker administrator, 10 March 1702 [22.pdf #22]. John Booker, petitioner, "about sixteen yeares since marryed Anne Price the widdow and relict of Richard Price deceased which said Anne is likewise lately deceased, that Richard Price, a younger sonne of Richard Price aforesaid, being about seaventeen yeares of age the last February, taking to ill company, doth absent himselfe from your petitioners house and doth endeavour to gett his freedom, that your petitioner, as is very well knowne in his neighbourhood, hath maintained the said Richard Price his sonne in law with all things necessary ever since he was a year or two old, and now when he is able to do your petitioner some service he absconds, and clandestinly endeavours to gett free before he is of full age," ordered by Court "that the said Richard Price continue with the said John Booker untill he shall arrive to the full and compleat age of twenty one years," 12 June 1705 [23.pdf #80]. Richard Price, orphan, parents not named, "being eighteen yeares old in February next," [23.pdf #104] "committed to the care and custody" of John Booker, 14 August 1705 [23.pdf #89], 11 September 1705 [23.pdf #100]. Edward Foster, servant to John Booker, "adjudged for runaway time," 8 November 1709 [Liber B Page 663, not microfilmed]. John Wright, grandson of John Booker, gift of livestock, 1711 [Liber C Page 250]. John Booker, will dated 14 October 1712, probated 25 March 1713, Elizabeth Booker executrix, [Liber AB No. 3 Folio 61]. Named in will: his wife Elizabeth Booker; Thomas Price; his son John Booker; his son in law Thomas Write & Mary his wife; his daughter Sarah; his daughter Ann. Age at death 57.

ENCYCLOPEDIA OF SURVIVORS

BURGES, JOHN, 28 January 1662, age not judged, James Waker (sic), sold by Humphrey Warring (Warren -- ed.) "of London, Marchant," four years [01.pdf #190] Expected date of freedom 1666. John Burgess, son in law of Richard Harris, gift of livestock, 1677 [08.pdf #47]. John Burgesse, parents not named, "hee now being fifteene yeares of age next March ensueing," "bound to Obadiah Dunn "of St. Maries County, 14 September 1680 [10.pdf #29]

BURGESSE, SAMUELL, 11 March 1690, age not judged, "Mr. John Bayne preferring to ye Court here an Indenture of one Samuell Burgesse a servant of Mrs. Elinor Bayne his mother," and "ye said Indenture not being under ye seale of any Office," ordered by Court "that ye said Samuell Burgesse serve his said Mrs. Elinor Bayne according to ye custome of ye country" [16.pdf #114]. Samuell Burgesse, servant to Mrs. Elinor Bayne, 10 June 1690, absent "severall times," 60 days in all, 600 days servitude [17.pdf #18]. John Ratclife v. Samuell Burgesse, judgment for plaintiff, 10 November 1696 [19.pdf #84]. Thomas Whichaley v. Samuell Burges, "concerning the said Samuell buying a certain guelding," judgment for plaintiff, 13 February 1700 [20.pdf #153]. Samuell Burgess, probate case, petition of Arthur Elie, "that the said Burgess lay very sick at your petitioners house who in the time of his sicknesse your petitioner nursed tended and cherished him to the utmost of his ability and soone after dyed," 13 January 1702 [21.pdf #174]. "An Accompt of Samuell Burgess's Cropp delivered to Court by Arthur Etie," 11 August 1702 [22.pdf #50].

CAMPBELL, JOHN, 14 November 1710, age 14, Edward Chapman [24.pdf #30]. Expected date of freedom 1718. John Campbell, "bayle bond assigned," 14 March 1721 [27.pdf #46], "tenn pounds sterling," & "ye aforesaid John Campbell although solemnly called came not but made default," 14 March 1721 [27.pdf #47]. Thomas Matthews v. John Campbell, "& the Sheriff to wit John Howard Gent." returns "that ye aforesaid John in his baliwick is not found," judgment for plaintiff, 14 March 1721 [27.pdf #61]. Stephen Mankin v. John Campbell, and "the Sheriff aforesaid returns to ye Court that ye said John Campbell is not found in his bayliwick," judgment for plaintiff, 13 June 1721 [27.pdf #89] and 14 November 1721 [27.pdf #113]. John Campbell, "concerning his breaking open a small chest or box belonging to Thomas Hatcher," "and ye same John though solemnly called comes not," judgment for plaintiff, by default, 13 March 1722 [27.pdf #152].

ENCYCLOPEDIA OF SURVIVORS

CANTLEY, JOHN, son of James Cantley, Baptized 12 August 1677, Rothiemay, Banff, Scotland. Canley, John, 12 August 1690, age 15, Raiph Smith, by John Duglas [17.pdf #30]. Expected date of freedom 1697. John Canele, List of Taxable Inhabitants, 51 squirrells heads, 12 November 1717 [26.pdf #18].

CAPSHAW, FRANCIS, 10 November 1674, age 15, Alexander Smith [07.pdf #19]. Expected date of freedom 1681. Francis Capshaw, probate case, George Junr. & Jemima Diamond executors, 12 January 1697 [29.pdf #101]. Age at death 37. John Capshaw, "sonn in law of George Diamond," "being sixteen yeares of age the sixth day of March last past," bound to John Mellor, he "to cause him to be learnt to read distinctly in the Bible" and "to find and allow him sufficient meat drinck washing and lodging and apparrell" and "to well cloathe him at the expiration of his time" and "to teach him the trade of a taylor" or "to give him a cow and calfe at the expiration of his time," 9 September 1707 [23.pdf #206]. Francis Capshaw (Junr.), "being fourteen yeares of age the thirteenth day of July last past," "bound in Court to his father in law George Diamond," he "to teach him the trade of a cooper and to find and allow him sufficient meat drinck washing lodging and apparrell" and "at the expiration of his time to well cloath him and to give him a good sett of coopers tooles," 9 September 1707 [23.pdf #206]. Francis Cabshaw (Junr.), List of Taxable Inhabitants, 75 squirrells heads, 12 November 1717 [26.pdf #19]. Frances Cabshaw (Junr.), List of Taxable Inhabitants, 6 crows heads, 12 November 1717 [26.pdf #19].

CARPENTER, HENRY, son of Henry and Mary Carpenter, Baptized 12 June 1659, All Hallows London Wall, London, England. Carpenter, Henry, 11 April 1676, age 16, William Perfitt [07.pdf #101]. Expected date of freedom 1682. Thomas Lewis v. Henry Carpenter, "the action was agreed," 10 March 1685 [12.pdf #61].

CHAMPE, STEEPHEN, 8 March 1664, age 14, William Marshall [02.pdf #322]. Expected date of freedom 1672. Stephen Champ, servant to William Marshall, 12 January 1669, "produceing an Indenture signed by William Barrett for five yeares," petitions for a discharge & for his corne & cloathes," ordered by Court "that the said servant be free & that the said William Marshall pay him his corn & cloathes he making the said Marshall satisfaction for two daies comeing to Court & for the amercement paid to the Court for judgeing his age" (ref. 8 March 1664 -- ed.) [Vol. 60:180]

ENCYCLOPEDIA OF SURVIVORS

CHANTLER, JOHN, 10 November 1696, age 18, William Wilkison [19.pdf #73]. Expected date of freedom 1703. John Chantler v. John Betts, agreed, 13 March 1705 [23.pdf #62]. Edward Kite, son of Anne Kite, "being two yeares old the twenty fourth day of July last past," bound to John Chandler, he "to learne him the trade of a shoe maker and to learne him to read distinctly in the Bible and to find and allow him sufficient meate drinck apparrell washing and lodging" and "at the expiration of his time to sett him out with a sett of shoe makers tooles and a good new suite of cloaths," 11 November 1707 [23.pdf #221]. Thomas Douglass, age not stated, presented by Capt. William Harbert, bound to John Chandler with "the consent of Thomas Douglass," he "to learne the trade of a tanner and shoomaker," 10 August 1708 [23.pdf #266]. John & Sarah Mellor to John Chandler, 66 acres, 13 June 1710 [Liber C Page 186]. John & Mary Mellor to John Chandler, 100 acres, 30 October 1719 [Liber H Page 310]. John & Ann Chandler to Mark Penn, 100 acres, 13 July 1720 [Liber H Page 380]. Michael Welsh, servant to Courts Keech, 8 August 1721, master's petition "sets forth that his servant named Michael Welsh has absconded from his service & that he is detained by John Chandler," and the Court summons John Chandler "to answer said complaint & ye aforesaid servant may be remanded to his service" [27.pdf #92]. John Chandler shoemaker, his mark of livestock, 5 April 1726 [Liber L Page 262]. Underwood, Charles, servant to John Chandler, 14 November 1727, 15 days absence, and "five hundred pounds of tobacco" expended "in takeing him up," ordered to serve "eight dayes for one of his runaway time" (120 days servitude), and "three months and a half for the expences aforesaid [31.pdf #18]. John Chandler, will dated 20 November 1735, probated 19 January 1736, Ann & John Chandler executors [Liber AC, No. 4, Folio 58]. Named in will: his wife Ann; his son John; his son William; his son Stephen; his daughter Ann Chandler; his daughter Mary Chandler; his daughter Sarah Hamel. Age at death 56.

CHESSON, JOHN, 12 May 1663, age 14 "and a half," John Meekes [02.pdf #177]. Expected date of freedom 1670. John Chesson, probate case, Barbary Chesson relict, 12 March 1678 [08.pdf #78]. Age at death 29. Mary Chesson, daughter of Barbary Chesson relict of John Chesson, gift of livestock, 11 November 1678 [09.pdf #46]

CHOMLEY, FRANCIS, 11 January 1670, age 16, Henry Adames [Vol. 60:230]. Expected date of freedom1677. Phillip Lynes v. Francis Chomley, "he hath absented himselfe out of the Province & left noe attorney behinde him," judgment for plaintiff, 12 March 1684 [11.pdf #203].

ENCYCLOPEDIA OF SURVIVORS

COB, SAMUEL, son of Henry Cob and Sarah Hinkley, Born 12 October 1654, Barnstable, Massachusetts. Cobb, Samuel, 8 June 1669, age 15, Thomas King [Vol. 60:196]. Expected date of freedom 1675. Samuel Cob married Elizabeth (surname not stated), 20 December 1680, Barnstable, Massachusetts.

COLE, JOHN, 8 August 1693, age 18, ROBERT BENSON [18.pdf #87]. Expected date of freedom 1700. The Grand Jury presented Philip Reyley for that he on 15 December 1700 "being the Sabbath day" "an assault in and upon the body of one John Cole did make and him did beat wound and evilly mistreat so that of his life it was despaired," found guilty, fined two hundred pounds of tobacco, 14 January 1701 [21.pdf #63]. Richard Byrth v. John Cole, judgment for plaintiff, 14 September 1708 [23.pdf #272]. William Elliott Senr. v. John Cole, agreed, 9 November 1708 [23.pdf #283]. John Cole, his "mark of cattel and hoggs," 8 February 1710 [Liber C Page 156]. John & Elizabeth Cole to Charles Musgrove, 125 acres, 25 April 1710, [Liber C Page 179]. John Cole v. Howards executor, March 1716 [Liber G Page 71]. John Cole v. Thomas Orrell, judgment for plaintiff, 10 November 1719 [26.pdf #146]. Thomas Turner to John Cole, 300 acres, 24 September 1721 [Liber H Page 458]. John Cole, will dated 28 May 1724, probated 18 June 1724, ____ Cole executor [Liber AB No. 3 Folio 180]. Named in will: his son William; his son John; his son Benjamin; his daughter Jemima; his daughter Elizabeth; his daughter Mary; his "loving wife" (not named). Age at death 49.

COMPTON, WILLIAM, son of William and Anne Compton, Baptized 14 February 1660, Little Compton, Gloucester, England. Cumpton, William, 11 January 1676, age 17, John Hatch [07.pdf #96]. Expected date of freedom 1683. William Compton v. Anthony Bankes, 1696 [Liber T Page 347]. James Neale v. William Compton, "maliciously intending him the said James of his good name fame creditt estimation and reputation totally to deprive him into scandall ignomey and reproach amongst all his neighbours and other honorable persons," judgment for plaintiff, 9 September 1701 [21.pdf #154]. William Compton v. Edward Sanders, agreed, 10 June 1707 [23.pdf #191]. William Darby, parents not named, master not stated, "arived to age of one and twenty years," "by the Deposition of Elizabeth Neale and William Compton," ordered by Court "that he be free and discharged from service," 13 November 1711 [25.pdf #16]. James Penny, parents not named, "being fourteen years of age the fourth day of February last," bound to William Compton, 11 March 1712

ENCYCLOPEDIA OF SURVIVORS

[25.pdf #33]. William Compton appointed Overseer for "Lower parts of William and Mary parish," 10 November 1713 [25.pdf #181]. William Compton v. Richard Smith, March 1716 [Liber G Page 87]. William Compton appointed Overseer for "Piles's Fresh East side upper precinct," 11 November 1718 [26.pdf #72]. William Cumpton appointed Overseer for Newport East side, 8 November 1720 [27.pdf #29] & 14 November 1721 [27.pdf #107]. Thomas Lutwidge v. William Compton, 14 March 1721 [27.pdf #66].

COOPER, JOHN, 14 January 1679, age 15, Capt. William Barton [09.pdf #62]. Expected date of freedom 1686. Elizabeth Shareman, orphan, "eight years of age the eighteenth day of October next," bound to John Cooper, "to read distinctly in the Bible" and be brought up "in the Established Religeon," 11 August 1713 [25.pdf #171]. Bead Sharman, orphan, "five years of age the first of November next," bound to John Cooper, "to read distinctly in the Bible" and be brought up "in the Established Religeon," 11 August 1713 [25.pdf #171]. John Cooper, List of Taxable Inhabitants, 30 squirrells heads, 12 November 1717 [26.pdf #18]. John Cooper, List of Taxable Inhabitants, 5 crows heads, 12 November 1717 [26.pdf #19]. "JOHN KING is appointed Constable of ye upper part of Durham hundred in ye room of John Cooper," 12 August 1718 [26.pdf #51]. John Cooper, his "proper brand mark," 26 May 1720 [Liber H Page 346].

COTTWELL (COTTERELL), JAMES, 13 March 1677, age 20, Thomas Gerrard [08.pdf #22]. Expected date of freedom 1683. Children of James & Elizabeth Cotterell of ye head of Wiccocomico River: Elizabeth, daughter, born 30 April 1689 [Liber Q Page 15]. Jane, daughter, born 15 August 1690 [Liber Q Page 17]. James, son, born 7 September 1694 [Liber Q Page 23]. James Cotterell v. John Duglas, agreed, 10 June 1690 [17.pdf #26]. James Cotterell v. William Marshall, taking of a "bay gelding," judgment for defendant, 11 November 1690 [17.pdf #74]. James Cottrell to Nicholas Wife, 100 acres, 5 December 1690 [17.pdf #137]. James Cotterell v. John Gale and CORNELIUS DONAHOWE garnishees of Anthony Smith, judgment for plaintiff, 12 January 1692 [17.pdf #205]. James Cotterell v. John Gale garnishee of Anthony Smith, judgment for defendant, 8 March 1692 [17.pdf #221]. WILLIAM HERBERT "together with James Cotterell his security," v. Philip Lynes, "and ye said Philip Lynes though solemnely called cameth not nor any for him," continued, 8 March 1692 [17.pdf #227]. Richard Edelen Junr. v. Thomas English, James Cotterell witness, 8 August 1693 [17.pdf 106]. James Cotterell v. Philip Lynes, judgment for plaintiff,

ENCYCLOPEDIA OF SURVIVORS

4 August 1694 [17.pdf #184]. HENRY HARDY, Thomas Baker & James Cotterell, named as witnesses against "Philip Lynes late of Charles County for forgery." 14 August 1694 [18.pdf #317]. William Dent v. Jame (sic) Cottrell, 1695 [Liber T Page 286]. James Cottrell v. John Wincele, 1696 [Liber T Page 344]. Francis Bullarye planter v. James Cotterell, judgment for plaintiff, 11 January 1698 [19.pdf #192]. LAWRENCE, JAMES, without indentures, 4 April 1699, age 17, James Cotteroll [20.pdf #26]. James Cotterell v. Jesse Doyne, judgment for plaintiff, 4 April 1699 [20.pdf #60]. James Cotterell v. Henry Perry & John Kirwood merchants, judgment for plaintiff, 14 November 1699 [20.pdf #105]. James & Elizabeth Cotterell v. John Beale, for "falsely feigned and scandalous and malicious words" intending to deprive "the said Elizabeth of her good name fame and credit estimation and reputation," "said and acknowledged in open Court to bee agreed," 12 November 1701 [21.pdf #165]. Smart, not named, daughter of Edward Smart, age not stated, presented by James Cottrell, who "desires shee may be bound to some one the mother being dead and the father runn away, the Court being credibly informed that Mrs. Anne Brandt the wife of Mr. Randolph Brandt being her God Mother would take her, therefore the same is referred untill the next Court," 8 June 1703 [22.pdf #107]. James Cotterrell v. John Baker, agreed, 8 June 1703 [22.pdf #117]. Madam Charity Courts v. James Cotterrell, agreed, 10 August 1703 [22.pdf #126]. "James Cottrell and Henry More appoynted Press Masters for Charles County," 12 June 1705 [23.pdf #80]. James Cottrell & Elizabeth his wife, "one of the daughters and coheires of Thomas Burford deceased," to George Plater, 200 acres, 2 November 1705 [Liber Z Page 240]. Edward Phillpott v. James Cottrell, agreed, 9 March 1708 [23.pdf #241]. William Crocker v. James Cotterill, 11 March 1712 [25.pdf #68]. James Cotterill appointed Overseer for "Upper parts of William and Mary parish," 10 November 1713 [25.pdf #181]. Henry Ossley v. James Cottrele, March 1717 [Liber G Page 187]. James Cottrell, confesses to "breach of the peace," 9 August 1720 [27.pdf #16]. "James Cottrell & Henry Barnes are by the Court here appointed press masters for ye ensuing year," 14 November 1721 [27.pdf #108]. James Cottrell, will dated 17 February 1723, probated 9 March 1723, Anne Cottrell and James Cottrell executors [Liber AB No. 3 Folio 155]. Named in will: his wife Anne; his son Thomas; his son James; his granddaughter Elizabeth Swan daughter of Thomas Swan; his daughter Anne Phillpott wife of John Philpott; his grandchildren James, Mary and Judith Swan children of Thomas Swan; George Plater; his daughter Jane Penn wife of Mark Penn; his daughter Hannah Lattimore. Age at death 65.

ENCYCLOPEDIA OF SURVIVORS

DAMER, THOMAS, 12 January 1669, age 17, John Cage. Expected date of freedom 1676. Thomas Damer, 11 March 1673, petition sets forth that on 21 August 1668 the said Thomas Damer did "covenant & agree with Thomas Tolson of London Merchant to serve him the said Tolson or his assignes for the term of fower yeares after his first & next arivall in Virginia or Maryland as by a Testimoniall from under the Seal of the Office here in Court produced it may appeare yet nevertheless Humphrey Warren Merchant Factor for the said Thomas Tolson did at his arrivall into this province contrary to the said Covenant sell your petitioner here for the custome of the countrey and took the said Testimoniall of the Office from your petitioner and blotted out your petitioners name and put in the name of another servant which was at the same tyme sold by him soe that your petitioner is thereby much injured and in danger of serveing seven yeares except your Worshipps" "grant him an order for his freedome together with his corne and cloathes" [06.pdf #135]; whereupon a jury was impaneled, which "brought in this ensueing verdict viz: that the Indenture belonged to Thomas Damour and by virtue of it he is free, whereupon the Commissioners ordered that Judgement should be entered against John Cage with costs of suite" [06.pdf #136]. "Richard New & Thomas Damer their marke of hogges & cattle," 1681 [10.pdf #55].

DARNELL, EDWARD, son of John and Anne Darnell, Baptized 26 September 1669, Saint Andrew, Enfield, London, England. Darnell, Edw., 13 March 1688, age 17, Phillip Lynes [14.pdf #176]. Expected date of freedom 1695. Edward Darnell, servant to Philip Lynes, 10 November 1691, with JAMES THORNBOROUGH & CATHERINE JONES, "came here into Court naked & made complaint that for want of clothes they were allmost starved, and ye said Philip Lynes being absent, itt is ordered that Major James Smallwood lett them have necessary clothes to preserve them from perishing with cold, and that Coll. Humphrey Warren sherife pay ye said Smallwood for what clothing they shall have of him out of what tobaccoe shall be allowed to ye said Lynes in ye County levy this yeare" [17.pdf #157]. Wee the Grand Jury "doe present Edward Darnall late of Charles County planter for entertaining a servant man belonging to Mr. John Smith of this County by information of the said Smith," 11 June 1706 [23.pdf #122]. It was presented that Edward Darnall on 28 March 1706 at Portobacco "did wittingly and willingly detaine and give entertainment to a certain man servant belonging to the said John Smith named William Mackeboy for the space of one night or twenty four hours without the leave or lycence of him the said John Smith," and "the said Edward Darnall prayeth that he may have

ENCYCLOPEDIA OF SURVIVORS

Councill assigned him before he pleads to the said presentment," "whereupon Cornelius White one of the attorneys of this Court is specially admitted and appoynted as Councill for the said Edward Darnall," jury "impannelled," verdict "that the said Edward Darnall be acquitted and discharged," 10 September 1706 [23.pdf #142]. "Elizabeth Darnall, daughter of Edward Darnall at Zachya, her marke of cattle & hoggs," 9 September 1707 [Liber Z Page 260]. John Darnall, son of Edward Darnall, gift of livestock, 8 July 1714 [Liber F Page 17]. Thomas Darnell, son of Edward Darnell, gift of livestock, 14 December 1726 [Liber L Page 312]. Sarah Darnell, daughter of Edward Darnell, gift of livestock, 14 December 1726 [Liber L Page 312]. Edward Darnal, will dated 1751, probated 4 May 1754, Edward Darnal executor [Liber AD No. 5 Folio 22]. Named in will: William Thomas; his son Edward; his son William; his son Isaac; his son Thomas; his daughter Mary; his daughter Sarah; his daughter Elizabeth. Age at death 84.

DAVERILL, THOMAS, 11 January 1670, age 20, Thomas Dent [Vol. 60:230]. Expected date of freedom 1676. Thomas Daverell, deposition, "that Richard Carpenter was to have ye one halfe of ye cattle that Mr. Thomas Dent bought of Mr. William Hatton," 12 June 1677 [08.pdf #37]. Elizabeth Deverell, daughter of Thomas & Anne Deverell, gift of livestock, 1682 [11.pdf #58]. Thomas Deverill v. John Reddish, "agreed before tryall," 13 June 1683 [11.pdf #127]. "Thomas Deverell his marke of cattle & hoggs," 1686 [14.pdf #106]. Anne Deverell wife of Thomas Deverell v. Joseph Harrison and Richard True, 9 August 1687 [14.pdf #152] and 13 September 1687 [14.pdf #158], defendants acquitted 8 November 1687 [14.pdf #161]. Thomas & Elizabeth Shuttleworth v. Thomas & Anne Deverill, suit for slander, 8 Novem,ber 1688, judgment for plaintiffs [16.pdf #33]. Thomas & Anne Deverill v. Thomas & Elizabeth Shuttleworth, assault "by force of armes the said Elizabeth upon ye said Anne at Nanjamey at ye house of THOMAS DICKISSON," judgment for plaintiffs, 8 November 1688 [16.pdf #34]. Thomas Deverell v. Thomas Parker, judgment for plaintiff, 10 March 1691 [17.pdf #106]. Charles Shepherd, indicted for assault "with force & armes upon ye body of Anne Deverell," "soe that of her life shee did despair," 11 August 1691 [17.pdf #137].

DAVIES, GRIFFIN, 8 June 1675, age 17, Nicholas Prodday, by Richard Fowke [07.pdf #63]. Expected date of freedom 1681. MATHEW DYKE and Griffith Davis, complaints against them dismissed, 8 November 1687 [14.pdf #161]. Richard Ward, MATHEW DYKE, Griffith Davis and Elinor Halee, summons issued 8 November 1687 [14.pdf #162]. Griffith Davis v. John Toney, judgment for defendant, 13 June 1693 [18.pdf #84]. Griffith & Elizabeth Davis v. John & Dorothy Toney, judgment for plaintiffs, 13 March 1694 [18.pdf #158]. Griffith Davis v. John Taney, "nonsuit," 1695 [Liber T Page 149]. John Stone v. Griffith Davis, judgment for plaintiff, 9 March 1697 [19.pdf #127].

DAVIES, HUGH, 12 August 1690, age 14, Raiph Smith, by John Duglas [17.pdf #30]. Expected date of freedom 1698. Hugh Davis, servant to Ralph Smith, 8 June 1697, servant confessing "here in Court," 17 days absence, 170 days servitude [19.pdf #130]. Expected date of freedom 1699. "Hugh Davies a criple his petition read the Court allowes him eight hundred pounds of tobacco in the next yeares Leavy and to bee henceforth Leavy free," 10 June 1701 [21.pdf #126]. "Hugh Davis a cripple allowed," Charles County Levy, 12 November 1701 [21.pdf #169]. Hugh Davis v. John Loftley, "the said Hugh by William Stone his attorney" petitions for freedom corn and clothes, quotes verbatim the relevant section of "an Act of Assembly made at the Port of Annapolis," 22 July 1699, "relateing to servants and slaves," ordered by Court "that the said Hugh Davis recover against the said John Loftley" "one good cloth suite either of kersey or broad cloth, one shift of white linning (linen -- ed.) to bee new, one paire of French falls shooes and stockings, two hoes, one axe, and one gunn of twenty shillings price, as also two hundred seaventy seaven pounds of tobacco for his cost and charges," "and the said John Loftley in mercy," 13 January 1702 [21.pdf #181]. "To Hugh Davis a Cripple on his Petition," Charles County Levy, 10 November 1702 [22.pdf #78]. Hugh Davis, former servant to John Lofton, 8 June 1703, master summoned "to show cause why execution should not pass against him at ye suite of Hugh Davis for his freedom clothes," and "ye said action was here in Court acknowledged to be agreed" [22.pdf #117]. "To Hugh Davis a Cripple on his Petition," Charles County Levy, 9 November 1703 [22.pdf #152], etc. "To William Warder for Hugh Davis's allowance and Burying him, 1706 [23.pdf #159]. Age at death 30.

DAVIES, WILLIAM, 12 November 1672, (age 18-22), John Stone, six years [06.pdf #94]. Expected date of freedom 1678. Edward Crouch v. William Davis, concerning the sale of a mare, acquitted, 9 August 1681 [10.pdf #98]. William Davis to Edward Frawner, 200 acres, 13 March 1684 [12.pdf #55]. William Davis v. John Clarke, agreed, 13 March 1688 [14.pdf #177]. William Davis v. Richard Wakelin, judgment for defendant, 9 June 1691 [17.pdf #122]. George Plater v. Charles Commaway & William Davis,

ENCYCLOPEDIA OF SURVIVORS

"hee will not further prosecute," judgment for defendants, 9 June 1691 [17.pdf #125]. Richard & Mary Wakelin v. William Davis, judgment for plaintiffs, 11 August 1691 [17.pdf #144]. William Davis v. Thomas Whichaley, dismissed, 10 November 1691 [17.pdf #170]. Richard Wakelin v. William Davis, 1694 [Liber T Page 87].

DAVIS, JOHN, 10 June 1674, age 13, Humphry Warren [06.pdf #158]. Expected date of freedom 1683. Children of John & Elizabeth Davis of Pyckyawaxon: Mary, daughter, born 25 December 1685 [Liber Q Page 11]. Elizabeth, daughter, born 15 January 1689 [Liber Q Page 14].

DAVISE, MARIE, 13 September 1687, age 17, Mr. Robert Doyne, "Sherife of this Countie" [14.pdf #158]. Expected date of freedom 1694. Mary Davis, servant to George Plater, 11 September 1694, "acquitt & discharged," "for that she hath made sufficient satisfaction for her haveing a bastard child in ye time of her servitude, because shee was not by Mr. Robert Doyne brought in time to ye Court to be adjudged of her age according to Act of Assembly, but was by him kept nine or ten months before shee was brought to Court to be adjudged" [18.pdf #195].

DICKISON, THOMAS, 13 March 1677, age 18-19, James Tyre, by Thomas Harris [08.pdf #22]. Expected date of freedom 1683. John Stone v. Thomas Dickison, 8 September 1685 [13.pdf #32] and 18 May 1686 [13.pdf #83] and 8 March 1687 [13.pdf #126]. Elizabeth Vinton, daughter of Richard Vinton, age not stated, bound to Thomas Dickson, 10 January 1688 [14.pdf #173]. Thomas Dickisson v. Daniel Bateman, agreed, 9 September 1690 [17.pdf #61]. Thomas & Anne Dickisson v. MOSES JONES, agreed, 10 March 1691 [17.pdf #106]. Mary Dickisson, daughter of Thomas Dickisson, gift of livestock, 1691 [17.pdf #137]. Thomas Dickson, fined, 1694 [Liber T Page 45], fine remitted [Liber T Page 77]. Ward, Richard, age not stated, servant to Joseph Ward, 10 January 1699, "complaineing to ye Court here against Joseph Ward his master for abusing of him and not allowing him sufficient & necessary clothing & bedding and it being averred here in Court that ye said Richard Ward is an orphan bound to ye said Joseph Ward," ordered by Court "that ye said Richard Ward," "naked without a shirt and never a bed to lie on, bee removed out of ye said Joseph Wards custody" "and serve Thomas Dickson untill he arrive to ye age of twenty one yeares, hee ye said Thomas Dickson findeing & allowing him sufficient meate drinke washing lodgeing

& clothing fitting & necessary for such a servant" [20.pdf #4]. DOANE, CHARLES, without indentures, 14 March 1699, age 14, Thomas Dickson [20.pdf #24]. Ebsworth Bayne to John Wilson and Thomas Diceson, 62 acres, 9 November 1716 [Liber H Page 27].

DIKE, MATHEW, 12 March 1672, age 20, Mathew Stone [06.pdf #59]. Expected date of freedom 1678. Mary Dike, wife of Mathew Dike, gift of livestock, 25 July 1684 [11.pdf #203]. Mathew Dike v. Richard Stevens, judgment for plaintiff, 13 January 1685 [12.pdf #54]. Richard New, probate case, Mathew Dyke executor, 13 September 1687 [15.pdf #15]. Mathew Dyke and GRIFFITH DAVIS, complaints against them dismissed, 8 November 1687 [14.pdf #161]. Richard Ward, Mathew Dyke, GRIFFITH DAVIS and Elinor Halee, summons issued 8 November 1687 [14.pdf #162]. Phillip Lynes v. Mathew Dyke executor of Richard New deceased, judgment for defendant, 12 March 1689 [16.pdf #37] and [16.pdf #68]. Elizabeth Dike, daughter of Matthew & Mary Dike, gift of livestock, 11 March 1690 [16.pdf #109]. Henry Brawner v. Matthew Dike, agreed, 11 November 1690 [17.pdf #72]. Matthew Dike v. ROBERT JONES, agreed, 8 September 1691 [17.pdf #155]. George Brent v. Mathew Dike, judgment foe plaintiff, 8 November 1692 [17.pdf #285]. Edward Ford v. Matthew Dike, agreed, 8 November 1692 [17.pdf #288]. "Itt is ordered that Matthew Dike upon his wifes administraccon of her late husband Thomas Allcocks estate, upon his acccount be allowed one penny & pound in tobaccoe," 8 November 1692 [Liber Q Page 62]. Mary Allen, servant to Matthew Dike, 14 November 1693, 11 days absence, "but two of ye said dayes shee went to Mr. Hinson one of ye Justices of this Court to Complaine, which said two dayes were not allowed by ye Court," 90 days servitude "from ye expiration of her time" which was 4 November 1693, and "ordered that Mary Allen serve Matthew Dike one whole yeare for ye damadges hee susteined by occasion of her having a bastard child in ye time of her servitude, or to pay to ye Matthew Dike ye sume of eight hundred pounds of tobaccoe," which "Thomas Plunkett did engage to pay" [18.pdf #115]. Matthew Dike v. Thomas Plunckett, judgment for plaintiff, 12 June 1694 [18.pdf #173]. Matthew Dike v. Samuel Edmonds, agreed, 1694 [Liber T Page 114]. Matthew Dike v. RICHARD MARSHALL, 1695 [Liber T Page 153]. MORRIS FITZ GERRALD & Rachell his wife v. Matthew Dike, agreed, 10 November 1696 [19.pdf #77]. "Matthew Dike to be overseer for ye cleareing of ye roads in ye Upper parts of Nanjemy Parish," 14 September 1697 [19.pdf #149]. Mathew Dyke, will dated 28 May 1697, probated 3 March 1698, Mary Dyke executrix [Liber A No. 2 Folio 172]. Named in will: his daughter

ENCYCLOPEDIA OF SURVIVORS

Elizabeth Dyke; Edward Rookwood son of Edward Rookwood; William Thomas; his son in law Thomas Allcock; his loveing wife Mary Dyke. Matthew Dike, probate case, Mary Dike executrix, 10 January 1699 [20.pdf #16]. Age at death 46.

DONOHAN, CORNELIUS, 11 August 1685, age 19, Thomas Hussey [12.pdf #96]. Expected date of freedom 1691. JAMES COTTERELL v. John Gale and Cornelius Donahowe garnishees of Anthony Smith, judgment for plaintiff, 12 January 1692 [17.pdf #205].

DOYLE (DOYNE), OWEN, 14 August 1683, age 20, Phillip Lynes [11.pdf #128]. Expected date of freedom 1689. Owen Doyne, servant to Philip Lynes, 10 March 1691, "being a servant lately free from Mr. Gerrard Fowke and formerly servant to Mr. Philip Lynes," petitions Court "to give Order which of his said masters shall pay him his corne & clothes they both refuseing," ordered by Court "that Mr. Philip Lynes shall pay ye said Owen Doyne his freedome corne & clothes hee ye said Owen Doyne haveing served ye first of his time & ye last of his time of servitude with ye said Philip Lynes" [17.pdf #102]; Owen Doyne, late servant to Philip Lynes, 9 June 1691, "petitioning this Court for an Order for his freedom & corne & clothes, itt is Ordered that Philip Lynes pay & satisfye unto ye said Owen Doyne three barrells of Indian corne, one suite of clothes of good broad cloth or kersey, one new shift of white linen, one pair of shoes & stockings two howes & one axe according to Act of Assembly in that case made & provided" [17.pdf #115]; Owen Doyne, by William Dent his attorney, 9 August 1692, pleads that Philip Lynes "render unto him a good cloth suite of clothes either of kearsey or broad cloth as shift of white linen to be new, one pair of shoes & stockins, two hoes, one axe and three barrells of Indian corne which hee oweth him & unjustly detaineth" ordered by Court "that ye said Owen Doyne recover against ye Philip Lynes" "his debt aforesaid" "and his damadges by occasion of deteining of ye said debt to three hundred & one pounds of tobaccoe" [17.pdf #245].

DREYDEN, GEORGE, 8 August 1699, age 20, Joseph Harrison, "hee saith that he had an Indenture but it was Lost" [20.pdf #79]. Expected date of freedom 1705. George Dryden, sworn as Constable, June 1717 [Liber G Page 219]. George Dryden, List of Taxable Inhabitants, 45 squirrells heads, 12 November 1717 [26.pdf #18]. John Pidgon v. George Dryden & Philip Cooper, judgment for plaintiff, 10 March 1719 [26.pdf #103].

ENCYCLOPEDIA OF SURVIVORS

DUNNINGTON, FRANCIS, 12 January 1686, age 20, Madam Mary Chandler [13.pdf #47]. Expected date of freedom 1692. Francis & Margaret Dunnington to Richard Nellson, 200 acres, 4 April 1704 [Liber Z Page 96].

EVENS, JOAN, 19 April 1698, age 17, Thomas Smoote [19.pdf #206]. Expected date of freedom 1705. The Grand Jurors "by the information of Michael Martin Constable of Portobacco" "doe present Joan Evan servant woman to Capt. Thomas Smoot for haveing a bastard child," 10 March 1702 [22.pdf #2]. "Joan Evan commeth into Court in her propper person and confesseth the fact," twelve lashes and one yeares service, 31 March 1702 [22.pdf #3]. Expected date of freedom 1706. The Grand Jurors "present Joane Evans liveing at Ralph Lomax for haveing a bastard child," 12 June 1711 [24.pdf #94].

FAARNANDEZ, PEDRO, 13 April 1669, age 17, Capt. James Neile [Vol. 60:188]. Expected date of freedom 1676. Wenefrett Fernandos, daughter of Peter Fernandos, gift of livestock, 1682 [10.pdf #165]. "Peter Fernandos his marke of cattle & hoggs," 1682 [10.pdf #165]. Elizabeth Farnandis, daughter of Peter Farnandis, gift of livestock, 1686 [13 pdf #104]. Peter Farnandis "cooper" to "Edward Branner sonne of Henry Branner," gift of livestock, 14 September 1686 [13.pdf #104]. William OBryan to Peter Fernandis, 200 acres, 13 March 1694 [18.pdf #145]. Agatha Ferdinandoe, daughter of Peter & Elinor Ferdinandoe of Portobaccoe, born 8 November 1694 [Liber Q Page 24]. John Kyrwood and Company v. Peter Ferdinando, "for divers goods and merchandizes to the said Peter sold and delivered," plaintiffs "take nothing by their said writt butt be in mercy for their false clamour," judgment for defendant, 13 February 1700 [20.pdf #167]. Peter Ferdinando v. John Lynwood and Comp., judgment for plaintiff, 11 March 1701 [21.pdf #106]. Thomas Wormely, servant to Peter Ferdinando, 8 June 1703, 38 days absence "proved by the Oath of John Paine," 380 days servitude [22.pdf #105]. Peter Ferdinando, father of Elizabeth Ferdinando, "offers to be her security to save the Parrish harmless by reason of her bastard child," 14 September 1703 [22.pdf #129]. William Puttuck, servant to Peter Ferdinando, 9 March 1708, servant confessing, 37 days absence, 370 days servitude [23.pdf #235]. Peter Farnando, List of Taxable Inhabitants, 127 squirrells heads, 12 November 1717 [26.pdf #18]. Peter Ferdinando, List of Taxable Inhabitants, 3 crows heads, 12 November 1717 [26.pdf #19]. Peter Ferdinando, aged 67 years, deposition, 5 August 1721 [Liber M Page 145]. Peter Ferdinando v. John Coombes, judgment confessed, 12 June 1722 [27.pdf #174]. Peter Ferdinando, aged 71 years,

ENCYCLOPEDIA OF SURVIVORS

deposition, 8 November 1726 [30.pdf #202]. Peter Fardinando, his mark of livestock, 1 December 1726 [Liber L Page 322]. Peter Fernandis, will dated 18 January 1734, probated 18 August 1736, no executor named [Liber AE No. 6 Folio 253]. Named in will: his grandson Peter Farnandis Junr. Age at death 84. Note: Peter Farnandis (Junr.), will dated 10 January 1775, probated 24 July 1775, Benedicta & Eleanor Farnandis, executors [Liber AE No. 6 Folio 253].

FARRELL, HUGH, 12 August 1701, age 18, William Moss [21.pdf #136]. Expected date of freedom 1708. Hugh Farrold v. Edward Rookwood, agreed, 12 June 1711 [24.pdf #106].

FEILD, CHARLES, 10 August 1680, age 20, Major William Boareman [09.pdf #182]. Expected date of freedom 1686. "Charles Feild dead & not worth a pound," the Public Levy "for Sundry persons Runaway and dead Insolvent in Charles County 1696," 9 November 1697 [19.pdf #179]. Age at death 37.

FITZ GERRALDS, JOHN, 4 April 1699, age 14, James Smallwood [20.pdf #26]. Expected date of freedom 1707. The Grand Jurors "present John Fitzgerrold for stealing a coat jacket & breeches from Thomas Costen," 14 March 1721 [27.pdf #42]. The Grand Jurors "do present John Fitzgerrard for stealing a hat & wigg from Thomas Costen," 8 August 1721 [27.pdf #91]. John Fitzgarrold, his recognizance, 8 August 1721 [27.pdf #92]

FITZ GERRALDS, PETER, 19 April 1698, age 12, Hugh Teares [19.pdf #206]. Expected date of freedom 1708. John Beale v. Peter Fitzgarrald, ordered by Court "that the said writt doe abate," judgment for defendant, 14 November 1710, [24.pdf #38].

FITZ GERRELD, MORRIS, 10 March 1685, age 17, John Wright [12.pdf #61]. Expected date of freedom 1692. Morris Fitzgarrald v. Serjeant, 1695 [Liber T Page 258]. Morris Fitz Gerrald & Rachell his wife v. MATTHEW DIKE, agreed, 10 November 1696 [19.pdf #77]. Elizabeth Smith executor of William Smith deceased v. Morris Fitz Gerrald, judgment for defendant, 10 November 1696 [19.pdf #79]. Morrice Fitzgarrald, son of Morrice Fitzgarrald, gift of livestock, 17 October 1709.

ENCYCLOPEDIA OF SURVIVORS

FOWTRELL, GEORGE, 13 June 1676, age 22-23, James Bowlinge, by Richard Edelen [07.pdf #111]. Expected date of freedom 1681. Fewtrill, George, servant to Samuell Raspin, 14 June 1681, "haveing truely & faithfully served out his time," petitions "for his corne & clothes," ordered by Court that "Thomas Marshall administrator of ye said Samuell Raspin deceased pay unto George Fewtrill three barrells of Indian corne, & freedome clothes, one axe & two howes out of ye estate of ye said Samuell Raspin deceased" [10.pdf #80]

FRANCES, JOHN, the son of Richard Frances and of Rebeca his wife, was borne the 15 of March, and baptisd the 18 of same, 1660, "Register of the Parish of Holy Trinity (Christ Church), Cork, Ireland." John Francis, 14 June 1681, age 21, Alexander Smith [10.pdf #79]. Expected date of freedom 1687. "John Francis his marke of his hogges & cattle," 1685 [13.pdf #19]. John Francis, probate case, ROBERT BENSON administrator, 9 September 1690 [17.pdf #52]. Age at death 30.

GIBBS, JOHN, 13 April 1669, age 19, Peter Carr [Vol. 60:188]. Expected date of freedom 1675. Thomas & Jane Tickerell v. John Gibbs, assault "with force & armes," LANCELOTT WILKINSON and SAMUEL SIMPSON witnesses, defendant acquitted, 10 January 1682 [10.pdf #136, 137]. John Gibbs v. John Fanning administrator of Robert Cooper deceased, judgment for plaintiff, 12 November 1684 [12.pdf #24]. John Gibbs v. John Carter, "who hath absented himselfe out of this County & left noe attorney behinde him," judgment for plaintiff, 11 August 1685 [12.pdf #96]. Cleborne Lomax v. John Gibbs, 14 September 1686 [13.pdf #113], agreed 9 November 1686 [13.pdf #131]. Gilbert Clarke v. John Gibbs, judgment for plaintiff, 14 September 1697 [19.pdf #157]. "John Gibbes fined for not attending as an evidences between John Emery and Anthoney Neale being legally summoned for the defendant," 10 November 1702 [22.pdf #64]. "Itt appeareing to the Court by the testimony of divers credible persons that the said John Gibbs was then sick and unable to travill, therefore his fine remitted," 12 January 1703 [22.pdf #80].

GIBSON, WILLIAM, 13 January 1680, age 11, Henry Adames, by Philip Mason [09.pdf #139]. Expected date of freedom 1691. George Leete v. William Gibson, judgment for plaintiff, 8 August 1693 [18.pdf #96]. Capt. John Bayne v. William Gibbson planter, judgment for plaintiff, 11 June 1700 [21.pdf #13]. William Gibson v. William White, judgment for plaintiff, 10 March 1713 [25.pdf #139] and 9 June 1713 [25.pdf #169].

ENCYCLOPEDIA OF SURVIVORS

GILL, ARGALUS, 8 June 1703, age 10, Coll. James Smallwood [22.pdf #105]. Expected date of freedom 1715. Archilaus Gill, servant to Col. James Smallwood, "lately deceased," 8 March 1715, servant "comes into Court & confesses" to 100 days absence, (1000 days servitude), to "serve ye Executor or Administrator of ye said Col. Smallwood" [25.pdf #266]. Expected date of freedom 1718. James Maddox v. Archelus Gill, agreed, 9 June 1719 [26.pdf #118]. Argulus Guill, servant to Ralph Shaw, 14 August 1722, 11 days absence, ordered to serve "eight days for one of his runaway time" (88 days servitude) [27.pdf #176].

GLASSON, JOHN, 12 September 1699, age 16, Joseph Manning [20.pdf #101]. Expected date of freedom 1705. Eleanor Haream (?), bound to John Glasson, March 1716 [Liber G Page 47]. Thomas Haream (?), bound to John Glasson, March 1716 [Liber G Page 47]. "To John Glashon for keeping an infant," List of Taxable Inhabitants, 12 November 1717 [26.pdf #20].

GRAY, JOSEPH, son of William and Margerett Gray, Baptized 18 May 1651, Plymouth: Charles, Devon, England. Gray, Joseph, 8 March 1664, age 13, Garrat Sennet [02.pdf #321]. Expected date of freedom 1673. Joseph Gray and Richard Newton to John Jones, son of MOSES JONES, gift of livestock, 10 September 1689 [16.pdf #109]. John Shackerley v. Joseph Gray, agreed, 8 March 1692 [17.pdf #215].

GRAY, RUTH, 13 June 1676, age 21, Richard Edelen [07.pdf #111]. Expected date of freedom 1682. Ruth Gray, servant to Henry Bonner, 10 March 1680, petitions that she "was by Capt. John Harrison transported brought over a servant by Indenture into this Province for ye tearme of foure years," and "by ye said Harrison sold & disposed of to Mr. Samuell Raspin for ye said terme, who afterwards disposed of your petitioner to Mr. Richard Edelen for ye remainder of ye said terme, & afterwards by ye said Edelen to Mr. Henry Bonner," and "ye petitioner arrived in this Province ye 24th day of February 1675/6 & hath fully served her time" according to her Indenture, and "upon ye 24th of February last past became a free woman," "but ye petitioners said master refused to sett her free, saying Mr. Edelen sold her to him for six yeares," whereupon Samuell Raspin "saith that hee told Richard Edelen when he bought her that shee had an Indenture for foure years" and "hee would not warrant her for any further time," and whereupon George Hodgson "saith that hee came in a servant in ye same ship along with her to ye said Samuell Raspin & has an Indenture from ye said John Harrison for ye said tearme, & was freed by ye same, soe were ye rest of ye servants," and "ye said Ruth Gray produceing her Indenture here in Court," ordered by Court to "bee free from her time of servitude" according to her Indenture [09.pdf #156].

GRAY, WILLIAM, 10 June 1684, age 13, Joseph Manning, by Adam Stone [11.pdf #204]. Expected date of freedom 1693. William Gray, servant to Joseph Manning, 13 June 1693, 32 days absence, 320 days servitude [18.pdf #80]; William Gray, servant to Joseph Manning, 13 March 1694, servant confessing "here in Court," 20 days absence, 200 days servitude [18.pdf # 144]. Expected date of freedom 1694. William Gray v. William Serjeant, 1695 [Liber T Page 133].

GREEN, JOHN, 8 September 1668, age 14, Benjamin Rozer [Vol. 60:142]. Expected date of freedom 1676. John Greene, servant to Philip Lines, 14 November 1676, "ye poore petitioner came in a servant in ye yeare 1668 & was sold to Mr. Benjamin Rozer who did present him to your Worshippfull Court in ye moneth of September in ye aforesaid yeare, where hee was adjudged to be fourteene yeares of age, & soe ordered to serve eight yeares, but ye poore petitioner afterwards being sold by Mr. Benjamin Rozer to Daniell Johnson," and after his decease "became servant to Francis Kilbourne, who married ye administratrix of ye said Daniell Johnson, and ye poore petitioner was by ye said Francis Kilbourne very hardly used, who being carried up upon a frontier plantation above Piscataway, was there like to be starved for want of victualls & cloathing, & there left alone in a strange place at a great distance from any neighbours to ye mercy of ye Indians; and ye poore petitioner, being reduced to these extremities was constrained to engage himselfe to serve Philip Lines above two years longer than the time your Worshipfull Court did adjudge him to serve, to ye end that hee might be freed from those injuries he was forced to undergoe, & ye poore petitioner haveing thus beene bought by ye said Philip Lines of ye said Francis Kilbourne hath truely & honestly served ye full time your Worshipfull Court did adjudge him to serve, ye said time being expired ever since May last past, and neverthelesse ye poore petitioner is still kept a servant by ye said Philip Lines who intends to make him serve two yeares longer;" and whereas Philip Lines saith "that ye said John was sett free, discharged & manumized by ye said Kilbourne, before hee did enter into Covenant with mee for any longer time of servitude," ordered by Court "that ye said John Greene be free according to ye time of his first servitude" [07.pdf #129]

ENCYCLOPEDIA OF SURVIVORS

GREENE, JAMES, 10 June 1674, age 15, Benjamin Rozer [06.pdf #158]. Expected date of freedom 1680. William Hutchison to JOHN THOMPSON, James Greene & Thomas Frederick, 422 acres, 11 November 1690 [17.pdf #70], survey from William Hutchisson, 29 December 1690 [17.pdf #83]. James Green, aged 69 years, depositions, stating that the plantation of Benjamin Rozer "was settled some time before this deponent came into this country which was about fifty four years ago," 8 November 1726 [30.pdf #197] and [30.pdf #199].

GWYNN, PETER, 13 June 1699, age 18, Robert Yates [20.pdf #69]. Expected date of freedom 1706. John Newman v. Peter Guynn, judgment for plaintiff, 14 June 1709 [23.pdf #314].

HAGAR, WILLIAM, son of William and Mary Hager, Born 12 February 1658, Watertown, Massachusetts. Hagar, William, 13 April 1669, age 14, Thomas Baker [Vol. 60:188]. Expected date of freedom 1676. William Hager married Sarah Benjamin, 31 March 1687, Watertown, Massachusetts.

HAMBYE, FRANCIS, 2 January 1686, age 19, Giles Blizard [13.pdf #47]. Expected date of freedom 1692. Francis Hanby, servant to Robert Thompson Junr., "proved to be ye father of two bastard children begotten on ye body of her ye said Elizabeth Hazlewood," ordered by Court that ye sherife carry ye said Francis Hanby "to ye whipping post and there to strip him naked from ye waist upwards and to give him thirteene lashes on his bare back well laid on for his offense to allmighty God," 9 June 1691 [17.pdf #114]. John Hanby, son of Francis Hanby "which he had by Elizabeth Hazleton," "hee ye said John Hanby being one yeare old ye tenth day of February last past," bound to EDWARD MILLSTEADE, "hee ye said EDWARD MILLSTEADE providing & alloweing necessary & convenient meate drinke washing lodgeing & clothing," 8 March 1692 [17.pdf #209]. Barker, Samuell, son of Alice Hanby wife of Francis Hanby, "now at ye age of seaven yeares ye second day of Aprill last," bound to Samuel Luckett "to be used & imployed in any manner of service," he promising to find & allow "sufficient meate drinke washing & lodgeing," 13 November 1695 [18.pdf #243].

HAMMOND, JOHN, son of John and Lidiah Hammond, Born 24 June 1654, Baptized 1 July 1654, Epping, Essex, England. Hammonde, John, 7 April 1668, age 15, Jeremiah Dickenson [03.pdf #310]. Expected date of freedom 1675. William Loveday to John Hamond, "one & equall halfe of

ENCYCLOPEDIA OF SURVIVORS

eighty five acres," 14 March 1676 [07.pdf #102]. "John Hammon his marke of hogges & cattle," 1677 [07.pdf #136]. William & Ruth Loveday to John Hamon, 85 acres, 13 November 1677 [08.pdf #57]. Abigail Hamond, servant to Thomas King deceased, 14 August 1678, "Richard Hodgshon & Johannah his wife Executors of ye Last Will & Testament of Thomas King deceased were attached to answer unto John Hamond & Abigail his wife," who "by ye name of Abigail Yates came from London a servant to this Province, & here arrived ye 2d day of June 1674 in ye good ship called ye Pelican of London Captn. John Bowman Comander & was a servant sold & disposed of by ye said Bowman to ye Honorable Benjamin Rozer Esqre. for ye tearme of foure yeares, shee ye said Abigail hath well & faithfully served, & upon ye 2d day of June 1678 & now last past became a free woman & soe of right ought to have delivered her by ye said Richard & Johannah three barrells of Indian corne, working tools, & freedom clothes," but the defendants "doth refuse as well ye same to doe, as allso to discharge her from her said service," and "these ensueing evidences were sworne in Court," Margaret Lines saith "that John Bowman hee never did nor would sell a servant for any longer time than ye tearme of foure yeares," Richard Perkins and James Berry both saith "that Mr. Thomas King bought ye said Abigail of ye Honorable Benjamin Rozer Esqre. but for foure yeares," ordered by Court "that ye said Abigail be free & discharged from her time of servitude," and "that ye said Richard Hodgshon & Johannah his wife" "pay unto ye said Abigail three barrells of Indian corne, working tools & freedome clothes according to ye custome of ye countrey, with cost of suite" [09.pdf #38]; see also 14 January 1679 [09.pdf # 62]. Hill, not named, orphan child of THOMAS HILL deceased, age not stated, "ordered by ye Court that John Hamond have ye sume of eight hundred pounds of tobaccoe allowed him out of ye next County Levy for ye maintenance" of the orphan child, 13 January 1680 [09.pdf #139]. "Itt is ordered by ye Court that John Hamond bee allowed in ye County Leavy ye next yeare sixteene hundred pounds of tobaccoe, for keepeing an orphan child of THOMAS HILL late of this County deceased one yeare past for which hee hath not yett received any satisfaction, & for ye keeping & mainteining of it (sic) one yeare more," 10 January 1682 [10.pdf #133]. "Itt is ordered by ye Court that John Hamond bee allowed out of ye next County Leavy eight hundred pounds of tobaccoe for ye keepeing & maintaineing Onsley Hill an orphan child of THOMAS HILL deceased for this ensueinge yeare," 9 January 1683 [11.pdf #59]. Onsley Hill, parents not named, age not stated, bound to John Hamond, 8 January 1684 [11.pdf #186]. George Riscorla, servant to Major Ninian Beale, 26 November 1689, "ye said George Riscorla produced in

ENCYCLOPEDIA OF SURVIVORS

Court this ensueing Deposition" of "Samuell Young of ye County of Ann Arundell," making oath that he "sold George Riscorla to Major Ninian Beale but for four yeares & noe longer time as witness our hands this 19th day of November 1689, Nicholas Gassaway & John Hammond," ordered by Court to "bee free & discharged from his said masters service" [16.pdf #110]. John Causeen v. John Hammond, agreed, 13 November 1711 [25.pdf #29]. John Hammond v. Paul Willet, "abated by the death of the defendant," 9 January 1713 [25.pdf #161]. Henry Netherton v. John Hammon blacksmith, agreed, 14 January 1707 [23.pdf #165]. "Ordered that John Hammon doe pay to WILLIAM RICHARDSON five hundred pounds of tobacco for keeping his wife's daughter Charity Thompson," 12 August 1707 [23.pdf #201]. John Hammond v. Nicholas Wattson, "the said action was abated by the death of the defendant," 14 June 1709 [23.pdf #312]. John Hammond, "fined one hundred pounds of tobacco," August 1715 [Liber G Page 4]. Philemon Hemsley v. John Hammond, judgment confessed, August 1716 [Liber G Page 147]. John Hammon to Francis Adams, 85 acres, 16 August 1716 [Liber H Page 17].

HARDY, HENRY, base child of Henry Howard & Issabell Hardy, Baptism 5 April 1646, St. Peter, Burnley, Lancashire, England. Hardy, Henry, 12 July 1664, age 20, Thomas Percei [02.pdf #377]. Expected date of freedom 1670. BENNETT, MARY, without indentures, 10 June 1679, age 22, Henry Hardy [09.pdf #84]. LENHAM, JOHN, without indentures, 10 June 1679, age 19, Henry Hardy [09.pdf #84]. "Henry Hardy Gentleman was sworne & admitted an atturney of this Court," 10 November 1691 [17.pdf #157]. Henry Hardy, Thomas Baker & JAMES COTTERELL, named as witnesses against "Philip Lynes late of Charles County for forgery." 14 August 1694 [18.pdf #317]. Capt. Henry Hardy and nine others "ordained and appointed" Worshippfull Commissioners for Charles County Court, 25 July 1696   [19.pdf #39]. (Capt. Henry Hardy served on the Court from 11 August 1696 through 12 June 1705 -- ed). Henry Hardy, will dated 21 December 1705, probated 20 September 1714, Walter Story executor [Liber AB No. 3 Folio 75]. Named in will: his wife Ann, his daughter Ann, his "kinsman" Henry Hardy the son of George Hardy; George Hardy the son of George Hardy; Philip Briscoe & his son John Briscoe. Henry Hardy, probate case, Anne Hardy administrator, 14 June 1715 [25.pdf #276]. Henry Hardy, probate case, Richard Ashman administrator, 9 June 1719 [26.pdf #112]. Age at death 68. (See full biography).

ENCYCLOPEDIA OF SURVIVORS

HAY, IZABEL, daughter of Patrick and Mary Hey, Born 31 August 1691, Charlestown, Massachusetts. Hays, Isabella, 8 June 1708, age 20, Mullinax Rattclife [23.pdf #253]. Expected date of freedom 1714. Isable Hay of Charlestown married Nathaniel Nichols of Reading, 26 September 1715, Charlestown, Massachusetts.

HAYS, JOHN, 10 June 1701, age 18, Coll. James Smalwood [21.pdf #125]. Expected date of freedom 1708. "Ordered that John Hayes's petition for being levy free be rejected," 8 March 1720 [26.pdf #160].

HENLEY, JOHN, 9 September 1701, age 14, William Smalwood [21.pdf #148]. Expected date of freedom 1709. The Grand Jurors "present Richard Sheppard and John Hendley for killing a stray heiffer the last of August last or thereabouts, William Williams and Ann Hall evidences," 12 June 1711 [24.pdf #94]. John Henly, his recognizance, "in the summe of tenn pounds sterling,"14 August 1711 [24.pdf #127]. John Henly, his recognizance "in the sum of five pounds sterling," 13 November 1711 [25.pdf #18], discharged, 11 March 1712, [25.pdf #39]. William Midelton v. John Henly, judgment for plaintiff, 10 March 1713 [25.pdf #133]. The Grand Jurors "present John Henly for stealing a certayne quantity of lining (linen -- ed.) cutt out into a shirt belonging to William Perry late deceased out of the house of George Elgin," 11 August 1713 [25.pdf #171]. Ralph Lomax v. John Hanly, March 1716 [Liber G Page 88], abated June 1716 [Liber G Page 126]. John Henly appointed Overseer "for amending & clearing the several roads & high ways" "from new bridges to Portobacco," 14 November 1721 [27.pdf #107].

HERBERT, JOHN, 13 March 1677, age 18, Capt. Josias Fendall, by Humphrey Warren [08.pdf #22]. Expected date of freedom 1684. William Herbert, son of John & Elizabeth Herbert of Zachyah hundred, born 6 July 1688 [16.pdf #121].

HERBERT, WILLIAM, son of William Herbert, Born 1 January 1658, Baptized 10 January 1658, Saint Michael Bassishaw, London, England. Herbert, William, 11 April 1676, age 17, Robert Rowlants [07.pdf #101]. Expected date of freedom 1683. Thomas Warren to William Herbert, 285 acres, 12 January 1690 [17.pdf #90]. William Herbert "together with JAMES COTTERELL his security," v. Philip Lynes, "and ye said Philip Lynes though solemnely called cameth not nor any for him," continued, 8 March 1692 [17.pdf #227]. Catherine, daughter of William & Mary Herbert of Pyckyawaxon, born 6 December 1692 [16.pdf #122].

ENCYCLOPEDIA OF SURVIVORS

HILL, THOMAS, 14 June 1670, age 16, Mr. Rozer [Vol. 60:256]. Expected date of freedom 1677. Onsley Hill, son of Thomas & Mary Hill, servants to Benjamin Rozer, born 5 May 1677, baptized 3 June 1677 [07.pdf #137] [16.pdf #120]. Thomas Hill, deceased, before 13 January 1680 [09.pdf #139]. Age at death 25. Hill, not named, orphan child of Thomas Hill deceased, age not stated, "ordered by ye Court that JOHN HAMOND have ye sume of eight hundred pounds of tobaccoe allowed him out of ye next County Levy for ye maintenance" of the orphan child, 13 January 1680 [09.pdf #139]. "Itt is ordered by ye Court that JOHN HAMOND bee allowed in ye County Leavy ye next yeare sixteene hundred pounds of tobaccoe, for keepeing an orphan child of Thomas Hill late of this County deceased one yeare past for which hee hath not yett received any satisfaction, & for ye keeping & mainteining of it (sic) one yeare more," 10 January 1682 [10.pdf #133]. "Itt is ordered by ye Court that JOHN HAMOND bee allowed out of ye next County Leavy eight hundred pounds of tobaccoe for ye keepeing & maintaineing Onsley Hill an orphan child of Thomas Hill deceased for this ensueinge yeare," 9 January 1683 [11.pdf #59]. Onsley Hill, parents not named, age not stated, bound to JOHN HAMOND, 8 January 1684 [11.pdf #186].

HILL, THOMAS, 8 June 1686, age 13, Giles Blizard [13.pdf #117]. Expected date of freedom 1695. Thomas Hills, servant to Robert Smallpage, 11 September 1694, absent "severall times" from service of Robert Smallpage "for ye space of 107 days, and absent 50 days "whilst he served" MARKE LAMPTON, 157 days in all, 1570 days servitude [18.pdf #195]. Expected date of freedom 1699. Thomas Hills v. Thomas Burford, verdict for plaintiff, 12 January 1697 [19.pdf #94]. William Stone v. Thomas Hills, verdict for plaintiff, 14 September 1697 [19.pdf #157]. James Muncaster v. Thomas Hill, agreed, 9 March 1708 [23.pdf #240]. Nichols, not named, "an infant child of a certayne JOHN NICHOLLS deceased," age not stated, complaint of Thomas Hill, who "contracted with the said Nicholls in his life tyme that for keeping & maintayneing the said child for one yeare he was to have an receive a cow & calfe & five hundred pounds of tobacco and that John Sanders of Mattawomann," "being Executor of ye Testament of the said Nichols," "will not deliver to him the said cow & calfe nor pay him the tobacco," ordered by Court "that the said John Sanders doe deliver and pay unto the said Thomas Hill the said cow & calfe and five hundred pounds of tobacco," 9 June 1713 [25.pdf #144]. Benjamin Nicholls, son of John & Bethsheba Nicholls deceased, "aged fifteen months," "is put under ye care of Thomas Hill to be maintained who is to be allowed in ye assessment of ye

ENCYCLOPEDIA OF SURVIVORS

next County Leavy one hundred pounds of tobacco," and "also two hundred pounds of tobacco for his care & charge in maintaining (during) two months past," 8 June 1714 [25.pdf #219]. Benjamin Nicholls "a minor orphan being two years of age ye eighth day of March last past," bound to Thomas Hill, he to instruct him "to read distinctly in ye Bible, to apparel him decently at ye expiration of his time of servitude and to discharge the County from any incumbrance or charge," 14 June 1715 [25.pdf #271] Thomas Hill, aged 49 years, deposition, declareth "that he saw & heard the above said MATTHEW SANDERS deceased lay his hand upon the above mentioned bounded white oak," 12 March 1725 [30.pdf #22].

HILL, VALL, 12 March 1672, age 12, William Hinsey [06.pdf #59]. Expected date of freedom 1682. Anne Hyde, daughter of Anne & Valentine Hill, "wee doe give our willing consent that our child Anne Hyde being aged seaven yeares doe serve Thomas Dixon untill shee bee eighteene yeares of age or ye day of marryage," 3 January 1690 [16.pdf #112]. "Valentine Hill his marke of cattle & hoggs," 1694 [18.pdf #191].

HINDLE, JOSHUA, 11 June 1678, age 21, Francis Goodrich [08.pdf #93]. Expected date of freedom 1684. Joshuah Hingle, probate case, MARKE LAMPTON executor, 10 March 1691 [17.pdf #108]. Age at death 34.

HOGG, FRANCES, daughter of William and Ann Hogg, Baptized 25 March 1683, Saint Mary Whitechapel, Stepney, London, England. Hogg, Frances, 14 January 1701, age 18, Major William Dent [21.pdf #67]. Expected date of freedom 1708. Turlough Obryan, servant to Major William Dent, "desires with ye approbation of this Court to bargaine with his said master, that in consideration ye his master will give his consent that hee may marry with one Frances Hogg a servant woman of ye said Major Dent, they will each of them serve ye said Major Dent two whole years upon which agreement they are both to bee free, ye fourteenth day of November in ye yeare 1705, and Major Dent promises to release ye rest of ye said Frances Hoggs service," 14 September 1703 [22.pdf #129].

HOLLIEWOOD, JAMES, 12 June 1688, age 18, William Smith [14.pdf #177]. Expected date of freedom 1695. James Hollywood, servant to William Smith, 13 March 1694, 62 days absence, 620 days servitude, and to "make satisfaction to ye said William Smith ye sum of six hundred pounds of tobaccoe disburst & expended for ye taking up & bringing home him twice out of ye Colony of Virginia," or else to serve three months [18.pdf #144]. Expected date of freedom 1697. James Hollywood, 1695, "his order for his freedom" [Liber T Page 289].

ENCYCLOPEDIA OF SURVIVORS

HOLMES, GRACE, daughter of Phillip Holmes, Baptized 12 June 1660, North Tawton, Devon, England. Holmes, Grace, 14 June 1681, age 22, Philip Lines [10.pdf #79]. Expected date of freedom 1687. Grace Holmes, servant to William Smith, 11 August 1686, 100 days absence, 1000 days servitude [13.pdf #119]. Expected date of freedom 1690. Grace Holmes, servant to John Gourely, 8 September 1691, "came here into Court & made her complaint that shee was naked & her said master would not her cloathe," ordered by Court that "ye sherife of this County" summon "ye said John Gourely that hee bee here at ye next Court" "and that hee bring ye said Grace Holmes along with him & there to answer to ye Complaint of ye said Grace Holmes" [17.pdf #154]. Grace Holmes, servant to John Goureley, 10 November 1691, absent "severall times," one year servitude, "and then to be free & discharged," provided "that shee ye said Grace Holmes doth not at any time within ye said yeare unlawfully absent herselfe & runaway out of her said masters service" [17.pdf #157]. Expected date of freedom 1692. Grace Holmes, servant to Stephen Mankin, 13 March 1694, "alledgeing here in Court that ye said Stephen Mankin did claime further service from her by vertue of an Indenture that was made between them before her time of servitude was expired," ordered by Court "that ye said Indenture thereupon was void & null by Act of Assembly in that case made & provided," "and that ye said Grace Holmes be manumitted & discharged from ye service of ye said Stephen Mankin and be thereof acquitt" [18.pdf #145].

HOSKINS, LAURAN, 13 April 1669, age 17, John Bowles [Vol. 60:188]. Expected date of freedom 1676. Larance Hoskins, will dated 9 January 1687, probated 14 June 1687, Rebecca Tyer executrix [Liber A No. 2 Folio 112]. Named in will: Rebekah Tyer; Mr. Tymothy; Michal Webb; Thomas Taylor; James Tyer, son of Rebekah Tyer. Lawrence Hoskins, probate case, Rebecka Tyre executrix, 14 June 1687 [14.pdf #123]. Age at death 35. "Robert Yates who married with Rebeckah ye relict of James Tyer who was executrix of ye Last Will & Testament of Lawrence Hoskins late of Charles County deceased," 8 September 1691 [Liber Q Page 42].

HOULT, WILLIAM, son of Henery Hoult, Abode Unsworth, Baptized 25 June 1665, Saint Mary the Virgin, Prestwich, Lancashire, England. Holt, William, 10 June 1684, age 20, Capt. Ignatius Causeene [11.pdf #204]. Expected date of freedom 1690. Robert Holt, son of William & Mary Holt of Portobaccoe, born 15 February 1695 [Liber Q Page 25]. Philip Cropper and William Holt, their recognizance, 12 January 1703 [22.pdf #80]. Godshall Barnes v. William Holt, March 1716 [Liber G Page 76].

ENCYCLOPEDIA OF SURVIVORS

William Holt appointed Constable for Newport hundred, 12 November 1717 [26.pdf #3] & 11 November 1718 [26.pdf #72] & 10 November 1719 [26.pdf #141] & 14 November 1721 [27.pdf #107].

HOWES, THOMAS, son of John Howes, Born 7 May 1663, Yarmouth, Massachusetts. Howes, Thomas, 12 March 1678, age 16, Capt. Josias Fendall, by Adam Weaver [08.pdf #73]. Expected date of freedom 1685. John Contee v. Thomas How, judgment for defendant, 13 August 1700 [21.pdf #36].

HUNT, JOHN, 13 April 1669, age 16, William Barton [Vol. 60:188]. Expected date of freedom 1676. "Thomas Tanney attachment against John Edenfield and attacht in ye hands of John Hunt," 29 November 1698 [court record lost, indexed at 19.pdf #14]. John Hunt, probate case, Dorothy Hunt "widdow" admininstrator, 3 December 1700 [21.pdf #60]. Age at death 47.

HUNTER, WILLIAM, 11 January 1676, age 14, Thomas Hussey [07.pdf #96]. Expected date of freedom 1684. "William Hunter his marke of hoggs & cattle," 1683 or 1684 [11.pdf #82]. William Hutchison to William Hunter, 392 acres, 18 April 1689 [18.pdf #85]. William Hunter v. Daniell Bateman, agreed, 9 September 1690 [17.pdf #61]. William Hunter v. Richard Agambrah, payment for "ye building of one forty foote house two & twenty foot wide for ye said Richard," judgment for plaintiff, 11 November 1690 [17.pdf #76]. William Hunter v. Daniell Bateman, agreed, 9 June 1691 [17.pdf #126]. Samuell Luckett v. William Hunter, agreed, 8 September 1691 [17.pdf #155]. Daniell Bateman v. William Hunter, agreed, 8 September 1691 [17.pdf #155]. Francis Bullane & James Smithson v. William Hunter, nonsuit, 1694 [Liber T Page 71]. William Hunter Gent. v. Mullinax Ratclife, judgment for defendant, 8 September 1696 [19.pdf #59]. William Hunter to ROBERT BENSON, 200 acres, 8 March 1697 [Liber Q Page 118]. The Grand Jurors, "by ye information of Thomas Orrell, doe present William Hunter late of Portobaccoe in Charles County Gentleman for that sometime in ye month of May 1699 an antient road or highway goeing & leading formerly to Church & Court hath inclosed & stopt up to ye evill & dangerous example of others, and to ye great damage & comon hurt of all ye good subjects thereunto nigh inhabiting who used to pass that way," 13 June 1699 [20.pdf #67]. Capt. Gerrard Sly v. William Hunter Gent., judgment for plaintiff, 14 November 1699 [20.pdf #122]. Gilbert Clarke v. William Hunter, judgment for plaintiff, 13 February 1700 [20.pdf #175]. William Hunter v. Joseph Lee, judgment for defendant,

ENCYCLOPEDIA OF SURVIVORS

14 January 1701 [21.pdf #80]. William Hunter v. John Wood, concerning timber for a "forty foot tobacco house," agreed, 10 November 1702 [22.pdf #69]. Notley Rozer to William Hunter, 150 acres, 20 November 1711 [Liber C Page 263], duplicated at [Liber C Page 265]. William Hunter v. Molleneaux Rattcliff, June 1717 [Liber G Page 230]. Thomas Dent v. William Hunter, agreed, 11 March 1718 [26.pdf #25]. William Hunter v. John Cooke, judgment for plaintiff, 11 March 1718 [26.pdf #30]. William Hunter v. Kennet Mackenzey, judgment for plaintiff, 10 June 1718 [26.pdf #49]. Ubgatt Reeves petitions "that he has a plantation next adjacent to the plantation of Mr. William Hunter who has so fenced him in that he is wholy without egresse," ordered by Court that Joseph Harrison, Robert Hanson & GUSTAVOUS BROWN inspect ye premises & report the same," whereupon the petition was adjudged "frivilous & groundless & thereupon the same is rejected," 14 March 1721 [27.pdf #45]. "William Hunters petition to be levy free is adjudged groundless," 13 November 1722 [28.pdf #7]. William Hunter, will dated 16 August 1723, probated 20 September 1723, George Thorold executor [Liber AB No. 3 Folio 170]. Named in will: George Thorold. Age at death 61.

HUNTSMAN, SAMUELL, 10 September 1678, age 14, Thomas Allanson [09.pdf #40]. Expected date of freedom 1686. JOHN WILKINSON v. Samuel Huntsman, 1694 [Liber T Page 21].

JACKSON, THOMAS, 22 April 1662, age 16, Thomas Gerrard Esq., by Samuel Dobson [01.pdf #211]. Expected date of freedom 1669. Thomas Jackson, probate case, Thomas & Margret Lenion executors, 8 January 1689 [16.pdf #54]. Thomas Jackson, probate case, Robert Yates executor, 10 November 1691 [17.pdf #162]. Age at death 43.

JONES, JOHN, 9 January 1694, age 14, John Wilder [18.pdf #128]. Expected date of freedom 1702. Matthew Mackeboy v. John Jones, judgment for plaintiff, 8 September 1702 [22.pdf #52]. John Jones, aged 51 years, deposition, 18 September 1731 [32.pdf #26].

JONES, MOSES, son of Phillip and Tomson Jones, Baptized 23 July 1655, Saint Stephen, Bristol, Gloucester, England. Jones, Moses, 8 June 1675, age 17, Zachary Wade [07.pdf #63]. Expected date of freedom 1682. Moses Jones, servant to Zachary Wade deceased, 10 June 1679, ordered to "be free from ye service of Randolph Hinson Executor of ye said Zachary Wade,

ENCYCLOPEDIA OF SURVIVORS

ye said Moses Jones his Indentures being produced in Court," "his time of servitude was fully expired" [09.pdf #84]. John Lemair v. Moses Jones, 11 August 1685 [12.pdf #90]. James Wheeler, probate case, Moses & Katherine Jones executors, 9 September 1685 [13.pdf #20]. JOSEPH GRAY and Richard Newton to John Jones, son of Moses Jones, gift of livestock, 10 September 1689 [16.pdf #109]. Moses Jones v. John Banckes, agreed, 11 November 1690 [17.pdf #76]. Mary Bartlett ye orphan child of Raiph Bartlett deceased which was in ye possession & tuition of William West," "being nine yeares of age January last past," bound to Moses Jones, 11 August 1691 [Liber Q Page 38]. THOMAS DICKISSON & Anne his wife v. Moses Jones, agreed, 10 March 1691 [17.pdf #106]. Jane Jones, daughter of Moses Jones of Portobaccoe, born 4 January 1692 [16.pdf #122]. "Itt is ordered that Moses Jones who marryed Catherine ye relict & executrix of James Wheeler late of this County deceased render his further accompt of ye administraccon of Catherine his late wife deceased," 8 March 1692 [Liber Q Page 53]. Anne Jenkins, sister in law of Moses Jones, gift of livestock, 15 March 1692 [17.pdf #294]. John Jenkins, brother in law of Moses Jones, gift of livestock, 15 March 1692 [17.pdf #294]. William Hutchison to Moses Jones, 90 acres, 13 September 1692 [17.pdf #259]. Moses Jones, witness against John Bayne, for bringing unloading & delivering severall liquors to his publick house at Chandler Towne, on ye Sabbath day, 25 September 1692 [17.pdf #276]. Moses Jones and six others, severally, gave security "in ye sume of five pounds of good & lawfull money of England apiece" upon condition that they appear "at ye next Provincial Court to be held at ye City of St. Maryes" and "there to give evidence against John Bayne of & concerning severall trespasses and contempts where of hee ye said John Bayne was presented by ye Grand Enquest for ye body of Charles County," 31 January 1693 [18.pdf #24]. Ignatius Wheeler v. Moses Jones, "nonsuit," 1694 [Liber T Page 57]. Morris Loyd to Moses Joanes, 200 acres, 18 February 1695 [Liber Q Page 76]. Thomas Jones, son of Moses Jones of Portobaccoe, born 2 March 1695 [Liber Q Page 24]. Michaell Lynn executor of Morris Loyd deceased v. Moses Jones, ordered by Court "that the writt be quashed," and plaintiff "take nothing," 9 June 1696 [19.pdf #25]. Robert Merryfield v. Moses Jones, judgment for defendant, 11 August 1696 [19.pdf #44].

JONES, ROBERT, 12 September 1682, age 21, Thomas Hussey [11.pdf #18]. Expected date of freedom 1688. Robert Jones, servant to Thomas Hussey, 12 June 1688, 26 days absence, 260 days servitude [14.pdf #177]. Expected date of freedom 1689. Edward Rookewood v. Robert Jones, agreed, 8 September 1691 [17.pdf #155]. MATTHEW DIKE v. Robert Jones, agreed, 8 September 1691 [17.pdf #155]. Robert Jones v. William Phillmore, judgment for plaintiff, 13 February 1700 [20.pdf #146].

KENNYDAY, NICHOLAS, 4 April 1699, age 22, Samuel Luckett [20.pdf #26]. Expected date of freedom 1705. Samuell Luckett v. Nicholass Kenneday, "Samuell Luckett by William Stone his attorney offered himselfe and the said Nicholass Kenneday cometh not," 9 January 1705 [23.pdf #44]. "Mr. Samuell Luckett discharged of his bond for Nicholas Kenedays appearance," 13 March 1705 [23.pdf #47].

KING, JOHN, 11 June 1700, age 11, Nicholas Cooper [21.pdf #9]. Expected date of freedom 1711. William & Mary Walker to John King, 300 acres, 14 March 1710 [Liber C Page 170]. John King v. Philemon Hemsley, agreed, March 1716 [Liber G Page 95]. John King, List of Taxable Inhabitants, 7 squirrells heads, 12 November 1717 [26.pdf #18]. John King, List of Taxable Inhabitants, 5 crows heads, 12 November 1717 [26.pdf #19]. "John King is appointed Constable of ye upper part of Durham hundred in ye room of JOHN COOPER," 12 August 1718 [26.pdf #51] & 11 November 1718 [26.pdf #72] & 10 November 1719 [26.pdf #141] & 8 November 1720 [27.pdf #29] & 14 November 1721 [27.pdf #107]. Thomas Barron, "a minor orphan of about fifteen years of age," bound to John King, he "to learn ye said Thomas ye art and mystery (sic) of a shipwright & to give him six months schooling," 8 March 1720 [26.pdf #161]. William Cleiveland v. John King, judgment for defendant, 13 June 1721 [27.pdf #86].

KINGE, THOMAS, son of John Kinge, Baptized 6 April 1664, Berkeley, Gloucester, England. Kinge, Thomas, 10 March 1685, age 20, Joseph Maning [12.pdf #61]. Expected date of freedom 1691. Henry Wharton to Thomas King, 50 acres, 5 September 1713 [24.pdf #198]. Thomas King, List of Taxable Inhabitants, 50 squirrells heads, 12 November 1717 [26.pdf #18]. "At ye request of Thomas King of Charles County shipwright ye following marks were recorded, Richard King's mark of cattle, William King's mark of cattle, Catherine King's mark of cattle," 26 May 1720 [Liber H Page 346].

KINIKEN, JAMES, 9 December 1685, age 13, Ralph Smith [13.pdf #47]. Expected date of freedom 1694. Thomas Reeves v. James Kennekin, 14 January 1707 [23.pdf #166] and 11 March 1707 [23.pdf #175].

ENCYCLOPEDIA OF SURVIVORS

LACKIMORE, EDWARD, 12 January 1686, age 14, Henry Hawkins [13.pdf #47]. Expected date of freedom 1694. The Grand Jurors "doe present Edward Lattimer planter for that" on 7 November 1699 "at Pickiawaxon" he "feloniously did pilfer steale & carry away" "one peck of potatoes of the value of twenty pounds of tobacco of ye propper goods of John Fendall," 14 November 1699 [20.pdf #98]. The Grand Jurors "doe present Joseph Andrews, Todde Gainer, and Edward Lattimer for that they did breake open a house belonging to Ellinor Teares widdow at Wiccocomico and from thence did pilfer steale take and carry away" untold gallons of cider, 11 June 1700 [21.pdf #9].

LAMPTON, MARKE, 10 January 1665, age 16, William Robbison, by Daniell Johnson [02.pdf #463]. Expected date of freedom: 1672. "Marke Lambton enters his marke of hogges & cattle," 1677 [07.pdf #136]. Children of Marke & Elizabeth Lampton of ye head of Portobacco Creeke: Mary, daughter, born 24 January 1678 [16.pdf #120]. Marke, son, born 6 October 1680 [16.pdf #120]. William, son, born 29 April 1682 [16.pdf #120]. Victoria, daughter, born 29 May 1685 [Liber Q Page 11]. John, son, born 16 October 1687 [Liber Q Page 13]. Anne, daughter, born 13 January 1690 [Liber Q Page 15]. Elizabeth, daughter, born 8 August 1692 [Liber Q Page 20]. Isable, daughter, born 15 December 1694 [Liber Q Page 24]. Marke Lampton v. John Charles Cushee, defendant "hath absented himselfe out of this Province," judgment for plaintiff, 9 August 1682 [10.pdf #189]. Marke Lampton v. John Tickpenny (?), "agreed by ye parties aforesaid, 10 June 1684 [11.pdf # 211]. Marke Lampton v. James Balis, who "absented himselfe & left noe attorney behinde him," judgment for plaintiff, 10 March 1685 [12.pdf #78]. Marke Lampton v. James Balis, 11 August 1685 [12.pdf #89]. KENES, MARY, without indentures, 12 June 1688, age 22, Mark Lampton, indenture judged "not to be good without further proofe" [14.pdf #177]. William Griffin v. Marke Lampton, judgment for plaintiff, 10 March 1691 [17.pdf #106]. JOSHUAH HINGLE, probate case, Marke Lampton executor, 10 March 1691 [17.pdf #108]. John Smallwood v. Marke Lampton planter, agreed, 11 August 1691 [17.pdf #149]. Charles Smith, servant to Marke Lampton, 14 June 1692, 56 days absence, 560 days servitude [17.pdf #233]. John Wall, servant to Marke Lampton, 14 November 1693, ordered by Court "that ye said John Wall returne to his master Marke Lampton & serve him according to ye tenour of his Indenture, ye said Marke Lampton engageing here in Court to use his uttmost endeavour in & about ye cure of him ye said John Wall of ye distemper" [18.pdf #115]. Marke & Elizabeth Lampton to William

Hutchison, 225 acres, 11 September 1694 [18.pdf #198]. Thomas Hills, servant to Robert Smallpage, 11 September 1694, absent "severall times" from service of Robert Smallpage "for ye space of 107 days, and absent 50 days "whilst he served" Marke Lampton, 157 days in all, 1570 days servitude [18.pdf #195]. Marke Lampton v. John Stewart, agreed, 1694 [Liber T Page 90]. Marke Lampton v. William Scott, 1695 [Liber T Page 127]. Marke Lampton to William Dent, 128 acres, 9 March 1697. [Liber Q Page 120]. Marke Lampton, petitioner, "hath a very antient Negroe woman that is past her labour and soe much decriped (decrepit -- ed.) that shee doth not earne her bread that she eates," ordered by Court "that ye said Negroe woman be putt out of ye list of taxeables," 14 September 1697 [19.pdf #152]. Marke Lampton, petitioner, "hath purchast a tract of land lying by Potomack River side, ye overseer appointed for cleareing ye high wayes in those parts hath marked & cleared a roade through ye middle of his plantation where never any roade nor highway was formerly cleared," asks "that ye said roade may be altered and cleared ye way that formerly it was used to bee cleared and marked," ordered by Court "that Mr. Richard Harrison one of ye Justices of this Court doe see that ye said roade be cleared with as little prejudice to ye petitioner as may be, and as convenient as may be," 1 February 1698 [19.pdf #187]. Marke Lampton v. Emanuel Rattcliffe, judgment for plaintiff, 13 June 1699 [20.pdf #74]. Mark Lampton v. James & Mary Sims, for "false feigned scandalous and malicious words" defaming "him the said Mark of his good name fame creditt and reputation," judgment for plaintiff, 14 January 1701 [21.pdf #83]. George Taylor, servant to Henry Tanner, 4 April 1704, 4 days absence, 40 days servitude, "and whereas the said Henry Tanner alledges that there was fourteen days more due when he was Marke Lamptons servant the same is continued till he makes due proofe of the same" [22.pdf #194]. "Wee the Grand Jury doe present Marke Lampton for saying that itt was noe more sinn to kill a Protestant than itt was to kill a catt," 13 March 1705 [23.pdf #46], "and it appeareing to the Court by the testimony of credible evidence that the words spoken were only in a jokeing way," ordered by Court "that the said Mark Lampton be acquitt and discharged," 12 June 1705 [23.pdf #89]. "Wee the Grand Jury doe present Marke Lampton and Anne his wife for being and suffering themselves to be marryed," 12 March 1706 [23.pdf #114], "and noe positive evidence appeareing against the said Marke Lampton," ordered by Court to "prosecute the said presentment no further," 12 November 1706 [23.pdf #156]. Marke Lampton (Junr.), will dated 13 December 1708, probated 7 February 1709, William Chandler executor [Liber AB No. 3 Folio 7]. Named in will: his sister Jesabell Lampton & her sister Ann;

his sister Sarah Lampton; his sister Jane Lampton; his son Mark; Mrs. Margeret Saule; William Chandler; John Lampton; his brother William Lampton. Refers to "the will of my father." Marke Lampton (Junr.), probate case, William Lampton executor, 8 November 1709 [23.pdf #351].

LAWSON, THOMAS, son of William Lawson, born 1 February 1681, Baptized 6 February 1681, Saint Peter, Heysham, Lancashire, England. Lawson, Thomas, 8 August 1699, age 18, William Newman. Expected date of freedom 1706. Thomas Lawson, will dated 10 December 1716, probated 12 March 1716, Elizabeth Lawson executrix [Liber AB No. 3 Folio 90]. Named in will: his wife Elizabeth; his son William; his daughter Mary. Age at death 35.

LAYNE, ANN, daughter of Richard and Ann Layne, Baptized 8 September 1644, Saint Bride Fleet Street, London, England. Lane, Anne, 17 March 1663, age 18, Humphery Warren, by William Heard [02.pdf #164]. Expected date of freedom 1670. Anne Lane, aged 25, deposition, 11 January 1670 [Vol. 60:235].

LEES, THOMAS, son of Thomas Lees and Martha Mellor, Baptized 11 September 1664, Saint Mary, Oldham, Lancashire, England. Lees, Thomas, 9 March 1686, age 22, John Court Jun., "produced an indenture which is found invalid" [13.pdf #49]. Expected date of freedom 1692. Thomas Lees, servant to John Courte, 10 June 1690, with six other servants, "it appeareing by ye Oath of Mr. John Bowman who transported them into this Countrey that hee had ye counterparts of their Indentures & did reade them aboard of his ship at Gravesend, and they were kidnappers Indentures but whether they were good or not hee could not tell, and noe proofe appearing here in Court that ye said Indentures were signed sealed & delivered by ye said John Williams with whom they did indent, & ye same not being under ye seale of an Office, or under ye hand of any Justice of ye peace," ordered by Court to "returne to their severall masters service & serve acording to ye Custome of ye Countrey, their Indentures being adjudged invalide by ye Courte" [17.pdf #18]. George Plater v. Thomas Lee, judgment for defendant, 9 June 1691, [17.pdf #126]. Thomas Lee v. Josiah Bridges, judgment for defendant, 12 January 1692 [17.pdf #195]. "Thomas Lees out of William & Mary Parish," the Public Levy "for Sundry persons Runaway and dead Insolvent in Charles County 1696," 9 November 1697 [19.pdf #179].

ENCYCLOPEDIA OF SURVIVORS

LENHAM, JOHN, 10 June 1679, age 19, Henry Hardy [09.pdf #84]. Expected date of freedom 1685. "The marke of John Lennam" for livestock, 1683 [11.pdf #149]. John Lannum, witness, 11 November 1690 [17.pdf #70]. John Lannam v. William Griffin, judgment for plaintiff, 9 August 1692 [17.pdf #250]. John Lannam v. John Hoppwell, agreed, 10 June 1707 [23.pdf #189].

LINGE, FRANCIS, male, 8 March 1664, age 17, Henry Adames [02.pdf #329]. Expected date of freedom 1670. Children of Francis & Mary Ling: William, son, born 11 March 1669. Michaell, son, born 22 January 1671. Mary, daughter, born 27 March 1673. Francis, son, born 9 October 1676 [16.pdf #120]. "Francis Ling his marke of cattle & hoggs," 9 November 1680 [09.pdf #191]. Mary Ling, "naturall borne daughter" of Mary Hall, gift of livestock, 1680 [10.pdf #33]. William Ling, "son in law" of Richard Hall and "ye naturall borne son of Mary his wife," gift of livestock, 1680 [09.pdf #164]. William Ling, "son of Francis & Mary Ling," gift of livestock, 1681 [10.pdf #78]

LUCCRAFT, JOHN, son of John Luccraft, Baptized 14 August 1690, Loddiswell, Devon, England. Lockraft, John, 1 April 1701, age 13, Francis Green [21.pdf #108]. Expected date of freedom 1710. Indenture between John Luecrafts and Richarde Combes, for "two thousand one hundred pounds of tobacco," ye said John Luecrafts "doth putt and bind himselfe of his own voluntary and free will a servant" "for & during ye full terme & tyme of four years" "in any lawful imployment," the said Richard Combes "to find and provide for him during the said term of tyme sufficient meat drink washing lodging apparell," and "at ye expiration of ye said tyme" "to give unto ye said John Luecrafts one decent suite of apparell viz: one kersie coate & breeches, one hatt, and one paire shoes and stockings," 27 September 1710 [Liber C Page 242] duplicated at [Liber C Page 242]. John Lucraft v. Leonard Green, March 1716 [Liber G Page 49]. George Mure v. John Lucraft planter, judgment for plaintiff, 10 March 1719 [26.pdf #106].

LOW, JAMES, 8 August 1699, age 14, John Gray [20.pdf #79]. Expected date of freedom 1707. James Low, servant to Thomas Jameson, 8 June 1708, servant confessing, 41 days absence, 410 days servitude, and six months "for four hundred pounds of tobacco expended for takeing him up" [23.pdf #253]. Expected date of freedom 1710. Philemon Hemsley v. James Lowe, March 1716 [Liber G Page 95]. Alexander Levistone v.

ENCYCLOPEDIA OF SURVIVORS

James Lowe planter, judgment for plaintiff, 11 March 1718 [26.pdf #35]. Richard Gray v. James Lowe planter, judgment for plaintiff 11 March 1718 [26.pdf #35]. Alexander Levistone v. James Lowe, judgment for plaintiff, 10 June 1718 [26.pdf #41]. Richard Grey v. James Lowe, judgment for plaintiff, 10 June 1718 [26.pdf #42].

LYALL, JOHN, son of John Lyall, Baptized 8 April 1649, Kilrenny, Fife, Scotland. Lyle, John, 8 March 1664, age 17, Mathias Obrian [02.pdf #320]. Expected date of freedom 1671. John Loyle, aged 20, deposition, 11 January 1670 [Vol. 60:233].

MACCLANNEN, MARGARETT, 13 August 1706, age 20, John Speake [23.pdf #138]. Expected date of freedom 1712. The Grand Jurors "present Margrett Macklanan servant to John Speake for haveing a bastard child," 12 June 1711 [24.pdf #94]. Elizabeth Macklanan, "a bastard child" of Margrett Macklanan, servant to John Speake, "two years of age next October," bound to John Speake and wife, 14 August 1711 [24.pdf #121]. (Her original term of servitude expired during this period). Margaret Macklanan, master not named, November 1716, "adjudged of her runaway time" on deposition of John Speake [Liber G Page 151]. Dorothy McLanan, daughter of Margaret McLanan, bound to John Speake, November 1716 [Liber G Page 151]. Margaret Maclanan, master not named, June 1717, "adjudged for runaway time" on deposition of John Speake [Liber G Page 220]. Margaret Maclanan, servant to George Thomas, 11 November 1718, 172 days absence, ordered to serve "four days for one" (688 days servitude), and four months "for his expence & charge in taking her up" [26.pdf #73].

MAC DANNELL, DANNIELE, 8 June 1708, age 19, John Manning [23.pdf #253]. Expected date of freedom 1714. Daniel Macdaniel v. Thomas Osborne, agreed, 10 November 1719. [26.pdf #158]. Samuel Perrie v. Daniel Macdaniel, agreed, 14 November 1721 [27.pdf #121]. Daniel McDaniel v. John Manning, judgment for defendant, 14 November 1721 [27.pdf #121]. Joseph Pillett, servant to Daniel McDaniel, 10 March 1724, 35 days absence, and "two hundred & eighty pounds of tobacco expended in taking him up," ordered to serve eight days for one of his runaway time (280 days servitude), and three months "for the charges aforesaid" [28.pdf #122]. Daniel McDaniel, his "marke of cattle & hoggs," 9 April 1726 [Liber L Page 262]. Daniel MacDaniel, will dated 25 May 1745, probated 13 August 1745, Ann MacDaniel executrix [Liber AC No. 4 Folio 212]. Named in will: his wife Ann; his son Daniel; his son Thomas; his son William; his daughter Esther; his "cousin" Catron Ryle. Age at death 57.

ENCYCLOPEDIA OF SURVIVORS

MACKDONAL, DANIELL, 4 April 1699, age 15, Thomas Hussey [20.pdf #26]. Expected date of freedom 1706. William Jackson, "a minor son of Elizabeth Jackson a single woman," "two years of age the thirteenth day of Aprill last, bound by his said mother unto Daniel Macdonald," he to cause him "to read distintly in ye Bible and when he comes of age to give him a cow & calfe and in ye mean tyme to bring him up in the Established Religeon," 9 June 1713 [25.pdf #144]. Daniel Macdonald v. Abram Barnes, November 1716 [Liber G Page 166]. Daniel Mackdonald, will dated 17 January 1741, probated 15 May 1741, Ann Rankin executrix [Liber AC No. 4 Folio 133]. Named in will: Mary Rankin; Margret Peacock; David Cagill; Peter Cagill; William Mitchel; John Pigen; James Mackintosh; Ann Rankin. Age at death 42.

MACLAINE, LAUGHLIN, 12 June 1705, age 17, Robert Green [23.pdf #79]. Expected date of freedom 1712. Thomas Combs v. Locklan Macklane planter, judgment for plaintiff, 10 June 1718 [26.pdf #46].

MADDOCK, WILLIAM, 9 February 1686, age 20, Thomas Gerrard [13.pdf #48]. Expected date of freedom 1692. "Ordered that ye Clarke issue out a Summons for William Warder and William Maddock to appear here next Court," 9 March 1703 [22.pdf #90]. "William Maddox petitions the Court that he may be admitted to fence in that part of his land that lyeth on or about the road that runneth downe Wiccocomico River he promiseing to keep up good and substantiall gates for the conveniency of travallers, the said petition is granted," 14 September 1708 [23.pdf #269]. Benonie & Hannah Fanning to William Maddox, 100 acres, 5 September 1710, [Liber C Page 197].

MAGRAH, HONOUR, 13 February 1700, age 18, George Tubman, by Henry Hawkins [20.pdf #142]. Expected date of freedom 1707. Honour Magrah, "In a matter between Honnour Magrauh and Juliana Price the wife of Robert Price, ordered that the said Juliana Price doe pay all costs & dues," 10 June 1707 [23.pdf #181]

MAHAWNEY, TYMOTHY, 8 August 1693, age 17, Coll. Humphrey Warren [18.pdf #87]. Expected date of freedom 1700. Henry Dreyden, probate case, Timothy Mahony, executor, 14 August 1705 [23.pdf #91]. Timothy Mahony v. William Shute, plaintiff "hath not prosecuted his said writt," judgment for defendant, 10 June 1707 [23.pdf #191]. Timothy Mahony v. Richard Stafford, agreed, 9 March 1708 [23.pdf #249]. Timothy Mahony v. Gervace Windsor, judgment for defendant, 11 August 1719 [26.pdf #125].

ENCYCLOPEDIA OF SURVIVORS

MAHONI, DANIELL, 10 March 1685, age 15, Thomas Craxon [12.pdf #61]. Expected date of freedom 1692. Daniell Mahoone, servant to Thomas Craxstone, 8 March 1692, absent twice, 5 days in all, 50 days servitude [17.pdf #209]. Expected date of freedom 1692. Philip Lynes v. Daniell Maloaney, complaineth that ye said Daniel on 20 December 1692 "without ye leave of lycense of ye said Philip and against his will & consent did take, ride, worke and may wayes vehemently labour" "a certain gray gelding," and "ye use & service of him" is "utterly lost," and "ye said Daniell Maloaney thereof without defense," judgment for plaintiff, damages awarded, 11 September 1694 [18.pdf #200].

MALBERRY, FRANCIS, 13 November 1677, age 18, Joseph Manninge [08.pdf #48]. Expected date of freedom 1684. "Francis Marberry his marke of cattle & hoggs," 1690 [16.pdf #118]. Francis Marberry v. Thomas Parker, judgment for plaintiff, 9 September 1690 [17.pdf #61]. Edward & Mary Scot to Francis Marbury & Morris Loyde, 200 acres, 28 November 1690 [17.pdf #83].

MARSH, WILLIAM, son of William Marsh, Born 11 January 1657/58, Fremington, Devon, England. Marsh, William, 11 August 1674, age 18, Thomas Gerrard [06.pdf #163]. Expected date of freedom 1681. William Marsh, will probated 18 February 1695, John Chittam executor [Liber A No. 2 Folio 133]. Age at death 37.

MARSHALL, RICHARD, son of Mathew Marshall, Baptized 23 June 1661, Tiverton, Saint Peter, Devon, England. Martiall, Richard, 12 April 1676, age 14, Benjamin Rozer [07.pdf #101]. Expected date of freedom 1682. Richard Marshall v. William Griffin, agreed, 10 June 1690 [17.pdf #28]. Robert Smallpage v. Richard Marshall, agreed, 12 January 1692 [17.pdf #195]. Thomas Mitchell v. Richard Marshall, judgment for plaintiff, 8 March 1692 [17.pdf #225]. Richard Marshall v. John Claxstone, judgment for plaintiff, 13 September 1692 [17.pdf #271]. Richard Marshall v. William Holland, judgment for plaintiff, 8 November 1692 [17.pdf #286]. Raiph Shaw v. Richard Marshall, judgment for plaintiff, 8 August 1693 [18.pdf #93]. William Elliott v. Richard Marshall, judgment for defendant, 8 August 1693 [18.pdf #102]. William Elliott v. Richard Marshall, agreed, 13 March 1694 [18.pdf #157]. William Dent v. Richard Marshall, judgment for plaintiff, 11 September 1694 [18.pdf #221], judgment affirmed, 1695 [Liber T Page 287]. MATTHEW DIKE v. Richard Marshall, 1695 [Liber T Page 153]. John Craxstone v. Richard Marshall,

ENCYCLOPEDIA OF SURVIVORS

"nonsuit," 1695 [Liber T Page 247]. "Richard Marshall runaway," the Public Levy "for Sundry persons Runaway and dead Insolvent in Charles County 1696," 9 November 1697 [19.pdf #179].

MASON, JOHN, 9 November 1680, age 21, John Redich, by John Hamilton [10.pdf #33]. Expected date of freedom 1686. John Mason v. William Griffin, agreed, 10 June 1690 [17.pdf #28]. John Mason v. Jesse Doyne, judgment for plaintiff, 8 June 1708 [23.pdf #257].

MAXFIELD, RICHARD, 10 August 1675, age 17, Francis Wine [07.pdf #74]. Expected date of freedom 1682. Richard Maxfeild, petition to Governor & Councill, against Mr. Henry Hawkins, "and ye Richard Maxfeild not appeareing here this day," ordered "that a summons be issued," 10 November 1696 [19.pdf #73]. Richard Maxfeild shoemaker v. Henry Hawkins, plaintiff summoned "to make good his complaint" and "came not," "ordered that ye petition be dismist," 12 January 1697 [19.pdf #92].

MILSTEAD, EDWARD, 12 January 1675, age 19, William Chandeler [07.pdf #33]. Expected date of freedom 1681. Edward Milsteade v. William Newman, 27 November 1683 [11.pdf #158]. Edward Milstead v. Thomas Kearsey, judgment for plaintiff, 13 January 1685 [12.pdf #51]; see also 10 March 1685 [12.pdf 78]. William Milstead, son of Edward & Susanna Milstead, born 20 July 1685 [16.pdf #121]. "The grand jurors doe present Edward Milstead for gitting Susannah Clarke with child of which she ye said Susannah is delivered," 9 March 1686 [13.pdf #52]. "Recognizance given by Phillip Hoskins & Edward Milstead for 50 pound sterling apeice to indemnify ye Court from a bastard child begotten one ye bodie of Susan Clarke by ye said Edward," 10 March 1686 [13.pdf #49]. William Milstead, William, "son of Edward Milstead begotten on ye bodie of Susannah Clarke by ye said Edward," age not stated, bound to Thomas Craxton "of Nangemie in Charles Countie," 9 November 1686 [13.pdf #120]. Edward Millsteade v. Samuell Jefferson, 12 August 1690 [17.pdf #34] and 8 March 1692 [17.pdf #222]. John Hanby, son of FRANCIS HANBY "which he had by Elizabeth Hazleton," "hee ye said John Hanby being one yeare old ye tenth day of February last past," bound to Edward Millsteade, "hee ye said Edward Millsteade providing & alloweing necessary & convenient meate drinke washing lodgeing & clothing," 8 March 1692 [17.pdf #209] Edward Millsteade v. George Athy, agreed, 9 January 1694 [18.pdf #138]. The Grand Jurors "doe present Edward Milstead planter for that" on or about 31 September 1700 "at Nanjemy" did assault "the body of

ENCYCLOPEDIA OF SURVIVORS

one William Grey," and "did beat wound and evilly mistreat so that of his life it was dispaired and other harmes to him did do," 12 November 1700 [21.pdf #50], tried and acquitted, 14 January 1701 [21.pdf #66].
SMITH, MARGRETT, without indentures, 14 November 1710, age 20, Edward Millstead [24.pdf #31]. Edward Milstead v. Pryor Smallwood, August 1715 [Liber G Page 13]. Edward Milstead v. Edward Sanders, March 1716 [Liber G Page 86]. Edward Milstead "presented for contempt," March 1717 [Liber G Page 180]. Edward Milstead, List of Taxable Inhabitants, 45 squirrells heads, 12 November 1717 [26.pdf #18]. Edward Milstead, List of Taxable Inhabitants, 2 crows heads, 12 November 1717 [26.pdf #19]. Edward Milstead v. Pryor Smallwood, judgment for plaintiff, 12 August 1718 [26.pdf #54]. James Ward, "an orphan lad born ye twenty seventh day of May seventeen hundred and five," parents not named, bound to Edward Milstead, he "to learn him to read distinctly in ye Bible" & at ye expiration of his time "to give him a good decent suit of broadcloth cloaths," 14 June 1720 [26.pdf #172]. Edward Milstead Junr., his mark, 22 January 1724 [Liber L Page 112]. John Manning to Edward Milstead, deed of real estate, 18 September 1724 [Liber L Page 200]. Edward Milstead, aged 70, deposition, 15 March 1726 [30.pdf #153]. "Edward Milsteads petition to be allowed for burying Edward Block is rejected," 14 November 1727 [31.pdf #19]. Thomas Milstead, his mark of livestock, 19 November 1728 [Liber L Page 450]. Edward Millstead Senr., will dated 14 December 1733, probated 17 January 1734, Mary Millstead executor [Liber AB No. 3 Folio 263]. Named in will: his wife Mary; his son Edward; "an orphan boy John Ettil"; John Millstead; William Millstead; James Mordock; John Grue (?). Age at death 77.

MIRES, CHRISTOPHER, 13 June 1682, age 21, Thomas Craxstone [10.pdf #165]. Expected date of freedom 1688. "Christopher Mayers his marke of catell & hoggs," 1688 [16.pdf #31]. "Itt is ordered by ye Court that ye sherife" carry Christopher Myers "to whipping post & give him twenty & one lashes on his bare back well laid on," "and that ye said Christopher Myers be & remaine in ye custody of ye sherife untill hee putt in sufficient security to save ye County harmlesse of & from ye maintenance of a bastard child begotten by him on ye body of ANNE RHENNICK," whereupon "came here into Court Christopher Myers late of Nanjemy planter in his proper person & did assume upon himselfe in ye sume of twenty pounds of good & lawfull money of England, 11 March 1690 [18.pdf #113]. Christopher & Mary Myers v. Thomas & Anne Craxon, whereas on 15 June 1689 "comunication was had concerning ye said Christopher marryeing ye said Mary then known by ye name of Mary Sellwood and dwelling at ye house in ye service of ye said Thomas & Anne," who "did affirme that shee ye said Mary was noe free woman but ye servant of them ye said Thomas & Anne for ye tearme of five yeares from her arrivall into this Province being shipt in London by ye said Anne and brought into this Province in ye ship Mary of London, John Harris Comander," "whereupon ye said Christopher & Mary did bargaine of buying ye time of service" for "five thousand four hundred seaventy & eight pounds if tobaccoe," and ye said Thomas accordingly did assigne over ye said Mary," "whereas in truth ye said Mary at ye time of ye comunication & sale aforesaid was not a servant to ye said Thomas & Anne but a free woman & as such came into this Province and soe ye said Thomas & Anne hath deceived & defrauded ye said Christopher & Mary," judgment for plaintiffs, 11 August 1691 [17.pdf #150]. Christopher & Mary Myers v. Thomas Craxon, judgment for defendant, 10 November 1691 [17.pdf #167]. Christopher Myers, probate case, Mary Myers administrator, 11 August 1696 [19.pdf #53]. Age at death 35.

MORAND, PATRICK, 1 August 1693, age 13, John Bayne, Saint Mary's County, Maryland [21.pdf #92]. Expected date of freedom 1702. "Patrick Cusacks petition reade, and he brings here into Court a coppy of the records of St. Marys County which hereafter followeth: Mr. John Bayne brings here into Court two Irish servants the one named Patrick Morand and the other named PATRICK CUSACK," adjudged by the St. Mary's County Court (with Mr. John Bayne present as Justice -- ed.) to be thirteen and seaventeen yeares of age respectively, copied into Charles County Court Record 11 March 1701 [21.pdf #92]. "Patrick Moreland his marke of cattle and hoggs," 3 March 1707 [Liber Z Page 267]. JOHN BRYAN, servant to Walter Bayne, 9 March 1708, "Patrick Moreland appeareing here to give evidence between JOHN BRYAN and Mr. Walter Bayne," ordered by Court "that the said JOHN BRYAN be free from the service of the said Walter Bayne," [23.pdf #236]. JOHN MAGRAH administrator of Patrick Moreland, 9 June 1719 [26.pdf #112]. Age at death 39.

MORRELL, CHRISTOPHER, 10 June 1673, age 20, Richard Chandler [Vol. 60:498]. Expected date of freedom 1679. Christopher Morrell v. John Martin, "agreed before tryall," 10 November 1680 [10.pdf #42]. James Wheeler v. Christopher Morrell, alleged theft of saddle, acquitted, 29 November 1681 [10.pdf #120].

ENCYCLOPEDIA OF SURVIVORS

MORRIS, ELLIS, 12 September 1682, age 19, James Neale Junior [11.pdf #18]. Expected date of freedom 1688. Morris, Ellice, servant to James Neale, 8 June 1686, 14 days absence, 140 days servitude, "and allsoe make such other sattisfacion for his trouble & charge" of bringing him home [13.pdf #117]. Expected date of freedom 1689. William Jenkinson v. Elias Morris, agreed, 9 June 1691 [17.pdf #133].

MORROUGH (MAGRAH), JOHN, 19 April 1698, age 12, Capt. John Bayne [19.pdf #206]. "a servant boy John Mograugh ye same time" (5 years), An Inventory of the Estate of Capt. John Bayne Deceased, 10 July 1702 [Vol. 22, Folio 34]. "John Magrah to serve 3 years next March," The Inventory of the Goods and Chattles of Madam Anne Bayne, 15 July 1703 [Vol. 24, Folio 140]. John Magrah administrator of PATRICK MORELAND, 9 June 1719 [26.pdf #112].

MURPHY, MAGLOUGHLIN, 9 November 1697, age 18, Capt. John Wilder [19.pdf #169]. Expected date of freedom 1704. "Wee of the Grand Jury doe present William Rawlings, John Jones, and Macklowling Merthey for stealeing a parcell of wheate a pott of butter and one turkey cock from Francis Wilder in the month of October. Witness Katherine Burke and Rebekah Gant," 13 June 1704 [22.pdf #226]. William Rawlings, John Jones, and Macklowling Merthey, jury "impannelled," "wee doe find Macklowling Murthey guilty of stealing the turkey and butter and John Jones for cutting off the head of the turkey and consealing the same for William Rawlings wee find nothing against him," ordered by Court "that the said John Jones and Macklowling Murthey doe pay the four fold of the goods soe stolen," and that the Sherriff "carry them to the pillory and put their necks therein for the space of half an hour and after that to take them to the whipping post and stripp them naked from the waste upwards and to give each of them twenty lashes well laid upon the bare back," and "that the said William Rawlings be acquitt and discharged from the presentment," 13 March 1705 [23.pdf #49]. "Mrs. Frances Wilders Indenture for Laughlin Merthy, itt is the opinion of the Court that the same be good and valid," 10 April 1705 [23.pdf #64].

MURPHY, MARY, 12 March 1700, age 22, Richard Combes [20.pdf #177]. Expected date of freedom 1706. Mary Murphey, her petition for allowance in ye County Levy for her maintenance rejected, 10 November 1719 [26.pdf #143].

ENCYCLOPEDIA OF SURVIVORS

NAILEE, JOHN, 10 August 1675, age 12, Thomas Matthewes [07.pdf #74]. Expected date of freedom 1685. John Dent executor of William Husculoe deceased v. John Naley, whereas on 30 May 1693 "John Naley by a certain writing of covenant" did lease for seven yeares from William Husculoe "a plantation of his lyeing in St. Maryes County," and "ye said William Husculoe made his Last Will & Testament" on 29 December 1693 and did "bequeath ye said tract of land unto ye said John Dent," "and ye said John Naley hath quietly & peaceable held & enjoyed ye said plantation byu virtue of ye lease aforesaid ye full time of two yeares since ye death of ye said William Husculoe and hath not paid to ye said John Dent ye yearly rent," "but ye said John Dent being solemnely called came not nor did prosecute his said writt," judgment for defendant, 10 August 1697 [19.pdf #137]. John Carty & Richard Bell administrators of John Seaman deceased v. John Nalley of St. Maryes County planter, judgments for plaintiffs, 10 August 1697 [19.pdf #147] and 4 October 1698 [19.pdf #257]. Capt. John Bayne v. John Nally planter, judgment for plaintiff, 11 June 1700 [21.pdf #12]. James Irving v. John Nalley planter, judgment for plaintiff, 13 August 1700 [21.pdf #29]. Mary Gary administratrix of Lawrence Gary deceased v. John Nally planter, judgment for plaintiff, 13 August 1700 [21.pdf #38]. John Nally v. Abraham Lemaister, 9 September 1701 [21.pdf #157]. Susannah Mason executrix of Robert Mason deceased v. John Nally, agreed, 12 January 1703 [22.pdf #86]. Walter Bayne administrator of Anne Bayne deceased v. John Nally, judgment for plaintiff, 13 June 1704 [22.pdf #230]. "Wee the Grand Jury doe present John Nalley planter & Jane his wife for stealing about four or five yards of fustaine (?) and sundry other goods from the said Benjamin Hall by information of Ditto," 11 March 1707 [23.pdf #168], and "they penitently owne the fact and submitt themselves to the mercy of the Court, upon whihc submission and the said Benjamin Halls Declaration in open Court that he freely forgave the fact," ordered by Court "to prosecute the said presentment no farther," 10 June 1707 [23.pdf #182]. John Nalley v. John Wattkins, "and the said John Wattkins is not found," judgment for plaintiff, 10 June 1707 [23.pdf #200]. Patrick Hepburn v. Thomas Lindzey, bailiff John Nally or Nalley, ordered that "the said writt be quashed," judgment for bailiff, 11 March 1712 [25.pdf #55]. John Nalley v. Patrick Hepburn, judgment for plaintiff, 10 June 1712 [25.pdf #85]. Patrick Hepburn v. John Nally, judgment for plaintiff, 9 June 1713 [25.pdf #163]. Patrick Hepburne v. John Nalley, 11 August 1713 [25.pdf #176]. Charles Higdon v. John Nayle, March 1716 [Liber G Page 86]. John Nalley, List of Taxable Inhabitants, 139 squirrells heads, 12 November 1717 [26.pdf #18]. John Nalley, List of Taxable Inhabitants,

ENCYCLOPEDIA OF SURVIVORS

2 crows heads, 12 November 1717 [26.pdf #19]. John Naile, his recognizance, 11 November 1718 [26.pdf #71]. Jonathan Scarth v. John Nally, judgment for plaintiff, 11 August 1719 [26.pdf #129]. Thomas Hargis, probate case, John Nalley administrator, 11 August 1719 [26.pdf #132]. John Nalley v. John Gibson, "struck off," 10 November 1719 [26.pdf #154]. "Ordered that a capias (bench warrant -- ed.) issue returnable" against John Nally & Thomas Harguiss, 14 November 1721 [27.pdf #108]. John Nally v. Thomas Harguiss, judgment for plaintiff, 14 November 1721 [27.pdf #123]. John Nally v. Thomas Harguiss, judgment for plaintiff, 13 March 1722 [27.pdf # 153]. Laurance McAvoy, servant to John Nalley, Gent., 13 June 1732, 16 days absence, on "oath in Court here" of "James Taylor his former master," ordered to "serve his present master John Nalley five days for each one of his runaway time aforesaid" (80 days servitude) [32.pdf #77]. John Nalley, will dated February 1733, probated 3 March 1734, William Nalley executor [Liber AB No. 3 Folio 257]. Named in will: his son Denis; his son Joseph; his son John; his son William. Age at death 70.

NEWMAN, ANN, daughter of Richard and Barbara Newman, Born 3 October 1653, Saint Nicholas, Bristol, Gloucester, England. Newman, Ann, 11 January 1670, age 17, William Barton [Vol. 60:230]. Expected date of freedom 1676. Anne Newman "demands a writt of subpoena for George Powell to testify ye truth of his knowledge betwixt Anne Newman plaintiff & Richard Price defendant," 10 August 1680 [09.pdf #180].

NICHOLS, JOHN, 8 November 1687, age not judged, John Court, produced Indentures "for four yeares," upon inspection, ordered to serve "according to ye Custom of ye Country" [14.pdf #160] Children of John & Bethsheba Nicholls: Jonathan, son, born c. 1702 [25.pdf #172]. William, son, born c. 1706 [25.pdf #144]. Solomon, son, born August 1710 [25.pdf #144]. Benjamin, son, born 8 March 1713 [25.pdf #219] [25.pdf #271]. John Contee v. John Nickollds, agreed, 14 March 1704 [22.pdf #169]. Philip Lynes to John Nicholls, 100 acres, 10 September 1706 [Liber C Page 19]. John & Bathsheba Nicholls to Philip Lynes, 400 acres, 10 September 1706 [Liber C Page 21]. Kate or Katherine, "being now of the age of two yeares," daughter of Elizabeth Edelin spinster, "being a free woman do on my owne free will and consent being poore and needy and haveing a female child" "begotten of my body by a Negro slave in Saint Maryes County and finding my disability to provide for the said child as to cloathing and provisions," bound "untill she shall arrive to the full age of thirty yeares and one" to John

ENCYCLOPEDIA OF SURVIVORS

Nicholls of Charles County and Batheshebah his wife," "my being given to the said John Nicholls by my master Mr. Edward Turner of St. Maryes County," "the above Indenture read in Court and the said Mollatto child is bound accordingly," 26 February 1708 [23.pdf #236]. Capt. William Harbert v. John Nicholls, judgment for plaintiff, 14 June 1709 [23.pdf #317]. The Grand Jurors "present John Nicholls planter for stoping ye main road by information of William Barton," 11 March 1712 [25.pdf #33], "discharged paying fees," 10 June 1712 [25.pdf #78]. Thomas Garret v. John Nicholls, judgment for plaintiff, 12 August 1712 [25.pdf #107]. George Banks v. John Nicholls, 11 November 1712 [25.pdf #112], "and the said John Nichols being sollemly called came not," judgment for plaintiff, 10 March 1713 [25.pdf #138]. Nichols, John, will dated 28 April 1713, probated 4 May 1713, John Sanders & Thomas Harris executors [Liber AB No. 3 Folio 63]. Named in will: his daughter in law Mary Ratcliff; Richard Ratcliff; Thomas Harris; his son Jonathan; his son William; his son Soloman; "and that all my children be free at the age of eighteen years." John Nicholls, probate case, John Sanders executor, 9 June 1713 [25.pdf #144]. Solomon Nichols, "an orphan boy," "being three years of age next August," bound to James Boyce "untill he arives to the age of eighteen years being left so by his fathers Will," he obleigeing himselfe that the boy "be instructed to read distinctly & to bring him up in ye Established Religion," 9 June 1713 [25.pdf #144]. William Nichols, orphan, "being seven years of age," bound to John Leverat, "he being left by his fathers Testament to be of age at eighteen years to the said Leverat," who "obleigs himselfe to instruct him to read and in the Established Religeon," 9 June 1713 [25.pdf #144]; "William Nichols petiton against John Leveret for schooling rejected," 13 November 1722 [28.pdf #8]. Nichols, not named (Benjamin -- ed.), "an infant child of a certayne John Nicholls deceased," age not stated, complaint of THOMAS HILL, who "contracted with the said Nicholls in his life tyme that for keeping & maintayneing the said child for one yeare he was to have and receive a cow & calfe & five hundred pounds of tobacco and that John Sanders of Mattawomann," "being Executor of ye Testament of the said Nichols," "will not deliver to him the said cow & calfe nor pay him the tobacco," ordered by Court "that the said John Sanders doe deliver and pay unto the said Thomas Hill the said cow & calfe and five hundred pounds of tobacco," 9 June 1713 [25.pdf #144]. Benjamin Nicholls, son of John & Bethsheba Nicholls deceased, "aged fifteen months," "is put under ye care of THOMAS HILL to be maintained who is to be allowed in ye assessment of ye next County Leavy one hundred pounds of tobacco," and "also two hundred pounds of tobacco for his care & charge in maintaining (during) two months

ENCYCLOPEDIA OF SURVIVORS

past," 8 June 1714 [25.pdf #219]. Benjamin Nicholls "a minor orphan being two years of age ye eighth day of March last past," bound to THOMAS HILL, he to instruct him "to read distinctly in ye Bible, to apparel him decently at ye expiration of his time of servitude and to discharge the County from any incumbrance or charge," 14 June 1715 [25.pdf #271]. Jonathan Nichols, "an orphan," "being about eleven years of age," bound to Thomas Harris, "to serve untill he arives at ye age of eighteen," "to be instructed to read and write, and to learne the art & trade of a cordwiner (cordwainer -- ed.)" and to be brought up "in the Established Protestant Religeon," 11 August 1713 [25.pdf #172].

OARD, PETER, 12 March 1672, age 18, Robert Henley [06.pdf #59]. Expected date of freedom 1679. Children of Peter & Anne Oard of Wiccocomicoe: Mary, daughter, born 24 March 1683 [16.pdf #121]. Thomas, son, born 19 November 1686 [16.pdf #121]. James, son, born 21 April 1690 [16.pdf #121]. Anne, daughter, born 19 September 1694 [Liber Q Page 23]. "Peter Ord his marke of cattle & hoggs," 1690 [16.pdf #118]. Nicholas Leigh merchant v. Peter Oard planter, judgment for defendant, 12 March 1700 [21.pdf #7]. John Courts Esqr. v. Peter Oard, agreed, 14 January 1701 [21.pdf #90]. "Peter Oard petitions the Court that he may be leavy free the said petition is rejected," 9 March 1708 [23.pdf #236]. Peter Oard deceased, 30 July 1709, Anne Oard administrator, Edward Turvey and Robert King, the two sons in law of Peter Oard.

PARKER, JOHN, 8 March 1670, age 18, Jeremiah Dickison [Vol. 60:242]. Expected date of freedom 1677. "John Parker enters his marke of hogges & cattle," 1677 [08.pdf #56]. John Parker v. "Humphrey Jones & Mary his wife," and "James Gallaway, John Slater & William Allridge servants to Richard Hodgson," "hogge stealers," 12 June 1679 [09.pdf #105]. John Parker v. Jane Price, Executrix of Edward Price deceased, judgment for plaintiff, 29 November 1681 [10.pdf #118]. Phillip Lynes v. John Parker, who "had absented himselfe out of this province & left no attorney behind him," judgment for plaintiff, 12 August 1684 [11.pdf #218]. James Smallwood Junr. v. John Parker, judgment for plaintiff, that he recover "two young piggs," 8 August 1693 [18.pdf #96]. Elizabeth Parker, daughter of John Parker, gift of livestock, 1694 [18.pdf #222]. John & Anne Parker to Thomas Chapman, 263 acres, 13 September 1695 [Liber Q Page 94]. William Stone v. Dennis Connell & John Parker, judgment for plaintiff, 11 August 1696 [19.pdf #53]. William Dent v. John Parker, "and ye said John Parker being dead," case dismissed, 14 September 1697 [19.pdf #153]. Age at death 45.

ENCYCLOPEDIA OF SURVIVORS

PARKER, JONAS, 8 June 1675, age 15, John Courtes, by Cleborne Lomax [07.pdf #63]. Expected date of freedom 1682. "Jonas Parker is appointed Constable in the room of WILLIAM BARKER for Benedict Leonard hundred," 12 November 1700 [21.pdf #51]. William Rowse v. Jonas Parker, for "falcely and malliciusly" calling him "a rogue and a cheat," "the said action was acknowledged to be agreed," 9 March 1703 [22.pdf #98]. Jonas Parker, aged 59, deposition, 30 August 1720 [Liber M Page 99].

PEACOCKE, WILLIAM, 13 March 1677, age 14, Philipp Lines [08.pdf #22]. Expected date of freedom 1685. The Grand Jurors "doe present William Peacock for that he" "at Portobacco" "one young heifer being in the marke & also properly the heifer of one John Payne feloniously did alter the marke of the said heifer into his owne marke," 10 June 1701 [21.pdf #124]. "Whereas att the last Court" on 9 September 1701 "Ralph Lomax of this County planter was found guilty for branding and ear marking a certaine horse belonging to one William Peacock" but "the said Lomax made his escape," "and now att this day" "the said Ralph Lomax not appearing," 12 November 1701 [21.pdf #163]. "And now came the said Ralph Lomax in his propper person," and "if there by any one that" "would prosecute him" "they should be heard and none came," ordered by Court "that the said Ralph Lomax be acquitt," 10 Mar 1702 [22.pdf #4]. Thomas Dent v. William Peacock, agreed, March 1716 [Liber G Page 78] and November 1716 [Liber G Page 160]. Philemon Hemsley v. William Peacock, August 1716 [Liber G Page 147].

PHILIPS, THOMAS, 13 March 1677, age 17, James Bowling [08.pdf #22]. Expected date of freedom 1684. Thomas Phillips v. John Church, debt "for one horse," 8 September 1685 [13.pdf #31]. Joseph & Margrett Cornall to William Griffine & Thomas Phillips, 234 acres, 2 June 1687 [14.pdf #113] and [16.pdf #15]. Thomas Phillips and Edward Ford, sureties for George Pouncey, 9 August 1687 [14.pdf #151].

PICKERING, MICHAEL, son of Michael Pickering, Baptized 6 March 1642, Witton Gilbert, Durham, England [near Durham]. Pickering, Michell, c. 13 March 1661, "beeing then" age 18, Charles County, Maryland, Robert Hendley, freed by court 13 March 1666, "hath sarved five years and upwards coming in without Indenturs beeing then 18 years of age and hath demanded his fredom with corne and cloaths," ordered by Court "that Michell Pickering shall bee free and that the defendant pay unto the plantive his corne and cloaths according to the custome of the contry" [02.pdf #600]

ENCYCLOPEDIA OF SURVIVORS

POTTS, JOHN, 8 June 1686, age 24, Capt. Bowling [13.pdf #117]. Expected date of freedom 1691. John Allward v. John Potts, 8 November 1692 [17.pdf #290].

POWELL, ROBERT, son of John Powell, Baptized 28 December 1655, Saint Stephan Coleman Street, London, London, England. Powell, Robert, 8 March 1670, age 16, Mr. Adams [Vol. 60:242]. Expected date of freedom 1677. "Robert Powell his marke of cattle & hoggs," 1687 [14.pdf #111]. Robert Powell, son of Robert Powell of Pyckyawaxon, born 17 November 1692, baptized 10 January 1693 [16.pdf #122]. Robert Powell v. John Carter, quashed, 1694 [Liber T Page 119].

RAYLEY, EDWARD, 13 March 1677, age 14, James Bowling [08.pdf #22]. Expected date of freedom 1685. Perrie Noeland v. Edward Ryley, agreed, 1695 [Liber T Page 143]. John Bayne v. Edward Reyley, 1696 [Liber T Page 353]. "Edward Ryley runaway," the Public Levy "for Sundry persons Runaway and dead Insolvent in Charles County 1696," 9 November 1697 [19.pdf #179].

REDMAN, CORNELIUS, 14 June 1698, age 20, Anne Taylor, "widdow" [19.pdf #217]. Expected date of freedom 1704. "Cornelius Reddman his marke of cattle and hoggs," 12 August 1708 [Liber C Page 116]. Walter Story v. Cornelius Redman, "and the said Cornelius though being sollemly called came not," judgment for plaintiff, 11 March 1712 [25.pdf #70]. William Nicholls v. Cornelius Redman, 11 March 1712 [25.pdf #70] and 12 August 1712 [25.pdf #102].

RENNICKE, ANNE, 10 November 1674, age 16, Elinor Beane, by John Long [07.pdf #19]. Expected date of freedom 1681. "The Grand Jurors by ye information of MOSES JONES Constable doe present Anne Rhenick late of Nanjemy of this County for haveing a bastard child," 26 November 1689 [16.pdf #110]. "Itt is ordered by ye Court that ye sherife take ye said Anne Rhennick into his custody & carry her to ye whipping post & strip her naked from ye waist upward & doe give or cause to given to her on her bare back twenty & one lashes well laid on," and "ye said Anne Rhennick did testifye in open Court that CHRISTOPHER MYERS late of Nanjemy planter was ye father of ye said child," 14 January 1690 [16.pdf #112].

ENCYCLOPEDIA OF SURVIVORS

RICHARDSON, JOSEPH, son of William Richardson, Born 18 May 1655, Newbury, Massachusetts. Richardson, Joseph, 12 January 1675, age 21, John Clarke [07.pdf #33]. Expected date of freedom 1681. Joseph Richardson married Margaret Godfrey, 12 June 1681, Newbury, Massachusetts.

RICHARDSON, WILLIAM, 14 June 1687, age 14, Capt. Randolph Brandt [14.pdf #142]. Expected date of freedom 1695. "Ordered that JOHN HAMMON doe pay unto William Richardson five hundred pounds of tobacco for keeping his wifes daughter Charity Thompson," 12 August 1707 [23.pdf #201].

ROBERTS, WILLIAM, 9 January 1677, age 20, Benjamin Rozer [08.pdf #14]. Expected date of freedom 1683. William Roberts, servant to Edward Saunders, 8 November 1681, five absences, 81 days "in all," 810 days servitude, assigned by Edward Saunders "unto Edward Gale for ye time of his servitude & for his runing away" [10.pdf #112]. Expected date of freedom 1685. Jane Roberds, "orphan of William Roberds (who) departed this Province," age not stated, bound to Phillip Mason, 14 June 1687 [14.pdf #141].

ROBINS, HENRY, 12 April 1676, age 17, Benjamin Rozer [07.pdf #101]. Expected date of freedom 1683. Phillip Lynes v. Henry Robins, "the said action is agreed," 10 March 1685 [12.pdf #61]. William Hutchison to Henry Robbins, 120 acres, 3 June 1689, [17.pdf #259]. "Henry Robins his marke of cattle & hoggs," 1691 [17.pdf #187]. William Robins, son of Henry Robins, gift of livestock, 1691 [17.pdf #187]. Gerrard Slye v. Henry Robins, judgment for defendant, 13 February 1700 [20.pdf #152]. James Robbins, son of Henry Robbins of Mattawoman, gift of livestock, 1704 [Liber Z Page 160]. Margarett Robbins, daughter of Henry Robbins of Mattawoman, gift of livestock, 1704 [Liber Z Page 161]. Thomas Robbins, son of Henry Robbins of Mattawoman, gift of livestock, 1704 [Liber Z Page 160]. Henry Robins v. Robert Taylor, judgment for plaintiff, 8 June 1708 [23.pdf #264].

ROBINSON, SAMUELL, son of George Robinson and Joanna Inhraham, Born 3 October 1654, Rehoboth, Massachusetts. Robinson, Samuell, 11 June 1678, age 21, Capt. Humphrey Warren [08.pdf #92]. Expected date of freedom 1684. Samuel Robinson married Mehitable Reed, 10 October 1688, New England.

ENCYCLOPEDIA OF SURVIVORS

ROSS, FRANCIS, 12 September 1699, age 11, Ubgatt Reeves [20.pdf #101]. Expected date of freedom 1710. Ross, Francis, servant to Ubgate Reeves, 13 June 1710, petition of Daniell Dullany, "the said Reeves suruptitiously obtayneing an Indenture or writing from under ye hand of the said Ross," which "was taken before the said Ross was free of his first tyme to the said Reeves," ordered by Court "that the Contract or Indenture be void and that the said Francis Ross be free" [23.pdf #402]. Francis Rosse v. Alexander Hamilton, June 1716 [Liber G Page 109]. Francis Rosse v. Henry Quando, June 1716 [Liber G Page 117].

SALT, MARY, 11 March 1679, age 20, Thomas Speeke, "of St. Maries County" [09.pdf #81]. Expected date of freedom 1685. The Grand Jurors "doe present Mary Salt living at William Fosters by information of Michaell Martin Constable for haveing a bastard child," 9 November 1697 [29.pdf #168]. "And ye said Mary Salt in her proper person came to answer unto ye presentment aforesaid and it appeareing to ye Court here that ye said bastard child was neither gott nor borne within ye jurisdiccion of this Court," ordered "that ye said Mary Salt be discharged & acquitt from ye presentment aforesaid," 11 January 1698 [19.pdf #181]. Mary Salt, "petition for an allowance in ye next County Levy whereby to support her in her poor & necessitous condition," 8 March 1720 [26.pdf #160]; "Mary Salt an antient indigent & lame woman, on her petition, is allowed five hundred pounds of tobacco," 8 November 1720 [27.pdf #29].

SAUNDERS, MATHEW, son of Mathew and Frances Saunders, Baptized 3 October 1647, Saint Dunstan, Stepney, London, England. Sanders, Mathew, 8 July 1662, age 15, John Cain [01.pdf #227]. Expected date of freedom 1669. John Boyden to William Boyden & Mathew Sanders, 80 acres, 14 March 1671 [06.pdf #40]. Garrett Sinnett to Matthew Saunders & Thomas Bryant, 150 acres, 9 March 1676 [08.pdf #24]. "Matthew Saunders enters his marke of hogges & cattle," 1677 [08.pdf #41]. Matthew Saunders v. Richard Taylor, 10 August 1680 [10.pdf #27]. Richard Capner, servant to Matthew Saunders, 13 March 1683, petitions that he "did covenant & agree with William Pennell to serve him his heirs & assigns for & dureing ye tearme of foure years after their first arrival in Virginia or Maryland, as by ye said Indenture," "and whereas you petitioner hath well & faithfully served Matthew Saunders of this County ye full tearme of foure yeares according to ye Indenture aforesaid, which tearme of time was fully expired on ye 7th day of February last past, & ye said Matthew Saunders doth refuse & deny to sett him free, but doth still deteine him in his service," "therefore your humble petitioner beggs & craves" "an order for his freedome, with satisfaction for ye time that hee hath served above, & for his freedome corne & clothes," "which Indenture being proved in open Court by ye oath of Jeremy Allanson that hee did see William Pennell at Barbados signe seale & deliver ye same as his act & deed to Richard Capner," ordered by Court "that ye said Richard Capner bee free from his said masters service, & that his master Matthew Saunders pay to him ye said Richard Capner his freedome corne & clothes" [11.pdf #84]. Philip Lynes to Matthew Sanders, 200 acres, 8 June 1683 [11.pdf #115]. Mathew Saunders v. Robert Goodrick, "agreed before tryall," 12 March 1684 [11.pdf #184]. John Saunders, son of Matthew Saunders, gift of livestock, 1690 [16.pdf #118]. George & Mary Pounsey v. Matthew Saunders, judgment for defendant, 13 March 1694 [18.pdf #155]. George Pounsey v. Matthew Sanders, 1694 [Liber T Page 81]. Matthew Sanders v. Samuel Edmonds, 1695 [Liber T Page 164]. William Dent v. Matthew Sanders, 1695 [Liber T Page 285]. CURRS, EDWARD, without indentures, 13 February 1700, age 17, Matthew Sanders [20.pdf #142]. "Matthew Sanders fined tenn shillings for vaine sweareing in Court," 14 January 1701 [21.pdf #69], not paid [22.pdf #103]. Notley Rozer v. Matthew Sanders, agreed, 9 March 1703 [22.pdf #96]. "William Sanders the son of Matthew Sanders did nott burne the house of Edward Tills," deposition of Thomas Mansfield, 11 November 1707 [23.pdf #222]. Mathew Sanders to "my dear & well beloved son William Sanders," gift of real estate, a "half part of a tract of land called Prichard purchased by me from Philip Lynes" by deed dated 8 June 1683 (see above), 100 acres, 6 August 1713 [Liber F Page 18]. Matthew Sanders Senr. to Francis Sanders "now Francis Robinson," 82 acres, 13 August 1717 [Liber H Page 76]. Archibald Smith v. Matthew Sanders, judgment for plaintiff, 12 August 1718 [26.pdf #65]. Robert and William Robertson, orphans of Francis Robertson deceased, ordered by Court to continue under ye care of their grandfather & grandmother Matthew & Eleanor Sanders, 9 June 1719 [26.pdf #113]. Matthew Sanders, aged 71, depositions, 4 November 1719 [Liber M Page 66] [Liber M Page 67]. Matthew Sanders Senr., Matthew, will dated 19 December 1719, probated 20 February 1720, Ellender Sanders executrix [Liber AB No. 3 Folio 137]. Named in will: his grandson Robert Roberson; his son John Sanders; his son William Sanders; his daughter Margat Ward; his "eldest son" Matthew Sanders; his wife Ellender Sanders. Age at death 71.

ENCYCLOPEDIA OF SURVIVORS

SEDGELY, SAMUELL, son of William and Ellen Sedgely, Baptized 13 December 1666, Saint Botolph without Aldersgate, London, England. Sigeley, Samuell, 9 November 1680, age 16, John Mun [10.pdf #33]. Expected date of freedom 1687. Sigley, Samuell, "an apprentice servant" to Mitchell Ashford, 14 June 1692, "came here into Court and made his complaint that his said master" "did turn him to common labor to ye axe and howe, but nothing appeareing to ye Court that hee did not keepe him to his trade, itt is ordered that ye Samuell Sigley returne to his said masters service, and his master imploy him at his trade according to ye tenour of his Indenture" [17.pdf #233]

SHAW, JOHN, 13 June 1682, age 17, Railph Smith [10.pdf #165]. Expected date of freedom 1688. The Grand Jury "by ye Information of Joseph Willson," presents John Shaw of Charles County planter "for that hee did feloniously pilfer steale take & carry away severall goods out of ye house of James Turner deceased," 10 August 1697 [19.pdf #134]; "and nothing appeareing against him that hee is guilty thereof," defendant acquitted, 14 September 1697 [19.pdf #151]. John Shaw, son of John Shaw, gift of livestock, 15 October 1709 [Liber C Page 148]. John Shaw, List of Taxable Inhabitants, 36 squirrells heads, 12 November 1717 [26.pdf #19]. John Shaw, Senr., aged 67, deposition, 25 October 1731 [32.pdf #26]. John Shaw, will dated 23 November 1739, probated 24 December 1739, John Shaw executor [Liber AC No.4 Folio 108]. Named in will: his son John; his daughter Mary Rock "wife of James Rock"; his daughter Sarah Gray "wife of William Gray"; his granddaughter Elizabeth Wakefield "wife of William Wakefield"; his daughter Elizabeth Freeman "wife of James Freeman"; his daughter Dorothy Orphen "wife of William Orphen"; his daughter Monacah Bateman "daughter of John Bateman." Age at death 74.

SHORT, GEORGE, 10 January 1671, age 17-18, Clement Theobalds [Vol. 60:281]. Expected date of freedom 1678. William Boreman v. George Short, judgment for plaintiff, 14 January 1701 [21.pdf #74]. The Grand Jurors "doe present George Short planter for that he" about 5 March 1701 at Newport hundred "a certain hoggs head of tobacco of one Sir John Rogers of Plymouth merchant faultily and deceitfully did pack and into the same hoggs head did put a considerable quantity of dirt or earth," 10 November 1702 [22.pdf #63]; George Short, his recognizance, 12 January 1703 [22.pdf #81]; jury "impannelled," defendant "acquitted and discharged," 9 March 1703 [22.pdf #92]. William Watts v. George Short, agreed, 14 March 1704 [22.pdf #180]. George Short Senr. v.

ENCYCLOPEDIA OF SURVIVORS

John Mansfeild, agreed 13 March 1711 [24.pdf #76]. See also George Short Junr. v. John Mansfeild, agreed, 13 March 1711 [24.pdf #75]. Edward Butler v. George Short, agreed, 13 November 1711 [25.pdf #29]. George Short Senr. of Newport Hundred, being antient and infirme, ordered to be razed out of ye List of Taxables, and likewise from hence forward leavey free, 12 August 1712 [25.pdf #90]. John Lemaster v. George Short, judgment for plaintiff, satisfied, 9 June 1713 [25.pdf #169]. George Short, will dated 5 October 1718, probated 14 March 1720, Ann Short executrix [Liber AB No. 3 Folio 136]. Named in will: his wife Ann; his son Daniell; his daughter Elizabeth Dent; his grandson George Dent. George Short, probate case, Anne Short executrix, 13 June 1721 [27.pdf #89]. Age at death 65.

SIMES, FRANCIS, son of William Simes, Baptized 10 December 1669, Saint Peter and Saint Paul, Milton by Gravesend, Kent, England. Simmes, Francis, 13 January 1686, age 17, Capt. William Barton [13.pdf #48]. Expected date of freedom 1693. Jonathan Scarth v. Francis Simms, judgment for plaintiff, 11 August 1719 [26.pdf #130]. Samuel Perrie & Comp. v. Francis Sims, agreed, 13 March 1722 [27.pdf #157]. Francis Sims, his mark of livestock, 21 November 1730 [Liber M Page 238]. Katherine Semmes, daughter of Francis Semmes, gift of livestock, 14 August 1733 [29.pdf #46].

SIMMONS, WILLIAM, 13 February 1700, age 12, Samuel Luckett [20.pdf #142]. Expected date of freedom 1710. Capt. Samuel Perrie v. William Symmons, March 1722 [27.pdf #8].

SIMPSON, ALEXANDER, 28 January 1662, age not judged, Edmond Tyler, sold by Humphrey Warrin, six years "from the 29th of September 1661 until the 29th of September 1667" [01.pdf #190]. Alexander Simpson, will dated 3 December 1669, probated 12 April 1670, Jane Wahob executrix [Liber A No. 2 Folio 11]. Named in will: Margrett Wahob and Elizabeth Wahob daughters of Archball & Jane Wahob; John Paine; Jacob Leah, brother of Mrs. Jane Wahob; Thomas Corker.

SIMPSON, SAMUELL, 12 August 1673, age 15, John Goodge, by Captn. Josias Fendall [06.pdf #140]. Expected date of freedom 1680. Thomas & Jane Tickerell v. JOHN GIBBS, assault "with force & armes," LANCELOTT WILKINSON and Samuel Simpson witnesses, acquitted, 10 January 1682 [10.pdf #136, 137].

144

ENCYCLOPEDIA OF SURVIVORS

SIMSON, JAMES, the son of Thomas Simson, sold(ie)r, and Elizabeth his mother, baptized 6th May 1680, "The Register of Derry Cathedral (Saint Columb's) Parish of Templemore, Londonderry, Northern Ireland." Sympson, James, 14 November 1699, age 19, Henry More [20.pdf #99]. Expected date of freedom 1705. James Sympson, aged 45, deposition, 12 March 1725 [30.pdf #21].

SKINNER, THOMAS, 11 June 1667, age 15, Robert Hunley [03.pdf #209]. Expected date of freedom 1674. John Maud v. Thomas Skinner, garnishee of William Crocker, "the said writt was quasht for want of security for cost," 9 June 1713 [25.pdf #163]. Thomas Skinner, List of Taxable Inhabitants, 60 squirrells heads, 12 November 1717 [26.pdf #18]. John & Mary Mellor to Thomas Skinner, 300 acres, 17 December 1720 [Liber H Page 410]. Thomas Skinner, son of Thomas Skinner, gift of livestock, 21 March 1723 [Liber L Page 78]. Thomas Skinner, will dated 8 October 1727, probated 19 February 1728, Constance & Thomas Skinner executors [Liber AB No. 3 Folio 198]. Named in will: his wife Constance; his son Thomas; his son William; his son James. Age at death 75.

SMITH, BENJAMIN, son of James Smith, Born 21 August 1681, Newbury, Massachusetts. Smith, Benjamin, 4 April 1699, age 19, William Dent [20.pdf #27]. Expected date of freedom 1705. Benjamin Smith married Hanna Somes, 2 April 1709, both of Newbury, Massachusetts.

SNOWDEN, WILLIAM, son of John and Johan Snowden, Baptized 20 March 1669/70, Loddiswell, Devon, England. Snowden, William, 11 March 1679, age 10, John Vandry, "of St. Maries County" [09.pdf #81]. Expected date of freedom 1691. Notley Warren v. William Snowden, 1695 [Liber T Page 249].

STEWART, DANIEL, 13 March 1722, age not judged, servant to William Penn, petitions to Court that "whereas he was taken in ye Rebellion at Preston and Transported into this Province without Indenture & was Sold unto Mr. John Walden of this County to whom he had served the full Term of five years, & that his said Master still Datained him in his Service -- Notwithstanding ye Petitioner was past the age of twenty two years at the Time of his Transportacion, and Praid that he might be Discharged from his said Master according to act of Assembly etc.," ordered by Court "that the petition aforesaid be rejected" (without explanation -- ed.) [27.pdf #126]. John Stuart, son of Daniel Stuart, gift of livestock, 1724 [Liber L

ENCYCLOPEDIA OF SURVIVORS

Page 119]. Daniel Steward, will dated 3 March 1766, probated 11 June 1766, James & Roby (?) Steward executors [Liber AD No. 5 Folio 342]. Named in will: his son James; his son Roby (?); his son Daniel; his granddaughter Edith Steward "daughter of William Steward"; his son Thomas; his son William; his daughter Ann Young; his daughter Sarah Hamelton; his daughter Charity McGraw; his daughter Rebeckah McDaniel. Refers to his wife Mary, who " while she was a widow" entered into a "treaty of marriage" on 16 January 1749.

STRINGER, GEORGE, son of George and Mary Stringer, Born 12 July 1664, Baptized 31 July 1664, Saint Giles Cripplegate, London, England. Stringer, George, 8 January 1678, age 15, Henry Hawkins [08.pdf #56]. Expected date of freedom 1685. John Bracher v. George Stringer planter, agreed, 9 September 1690 [17.pdf #58].

THOMPSON, HENRY, 11 March 1679, age 16, Thomas Clipsham [09.pdf #82]. Expected date of freedom 1686. "Henry Thompson comes in Court & acknowledgeth to serve Capt. Humphrey Warren from this time to Chrismas come a twelve month," 10 August 1686 [13.pdf #119]. "Henry Thompson his marke of cattle & hogges," 11 March 1690 [16.pdf #109]. Henry Thompson v. Edward Turner, judgment for plaintiff, 9 June 1691 [17.pdf #126]. CATHERINE JONES, servant to Philip Lynes, 11 August 1691, complaining "of her hard useage by Henry Thompson one of ye overseers of ye said Lynes, ordered that ye said Philip Lynes take his said servant CATHERINE JONES and remove her from her overseer Henry Thompson to another plantation and to cloth her well" [17.pdf #139]. Edward Turner v. Henry Thompson, agreed, 10 November 1691 [17.pdf #170]. Henry Thompson to Margarett Mankin daughter of Stephen & Mary Mankin, gift of livestock, 10 January 1693 [17.pdf #292]. Cornelius Maddock v. Henry Thompson, judgment for plaintiff, 14 March 1693 [18.pdf #67]. William Spikeman v. Henry Thompson, judgment for defendant, 9 January 1694 [18.pdf #139]. Henry Thompson v. William Spikeman, judgment for plaintiff, 14 August 1694 [18.pdf #184]. Henry Thompson v. Richard Wade, agreed, 1695 [Liber T Page 273]. Henry Thompson v. William Frost, agreed, 8 September 1696 [19.pdf #58]. The Grand Jurors "doe present Henry Thompson late of Charles County planter for markeing and selling a horse belonging to William Thomas," 29 November 1698 [19.pdf #259], "and nothing appeareing that ye said Henry Thompson was guilty," ordered that Henry Thompson be acquitted, 10 January 1699 [20.pdf #4]. Henry Thompson, probate case, Isabella Thompson, administrator, 8 August 1699 [20.pdf #85]. Age at death 36.

ENCYCLOPEDIA OF SURVIVORS

THOMPSON, JAMES, 12 January 1675, age 12, Francis Goodrich [07.pdf #33]. Expected date of freedom 1685. "James Thompson his mark of cattle & hoggs," 1688 [16.pdf #30]. James Thompson, "nominated & appointed to bee a Justice of ye peace," 12 August 1690 [17.pdf #30]. Philip Lynes v. James Thompson, agreed, 14 August 1694 [18.pdf #183]. Robert Ferguson v. James Thompson, 1694 [Liber T Page 68]. James Thompson v. Robert Ferguson, judgment affirmed, 1696 [Liber T Page 347]. Christopher Gregory v. James Thompson, judgment for plaintiff, 11 August 1696 [19.pdf #45]. Gillroy, Catherine, daughter of Richard Gillroy deceased, age not stated, bound to James Thompson, "hee bringing her up in ye Protestant religion," 8 September 1696 [19.pdf #56]; the Grand Jurors "by ye information of William Thomas & Peter Mackmillian upon their oath doe present James Thompson for not keeping & maintaineing orphan child of Richard Gillroy deceased named Catherine Gillroy in his custody but sufferring her to want for lookeing after as she ought to bee," 14 June 1698 [19.pdf #219]; ordered by Court "that ye said James Thompson deliver Catherine Gillroy ye orphan daughter of Richard Gillroy to Joseph Harrison," and "if ye said Joseph Harrison doth like ye said orphan & thinke fitt to take her into his care custody or else to make a report to ye Court here in what condition ye said orphan girl is in," 4 October 1698 [19.pdf #239]. John Contee v. James Thompson, judgment for plaintiff, 1 April 1701 [21.pdf #121]. GUSTAVUS BROWN v. James Thompson, agreed, 14 November 1721 [27.pdf #124]. James Thompson, will dated 30 March 1734, probated 14 August 1734, Jane Thompson executrix [Liber AC No. 4 Folio 29]. Named in will: his wife Jane; John McPherson; Richard McPherson. Age at death 71.

THOMPSON, JOHN, 11 June 1678, age 15 "ye first day of next January," Robert Greene. Expected date of freedom 1686. William Hutchinson to John Thompson, JAMES GREENE & Thomas Frederick, 422 acres, 11 November 1690 [17.pdf #70], survey from William Hutchisson, 29 December 1690 [17.pdf #83]. Mary Thompson, daughter of John & Mary Thompson of Portobaccoe, born 8 January 1695 [Liber Q Page 25]. Benjamin Legg, former servant to John Thompson, 13 January 1702, "whereas your petitioner came into Maryland a servant and sold to John Thompson of Portobacco and by carrying of a piece of timber fell downe and broke his back and his master finding him not fitt for service sett him free about nine months since and your poore petitioner having noe friend nor relation to take care of him now is not capable of doing any manner of labour whereby to gett a livelyhood, humbly desires your Worshipps to allow him somewhat towards a maintenance," allowed by Court "foure hundred pounds of tobacco in the next yeares Leavy" [21.pdf #173]. John & Mary Thompson to John Clemons Junr. & William Clemons, 183 acres, 11 August 1713 [24.pdf #185]. John Thompson, aged 63, deposition, 8 November 1726 [30.pdf #202]. John Thompson, will dated 2 March 1734, probated 8 May 1739, Thomas & William Thompson executors [Liber AC No. 4 Folio 99]. Named in will: his son Thomas; his son William; his son John; his daughter Winefred; his grandson Joseph "son of my son William"; his daughter Ann; his daughter Magdalen; his daughter Susannah. Age at death 75.

THORNEBROOKE, JAMES, 11 August 1686, age 21, Phillip Lynes [13.pdf #120]. Expected date of freedom 1692. James Thornborough, servant to Philip Lynes, 10 November 1691, with EDWARD DARNELL & CATHERINE JONES, "came here into Court naked & made complaint that for want of clothes they were allmost starved, and ye said Philip Lynes being absent, itt is ordered that Major James Smallwood lett them have necessary clothes to preserve them from perishing with cold, and that Coll. Humphrey Warren sherife pay ye said Smallwood for what clothing they shall have of him out of what tobaccoe shall be allowed to ye said Lynes in ye County levy this yeare" [17.pdf #157]. James Thornborrow, servant to Philip Lynes, 12 January 1692, "alledgeing here in Court that hee had served ye said Lynes ye tearme of six yeares, and it being testifyed here in Court that ye said James Thornborrow had beene in ye Countrey six yeares or thereabouts and in ye service of ye said Lynes, and that ye said Philip Lynes kept ye said James Thorneborrow from January until August Court following before he brought him to Court to be adjudged which was above six moneths contrary to ye Act of Assembly in that case made & provided," ordered by Court "that ye said James Thorneborrow be free & discharged from ye service of ye said Philip Lynes" [17.pdf #190]; James Thornborrow, servant to Philip Lynes, 8 November 1692, petition of Philip Lynes, "that a man servant named James Thornborrow of your petitioner in ye absence of your petitioner when in Virginia made application to this Court for his freedome," but hath service due "for runaway time according to law which can prove by ye overseer with whom hee then lived," and tobacco hath been "paid for his takeing up," ordered by Court that "James Thornborrow bee sumoned to appeare here at ye next Court to be held here on ye tenth day of January next to answer to ye complaint of ye said Philip Lynes" [17.pdf #277]; James Thornburrough, servant to Philip Lynes, 31 January 1693, "ye said Philip Lynes by William Stone his attorney" alleadging that "ye said James Thornburrough ought to make satisfaction to ye said Philip Lynes for severall dayes" absence "at severall times," "and ye said James Thornburrough by William Dent his attorney cometh & saith that hee being formerly discharged & sett free from ye service of ye said Philip Lynes by this Court hee ought not to make any further satisfaction," "and ye said Philip Lynes not proveing any thing against ye said James Thornburrough that hee had at any time absented himselfe out of his ye said Lynes his service as is above alledged," ordered by Court "that ye said James Thornburrough is free & discharged from ye service of ye said Lynes," "and ought to be free by reason of his hard useage that hee ye said James Thornburrough did undergoe in ye time of his servitude with ye said Philip Lynes" [18.pdf #25].

TIPTON, EDWARD, 11 August 1668, age 18, Humphrey Warren Junr. [Vol. 60:139] Expected date of freedom 1675. Edward Typton, servant to Humphry Warren, 10 June 1673, "petitioninge the Court for his freedome, his maister Mr. Humphry Warren makeinge it appear that he had not served his full tyme according to the former Judgment of ye Court, it is Ordered that the said Typton goe home & follow his maisters busines untill his tyme be expired as he was first adjudged" [06.pdf #139]. Thomas Patrick, servant to Philip Lynes, 11 November 1690, petitions that "ye said Philip Lynes being now absent & those who lookes after his consernes refuseing to sett him free, itt being proved here in Court by ye Oath of Edward Thypton his master who sold him to ye said Philip Lynes that his time of servitude was fully expired, itt is ordered that ye said Thomas Patrick be discharged from ye service of his said master Philip Lynes" [17.pdf #69]. Edward Thypton v. Philip Lynes, judgment for plaintiff, 13 January 1691 [17.pdf #97]. Edward Typton v. Thomas Warren, judgment for plaintiff, 12 January 1692 [17.pdf #200]. Edward Typton v. William Groome, judgment for plaintiff, 14 November 1693 [18.pdf #123].

TOY, WALTER, 9 June 1702, age 13, Benjamin Smallwood [22.pdf #31]. Expected date of freedom 1711. Walter Toy, servant to John Frazier, 12 June 1711, servant confessing, 8 days absence, 64 days servitude, and two months "for what his said master makes appear to ye Court to have laid out and expended" [24.pdf #97]. Walter Toy, his recognizance, 13 June 1721 [27.pdf #73]. Walter Toy, witness against William Groves who "did kill one hogg of Walter Winter on the out side of William Groves fence of his cornfeild," 13 June 1721 [27.pdf #75]. The Grand Jurors do present Walter Toy for that on 10 December 1720 with force of arms at Nanjemy parish a bagg of Indian corne containing two bushels & an halfe the proper goods of

ENCYCLOPEDIA OF SURVIVORS

Walter Winter felonioiusly did steal take & carry away, defendant acquitted, 8 August 1721 [27.pdf #94]. Walter Toy, "being legally summoned as an evidence, although solemly called comes not but makes default, fined five hundred pounds of tobacco," 13 March 1722 [27.pdf #125].

TYMOTHIE, WILLIAM, 11 June 1667, age 15, John Bowles [03.pdf #209]. Expected date of freedom 1674. AUSTRICH, WILLIAM, without indentures, 13 June 1676, age 13, James Tyre, by William Tymothy [07.pdf #111]. KINGSTONE, THOMAS, without indentures, 13 June 1676, age 14, James Tyre, by William Tymothy [07.pdf #111]. Petition of William Tymothy, "that your petitioner ye 26th of February 1679/80 agreed with Capt. Warren to nurse a bastard child for one whole yeare at ye rate of twelve hundred pounds of tobaccoe which time was expired in February last past for which ye said Warren hath made satisfaccon according to agreement, since which ye said child hath & doth remaine in custody of ye petitioner," seeks satisfaction for "future care & trouble," ordered by Court "that William Tymothy be allowed ye next yeare ye sume of twelve hundred pounds of tobaccoe out of ye Leavy of this County for ye nurseing ye said child one yeare," 8 March 1681 [10.pdf #60]. Madam Mary Chandler executrix of Coll. William Chandler v. William Timothy, 8 September 1685 [13.pdf #45]. Stephen Bridges, servant to William Tymothy, 9 September 1690, absent "severall times," 38 days in all, 380 days servitude [17.pdf #36]. Mabella, daughter of William & Mabella Tymothy of Pyckyawaxon, born 12 October 1693 [Liber Q Page 22]. William Tymothy, fined, 1694 [Liber T Page 44], fine remitted, 1694 [Liber T Page 77]. Smith, not named, orphans of Richard Smith late of Charles County deceased, the Grand Jury "presented that Joseph Wilson of Charles County planter who married Anne ye Relict & Executrix of Richard Smith deceased at Pyckyawaxon hath made waist & destruction of ye timber on the lands belonging to ye orphans of ye said Richard Smith," "and ye said Joseph Wilson here in Court alledgeing that hee had built severall good & substantiall houses on ye said plantation for ye good & benefitt of ye said orphans, and in ye building of which hee hath made no waist nor destruction of ye timber more than what was necessary & convenient for ye building of ye said houses," ordered by Court that Richard Maston, William Tymothy, and one of ye Commissioners of this Court "enter into ye lands & plantation & view ye dwelling houses outhouses lands orchards & fences," and "see what land ye said Joseph Wilson hath cleared" and "whether hee hath made any waist or destruction of timber," 19 April 1698 [19.pdf #209]; Affidavit of William Tymothy and Richard Marston, dated 8 June 1698, stating that

ENCYCLOPEDIA OF SURVIVORS

Joseph Wilson "haveing erected & built one fifty foot tobaccoe house, one thirty foot dwelling house, one twenty five foot kitchin, putt a new roof to an old twenty & five foot dwelling house standing in ye orchard," and "haveing made a good & sufficient new corne feild fence containeing about five thousand corne hills," "wee find no waist of timber made by ye said Wilson," defendant "acquitt & discharged" by Court, 14 June 1698 [19.pdf #220]. MORRIS, JAMES, without indentures, 14 March 1699, age 15, William Tymothy [20.pdf #24]. William Tymothy, death notice, 13 February 1700 [20.pdf #166]. Age at death 48.

VAUX, JOSEPH, son of George Vaux, Baptized 24 April 1667, Wigton, Cumberland, England. Vaux, Joseph, 8 June 1686, age 19, Phillip Lynes [13.pdf #118]. Expected date of freedom 1692. Lewis Watkins, "his bayle from Joseph Voax," 1695 [Liber T Page 208]. Thomas Hussey executor of Langworth v. Joseph Vaux, agreed, 1696 [Liber T Page 351]. "Mary Brawner, widdow, petitioning ye Court here for an alloweance for her trouble in lookeing after and takeing care of one Joseph Voux and his wife in ye time of their sicknes ye one being eight dayes ye other sixteene dayes sick and for her trouble in burying of them," ordered by Court "that ye said Mary Brawner be allowed ye sume of eight hundred pounds of tobaccoe in ye County Levy," 19 April 1698 [19.pdf #207]. Age at death 30.

WAEDMAN, RICE, 14 March 1665, age 21, Archibell Whahob [02.pdf #509]. Expected date of freedom 1671. "Richard Midgely & Rice Wainman doe acknowledge all their right of a tract of land unto Edward Knight," 12 March 1672 [06.pdf #59]. "Rice Wayneman his marke" of livestock, 1672 [06.pdf #78]. Beteres Clarke, daughter of Robert Clarke "who is runaway" & Mary Clarke deceased, age not stated, bound to Richard Midgeley, 11 January 1676 [07.pdf #96]; ordered by Court "that John Hanson administrator of Richard Midgeley deceased pay unto Rice Wayman ye sume of foure hundred pounds of tobaccoe out of ye estate of ye said Richard Midgeley deceased in his hands, for ye maintenance of an orphan child of Robert Clarkes late of this County deceased bound to ye said Midgeley by ye Court," 13 March 1677 [08.pdf #22]; ordered by Court "that Rice Wayman have one thousand pounds of tobaccoe allowed him out of the County Levy this yeare for ye maintenance of Veteres Clarke an orphan child of Robert Clarke late of this County deceased till March Court next ensueinge," 12 June 1677 [08.pdf #37]; Veteres Clarke, daughter of Robert Clarke deceased, "now adjudged to be five yeares of age," bound to Rice Wayman, 12 March 1678 [08.pdf #73]. John & Margarett Cassock to

ENCYCLOPEDIA OF SURVIVORS

Rice Wayman & JOSEPH WOLPH, 200 acres, 12 October 1678 [09.pdf #64]. Henry Adams to Veteres Clarke ye daughter of Robert Clarke deceased," 1682 [10.pdf #143]. Rice Wayman to "Mary Wolph ye daughter of JOSEPH WOLPH," gift of livestock, 8 August 1682 [10.pdf #177]. John Martine v. Rice Wayman, dismissed, 8 September 1685 [13.pdf #17]. Madam Mary Chandler executrix of Coll. William Chandler v. Rice Waynman administrator of Joseph Wolph, 8 September 1685 [13.pdf #31]. JOSEPH WOLPH, probate case, Rice Waynman, administrator, 9 September 1685 [13.pdf #31]. Mary Wolfe, probate case, Rice Waynman executor, 12 January 1686 [13.pdf #68]. Mary Wolfe, probate case, Mary Waynman executrix, 9 February 1686 [13.pdf #48].

WARD, HENRY, son of Lawrance Ward, Baptized 28 July 1658, Mickleton, Gloucester, England. Ward, Henry, 8 June 1675, age 15, Richard Smoote, by William Barton [07.pdf #63]. Expected date of freedom 1682. "Henry & Katherine Ward their mark of cattell & hoggs," 1688 [16.pdf #30]. Henry Ward, List of Taxable Inhabitants, 76 squirrells heads, 12 November 1717 [26.pdf #18]. Edward Lawn & Henry Ward, security for John Dempsey, 13 June 1721 [27.pdf #73]. Henry Ward, his recognizance, 13 June 1721 [27.pdf #73]. William & Elizabeth Groves, their recognizance, "concerning the stealing of three hoggs from Henry Ward," 13 June 1721 [27.pdf #75]. Ward, John Ward, son in law of Henry Ward, gift of livestock, 14 June 1722 [Liber L Page 89].

WARD, RICHARD, 11 April 1676, age 12, Humphrey Warren [07.pdf #101]. Expected date of freedom 1686. Richard Warde aged 62, deposition, 8 June 1725 [30.pdf #24].

WARNER, CHRISTOPHER, son of John Warner, Born 28 October 1648, Baptized 7 November 1648, Saint John, Hackney, London, England. Warner, Christopher, 13 April 1669, age 20, Robert Downes [Vol. 60:188]. Expected date of freedom 1675. "It is ordered by ye Court that John Wright & Richard Pinner appraise ye estate of Christopher Warner gathered together by Phillip Lines," 15 January 1679 [09.pdf #70]. Age at death 30.

WATTERS, EDWARD, son of James and Dorcas Watters, Baptized 24 April 1687, Saint Sepulchre, London, England. Waters, Edward, 9 June 1702, age 15, Richard Wade [22.pdf #31]. Expected date of freedom 1709. Edward Waters, servant to Richard Wade, 9 November 1708, 62 days absence, 620 days servitude, and two months "for two hundred and fifty pounds of tobacco paid and expended for the takeing him upp" [23.pdf #279]. Expected date of freedom 1711. Arthur Johnson v. Edward Waters, agreed, March 1716 [Liber G Page 72].

WELCH, JAMES, 13 June 1693, age 15, Major James Smallwood [18.pdf #81]. Expected date of freedom 1700. James Welch, servant to Major James Smallwood, 10 January 1699, servant confessing "here in Court," absent "severall times," 85 days in all, 850 days servitude [20.pdf # 4]. Expected date of freedom 1702. Thomas Combes v. James Welsh, agreed, March 1716 [Liber G Page 81]. John Hyde v. James Welch, judgment for plaintiff, 11 August 1719 [26.pdf #132]. Henry Darnall v. James Welsh, judgment for plaintiff, 11 August 1719 [26.pdf #137]. Philip Dove v. James Welch, agreed, 14 March 1721 [27.pdf #67]. Eleanor Rumney v. James Welsh, judgment for plaintiff, 13 March 1722 [27.pdf #144].

WELCH, THOMAS, 14 June 1698, age 16, Philip Briscoe [19.pdf #217]. Expected date of freedom 1705. Thomas Welch v. John Maud, judgment for plaintiff, 11 March 1712 [25.pdf #47].

WHITTIMORE, CHRISTOPHER, servant to Henry Hawkins, 11 March 1690, "petitioning this Court for his freedome & hee not proveing his Indenture to be authentick & good," ordered by Court to "serve his said master according to ye custome of ye country" (age not judged -- ed.) [16.pdf #114]. Whitworth (sic), Christopher, servant to Henry Hawkins, 10 June 1690, with six other servants, "it appeareing by ye Oath of Mr. John Bowman who transported them into this Countrey that hee had ye counterparts of their Indentures & did reade them aboard of his ship at Gravesend, and they were kidnappers Indentures but whether they were good or not hee could not tell, and noe proofe appearing here in Court that ye said Indentures were signed sealed & delivered by ye said John Williams with whom they did indent, & ye same not being under ye seale of an Office, or under ye hand of any Justice of ye peace," ordered by Court to "returne to their severall masters service & serve acording to ye Custome of ye Countrey, their Indentures being adjudged invalide by ye Courte" (age not judged -- ed.) [17.pdf #18]. Children of Christopher & Anne Whittymore of Portobaccoe: Anne, daughter, born 5 September 1690 [Liber Q Page 16]. Richard, son, born 2 September 1694 [Liber Q Page 25]. Anne Whittymore, daughter of Christopher Whittymore, gift of livestock, 1693 [18.pdf #78].

ENCYCLOPEDIA OF SURVIVORS

WILDER, ROBERT, son of Robert Wilder, Baptized 20 September 1653, Saint Andrew by the Wardrobe, London, England. Wilder, Robert, 8 August 1671, age 16-17, John Bowles [06.pdf #46]. Expected date of freedom 1678. "It is ordered by ye Court that Robert Wilder bee allowed in ye County Leavy ye next yeare one thousand pounds of tobaccoe for keepeing & mainteininge an orphan child one whole yeare," 10 January 1682 [10.pdf #133].

WILKINSON, JOHN, 10 June 1674, age 18, John Taylor [06.pdf #158]. Expected date of freedom 1680. John Wilkinson, servant to Thomas Taylor, 10 March 1680, petitions "that he hath served six yeares according to ye judgment Court, sometime in February last past at which time ye ship he came in arrived here in Maryland, & was adjudged at Court in June Court following," ordered by Court to "serve his master Thomas Taylor untill ye time of his judgment at Court be fully finished compleated & ended" [09.pdf #156] "John Wilkinson his marke of cattle & hoggs," 1681 [10.pdf #143] and 1683 [11.pdf #133]. John Wilkinson to Thomas Jenkins, "one brown cow" for "a young horss," 23 October 1683 [11.pdf #144]. John Wilkinson v. William Standiford, "agreed before tryall," 12 March 1684 [11.pdf #184]. "John Wilkinson his mark of cattell & hoggs," 1688 [16.pdf #30]. John Wilkinson, witness against John Bayne for keeping a "publick house of entertainment" where he "comonly & publickly did sell & retayle wyne, cyder & other liquors," 20 September 1692 [17.pdf #296]. William Sarjeant v. John Wilkinson, agreed, 12 June 1694 [18.pdf #173]. John Wilkinson, "his order about taking up Colo. Courts's runaway servant," 1694 [Liber T Page 7]. John Wilkinson v. SAMUEL HUNTSMAN, 1694 [Liber T Page 21]. Charles Jones v. John Wilkinson, 4 April 1699 [20.pdf #51]. John Allen v. John Wilkinson, 4 April 1699 [20.pdf #52]. "Wee the Grand Jury doe present Henry Wharton and John Wilkinson his Overseer by force of armes broke open the house of Henry Tanner and turned his wife and children out of doores in his absence by the Information of the said Henry Tanner the 12th of January," 9 March 1708 [23.pdf #244] and 14 September 1708 [23.pdf #269]. William Kerran v. John Wilkinson, agreed, 9 November 1708 [23.pdf #283]. John Wilkinson v. William Kerren, 12 June 1711 [24.pdf #103]. Henry Ossley v. John Wilkinson, judgment confessed, March 1716 [Liber G Page 53]. Isaac Langton v. John Wilkinson, agreed, March 1716 [Liber G Page 59]. John Radcliff v. John Wilkinson, judgment for plaintiff, 11 August 1719 [26.pdf #135]. The Grand Jurors "do present John Wilkinson for nonappearance on ye highways by information of Josiah

ENCYCLOPEDIA OF SURVIVORS

Mankin appoynted overseer of the highways," 14 June 1720 [26.pdf #172], defendant confessing, "fined one hundred pounds of tobacco," 9 August 1720 [27.pdf #16]. "John Wilkinsons petition concerning his servant Michael Welsh rejected," 8 November 1720 [27.pdf #29]. Michael Welsh, servant to John Wilkinson, 8 November 1720, servant confessing "in Court," 4 days absence, 40 days servitude, and two months for "two hundred pounds of tobacco" expended "in taking up the said servant" [27.pdf #30]. William Nelm, late servant to John Wilkinson, 14 November 1721, "by his petition to the Court sets forth that he has not yet received but one pair of shoes stockings & shirt from his late master John Wilkinson and humbly praies ye Court here to order the said Wilkinson to pay ye remaining part of his freedom dues," ordered by Court "that ye aforesaid William have the effect of his petition" [27.pdf #109]. Michael Welsh, servant to John Wilkinson, 14 August 1722, "by his petition to the Court sets forth that his late master John Wilkinson refuses to deliver him a suit of clothes which he ought to pay him," and "it seemed to ye Court here that ye facts" "are sufficiently proved," ordered by Court "that the said Wilkinson deliver to ye said Welsh ye cloaths aforesaid that is to say: a coat jacket & breeches of kersy & pay ye costs of ye petitioner aforesaid" [27.pdf #177]. John Wilkinson, his mark, 11 February 1723 [Liber L Page 73].

WILKINSON, LANCELOT, 9 January 1672, age 18, Humphry Warren [06.pdf #55]. (From Hesket in the Forest, Cumberland, England, baptismal record has not survived). Expected date of freedom 1678. "Lancellott Wilkinson entreth his marke of cattle & hoggs," 10 August 1680 [09.pdf #181]. JOHN BOOTH v. Lancelott Wilkinson, agreed before trial, 11 January 1681 [10.pdf #49]. John Mouldin, probate case, Lancelot & Margery Wilkinson executors, 8 March 1681 [10.pdf #53]. Thomas & Jane Tickerell v. JOHN GIBBS, assault "with force & armes," Lancelott Wilkinson and SAMUEL SIMPSON witnesses, acquitted, 10 January 1682 [10.pdf #136, 137]. Mary Wilkinson, daughter of Lancelott & Mary Wilkinson of Mattawoman, born 15 October 1687 [Liber Q Page 13]. Lancelott Wilkinson, his recognizance, 11 March 1690 [30.pdf #113]. Joshuah Graves v. Lanselott Wilkinson, agreed, 9 September 1690 [17.pdf #61]. "Magdalen Tayler ye wife of William Tayler" to "Mary Wilkinson daughter of Lancelott & Mary Wilkinson," gift of livestock, 14 November 1693 [18.pdf #107]. Emannuell Ratclife v. Lancelott Wilkison, judgment for plaintiff, 12 June 1694 [18.pdf #173]. Mary Wilkinson, daughter of Lance and Mary Wilkinson deceased, age not stated, bound to Francis Miller "by hir owne free consent," 3 December 1700 [21.pdf #57]. Age at death 46.

ENCYCLOPEDIA OF SURVIVORS

WILLIAMS, EDWARD, son of William and Elizabeth Williams, Baptized 21 November 1659, Dartington, Devon, England. Williams, Edward, 11 March 1679, age 20, Henry Hawkins [09.pdf #81]. Expected date of freedom 1685. George & Sarah Athy to Edward Williams, 91 acres, 11 March 1689 [16.pdf #116]. Edward Williams v. John Gray, their recognizance, 10 June 1690 [17.pdf #30] and 13 January 1691 [17.pdf #88]. William Hutchisson v. Edward Williams, "and ye said Edward Williams though solemnely called came not nor any for him," judgment for plaintiff, 11 August 1691 [17.pdf #151]. Edward Williams v. Molleneux Rattcliff, agreed, 1695 [Liber T Page 156]. Griffith Morris, servant to Edward Williams, 13 August 1700, servant confessing "in Court," absent 80 days "when he was Jesse Doynes servant," and 38 days "since he was the said Williams's servant," 118 days in all, 1180 days servitude [21.pdf #19]; sold or assigned to Major William Barton, before 4 April 1704 [22.pdf #194]. John Miller v. Edward Williams, judgment for plaintiff 11 March 1701 [21.pdf #105]. Jesse Doyne v. Edward Williams, judgment for defendant, 10 November 1702 [22.pdf #76]. The Grand Jurors "doe present Edward Williams planter" for "willfull and corrupt perjury, 10 November 1702 [22.pdf #63]. John Wood and Edward Williams, their recognizance, 12 January 1703 [23.pdf #81]. The Grand Jurors "presented Edward Williams for that" on 8 September 1702 at Portobacco "not haveing the feare of God before his eyes but being ledd by the persuasion and instagation of the Devill did sweare to a certain accompt against one Jesse Doyne that the said accompt was just and true," "the said accompt being alltogether false and untrue," "and the said Edward Williams in his propper person cometh and saith that hee is an illetterate person and ignorant in the laws and therefore desires that hee may have councill assigned before he pleads farther," "whereupon Cornelius White one of the attorneys of this Court is specially admitted and appoynted as Councill for the said Edward Williams," jury "impannelled," defendant acquitted, 9 March 1703 [22.pdf #92]. John Contee v. Edward Williams, agreed, 9 March 1703 [22.pdf #101]. Edward Williams v. Jesse Doyne, agreed, 8 June 1703 [22.pdf #117]. Edward Williams named as Overseer for the High Wayes, "for ye Lower parts of Durham Parrish," 14 September 1703 [22.pdf #130]. Thomas Hunt v. Edward Williams, judgment for plaintiff, 9 January 1705 [23.pdf #44]. "Edward Williams's recognizance continued till next Cort for the appearance of John Welch," 12 June 1705 [23.pdf #89], whereupon appeares Edward Williams his security and saith that the said John Welch at presant hath eloyned himselfe out of the jursidiction of this Court," therefore the said Edward Williams forfeits "the summe of five pounds sterling,"

ENCYCLOPEDIA OF SURVIVORS

11 June 1705 [23.pdf #124]. Edward Williams v. John Jenckins, 30 January 1708 [23.pdf #232] and 9 March 1708 [23.pdf #250]. Charles Regon, orphan, parents not named, age not stated, bound to Edward Williams, he "to learn him the said Charles Regon the trade of a cooper (viz.) to make tobacco hogs heads, and to "find and allow to the said Charles Regon sufficient meat, drink, apparrell and lodgeing," "and at the expiration" of his time "to give him a sett of coopers tooles and a new suit of cloaths either of broad cloath or of kersey with hat shoes and stockings," she "to learn him the said Charles Regon to read distinctly in the Bible," 8 June 1708 [23.pdf #253]. Charles Jones v. Edward Williams, judgment for plaintiff, 8 March 1709 [23.pdf #303]. Thomas Honeam (?) v. Edward Williams, agreed, 12 August 1712 [25.pdf #105], 9 June 1713 [25.pdf #167]. John Sanders v. Edward Williams, judgment confessed, 11 August 1713 [25.pdf #178]. John Sanders v. Edward Williams, March 1716 [Liber G Page 58]. Diggs executor v. Edward Williams, June 1716 [Liber G Page 125]. John Speake v. Edward Williams, judgment confessed, June 1716 [Liber G Page 127]. Keleys administrator v. Edward Williams, judgment & confession, June 1716 [Liber G Page 163]. Robert Hanson administrator of Cornelius Kelly deceased v. Edward Williams, judgment for plaintiff, 11 November 1718 [26.pdf #87].

WILLIAMS, JOHN, 13 March 1677, age 21, Thomas Gerrard [08.pdf #22]. Expected date of freedom 1683. "John Williams his marke of hoggs & cattle," 1685 [12.pdf #106]. Children of John & Sarah Williams of ye Riverside: William, son, born 2 October 1685 [16.pdf #121]. John, son, born 2 August 1688 [16.pdf #121]. Henry Frankam to John Williams, 250 acres, 11 June 1689 [16.pdf #104]. John Williams "labourer" was presented by ye Grand Enquest for markeing of a heifer belonging to Coll. William Diggs," 13 January 1691 [17.pdf #87], "John Williams is guilty of ye felony aforesaid," 10 March 1691 [17.pdf #101]. Edward Rookwood v. John Williams, judgment for defendant, 8 August 1693 [18.pdf #101]. Elizabeth Smith widdow (of William Smith deceased -- ed.) v. John Williams, agreed, 8 March 1697 [19.pdf #201]. FORDICE, ALEXANDER, without indentures, 13 June 1699, age 19, John Williams [20.pdf #69]. John Smoote, son of James and Joan Smoote, age not stated, bound to John Williams, he "provideing him sufficient meate apparrell & lodgeing" and "well to cloath him when free," 11 November 1701 [21.pdf #160]. William Stone v. John Williams judgment for plaintiff, 9 March 1703 [22.pdf #101]. John Williams v. John Rowley, agreed, 14 March 1704 [22.pdf #181]. "Wee of the Grand Jury doe present John Williams for not

157

ENCYCLOPEDIA OF SURVIVORS

giveing an accompt of a taxable person named Henry Lynsey by information of WILLIAM BISHOP Constable," 14 November 1704 [23.pdf #35], "and the said John Williams in his propper person cometh and confesseth the fact and submitts himselfe to the Court and itt appeareing to the Court here that it was rather out of ignorence than contempt," ordered by Court that the said John Williams "pay the leavy concealed as aforesaid," and the fine "is hereby remitted," 13 March 1705. [23.pdf #54]. "John Williams petitions the Court to be leavy free," so ordered by the Court, 10 June 1707 [23.pdf #181]. John Williams v. William Roberts, 10 August 1708 [23.pdf #265]. Edward Rookwood v. John Williams, agreed, 9 November 1708 [23.pdf #281] and [23.pdf #282]. John Williams, will dated 10 April 1709, probated 18 April 1709, Sarah & William Williams executors, [Liber AB No. 3 Folio 23]. Named in will: his wife Sarah; his son Jon; his "eldest son" William; his daughter Elizabeth Mackey; his daughter Anne; his daughter Mary; his Godson John Smoot. Age at death 53. John Smoote, parents not named, age not stated, petitions "that Gerrard Ocaine his father in law refuses to deliver him his land being att age to receive the same," and "the said John Smoot declared the said difference to be agreed," 9 March 1708 [23.pdf #236]. John Smoote "an orphant formerly bound to John Williams att Potomack River side the former order of Court confirmed and ye said orphant bound to William Williams son of ye said John Williams," 14 June 1709 [23.pdf #305]; John Smoot his petition aledging that William Williams "will not instruct him in ye trade of a cooper as by the condition that he was bound by this Court," "the said petition was rejected ye former order againe confirmed," 9 August 1709 [23.pdf #321].

WILSON, JOHN, son of Jacob and Susanna Wilson, Born 25 January 1697, Malden, Massachusetts. Willson, John, 10 June 1707, age 10, Thomas Plunkett [23.pdf #180]. Expected date of freedom 1719. John Wilson married Mary Green, 31 December 1719, Malden (?), Massachusetts, ref. Jacob Green's "Writing Book."

WILSON, JOSEPH, son of Jacob and Susanna Wilson, Born 19 December 1701, Malden, Massachusetts. Willson, Joseph, 10 June 1707, age 7, Leonard Greene [23.pdf #180]. Expected date of freedom 1722. Joseph Wilson married Rachel. First child born 14 December 1728, Malden, Massachusetts.

ENCYCLOPEDIA OF SURVIVORS

WINTER, JOHN, 11 March 1679, age 15, Capt. Ignatius Causin [09.pdf #82]. Expected date of freedom 1686. William Harbert v. John Winter, judgment for plaintiff, 10 November 1702 [22.pdf #72]. "Wee the Grand Jury doe present William Crocker, John Winter, John Brayfield and Edward Phillpott for nott giveing due attendance and lending their hands to claere the high wayes by information of JAMES COTTRELL," 11 March 1707 [23.pdf #167], "and the said John Winter in his propper person cometh and saith nothing in barr of the said presentment," fined "the summe of one hundred pounds of tobacco," 10 June 1707 [23.pdf #183]. John Winter v. Walter Bayne, agreed, 9 November 1708 [23.pdf #288]. Thomas Orrell v. John Winter, judgment for defendant, 14 November 1710 [24.pdf #37]. The Grand Jurors "present John Winter planter for a breach of Sabbath comitted by the said Winter at Portobacco on ye 8th day of July last past, evidences Richard Dod, John Rogers, John Bruce," 14 August 1711 [24.pdf #121]. John Winter, presented for breach of Sabbath, "struck off," 11 March 1712 [25.pdf #38]. Daniell Dullany v. John Winter, "struck off," 11 March 1712 [25.pdf #59]. Philemon & Mary Hemsley v. John Winter, 12 August 1712 [25.pdf #106]. Joseph Manning v. John Winter, 12 August 1712 [25.pdf #108]. Cornelius White v. John Winter, 11 November 1712 [25.pdf #113].

WOLFE, JOSEPH, son of Nicholas Wolfe, Baptized 3 July 1651, Bideford, Devon, England. Woolf, Joseph, 8 March 1664, age 13, Robert Perkins [02.pdf #321]. Expected date of freedom 1673. John & Margarett Cassock to RICE WAYMAN & Joseph Wolph, 200 acres, 12 October 1678 [09.pdf #64]. "Joseph Wolph enters his marke of hogges & cattle," 1678 [08.pdf #96]. Mary Wolph, daughter of Joseph Wolph, gifts of livestock, from her father, 1678 [08.pdf #96], and from RICE WAYMAN, 8 August 1682 [10.pdf #177]. Joseph Wolph v. Edward Knight, 11 June 1679 [09.pdf #89]. Joseph Wolph, probate case, RICE WAYNMAN, administrator, 9 September 1685 [13.pdf #31]. Age at death 34. Mary Wolfe, probate case, Rice Waynman executor, 12 January 1686 [13.pdf #68]. Mary Wolfe, probate case, Mary Waynman executrix, 9 February 1686 [13.pdf #48].

WOOD, JONATHAN, son of Jonathan and Mary Wood, Baptized 27 June 1687, Saint Paul Covent Garden, Westminster, London, England. Wood, Jonathan, 14 January 1701, age 14, Capt. William Barton [21.pdf #67]. Expected date of freedom 1709. Johanna Bawdry, "petition for an allowance in ye next County Levy for burying Jonathan Wood," 8 March 1720 [26.pdf #160]. Age at death 33. "Johannah Bawdry's petition to be allowed for burying Jonathan Wood adjudged frivilous & therefore rejected," 8 November 1720 [27.pdf #29].

ENCYCLOPEDIA OF SURVIVORS

WORTHINGTON, JOSEPH, son of William & Allice Worthington, Abode Adlington, Baptized 9 December 1667, Saint Wilfrid, Standish, Lancashire, England. Worthington, Joseph, 11 August 1685, age 15, Edw. Rookard [12.pdf #96]. Expected date of freedom 1692. Thomas Dison v. Joseph Witherington, agreed, 10 August 1703 [22.pdf #128].

WRIGHT, GEORGE, son of George Wright, Baptism 1 March 1656/7, Saint Elphin, Warrington, Lancashire, England. Wright, George, 13 June 1676, age 18-19, Benjamin Rozer, by Alexander Gallant [07.pdf #111]. Expected date of freedom 1682. Ellinore / Elinor Wright, daughter of George Wright, born 7 October 1683 [16.pdf #120] [Liber Q Page 9]. Robert Smallpage v. George Wright, "ye said writt be quashed," judgment for defendant, 10 June 1690 [17.pdf #26]. William Moss v. George Wright, dismissed, 13 September 1692 [17.pdf #261].

YAPPE, ROGER, 12 January 1686, age 21, Henry Hawkins [13.pdf #47]. Expected date of freedom 1692. Yappe, Roger, servant to Henry Hawkins, 10 June 1690, with six other servants, "it appeareing by ye Oath of Mr. John Bowman who transported them into this Countrey that hee had ye counterparts of their Indentures & did reade them aboard of his ship at Gravesend, and they were kidnappers Indentures but whether they were good or not hee could not tell, and noe proofe appearing here in Court that ye said Indentures were signed sealed & delivered by ye said John Williams with whom they did indent, & ye same not being under ye seale of an Office, or under ye hand of any Justice of ye peace," ordered by Court to "returne to their severall masters service & serve acording to ye Custome of ye Countrey, their Indentures being adjudged invalid by ye Courte" [17.pdf #18]. William Davis v. Roger Yapp, 1695 [Liber T Page 208]. Thomas Davis v. Roger Yapp, "and ye said Roger Yapp being solomnely called here in Court came not," judgment for plaintiff, 9 March 1697 [19.pdf #204]. John Bayn v. Roger Yapp, judgment for defendant, 11 March 1701 [21.pdf #95]. Waples administrator v. Roger Yopp, judgment confessed, June 1716 [Liber G Page 131]. Thomas Dent v.Roger Yapp, agreed, November 1716 [Liber G Page 160]. Jane Yopp, parents not named, age not stated, "makes choice of John Craxon" as her guardian, 13 March 1722 [27.pdf #125].

WITHOUT INDENTURES, ELSEWHERE IN RECORD, NOT YET FREE

ARCHIBALL, JOHN, 9 February 1686, age 22, Alexander Smith [13.pdf #48].
John Archbald, servant to Henry Hawkins Junior, Petitions for Freedom, adjudged to have "kidnappers Indentures," 10 June 1690 [17.pdf #18].

BAEN (?), THOMAS, 13 June 1699, age 11, Thomas Harguesse [20.pdf #68].
Thomas Bayhan, servant to Henry Netherton, Recaptured Runaways, 12 November 1706 [23.pdf #153]

BONNERE, ELIZABETH, daughter of Thomas and Elizabeth Bonnere, Baptized 3 September 1658, Clayhanger, Devon, England. Bonner, Elizabeth, 10 August 1675, age 19, Richard Harrison [07.pdf #74]. Elizabeth Bonner (or Hodges), servant to James Tyer, Recaptured Runaways, 8 March 1681, [10.pdf #59].

BRENAN, KATHERINE, 14 November 1699, age 20, Edward Phillpott [20.pdf #101]. Katherine Brennon, servant to Edward Phillpott, Presentment by Grand Jury, 13 March 1705 [23.pdf #46] & [23.pdf #48].

BRIDGES, STEPHEN, 9 March 1686, age 25, John Court Junr. [13.pdf #49].
Stephen Bridges, servant to WILLIAM TYMOTHY, Recaptured Runaways, 9 September 1690 [17.pdf #36].

CAMELL, MARY, parents not named, Baptized 28 April 1685, Saint Martin in the Fields, Westminster, London, England. Cammelle, Mary, 11 June 1706, age 20, Samuell Luckett [23.pdf #123]. Mary Cammell, servant to Samuell Luckett, Abuse and Neglect, 11 March 1707 [23.pdf #169].

CHAPMAN, ELIZABETH, 13 June 1699, age 16, John Vandry [20.pdf #68].
Elizabeth Chapman, servant to John Va(n)dry, Presentment by Grand Jury, 11 November 1701 [21.pdf #158] & 10 March 1702 [22.pdf #6].

COOKE, JOHN, 9 February 1686, age 14, Richard Newman [13.pdf #48].
John Cooke, servant to Richard Newton, Recaptured Runaways, 9 August 1692 [17.pdf #238] & 12 June 1694 [18.pdf #165].

CUSACK, PATRICK, 1 August 1693, age 17, John Bayne, Saint Mary's County, Maryland [21.pdf #92]. Recaptured Runaways: Patrick Casey, 12 March 1700 [20.pdf #177]; Patrick Cusy, 3 December 1700 [21.pdf #57]; Patrick Cusack, 11 March 1701 [21.pdf #92].

WITHOUT INDENTURES, ELSEWHERE IN RECORD, NOT YET FREE

DRUNCORE, JAMES, 10 March 1686, age 15, Thomas Burford [13.pdf #49].
James Drunckore, servant to William Forster, Recaptured Runaways,
13 September 1692 [17.pdf # 255] & 13 March 1694 [18.pdf #144].

FARREL, BRYAN, 8 November 1687, age 17, John Speake [14.pdf #160].
Bryan Farrell, servant to John Speake, Recaptured Runaways,
8 August 1693 [18.pdf #87].

FORSTER, EDWARD, 14 September 1703, age 13, George Brett [22.pdf #130].
Edward Foster, servant to John Booker, Recaptured Runaways,
8 November 1709 [Liber B # 2 Page 663].

GILBARD, JAMES, 10 June 1679, age 21, Philip Linos [09.pdf #84]. James
Gilbard, servant to Philip Lines, Recaptured Runaways, 10 January
1682 [10.pdf #134].

GLEEVES, GEORGE, 10 August 1680, age 20, Capt. James Neale [09.pdf #182].
George Gleive, servant to James Neale, Recaptured Runaways,
8 June 1686 [13.pdf #117].

HALL, JOHN, 10 June 1690, age not judged, Henry Hawkins, Petitions for
Freedom, adjudged to have "kidnappers Indentures," 10 June 1690
[17.pdf #18].

HARRIS, WILLIAM, 13 June 1693, age 13, Capt. John Courts [18.pdf #81].
William Harrison, servant to Coll. John Courts, Recaptured Runaways,
10 August 1697 [19.pdf #136].

HINSEY, JOHN, 10 June 1701, age 18, Francis Goodrick Junr. [21.pdf #126].
Petitions for Freedom, 10 & 11 June 1701 [21.pdf #126].

HOLBERTON, ELIZABETH, daughter of Thomas Holberton, Baptized
30 November 1686, Holbeton, Devon, England. Halliburton,
Elizabeth, 12 June 1705, age 19, Capt. William Barton [23.pdf #80].
Elizabeth Halleburton, alias Morris, servant to Capt. William Barton,
Recaptured Runaways, 13 June 1710 [23.pdf #401]. Presentment
by Grand Jury, 14 June 1709 [23.pdf #304].

JONES, KATHERINE, 8 June 1686, age 16, Phillip Lynes [13.pdf #118].
Catherine Jones, servant to Philip Lynes, Abuse and Neglect,
11 August 1691 [17.pdf #139], 8 November 1691 [17.pdf #157],
10 November 1692 [17.pdf #276].

WITHOUT INDENTURES, ELSEWHERE IN RECORD, NOT YET FREE

KENADY, JAMES, son of James Kenady, labourer, & Isabell, his wife. Baptized April ye first, 1688, Parish Registers of St. Michan, Dublin, Ireland. Kenneday, James, 9 January 1700, age 12, Thomas Hussey [20.pdf #131]. James Kenneday, servant to Matthew Tennison, Recaptured Runaways, 3 August 1706 [23.pdf #138]. James Kenneday, servant to Michaell Martin, Recaptured Runaways, 8 June 1708 [23.pdf #254].

KILLPATRICK, ALEXANDER, 4 April 1699, age 14, George Tubman [20.pdf #26]. Allexander Killpatrick, William Smallwood, Recaptured Runaways, 12 March 1706 [23.pdf #114].

KNIGHTSMITH, HANNAH, 14 June 1681, age 20, Thomas Taylor [10.pdf #79]. Hannah Knightsmith, servant to Thomas Fuller, Petitions for Freedom, 16 December 1686 [14.pdf #10].

LACKEY, JAMES, son of Henry and Mary Lackey, Baptized 22 April 1690, Crediton, Devon, England. Lacquey, James, 8 June 1708, age 18, Francis Goodrich [23.pdf #253]. James Leckie, servant to Francis Goodrick Senr., Recaptured Runaways, 9 March 1714 [25.pdf #198].

LALLEE, CORNELIUS, 19 April 1698, age 12, Thomas Smoote [19.pdf #206]. Cornelius Loller, servant to Capt. Thomas Smoot, Presentment by Grand Jury, 14 March 1704 [22.pdf #163].

LEACH, JAMES, illegitimate son of Alexander Roads et Susan Leach, Baptized 19 July 1663, Saint Chad, Rochdale, Lancashire, England. Leech, James, 8 June 1675, age 11, Edmund Taylor [07.pdf #63]. James Leech, servant to Elinor Boice, Recaptured Runaways, 9 February 1686 [13.pdf #48].

MACDANIEL, JAMES, 11 August 1719, age 21, Thomas Hussey Luckett [26.pdf #123]. James McDaniel, servant to Thomas Hussey Luckett, Petition for Freedom, 9 June 1724 [28.pdf #158].

MACKONTOSH, JAMES, 13 March 1722, age not judged, Henry Hawkins, "taken in ye Rebellion at Preston," "had served the full Term of five years" [27.pdf #126]. See James Mcantosh, 8 August 1721 [27.pdf #92].

MEGROUGH (MAGRAH), ALICE, 19 April 1698, age 19, Hugh Teares [19.pdf #206]. Alice Magrah (Magraugh), servant to John Beale, Recaptured Runaways, 9 March 1703 [22.pdf #89], 14 March 1704 [22.pdf #144], 14 August 1705 [23.pdf #88], 13 August 1706 [23.pdf #138].

WITHOUT INDENTURES, ELSEWHERE IN RECORD, NOT YET FREE

MAYBANCK, ELIZABETH, 10 June 1674, age 13, John Wood [06.pdf #158].
  Recaptured Runaways: Elizabeth Maybanke, servant to Philip Lynes, 13 June 1683 [11.pdf #128]. Elizabeth Maybancke, servant to Edward Mings, 10 June 1684 [11.pdf #204].

MILL, ISABELLA, 14 November 1710, age 21, Barton Hungerford [24.pdf #29].
  Isabella Mills, servant to Thomas Skinner, Presentment by Grand Jury, 11 March 1712 [25.pdf #33] & 10 June 1712 [25.pdf #78].

NEWTON, JOHN, 14 June 1681, age 20, Henry Hawkins [10.pdf #79].
  John Newton, servant to Henry Hawkins, Recaptured Runaways, 14 June 1687 [14.pdf #142].

OLIVER, ELIZABETH, 1 April 1701, age 20, Ubgatt Reeves [21.pdf #108].
  Elizabeth Oliver, servant to Mr. Ubgatt Reeves, Presentment by Grand Jury, 11 June 1706 [23.pdf #122] & 13 August 1706 [23.pdf #139].

PATTERSON, WILLIAM, 14 June 1698, age 16, William Dent [19.pdf #217].
  William Patterson, servant to William Dent, producing his Indenture in Court, Petitions for Freedom, 29 November 1698 [19.pdf #261].

PERRY, THOMAS, 13 June 1699, age 11, Philip Briscoe [20.pdf #68].
  Perry, Thomas, servant to Cornelius White, Recaptured Runaways, 14 November 1710, [24.pdf #32]

ROBERTSON, PETER, 9 June 1719, age 15, Col. Walter Story [26.pdf #112].
  Peter Robinson, servant to Mrs. Anne Story, "Relict of Col. Walter Story," Recaptured Runaways, 8 March 1726 [30.pdf #64].

SMITH, JAMES, 9 February 1686, age 21, Samuell Luckett, "ye servant produced an Indenture ye Court adjudgeth ye same Invalid" [13.pdf #48].
  James Smith, servant to Samuell Luckett, Petitions for Freedom, adjudged to have "kidnappers Indentures," 10 June 1690 [17.pdf #18].

SPURLING, JEREMIAH, 12 January 1686, age 18, Henry Hawkins [13.pdf #47].
  Jeremiah Spurling, servant to Henry Hawkins, Petitions for Freedom, adjudged to have "kidnappers Indentures," 10 June 1690 [17.pdf #18].

WITHOUT INDENTURES, ELSEWHERE IN RECORD, NOT YET FREE

TOD, JEREMIAH, son of Jeremiah and Anne Tod, Baptized 14 December 1684, Epping, Essex, England. Todd, Jeremiah, 14 June 1698, age 14, Elinor Stone [19.pdf #217]. Jeremiah Todd, servant to John Beale, Recaptured Runaways, 12 January 1703 [22.pdf #80], 14 September 1703 [22.pdf # 130] & 12 March 1706 [23.pdf #115].

TOD, THOMAS, 10 January 1671, age 13, William Love [Vol. 60:281]. Thomas Tod, deposition about William Love's heifer, 12 June 1677 [08.pdf #36].

WADE (WARE), ALLEXANDER, 14 November 1699, age 11, John Godshall [20.pdf #99]. Recaptured Runaways: Alexander Ware, servant to John Godshall, 14 March 1710 [23.pdf #372]; Alexander Waire, servant to Pryor Smallwood, 14 November 1710 [24.pdf #29].

RECAPTURED RUNAWAYS

"The Court declares that a Runnaway shall serve 10 dayes for one & receive punishment of whipping likewise" -- 10 August 1686 [13.pdf #119]

Allen, Mary, servant to Matthew Dike, 14 November 1693, 11 days absence, "but two of ye said dayes shee went to Mr. Hinson one of ye Justices of this Court to Complaine, which said two dayes were not allowed by ye Court," 90 days servitude "from ye expiration of her time" which was 4 November 1693 [18.pdf #115]

Alper, Thomas, servant to William Kingsland, 13 November 1722, 23 days absence, ordered to serve "eight days for one" (184 days servitude), and 30 days absence from his former master John Donaldson, "and ten shillings expended in taking him up," ordered to serve "eight days for one of his runaway time" (240 days servitude), and one month "for the expence aforesaid," and [28.pdf #7]

Anderson, Jane, servant to Michaell Martin, 10 August 1708, servant confessing, 32 days absence, 320 days servitude [23.pdf #266]

Andrews, John, servant to Martha Peters, 12 June 1705, servant confessing, 80 days absence, 800 days servitude, and two months "for four hundred pounds of tobacco paid for takeing him up" [23.pdf #79]

Archer, Christian, female, servant to John Dodson, 14 September 1708, servant confessing, 12 days absence, 120 days servitude [23.pdf #269]

Atterberry, John, servant to Thomas Coleman, 13 November 1705, servant confessing, 50 days absence, 500 days servitude [23.pdf #104]

Babberry, William, servant to William Hall, "Chyrurgion" (Surgeon), 9 June 1696, servant confessing "here in Court," absent from ye seaventh day of January (1693) until ye fourth day of May 1696," 1213 days in all, 12,130 days servitude (33 years and 2 months), master acknowledging "here in Court" to be "content with five yeares service to commence ye fourth day of May 1696 and doth hereby acquit & discharge him from ye remaineing part of ye Judgment aforesaid, if ye said William Babberry shall well & faithfully serve him and doth not again unlawfully absent himself" [19.pdf #20]

Bacon, John, "formerly" servant to Henry Hawkins "and now" servant to Maj. Andrew Gibson, 15 December 1686, "did in time of his service with his master Hawkins absent himselfe" 235 days, "seven years nine months three weeks & five days" servitude (equals 2850 days servitude) [14.pdf #9]

RECAPTURED RUNAWAYS

Ball, Silent, servant to William Thompson, 11 November 1690, servant
    confessing "here in Court," absent "severall times," 132 days in all,
    1320 days servitude [17.pdf #69]; Silent Balls, servant to
    Benjamin Posey, 11 September 1694, servant confessing "here in
    Court," 11 days absence "whilst shee lived with Mr. William
    Thompson," absent "severall times for ye span of thirty days" from
    "ye said Benjamin Posey," 41 days in all, 410 days servitude
    [18.pdf #194]; Silent Ball, servant to Benjamin Posey, 11 August
    1696, servant confessing "here in Court," 41 days absence, 410 days
    servitude, "and afterwards ye said Benjamin Posey acknowledged
    that in case ye said Silent Ball doth well & truely serve him until
    Christmas next come twelve month," "then hee will discharge &
    acquitt her" [19.pdf #41]; Silent Ball, servant to Thomas Davis,
    8 June 1697, "assigned over to him ye said Davis by Benj. Posey,"
    50 days absence, 500 days servitude [19.pdf #130]; Silent Ball,
    servant to John Ward, 10 January 1699, petition "to gett Copyes of
    ye severall Judgments entered against her for her Runaway time"
    [20.pdf #4]; The Grand Jurors "doe present Silence Balls liveing
    att Francis Wheatley's for haveing a bastard child," 10 November
    1702 [22.pdf #63]. Twelve lashes [22.pdf #90]
Barker, Thomas, servant to Benjamin Haddock, 12 August 1690, 30 days
    absence, 300 days servitude [17.pdf #30]
Barlowe, Anne, servant to William Browne, 9 September 1690, absent
    "severall times," 36 days in all, 360 days servitude [17.pdf #36]
Bartin, Robert, servant to William Keele, 8 January 1684, 28 days absence,
    ordered to serve "such proportion of time in consideration of his
    said running away as by act of Assembly in ye case made &
    provided is required," (280 days servitude) [11.pdf #187]
Bayhan, Thomas, servant to Henry Netherton, 12 November 1706,
    57 days absence "proved by the Oath of Philip Reyley,"
    and 24 days absence "proved by the Oath of Mr. Thomas Orrell,"
    81 days in all, 810 days servitude [23.pdf #153]
Bayley, Bryan, servant to Samuel Love, 10 March 1724, 17 days absence,
    and "six hundred pounds of tobacco" expended "in taking him up,"
    ordered to serve "eight days for one" (136 days servitude), and
    eight months for the expenses aforesaid" [28.pdf #122]
Bene, Andrew, servant to Randolph Brandt, 12 November 1728,
    12 days absence, and "seven hundred pounds of tobacco and
    fifteen shillings" expended "in takeing him up," ordered to serve

"five dayes for one of his runaway time (60 days servitude) and eight months for the expences" [31.pdf #96]

Benjer, Thomas, servant to John Gwynn, 8 August 1704, "the said John Gwynn alledges that he bought the said servant of John Wathen and that there was some runnaway time due whilst he was the said Wathens servant which the said Wathen hath Assigned and made over unto him," "whereupon the said Thomas Benjer makes itt appeare to the Court that the occasion of his Running away from the said Wathen was by Harsh Usage," ordered that "Thomas Benjer be Accquitt and Discharged from any forfietture for runnaway time dureing the time that hee was the said John Wathens servant," but "Thomas Benjer doth here in Court owne that he hath absented himselfe from the said John Gwynns service 17 days," 170 days servitude [23.pdf #20, 21]

Bennett, John, servant to Major James Smallwood, 11 January 1698, 20 days absence, 200 days servitude [19.pdf #180]

Berry, John, servant to George Gower, 12 June 1688, on oath of Ralph Shaw, 57 days absence, 570 days servitude [14.pdf #178]

Bevins, Mary, servant to James Neale, 8 September 1696, servant confessing "here in Court," 8 days absence, 80 days servitude [19.pdf #55]

Boareman, James, "an Indian servant to Capt. John Dent of St. Maryes County," 11 August 1691, ordered to be taken into custody and "be delivered to his said master" [17.pdf #138]

Bonner (or Hodges), Elizabeth, servant to James Tyer, 8 March 1681, "upon pretense of being a free woman hath absented her selfe," master alleging "that shee is not free untill August," 15 days absence, 150 days servitude [10.pdf #59]

Boyd, Robert, servant to Thomas Dixon, 11 January 1709, servant confessing, 10 days absence, 100 days servitude [23.pdf #293]

Bradey, Joseph, servant to Capt. Randolph Brandt Senior, 26 January 1692, absent seven times, 26 days in all, account filed, servant not appearing, no order or judgment by Court [17.pdf #254]

Brayber, William, servant to Thomas Hussey "who married Jane Broade ye Relict of John Broad deceased," 11 November 1690, absent "severall times," 31 days in all, 310 days servitude [17.pdf #69]

Bridges, Stephen, servant to William Tymothy, 9 September 1690, absent "severall times," 38 days in all, 380 days servitude [17.pdf #36]

Brockwell, Elias, servant to William Barton Junr., 9 September 1690, absent "severall times," "from Francis Goodrich his first master 106 days,

RECAPTURED RUNAWAYS

from William Hungerford 20 days, & from ye said William Barton 20 days," 146 days in all, 1460 days servitude [17.pdf #36]

Browne, John, servant to Thomas Hussey "who marryed Jane Broade ye Relict of John Broade deceased," 11 November 1690, absent "severall times," 16 days in all, 160 days servitude [17.pdf #69]

Browne, William, servant to Jacob Miller, 12 August 1712, 30 days absence, (300 days servitude) [25.pdf #90]

Bryan, John, servant to Thomas Jenckins, 9 January 1700, servant confessing "in Court," 29 days absence, 290 days servitude [20.pdf #131]

Buckner, Richard, servant to Thomas Tayler "of Charles County," 14 March 1721, servant confessing, 88 days absence, ordered to serve "ten days for one of his runaway time" (880 days servitude), "in full of all damages & expences" [27.pdf #43]; Richard Bucknam, servant to Thomas Mercer, 12 November 1723, servant "here in Court confesses that he absented himself from ye service of his former master Thomas Taylor fifteen days over & above what he has been formerly adjudged of," ordered to serve "his present master five days for one of the runaway time aforesaid" (75 days servitude) [28.pdf #91]

Bunn, Anthony, servant to Thomas Matthews, 11 March 1729, 108 days absence, and "two thousand one hundred and twenty pounds of tobacco" expended "in takeing him up," ordered to serve "seven dayes for one of his runaway time" (756 days servitude), and three years "for the expences aforesaid" [31.pdf #118]

Burdett, Thomas, servant to Ralph Gwynn, 10 March 1702, "for Runnaway time," 10 days "being proved by the Oath of Benjamin Wheeler his late master" and 10 days "acknowledged by the said Thomas Burdett from his former master Thomas Fletcher," 20 days in all, 200 days servitude, to "serve the said Ralph Gwynn" [22.pdf #22]; Thomas Burdett, servant to Doctor Francis, "Seargen," 13 March 1705, presented by Ralph Gwynn, servant confessing, 3 days absence, 30 days servitude, and two months "for two hundred pounds of tobacco paid for takeing him up" [23.pdf #46]

Burgesse, Samuell, servant to Mrs. Elinor Bayne, 10 June 1690, absent "severall times," 60 days in all, 600 days servitude [17.pdf #18]

Bushell, Jane, servant to John Beale, 9 September 1707, 36 days absence "proved by the Oath of the said John Beale in Court," and 9 days absence "proved by the Oath of Elinor" his wife before "Gerrard Fowke one of her majesty's justices of the peace," 45 days in all, 450 days servitude [23.pdf #206]

RECAPTURED RUNAWAYS

Butler, John, servant to Peter Garrett, 14 November 1721, 60 days absence "proved by the Oath of Archibald Johnson his former master," ordered to serve "seven dayes for one of his runaway time" (420 days servitude), and six months "for four hundred pounds of tobacco expended in taking him up" [27.pdf #108]

Butterfeild, John, servant to Thomas Harris, 11 August 1724, 3 days absence, and "five hundred pounds of tobacco" expended "in taking him up," ordered to serve "tenn days for one of his runaway time" (30 days servitude), and four months "for the charges" [28.pdf #185]

Caddick, William, servant to John Ensey, 14 June 1720, 39 days absence, ordered to serve "tenn days for one" (390 days servitude), and one month "for two hundred pounds of tobacco expended in taking him up" [26.pdf #172]

Capper, Anne, servant to Thomas Hussy, 15 March 1682, 42 days absence "at severall times," (420 days servitude), "and ye said Thomas Hussy doth in open Court assigne all his right title & interest of ye above named woman servant Anne Capper unto Mr. Henry Hawkins" [10.pdf #161]; Ann Capher (?), master not named, 12 November 1684, ordered to "serve for seaventy five days runing away," (750 days servitude) [12.pdf #23]; Ann Capard, master not named, 12 August 1685, ordered to serve "for runing away forty seaven days," (470 days servitude) [12.pdf #97]

Careless, Mary, servant to James Gallwith, 14 November 1721, 52 days absence, and "three hundred pounds of tobacco" expended "in taking her up," ordered "that shee serve two years & a half" [27.pdf #108]; Mary Careless, servant to Mary Miller, 8 March 1726, 14 days absence, ordered to serve "five days for one of her runnaway time" (70 days servitude) [30.pdf #64]

Casey, Patrick, servant to Capt. John Bayn, 12 March 1700, 23 days absence, 230 days servitude [20.pdf #177]; Patrick Cusy, servant to Capt. John Bayne, 3 December 1700, presented by Thomas Whichaley, 7 days absence "proved by oathe of James Lattimar," (70 days servitude), "and whereas the said Patrick Cusy alleadges that he was adjudged last March court for Runaway time, ordered therefore that what time was then entered be deducted out of this Judgment [21.pdf #57]; Patrick Cusack, petitioner, 11 March 1701, "brings here into Court a coppy of the records of St. Marys County which hereafter followeth to wit: Att a Court holden at Newtowne," 1 August 1693, (with Mr. John Bayne present as Justice),

RECAPTURED RUNAWAYS

"Mr. John Bayne brings here into Court two Irish servants the one named Patrick Morand and the other named Patrick Cusack the Morand was judged by the Court to be thirteen yeares of age and the said Cusack to be seaventeen yeares of age" [21.pdf #92]; Patrick Cusack, servant to John Bayne, 11 March 1701, 47 days absence, ordered "that the 23 dayes moved by the said Capt. Bayne in March court last is disallowed, being part of the 47 days," ordered to serve "till the tenth day of May next and from thence 105 days and after that to be discharged" [21.pdf #92]

Cavenaugh, William, servant to Francis Goodrick Senr., 8 September 1702, 7 days absence, 70 days servitude, "but if hee payes his said master four hundred pounds of tobacco, then to be free" [22.pdf #50]

Cheatham, Joseph, servant to John Marten, March 1716, "judgment of his runaway time" [Liber G Page 47]

Chiston (?), Valentine, servant to Thomas Dixon, November 1716, "adjudged for runaway" [Liber G Page 173]

Clampett, Abigail, servant to Robert Coleson, 9 November 1703, servant confessing "in Court," 10 days absence, 100 days servitude [22.pdf #144]

Cliford, John, servant to John Parry, 10 November 1713, servant confessing, 45 days absence, (450 days servitude) [25.pdf #181]

Cocks, Elizabeth, servant to Thomas Coleman, 12 November 1706, servant confessing, 25 days absence, 250 days servitude [23.pdf #152]

Coherin, Patrick, servant to Coll. James Smallwood, 12 November 1706, servant confessing, 31 days absence, 310 days servitude [23.pdf #152]

Coho, James, servant to John Smith, 12 January 1703, servant confessing, 45 days absence, 450 days servitude [22.pdf #80]

Cole, Nicholas, servant to James Neale, 8 June 1686, 14 days absence, 140 days servitude, "and allsoe make such other sattisfacion for his trouble & charge" of bringing him home [13.pdf #117]

Coleman, William, servant to Nathaniell Freeman, 14 August 1705, 11 days absence, 110 days servitude [23.pdf #89]

Collens, Mary, presented by Cornelius Maddock "to be adjudged for runaway time," 13 August 1700, 60 days absence, 600 days servitude [21.pdf #19]; "William Moss produces the said Mary Collins," 13 August 1700, 30 days absence, 300 days servitude [21.pdf #19]

RECAPTURED RUNAWAYS

Collins, Christopher, servant to Samuel Hanson, 11 March 1729, 7 days absence, and "forty shillings" expended "in takeing him up," "besides his own trouble in pursueing him," ordered to serve "ten dayes for one of his runaway time," (70 days servitude), and eight months "for the expences and trouble aforesaid" [31.pdf #118]; Christopher Collins and Daniel Russell, servants to Humphrey Bell "of London, Merchant," 11 August 1730, presented by John Parnham, servants confessing, "the said Parnham makes oath that acording to Capt. Reynolds information they absented themselves seven days from said Bells service, and that he paid on behalf of the said Bell four hundred pounds of tobacco and twenty shillings in charges and expences in takeing them up," ordered to serve "seven days for one of their runaway time" (49 days servitude), and four months "for the expences aforesaid" [31.pdf #210]

Colum, Thomas, servant to George Plater, 8 November 1692, 91 days absence, 910 days servitude [17.pdf #276]

Coney, Elizabeth, servant to John Hanson, 14 March 1721, servant confessing, 40 days absence, ordered to serve "eight days for one of her runaway time" (320 days servitude) [27.pdf #44]

Connor, John, servant to Isaac Gilpin, 10 November 1719, for two days absence "and for two hundred pounds of tobacco expended in regaining him," two months servitude [26.pdf #141]

Coody, Charron, servant to John Allen, 8 March 1715, 6 days absence, ordered "that he serve according to law" (60 days servitude), and "eighteen months in consideration of" "sixteen hundred pounds of tobacco which the said John had paid" [25.pdf #265]

Cooke, Joane, servant to Francis Greene, 9 June 1696, "purchased of Samuel Luckett," servant confessing "here in Court," 30 days absence, 300 days servitude [19.pdf #20]

Cooke, John, servant to Richard Newton, 9 August 1692, 10 days absence, 100 days servitude [17.pdf #238]; John Cooke, servant to Richard Newton, 12 June 1694, 11 days absence, 110 days servitude [18.pdf #165]

Cooke, John, servant to Samuel Luckett, 14 November 1699, servant confessing in Court, 26 days absence, 260 days servitude, "and for takeing him up in Virginia" either four hundred pounds of tobacco or two months service [20.pdf #101]

Corder, Richard, servant to Major James Smallwood, 11 November 1690, servant confessing "here in Court," absent "severall times," 60 days in all, 600 days servitude [17.pdf #69]

RECAPTURED RUNAWAYS

Couch, Richard, servant to Thomas Truman Davie, 11 November 1718, 31 days absence while servant of Thomas Swann, and "he has expended 800 pounds of tobacco about taking him up at several times," and 14 days absence while servant of Philip Brisco, and "he has expended 200 pounds of tobacco about taking him up," 45 days in all, 450 days servitude, and ten months "for ye said" tobacco, to "serve his present master Thomas Truman Davie" [26.pdf #72]

Cowley, Abraham, servant to Gabriel Moran, 12 June 1722, 16 days absence, ordered to serve "ten days for one" (160 days servitude), and nine months "for eight hundred seventy five pounds of tobacco expended in takeing him up" [27.pdf #163]

Coyne, Thomas, servant to Richard Land, 10 November 1691, servant confessing "here in Court," absent "severall times," 28 days in all, 280 days servitude, and "to pay and satisfy his master for his being taken up, either by servitude or otherwise" [17.pdf #157]

Crackingdale, Henry, servant to Edward Jenkins, 14 June 1715, 27 days absence, ordered to "serve his said master according to law" (270 days servitude), and "two months for two hundred pounds of tobacco expended" "in regaining him to his serveice" [25.pdf #271]

Craxon, James, servant to Samuel Luckett, 10 June 1701, "for Runaway time acknowledged by the said servant and allowed by the Court. Ordered to serve, when his time of servitude is expired, five months for Mr. Luckett's charge in takeing him upp" [21.pdf #126]

Crocker, William, servant to Henry Hardy, 1695, "judgment for runaway time" [Liber T Page 290]; William Crocker, servant to Capt. Henry Hardy, 12 March 1700, "Upon a Complaint alleadging that he was free," "the said Hardy proveing in Court that he had unlawfully absented himselfe nineteen days," 190 days servitude [20.pdf #177]

Crommy, John, servant to Thomas Coleman, 8 November 1720, servant confessing, 26 days absence, ordered to serve "six days for one of his runaway time" (156 days servitude), and three months "for charges in taking him up" [27.pdf #31]; John Crammy, servant to Thomas Coleman, 8 August 1721, 10 days absence, ordered to serve "eight days for one of his runaway time" (80 days servitude) [27.pdf #91]; John Crummy, 14 August 1722, "binds himself to William Middleton for ye term of four years and five months in consideration of ye said Middleton paying two thousand four hundred pounds of tobacco for said Crummy & giving him a decent suit of apparel at ye expiration of the aforesaid term" [27.pdf #176]

Crouch, Edmund, servant to William Wilkinson, 10 November 1713, servant confessing, 19 days absence, (190 days servitude), and "two whole years" for "tymes and expenses" [25.pdf #181]

Crowson, Thomas, servant to Richard Barber, 14 November 1727, 124 days absence, and "twelve hundred seventy eight pounds of tobacco & thirteen shillings" expended "in takeing him up," ordered to serve "four dayes for one of his runaway time" (496 days servitude), and "one year for one thousand pounds of tobacco, expenses allowed by the Court [31.pdf #18]

Cruckshanks, Christopher, servant to Edward Anderson, 8 August 1732, 46 days absence, and "five hundred pounds of tobacco" expended "in takeing him up," ordered to serve "ten days for each one of his runaway time" (460 days servitude), and "three months for the expenses aforesaid" [32.pdf #100]

Dallyson, Mary, servant to Thomas Mason "of Nomyny in ye Colony of Virginia," 8 June 1680, ordered by Court "to remaine in ye custody of George Symons & Elinor his wife, untill hee either come or send for her, & make satisfaction to them for takeing her up shee being runaway" [09.pdf #167]

Davis, Hugh, servant to Ralph Smith, 8 June 1697, servant confessing "here in Court," 17 days absence, 170 days servitude [19.pdf #130]

Davison, Anne, servant to John Beale, 10 August 1725, 8 days absence, ordered to serve "five days for one of her runaway time" (40 days servitude) [30.pdf #28]

Davison, Peter, servant to John Beale, 10 March 1724, 24 days absence "proved by the oath of John Pidgeon his former master," and 20 days absence "by the oath of Richard Beale," 44 days in all, and "four hundred pounds of tobacco expended in taking him up," ordered to serve "eight days for one of his runaway time" (352 days servitude), and four months "for the charges aforesaid" [28.pdf #122]; On the complaint of John Beale, 9 June 1724, "It is ordered that the Sheriff take his servant Peter Davison to the whipping post & there give him twelve lashes on the bare back for his insolent behaviour towards his said master" [28.pdf #163]; Peter Davison, servant to John Beale, 10 November 1724, "John Pidgeon makes oath (to) the Court that he expended two hundred pounds of tobacco in taking up Peter Davidson while he was his servant before he sold him to Mr. Beale" [29.pdf # 7]; Peter

RECAPTURED RUNAWAYS

Davison, servant to John Beale, 9 March 1725, ordered to "serve the Beale two months for two hundred pounds of tobacco expended in taking him up when runaway & proved by the oath of John Pidgeon" [29.pdf #25]

Dewell, John, servant to Francis Person, 14 November 1710, servant confessing, 16 days absence, (160 days servitude), and one month "for one hundred pounds of tobacco expended" [24.pdf #31]

Dickins, Henry, servant to Mr. Hatch, 10 January 1688, 40 days absence, 400 days servitude [14.pdf #173]

Digginer, James, servant to Hugh Teares, 9 March 1697, 170 days absence, 1700 days servitude [19.pdf #111]

Douglass, Margarett, servant to Edward Clements, 8 June 1708, servant confessing, 14 days absence, 140 days servitude, and six months "for three hundred and sixty pounds of tobaccoe for takeing her up" [23.pdf #253]

Douglass, Patrick, servant to John Wilder, 8 August 1727, 101 days absence, and "five hundred and sixty pounds of tobacco" expended "in takeing him up," ordered to serve "five days for one of his runaway time" (505 days servitude) and eight months "for the expences aforesaid" [31.pdf #4]

Doulton, Anne, servant to Thomas Lyndsey, 14 June 1692, 56 days absence, 560 days servitude, and for her "abuse" of "severall of ye Commissioners belonging to this Court," "Ordered that ye sherife take ye said Anne Dolton into his Custody and carry her to ye whipping post and there to strip her naked from ye waist upwards and on her bare back to give her twelve lashes well laid on" [17.pdf #233]

Downes, Jane, servant to Edward Rockwood, 9 November 1703, presented by William Moss, servant confessing "in Court," 22 (sic) days absence, 240 (sic) days servitude [22.pdf #143]

Drunckore, James, servant to William Forster, 13 September 1692, by Mrs. Anne Burford, "formerly her servant and by her sold to Michael Minock in his life time," "did in time of his servitude with her ye said Anne Burford absent himself & runaway at severall times," 112 days in all, 1120 days servitude [17.pdf # 255]; James Drunckore, servant to William Forster, 13 March 1694, absent 8 days from "his wife Dorothy Forster before marryage," absent 33 days from William Forester, 41 days in all, 410 days servitude, "for which Mrs. Anne Burford did assign him over to predecessor Michaell Minock [18.pdf #144]; James Drunkore, servant to William Foster, 1694, "judgment of his runaway time" [Liber T Page 110]

Ducker, Elizabeth, servant to John Higton Senr., 14 March 1721, servant confessing, 19 days absence, ordered to serve "eight days for one" (152 days servitude), and four months "for two hundred pounds of tobacco expended in taking her up" [27.pdf #43]; Elizabeth Ducker, servant to Millisent Higton, 11 June 1723, 7 days absence, ordered to serve three days for one of her runaway time" (21 days servitude) [28.pdf #53]

Dunstan, Michael, servant to Richard Wheeler, 14 November 1721, servant confessing, 7 days absence, and twenty shillings "expended in taking him up," ordered to serve "eight days for one of his runaway time" (56 days servitude), and two months "for ye expenses aforesaid" [27.pdf #108]

Edge, Edward, servant to Josha Doyne, 11 March 1729, 7 days absence, and "forty shillings" expended "in takeing him up," "besides his own trouble in pursueing him," ordered to serve "ten dayes for one of his runaway time" (70 days servitude), and eight months "for the expences and trouble aforesaid" [31.pdf #118]

Edgerley, John, servant to Robert Green, 9 March 1703, servant confessing "here in Court," 3 days absence "from Mr. William Peale," and 8 days absence from "Robert Greens service," 11 days in all, 110 days servitude, and six weeks "for what tobacco the said William Peale paid for takeing him up in Virginia" [22.pdf #89]

Edwards, John, servant to Randolph Garland, 11 November 1718, servant confessing, 11 days absence, ordered to serve "tenn for one" (110 days servitude), "including sixteen shillings & eight pence expences in taking him up" [26.pdf #73]

Ellison, Jeremiah, servant to Henry Hawkins, 8 January 1684, 149 days absence, ordered by Court "with ye consent & agreement of ye said Mr. Hawkins that upon condition that ye said Jeremiah Ellison shall faithfully & truely serve his said master ye half of such proportion of tyme in consideration of his running away as is by act of Assembly allowed," (745 days servitude), "ye said master shall & will remitt ye residue & remainder of ye said runaway time" [11.pdf #187]

Elswood, Anne, servant to James Neale, 14 June 1692, 9 days absence, 90 days servitude [17.pdf #233]; Anne Ellswood, servant to James Neale, 1694, "judgment for runaway time [Liber T Page 101]

RECAPTURED RUNAWAYS

Ethue, Rachel, servant to Capt. Ashford, 13 March 1688, her indenture judged "to be good," but "ye said Rachell thrice hath run away," 40 days absence, 400 days servitude [14.pdf #176]

Evans, Evan, servant to John Higgins, 9 March 1703, "bought of Thomas Wheeler, 62 days absence "proved by the Oath of Thomas Wheeler," and 8 days absence "dureing the time of Higgens's service," 70 days in all, 700 days servitude, and six months "for seaven hundred and fifty pounds of tobacco paid for takeing him up when Runaway" [22.pdf #89]

Evans, Grace, servant to John Peggeon, 13 March 1711, 15 days absence, (150 days servitude) [24.pdf #59]; Grace Evans, servant to John Beale, 13 March 1711, 8 days absence, (80 days servitude) [24.pdf #59]; Grace Evans, servant to John Beale, 10 March 1713, 45 days absence "proved by Oaths of her said master and William Smith, 450 days servitude) [25.pdf #120]

Evans, alias Jones, Margarett, servant to Thomas Wheeler, 9 March 1703, 60 days absence, 600 days servitude, and six months "for seaven hundred and fifty pounds of tobacco paid for takeing her up when Runn away" [22.pdf #89]

Evers, Henry, servant to Francis Greene, 14 June 1698, absent 3 days "from Mr. William Peale," and 5 days from "ye said Francis Greene," 8 days in all, 80 days servitude, and six weeks "for what tobaccoe ye said William Peale paid for ye takeing him up in Virginia," "which said time of service ye said William Peale doth here in Court assigne over to ye said Francis Greene" [19.pdf #219]

Farrald, Anne, servant to William Whitter, 8 November 1709, "adjudged for runaway time," [Liber B # 2 Page 662, page not microfilmed]

Farrell, Bryan, servant to John Speake, 8 August 1693, absent "severall times," 33 days in all, servant confessing "here in Court" to 6 days only, 330 days servitude; "Whereas Bryan Farrell hath abused this Court -- Itt is ordered that ye Sherife take ye said Bryan Farrell into his custody and carry him to ye whipping post and there strip him naked from ye waist upward and give him twelve lashes on his bare back well laid on," [18.pdf #87]

Fenn, Francis, servant to William Harbert, 13 March 1705, 40 days absence "proved by the Oath of Mr. John Rowland his former master," and 2 days absence "proved by the Oath of the said William Harbert," 42 days in all, 420 days servitude [23.pdf #47]

Ferril, Robert, servant to Thomas Plunket, 11 August 1713, nine months absence, (ninety months servitude), "and the said Plunket" saith

RECAPTURED RUNAWAYS

"that if the said Ferril does not absent himselfe any more out of his service that he will release all the above time, and discharge him after five years for the full service" [25.pdf #171]

Flanagen, David, servant to John Smith, 13 November 1705, 47 days absence, 470 days servitude [23.pdf #104]; David Flannagin, servant to John Smith, 9 March 1708, servant confessing, 18 days absence, 180 days servitude, and six months "for six hundred pounds of tobacco expended for takeing him up" [23.pdf #235]

Fletcher, Catherine, servant to Philip Lines, 10 January 1682, absent "severall times," 176 days absence, 1760 days servitude, assigned to Derby Dunnavan of St. Maries County for ye tearme of time" remaining, "five yeares from ye Eighth day of November last past" and "for her runing away" [10.pdf #134]

Forster, Elizabeth, servant to Charles Shepherd, 13 January 1691, absent "severall times," 19 days in all, 190 days servitude [17.pdf #89]; Elizabeth Forster, servant to Samuell Luckett, 9 January 1694, 9 days absence, 90 days servitude [18.pdf #128]

Foster, Edward, servant to John Booker, "adjudged for runaway time," 8 November 1709 [Liber B # 2 Page 663, not microfilmed]

Fountain, Thomas, "a Mallatto servant" to Captain Joseph Douglass, 11 March 1729, 30 days absence "whilst John Snoggen was his overseer," and nine months from "the said Douglass," ten months in all, and "four hundred and fifty pounds of tobacco" expended "in taking him up," ordered to serve "ten dayes for one of his runaway time" (one hundred months servitude) "in full for that and the expences aforesaid" [31.pdf #118]

Fox, Robert, servant to John Howard, 10 August 1731, absent "several times," 20 days in all, ordered to serve "two days for each one of his runaway time aforesaid" (40 days servitude) [32.pdf #5]

Fuller, James, 10 August 1697, "seized & taken up as a Runnaway" and "comitted into ye Custody of ye Sherife," but "nothing appeareing to ye Court here that hee is a runaway servant," it is "Ordered that ye said James Fuller be discharged hee makeing satisfaction to ye persons seizeing & taking up as a Runaway ye sum of two hundred pounds of tobaccoe" [19.pdf #136]

Gaba, Joseph, servant to John Beale, 11 June 1723, 11 days absence, "adjudged that he serve fifty-five days therefore" [28.pdf #53]; Joseph Gaby, servant to John Hanson, 11 November 1729,

33 days absence, and "twenty shillings" expended "in takeing him up," ordered to serve "nine days for one of his runaway time" (297 days servitude), and two months "for the expences aforesaid" [31.pdf #173]

Gains, Grizzle, servant to Samuel Hanson, 10 March 1719, 50 days absence, ordered to serve "three days for one" (150 days servitude), and three years "for three pounds current money & eleven hundred & fifty pounds of tobacco expended about her" [26.pdf #96]

Ganer, Taddy, servant to Hugh Teares, 9 March 1697, 43 days absence, 430 days servitude [19.pdf #111]

Gibson, Thomas, servant to Thomas Green, 12 March 1723, 15 days absence, and "two hundred pounds of tobacco expended in taking him up," ordered to serve "three days for one of his runaway time" (45 days servitude), and five weeks to "repay his said master" [28.pdf #24]

Gilbard, James, servant to Philip Lines, 10 January 1682, servant confessing "in Court," 40 days absence, 400 days servitude, and "six months for eight hundred pounds of tobaccoe disburst for his twice takeing up in Virginia" [10.pdf #134]

Gill, Archilaus, servant to Col. James Smallwood, "lately deceased," 8 March 1715, servant "comes into Court & confesses" to 100 days absence, (1000 days servitude), to "serve ye Executor or Administrator of ye said Col. Smallwood" [25.pdf #266]; Argulus Guill, servant to Ralph Shaw, 14 August 1722, 11 days absence, ordered to serve "eight days for one of his runaway time" (88 days servitude) [27.pdf #176]

Gleive, George, servant to James Neale, 8 June 1686, 14 days absence, 140 days servitude, "and allsoe make such other sattisfacion for his trouble & charge" of bringing him home [13.pdf #117]

Glover, John, "a mollato," servant to John Hanson Junr., 13 November 1711, servant confessing, 80 days absence, 800 days servitude, and four months "for four hundred pounds of tobacco expended for takeing him up" [25.pdf #16]

Goddard, Edward, servant to John Blee, 9 November 1708, "by consent they both agree in Court that if the said Edward Goddard doe serve the said John Blee five years from this present day that then hee is willing to accquitt him of all Runaway time" [23.pdf #279]; Edward Goddart, servant to John Blee, 14 June 1709, 15 days absence, "contrary to the covenant" made "on the ninth of November last past," 150 days servitude [23.pdf #305]

RECAPTURED RUNAWAYS

Goffe, Patrick, servant to John Jackson, 10 November 1730, "to be adjudged for what said Jackson expended in takeing hime up when runaway," "five shillings and one hundred pounds of tobacco," ordered to serve two months [31.pdf #225]

Goles, John, servant to Henry Hardy, 1694, "judgment of his runaway time" [Liber T Page 111]

Gordian, Ruth, servant to James Raye, 8 March 1715, 84 days absence, (840 days servitude) [25.pdf #265]

Gray, William, servant to Joseph Manning, 13 June 1693, 32 days absence, 320 days servitude [18.pdf #80]; William Gray, servant to Joseph Manning, 13 March 1694, servant confessing "here in Court," 20 days absence, 200 days servitude [18.pdf # 144]

Greenwood, Edward, servant to Mark Penn, June 1716, "judgment of his runaway time" [Liber G Page 100]

Gregory, John, servant to Ralph Lomax, 14 June 1709, "being runaway comes into Court and being assigned by the said Ralph Lomax to Richard Lemaster acknowledgeth that he is willing to serve the said Richard Lemaster two whole yeares to commence from the foure and twentyeth day of May last past" [23.pdf #305]

Grenham, Margret, servant to Henry Darnes, 11 June 1723, 20 days absence "proved by the Oath of Daniel Bryant her former master," ordered to serve "five days for one of her runaway time" (100 days servitude) [28.pdf #53]

Grey, Charles, servant to James Neale, 8 June 1686, 14 days absence, 140 days servitude, "and allsoe make such other sattisfacion for his trouble & charge" of bringing him home [13.pdf #117]

Groves, William, servant to Thomas Smallwood, 14 January 1707, presented by James Maddocks, "by vertue of a warrant under the hand of Thomas Tench Esqr, which said warrant followeth in these words, Anarundel (sic) County December 31 1706, James Stone and Edward Webb of this County brought before me one William Groves upon suspicion of being a runnaway who upon examination acknowledged that he had been a servant to one Thomas Smallwood of Charles County and had lived with him nigh six years but before the expiration of his full indented time James Maddocks of the same County and a relation of the said Smallwoods prevailed with the above said William Groves to signe an Indenture to serve the said Maddocks the terme of four yeares more which is contrary to the good lawes of this Province," ordered

RECAPTURED RUNAWAYS

by Court "that the said William Groves returne to his said master James Maddocks's service dureing his indented time" [23.pdf #161]

Gubbins, Mary, master not named, 10 March 1686, three absences in 1685, 87 days in all, "Runaway at severall times in ye year 1684," 12 weeks in all, (1710 days servitude) [13.pdf #50]

Gulley, Robert, servant to Thomas Plunckett, 9 November 1703, servant confessing "here in Court," 9 days absence, 90 days servitude [22.pdf #143]; Robert Gulley, servant to Thomas Plunckett, 14 March 1704, two months servitude "for two hundred pounds of tobacco expended for takeing upp Robert Gulley when he Rann away" [22.pdf #163]; Robert Gulley, servant to Thomas Plunckett, 12 September 1704, 18 days absence, 180 days servitude [23.pdf #33]

Ha___, William, servant to George Dent, 11 November 1718, 87 days absence "by ye oath of Benjamin Doughlasse," ordered to serve "tenn days for one" (870 days servitude), and four months "for fifty shillings expended in taking him up" [26.pdf #73]

Hagon, John, servant to John Smith "of Jurden," 13 March 1705, 5 days absence, 50 days servitude [23.pdf #47]

Haley, Elizabeth, servant to John Smith, 10 June 1718, "adjudged for absenting herself out of her late master Bowling Speake's service," 20 days absence, ordered to "serve her present master John Smith the assignee of ye said Bowling tenn days for every one of ye time aforesaid," 200 days servitude [26.pdf #38]

Halleburton, alias Morris, Elizabeth, servant to Capt. William Barton, 13 June 1710, 20 days absence, ordered by Court "to serve according to act of assembly" (200 days servitude) [23.pdf #401]

Hamilton, David, servant to Ubgatt Reeves, 9 March 1714, servant confessing, 14 days absence, (140 days servitude), and three months "for three hundred pounds of tobacco expended in taking him up twice" [25.pdf #197]

Harrison, Bryan, servant to Robert Thompson, 9 September 1690, absent "severall times," 98 days in all, 980 days servitude, and four months "for four hundred pounds of tobaccoe expended for ye takeing him up in ye Colony of Virginia (or to reimburse at ye expiration of his time) [17.pdf #37]; Bryan Harrisson, servant to Jefferry Cole, 9 June 1691, "formerly belonging to Robert Thompson Junr.," absent "severall times," 10 days in all, 100 days servitude, and three months "for four hundred pounds of tobaccoe for ye takeing up" [17.pdf #114]; Bryan Harrison, servant to Jeoffrey Cole, "his order for runaway time & order for sattisfaction for his taking him up in Virginia," 1694 [Liber T Page 30]; Bryan Harrison, servant to Jeoffry Cole, "his judgment for runaway time," 1695 [Liber T Page 290]; Bryan Harrison, servant to Jefferry Cole, 10 November 1696, 45 days absence, 450 days servitude [19.pdf #73]

Harrison, William, servant to Coll. John Courts, 10 August 1697, absent "severall times," 37 days in all, 370 days servitude [19.pdf #136]

Haslewood, Anne, servant to James Neale, 13 June 1693, 9 days absence, 90 days servitude [18.pdf #80]

Hawkins, John, servant to Philip Lines, 10 January 1682, servant confessing "in Court," 164 days absence, 1640 days servitude, and "three months for foure (hundred) pounds of tobaccoe disburst for his takeing up in Virginia" [10.pdf #134]

Haylee, Ellinor, servant to Phillip Lynes, 13 March 1688, her "Indenture is not good," ordered to "remain with Mr. Lynes as his servant for one yeare more," and 26 days absence, 260 days servitude [14.pdf #177]

Hedges, Mary, servant to Edward Minggs, 13 June 1683, 10 days absence, ordered to serve "such proportion of time in consideration of her running away as by act of Assembly in ye case made and provided is required, (100 days servitude) [11.pdf #128]

Herauld (?), William, servant to John Manning, 62 days absence, ordered "to serve him eight days for one," (496 days servitude), 11 March 1718 [26.pdf #21]

Hills, Thomas, servant to Robert Smallpage, 11 September 1694, absent "severall times" from service of Robert Smallpage "for ye space of 107 days, and absent 50 days "whilst he served" Marke Lampton, 157 days in all, 1570 days servitude [18.pdf #195]

Hine, Ann, servant to Joseph Manning, 10 March 1713, servant confessing, 20 days absence, (200 days servitude) [25.pdf #118]

Hodsworth, Robert, servant to Godshall Barnes, 9 March 1731, 10 days absence, ordered to serve "eight days for each one of his runaway time" (80 days servitude) [31.pdf #245]

Hogg, Jane, servant to Gerard Fowke, 14 June 1715, 36 days absence, (360 days servitude) [25.pdf #272]

Hollywood, James, servant to William Smith, 13 March 1694, 62 days absence, 620 days servitude, and to "make satisfaction to ye said William Smith ye sum of six hundred pounds of tobaccoe disburst & expended for ye takeing up & bringing home him twice out of ye Colony of Virginia," or else to serve three months [18.pdf #144]

RECAPTURED RUNAWAYS

Holmes, Grace, servant to William Smith, 11 August 1686, 100 days absence, 1000 days servitude [13.pdf #119]; Grace Holmes, servant to John Goureley, 10 November 1691, absent "severall times," one year servitude, "and then to be free" if "she doth not at any time within ye said yeare unlawfully absent herselfe & runaway" [17.pdf #157]

Hoskins, William, servant to Thomas Dixon, 11 August 1713, servant confessing, 26 days absence, (260 days servitude) [25.pdf #172]

Howard, Mary, servant to John Symms, 13 November 1705, servant confessing, 12 days absence, 120 days servitude [23.pdf #104]

Hughs, Timothy, servant to Allexander Willson, 14 March 1704, 77 days absence "proved by the Oath of John Smith of Jorden," 770 days servitude [22.pdf #163]; Timothy Hughs, servant to Allexander Willson, 11 June 1706, servant confessing, 8 days absence, 80 days servitude [23.pdf #123]

Humphreys, Anne, servant to Samuel King, 14 March 1721, 24 days absence from "Jane Chapman her former mistress," "her husband paid two hundred pounds of tobacco for taking up said servant," and 12 days absence from "her present master," 36 days in all, ordered to serve "her said master five days for one of her runaway time" (180 days servitude), and three months "for the charge in taking her up" [27.pdf #43]; Anne Humphreys, servant to Richard Stevens, 11 June 1723, 46 days absence "proved by the oath of Elizabeth King her late mistress," ordered to serve "five days for one of her runaway time" (230 days servitude) [28.pdf #53]

Inscoe, Andrew, servant to Capt. Randolph Brandt, 10 November 1691, 4 days absence, 40 days servitude [17.pdf #157]

Jeffries, William, servant to Robert Gates, 9 June 1719, "late servant to William Fenwick," two months servitude for "two hundred pounds of tobacco" "expences paid in taking him up" [26.pdf #112]

Johnson, Jacob, servant to John Barker, 10 November 1719, "late servant to Richard Hodgson," "for 96 days runaway time & two hundred pounds of tobacco expended in taking him up," twelve months servitude [26.pdf #141]; Jacob Johnson, servant to John Barker, 13 November 1722, 65 days absence, ordered to serve "eight days for one of his runaway time" (520 days servitude) [28.pdf #7]

Johnson, Mary, servant to Doctor Gustavus Brown, 14 March 1732, 38 days absence, and "four hundred pounds of tobacco" expended "in takeing her up," ordered to serve "five days for each one of her runaway time" (190 days servitude), and "six months for the expences aforesaid" [32.pdf #51]

Johnson, William, servant to Thomas Mudd, 1694, "his judgment for runaway time" [Liber T Page 112]

Jones, Elinor, servant to Mary Matthewes, 29 November 1698, absent "out of her husbands service in his lifetime and since his death out of her service," 39 days in all, 390 days servitude [19.pdf #261]

Jones, John, servant to Jonathan Walker, 10 March 1724, servant confessing, 30 days absence, ordered to serve "six days for one" (180 days servitude), and two months "for two hundred pounds of tobacco expended in taking him up" [28.pdf #122]

Jones, Mary, servant to Mary Hall, "ye Relict & Executor of Doctor William Hall," 10 August 1697, absent "out of William Halls service in his lifetime" 14 days, "and allsoe out of Mary Halls service since his death" one day, "which was proved by ye Oath of Benjamin Jones & ye said Mary Hall before Capt. Philip Hoskins," 15 days in all, 150 days servitude [19.pdf #135]

Jones, Robert, servant to Thomas Baker, 14 June 1681, his master not finding him "by reason hee changed his name," servant confessing "in open court," 169 days absence, 1690 days servitude [10.pdf #79]

Jones, Robert, servant to Thomas Hussey, 12 June 1688, 26 days absence, 260 days servitude [14.pdf #177]

Kelley, Daniel, servant to James Maddox, 14 November 1727, 20 days absence, and "ten shillings" expended "in takeing him up," ordered to serve "five dayes for one of his runaway time" (100 days servitude), and one month for the expences aforesaid [31.pdf #18]

Kelly, Daniel, servant to Thomas Jameson, 11 August 1702, "upon hard usage did runn away eight days and the said Mr. Jameson being in England his wife doe appear against your petitioner for the said runnaway time, but charges more there is due, notwithstand hee has been lasht, and beate for the same," "Mrs. Jameson sweares to eleaven days runnaway time and desires that Mr. Jameson may prove the rest when he comes, and whereas the said Danniell Kelly in open Court produces his masters pockett book which his said mistress disownes that shee has ever any knowledge of his takeing of the same and itt appearing to the Court that severall of the leaves are imbezzled and torne out of the said book which his mistress alledges to be done by the said Danniel Kelly," ordered by Court "that the said Daniel Kelly" be given twenty four lashes, and

RECAPTURED RUNAWAYS

"that the said Daniell Kelly doe serve the said James" "for the eleaven days runnaway time," 110 days servitude [22.pdf #38]; Danniell Kelly, servant to Thomas Jameson, master "sweares to twenty days more besides the eleaven days his wife formerly swore to," 200 days servitude, and "two months time for two hundred pounds of tobacco payd for takeing him up" [22. pdf #80]

Kenneday, James, servant to Matthew Tennison, 3 August 1706, "ordered that George Atkin pay him two hundred pounds of tobacco for takeing up his servant James Kenneday in Virginia when runnaway" [23.pdf #138]; James Kenneday, servant to Michaell Martin, 8 June 1708, "itt appeareing to the Court the runaway time aforesaid to be uncertaine and ye said James Kenneday declaring in Court that he is willing to serve the said Michaell Martin foure yeares to commence from ye first day of October next ensueing which the said Michaell Martin accepts of in Court in leiw of the runaway time aforesaid" [23.pdf #254]

Killpatrick, Allexander, servant to William Smallwood, 12 March 1706, presented by Mrs. Ellinor Smallwood "in the behalfe of her husband," 27 days absence "proved by the Oath of the said Mrs. Smallwood," ordered to "serve the said William Smallwood" 270 days [23.pdf #114]

King, John, servant to William McFerson, 10 November 1730, 10 days absence, and "two hundred pounds of tobacco" expended "in taking him up," ordered to serve "four days for each one of his runaway time" (40 days servitude), and two months "for the expences aforesaid" [31.pdf #226]

Kirweather, Amy, servant to John Mellor, 11 March 1718, servant confessing, 16 days absence, "adjudged by ye Court here that she serve Tenn for one" 160 days servitude [26.pdf #22]

Knelin, William, servant to John Wilkinson, 10 November 1719, servant confessing, 50 days absence, 250 days servitude, and eight months "for ye charges his said master has been at in taking him up several times," "Ordered also at same time on ye Complaint of ye said Servant that ye said John Wilkinson his master provide for him a good & sufficient bedd to lye on" [26.pdf #141]

Law, Rosomon, servant to Robert Hagar, 12 November 1706, 148 days absence, 1480 days servitude [23.pdf #152]; Rosamond Law, servant to Alexander Wilson, 14 June 1715, 338 days absence, ordered "to serve her said master according to law for ye runaway time" (9 years and 92 days servitude) [25.pdf #271]

RECAPTURED RUNAWAYS

Lauler, John, servant to Henry Buttridge, 13 June 1727, by "Deposition of Charles Byrne, late master to the said Lauler," "the servant had absented himself out of his service from about the 20th of August 1722 to the date of the said Deposition being the 16th May 1727" (1730 days absence), ordered to serve "two dayes for one of his runaway time" (9 years & 172 days) and "one year and a half in consideration of two Guineas expended in takeing said servant up, imprisonment fees, &c., which expence was proved by the Oath of said Butridge," "whereupon the said Henry Butridge in Court releases all the service aforesaid except five years on condition that he serve that time faithfully and truely" [30.pdf #244]

Leckie, James, servant to Francis Goodrick Senr., 9 March 1714, 36 days absence, (360 days servitude) [25.pdf #198]

Lee, James, 11 June 1706, presented by "Capt. Walter Story high sherriff of this County," "committed into his custody by vertue of a warrant from under the hand and seale of Mr. Joseph Manning one of the Justices of this Court beareing date the one and twentieth day of March 1706 upon suspition of being a runaway and no master being found for the said James Lee the said Capt. Story desires that the Court order some sattisfaction for his fees either by service or otherwise," ordered by Court "that the said James Lee doe remaine with the said Capt. Walter Story two yeares fully to be compleated and ended to commence from the last of October next for his fees aforesaid" and then to be free [23.pdf #123]

Lee or Lees, Edward, servant to John Court, 9 November 1686, 36 days absence, 360 days servitude, and ordered "that in case ye said Edward at ye compleating his full time of servitude shall not immediatelie sattisfie & pay to his said master ye sume of seaven hundred pounds of tobaccoe expended by his said master for taking him up then ye said Edward in consideration of ye said runaway time to serve his said master for ye full terme & space of foure monthes to be complete & ended before ye said Edward Lees shall goe free from his said master" [13.pdf #120]

Leech, James, servant to Elinor Boice, 9 February 1686, servant "confesseth his runing away from his Mistrisse 18 days," ordered "to serve according to Act of Assembly," (180 days servitude) [13.pdf #48]

Leman, Joseph, servant to Samuell Luckett, 8 August 1704, 20 days absence, 200 days servitude, and nine months "for twice takeing him up in Virginia" [23.pdf #22]

RECAPTURED RUNAWAYS

Lematt, Paul, servant to Ellinor Smallpage, 12 March 1706, servant confessing, 15 days absence, ordered to serve "five and twenty months time and then to be free" [23.pdf #115]

Levalley, Richard Michael, servant to John Payne, 10 November 1730, 21 (?) days absence, and "two hundred pounds of tobacco" expended "in takeing him up," ordered to serve "eight days for each one of his runaway time" (168 days servitude), and two months "for the expences aforesaid" [31.pdf #225]

Lewis, Edward, servant to Thomas Stone, "one of ye Executors of Mr. John Stone deceased, 10 January 1699, servant confessing "here," absent 12 days "in ye lifetime of ye said John Stone out of his service," 120 days servitude [20.pdf #4]

Lonsdon, Nicholas, servant to Edward Maddock, 13 March 1683, servant confessing "in open Court," 109 days absence, 1090 days servitude, master agrees if servant "doth well and truely serve him twelve moneths more without runing away, then hee shall be discharged" [11.pdf #83]

Low, James, servant to Thomas Jameson, 8 June 1708, servant confessing, 41 days absence, 410 days servitude, and six months "for four hundred pounds of tobacco expended for takeing him up" [23.pdf #253]

Lowry, Jennet, servant to Cornelius White, 14 November 1710, 60 days absence, (600 days servitude) [24.pdf #31]

Lyne, James, servant to Philip Lynes, 10 November 1696, servant confessing "here in Court," absent "severall times," 34 days in all, 340 days servitude [19.pdf #73]

M(?)oat, Daniel, servant to Hudson Wathen, 9 November 1731, 11 days absence, and "two hundred pounds of tobacco" expended "in takeing him up," ordered to serve "eight days for each one of his runaway time" (88 days servitude), and three months "for the expences aforesaid" [32.pdf #15]

Macdonnell, William, servant to Thomas Wheeler, 1 April 1701, 45 days absence "proved by the said Wheeler and owned by the servant," 450 days servitude [21.pdf #107]

MacFail, Alexander, servant to Benjamin Reader, 9 March 1731, 44 days absence, and "two hundred pounds of tobacco" expended "in takeing him up," ordered to serve "seven days for each one of his runaway time" (308 days servitude), and two months "for the expences aforesaid" [31.pdf #238]

RECAPTURED RUNAWAYS

Mackaboy, William, servant to John Smith, 11 June 1706, 2 days absence, 20 days servitude, and one month "for two hundred pounds of tobacco paid for takeing him up" [23.pdf #123]

Mackdonnell, Nehemiah, servant to John Gwynn, 12 November 1706, servant confessing, 20 days absence, 200 days servitude, and four months "for two hundred pounds of tobacco paid for takeing him up" [23.pdf #152]

Mackdonnell, Owen, servant to John Smith, 14 March 1704, servant confessing, 20 days absence, 200 days servitude [22.pdf #163]

Mackenny, Keeny, servant to Robert Greene, 9 November 1703, 31 days absence, 310 days servitude [22.pdf #143]

Macknamarre, Eleanor, servant to Robert Doyne, 8 January 1684, 51 days absence, ordered to serve "such proportion of time in consideration of her running away as by act of Assembly in ye case made & provided is required," (510 days servitude) [11.pdf #187]

Macknew, Lomax, servant to Walter Winter, 25 April 1710, "to be adjudged for runaway tyme, which although it be considerable," if he "doe serve nine months and twenty six days faithfully and truly, which is only the tyme he absented himselfe, after the expiration of his first tyme ended, he the said Walter Winter consents he should be" free [23.pdf #391]

Macklanan, Margaret, master not named, November 1716, "adjudged of her runaway time" on deposition of John Speake [Liber G Page 151]; Margaret Maclanan, master not named, June 1717, "adjudged for runaway time" on deposition of John Speake [Liber G Page 220]; Margaret Maclanan, servant to George Thomas, 11 November 1718, 172 days absence, ordered to serve "four days for one" (688 days servitude), and four months "for his expence & charge in taking her up" [26.pdf #73]

MackQueen, Timothy, servant to John Hanson, 14 September 1703, presented by Robert Hanson "in ye behalfe of his father," 71 days absence "proved by ye Oath of John Theobalds," 710 days servitude [22.pdf #130]

Magrah, Alice, servant to John Beale, 9 March 1703, 18 days absence "proved by the Oath of the said John Beale," and 5 days absence "in the time of Mrs. Teares's widdowhood proved by the Oath of William Holt," and 10 days absence "proved by the Oath of John Pidgeon," 33 days in all, 330 days servitude [22.pdf #89]; Alice Magraugh, servant to John Beale, 14 March 1704, 16 days absence, 160 days servitude [22.pdf #163]; Alice Magraugh, servant to

RECAPTURED RUNAWAYS

John Beale, 14 August 1705, 28 days absence, 280 days servitude, and four months for "four hundred pounds of tobacco paid for twice takeing her up" [23.pdf #88]; Alice Magrah, servant to John Beale, 13 August 1706, ordered to "serve Mr. John Beale untill the twenty ninth day of September next for fees paid for her" [23.pdf #138]

Magrah, Richard, servant to Francis Goodrick, 9 November 1725, 32 days absence, ordered to serve "eight days for one of his runaway time" (256 days servitude) [30.pdf #49]

Mahoone, Daniell, servant to Thomas Craxstone, 8 March 1692, absent twice, 5 days in all, 50 days servitude [17.pdf #209]

Mandam, Charles, servant to George Brett, 14 November 1704, servant confessing, 20 days absence, 200 days servitude [23.pdf #36]

Marden, John, servant to Samuel Williams, 8 June 1725, 4 days absence, ordered to serve "three days for one of his runaway time" (12 days servitude) [30.pdf # 4]

Martin, Thomas, servant to John Leverat, 10 March 1713, 36 days absence, (360 days servitude) [25.pdf #118]

Mattock, George, servant to Andrew Clarke, 13 September 1687, servant confessing, 45 days absence, ordered to serve "tenne dayes for one according to act of assemblie" (450 days servitude), "and further ordered that in consideration of ye said Andrews trouble & charge in taking up ye said runaway servant & bringing him home he ye said Andrew shall be allowed three hundred pounds of tobaccoe to be paid by ye said servant immediately upon his freedome or for default of such payment ye said servant to serve his said master three months for & in consideration of ye same" [14.pdf #158]

Maybanke, Elizabeth, servant to Philip Lynes, 13 June 1683 "hath severall times runn away & absented her selfe from her said masters service without his leave or license," ordered to serve "her said master or his assignes ye full & just tearme of three yeares & noe more" [11.pdf #128]; "Elizabeth Maybancke released from Mr. Lynes to Edward Mings all manner of crymes released onely five yeares to Edward Mings," 10 June 1684 [11.pdf #204].

McAvoy, Laurance, servant to John Nalley, Gent., 13 June 1732, 16 days absence, on "oath in Court here" of "James Taylor his former master," ordered to "serve his present master John Nalley five days for each one of his runaway time aforesaid" (80 days servitude) [32.pdf #77]

RECAPTURED RUNAWAYS

Miles, Daniel, servant to William Morphy, 14 November 1727, 34 days absence upon oath of "Doctor Alexander Adair his late master," ordered to "serve said Morphy eight dayes for one of his runaway time" (272 days servitude) [31.pdf #18]

Miles, Francis, servant to Philip Lynes, 1695, "judgment of runaway time" [Liber T Page 216]

Mohoy, James, servant to Thomas Stonestreet, 13 March 1705, 9 days absence, 90 days servitude [23.pdf #47]

Moldoone, Laughlin, servant to Ignatius Wheeler, 9 March 1697, 25 days absence, 250 days servitude [19.pdf #110, 111]

Mollatto Will, servant to Capt. Benoni Thomas, 11 June 1706, servant confessing, 180 days absence, 1800 days servitude, and "four yeares more for eighteen hundred pounds of tobacco and two pounds and sixpence sterling paid for takeing him up" [23.pdf #123]

Moody, William, servant to John Hawkins, 9 January 1694, "ye said Hawkins appearing here & testifying in Court that had not any wayes abused or wronged him but only desired & requested that hee might serve him seaven moneths after ye expiration of his time of servitude, for seaven moneths time that hee had run away & absented himselfe out of his service," ordered by Court that William Moody "serve ye said John Hawkins till his time of servitude is expired which is in March next coming," and "seaven moneths more for seaven monthes hee was absent of ye service of ye said John Hawkins hee ye said William Moody owneing ye same here in Court" [18.pdf #129]

Morden, Roger, servant to Thomas Matthews, 9 March 1725, 11 days absence, 77 days servitude [29.pdf #25]

Morgan, Elizabeth, servant to John Bowld, 14 March 1693, absent "severall times," 100 days in all, 1000 days servitude, and ordered that "ye said John Bowld bring a coppy of ye records from Newtown Court for what runaway time shee was adjudged for there" [18.pdf #72]

Morgan, Roger, servant to William Macferson, 12 March 1728, 10 days absence, ordered to serve "seven days for one of his runaway time" (70 days servitude), and "three months for what it appears he expended in takeing him up" (31.pdf #36]

Morris, Ellice, servant to James Neale, 8 June 1686, 14 days absence, 140 days servitude, "and allsoe make such other sattisfacion for his trouble & charge" of bringing him home [13.pdf #117]

RECAPTURED RUNAWAYS

Morris, Griffith, servant to Edward Williams, 13 August 1700, servant confessing "in Court," absent 80 days "when he was Jesse Doynes servant," and 38 days "since he was the said Williams's servant," 118 days in all, 1180 days servitude [21.pdf #19]; ordered by Court "that Jesse Doyne pay to Jonas Farloe the summe of two hundred pounds of tobacco for bringing home his runnaway servant Griffith Morris, 14 November 1699 [20.pdf #101]; Griffith Morris, servant to Jesse Doyne, 9 January 1700, given thirty nine lashes on the bare back [20.pdf #133]

Munroe, Andrew, servant to William Annis, 11 June 1728, 50 days absence from "the Reverend Mr. Hugh Jones his late master," ordered to serve "six days for one of his runaway time" (300 days servitude), and six months "for what appears to have been expended in takeing him up" [31.pdf #61]

Murfey, Owen, servant to Gerrard Fowke, 13 March 1705, 10 days absence, 100 days servitude "to commence from the fifteenth of February last" [23.pdf #46]

Newton, John, servant to Henry Hawkins, 14 June 1687, 10 days absence, 100 days servitude [14.pdf #142]

Norris, Caleb, servant to Henry Norris, 9 March 1698, 42 days absence, 420 days servitude [19.pdf #200]

Oliver, John, servant to Stephen Mankin, 10 August 1697, two years absence, twenty years servitude, "Stephen Mankin doth acknowledge to be content with four yeares service from ye last day of October next ensueing in case ye said John Oliver shall not unlawfully absent himselfe out of his service during that time" [19.pdf #136]

Palmer, John, servant to Dr. Gustavus Brown, 10 November 1724, 148 days absence, and "two hundred pounds of tobacco expended in taking him up," ordered to serve "tenn days for one of his runnaway time (1480 days servitude) & tenn weeks for the expences aforesaid [29.pdf # 7]; John Palmer, servant to James Maddox, 14 November 1727, 3 days absence, ordered to serve "five dayes for one of the runaway time" (15 days servitude) [31.pdf #18]

Palmer, Martha, servant to Edward Daviss, 9 August 1720, 23 days absence from "her former master William Chapman," ordered to serve "eight days for one of her runaway time" (184 days servitude) [27.pdf #13]

Paul, Elizabeth, servant to Philip Mason, 10 November 1691, absent "severall times," 170 days in all, 1700 days servitude [17.pdf #157]

RECAPTURED RUNAWAYS

Pears (?), Mary, servant to Randolph Garland, 8 March 1720, 12 days absence "out of his service," ordered to serve "tenn days for one" (120 days servitude), and three months for "two hundred pounds of tobacco" expended "in regaining her," adjudged also for 6 days absence "from her late master Thomas Orrell of whom ye said Randolph Garland purchased her," 60 days servitude [26.pdf #161]

Pell, William, servant to Samuel Barber, 13 March 1722, servant confessing, 14 days absence, ordered to serve "five days for one of his runaway time" (70 days servitude), and six weeks "for two hundred pounds of tobacco expended in taking him up" [27.pdf #126]

Penney, Ann, servant to Prudence Standish, 11 November 1701, servant confessing, 37 days absence, 370 days servitude [21.pdf #159]

Perrie, Mathew, servant to James Neale, 8 June 1686, 14 days absence, 140 days servitude, "and allsoe make such other sattisfacion for his trouble & charge" of bringing him home [13.pdf #117]

Perry, Thomas, servant to Cornelius White, 14 November 1710, servant confessing, 70 days absence, "adjudged to serve according to act," (700 days servitude), "and for foure hundred pounds of tobacco, which the said Cornelius White hath expended for the recovery of him, he is adjudged to serve foure months" [24.pdf #32]

Pillett, Joseph, servant to Daniel McDaniel, 10 March 1724, 35 days absence, and "two hundred & eighty pounds of tobacco expended in taking him up," ordered to serve eight days for one of his runaway time (280 days servitude), and three months "for the charges aforesaid" [28.pdf #122]

Poore, Ellinor, servant to Peter Mills, 13 February 1700, servant confessing "in Court," 30 days absence, 300 days servitude [20.pdf #142]

Powell, Elizabeth, servant to Philip Lines, 10 August 1681, arrived in Maryland "ye 21st day of December last past" and "five yeares agoe," 12 days absence, (120 days servitude) [10.pdf #94]; Elizabeth Powell, servant to Philip Lines, 10 January 1682, 4 days absence, 40 days servitude, and three months for "foure hundred pounds of tobaccoe for taking her up "in Virginia" [10.pdf #135]

Powell, Thomas, servant to Philip Lines, 10 August 1681, arrived in Maryland "ye 21st day of December last past" and "five yeares agoe," 15 days absence, (150 days servitude) [10.pdf #94]; Thomas Powell, servant to Philip Lines, 10 January 1682, 4 days absence, 40 days servitude, and three months for "foure hundred pounds of tobaccoe for taking him up "in Virginia" [10.pdf #135]

RECAPTURED RUNAWAYS

Price, John, servant of Joshuah Graves "by assignment" of Thomas Hussey, 14 June 1687, "did in time of his service with his master Hussey absent himselfe" 23 days, 230 days servitude [14.pdf #142]

Procter, Elizabeth, servant to William Boreman, 14 August 1705, servant confessing, 18 days absence, 180 days servitude [23.pdf #89]

Puttuck, William, servant to Peter Ferdinando, 9 March 1708, servant confessing, 37 days absence, 370 days servitude [23.pdf #235]

Read, Anne, servant to Doctor Gustavus Brown, 8 March 1715, 65 days absence, (650 days servitude), and eight months for "six hundred pounds of tobacco" "expended in regaining her" [25.pdf #265]

Richardson, John, servant to William Witter, June 1716, "judgment of his runaway time" [Liber G Page 100]

Rigby, Alexander, servant to Thomas Jannson (?), 13 March 1711, 57 days absence, (570 days servitude) [24.pdf #58]

Rigby, Edward, servant to Thomas Jannson (?), 14 March 1710, 19 days absence, 190 days servitude, "and for two hundred pounds of tobacco which he hath expended the said Rigby is to serve two months by the Court here likewise adjudged" [23.pdf #375]

Roberds, William, servant to William Clerk, 13 March 1688, 143 days absence, 1430 days servitude [14.pdf #176]

Roberts, Ellnor, servant to William Newman, 14 November 1710, 15 days absence, (150 days servitude) [24.pdf #29]

Roberts, William, servant to Edward Saunders, 8 November 1681, five absences, 81 days "in all," 810 days servitude, assigned by Edward Saunders "unto Edward Gale for ye time of his servitude & for his runing away" [10.pdf #112]

Robbinson, John, servant to Capt. James Keech, 12 September 1704, 10 days absence "proved by the oath of the said Capt. James Keech," and 28 days absence "proved by the oath of James Mackoy," 38 days in all, 380 days servitude [23.pdf #33]; ordered by Court that six days runaway time be deducted "amounting to sixty days at tenn days per one," 12 June 1705 [23.pdf #79]

Robinson, Peter, servant to Mrs. Anne Story, "Relict of Col. Walter Story," 8 March 1726, 30 days absence, ordered to "serve the legal representatives of said Walter Story four days for one of his runaway time" (120 days servitude) [30.pdf #64]

Robinson, Thomas, servant to Phillip Lynes, 12 June 1688, "ye full space of" two years absence, "ye said Mr. Lynes came into Court & declared himselfe to be sattisfied with seaven yeares service provided ye said Thomas Robinson shall serve ye same duely & truely without runing away," and "in case ye said Robinson shall not serve ye said seaven yeares duely & truely as aforesaid that then ye said Robinson shall serve his said master" according to Act of Assembly" (twenty years servitude) [14. pdf #178]

Roder, John, servant to Charles Phillpot, 9 November 1725, 57 days absence, and "two hundred pounds of tobacco" expended "in taking him up," ordered to serve "four days for one of his runaway time" (228 days servitude), and "six months for the expences aforesaid" [30.pdf #49]

Ross, Angus, servant to Thomas Coombs, 9 November 1731, 65 days absence, and "eight hundred and forty pounds of tobacco" expended "in takeing him up," ordered to serve "two days for each one of his runaway time" (130 days servitude), and "one month for each hundred pounds of tobacco for his expences aforesaid" [32.pdf #15]

Rouz, James, servant to Capt. Ignatius Causin, 8 March 1681, 221 days absence, 2210 days servitude, master agrees to set him free in four years if "his servant serve him faithfully without running away" [10.pdf #59, 60]

Rowaine, John, servant to Thomas Hackett, 10 August 1703, 40 days absence, 400 days servitude, and "two hundred pounds of tobacco or two months service more for takeing him up when Runn away" [22.pdf #125]

Rue, Elizabeth, servant to Richard Clowder, 13 March 1688, "hath absented herselfe four months at 28 dayes per month," 1120 days servitude [14.pdf #175]

Russell, Daniel, and Christopher Collins, servants to Humphrey Bell "of London, Merchant," 11 August 1730, presented by John Parnham, servants confessing, "the said Parnham makes oath that acording to Capt. Reynolds information they absented themselves seven days from said Bells service, and that he paid on behalf of the said Bell four hundred pounds of tobacco and twenty shillings in charges and expences in takeing them up," ordered to serve "seven days for one of their runaway time" (49 days servitude), and four months "for the expences aforesaid" [31.pdf #210]

Ruth, Thomas, servant to Jacob Morris, 11 March 1701, "to be adjudged for runaway time, continued untill the next court then both partyes to appear" [21.pdf #94]. Thomas Ruth, servant to James Morris, 11 November 1701, 20 days absence, "ordered to serve according to Act," (200 days servitude) [21.pdf #160]

RECAPTURED RUNAWAYS

Sall, John, servant to William Marloe, 14 November 1721, 2 days absence "proved by the Oath of his former master Henry Acton and two hundred pounds of tobacco paid for taking him up," 35 days servitude [27.pdf #108]

Scott, Thomas, servant to William Thompson "by assignment of George Geer," 110 days absence, "confessed by ye said servant," 1100 days servitude [14.pdf #142]

Sidney, Nathaniell, servant to Margarett Hungerford, 13 March 1705, servant confessing, 5 days absence, 50 days servitude, and two months "for two hundred pounds of tobacco paid for takeing him up" [23.pdf #47]

Smith, Charles, servant to Marke Lampton, 14 June 1692, 56 days absence, 560 days servitude [17.pdf #233]

Smith, John, servant to William Hardy, 13 January 1708, servant confessing, 26 days absence, 260 days servitude, and thirty days "for two hundred pounds of tobacco paid for takeing him up" [23.pdf #230]

Smith, Mary, "formerly" servant to James Smallwood "and now" servant to Humphrey Jones, 15 December 1686, "did in time of her service with her master Smallwood absent herselfe" 60 days, 600 days servitude [14.pdf #8, 9]

Smith, William, servant to Richard Land, 12 January 1692, "Came here into Courte and acknowledged to serve three years & eight moneths wanting thirteen dayes" [17.pdf #190]

Southerly, David, servant to Mrs. Elizabeth Hawkins, 14 August 1705, 7 days absence, 70 days servitude [23.pdf #88]

Steele, John, servant to William Stone, 8 June 1725, 18 days absence, and "two hundred pounds of tobacco" expended "in taking him up," ordered to serve "ten days for one of his runaway time" (180 days servitude), and "three months for the expences aforesaid" [30.pdf #4]

Stephens, James, servant to Charles Musgrave, 13 August 1728, 8 days absence, and "one hundred seventy four pounds of tobacco," ordered to serve "six dayes for one of his runaway time" (48 days servitude), and two months "for the expenses aforesaid" [31.pdf #77]

Stevens, James, servant to Ignatius Lucket, 10 August 1725, 4 days absence, ordered to serve "five days for one of his runaway time" (20 days servitude) [30.pdf #28]

Sumerton, William, servant to Gilbert Clarke, 10 August 1697, absent "severall times," 34 days in all, 340 days servitude, and also two months for "four hundred pounds of tobaccoe paid for ye takeing up ye said William Sumerton in ye Colony of Virginia," or else to pay four hundred pounds of tobacco ready down" [19.pdf #135, 136]

Sutton, John, servant to Eleanor Philpot, 8 March 1720, 6 days absence, ordered to serve "tenn days for one of ye runaway time" 60 days servitude [26.pdf #161]

Symmons, Mary, servant to Capt. Henry Hardy, 10 September 1706, "to be adjudged for runaway time," whereupon the matter in controversy was heard, and the Court ordered "that the said Mary Symmons be free from the said Capt. Henry Hardys service" [23.pdf #141]

Taylor, Daniel, servant to Philip Lynes, 8 November 1687, 13 months absence, ordered by Court that "provided ye said Daniel Taylor shall & doe serve his said master or his assignes duelie & truely six yeares from this present day ye same shall suffice & be accepted of by ye said Mr. Lynes for his whole servitude & ye said Daniel to be set free or otherwise ye said Daniel over & above his first time of servitude due shall serve his said master or his assignes for ye whole runaway time according to act of Assemblie in ye case made & provided without remission of one day or houre thereof" [14.pdf #160]

Taylor, George, servant to Henry Tanner, 4 April 1704, 4 days absence, 40 days servitude, "and whereas the said Henry Tanner alledges that there was fourteen days more due when he was Marke Lamptons servant the same is continued till he makes due proofe of the same" [22.pdf #194]

Taylor, Henry, servant to John Club, 8 June 1725, 20 days absence "proved by the oath of Alexander Contee his former master," and 7 days absence "by the oath of said Clubb," 27 days in all, ordered to serve "six days for one of his runaway time" (162 days servitude) [30.pdf #4]

Thompson, John, servant to Capt. John Hany "of ye head of Chococeone in Virginia," 10 June 1690, taken up by William Sarjeant [17.pdf #18]

Thornley, Thomas, servant to Thomas Green, 10 June 1707, servant confessing, 6 days absence, 60 days servitude [23.pdf #180]

Todd, Jeremiah, servant to John Beale, 12 January 1703, "being lately hired to John Bannister," servant confessing, 8 days absence, 80 days servitude, to "the said John Bannister" "after ye expiration of his time to Mr. Beale [22.pdf #80]; Jeremiah Todd, servant to John Beale, 14 September 1703, servant confessing "here in Court,"

RECAPTURED RUNAWAYS

37 days absence, 370 days servitude [22.pdf # 130]; Jeremiah Todd, servant to John Beale, 12 March 1706, "alledging in Court that he hath paid one thousand and tenne pounds of tobacco for takeing his servant Jeremiah Todd up when runaway and also two hundred pounds of tobacco more paid by John Bannister," ordered by Court that "Jeremiah Todd doe serve the said John Beale one whole yeare and a halfe for the tobacco fee paid" [23.pdf #115]

Toy, Walter, servant to John Frazier, 12 June 1711, servant confessing, 8 days absence, 64 days servitude, and two months "for what his said master makes appear to ye Court to have laid out and expended" [24.pdf #97]

Turlayes, Teague, servant to Philip Lynes, 10 November 1696, absent "severall times," "proved here in Court by ye said Philip Lynes his oath and ye oathes of John Wincell & Christopher Gregory," 240 days in all, "but ye said Teague Turlayes went severall times to complaine," and "ye Court here doth thinke fitt to deduct forty dayes out of ye said amount," 2000 days servitude [19.pdf #73]

Turner, Thomas, servant to Thomas Coombes, 10 November 1724, 4 days absence, and "two hundred pounds tobacco" expended "in taking him up," ordered to serve "tenn weeks in satisfaction of the runaway time & expences aforesaid" [29.pdf #7]

Tytchett, Mary, servant to John Davis, 10 March 1719, servant confessing, 17 days absence from "her late master John Pigeon," ordered to serve "five days for one" (85 days servitude) [26.pdf #96]

Underwood, Charles, servant to John Chandler, 14 November 1727, 15 days absence, and "five hundred pounds of tobacco" expended "in taking him up," ordered to serve "eight dayes for one of his runaway time" (120 days servitude), and "three months and a half for the expences aforesaid" [31.pdf #18]

Vearly, William, servant to George Plater, 8 January 1706, presented by Daniell Dunn, servant confessing "in Court," 2 days absence, 20 days servitude [23.pdf #111]

Walker, Edward, servant to Richard Wade, 14 November 1710, servant confessing, 97 days absence, (970 days servitude), and four months "for foure hundred pounds of tobacco expended for recovering him" [24.pdf #29]

Ware, Alexander, servant to John Godshall, 14 March 1710, servant confessing, 7 days absence, 70 days servitude, and six months "for seven hundred pounds of tobacco expended towards the obtaineing the said servant [23.pdf #372]; Alexander Waire, servant to Pryor Smallwood, 14 November 1710, 69 days absence, (690 days servitude), and two months "for two hundred pounds of tobacco which the said Smallwood hath laid out and expended for recovering him" [24.pdf #29]

Waters, Edward, servant to Richard Wade, 9 November 1708, 62 days absence, 620 days servitude, and two months "for two hundred and fifty pounds of tobacco paid and expended for the takeing him upp" [23.pdf #279]

Waters, James, servant to John Fairfax, 11 August 1724, 13 days absence, and "two hundred pounds of tobacco" expended "in taking him up," ordered to serve "tenn days for one of the runaway time" (130 days servitude), and sixty days "for the expenses aforesaid" [28.pdf #185]

Watkins, John, servant to Philemon Hemsley, "formerly belonging to Edward Clements," 11 March 1712, servant confessing, 13 days absence, 130 days servitude [25.pdf #34]

Webb, Hugh, servant to Coll. Humphrey Warren, 8 November 1692, servant confessing "here in Court," 42 days absence, 420 days servitude [17.pdf #276]

Welch, James, servant to Major James Smallwood, 10 January 1699, servant confessing "here in Court," absent "severall times," 85 days in all, 850 days servitude [20.pdf # 4]

Welsh, Michael, servant to John Wilkinson, 8 November 1720, servant confessing "in Court," 4 days absence, 40 days servitude, and two months for "two hundred pounds of tobacco" expended "in taking up the said servant" [27.pdf #30]

Welsh, Michael, servant to Courts Keech, 8 August 1721, master's petition "sets forth that his servant named Michael Welsh has absconded from his service & that he is detained by John Chandler," and the Court summons John Chandler "to answer said complaint & ye aforesaid servant may be remanded to his service" [27.pdf #92]

Whit(e)head, John, servant to Captain Humphery Warren, 8 January 1684, 16 days absence, ordered to serve "such proportion of tyme (in consideration of his said running away as by act of Assembly is required)," (160 days servitude), and to "reimburse his said master 200 pounds of tobacco by him expended for his taking up according to agreement between said master & servant [11.pdf #187]

Wiggsby, George, servant to William Herbert, 10 September 1700, "formerly John Loftans servant," confessing "in Court," 20 days absence, 200 days servitude [21.pdf #41]

RECAPTURED RUNAWAYS

Wild, Catherine, servant to John Smoot, 9 March 1725, "formerly servant to Thomas Sharp of Virginia," 223 days absence "proved by the oath of said Sharpe her former master & six hundred & twenty pounds of tobacco expended in taking her up," ordered to serve "two days for one of her runaway time according to the Directions of the Virginia Law" (446 days servitude), and "ten months for the tobacco aforesaid," and "six weeks for ten shillings proved by the oath of said Sharpe to have likewise expended" [29.pdf #25]

Williams, Eleanor, servant to Justinian Birch, 14 November 1721, 14 days absence, and "two hundred pounds of tobacco expended in taking her up," ordered to serve "six dayes for one" (84 days servitude), and three months "for ye expences aforesaid" [27.pdf #108]

Williams, Henry, servant to Coll. James Smallwood, 9 March 1708, servant confessing, 180 days absence, master states "in Open Court that if the said Henry Williams doth well and truely serve him three years from this instant March" "he will remitt the runaway time aforesaid and all charges accrewing thereon" [23.pdf #235]

Williams, Hugh, servant to Robert Henly, 10 January 1682, servant confessing "in open court," 164 days absence, 1640 days servitude, and "three months for foure hundred pounds of tobaccoe disburst for his takeing up "in Virginia" [10.pdf #133]

Williams, Mary, servant to John Marten, 10 March 1724, 35 days absence, and "two hundred pounds of tobacco expended in taking her up," ordered to serve "eight days for one of her runaway time" (280 days servitude), and three months "for the charges aforesaid" [28.pdf #122]; Mary Williams, servant to James Parrandier, 14 March 1727, 50 days absence, and "four hundred pounds of tobacco" expended "in taking her up," by oath of "John Marten, with whom the said Mary had served part of her time," and 6 days absence from "John Hanley her late master," 56 days in all, ordered to serve "six days for each one of her runaway time," (336 days servitude), and eight months "for the expences aforesaid" [30.pdf #209]

Williamson, Mary, servant to one Goffe in Virginia, 14 November 1699, "by Capt. Richard Hill conveyed to Thomas Coleman Constable of Benedict Hundred in Charles County," "Ordered That ye said Thomas Coleman send to her Master Mr. Goffe in Virginia to give him notice of his said Servant to fetch her away & soe that he may have sattisfaction for his trouble in looking after her" [20.pdf #99]

RECAPTURED RUNAWAYS

Willson, James, servant to Robert Greene, 10 April 1705, servant confessing, 5 days absence, 50 days servitude, and two months for "two hundred pounds of tobacco paid for takeing him up" [23.pdf #63]

Wood, Anne, servant to Henry Tanner, 14 June 1709, servant confessing, 8 days absence, 80 days servitude [23.pdf #305]

Wood, Susanna, servant to Richard Land, 9 September 1690, 7 days absence, 70 days servitude [17.pdf #36]

Wormely, Mary, servant to Thomas Price, 11 June 1723, 15 days absence "proved by the oath of John Barker her former master," and "six hundred pounds of tobacco expending in taking her up," ordered to serve "five days for one of her runaway time" (75 days servitude), and one year for the expences aforesaid" [28.pdf #53]

Wormely, Thomas, servant to Peter Ferdinando, 8 June 1703, 38 days absence "proved by the Oath of John Paine," 380 days servitude [22.pdf #105]

Wright, William and wife, servants to Jonathan White, 13 November 1711, presented by Cornelius White his brother "by vertue of a warrant to the Constable of Benedict Hundred directed," 11 days absence, 110 days servitude [25.pdf #15]

Youngsen, John, servant to Major Robert Hansen, 12 November 1728, 35 days absence, and "two hundred pounds of tobacco and three shillings" expended "in takeing him up," ordered to serve "ten dayes for one of his runaway time" (350 days servitude), and two months "for the expences aforesaid" [31.pdf #96]

(illegible), Thomas, servant to Joseph Manning, 10 March 1713, servant confessing, 20 days absence, "adjudged to serve according to law" (200 days servitude) [25.pdf #118]

__ ain, John, servant to Alexander McFearson, 13 November 1722, presented by John Cornwell, 21 days absence, and "fifty two shillings expended in taking up the said servant proved by the oath of John Cornwell, and 5 days absence, and "two hundred pounds of tobacco in like manner proved by ye oath of Samuel Warren," 26 days in all, ordered to serve "eight days for one" (208 days servitude), and six months "for the charges aforesaid" [28.pdf #7]

___ ie, William, servant to William Roch, 14 March 1710, servant confessing, 33 days absence, 330 days servitude, and two months for "two hundred pounds of tobacco which the said Roch has expended towards ye obtaineing his said servant" [23.pdf #372]

_____ , ____ , servant to William Smallwood, 14 January 1701, servant confessing "in Court," 200 days absence, 2000 days servitude [21.pdf #69]

RECAPTURED RUNAWAYS, ELSEWHERE IN THE RECORD

Ball, Silent, 11 November 1690 [17.pdf #69]; 11 September 1694 [18.pdf #94]; 11 August 1696 [19.pdf #41] & 8 June 1697 [19.pdf #130]. Presentment by Grand Jury, 10 November 1702 [22.pdf #63, #90].

Barker, Thomas, 12 August 1690 [17.pdf #30]. Deaths and Estates, 13 August 1700 [21.pdf #33].

Browne, William, 12 August 1712 [25.pdf #90]. Gifts of Livestock, 1690 [16.pdf #118].

Cheatham, Joseph, March 1716 [Liber G Page 47]. Gifts of Livestock, 28 October 1731 [Liber M Page 266].

Fountain, Thomas, "a Mollottoe," 11 March 1729 [31.pdf #118]. Index to Orphans, 14 March 1704 [22.pdf #163].

Ganer, Taddy, 9 March 1697 [19.pdf #111]. Presentment by Grand Jury, 11 June 1700 [21.pdf #9].

Glover, John, "a mollato," 13 November 1711 [25.pdf #16]. Vital Records, February 1680 [22.pdf #125].

Groves, William, 14 January 1707 [23.pdf #161]. Vital Records, 24 May 1690 [Liber Q Page 16].

Hagon, John, 13 March 1705 [23.pdf #47]. Probably the brother of Ann Hagon, Vital Records, 3 November 1713 [24.pdf #195].

Hawkins, John, 10 January 1682 [10.pdf #134]. Deaths and Estates, 9 August 1709 [23.pdf #344].

Hoskins, William, 11 August 1713 [25.pdf #172]. Index to Deeds, 12 December 1717 [Liber H Page 120].

Jones, Mary, 10 August 1697 [19.pdf #135]. Vital Records, 27 May 1677 [16.pdf #120].

Lewis, Edward, 10 January 1699 [20.pdf #4]. Deaths and Estates, 10 March 1702 [22.pdf #4].

Moody, William, 9 January 1694 [18.pdf #129]. Index to Orphans, 3 December 1700 [21.pdf #57].

Penney, Ann, 11 November 1701 [21.pdf #159]. Index to Orphans, 22 December 1703 [Liber C Page 82].

Roberds, William, 13 March 1688 [14.pdf #176]. Index to Orphans, 14 June 1687 [14.pdf #141].

Rue, Elizabeth, 13 March 1688 [14.pdf #175]. Index to Orphans, 8 March 1692 [17.pdf #209].

Ruth, Thomas, 11 November 1701 [21.pdf #160]. Probably the father of Elizabeth Ruth, Index to Orphans, 8 June 1714 [25.pdf #219].

Thompson, John, 10 June 1690 [17.pdf #18]. Vital Records, 8 January 1695 [Liber Q Page 25].

PETITIONS FOR FREEDOM

Adames, James, servant to Philip Lynes, 11 March 1690, "produceing an Indenture in Court that hee had but ye tearme of four yeares to serve," and "alledgeing here that Mr. William Settle who sold him to ye said Philip Lynes could testify upon oath that hee ye said Settle sold him for noe longer time to ye said Philip Lynes then ye tearme of four yeares," "and that ye said William Settle did see ye said Indenture signed sealed & delivered," "and requesting that some time might be allowed him to goe up into Ann Arundell County to ye said William Settle to gett his deposition to testifye ye same," "his said master consenting thereunto in Court," ordered by Court "to have tenne dayes liberty" "to get ye said William Settles deposition attested before two Justices of ye peace" [16.pdf #114]; James Adames, servant to Philip Lynes, 10 June 1690, "produceing here ye deposition of ye said William Settle that he sold him but for ye tearme of four yeares & noe longer, and it appearing to ye Court here that ye said James Adames had served ye said Philip Lynes two months over & above ye four yeares hee was sold for," ordered by Court "that ye said Philip Lynes doe pay unto ye said James Adames ye sume of two hundred pounds of tobacco" [17.pdf #18]

Ambros, David, servant to Philip Lynes, 9 June 1691, "produced this ensueing certificate here in Court" -- "These are to certify that on or about ye 24th day of May in ye yeare of our Lord 1689 came in a vessell belonging to mee, one Kelley Inerehaut (?) brought with him four passengers as servants three of them hee sold for two yeares each of them and furthermore one David Ambros was to my certaine knowledge disposed of unto Philip Lynes for noe more then for ye tearme of two yeares from his arrivall here in testimony of which I have sett my hand & seale this fifth day of June 1691, John Edmondson, delivered in ye presence of David Small & Archibald Edmonston," ordered by Court "that ye said David Ambros be discharged & acquitt from ye service of ye said Philip Lynes" [17.pdf #115]

Andrews, Elizabeth, servant to Patrick Connolley, 9 June 1724, petition "for her freedom is rejected" [28.pdf #157]

Archbald, John, servant to Henry Hawkins Junior, 10 June 1690, with six other servants, "it appeareing by ye Oath of Mr. John Bowman who transported them into this Countrey that hee had ye counterparts of their Indentures & did reade them aboard of his ship at Gravesend, and they were kidnappers Indentures but whether they were good or not hee could not tell, and noe proofe appearing here in Court that

PETITIONS FOR FREEDOM

ye said Indentures were signed sealed & delivered by ye said John Williams with whom they did indent, & ye same not being under ye seale of an Office, or under ye hand of any Justice of ye peace," ordered by Court to "returne to their severall masters service & serve acording to ye Custome of ye Countrey, their Indentures being adjudged invalide by ye Courte" (age not judged -- ed.) [17.pdf #18]

Arrington, Francis, servant to Thomas Thompson, 12 November 1728, "on the complaint of Francis Arrington that Thomas Thompson unjustly detains him as a servant by an Indenture entered into by the said Francis in time of his minority and without the consent of either parent or guardian," ordered by Court "that ye said Arrington be discharged from his service aforesaid" [31.pdf #96]

Attkinson, Margarett, servant to Richard Hodgson, 13 January 1680, "whereas your petitioner upon ye 23d day of November 1675 arrived in this Province in ye ship Antilope of Liverpoole, Capt. Crosman Comander, as a servant by Indenture for ye tearme of foure yeares, to begin from & after ye said arrivall, which tearme of foure yeares on ye 23d day of November last was expired, & your petitioner became a free woman, as by a discharge under ye hand of Richard Hodgson, with whome shee served ye last part of her time," ye said Richard Hodgson "refuseth to pay & deliver unto her freedome corne cloathes workeing tools," "and ye said Richard Hodgson appeares by Thomas Lomax his attorney & produces another Indenture wherein ye said Margarett Attkinson had covenanted with ye said Richard Hodgson for one yeares service more, & pleads that in satisfaction of her corne & clothes that hee had discharged ye said Margarett Attkinson from her first time of servitude above one moneth before it was expired," but ye said Margarett Attkinson "having proved her time to be fully expired by ye oath of Mr. John Addisson, and it being contrary to ye Lawes of this Province that any master should make any bargaine with any servant for any time longer, not untill his first time of servitude be fully expired," ordered by Court "that Margarett Attkinson bee freed & discharged from ye service of Richard Hodgson, & that Richard Hodgson pay unto ye said Margarett Attkinson her freedome corne cloathes & workeing tooles that are due unto her by ye Law & according to ye custome of this Province, with cost of suite" [09.pdf #141]; see also [09.pdf #152]

PETITIONS FOR FREEDOM

Bald, Sarah, servant to Philip Lines, 11 June 1678, "your petitioner had Indentures for foure yeares, which now is lost, & have good wittnes to testifie it," "and ye said Sarah Bald haveing made it appeare by ye oathes of Thomas Hussy & Johannah his wife that they did heare Joseph Pearse upon his death bed declare that hee sold her to Philip Lines but for foure yeares & that shee should serve noe longer, & further that ye said Pearse did declare that shee had an Indenture for ye tearme of foure yeares & noe longer," ordered by Court "that Sarah Bald be free from ye service of Philip Lines" [08.pdf #93]

Barnes, Thomas, servant to Thomas Baker, 8 June 1686, ordered by Court to "returne to his present master John Harrison & serve him till ye tenth of November next & that then the said servant goe free and to have sattisfaction for what is his due out of ye deceased Bakers Estate" [13.pdf #117]

Bass, John, servant to Robert Thompson Junr., 11 November 1690, "produceing an Indenture here in Court," "and noe sufficient testimony of ye same appeareing," ordered by Court to serve "according to ye custome of ye countrey, unless hee can produce better pooofe to his Indenture" [17.pdf #69]

Benlow, George, late servant to William Harbert, 13 March 1705, "petitions the Court for corne and cloaths and a sett of taylors tools, the said Mr. Harbert being then in Court saith he will give him what the law in such cases requires, therefore the said petition is rejected" [23.pdf #47]

Bennett, John, servant to Hugh French, see Encyclopedia of Survivors

Bennet, John, servant to George Godfrey see Encyclopedia of Survivors

Bennett, Richard, former servant to George Godfrey, 10 March 1702, "whereas your petitioner came into this country a servant for five yeares and was sold to Lt. Coll. James Smallwood and then sold and assigned over to George Godfrey to whome he hath well and truely served his full time of servitude yett nevertheless the said George Godfrey to pay your petitioner his corne and cloaths and other things which the law allowes him doth refuse by reason he saith he is not oblidged to pay the same because he was first sould to Collonell Smallwood soe between them boath your petitioner is like to be defrauded of his just rights," ordered by Court "that the last master ought to pay itt" [22.pdf #22]

PETITIONS FOR FREEDOM

Bennett, Thomas, servant to Philip Lynes, 11 August 1691, "whereas your petitioner hath honestly & faithfully served his time with Mr. Philip Lynes long since, notwithstanding ye said Lynes hath detained your petitioner as his servant for near these two yeares for what reason your petitioner knoweth not," "whereupon ye wittnesses here in Court being produced sworne heard & examined," "it is ordered that ye said Thomas Bennett bee free & discharged from ye servitude of ye said Philip Lynes" [17.pdf #138]

Benson, Patrick, servant to Capt. William Barton, 11 November 1679, "William Barrett of ye City of London merchant did transport your petitioner into this Province of Maryland, and your humble petitioner" "did covenant & agree with ye said William Barrett at Gravesend to serve him or his assignes ye full tearme of foure yeares next after his arrivall here into this Province, & for ye performance of which ye said William Barrett did give your petitioner a noate under his hand at Gravesend that hee should serve noe longer time," "and whereas your petitioner hath faithfully & truely served Capt. William Barton one of his Lordshipps Justices for this County ye assignee of ye said William Barrett ye full & just tearme of foure yeares," "& ye said William Barton doth refuse to lett your petitioner have his freedome," "your humble petitioner humbly craves" that "hee might have his freedome, & his corne & cloathes & other things that are his due according to ye custome of ye country" "and ye said Patrick Benson haveing made appeare by ye oathes of John Raines & David Dickson that hee had a noate from under William Barretts hand that hee should serve noe longer than foure yeares, & that they did see & reade ye said noate, & William Barrett being about to sell him to Mr. Henry Adames, Mr. Adames understanding of ye noate, hee would not buy him," ordered by Court "that ye said Patrick Benson bee free from ye service of Capt. William Barton his time being fully expired according to his agreement with William Barrett" [09.pdf #130]

Birke, John, "a Mollatto," servant to Mrs. Elizabeth Hawkins, 10 June 1707, "desires that he may be free being twenty one yeares and produceth for evidence Mary the wife of William Elliot formerly the wife of Henry Brawner who sold the said Mollatto to Mr. Henry Hawkins deceased," ordered by Court "that the said Mollatto is free att twenty one yeares of age" [23.pdf #181]

PETITIONS FOR FREEDOM

Bowles, Mary, servant to Philip Lynes, 10 November 1691, "produceing here in Court an indenture under ye hand of ye Register & Seale of ye Office that shee had but ye tearme of four yeares to serve," ordered by Court "that ye said Mary Bowles be acquitted & discharged from ye service of ye said Philip Lynes" [17.pdf #157]; Mary Bowles, by William Dent her attorney, 8 November 1692, pleads "that Philip Lynes "render unto her one good cloth suite of clothes either of kersey or broad cloth a shift of white linen to be new one pair of shoes & stockins and three barrells of Indian corne which hee oweth her and unjustly detaineth," ordered by Court "that ye said Mary Bowles recover against ye said Philip Lynes" "her debt aforesaid" "and her damadges by occasion of detaineing ye said debt to three hundred & nine pounds of tobaccoe" [17.pdf #280]

Boys, John, servant to Samuel Sherrill deceased, 8 August 1676, "ye petitioner hath well & truely served five yeares in this County ye fifth day of November last, & haveing his freedome corne due from Samuel Sherrill, ye petitioner humbly craves your Worships to order Thomas Kingadon Executor of Samuel Sherrill deceased to pay petitoner his freedome corne without which your petitioner will bee inevitably ruined," ordered by Court that Thomas Kingadin "pay unto John Boys three barrells of corne for his freedome out of ye estate of ye said Samuel Sherrill deceased" [07.pdf #114]

Browne, Alice, former servant to Sarah Harbert, 9 June 1702, petition presented by her husband John Brown "for her corne and cloathes &c. she haveing finnished and compleated her time of servitude with Ralph Smith the predecessor and Sarah the now wife of William Harbert one of the Justices of this Court," ordered by Court "that the said William Harbert doe pay the said Alice Browne her corne cloaths &c. that doe justly belong unto her" [22.pdf #32]

Brunon, Edmond, master not named, 16 December 1686, "it having been formerly made appear to this Court by ye personal attestation of Richard Land of this Countie that ye said Brunon was brought into these parts as a cabbin boy by a master of a ship who had noe disposing power of him otherwise than by his primary contract as a cabbin boy," ordered by Court "that ye said Edmond Brunon be free to all intents & purposes" [14.pdf #10]

Bryan, John, servant to Walter Bayne, see Encyclopedia of Survivors

PETITIONS FOR FREEDOM

Burchner, James, servant to Philip Lynes, 8 March 1692, "produceing an Indenture here in Court under ye seale of ye office that hee had but four yeares to serve, and it appeareing to ye Court here that hee had served ye said Lines four yeares & five & thirty dayes over & above his said time," ordered by Court "that ye said James Burchner be acquitted & discharged from ye service of ye said Philip Lynes," and "that by reason of his hard useage & un-Christian like dealeing with him in ye time of his servitude hee hath sustained, ye said James Bourchner bee allso acquitted & discharged from any service that ye said Lynes can claime for his runaway time" [17.pdf #209]

Burgesse, Samuell, servant to Elinor Bayne, see Encyclopedia of Survivors

Burroughes, Sarah, servant to Robert Downes, 12 January 1675, "ye plaintife Robert Downes petitioning ye Court ye defendant Sarah Burroughes might serve him ye custome of ye countrey, ye defendant produces this ensueing deposition -- Captaine Edward Blagg Junior came before mee this day made oath that one Sarah Burroughes now a servant with Robert Downes was a passenger in ye ship Industry whereof he was Comander in November 1670 and that shee had an Indenture wherein to ye best of his knowledge it was exprest shee was but to serve foure years, & noe more," sworn before Zachary Wade 14 December 1674, "likewise the defendant produces an Indenture in Court which did testifie shee had butt foure yeares to serve," ordered by Court "that the said Sarah Burroughes be free & that Robert Downes pay her one hundred pounds of tobacco for ye time shee hath served above what was specified in her Indenture & her corn & cloathes according to ye custome of ye countrey with cost of suite" [07.pdf #41]

Burroughs, Paul, servant to Edward Ford, 8 August 1710, having "come to the age of 21 years the Aprill last," petitions that he "in January last was persuaded by Edward Ford to bind himselfe to him to learne the trade of shoemaking for 3 years and 3 months and to be provided for with sufficient dyet logeing & (illegible)," "butt keeps to slaverey contrary to the true intent and meaning of the said agreement," "which said pettition is rejected and the said Indenture adjudged good and sufficient," "itt appeareing that he did volluntarily bind himselfe, before two of her majesty's Justices of the Court" [23.pdf #410]

Butler, Anne, servant to John Neale, 10 November 1730, "by her petition to the Court here setts forth that she was an Indented servant to one

Dunkan Murray, that the said Murray sold her to a certain John Neale of Charles County and delivered her Indentures to said Neale," who immediately "delivered the Indentures aforesaid to the petitioner and told her before several evidences that she was a free woman," all that notwithstanding "the petitioner is still detained as a servant by the said Neale," and whereas "it appears to the Court here by sufficient testimony that the facts aforesaid are true," ordered by Court "that the said Anne Butler from the service aforesaid be immediately discharged," and "that the said Anne do recover against the said John two hundred eighty two pounds of tobacco for her costs and damages" [31.pdf #227]

Butterfield, John, servant to Thomas Harris, 11 August 1724, "by his petition to the Court here setts forth that he was brought into this province by Capt. John Lurting last July was five years and sold to a certain Thomas Harris, that the petitioner was of the age of twenty one years before his coming hither and entred into no Indenture 'till he was obliged so to do on board the said Ship by Mr. Henry Smith, that he has faithfully served the term of five years, & praies the Court to adjudge him his freedom which by the good laws of this province he conceives he has a right to," whereupon "it seems to the Court here that ye petition aforesaid is groundless and frivilous, it is therefore rejected," and ordered by Court "that the said John do either pay" to his said master "three hundred fifty seven pounds of tobacco being the costs accrued" or serve him "at the rate of five pounds of tobacco per day" (72 days servitude) [28.pdf #186]

Capner, Richard, servant to Matthew Saunders, 13 March 1683, petitions that he "did covenant & agree with William Pennell to serve him his heirs & assigns for & dureing ye tearme of foure years after their first arrival in Virginia or Maryland, as by ye said Indenture," "and whereas you petitioner hath well & faithfully served Matthew Saunders of this County ye full tearme of foure yeares according to ye Indenture aforesaid, which tearme of time was fully expired on ye 7th day of February last past, & ye said Matthew Saunders doth refuse & deny to sett him free, but doth still deteine him in his service," "therefore your humble petitioner beggs & craves" "an order for his freedome, with satisfaction for ye time that hee hath served above, & for his freedome corne & clothes," "which Indenture being proved in open Court by ye oath of Jeremy Allanson that hee did see William Pennell at Barbados signe seale & deliver ye same as his act & deed to Richard Capner," ordered by

PETITIONS FOR FREEDOM

Court "that ye said Richard Capner bee free from his said masters service, & that his master Matthew Saunders pay to him ye said Richard Capner his freedome corne & clothes" [11.pdf #84]

Carter, George, and Margarett his wife, servants to Charles Jones, 9 March 1708, "Charles Jones produceth a certaine Indenture under the hand and seale of the said George Carter," which he "alledges he was forced to signe seale and deliver whilest he was a servant to the said Charles Jones which is contrary to contrary to the Act of Assembly," ordered by Court "that the said Indenture be reckoned invallid and that the said George Carter and Margarett his wife be free from any service (to) the said Charles Jones, they quitting their freedom dues" [23.pdf #237]

Champ, Stephen, servant to William Marshall, see Encyclopedia of Survivors

Charleson, Charles, servant to Philip Lines, 9 November 1680, "arrived in this Province on ye first day of November 1675 and was sold as servant unto ye aforesaid Philip Lines, since which time for ye space of five yeares according to ye Custome of this Province" he has "served ye said Lines," except "for ye space of tenne dayes in ye first yeare" of his servitude, "being nott accustomed to such severities" as he did "meete with in ye said Lines in his service," he did absent himself, for which he received "just & publick punishment," yet notwithstanding his "time of servitude being expired ye first day of this present moneth of November," he has "demanded of Margarett Lines ye now wife ye said Philip Lines in his absence" his freedome, "which she doth deny to grant" him, ordered by Court to "serve ye said Philip Lines one hundred dayes for ye ten dayes that hee had absented himself" [10.pdf #35]; Charles Charleson, servant to Philip Lines, 9 March 1681, ordered by Court that he "bee free hee haveing served ye full time allotted him in November Court to serve ye said Lines, but upon ye request of George Thompson attorney of ye said Philip Lines to ye Court to have ye said Charles Charleson comitted for severall misemeanours that he comitted in ye time of his servitude," whereupon he "was taken into custody by ye sherife," "ye said Charles Charleson doth in open Court engage to serve Philip Lines one whole yeare from this day next ensueinge faithfully for what misdemeanours hee hath comitted, ye said Philip Lines at ye expiration of ye said yeare paying unto him corne & cloathes & what is his due according to ye custome of ye country" [10.pdf #60]

PETITIONS FOR FREEDOM

Clash, Nicholas, late servant to Coll. Edward Pye, 9 August 1687, "this Court upon hearing & full understanding ye severall attestacons of Mistris Jane Bread, Robert Midleton, & Stephen Mankin," "doe declare him ye said Nicholas Clash to be free" "to all intents & purposes" [16.pdf #22]; Nicholas Clash, servant to Stephen Mankin, 13 June 1688, whose petition sets forth "that whereas Nicholas Clash an Indian was in August Court last discharged of his servitude by your Worships from Coll. Edward Pye, the said Clash since contracted to serve ye petitioner untill Christmas next come twelve month," ordered by Court "that ye said Nicholas Clash shall be & remaine in ye service of ye petitioner until he be fetch away from ye said service either by a speciall writt from his Lordships Provinciall Court or from one of his Lordship's Honorable Councell besides Coll. Edward Pye late master of ye said Nicholas Clash" [16.pdf #22]; Nicholas Cloyce, servant to Coll. Edward Pye, 11 March 1690, "haveing served several yeares longer than his just time," prayes "for his corne & cloathes," ordered by Court to "recover against ye said Coll. Edward Pye his debt aforesaid: three barrells of Indian corne, a good cloth suite either of kersey or broad cloth, a shift of white linen to be new, one pair of shoes & stockins, two hoes & one axe," and "his damadges by occasion of detaineing ye said defendant to one hundred ninety & six poundes of tobaccoe" [16.pdf #114]; see also [20.pdf #65]

Clifford, John, servant to Anne Dixon, "the relict of Samuel Compton now ye wife of Thomas Dixon, it appeareing to the Court by an Indenture produced & read in Court that the said John Clifford was bound to Samuel Compton & his assignes therefore ye said petition is rejected," 14 September 1703 [22.pdf #129]

Comorains, John, servant to William Penn, 13 March 1722, "his petition to the same effect is likewise rejected" (refers to petition of Markam Mackollom -- ed.) [27.pdf #126]

Conders, David, servant to John Hanson Junr., 13 August 1706, ordered by Court "that Mr. John Hanson Junr. their last master doe pay them their (freedom) dues" [23.pdf #138]

Conders, Richard, servant to John Hanson Junr., 13 August 1706, ordered by Court "that Mr. John Hanson Junr. their last master doe pay them their (freedom) dues" [23.pdf #138]

Conyers, Richard, servant to Edward Pye, 9 January 1683, late servant to Coll. Benjamin Rozer deceased, "his Indenture being in open Court proved by ye oath of Jane Higans, ordered by Court to "be free &

PETITIONS FOR FREEDOM

discharged from his said master's service," and "that ye said Edward Pye" pay unto him "freedome clothes & corne" [11.pdf #59]

Crandall, Francis, servant to Mrs. Elizabeth Hawkins, 10 March 1702, "comes into Court and alledges that he hath served his full time of servitude and produces an Indenture which is allowed of by the Court his time being out this day" [22.pdf #22]

Damer, Thomas, servant to John Cage, see Encyclopedia of Survivors

Davies, Hugh, servant to John Lofton, see Encyclopedia of Survivors

Davis, Mary, servant to George Plater, see Encyclopedia of Survivors

Davison, Anne, servant to John Beale, 9 June 1724, "by her petition to the Court here setts forth that she was indented a servant to Richard Beale 'till ye expiracon of Peter Davisons indented time, which time being expired last April demands her freedom of John Beale which he refuses" "and the aforesaid John Beale produces to the Court here the Indenture of the said Anne which Indenture was assigned" to John Beale by Richard Beale "and it appearing to the said Court that ye time of service of the aforesaid Peter is not expired," ordered by Court "that the aforesaid Anne return to the service of the aforesaid John & serve her said master 'till the expiration of said Peters time of servitude," and "for one hundred seventy pounds of tobacco for costs on the above petition" "at the rate of ten pounds of tobacco per diem" (17 days servitude) [28.pdf #158]

Deane, Elinor, servant to Robert Doyne, 13 November 1685, ordered by Court to "be sett free & discharged from all manner of services" [13.pdf #46]

Deane, John, servant to Michaell Minoake, 11 March 1690, "produceing an Indenture in Court that hee had but ye tearme of four yeares to serve, and allsoe it appearing by ye oath of Mr. Walter Story that hee sould him but for ye tearme if four yeares, & ye said Walter Story produceing here in Court a letter from under ye hand of his uncle Samuell Story & Mr. Thomas Ellsinge that ye most of ye servants then sent in had noe longer time to serve than ye tearme of four yeares according to ye tenour of their Indentures," ordered by Court "that ye said John Deane be free & discharged from his said master" [16.pdf # 114]

Doyne Owen, servant to Philip Lynes, see Encyclopedia of Survivors

PETITIONS FOR FREEDOM

Eingle, John, servant to Anne Smith, 1694, "order to return to her servitude" [Liber T Page 78]

Elliott, John, servant to Capt. John Bayne, 29 November 1698, "produceing an Indenture here in Court under ye hand & seale of ye said John Elliott which said Indenture by ye Court here was adjudged to be good & valid," ordered by Court "that ye said John Elliott returne to ye said Capt. John Bayne his master and to serve him for & dureing ye tearme of time mentioned in ye said Indenture," "three whole yeares and six moneths" commencing 21 March 1696 [19.pdf #261]

Elswood, Anne, master not named, 1694, "her order for her freedom corne & cloaths" [Liber T Page 112]

Evans, Peter, servant to Ruth Chandler, 11 November 1684, ordered by Court to "have corne & cloathes" [12.pdf #23]; said Indenture dated 4 June 1680 between Richard Batts Merchant and Peter Evans "aged twenty five years from the County of Denby" acknowledged in open Court, to serve "ye terme of foure yeares" [12.pdf #22]

Evens, Elizabeth, servant to Mrs. Anne Burford, 10 November 1696, "produceing here in Court" her servant's Indenture, adjudged "to be good & valid," ordered "that ye said Elizabeth Evens ought to be free according to ye tenour of ye same," and "that ye said Anne Burford" pay "her freedome corne & clothes," and "deliver her to ye Vestry of William & Mary Parish to serve according to Act of Assembly for haveing a bastard child by a Negroe" [19.pdf #73]

Farmer, Price, servant to Jane Price, 8 June 1680, "in a plea that shee render unto him his freedome corne & clothes & what is his due by Act of Assembly which to him shee oweth & from him unjustly detaineth [09.pdf #181]

Feild, Charles, 14 June 1709, ordered by Court "that Hugh Mee who married the widdow of Philip Cropper deceased doe pay unto Charles Feild his dues according to a certain Indenture betweene them viz: one broad cloathe coat, one pair leather breeches, one pair of shoes and one hatt," [23.pdf #305]

Fewtrill, George, servant to Samuell Raspin, see Encyclopedia of Survivors

Field, Katherine, servant to Thomas Sympson, 8 August 1704, petitions for "her corne and cloaths according to the forme of a certain Indenture which shee produceth here in Court," ordered that Thomas Sympson be summoned "to appeare here next Court to answer the complaint of the said Katherine Field" [23.pdf #21]; Katherine

PETITIONS FOR FREEDOM

Fields, servant to Thomas Sympson, 13 March 1705, "petition read, Thomas Sympson appears, the Judgment of the Court is that he pay her dues mentioned in the Indenture and four hundred pounds of tobacco in liew of her schooleing" [23.pdf #47]

Fitzgerald, Mary, servant to William Whitter, 13 August 1723, "by her petition to the Court sets forth that she is detained by a certain William Whitter as a servant notwithstanding she is country born, now nineteen years of age & never bound or contracted to him," "ordered that the said Mary be discharged from the service of the said William & that he pay all costs which have accrued" [28.pdf #76]

Fitzgerrald, Morris, servant to Thomas Jenckins, ordered by Court to "serve out the remainder of his time according to Indenture and that if the said Morris Fitzgerald had made a foolish bargaine they could not releive him," 14 June 1709 [23.pdf #307]; see also [23.pdf #321]

Fowke, Richard, orphan of Richard Fowke deceased, "is become of ye full age of one & twenty years, ordered that ye said Richard Fowke goe free from ye service of Henry Hardy to whom he hath been bound an apprentice by this Court," 13 March 1688 [14.pdf #175]

Fox, Robert, servant to John Howard, 12 August 1729, petition "for his freedom is rejected" [31.pdf #155]

Fraizer, William, servant to Michaell Minock, 26 November 1689, "by ye consent of his master" presenting his Indenture "for ye tearme of four yeares," and "it appearing that hee was bound & examined by one Clement Armstrong one of his majesty's Justices of ye peace for Middlesex," ordered by Court "that ye said Indenture is good & valid & that ye said William Fraizer bee free & discharged from his masters service" [16.pdf #110]; William Fraizer, servant to Michael Minocke, 11 March 1690, master "petitioning this Court to reverse a Judgement" of "ye 26th day of November last past," alleging "that ye said William Fraizer had hired one to counterfeite a Justice of peace his hand & seale to his Indenture then produced in Court," ordered by Court that Michael Minocke take out a writt of error for ye reverseing ye judgment aforesaid" [16.pdf #114]

Frawner, Dorothy, late servant to Robert Doyne deceased, 11 August 1691, "your petitioner was ye daughter of a freeborne subject of England and shee has faithfully served severall persons untill this time and being now at age of two & twenty yeares," "whereupon ye wittnesses here in Court being produced swome heard & examined," "it is ordered that ye said Dorothy Frawner be free

PETITIONS FOR FREEDOM

& discharged from ye servitude of Mr. George Plater & Anne his wife Executrix of ye last will & testament of Mr. Robert Doyne deceased" [17.pdf #139]

French, Catherine, servant to Thomas Cooke, 13 March 1683, petitions that she "did covenant & agree with William Pennell on ye behalfe of Thomas Cooke" to serve "ye said Thomas Cooke his heires & assigns for & during ye tearme of four yeares," and "whereas your petitioner hath well & faithfully served Mrs. Anne Fowkes" four years, "which tearme of time was fully expired & ended ye 7th day of February last past, but ye said Anne Fowkes doth deny to sett your petitioner free, but as yett doth detaine her in her service," ordered by Court that "ye said Catherine French not being able to prove that ye said Indenture was signed sealed & delivered by William Pennell," therefore "ye said Catherine French remaine in ye service of Mrs. Anne Fowkes untill five yeares bee fully expired, or till such time as shee can prove herselfe free" [11.pdf #86, 87]

Gallaway, James, servant to Richard Hodgson, 14 March 1682, having "truely & honestly served him & being now free, hee cannot gett his corne & clothes," ordered by Court to "recover of ye aforesaid Richard Hodgson, three barrells of Indian corne, one new kersey suite of broad cloath, one new white linene shift, one new pair of shoes & stockins, two hoes & one axe, according to Act of Assembly," "with cost of suite" [10.pdf #150]

Gamon, Charles, servant to Philip Lynes deceased, 9 March 1725, "by his petition to the Court here setts forth that he was born of a free white woman & a Mullatto & that he was taken into the house of the late Mr. Lynes when he was very young & that he has served ye said Mr. Lynes & Mr. John Marten Executor of said Lynes ever since which is above thirty one years, that he was not bound by any Indenture & that he humbly conceives he is not obliged to serve the said master any time longer," ordered by Court that "ye said John Marten" be summoned "to appear and answer ye complaint," whereupon it is judged "that the same Charles be free" [29.pdf #26]

Glass, John, servant to Anne Smith, 1694, "order to return to her servitude" [Liber T Page 78]

Glew, Robert, servant to Philip Lines, 10 March 1680, petitions that after his "arrival in this Province was sold as a servant unto Philip Lines with whom hee served his full time, & from his said service hath ye said Lines his discharge, but before hee could obtaine or gett that discharge delivered him, by ye said Lines his threatenings, was

PETITIONS FOR FREEDOM

constrained to sett his hand & seale to an Indenture to serve ye said Lines eighteene moneths more, under pretence of runing away & charges ensueing thereon," ordered by Court to "returne to his said masters service untill ye time of his Indenture for eighteene moneths bee fully expired" [09.pdf #156, 157]

Glover, John, "a Mollatto," servant to Samuell Luckett, 9 March 1703, "petitions the Court for his freedom alledgeing that he was borne of an English woman and that he is past twenty one years of age and that att the time of his birth there was a Law of this Province that Mollattoes born of white women should be free at that age, Mr. Samuell Luckett being then in Court consents to and desires that the matter may come to a heareing," ordered by the Court that, "noe such law appeareing," the said John Glover shall "remaine a servant until he shall arrive to the age of thirty and one yeares unless the said John Glover shall produce a law to the contrary" or lawful evidence "agreeing with the time of his birth" [22.pdf #90]; John Glover, "Mollatto," servant to Samuel Luckett, 10 August 1703, "moves the Court againe about his freedom ye former Judgment in March last past confirmed" "Sarah Smith ye Mother of ye said John Glover maketh Oath in Court that her said sonn was borne in ye month of February" 1680 [22.pdf #125]; John Glover, "Mollatto servant" to John Hanson, 9 March 1708, ordered by Court "to appeare here to morrow morning to shew cause why the said Glover should not be free" [23.pdf #237]; the "matter depending between John Hanson and John Glover a Mulatto continued till next Court," 8 June 1708 [23.pdf #253]

Gluffur, Robert, servant to William Marshall, 14 January 1690, "did in open Courte preferre a certaine Indenture" between "ye said Robert Gluffur" and "one John Williams" "to serve him or his assigns for ye tearme of four yeares," and it "appeareing that ye said Robert Gluffur or some other person by his procurement & means had counterfeited a Justice of the peace his hand & seale to ye said Indenture," ordered by Court "that ye said Robert Gluffur serve his said master William Marshall according to ye custome of ye country" (age not judged -- ed.) [16.pdf #111]

Gordan, Stephen, servant to Moses Bell, 11 March 1729, "by his petition to the Court here sets forth that he is detained as a servant by Moses Bell contrary to law and justice," "whereupon it is ordered that John Smith be summoned to testify for the said Stephen Gordon," and ordered by Court "that the said Stephen be discharged from the

PETITIONS FOR FREEDOM

service aforesaid and that the said Moses pay the several fees due to the officers and ministers of the Court" [31.pdf #118]

Grant, William, servant to Col. Gerrard Fowke, 8 September 1668, "in a plea of debt for three barrells of corne and his freedome cloaths, writt of summons to the Sherrife returnable the first day of the following Court" [Vol. 60:142]

Gray, Ruth, servant to Henry Bonner, see Encyclopedia of Survivors

Greene, John, servant to Philip Lines, see Encyclopedia of Survivors

Halfway, William, master not named, 10 November 1719, ordered by Court that his "petition of & concerning his freedom be rejected" [26.pdf #143]

Hall, John, servant to Henry Hawkins, 14 January 1690, "did in open Courte preferre a certaine Indenture" between "ye said John Hall" and "one John Williams" "to serve him or his assigns for ye tearme of four yeares," ordered by Court "that ye said John Hall bring an evidence here ye next Court to be held on ye eleaventh day of March next to testifye upon oath that hee did see ye John Williams signe & seale ye said Indenture, then ye said John Hall to be free & discharged from his servitude" [16.pdf #111]; John Hall, servant to Henry Hawkins, 11 March 1690, "and now here at this Court ye said John Hall did bring his evidence into Court & ye same not fully proveing ye said Indenture to ye Court," "the said Indenture is judged by ye Court invalid, and it is ordered that ye said John Hall doe serve his said master according to ye custome of ye countrey" (age not judged -- ed.) [16.pdf #114]; John Hall, servant to Henry Hawkins, 10 June 1690, with six other servants, "it appeareing by ye Oath of Mr. John Bowman who transported them into this Countrey that hee had ye counterparts of their Indentures & did reade them aboard of his ship at Gravesend, and they were kidnappers Indentures but whether they were good or not hee could not tell, and noe proofe appearing here in Court that ye said Indentures were signed sealed & delivered by ye said John Williams with whom they did indent, & ye same not being under ye seale of an Office, or under ye hand of any Justice of ye peace," ordered by Court to "returne to their severall masters service & serve acording to ye Custome of ye Countrey, their Indentures being adjudged invalide by ye Courte" (age not judged -- ed.) [17.pdf #18]

PETITIONS FOR FREEDOM

Hamilton, David, servant to Ubgate Reeves, 8 March 1715, "by his petition to ye Court showeth that his late master Ubgate Reeves, notwithstanding he hath served his time with him according to the custom of this country, refuses to give him his freedom dues payeable by Act of Assembly," ordered by Court "that ye said Ubgate pay the said David one kersey coat & britches two hoes & one ax and one gun of twenty shillings value" [25.pdf #266]

Hammon, Edward, late servant to William Stone, 13 March 1705, "comes into Court and claims his freedom and produces an Indenture that he is free, Mr. Stone alledges the insufficiency of the Indenture," ordered by Court "that the said Edward Hammon be free from the said William Stone his Indenture appearing to the Court to be good and valid" [23.pdf #46]

Hamond, Abigail, servant to Thomas King deceased, 14 August 1678, "Richard Hodgshon & Johannah his wife Executors of ye Last Will & Testament of Thomas King deceased were attached to answer unto John Hamond & Abigail his wife," who "by ye name of Abigail Yates came from London a servant to this Province, & here arrived ye 2d day of June 1674 in ye good ship called ye Pelican of London Captn. John Bowman Comander & was a servant sold & disposed of by ye said Bowman to ye Honorable Benjamin Rozer Esqre. for ye tearme of foure yeares, shee ye said Abigail hath well & faithfully served, & upon ye 2d day of June 1678 & now last past became a free woman & soe of right ought to have delivered her by ye said Richard & Johannah three barrells of Indian corne, working tools, & freedom clothes," but the defendants "doth refuse as well ye same to doe, as allso to discharge her from her said service," and "ye said Richard Hodgshon & Johannah his wife by Philip Lines their attorney" "saith that ye said John & Abigail ought not to have their attachment" because ye said Johannah and Richard "hath not as yet provided ye Will of Thomas King deceased, nor given security to ye Honorable ye Chancellor for ye said Executrixship," "but it being ye judgment of this Courte that ye said John Hamond & Abigail his wife ought not to be debarred of this their attachment thereby, these ensueing evidences were sworne in Court," Margaret Lines saith "that John Bowman hee never did nor would sell a servant for any longer time than ye tearme of foure yeares," Richard Perkins and James Berry both saith "that Mr. Thomas King bought ye said Abigail of ye Honorable Benjamin Rozer Esqre. but for foure yeares," ordered by Court "that ye said Abigail be free &

discharged from her time of servitude," and "that ye said Richard
Hodgshon & Johannah his wife" "pay unto ye said Abigail three
barrells of Indian corne, workeing tools & freedome clothes
according to ye custome of ye countrey, with cost of suite"
[09.pdf #38]; see also 14 January 1679 [09.pdf # 62]

Handerkin, John, servant to Michaell Ashford, 13 March 1683, "produceing
his Indenture in open Court, it was proved by ye oathes of William
Thatcher & Oliver Rockford that ye said John Handerkin did urge
& perswade them to alter his Indenture from five yeares to four
yeares, & afterwards in open Court owned by ye said John
Handerkin," ordered by Court to "serve ye said Michaell Ashford
until ye tearme of five yeares be fully expired" [11.pdf #87]

Harriss, Joane, servant to John Smith, 8 January 1706, "petition concerning
her freedom cloaths read and ordered that Mr. John Smith doe pay
the same according to Act of Assembly" [23.pdf #111]

Harrison, John, "and Mary his wife," servants to Edward Pye, Esq.,
11 November 1684, ordered to "have their corne & cloathes by
virtue of theire Indentures which are judged by ye Court to be good
& lawfull Indentures [12.pdf #23]; said Indenture dated 26 August
1680 between Benjamin Rozer Merchant and John Harrison &
Mary his wife acknowledged in open Court, to serve "for & dureing
ye terme of four yeares" [12.pdf #22]

Harrison, Mary, wife of John Harrison, servants to Edward Pye, Esq.,
11 November 1684, ordered to "have their corne & cloathes by
virtue of theire Indentures which are judged by ye Court to be good
& lawfull Indentures [12.pdf #23]; said Indenture dated 26 August
1680 between Benjamin Rozer Merchant and John Harrison &
Mary his wife acknowledged in open Court, to serve "for & dureing
ye terme of four yeares" [12.pdf #22]

Hayes, John, "a Negro," servant to Thomas Crabb, 14 June 1720, "by his
petition sets forth that he came in a servant to Capt. Crabb with
indenture out of England for seven years & that giving his Indenture
to his master to keep could never get again, supposing he has
destroyed it to keep him a slave and has kept him almost sixteen
years and do intend to keep him all the days of his life if they can
being unfair dishonest & contrary to law that any serve above what
their Indenture specifies and hopes the Court here will consider his
case & grant him his freedom & likewise satisfaction for ye time he
has been kept it is eight or nine years above his indenture time,"
comes here as well "Elizabeth Crabb Executrix of ye last will &

testament of ye said Thomas Crabb now deceased, and for that it sufficiently appears to ye Court here that ye above recited petition is frivolous and altogether groundless, it is considered that the same be rejected & that ye above named John Hayes be a slave during life by ye Court here adjudged" [26.pdf #173]; John Hayes, "a Negroe," servant to Randolph Morris, 13 August 1728, "by his petition to the Court here sets forth that he was brought into this Country from old England anno 1703 and has ever since been kept in slavery though Indented to serve but seven years, that his Indentures are unfortunately lost, that he has sufficient evidence to prove the said Indentures," "whereupon into Court here in his proper person comes the said Randolph," whereas "it is manifest to the Court here that the petitioner has formerly been heard in this Court on alike petition and by the Justices then adjudged a slave, it is considered that the petition aforesaid be rejected" [31.pdf #77]

Hilton, William, servant to Elizabeth Hawkins, 10 August 1714, William Hilton by Daniel Dullany his attorney showeth "that by the instigation of Mrs. Hawkins & Mr. Henry Hawkins he was prevayled on to enter into an indenture to serve the said Mrs. Hawkins six years before ye expiracion of his first term of service," ordered by Court "that the said William Hilton from the force & effect of ye aforementioned Indenture be acquitted & discharged," [25.pdf #243]

Hinsey, John, servant to Francis Goodrick, Junr., 10 June 1701, "alleadging that hee had Indentures in Ireland before hee came on board the Shipp which are casually or accidentally lost or imbezzelled," ordered that summons be issued "for Capt. William Broadhead Master of the said Shipp, Joseph Howell the Mate, and William Beard the Carpenter of the said Shipp" to appear before "his Majestyes Justices on Satturday next" to give their depositions [21.pdf # 126]; "And on the next day," 11 June 1701, "The Deposition of Capt. William Broadhead Master of the America upon his Oath saith that John Hinson had never noe Indenture some few others had a sort of an Indenture for to serve the Custome of the Countrey and further saith not" [21.pdf #126]

Hogin, Thomas, servant to John Meekes, 13 October 1663, "the said Meekes in open Court declared him to bee a free man" "by vertue of an Act of Assembly prohibiting masters to covenant with their servants for any longer time" of service than the "custom of the country," his Indenture being "no valid" [02.pdf #242]

PETITIONS FOR FREEDOM

Hollywood, James, 1695, "his order for his freedom" [Liber T Page 289]

Holmes, Grace, servant to Stephen Mankin, see Encyclopedia of Survivors

Hughs, Evan, 10 Mar 1702, "petitions the Court here about some cloaths linnen & corne left in the hands of James Stigeleer by one John Clift," ordered by Court "that is not within their jurisdiction therefore the said Evan Hughs is left to his remedy at the common law" [22.pdf #4]

Inskip, Sarah, former servant to Robert Smallpage, 13 March 1694, "your petitioner hath served her time of servitude with Robert Smallpage, and according to Act of Assembly" is allowed & given "a good cloth suite either of kersey or broad cloth, a shift of white linen to be new, one pair of shoes & stockins, two hoes & one axe and three barrells of Indian corne," and "your petitioner hath several times demanded her due for ye like provisions of corne & clothes as aforesaid to be allowed & given her by ye said Robert Smallpage yett hee hath denyed & doth still deny to allow & give unto your petitioner her freedome corne & clothes," ordered by Court that ye said Sarah Inskip recover against ye said Robert Smallpage her debt aforesaid, and for damadges by occasion of detaineing ye said debt to one hundred eighty & two pounds of tobaccoe" [18.pdf #145]

Jackson, Thomas, servant to Henry Hardy, 4 April 1699, "your petitioner was by fair pretenses of Capt. Henry Hardy sent into him to learne ye affaires of this Cuntrey," "which hee hath not in any way performed," and "although your petitioners father paid his passage," and "clothing sufficient to last him a considerable time," and your petitioner "haveing served him full four yeares, hee ye said Hardy claimes three yeares service more," petitions "to be sett free to worke for himselfe," and "to have satisfaction for his clothes," ordered by Court "that Capt. Henry Hardy not fullfilling his promise to ye said Thomas Jackson and hee being under age," he "make choice of his guardian," "and afterwards ye said Thomas Jackson came here into Court and made choice of John Cumpton ye Elder to be his guardian [20.pdf #29]

Jones, Catherine, servant to George Thomas, 9 November 1725, and John her husband, "by their petition to the Court here sett forth that they were free from their late master George Thomas on the 20th day of October last & have not as yet received all their freedom dues although they have demanded them," ordered by Court "that the said George within a fortnights time deliver the petitioners a coat

PETITIONS FOR FREEDOM

& one pair of breeches one shirt one pair mens stockings one gun three barrels of Indian corn two capps an apron one pair womens stockins & a shift such as the Act of Assembly in that case directs & provides" [30.pdf #50]

Jones, John, servant to George Thomas, 9 November 1725, and Catherine his wife, "by their petition to the Court here sett forth that they were free from their late master George Thomas on the 20th day of October last & have not as yet received all their freedom dues although they have demanded them," ordered by Court "that the said George within a fortnights time deliver the petitioners a coat & one pair of breeches one shirt one pair mens stockings one gun three barrels of Indian corn two capps an apron one pair womens stockins & a shift such as the Act of Assembly in that case directs & provides" [30.pdf #50]

Jones, Moses, servant to Zachary Wade, see Encyclopedia of Survivors

Kelly, Mary, late servant to John Hanson, 8 June 1703, "her petition, concerning her corne & cloathes is read, it is ye Courts opinion that it lyes not before them therefore shee is left to her remedy at the common law" [22.pdf #106]

King, Samuell, former servant to Joseph Manning, 14 January 1707, "petitions the Court that Mr. Joseph Manning may pay him the remainder of his freedom dues, Mr. Manning makeing itt appeare that he hath paid him therefore his petition is rejected [23.pdf #160]

Kite, Anne, former servant to John Payne, 11 November 1707, ordered by Court "that Capt. William Harbert doe order John Payne to pay her her freedome dues [23.pdf #221]

Knightsmith, Hannah, servant to Thomas Fuller, 16 December 1686, ordered to "returne to her masters service & serve her full time according to ye adjudgment of her age by this Court to be found upon record" [14.pdf #10]

Lees, Thomas, servant to John Courte, see Encyclopedia of Survivors

Legg, Benjamin, servant to John Thompson, 12 January 1703, petitions "that he render unto him one new hatt, a good cloath suite either of kersey or broad cloath, a shift of white linning (linen -- ed.) to be new, one paire of French fall shooes and stockins, two howes and one ax and one gunn of twenty shillings price which to him he oweth and unjustly detaineth," complains that "the time of the service of the said Benjamin with the said John was expired and ended" on 23 March 1701, "and the said John Thompson saith that he hath made full satisfaction for the same," ordered by Court "that the said Benjamin Legg take nothing" [22.pdf #84]

Lindsey, Margaret, late servant to John Scot, 14 March 1721, "by her petition to the Court sets forth that she served her time according to the custom of the country with John Scot & she has been free ever since November last & that her said master refuses to pay her freedom dues although he hath often thereunto required," ordered by Court "that the said Scot pay ye said petitioner her freedom dues aforesaid" "without delay" [27.pdf 45]

Linghams, Daniell, servant to John Bayne, 11 March 1690, his "Indenture being not under ye seale of any office," ordered by Court to "serve his said master John Bayne according to ye custome of ye countrey" (age not judged -- ed.) [16.pdf #114]

Lloyd, Rodricke, servant to Allexander Smith, 10 September 1672, petitions that he "has served the terme of four compleat years" according to his Indenture made between him the said Lloyd "and John Davies of the Island of Cricke (?) of the Eastern Shore," "being assigned unto Mr. John Allen Merchant and from the said Allen unto Allexander Smith," who "under pretense of being sold to him for the custom of the country refuseth to lett ye petitioner have his freedome according to the conditions expressed in the aforesaid Indenture," whereupon the Jury found the Indenture to be good and the servant to be free [06.pdf #86]; affidavit dated 28 February 1669, recorded 12 August 1673, to wit: "I John Allen of London merchant doe acknowlege to have sold unto Allexander Smith of Charles County planter a man servant named Theodrike Lloyd for ye terme of five yeares" [06.pdf #140]

Lowe, Mary, servant to Raiph Smith, 26 November 1689, "complaint of Mary Lowe for detainment of her clothes," and ye said Raiph Smith alledgeing that shee was endebted unto him for two years & nine months dyett & untill hee had satisfaction for ye same hee would not deliver her clothes," ordered by Court "that ye said Raiph Smith doe deliver unto her ye said Mary Lowe her cloathes" [16.pdf #110]

Lyle, James, and John Pigman, servants to Edward Pye, Esq., 11 November 1684, ordered by Court to "bee free & have theire corne & cloathes from said Pye" [12.pdf #23]

Lyle, James, servant to Philip Lynes, 29 November 1698, "your petitioner hath duely served Mr. Philip Lynes his time of servitude yett notwithstanding ye law he refuses to pay your petitioner his corne

PETITIONS FOR FREEDOM

& clothes due by law as allsoe six moneths time of servitude more," ordered by Court "that ye said James Lyle be admitted to prosecute ye said Philip Lynes in forma pauperis, and Mr. William Shaw one of ye atturneys of this Court is assigned to him for his Councell here in Court" [19.pdf #261]

Mackey, Daniel, servant to Robert Cowerd, 13 March 1733, "his petition for his freedom is rejected" [32.pdf #143]

Mackcloud, Norman, servant to John Landers, 10 November 1702, "complaining against his master," ordered by Court "to returne to his masters service," [22.pdf #63]

Macknew, Lomax, "pretended servant" of Capt. Francis Harrison, "being bound over by recognizance from under the hand of Coll. Phillip Hoskins," ordered by Court "that the said Lomax Macknew is no servant," 9 September 1707 [23.pdf #206]

Mackollom, Markam, servant to John Walden, 13 March 1722, "by his petition to the Court here in November last sets forth that whereas he was taken in ye Rebellion at Preston and Transported into this Province without Indenture & was Sold unto Mr. John Walden of this County to whom he had served the full Term of five years, & that his said Master still Datained him in his Service -- Notwithstanding ye Petitioner was past the age of twenty two years at the Time of his Transportacion, and Praid that he might be Discharged from his said Master according to act of Assembly etc.," ordered by Court "that the petition aforesaid be rejected" (without explanation -- ed.) [27.pdf #126]

Mackontosh, James, servant to Henry Hawkins, 13 March 1722, "his petition of ye same purpose is likewise rejected" (refers to petition of Markam Mackollom -- ed.) [27.pdf #126]

Macmillian, Margaret, servant to Thomas Green, 13 June 1721, "by her petition sets forth that one William Blare sold the petitoner to Thomas Green for five years and two months which the said Blare had no authority to do she haveing never been lawfully bound to him," ordered by Court "that the aforesaid Margaret be discharged from the service aforesaid" [27.pdf #74]

Magrah, Honour, servant to Juliana Price, see Encyclopedia of Survivors

Mancaster, James, servant to Richard Waye, 1694, "order to return to his service" [Liber T Page 45]

Mancaster, William, servant to Richard Waye, 1694, "order to return to his service" [Liber T Page 45]

PETITIONS FOR FREEDOM

Mankin, Tubman, "ordered that his petition about his freedom dues detained by Edward Philpot as he therein setts forth be rejected," 11 March 1718 [26.pdf #22]

Mcantosh, James, servant to Henry Hawkins, 8 August 1721, "petition to be free appearing to ye Court to be groundless & frivilous is therefore rejected" [27.pdf # 92]

McDaniel, James, servant to Thomas Hussey Luckett, 9 June 1724, petition "for his freedom is rejected" [28.pdf #158]

McDaniels, Miles, servant to Michael Marten, 8 August 1721, his "petition to be free appearing to ye Court to be groundless & frivilous is therefore rejected" [27.pdf # 92]

Miller, John, servant to William Forster, 13 November 1694, "it appearing to ye Court here by his Indenture that his time of servitude was not fully expired," ordered to "return to his master William Forster, and to serve out his time according to ye tenour of his Indenture" [18.pdf #229]; John Miller, order for his freedom, 1694 [Liber T Page 7]

Mingoe, "a Negro man belonging to Mr. William Stone," 10 November 1702, "whereas your petitioner was a slave to Mr. Joshua Doyne late of this County Gent. deceased" who "did in his lifetime, haveing experienced and found ye fidellity and uprightness of your petitioner as to his service," "did ordain and appoynt that your petitioner should serve his sonn Dennis Doyne for the full and compleate terme of seaven yeares" and after that "freed from any farther servitude, and your petitioner" "did with alacrity and fidelity serve" Dennis Doyne "untill that itt did please God to call" him, "and after the decease of the said Dennis Doyne contrary to the Deed of Guift" "William Doyne brother to the aforesaid Dennis Doyne did claim a right and intrest in your petitioner as his propper chattell and servant comeing to him by descent soe that your petitioner hath continued with him the said William Doyne in the station of a slave" until your petitioner told William Doyne "that he was no slave to him nor to none other" "and afterwards the said William Doyne did make sale of your petitioner to Mr. William Stone so that your petitioner is likely to continue in the same condition dureing his life," "whereupon the evidence being heard and examined" and "nothing of the allegations appeareing to be true," ordered by Court "that the said Negroe Mingoe returne to Mr. William Stones service and that he be continued as a servant dureing life" [22.pdf #64]

PETITIONS FOR FREEDOM

Monroe, John, servant to John Beale, 8 August 1732, "by his petition to the Court here setts forth that he has served said Beale five years from his arrival into this province the sixteenth day of April last, that he had no Indentures nor was adjudged at the Court, that the said Beale declares he will force the petitioner to serve seven years against the laws and customs of this province, and he prays he may be discharged from his said service," whereupon the said John Beale "produces to the Court here a certain Indenture whereby it appears that the said Monroe was bound at Inverness in Great Britain to a certain Macky or his assigns for the space of seven years," ordered by Court "that the petition aforesaid be rejected and that the said John Monroe serve his said master according to the effect of said Indentures" [32.pdf #114]

Moody, William, servant to Richard Hodgson, 13 January 1680, "whereas your petitioner in ye moneth of November 1675 came over to this Province as a servant to serve foure yeares by Indenture which tearme of foure yeares on ye 13th day of November last being expired, your petitioner became a freeman as by a discharge under ye hand of Richard Hodgson, with whom your petitioner served ye last part of his time," ye said Richard Hodgson "refuseth to pay & deliver unto him his freedome corne clothes & working tooles," "and ye said Richard Hodgson appeares by Thomas Lomax his attorney & produces another Indenture wherein ye said William Moody had engaged with ye said Richard Hodgson for one yeares service more, & pleads that in leiw of his corne & cloathes that hee had discharged ye said William Moody from his first time of service above one moneth before it was expired," but "it being contrary to ye Lawes of this Province that any master should make any bargaine with any servant for any time longer, not untill his first time of servitude be fully expired," ordered by Court "that William Moody be freed & discharged from ye service of Richard Hodgson, & that Richard Hodgson pay unto ye said William Moody his freedome corne & cloathes & workeing tooles that are due unto him by ye law according to ye custome of this Province with cost of suite" [09.pdf #141]; William Moody, servant to Richard Hodgson, 15 March 1682, "having received full satisfaction for his corne of Coll. Benjamin Rozer," but Richard Hodgson "haveing not paid ye said William Moody" his freedom clothes, ordered by Court that "William Moody doe recover of ye aforesaid Richard Hodgson, one new shift of white linen, one new pair of shoes & stockins,

PETITIONS FOR FREEDOM

one new hat or cap, two hoes & one axe, & ye sume of two hundred twenty & one pounds of tobaccoe for ye former cost of suite by him expended, with cost of suite now [10.pdf #152]

Moore, Henry, servant to John Beale, 12 August 1701, "petitioner hath heretofore been a servant to Capt. John Bayne and by him signed over to Mrs. Ellinor Stone in the time of her widowhood and by intermarriage became a servant to Mr. John Beale who was his last master with whom hee hath served his full time of servitude according to the judgment of St. Maryes County Court" "and one month more," "yet the said Beale doth deny and refuse to pay and deliver to your petitioner his cloathes and such like other things as are his due according to Act of Assembly or to make him any satisfaction for the overplus of service as aforesaid," ordered by Court "that the said Henry Moore be discharged of his service & the Court being satisfyed that hee hath served his full time" [21.pdf #137]

Murphey, Owen, servant to Gerrard Fowke, 12 June 1705, "sett free itt appearing to the Court that he hath served his full time" [23.pdf # 79]

Murphy, William, servant to Francis Goodrick Senr., 8 September 1702, "petitioning the Court about his freedome," continued "from the tenth of March to the eighth day of September," on which day the said William Murphy "came into Court and acknowledged that hee & his said master were agreed" [22.pdf #62]

Neale, John, servant to Coll. Humphrey Warren, 12 January 1692, "and ye said Warren here in Court affirmeing that hee bought ye said servant of Capt. John Harris for ye tearme of six yeares and that ye said John Harris hath ye Indenture," and "ye said John Neale did own himselfe that hee had an Indenture for six yeares & was sold for ye said tearme of six yeares," ordered by Court to "returne to his said masters service and serve out ye six yeares according to ye tenour of his Indenture that hee was sold by" [17.pdf #189]

Negro Jupitter, 4 April 1704, "Petitions the Court Concerning Cloaths, Mr. Contee being then in Court says he Never Denyed to pay his just Debts, Ordered that the Petitioner Pay all the Charge, Mr. Contee to pay him his Due According to his Indenture" [22.pdf #194]

Nelm, William, late servant to John Wilkinson, 14 November 1721, "by his petition to the Court sets forth that he has not yet received but one pair of shoes stockings & shirt from his late master John

PETITIONS FOR FREEDOM

Wilkinson and humbly praies ye Court here to order the said Wilkinson to pay ye remaining part of his freedom dues," ordered by Court "that ye aforesaid William have the effect of his petition" [27.pdf #109]

Newman, William, Junr., servant to Coll. James Smallwood, 14 June 1709, ordered by Court "that the said Newman doe serve the said Coll. Smallwood his full time according to Indenture between them" [23.pdf #304]

Nichols, Margarett, master not named, 1696, "ordered to be whipt & her discharge from her servitude" [Liber T Page 253]

Owen, John, "Taylor," servant to Samuel Fendall, 8 March 1670, "is now his own man, and noe way is farther obliged to me" [06.pdf #29]

Parker, Abram, servant to Benjamin Rozer, 8 March 1681, "having served Coll. Benjamin Rozer according to (his) Indentures foure yeares, which Indentures being stolne out of your petioner Abram Parkers chest, are denied by ye Attorney of ye said Rozer, Mr. William Chandler, their freedome with their corne & cloathes," William Sunley "in open Court saith that hee saw ye Indentures" "signed sealed & delivered & that he saw ye Mayor of ye Citty of Yorke sett his hand & seale to ye same," William Webb "in open Court saith that hee saw ye Indentures & read the & they were written Indentures & were for foure yeares & dated Anno. 1676," William Theobald "in open Court saith that his butler Rowland Place told him that all ye servants that came out of Yorkeshire Anno 1676 were but to serve foure yeares," ordered by Court "that Abram Parker be free" [10.pdf # 60]

Parry, Thomas, servant to Robert Scott, November 1716, "his petition v. Robert Scott & judgment thereon" [Liber G Page 151]; Thomas Parry, "ordered to return to the service of Robert Scott till appeale be determined" [Liber G Page 152]

Patrick, Thomas, servant to Philip Lynes, 11 November 1690, petitions that "ye said Philip Lynes being now absent & those who lookes after his consernes refuseing to sett him free, itt being proved here in Court by ye Oath of Edward Thypton his master who sold him to ye said Philip Lynes that his time of servitude was fully expired, itt is ordered that ye said Thomas Patrick be discharged from ye service of his said master Philip Lynes [17.pdf #69]

Patterson, William, servant to William Dent, 29 November 1698, adjudged of his age "on ye fourteenth day of June last past," "and then ye said William affirmeing that hee had an Indenture and was but to serve foure yeares," "the said Indenture being here in Court this day" "produced all ragged & torne soe that it could not be well read, and Jefferry Cockshott his master who brought him in being present here in Court" "he did own the same to be his name and to be subscribed by him," ordered by Court "that ye said William Patterson serve ye tearme of four yeares and no longer according to ye tenour of ye paper of Indenture here in Court produced" [19.pdf #261]

Perrey, Abraham, "your petitioner hath duly and truely served with Mr. Joseph Manning one of the Commissioners of this Court and hath been discharged from the said Mr. Joseph Mannings service near two yeares last past," and now "one Stephen Gray a shipp mate of your petitioners by false fraudulent and deceitfulle promises and pretences doth endeavour to bring your petitioner in a servant for four yeares more, ordered by Court "that the said Abraham Perry be accquitted and discharged and that the said Stephen Gray nor noe other hath any right to the said Abraham Perry," 14 November 1704 [23.pdf #36]

Pickering, Michaell, servant to Robert Hendly, see Encyclopedia of Survivors

Pigman, John, and James Lyle, servants to Edward Pye, Esq., 11 November 1684, ordered by Court to "bee free & have theire corne & cloathes from said Pye" [12.pdf #23]

Pillion, Peter, servant to John Maddox, 14 June 1715, "concerning his freedom," "ordered that ye same be continued till ye next Court in order for ye petitioner to produce his evidence" [25.pdf #271]

Posey, Humphrey, and Posey, John, servants to Edward Philpott, 1 February 1698, "complaint was made by Edward Philpott that Susanna Austin ye wife of Thomas Austin hath taken & carried away with her two servant boys belonging to him ye said Edward Philpott named Humphrey Posey and John Posey," and "Indentures made betweene ye said Susanna Austin of ye one part and ye said Edward Philpott & Susanna his wife of ye other part for & on ye behalfe of ye said Humphrey Posey & John Posey to serve being produced," "said Indentures by ye Court here was adjudged void & of noe effect," ordered by Court "that ye said Humphrey Posey & John Posey be acquitt & discharged from any service," and "they return to their mother Susanna Austin again," [19.pdf #187]

Powell, Anne, servant to Philip Lynes, 31 January 1693, "alledgeing here in Court that shee had an Indenture for ye tearme of four yeares which said Indenture shee lost, and her said master Philip Lynes would not discharge her nor sett her free pretending that shee was judged here at Court and had six yeares to serve, whereupon it being testifyed here in Court by ye Oath of John Wooden that all ye servants that came in that yeare in ye ship that hee came in had Indentures for four yeares under ye Seal of ye Office except one Edward Darley that was sold to ye said Philip Lynes who had noe Indenture" ("Edw. Darnell," servant to Philip Lynes, was adjudged age 17 on 13 March 1688 -- ed.), ordered by Court "that ye said Anne Powell bee free & discharged from ye service of ye said Philip Lynes, shee haveing served ye said Lynes one year wanting two days above ye time of her Indenture" [18.pdf #24]

Powell, Elizabeth, and Thomas Powell her husband, servants to Philip Lynes, 11 September 1683, having "served ye said Philip Lynes (their) full terme of service," petitions "that hee render unto them, three barrells of corne, one suite of new clothes, one new shift of white linen, one pair of shoes, one pair of stockins, two hoes & one ax which to them he oweth & unjustly detaineth," and ye said Philip Lynes "saith that hee oweth ye plaintives nothing," ordered by Court that petitioners "doe recover" ye aforesaid, and "allsoe ye sume of two hundred & fifty seaven pounds of tobaccoe for their costs & charges of suite" [11.pdf #135]

Powell, Thomas, and Elizabeth Powell his wife, servants to Philip Lynes, 11 September 1683, having "served ye said Philip Lynes (their) full terme of service," petitions "that hee render unto them, three barrells of corne, one suite of new clothes, one new shift of white linen, one pair of shoes, one pair of stockins, two hoes & one ax which to them he oweth & unjustly detaineth," and ye said Philip Lynes "saith that hee oweth ye plaintives nothing," ordered by Court that petitioners "doe recover" ye aforesaid, and "allsoe ye sume of two hundred & fifty seaven pounds of tobaccoe for their costs & charges of suite" [11.pdf #135]

Pratt, Elizabeth, "a malloto girle," 12 August 1712, master not stated, "pettitions the Court "that notwithstanding shee being arrived to ye age of eighteen years is still detayned as a servant by ye widdow & relict of John Southeron," ordered by Court "that the said Elizabeth Pratt be discharged according to pettition" [25.pdf #91]

Rawlins, William, servant to Capt. John Bayne, 9 November 1697, "alledging here in Court that by his Indenture ye time that he came in for is expired, & ye said Rawlins not haveing his Indenture here," ordered by Court to "returne to his master John Bayne and remaine in his service untill ye next Court to be held here on ye eleaventh day of January next, and in case ye said Rawlins then appeare to be free by his Indenture then produced, the said John Bayne is to make him satisfaction fore his time that hee shall serve said John Bayne over & above," and "ordered that Edward Rookwood who assigned him to ye said John Bayne bring here to ye Court" "his Indenture which hee had delivered to him when hee bought him of Robert Duglas" [19.pdf #169]; William Rawlins, servant to Capt. John Bayne, 11 January 1698, "coming here this Court again to petition about his freedome," and "Edward Rookwood not heveing his Indenture here," ordered by Court "that ye said William Rawlins returne again to his said masters service untill ye next Court to be held here on ye first day of February next" [19.pdf #180]; William Rawlins, servant to Capt. John Bayne, 1 February 1698, "came here again" "to petition ye Court about his freedome and ye said William Rawlins his Indenture was produced here in Court by Edward Rookwood and it appeareing to ye Court here by ye said Indenture that hee had fully finished & compleated his time of servitude," ordered by Court "that ye said William Rawlins bee acquitt & discharged from ye service of his said master," and that Capt. John Bayne "pay unto ye said William Rawlins ye sume of one hundred pounds of tobacco for ye time that hee hath served him since ye expiration of ye time of his servitude" [19.pdf #186]

Reynolds, Honor, formerly servant to Philip Lynes, 11 March 1690, "was taken from ye said Lynes & sold to Mr. John Speake for ye remaineing part of her time, your petitioner haveing fully compleated her time of service," "prayes for her corne & clothes," ordered by Court that ye said Honor Reynolds bee a free woman & discharged from ye service of any person whatsoever and that John Speake pay unto her her corne & cloathes: a good cloth suite either of kersey or broad cloath, a shift of white linen to be new, one pair of shoes & stockins & three barrells of Indian corne," and "her damadges by occasion of deteineing of ye said debt to one hundred seventy & six pounds of tobaccoe" [16.pdf #114]

Riardine, Dennis, servant to Major James Smallwood, 10 January 1699, "there not being Commissioners enough to adjudge" his Indenture "without ye said Smallwood, itt is referred untill ye next court to be held here on ye fourteenth day of March next" [20.pdf # 4]

PETITIONS FOR FREEDOM

Riscorla, George, servant to Ninian Beale "of Calvert County," 12 November 1689, whose petition sets forth that he "hath a man servant named George Riscorla transported into this Province by Mr. Samuell Young then Merchant in Petuxant, & by ye said Mr. Young sold to ye said petitioner but did (not) mention any time of servitude, which said servant haveing served four yeares produceth a forged Indenture for soe long time & thereupon demanded his freedom, whereupon your petitioner ordered him to goe to ye said Mr. Young & gett a noate from him whether hee know of such an Indenture," and "if ye Court judged ye Indenture good & sufficient your petitioner would satisfye him" notwithstanding "ye said servant hath absented himselfe" and "liveth in Charles County," whereupon ye said George Riscorla appearing in Court produced a letter under ye hand of ye said Mr. Samuell Younge which did testify that hee sold ye servant to Major Ninian Beale for noe longer time then four yeares," continued by Court until "ye 26th day of this instant November" as "it is not certainely knowne whether ye said letter be ye handwriting of ye said Young," ordered by Court "to bring ye deposition of ye said Samuell Younge attested by two Justices of ye peace" [16.pdf #109]; George Riscorla, servant to Major Ninian Beale, 26 November 1689, "ye said George Riscorla produced in Court this ensueing Deposition" of "Samuell Young of ye County of Ann Arundell," making oath that he "sold George Riscorla to Major Ninian Beale but for four yeares & noe longer time as witness our hands this 19th day of November 1689, Nicholas Gassaway & John Hammond," ordered by Court to "bee free & discharged from his said masters service" [16.pdf #110]

Ross, Daniel, servant to Alexander Hambleton, 13 June 1727, "complains to the Court that he was sold by Mr. Mackey Merchant for the term of seven years contrary to the intent & meaning of his Indentures entered into at Inverness upon which the said Hamilton produced the said Indentures to the Court on inspection whereof the Court here adjudged the Indentures aforesaid to be good and valid for the space and term of seven years" [30.pdf #244]; Daniel Ross, servant to Elizabeth Hambleton, 8 August 1732, "petitions to the Court here for his freedom on hearing whereof the same is rejected and ordered that the petitioner pay the costs therein accrued to his said mistriss" [32.pdf #114]

Ross, Francis, servant to Ubgate Reeves, see Encyclopedia of Survivors

PETITIONS FOR FREEDOM

Ruby, Joan, servant to Benjamin Carpenter, 14 March 1721, "by her petition sets forth that notwithstanding she had served her time according to the tennour of her Indenture she was still witheld by her master on pretext of a contract made by her dureing the force of her first Indentures," "the facts therein appearing to be true," ordered by Court that she "be forthwith discharged & that Benjamin Carpenter her last master paye her freedom dues & all the fees deriveing on this petition" [27.pdf 45]

Russell, James, "a Mallatto," servant to Notley Rozier, 13 March 1722, "by his petition to ye Court setts forth that he was born of a white woman & conceives himself to be above the age of thirty one years & ought to be free pursuant to Act of Assembly" and "praies the Court to here his evidence relating thereto that he may be discharged if one & thirty or else be sattisfyed how long he has to serve," "whereupon it is ordered that the deposition of Mary Semmes be taken & lodged with the Clerk, which deposition follows in these words viz." "This Deponent makes Oath that a Mullatto named James belonging to Notley Rozier was born some time before her son Edward Anderson who is thirty one years of age sometime in August next & further this Deponent saith not," (no decision recorded -- ed.) [27.pdf #127]

Russell, Thomas, "a Mallatto servant of Mr. Notley Rozier," 14 August 1722, petitions "that he is past ye age of thirty one years & is still detained by his said master and praies that he may be set at liberty," "and the said Notley Rozier acknowledges that the said Thomas is at age," ordered by Court "that the said Thomas be free & discharged from his service, & that the aforesaid Notley pay all" court costs [27.pdf #178]

Sarah "a Molattoe girl belonging to ye Estate of William Smith deceased," 4 April 1699, "alledgeing that shee was sixteene yeares of age," ordered by Court "that Sarah a Molattoe bee discharged from ye service of ye administrators of ye said William Smith at ye age of sixteene yeares," and if "Mary Perry who was her mothers midwife "take her oath that shee is now sixteene yeares of age, then ye said Sarah to be discharged & sett free" [20.pdf #29]

Smallpage, Robert, servant to Benjamin Rozer, 8 March 1681, "having served Coll. Benjamin Rozer according to (his) Indentures foure yeares, which Indentures being stolne out of your petioner Abram Parkers chest, are denied by ye Attorney of ye said Rozer, Mr. William Chandler, their freedome with their corne & cloathes,"

232

PETITIONS FOR FREEDOM

William Sunley "in open Court saith that hee saw ye Indentures" "signed sealed & delivered & that he saw ye Mayor of ye Citty of Yorke sett his hand & seale to ye same," William Webb "in open Court saith that hee saw ye Indentures & read the & they were written Indentures & were for foure yeares & dated Anno. 1676," William Theobald "in open Court saith that his butler Rowland Place told him that all ye servants that came out of Yorkeshire Anno 1676 were but to serve foure yeares," ordered by Court "that Robert Smallpage be free" [10.pdf # 60]

Smith, James, servant to Samuell Luckett, 10 June 1690, with six other servants, "it appeareing by ye Oath of Mr. John Bowman who transported them into this Countrey that hee had ye counterparts of their Indentures & did reade them aboard of his ship at Gravesend, and they were kidnappers Indentures but whether they were good or not hee could not tell, and noe proofe appearing here in Court that ye said Indentures were signed sealed & delivered by ye said John Williams with whom they did indent, & ye same not being under ye seale of an Office, or under ye hand of any Justice of ye peace," ordered by Court to "returne to their severall masters service & serve acording to ye Custome of ye Countrey, their Indentures being adjudged invalide by ye Courte" (age not judged -- ed.) [17.pdf #18]

Spurling, Jeremiah, servant to Henry Hawkins, 10 June 1690, with six other servants, "it appeareing by ye Oath of Mr. John Bowman who transported them into this Countrey that hee had ye counterparts of their Indentures & did reade them aboard of his ship at Gravesend, and they were kidnappers Indentures but whether they were good or not hee could not tell, and noe proofe appearing here in Court that ye said Indentures were signed sealed & delivered by ye said John Williams with whom they did indent, & ye same not being under ye seale of an Office, or under ye hand of any Justice of ye peace," ordered by Court to "returne to their severall masters service & serve acording to ye Custome of ye Countrey, their Indentures being adjudged invalide by ye Courte" (age not judged -- ed.) [17.pdf #18]

Stephens, James, master not named, 8 March 1726, "petition for his freedom being adjudged frivilous & therefore rejected" [30.pdf #65]

Stewart, Daniel, servant to Mrs. Jane Lewellin, 13 March 1722, "his petition to the Court here to ye same purpose is likewise rejected" (refers to petition of Markam Mackollom -- ed.) [27.pdf #126]

PETITIONS FOR FREEDOM

Sutorne, Mary, servant to Daniell Murphy, 14 January 1701, "your petitioner came in a servant about three yeares since and was first sold to Mr. Van Swearingen deceased, and by him sold to one William Neagle, and by two or three assignments since sold to one Daniell Murphy, of whom she lately purchased hir freedome, and demanding her corne and clothes according to act of assembly he utterly refuses to pay hir," "the petition read Daneill Murphy being then in Court, she ownes in Court that shee had rather quit ye corne & cloathes than serve out her time" [21.pdf #69]

Thornborrow, James, servant to Philip Lynes, see Encyclopedia of Survivors

Thornely, Thomas, master not named, 10 August 1708, "adjudged by the Court to be free having fully served his indented time and ordered by the Court that his master pay him his freedome dues" [23.pdf #266]

Thorrowgood, John, "his discharge from Notley Warren," 1695 [Liber T Page 253]

Typton, Edward, servant to Humphry Warren, see Encyclopedia of Survivors

Walker, Dearman, servant to Henry Hawkins, 8 March 1692, petitioning "for his freedome corne it being denied him by Henry Hawkins Junior with whom hee served his time honestly & truely," ordered by Court "that ye said Dearman Walker recover against ye said Henry Hawkins three barrells of Indian corne" [17.pdf #209]

Walker, Katherine, servant to John Miller, 20 January 1680, "in a plea of debt that hee render unto her, her freedome corne & cloathes according to ye custome of ye country which to her hee oweth & unjustly detaineth," [09.pdf #152]; Katherine Walker, servant to John Miller, 10 March 1680, demands "that hee ye said John forthwith render & pay unto ye said Katherine three barrells of good Indian corne, one good cloth suite of kersey or broad cloath, one new white linen shift, one new pair of shoes & stockins, two howes & one axe, which to her he oweth according to an Act of Assembly, intitled an Act relateing to servants & slaves, & from her unjustly doth deteine, for that whereas ye said Katherine on ye 25th day of December 1674 arrived in this Province, & was disposed of as a servant for ye tearme of five years, & upon ye 25th of December 1679 became a free woman serveing ye last part of her time with ye said John Miller, but although ye said John Miller hath beene often required to deliver & pay to ye said Katherine ye said corne &

PETITIONS FOR FREEDOM

clothes & tooles hath hitherto refused, & still denieth to ye damadge of ye said Katherine 2000 pounds of tobacco & thereupon free brings this suite," and ye said John Miller "saith that hee oweth nothing by law," ordered by Court "that John Miller pay unto Katherine Walker her freedome corne & clothes & what is her due according to Act of Assembly with cost of suite" [09.pdf #162]

Wallis, Richard, servant to Philip Lines, 9 November 1680, "arrived in this Province on ye first day of November 1675 and was sold as servant unto ye aforesaid Philip Lines, since which time for ye space of five yeares according to ye Custome of this Province" he has "served ye said Lines," except "for ye space of (thirteene) dayes in ye first yeare" of his servitude, "being nott accustomed to such severities" as he did "meete with in ye said Lines in his service," he did absent himself, for which he received "just & publick punishment," yet notwithstanding his "time of servitude being expired ye first day of this present moneth of November," he has "demanded of Margarett Lines ye now wife ye said Philip Lines in his absence" his freedome, "which she doth deny to grant" him, ordered by Court to "serve ye said Philip Lines one hundred & thirty dayes for ye thirteene dayes that hee had absented himself" [10.pdf #35]; William Herbert v. Richard Wallis, former servant to Philip Lines, 12 September 1682 [11.pdf #19].

Walsh, Richard, servant to Matthew Barnes, 13 November 1722, "was lawfully bound by Indenture for the term of four years which your petitioner can prove by severall of his ship mates & by his first master William Theobalds who by enquiry made was told by Nathaniell Milles marriner of our ship," ordered by Court "that ye petitioner be instantly free from his said master" [28.pdf #7]

Warner, Thomas, servant to Thomas Baker, 8 June 1686, ordered by Court to "returne to his present master John Harrison & serve him tell ye tenth of November next & that then the said servant goe free and to have sattisfaction for what is his due out of ye deceased Bakers Estate" [13.pdf #117]

Warren, Alice, master not named, 10 January 1677, "petitioning ye Court for her freedome, it is ordered that ye said Alice Warren bee free according to ye time of her first servitude from her last master" [08.pdf #18]

Webster, Edward, servant to Capt. Richard Hodgson, 30 November 1681, petitioning for "freedome corne & clothes & what is due according to ye Custome of this Province, & according to ye Law

PETITIONS FOR FREEDOM

[10.pdf #129]; "Att ye request of Edward Webster these ensueing depositions were taken in open Court," 14 March 1682 -- Richard Raston "saith that hee came into ye Countrey in ye ship called ye Vine along with Edward Webster & that they did cast anchor ye twenty sixth day of December within ye capes, & then they came up to Coll. Calverts, & on new yeares day Edward Webster went ashoare with his master Marke Cordea," William Shellson "saith as above written," John Hodisson "saith that hee did see ye Indentures between Marke Cordea & Edward Webster signed sealed & delivered," John Redick "saith that there was an Indenture betwixt Marke Cordea & Edward Webster for foure yeares," no judgment by Court [10.pdf #151]; Richard Hodgson summoned by Court, 15 March 1682, ordered by Court that "Edward Webster doe recover of ye aforesaid Richard Hodgson what is due unto him according to Act of Assembly," viz: "three barrells of Indian corne, one new suite of clothes either of good kersey or broad cloath, one new white linen shift, one new pair of shoes & stockins, two hoes & one axe with cost of suite " [10.pdf #157]

Welsh, Michael, servant to John Wilkinson, 14 August 1722, "by his petition to the Court sets forth that his late master John Wilkinson refuses to deliver him a suit of clothes which he ought to pay him," and "it seemed to ye Court here that ye facts" "are sufficiently proved," ordered by Court "that the said Wilkinson deliver to ye said Welsh ye cloaths aforesaid that is to say: a coat jacket & breeches of kersy & pay ye costs of ye petitioner aforesaid" [27.pdf #177]

Welsh, Richard, master not named, 14 August 1722, "his petition for his freedom is rejected" [27.pdf #177]

Whittimore, Christopher, servant to Henry Hawkins, 11 March 1690, "petitioning this Court for his freedome & hee not proveing his Indenture to be authentick & good," ordered by Court to "serve his said master according to ye custome of ye country" (age not judged -- ed.) [16.pdf #114]

Whitworth (sic), Christopher, servant to Henry Hawkins, 10 June 1690, with six other servants, "it appeareing by ye Oath of Mr. John Bowman who transported them into this Countrey that hee had ye counterparts of their Indentures & did reade them aboard of his ship at Gravesend, and they were kidnappers Indentures but whether they were good or not hee could not tell, and noe proofe appearing here in Court that ye said Indentures were signed sealed & delivered by ye said John Williams with whom they did indent, & ye same

PETITIONS FOR FREEDOM

not being under ye seale of an Office, or under ye hand of any Justice of ye peace," ordered by Court to "returne to their severall masters service & serve acording to ye Custome of ye Countrey, their Indentures being adjudged invalide by ye Courte" (age not judged -- ed.) [17.pdf #18]

Wilkinson, John, servant to Thomas Taylor, see Encyclopedia of Survivors

William, John, "an East Indian," servant to Richard Hodgson, 12 November 1706, former slave to Mrs. Johannah Hodgson the mother of the said Richard Hodgson," purchased "about fifteen or sixteen yeares since," [23.pdf # 153]; 14 January 1707, ordered by Court "that the said John William be free from the said Richard Hodgsons service" [23.pdf #161]

Williams, Giles, servant to (illegible) Newman, 11 March 1707, "your poore petitioner has been these twelve yeares a servant to one (illegible) Newman of this County and became a servant to be imployed and to learne the taylor trade which they have not done and your poore petitioner desires that he may be imployed in that trade the remaineing part of his time," "the above petition read in Court Mrs. Newman being there present," ordered by Court "to learne him the trade of a taylor and declareing that she was allwayes willing thereto" [23.pdf #168]

Williams, Hugh, servant to Capt. Richard Hodgson, 30 November 1681, petitioning for "freedome corne & clothes & what is due according to ye Custome of this Province, & according to ye Law [10.pdf #129]; Richard Hodgson summoned by Court, 15 March 1682, ordered by Court that "Hugh Williams doe recover of ye aforesaid Richard Hodgson what is due unto him according to Act of Assembly," viz: "three barrells of Indian corne, one good new suit of kersey or broad cloath, one new white linen shift, one new pair of shoes & stockins, two hoes & one axe with cost of suite [10.pdf #158]

Yappe, Roger, servant to Henry Hawkins, see Encyclopedia of Survivors

PETITIONERS FOR FREEDOM, ELSEWHERE IN THE RECORD

Boyce, John, 8 August 1676 [07.pdf #114]. Son of John & Eleanor Boyce. Index to Deeds, 25 December 684 [12.pdf #85]. Gifts of Livestock, 12 June 1686 [13.pdf #61].

Charleson, Charles, 9 November 1680 [10.pdf #35] & 9 March 1681 [10.pdf #60]. Married Dorothy Musgrave, widow. Vital Records, 14 November 1689 [16.pdf #121] & 9 January 1694 [18.pdf #140].

Clash, Nicholas, "an Indian," 9 August 1687 [16.pdf #22] & 11 March 1690 [16.pdf #114]. Vital Records, 20 September 1693 [Liber Q Page 21].

Conyers, Richard, 9 January 1683 [11.pdf #159]. Conner, Richard, Witnesses Who Stated Their Ages, 17 July 1706 [23.pdf #136].

Evans, Peter, 11 November 1684 [12.pdf #23]. Indenture on Record, dated 4 June 1680 [12.pdf #22]. Peter Evans "aged twenty five years from the County of Denby" to serve "ye terme of foure yeares"

Fitzgerald, Mary, 13 August 1723 [28.pdf #76]. Index to Orphans, 9 March 1708 [23.pdf #236].

Fitzgerrald, Morris, 14 June 1709 [23.pdf #307]. Son of Morrice Fitzgarrald, Gifts of Livestock, 17 October 1709 [Liber C Page 148].

Fowke, Richard, 13 March 1688 [14.pdf #175]. Index to Orphans, 8 June 1686 [13.pdf #117].

Glass, John, 1694 [Liber T Page 78]. Index to Deeds, 28 May 1713 [24.pdf #180].

Glover, John, "a Mollatto," 9 March 1703 [22.pdf #90] et seq. Son of Sarah Smith. Vital Records, February 1680 [22.pdf #125].

Grant, William, 8 September 1668 [Vol. 60:142]. Index to Deeds, 4 January 1673 [06.pdf #115].

Kite, Anne, 11 November 1707 [23.pdf #221]. alias Ann Beaumont. Index to Orphans, 8 January 1706 [23.pdf #111], 11 November 1707 [23.pdf #221], 8 June 1714 [25.pdf #219].

Macknew, Lomax, 9 September 1707 [23.pdf #206]. Mackune, Lomax, Witnesses Who Stated Their Ages, 20 May 1721 [Liber M Page 123].

Mankin, Tubman, 11 March 1718 [26.pdf #22]. Son of Stephen & Mary Mankin. Vital Records, 9 April 1696 [Liber Q Page 26]. Index to Orphans, 11 November 1701 [21.pdf #160] & 9 November 1714 [25.pdf #257].

Miller, John, 13 November 1694 [18.pdf #229] & 1694 [Liber T Page 7]. Son of John & Grace Miller of Nanjamey. Vital Records, 5 November 1673 [16.pdf #121].

Moody, William, 13 January 1680 [09.pdf #141] & 15 March 1682 [10.pdf #152]. Vital Records, 20 March 1692 [16.pdf #123]. Index to Orphans, 3 December 1700 [21.pdf #157].

Moore, Henry, 12 August 1701 [21.pdf #137]. More, Henry, Index to Deeds, 20 July 1705 [23.pdf #114].

PETITIONERS FOR FREEDOM, ELSEWHERE IN THE RECORD

Neale, John, 12 January 1692 [17.pdf #189]. Index to Deeds, 18 November 1712 [24.pdf #174]. Gifts of Livestock, 21 June 1721 [Liber H Page 441].

Newman, William, Junr., 14 June 1709 [23.pdf #304]. Son of William Newman Senr., Index to Deeds, 5 August 1684 [14.pdf #115].

Parry, Thomas, November 1716 [Liber G Pages 151 & 152]. Son of Dorothy Parry widow, now wife of Robert Hanson. Index to Deeds, 13 March 1721 [Liber H Page 425] & 13 July 1721 [Liber H Page 442].

Patrick, Thomas, 11 November 1690 [17.pdf #69]. Deaths and Estates, 11 August 1691 [Liber Q Page 39] & 12 January 1692 [17.pdf #198].

Posey, Humphrey, 1 February 1698 [19.pdf #187]. Son of John & Susanna Posey. Vital Records, 1 February 1683 [16.pdf #122]. Gifts of Livestock, 16 August 1717 & 17 February 1718 [Liber H Page 126]. Deaths and Estates, 10 March 1719 [26.pdf #105].

Smallpage, Robert, 8 March 1681 [10.pdf #60]. Index to Deeds, 24 March 1687 [17.pdf #258], 9 June 1691 [17.pdf #117], 10 November 1691 [17.pdf #158].

Warner, Thomas, 8 June 1686 [13.pdf #117]. Index to Deeds, 20 February 1691 [17.pdf #293]. Deaths and Estates, 14 November 1676 [08.pdf #32]. Index to Orphans, 27 March 1677 [08.pdf #32]. Deaths and Estates, 16 May 1688 [16.pdf #28]. Index to Deeds, 20 February 1691 [17.pdf #293].

Some of these kids had lengthy chains of title, as revealed in their petitions:

John Green arrived as a servant in 1668 and was sold to Benjamin Rozer, Sheriff of Charles County; he was adjudged to be fourteen and ordered to serve eight years; he was then sold to Daniell Johnson who died before 10 March 1671; he then became a servant to Francis Kilbourne, and thence to Philip Lynes, who refused to set him free, claiming him for two years longer than the Court had ordered him to serve.

Abigail Hamond, formerly Yates, arrived on 2 June 1674 in the Pelican of London as an indentured servant for the term of four years; the ship's commander, Capt. John Bowman, sold her to Benjamin Rozer, Sheriff of Charles County, who sold her to Thomas King; he died before 14 August 1678, and the executors of his will, Richard and Johannah Hodgshon, with Philip Lynes as their attorney, refused to set her free.

Ruth Gray, transported by Capt. John Harrison, arrived on 24 February 1676 as an indentured servant for the term of four years; she was brought to Court, adjudged to be twenty-one, and ordered to serve six years according to the custom of the country; she was sold to Samuell Raspin, and then to Richard Edelen, and then to Henry Bonner, who refused to set her free, saying he bought her for six years.

ABUSE AND NEGLECT

Adams, Joseph, servant to Mr. Welsh, 13 June 1732, "by his petition sets forth that sometime since he bound himself a servant to Mr. Morris high sherife of this County who hired him out to a certain Mr. Welsh a boat builder or ship carpenter of Prince Georges County, that Mr. Morris and Mr. Welsh having differed about their bargain and the petitioner being now very ill, Mr. Welsh utterly denys him as his servant and neither of them will receive him into his house," ordered by Court that "the said Morris take care of and provide necessarys for the petitioner [32.pdf #78]

Battersby, Hugh, servant to George Plater, 14 June 1692, "came here into Court and made his complaint that hee had a very sore legg and was not able to worke and (neither) his master nor Michaell Martin his overseer would take any care for ye cure of ye same because hee had but a short time to serve, and it appeareing here in Court that if some speedy care be not taken for ye care of ye same hee may be thereby rendered uncapable of getting his livelyhood and become a charge to ye County to maintaine him, it is ordered that Michaell Martin overseer to Mr. George Plater under whose charge hee is take care for ye cure of ye said Hugh Battersbyes legg or else to sett him free that hee may take care for ye cure of ye same himselfe" [17.pdf #233]

Brown, Daniel, servant to John Smallwood, 14 August 1722, "complains to the court that he is greivously afflicted with a fistula and that his master neglects to endeavour his care so that the said servant is likely to perish, whereupon the said John Smallwood being called before ye Court on the complaint aforesaid he confesses that he is willing to discharge him from his service rather than be at ye expence and hazard of his care and thereupon ye same servant is by the Court here discharged" [27.pdf #177]

Bryan, Turlough, servant to William Dent, 13 June 1699, "came here into Court and made complaint against William Wilson late of Charles County planter his overseer for abuseing of him and that hee had unreasonably beaten & wounded him," ordered by Court that "ye sherife to take ye said William Wilson and him in safe custody keepe untill hee putt in good & sufficient security for his appearance her att ye next Court to be held here on ye eighth day of August next to answer unto ye complaint of ye said Turlough Bryan, and for his good behavior in ye meanetime" [20.pdf #68]; Turlough Brian, servant to William Willson, 12 September 1699, complaint "for unreasonable beateing & wounding him the said

ABUSE AND NEGLECT

Turlough Brian," and "the said William Willson cometh & saith that he is in no wise guilty," whereupon "the wittenesses respectively being produced sworne heard & examined," "the said William Willson by the Court here was adjudged guilty," and fined "two hundred pounds of tobacco" [20.pdf #90]. See Encyclopedia of Survivors.

Cammell, Mary, servant to Samuell Luckett, 11 March 1707, "comes into Court and compaines against her said master for unreasonably beateing and abuseing her, the said Samuell Luckett being then in Court" "and being admonished by the Justices here for his more milder usage and correction towards the said Mary Cammell for the future," ordered by Court "that the said Mary Cammell doe returne to the said Samuell Lucketts service" [23.pdf #169]

Carr, Owen, servant to Philip Lynes, 11 November 1690, "Whereas James Lewis" "on ye fourteenth day of January last past (being presented by ye grand Enquest upon suspicion of murthering one Owen Carr servant to Mr. Philip Lynes) was comitted to ye custody of ye Sherife of this County," and "ye said James Lewis remaineing still in custody of ye said Sherife and being allmost naked & ready to perish for want of clothing," ordered by Court "that ye Sherife discharge ye said James Lewis hee takeing his own bond for his good behavior & appearance at ye next Provintiall Court" [17.pdf #83]

Chandler, Ann, servant to Ignatius Causeen, 13 March 1711, "being hired for one year from the sixth of January, has been soe unreasonably used, by beating threatening and such usage that your pettitioner is not able to serve the said Ignatius Causeen," asks for "release," ordered by Court "that shee be free and discharged from the said Causeen" and that he "deliver unto ye complaynant what belongs to her" [24.pdf #60]

Clampett, Abigail, servant to Robert Coleson, 9 November 1703, servant confessing "in Court," 10 days absence, 100 days servitude, "and whereas the said Robert Coleson "alledges that he Bought the said woman servant from Cornelius Maddock & there is some Runnaway time due whilest shee was servant to the said Cornelius Maddock," "Whereupon ye said Abigail Clampett in Open Court in ye presence of ye said Cornelius Maddock did stripp herselfe naked from ye Waist upwards and Exposed to ye Justices view both on her Back, Belly, Armes & Wrists many Markes of Seveare & Cruel Whippings & Tyings whilest shee was ye said Maddocks servant," ordered that "ye said Abigail Clampett be acquitt & Discharged" from any runaway time "whilest shee was servant to the said Cornelius Maddock" [22.pdf #144]

Constable, John, servant to William Heard, 12 July 1664, "a jury impannelled" "to vew the bodie of John Constable." "the verdict is that having vewed the dead bodie of the above said Constable that we find itt cleare and without stripes and to the best of our judgments was the cause of his own death by wilfully drownding of himself" [02.pdf #405]

Darnell, Edward, see Catherine Jones, and Encyclopedia of Survivors

Dempsey, John, servant to John Eaton, 12 June 1722, "on the petition of Mary Dempsey setting forth the barbarous & inhumane usage of her husband John Dempsey," ordered that John Eaton stand indebted "in the sum of twenty pounds" recognizance [27.pdf #163]

Edwards, Humphrey, servant to Stephen Mankin, 9 January 1693, "complaineing to ye Court here that hee wanted clothing and that his master would not find or provide any for him although hee was bound in his Indentures" to do so, ordered by Court "that his master Stephen Mankin forthwith provide & allow necessary & fitting clothing," "and if ye said servant come again ye next Court to complaine," "ye said Humphrey Edwards to be discharged from ye service of ye said Stephen Mankin" [18.pdf #129]

Evans, Margarett, servant to Thomas Wheeler, 11 September 1705, "complains against her master for harsh usage, the said Thomas Wheeler fined five hundred pounds of tobacco for contempt" [23.pdf #100] "for unlawfully beating his servant Margaret Evans after due admonishment given him to the contrary by Coll. James Smallwood one of the Justices of this Court, whereupon the said Thomas Wheeler petitions the Court that the fine may be remitted, confessing that it was ignorantly done being urged thereto by the ill language of the said servant," ordered by Court "that the said petition be rejected," 13 November 1705 [23.pdf #104]

Fisher, Peter, servant to Capt. Samuel Perrie, 12 June 1722, "complains that his master does not provide sufficient cloathing," ordered by Court "that ye said servant return to his masters service & his said master take care to provide" [27.pdf #163]

Fitz Gerralds, Joan, servant to William Sarjeant, 11 September 1694, "making complaint to ye Court of & concerning her masters harsh & rigorous dealing towards her and misuseing of her, itt is commanded the sherife that hee cause to come here before ye Justices" "ye said William Sarjeant" "to answer unto ye complaint" "at ye next Court to be held here on ye thirteenth day of November next and in ye meantime" "not rigorously to use his said servant Joan Fitz Gerralds" [18.pdf #195]

Gibson, Thomas, servant to Thomas Green, 13 June 1721, petitions that he has been "most cruely and barbarously abused by his master Thomas Green and contrary to his agreement with Capt. James Norris has put him to work at the hoe where he is not sattisfyed with ye utmost endeavours," "neither will he sell" your poor petitioner "but keeps him purposely to plague him," "the bad usage that he gives your poor petitioner has brought him into a weak condicion already and will shortly be the death of him," petition adjudged "false malicious scurrilous & groundless, it was therefore rejected," "ordered likewise that the Sheriff take the said Gibson to the whipping post & give him six lashes on his bare back well laid on for the unjust & scandalous abuse given his said master by ye petition aforesaid" [27.pdf #74]; Thomas Gibson, servant to Thomas Green, 8 August 1721, "petition setting forth ye cruel & severe usage of his master" is rejected" [27.pdf #92]

Griffin, Charles, "an indented servant" to Thomas Barton, 13 March 1722, "sets forth that" his master "is gone out of the government whereby ye petitioner is disabled from getting his living by reason no person will employ him he being a servant," ordered by Court "that any person have the liberty of employing ye said petitioner untill his master return" [27.pdf #126]

Harris, Thomas, "a hired servant" to Kenneth Mackenzy, 8 September 1720, "setting forth that his said master does not provide sufficient victuals or cloathing for said servant," and "ye said McKenzy had notice of said complaint & was ordered by the worshippful Dr. Brown to appear but did not, 'twas ordered that the said servant be discharged from his service" [27.pdf #31]

Hasell, Elizabeth, servant to Nicholas Emanson, 11 January 1670, "having served out the time she was att her first arrival obliged to serve" six years), she had "severall times" run away "during the time of her service," for which her master demanded punishment according to Act of Assembly; whereupon Richard Boughton her attorney alleged that she "could not be punished by that Act of Assembly, having for every such time of her running away received corporall punishment; whereupon a jury was impanelled and the following

ABUSE AND NEGLECT

witnesses heard: Joseph Dorosall "saith that Mrs. Emanson did beat the defendant for runing away," Richard Beck saith that his mother "beat her & putt her in irons," Edmond Lambert saith that "he carried her home & she was then pardoned for her running away & after that she run away again & her mistris tyed her to a bed post & whipped her," Anne Lambert "saith that once when the said defendant had run away her mistris took her & whipt her," Anne Lane saith that "the said defendant was brought home by James Mackey & her mistris tooke her & whipt her & goeing in afterwards to sweep the roome there was a puddle of blood in the room & great wounds in her back," Lewis Beck saith "when she came home his mother put her in irons & another time his mother whipt her & severall times she hath been beaten for running away;" whereupon the jury "found for the defendant" Elizabeth Hasell [Vol. 60:233]

Holmes, Grace, servant to John Gourely, 8 September 1691, "came here into Court & made her complaint that shee was naked & her said master would not her cloathe," ordered by Court that "ye sherife of this County" summon "ye said John Gourely that hee bee here at ye next Court to be held here on ye tenth day of November next and that hee bring ye said Grace Holmes along with him & there to answer to ye Complaint of ye said Grace Holmes" [17.pdf #154]; Grace Holmes, servant to John Goureley, 10 November 1691 "it appeareing here to this Court that ye said Grace Holmes had at severall times absented her selfe out of her said masters service," ordered by Court that ye said Grace Holmes serve ye said John Gourely from this day one whole yeare next ensuing and then to be free & discharged from her said masters service," provided "that shee ye said Grace Holmes doth not at any time within ye said yeare unlawfully absent herselfe & runaway out of her said masters service" [17.pdf #157]. See Encyclopedia of Survivors.

Ingram, Thomas, servant to William Coody, 8 November 1726, "it appearing to the Court here that William Coody has most barbarously and inhumanely treated his hired servant Thomas Ingram on the motion of the aforesaid Thomas, it is ordered that he be forthwith discharged from the said Coody's service" [30.pdf #175]

Johnson, Elisabeth, servant to Daniell Johnson, 12 July 1664, "a jury impannell" to determine "the cause of her death," "who brought in thear verdict that Elizabeth Johnson hath hanged and murdered herself with a bridell raine" [02.pdf #405]

ABUSE AND NEGLECT

Jones, Catherine, servant to Philip Lynes, 11 August 1691, complaining "of her hard useage by Henry Thompson one of ye overseers of ye said Lynes, ordered that ye said Philip Lynes take his said servant Catherine Jones and remove her from her overseer Henry Thompson to another plantation and to cloth her well; and for her hard servitude & ye abuses that shee hath received therein be discharged from her damadges of haveing a bastard child; and be free according to her Judgment in Court" (adjudged on 8 June 1686 to be age 16, seven years servitude -- ed.) [17.pdf #139]; Catherine Jones, servant to Philip Lynes, 8 November 1691, with James Thornborough & Edward Darnell, "came here into Court naked & made complaint that for want of clothes they were allmost starved, and ye said Philip Lynes being absent, itt is ordered that Major James Smallwood lett them have necessary clothes to preserve them from perishing with cold, and that Coll. Humphrey Warren sherife pay ye said Smallwood for what clothing they shall have of him out of what tobaccoe shall be allowed to ye said Lynes in ye County levy this yeare" [17.pdf #157]; Catherine Jones, servant to Philip Lynes "gentleman," 10 November 1692, "a poor distressed & almost naked servant," "haveing endured a long & hard servitude under severall overseers of ye said Lynes and being kept soe bare of clothes that shee was allmost perrished with cold and constantly compelled to doe her labour allmost naked," ye last November Court did then order that shee should have reliefe; "from that time to this shee hath never had any clothes from ye said Lynes except one shift & one linen petticoate with which shee endured all last winter & this last summer & constantly forced to worke out of doores," and "she is in apparent danger of perishing this winter with cold if not releived by your worshipps in dischargeing her from her intollerable servitude as aforesaid, her time being till next June to serve ye said Lynes, for shee findes by experience that ye said Lynes gives noe manner of obedience to your worshipps order," ordered by Court "that ye said Philip Lynes cloth ye said Catherine Jones his servant with good woollen clothes shoes & stockings" "to keep her from ye cold," "and in case ye said Philip Lynes doe not provide" within twenty dayes, "upon her complaint thereof to any one of ye Justices of this Court he is to discharge her & sett her free" [17.pdf #276]

ABUSE AND NEGLECT

Jones, John, and Katherine Jones servants to Walter Pye, 11 June 1723, "their petition setting forth their hard & severe usage appearing to the Court to be groundless is therefore rejected," ordered by Court "on the motion of the said Walter Pye that the sheriff take the aforesaid John Jones to the whipping post & there give him six lashes on the bare back for his insolent behaviour to his said master" [28.pdf #54]

Jones, Katherine, and John Jones, servants to Walter Pye, 11 June 1723, "their petition setting forth their hard & severe usage appearing to the Court to be groundless is therefore rejected," [28.pdf #54]

Legg, Benjamin, former servant to John Thompson, 13 January 1702, "whereas your petitioner came into Maryland a servant and sold to John Thompson of Portobacco and by carrying of a piece of timber fell downe and broke his back and his master finding him not fitt for service sett him free about nine months since and your poore petitioner having noe friend nor relation to take care of him now is not capable of doing any manner of labour whereby to gett a livelyhood, humbly desires your Worshipps to allow him somewhat towards a maintenance," allowed by Court "foure hundred pounds of tobacco in the next yeares Leavy" [21.pdf #173]

Leport, Francis, servant to Samuel Williams, 13 June 1732, on the complaint "that he is misused by his said master and not allowed sufficient dyet," ordered by Court that the said Samuel Williams "allow his said servant sufficient provisions and accomodations for the future" [32.pdf #77]

Lew, John, servant to Philip Lynes, 14 September 1686, "ordered that a sumons issue to Henrie Goodrick Overseer to Mr. Lynes to appear next Court to answer ye complaint of John Lew servant to ye said Lynes and moreover that there be an express order of this Court delivered to ye said Goodrick forbidding him at his perill to offer anie abuse to ye said Lew or soe much as to give him any correction till further order from this Court" [13.pdf #120]

Line, James, see Teague Turlayes.

Mackontosh, Mark, servant to Dorothy Graves, 12 November 1706, "being greviously afflicted with hard usage in my service," and "John Wheeler sone in law to ye aforesaid Dorothy Graves" "came to me and by faire speeches and deludeing way inveighed me to consent in case he would purchase me of my mistress to serve him the said Wheeler four yeares without any consideration of being sett free from ye petitioner's first mistress's service," ordered by Court "to serve the said John Wheeler according to his Indenture and that the same be kept amongst the records of this Court" [23.pdf #152]

McMillian, William, servant to Thomas Green, 8 June 1725, "complains to the Court here that notwithstanding ye admonition given his master by some of the Justices of the Court here on the said William he complaining to them of the barbarous usage & treatment he had received from his master, he still continues to abuse the said William by beating," "whereupon "it seemeth to the Court here by sufficient testimony that the said Thomas has abused his said servant," ordered by Court "that the said Thomas be fined two hundred (pounds of) tobacco" [30.pdf #4]

Parry, Thomas, servant to Richard Barber, 14 August 1722, "by his petition to the Court setts forth that he is greivously afflicted with a sore legg which renders him incapable of working & yet his master Richard Barber, to whom he had about eighteen months to serve, has set him free under pretense of getting himself cured and that ye petitioner must inevitably perish unless the Court will" "bestow something on him toward his releif," ordered by Court that "Colo. John Fendall take care to place ye petitioner conveniently and provide" for his support and care, "which is to be paid in ye county levy" [27.pdf #177]

Rogers, Peter, "an indented servant" to Thomas Barton, 13 March 1722, "sets forth that" his master "is gone out of the government whereby ye petitioner is disabled from getting his living by reason no person will employ him he being a servant," ordered by Court "that any person have the liberty of employing ye said petitioner untill his master return" [27.pdf #126]

Shalter, Henry, servant to Philip Lynes, 13 January 1691, "was ordered by ye said Lynes to live with John Bould who doth very much beate & abuse your Petitioner," prays "that hee may serve ye remaineing part of his time with some other person in ye said Lynes his employ," ordered by Court "that hee be putt by Mr. James Mackewen who doth now looke after ye businesse & concernes of ye said Philip Lynes where hee ye said Mackewen shall thinke fitt & see convenient to employ him in ye said Lynes his service," [17.pdf #89]

Thornborough, James, see Catherine Jones, and Encyclopedia of Survivors

ABUSE AND NEGLECT

Turlayes, Teague, and James Line, servants to Philip Lynes, 9 March 1697, "did make their complaint against ye said Philip Lynes their master for want of clothing & lodgeing," ordered by Court "that ye said Philip Lynes forthwith cloth his said two servants with necessary & convenient clothing, and to provide them a bed to lie on," and in case "ye said Teague Turlayes and James Lyne come again to complain for want of ye same ye next Court, then ye said two servants to be sett free & discharged from ye said Lynes his service" [19.pdf #111]; Teague Turlayes and James Line, servants to Philip Lynes, 8 June 1697, "came here this day to make their further complaint against ye said Philip Lynes their master for not complyeing with a former order of this Court upon their former complaint made," ordered by Court that ye said Teague Turlayes and James Lyne appear here at ye next Court to be held here on ye tenth day of August next," "for that ye said Philip Lynes is not here" "and allsoe that there may be a full Court [19.pdf #131]; Teague Turlayes, Teague, servant to Philip Lynes, 9 November 1697, "came here severall Courts to complain against his said master and he allsoe comeing here this day, the said complaint of ye said Teague Turlayes by ye Court by ye Court being heard and hee not being able to make good his said complaint," ordered by Court "that ye said Teague Turlayes return to his masters service and to serve him according to ye judgment of this Court for his runaway time that hee was here adjudged to serve," (2000 days servitude -- ed.) [19.pdf #170]. See Recaptured Runaways.

Ward, John, servant to Arthur Turner, 3 November 1663, "Mr. Arthur Turner being summoned to give a reason why the orphant John Ward hath bin so ill treated in his hows in so much that the voyce of the people crieth shame thereat and also to bring the sayd Ward and his indentur to the Court with him all which accordingly hear wear produced: The sayd Ward with a most rotten filthy stincking lodge that even loathed all the beholders thearof his apparrell beeing all ragged and torne and his haer seemed to bee raked of with ashes," ordered by Court "that the sayd Ward shoold bee free from the sayd Turner" [02.pdf #255, 256, 257]

Ward, Richard, servant to Joseph Ward, 10 January 1699, "complaineing to ye Court here against Joseph Ward his master for abusing of him and not allowing him sufficient & necessary clothing & bedding and it being averred here in Court that ye said Richard Ward is an orphan bound to ye said Joseph Ward," ordered by Court "that ye

248

ABUSE AND NEGLECT

said Richard Ward," "naked without a shirt and never a bed to lie on, bee removed out of ye said Joseph Wards custody" "and serve Thomas Dickson untill he arrive to ye age of twenty one yeares, hee ye said Thomas Dickson findeing & allowing him sufficient meate drinke washing lodgeing & clothing fitting & necessary for such a servant" [20.pdf #4]

Webster, Edward, servant to Richard Hodgson, 13 January 1680, "upon ye petition & complaint of Edward Wheeler to ye Court concerning his master Richard Hodgson unlawfully & unreasonable beateing & woundeinge of him," and ye said Richard Hodgson "not appeareing here this Court," ordered by Court "that a speciall warrant directed to ye Constable bee issued forth to take ye body of ye said Richard Hodgson, soe that hee may make his personall appearrance before his Lordshipps Justices at ye next Court to be held in this County on ye ninth day of March next there to answer to ye Complaint of ye said Edward Webster [09.pdf #143]

Wharton, Adam, servant to Phillip Lynes, 9 December 1685, "being lately found in Capt. Warren's quarter naked of all cloaths & in a perishing condition hath by Capt. Warren exhibited his greiveous complaint against his said Master for want of necessary cloathing, the Court comisserating ye miserable condition of ye said servant, orders that ye said Capt. Warren in charity provide things necessary for ye said servant till ye said Lynes shall give good security to make better provision for his said servant & that ye said Capt. Warren be by ye said Lynes sattisfied for what he shall expend in this behalfe [13.pdf #47]; "As to ye servant Adam Horton, Capt. Warren to sattisfye 400 pounds of tobacco to Phillip Lynes & then ye said Philip to have ye said servant," 10 August 1686 [13.pdf #119]

Willkinson, Mary, servant to Francis Miller, 8 June 1703, "haveing a sore mouth and throat petitions the Court and alledges that her master neglects or is not of ability to gett her cured," ordered by Court "that a summons be sent for Francis Miller to be here on the morrow," and "the said Francis Miller appearing," "it is ordered that the said Mary Willkinson doe returne to her said master Francis Millers service untill her time of servitude be fully expired, hee promiseing and ingageing here in Court to use his best endeavour to cause her mouth & throat to be cured" [22.pdf #107]

Wood, Thomas, servant to Hugh French, 8 March 1681, "upon ye complaint" "for want of necessary cloathing," ordered by Court "that Thomas Wood returne to his master & that hee provide necessary cloathing for him as soone as possibly hee can" [10.pdf #59]

ABUSE AND NEGLECT

9 March 1680

The grand jurors for ye Right Honorable ye Lord Proprietary doe present Philip Lines of this County planter, for that this day hee did sett upon, beate & sorely abuse Thomas Smith his hirelinge, comeinge on his way to this present Court, to testify ye truth of his knowledge on ye behalfe of ye Right Honorable ye Lord Proprietary against Thomas Powell & John Dyall servants to ye above said Lines, Contrary to ye peace of ye Right Honorable ye Lord Proprietary of this Province [09.pdf #154]

To ye honorable Coll. Benjamin Rozer Esqre. & ye worshipfull his Lordshipps Commissioners Justices of this County. The humble petition of Thomas Smith. Humbly sheweth. That whereas ye petitioner yesterday being ye Eighth day of this instant March, gave in Evidence (before Mr. Robert Henley one of his Lordshipps Justices for this County) against Thomas Powell & John Dyall two servants belonging to Philip Lines for & on ye behalfe of ye Right Honorable ye Lord Proprietary ye said Lines overtakeing ye petitioner on ye roade this day Comeinge to Court to give in ye same Evidence to ye grand Jury, did beate him with a great cane many blowes soe that ye said cane with beateinge him hee ye said Lines broke to your petitioners great damadge, your petitioner prayes your honor & worships to Consider of your petitioners Complaint, & therein releive him as to you shall seeme meete, And your petitioner shall pray. [09.pdf #154]

And ye said Philip Lines appeares in his proper person & saith that yesterday morning Thomas Smith (being hired to him) did absent himselfe from his service, not knowing whether hee was gone, this morning Comeing to Court hee did overtake him, & askt him whether hee was goeing, hee replyed hee was goeing to Court, but would not resolve him what hee was goeing about therefore hee did strike him two or three blowes with his caine, & ye head of ye Cane came off. Hereupon it is ordered by ye Court that Philip Lines bee not fined for beateing of Thomas Smith, because hee did it ignorantly not knoweinge what hee was comeinge to Court about. [09.pdf #154]

Whereas Thomas Powell servant to Philip Lines was bond to appeare at this Court, Proclamacon being made & no person appeareinge to prosecute him, Itt is ordered by ye Court that ye said Thomas Powell be cleared

[See also 10.pdf #94]

VITAL RECORDS

Acton, Mary, daughter of Mary Acton, born 2 May 1708 [23.pdf #400]

Agborough, Thomas, servant to Alexander Simpson, died 10 August 1667
[03.pdf #298] [16.pdf #119]

Allen, John & Elinor, of Portobaccoe
Anne, daughter, born 28 January 1695 [Liber Q Page 25]

Allen, William, alias Gill, bastard son of Joseph Allen, born 9 July 1699
[24.pdf #96]

Allison, Elizabeth, daughter of Thomas Allison, born c. 1673 [Liber M Page 66]

Allward, John & Mary, of ye head of Portobacco Creeke
Mary, daughter, born 20 December 1676 [16.pdf #120]
John, son, born 18 December 1678 [16.pdf #120]
Margarett, daughter, born 4 March 1680 [16.pdf #120]

Anderson, John & Mary, of Portobaccoe
Edward, son, born 13 August 1691 [Liber Q Page 20]
John, son, born 14 April 1693 [Liber Q Page 22]
George, son, born 22 March 1694 [Liber Q Page 25]

Andras, Elizabeth, daughter of Lawrence & Mary Andras, born 14 August 1716
[Liber H Page 366]
Andras, Henry, son of Lawrance & Mary Andras, born 27 January 1718
[Liber H Page 366]
Andross, Benjamin, son of Lawrence Andross, born 2 May 1722 [Liber L Page 233]
Andross, William, son of Lawrence Andross, born 23 June 1724

Ashbrooke, John, married "in the yeare 1667" [03.pdf #267]

Ashman, Richard & Anne, of Wiccocomicoe
Elizabeth, daughter, born 29 June 1680 [16.pdf #121]
Richard, son, born 4 February 1682 [16.pdf #121]
Mary, daughter, born 3 August 1685 [16.pdf #121]
Standidge, son, born 1 October 1687 [16.pdf #121]
Allward Hardy, son, born 12 June 1691 [16.pdf #121]
John, son, born 4 February 1694 [22.pdf #129]

Baddoe, James, son of Martha Baddoe, born c. April 1713 [25.pdf #172]

Baker, Thomas & Martha, of Potomack River side
Martha, daughter, born 31 March 1675 [07.pdf #50] [16.pdf #119]
Andrew, son, born 29 March 1679 [16.pdf #120]

VITAL RECORDS

Baker, Martha, orphan of Thomas Baker deceased, married Anthony Smith, before 8 November 1692 [17.pdf #277]

Barker, John & _____ , of Nanjemy
    John, son, born 3 April 1691, baptized 17 April 1691 [16.pdf #122]

Barker, Margaret, married John Smyth / Smith, 14 February 1666/7 [03.pdf #297] [16.pdf #119]

Barker, Samuell, son of Alice Hanby, born 2 April 1688 [18.pdf #243]

Barker, Sarah, intention to marry John Lambert, 12 April 1676 [07.pdf #105]

Barnes, Matthew & Elizabeth, of Portobaccoe
    Godshall, son, born 20 December 1692 [16.pdf #123]
    Jane, daughter, born 19 December 1694 [Liber Q Page 24]

Baron, John & Mary, of Portobaccoe
    Martha, daughter, born 15 January 1695 [Liber Q Page 24]

Baron, Richard, servant to Humphrey Warren, died 27 July 1667 [03.pdf #297]

Bartlett, Mary, daughter of Raiph Bartlett, born January 1682 [Liber Q Page 38]

Barton, William Junr.
    Grace, daughter, born 26 August 1659 [01.pdf #77] [16.pdf #119]
    Grace, daughter, died 31 August 1659 [01.pdf #77] [16.pdf #119]
    William, son, born 29 June 1662 [01.pdf #247] [16.pdf #119]
    William, son, born 27 February 1667 [03.pdf #305]
    Elizabeth, daughter, born 27 February 1672 [06.pdf #78]

Barton, William & Elizabeth, of Mattawoman
    Thomas, son, born 17 July 1689 [Liber Q Page 14]
    William, son, born 11 November 1690 [Liber Q Page 14]
    David, son, born 25 June 1695 [Liber Q Page 26]

Barton, Nathan
    William, son, born 19 February 1667 [03.pdf #297] [16.pdf #119]

Bateman, George & Elizabeth, of Pyckyawaxon
    George, son, born 7 December 1692 [16.pdf #122]

Bayly, John & Mary
    John, son, born 20 January 1680 [16.pdf #120]
    James, son, born 10 January 1683 [16.pdf #120]

VITAL RECORDS

Beck, Richard & Elizabeth
    Elizabeth, daughter, born 2 October 1669 [08.pdf #92] [16.pdf #120]
    Mary, daughter, born 15 November 1672 [08.pdf #92] [16.pdf #120]
    Margarett, daughter, born 1 May 1674 [08.pdf #92] [16.pdf #120]

Belayne / Belaine, Nicholas & Mary, of ye head of Wiccomico River
    Jemima, daughter, born 21 March 1686 [16.pdf #122]
    Elizabeth, daughter, born 25 February 1688 [16.pdf #122]

Blizard, Giles, intention to marry Susanna Caine, daughter of John Caine, 4 August 1684 [12.pdf #13]

Bowld, John & Jane, of Pyckyawaxon
    John, son, born 25 June 1686 [Liber Q Page 12]
    Elizabeth, daughter, born 27 October 1690 [Liber Q Page 16]
    Mary Anne, daughter, born 3 April 1694 [Liber Q Page 23]

Bramhall, Thomas
    Ann, daughter, born 1706 [25.pdf #110]
    William, son, born 7 December 1708 [25.pdf #110]
    Thomas, son, born 1711 [25.pdf #110]

Brawner, Henry & Mary, of Mattawoman
    John, son, born 2 April 1693 [Liber Q Page 19]

Browne, Elizabeth, married John Robinson, 21 March 1666
    [03.pdf #298] [16.pdf #119]
    Browne, John, son of Elizabeth Browne, born 5 June 1666
    [03.pdf #297] [16.pdf #119]
    Browne, John, died 7 November 1666 [03.pdf #298] [16.pdf #119]

Browne, Thomas, married Alice Horton, 26 July 1692 [16.pdf #122]
Browne, Thomas & Alice, of Pyckyawaxon Parish [Liber Q Page 21]
    Thomas, son, born 21 December 1693 [Liber Q Page 21]

Bullett / Bullott, Joseph & Elizabeth, of Mattawoman
    Joseph, son, born 8 February 1688 [16.pdf #123]
    Benjamin, son, born 28 April 1693 [16.pdf #123]

Burdett, Sarah, "youngest daughter of Mr. Thomas Burdett deceased, married Gerrard Fowke of Portobaccoe, 31 December 1686 [Liber Q Page 12]

Burroughs, Paul, indentured servant, born April 1689 [23.pdf #410]

VITAL RECORDS

Caine, Susanna, daughter of John Caine, intention to marry Giles Blizard,
 4 August 1684 [12.pdf #13]

Capshaw, John, son in law of George Diamond, born 6 March 1691 [23.pdf #206]
Capshaw, Francis, son in law of George Diamond, born 13 July 1693 [23.pdf #206]

Carr / Carre, Grace, married George Mackmillion, January 1669
 [Vol. 60:221] [16.pdf #119]

Carr, Owen, servant to Philip Lynes, murdered, before 11 November 1690
 [17.pdf #83]

Carver, John, parents not named, born 19 September 1710 [27.pdf #108]
Carver, Ann, parents not named, born 12 May 1713 [27.pdf #108]
Carver, Richard, parents not named, born 8 May 1716 [27.pdf #108]

Causin, Ignatius & Jane, of Portobaccoe
 Jane, daughter, born 11 July 1682 [Liber Q Page 9]
 Ignatius, son, born 10 September 1685 [Liber Q Page 11]
 John, son, born 12 April 1690 [Liber Q Page 15]
 William, son, born 20 February 1693 [Liber Q Page 20]

Chandler, William & Jane, of Portobacco
 William, son, born 13 October 1678 [16.pdf #120]

Chapman, Thomas & Elizabeth, of Nanjemy
 Thomas, son, born 26 March 1690 [Liber Q Page 16]
 Mary, daughter, born 19 August 1693 [Liber Q Page 21]

Charleson, Charles, married Dorothy Musgrave, widow, 14 November 1689
 [16.pdf #121]
Charleson, Dorothy, widow, married John Toney, before 9 January 1694
 [18.pdf #140]

Cherrybub, John & Mary, of Pyckyawaxon
 Elizabeth, daughter, born 28 March 1687 [16.pdf #123]
 John, son, twin, born 20 March 1690 [16.pdf #123]
 William, son, twin, born 20 March 1690 [16.pdf #123]
 Walter, son, born 25 February 1694 [Liber Q Page 22]

Clash, Nicholas & Mary, of Portobaccoe
 John, son, born 20 September 1693 [Liber Q Page 21]

VITAL RECORDS

Clerke / Clark, John
    Ambrose, son, born 13 September 1666 [03.pdf #297] [16.pdf #119]
    Ambros, son, buried 18 February 1667 [03.pdf #297] [16.pdf #119]

Clouder, Elizabeth, "ye daughter of Richard & Temperance Clouder of Nanjemy,"
    married Thomas Davis, taylor, 1693 [Liber Q Page 21]

Cofer / Coffer, John
    John, son, born 25 November 1663 [03.pdf #298]
    Thomas, son, born 15 August 1667 [03.pdf #298]

Cofer, John & Elizabeth, of Portobaccoe
    John, son, born 5 March 1695 [Liber Q Page 25]

Cofer, Thomas & Mary, of Portobaccoe
    Sarah, daughter, born 28 October 1694 [Liber Q Page 24]

Coghill, William & Christian, of Portobaccoe
    James, son, born 10 January 1692 [16.pdf #123]

Cogwell, James & Anne, of Nanjemy
    James, son, born 11 July 1693 [Liber Q Page 21]

Cole, Edward, Junr., "of St. Marys County," married Ann Neale, daughter of
    James Neale Senr., "of Charles County," before 10 January 1716
    [Liber F Page 85]

Cole, Phillip & Mary, of ye head of Wiccocomico River
    John, son, born 10 January 1678 [16.pdf #120]
    Phillip, son, born 4 December 1680 [16.pdf #120]

Collier, William, brother to Giles Collier, born May 1693 [23.pdf #305]

Cone, Benjamin, son of Elizabeth Cone, born 17 September 1697 [23.pdf #20]

Connel, William, son of Dennis & Mary Connel, born 2 April 1693 [Liber L Page 96]

Cooksey, Thomas, son of Philip Cooksey deceased, born August 1689 [19.pdf #207]

Cooper, Nicholas & Penellepy / Penelope, of ye Riverside [Liber Q Page 20]
    John, son, born ____ [16.pdf #121]
    Anne, daughter, born 15 March 1688 [16.pdf #121]
    Prudence, daughter, born 11 April 1692 [Liber Q Page 20]

Corner, unnamed, child of Gilbert Corner, born 4 June 1667 [03.pdf #297]

VITAL RECORDS

Cornish, John & Martha, of Mattawoman
    Elizabeth, daughter, born 18 August 1678 [16.pdf #121]
    Richard, son, born 11 December 1679 [16.pdf #121]
    Edward, son, born 10 October 1682 [16.pdf #121]
    Martha, daughter, born 4 May 1687 [16.pdf #121]
    Margarett, daughter, born 30 November 1690 [16.pdf #121]
    John, son, born 27 May 1693 [Liber Q Page 21]

Cosleton, Robert
    Marie, daughter, born 6 February 1667 [03.pdf #305]

Cotterell, James & Elizabeth, of ye head of Wiccocomico River
    Elizabeth, daughter, born 30 April 1689 [Liber Q Page 15]
    Jane, daughter, born 15 August 1690 [Liber Q Page 17]
    James, son, born 7 September 1694 [Liber Q Page 23]

Court / Courts, John & Margarett [Liber Q Pages 1 & 2]
    John, son, born 19 February 1655 [Vol. 60:221] [16.pdf #119]
    Elizabeth, daughter, born 16 May 1663 [Vol. 60:221] [16.pdf #119]
    Margarett, daughter, born 15 January 1665 [Vol. 60:221] [16.pdf #119]

Courtes, John & Charity, of Pyckyawaxon
    Charity, daughter, born 4 October 1680 [16.pdf #122]
    John, son, born 3 March 1691 [16.pdf #122]
    Anne, daughter, born 29 August 1693 [Liber Q Page 22]

Cox, James & Margarett, of Pyckyawaxon
    Margarett, daughter, born 2 November 1680 [Liber Q Page 7]

Cox, James & Anne, of Pyckyawaxon
    Thomasine, daughter, born 27 December 1690 [Liber Q Page 16]

Crompton, Francis, parents not named, born 8 October 1685 [23.pdf #141]

Cumpton, Elinor, "ye daughter of John Cumpton of St. Maryes County," married
    Henry Hardy, of Pyckyawaxon, 21 August 1694 [Liber Q Page 23]

Danson (?), James, son in law of Thomas Bramhall, born 15 November 1703
    [25.pdf #110]

Davis, John & Elizabeth, of Pyckyawaxon
    Mary, daughter, born 25 December 1685 [Liber Q Page 11]
    Elizabeth, daughter, born 15 January 1689 [Liber Q Page 14]

VITAL RECORDS

Davis, Thomas, taylor, married Elizabeth Clouder, "ye daughter of Richard & Temperance Clouder of Nanjemy," 1693 [Liber Q Page 21]

Dawson, John, married Elizabeth Thirst, 16 September 1690 [16.pdf #122]
Mary, daughter, born 22 September 1692 [16.pdf #122]

Dawson, Anne, daughter of Matthias Dawson, granddaughter of John Dawson, born 26 (?) September 1695 [20.pdf #69]

Dent, William, married Elizabeth Fowke, daughter of Anne Fowke, 8 February 1684, "at ye house of Mrs. Anne Fowke at Portobacco" [16.pdf #121]

Dent, William & Elizabeth, of Nanjemy
 Thomas, son, baptized 19 December 1685 [16.pdf #121]
 William, son, baptized 25 December 1687 [16.pdf #121]
 Gerrard, son, baptized 3 February 1688 [16.pdf #121]
 George, son, born 27 September 1690, baptized 16 April 1691
  [16.pdf #121]
 Anne, daughter, born __ March 1692, baptized 16 March 1692
  [16.pdf #123]
 Peter, son, baptized 13 January 1695 [Liber Q Page 24]

Deverell, Thomas & Anne
 Elizabeth, daughter, born 1 January 1679 [16.pdf #120]

Dixon, Thomas
 Thomas, son, born 8 June 1692 [16.pdf #122]

Dod, Richard & Mary, of Potomack River
 Mary, daughter, born 25 February 1656 [02.pdf #420] [16.pdf #119]
 Richard, son, born 4 January 1662 [02.pdf #420] [16.pdf #119]
 John, son, born 2 July 1666 [16.pdf #120]
 Richard, son, born 13 January 1670 [16.pdf #120]

Dod, Richard & Jane, at ye head of Bakers Creeke
 Anne, daughter, born 24 September 1692 [16.pdf #122]

Doughaley, Robert, son of Grace Mackdonnel, born 21 June 1695 at Nanjemy Parish [20.pdf #131]

Douglas, John
 Elizabeth, daughter, born 26 April 1673 [16.pdf #119]

Duglas, John & Catherine, of Pyckyawaxon [Liber Q Page 12]
 John, son, born 29 October 1686 [16.pdf #122]

VITAL RECORDS

Dowell, John, parents not named, born c. 25 December 1705 [25.pdf #110]

Downes, Robert, son of Robert Downes, born 4 February 1670 [16.pdf #120]

Dunkin, Nimrod, son of John Dunkin, born February or March 1702
    [23.pdf #305] [24.pdf #96]

Dutton, Thomas & Elizabeth, of Wiccocomico
    Matthew, son, born 28 September 1692 [16.pdf #122]
    Notley, son, born 19 December 1694 [Liber Q Page 24]

Edgar, Richard & Joanna / Johannah
    William, son, born 24 June 1693 [Liber Q Page 19]
    John, "ye third sonne," born 30 August 1699 [Liber Q Page 19]
    Elizabeth, daughter, twin, born 28 October 1706 [Liber Q Page 26]
    Sarah, daughter, twin, born 28 October 1706 [Liber Q Page 26]

Effye, Arthur
    Arthur, son, born c. 1665, aged 26 on 11 August 1691 [17.pdf #138]

Elliott, William & Joan, of ye head of Wiccocomico River
    William, son, born 10 August 1682 [Liber Q Page 9]

Emerson, Nicholas
    William, son, born 17 November 1666 [03.pdf #267] [16.pdf #119]

Ettye, Arthur & Elizabeth, of Wiccocomicoe
    Rachell, daughter, born 30 July 1694 [Liber Q Page 23]

Evans, Roger, servant to Thomas Baker, died c. 16 September 1661 [01.pdf #156]

Farloe / Farlowe, Ambrose
    William, son, born 15 February 1671 [06.pdf #155] [16.pdf #119]

Ferdinandoe, Peter & Elinor, of Portobaccoe
    Agatha, daughter, born 8 November 1694 [Liber Q Page 24]

Fitz Gerralds, Edward & Margarett
    Elizabeth, daughter, born 30 April 1695 [19.pdf #231]

Ford, Edward & Elizabeth, of Chingoemaxon
Ford, Edward, of Chingoemaxon, died 6 January 1694 [Liber Q Page 22]
    Posthuma, daughter, born 29 July 1694 [Liber Q Page 25]

VITAL RECORDS

Ford, Elizabeth, widow of Edward Ford deceased, "who was ye daughter of Thomas Allanson of Chingoemuxon deceased," married Thomas Whichaley, 25 April 1694 [Liber Q Page 23]

Ford, Thomas, son of Christopher Ford, born 29 March 1699 [23.pdf #300]

Fowke, Elizabeth, daughter of Anne Fowke, married William Dent, 8 February 1684, "at ye house of Mrs. Anne Fowke at Portobacco" [16.pdf #121]

Fowke, Gerrard, of Portobaccoe, married Sarah Burdett, "youngest daughter of Mr. Thomas Burdett deceased, 31 December 1686 [Liber Q Page 12]

Fowke, Gerrard & Sarah, of Nanjemy
 Gerrard, son, born 16 October 1687 [Liber Q Page 13]
 Anne, daughter, born 30 January 1690 [Liber Q Page 15]
 Francis, daughter, born 2 February 1692 [Liber Q Page 17]
 Katherine, daughter, born 8 April 1694 [Liber Q Page 23]

Francklin, Henry & Mary, of Wiccocomico
 Mary, daughter, born 12 October 1689 [16.pdf #123]
 Jane, daughter, born 31 January 1692 [16.pdf #123]

Garrett, Charles & Joyce, of ye head of Wiccocomico River
 Charles, son, born 7 May 1684 [16.pdf #121]

Gates, John, son of Catherine Ellory, born April 1709 [25.pdf #266]

Gibson, Thomas & Elizabeth, of Pyckyawaxon
 Thomas, son, born 30 May 1694 [Liber Q Page 23]

Glover, John, "Mollatto," son of Sarah Smith, born February 1680 [22.pdf #125]

Goer, George & Anne, of ye head of Wiccocomico River
 Mary, daughter, born 12 June 1683 [16.pdf #121]
 Sarah, daughter, born 1 May 1686 [16.pdf #121]
 George, son, born 13 July 1689 [16.pdf #121]

Goodrick, Robert
 Mary, daughter, born 13 March 1673 [06.pdf #154] [16.pdf #119]

Goureley, John & Barbary, of Cedar Point Neck
 Thomas, son, born 4 April 1686 [Liber Q Page 12]
 Elizabeth, daughter, born 20 October 1690 [Liber Q Page 17]
 John, son, born 23 April 1693 [16.pdf #123]

VITAL RECORDS

Green, Elizabeth, daughter of Robert Green, married Andrew Sympson, before 9 November 1702 [Liber Z Page 27]

Greene, Francis & Elizabeth, of Portobaccoe
    Leonard, son, born 30 May 1691 [Liber Q Page 20]
    Verlinda, daughter, born 16 August 1692 [Liber Q Page 20]
    Francis, son, born 23 April 1694 [Liber Q Page 25]

Greene, Robert & Mary, of Portobaccoe
    William, son, born 28 December 1694 [Liber Q Page 25]

Groves, George & Alice, of ye head of Wiccocomico River
    George, son, born 2 June 1687 [Liber Q Page 13]
    William, son, born 24 May 1690 [Liber Q Page 16]
    Elizabeth, daughter, born 1 February 1692 [16.pdf #122]
    John, son, born 9 February 1695 [Liber Q Page 25]

Guy, Charles & Elizabeth, of Wiccocomico
    Elizabeth, daughter, born 1 July 1693 [Liber Q Page 21]

Gwinn, Ralph, son of Ralph Gwinn, born 31 May 1695 [24.pdf #96]

Gwynn, Christopher & Susanna Gwynn
    Anne, daughter, born 27 July 1692 [16.pdf #122]

Hadlowe, Edith or Headlow, Idy married William Hills, June 1667, at Mr. Montagues [03.pdf #298] [16.pdf #119]

Hagon, Ann, daughter of Thomas Hagon, married John Smith Junr., son of John Smith Senr., before 3 November 1713 [24.pdf #195]

Hall, Richard & Mary, of Portobacco
    Richard, son, born 28 July 1679 [16.pdf #120]

Hall, William & Mary, of Portobaccoe
    John, son, born 4 November 1692 [16.pdf #122]

Hanby, Francis & Hazleton, Elizabeth
    son John, born 10 February 1691 [17.pdf #209]

Hanson, John & Mary, of Portobaccoe
    Anne, daughter, born 18 January 1692 [16.pdf #123]

VITAL RECORDS

Hanson, John, Junr., married Elizabeth, "the widdow Luckett," before 12 March 1706
[23.pdf #114] [23.pdf #155]

Hanson, Samuel, son of Robert and Benedicta Hanson, born 26 December 1705
[Liber L Page 199]

Hanson, Samuel & Elizabeth [Liber L Page 200]
    Elizabeth, daughter, born Sunday 9 November 1707 "about 1 or 2 oclock
        in ye morning"
    Mary, daughter, born Saturday 6 February 1710 "about 8 oclock at night"
    Walter, son, born Tuesday 11 March 1712 "about 6 in ye morning"
    Sarah, daughter, born Thursday 29 July 1714 "about 3 in ye afternoon"
    Samuel, son, born Thursday 20 December 1716 "about 2 or 3
        in ye morning"
    William, son, born Wednesday 18 March 1719 "about half an hour
        after 11 at night"
    John, son, born Monday 3 April 1721 "about 2 or 3 in ye afternoon"
    William, son, "above mentioned," died Saturday 2 September 1721
    Jane, daughter, born Saturday 18 February 1722 "about 2 or 3
        in ye afternoon"
    Charity, daughter, born Saturday 15 August 1724 "about 7 at night"
    William, son, born Thursday 29 September 1726 "about six in the morning"

Hardy, Henry, of Pyckyawaxon, married Elinor Cumpton, "ye daughter of
    John Cumpton of St. Maryes County," 21 August 1694 [Liber Q Page 23]

Harguess, Sarah, daughter of Isbell Harguess, born 12 November 1696 [22.pdf #63]

Harmon, Francis, female, parents not named, born 29 January 1695 [24.pdf #60]

Harris, Thomas & Mary, of Pyckyawaxon
    Mary, daughter, born 16 November 1680 [16.pdf #123]
    Thomas, son, born 26 February 1682 [16.pdf #123]
    John, son, born 5 March 1684 [16.pdf #123]

Harrison, Joseph
    Richard, son, born 13 October 1659 [01.pdf #224] [16.pdf #119]
    Mary, daughter, born 21 December 1661 [01.pdf #224] [16.pdf #119]
    Elizabeth, daughter, born 11 March 1663 [03.pdf #297] [16.pdf #119]
    Katherine, daughter, born 4 January 1666 [03.pdf #297] [16.pdf #119]

VITAL RECORDS

Harrisson, Richard & Jane, of Nanjemy
    Elizabeth, daughter, born 24 July 1685 [Liber Q Page 11]
    Joseph, son, born 27 October 1687 [Liber Q Page 13]
    Richard, son, born 31 January 1690 [Liber Q Page 15]
    Tabitha, daughter, born 23 June 1693 [Liber Q Page 22]

Hawkins, Henry Junior & Sarah, of Zachyah hundred
    Henry, son, born 5 January 1689 [16.pdf #121]
Hawkins, Henry Junior, & Sarah, of ye head of Wiccomico River
    Alexander Smith Hawkins, son, born 20 January 1692 [Liber Q Page 17]

Hawling, William & Mary, of Portobaccoe
    Mary, daughter, born 29 June 1687 [16.pdf #121]
    William, son, born 18 March 1689 [16.pdf #121]

Hedges, Ralph, parents not named, born 23 October 1709 [25.pdf #181]

Hedges, Thomas, son of Ralph & Mary Hedges, born 19 December 1717
    [27.pdf #92]

Herbert, John & Elizabeth, of Zachyah hundred
    William, son, born 6 July 1688 [16.pdf #121]

Herbert, William, born 2 May 1680 [21.pdf #93]

Herbert, William & Mary, of Pyckyawaxon
    Catherine, daughter, born 6 December 1692 [16.pdf #122]

Higgins, John & Ellinor
    Elizabeth, daughter, born 27 January 1693 [22.pdf #153]
    Richard, son, born 28 February 1694 [22.pdf #153] [25.pdf #181]
    Mary, daughter, born c. 1696 [22.pdf #153]
    Margarett, daughter, born c. 1697 [22.pdf #153]

Hill, Thomas & Mary, servants to Benjamin Rozer
    Onsley, son, born 5 May 1677, baptized 3 June 1677
        [07.pdf #137] [16.pdf #120]

Hills, William, married Idy Hadlowe or Edith Headlow, June 1667,
    at Mr. Montagues [03.pdf #298] [16.pdf #119]
    Hills, unnamed, daughter, born 7 August 1667 [03.pdf #298]

Hogg, Frances, servant to Maj. William Dent, consent to marry Turlough Obryan,
    14 September 1703 [22.pdf #129]

VITAL RECORDS

Holt, James & Margarett, of Pyckyawaxon Parish
    Jane, daughter, born 19 November 1693 [Liber Q Page 21]

Holt, William & Mary, of Portobaccoe
    Robert, son, born 15 February 1695 [Liber Q Page 25]

Horton, Alice, married Thomas Browne, 26 July 1692 [16.pdf #122]

Hoskins, Philip & Elizabeth, of Portobaccoe
    Jane, daughter, born 1 March 1682 [Liber Q Page 8]
    Benedicta, daughter, born 18 December 1685 [Liber Q Page 11]
    Elizabeth, daughter, born 9 February 1688 [Liber Q Page 13]
    William, son, born 18 March 1691 [Liber Q Page 17]
    Mary, daughter, born 24 March 1692 [Liber Q Page 20]
    Margarett, daughter, born 15 August 1694 [Liber Q Page 23]

Howard, Thomas, son of Thomas & Mary Howard, born 17 July 1699 [22.pdf #4]

Hungerford, William & Margarett, of Portobaccoe
    Elizabeth, daughter, born 14 February 1692 [Liber Q Page 20]
    William, son, born 12 June 1694 [Liber Q Page 23]

Hunt, Alice, married Garret Synnet / Sinnett, 21 November 1666
    [03. pdf #298] [16.pdf #119]
Hunt, Mary, daughter in law of Garrett Synnet / Sinnett, born 24 March 1665
    [16.pdf #119]

Hus, Robert, "liveing at Edward Tills at Mattawoman formerly belonging to
    Robert Smallpage," died 24 July 1694 [Liber Q Page 23]

Jackson, William, son of Elizabeth Jackson "a single woman," born 13 April 1711
    [25.pdf #144]

Jenkins, Daniell & Elizabeth, of Pyckyawaxon
    Enock, son, born 31 July 1694 [Liber Q Page 23]

Jenkins, Philip & Fantalina
    Philip, son, born 7 March 1709 [Liber F Page 10]
    John, son, born 2 April 1711 [Liber F Page 10]

Jenkinson, William & Mary, of Wiccocomico
    Ignatius, son, born 2 May 1693 [Liber Q Page 22]

Jennians, Ignatius, parents not named, born 29 April 1716 [27.pdf #125]

VITAL RECORDS

Johnson, Diana, daughter of Mary Acton, born 25 July 1705 [23.pdf #400]

Jones, Moses & _____, of Portobaccoe
    Jane, daughter, born 4 January 1692 [16.pdf #122]
    Thomas, son, born 2 March 1695 [Liber Q Page 24]

Jones, Richard & Elizabeth, of Mattawoman
    Margarett, daughter, born 6 May 1673 [16.pdf #120]
    Mary, daughter, born 27 May 1677 [16.pdf #120]
    Elizabeth, daughter, born 27 April 1679 [16.pdf #120]

Jones, Richard & Jane
    Richard, son, born 1 April 1680 [16.pdf #121]
    Anne, daughter, born 25 December 1684 [16.pdf #121]

Karnes, Robert & Mary, of Portobaccoe
    Henry, son, born 3 September 1688 [16.pdf #121]
    William, son, born 3 April 1691 [16.pdf #122]

Ketton, Charles, son of Mary Ketton, born 28 May 1707 [23.pdf #323]

Kingersley, George & Elizabeth, of Portobaccoe
    Mary, daughter, born 15 February 1693 [Liber Q Page 20]
    Elizabeth, daughter, born 25 March 1694 [Liber Q Page 25]

Kirkley, Christopher & Catherine, of ye head of Wiccocomico River
    Susanna, daughter, born 17 March 1681 [16.pdf #122]
    Christopher, son, born 23 February 1684 [16.pdf #122]

Kite, Ann, alias Ann Beaumont
    John, son, born c. 1701 [23.pdf # 111]
    Edward, son, born 24 July 1705 [23.pdf #221]
    Elizabeth, daughter, born October 1708 [25.pdf #219]

Knight, John & Jennett, of Cedar Point Neck
    Anne, daughter, born 25 March 1688 [Liber Q Page 14]
    John, son, born 30 September 1691 [Liber Q Page 17]
    Mary, daughter, born 27 March 1694 [Liber Q Page 23]

Lambert, John
    John, son, born 5 February 1664 [06.pdf #78] [16.pdf #119]
    Elinor, daughter, born January 1667 [06.pdf #78] [16.pdf #119]
    William, son, born 27 February 1669 [06.pdf #78] [16.pdf #119]
    Samuell, son, born 10 March 1671 [06.pdf #78] [16.pdf #119]

VITAL RECORDS

Lambert, John, intention to marry Sarah Barker, 12 April 1676 [07.pdf #105]

Lampton, Marke & Elizabeth, of ye head of Portobacco Creeke
    Mary, daughter, born 24 January 1678 [16.pdf #120]
    Marke, son, born 6 October 1680 [16.pdf #120]
    William, son, born 29 April 1682 [16.pdf #120]
    Victoria, daughter, born 29 May 1685 [Liber Q Page 11]
    John, son, born 16 October 1687 [Liber Q Page 13]
    Anne, daughter, born 13 January 1690 [Liber Q Page 15]
    Elizabeth, daughter, born 8 August 1692 [Liber Q Page 20]
    Isable, daughter, born 15 December 1694 [Liber Q Page 24]

Lampton, Marke, married Anne Taunt, before 12 March 1706 [23.pdf #114] [23.pdf #156]

Land, Richard & Penelope, of Pyckyawaxon
    Richard, son, born 8 October 1687 [16.pdf #123]
    John, son, born 12 January 1689 [16.pdf #123]
    Elizabeth, daughter, born 4 April 1691 [16.pdf #123]
    Susanna, daughter, born 8 November 1694 [Liber Q Page 25]

Lange, William, parents not named, born 21 May 1699 [25.pdf #119]
Lange, John, parents not named, born 15 November 1702 [25.pdf #119]
Lange, Robert, parents not named, born September 1705 [25.pdf #119]

Langham, Jane, daughter of George Langham, born 21 August 1698 [23.pdf #89]

Leete, George & Elinor, of Portobaccoe
    John, son, born 15 January 1688 [Liber Q Page 12]

Lemaistre, Abraham, son of John & Sarah Lemaistre, born c. 1640 [Liber H Page 415]

Lewis, David & Jane, of Pyckyawaxon
    Henry, son, born 16 October 1687 [16.pdf #122]
    Isable, daughter, born 4 August 1690 [16.pdf #122]
    Mary, daughter, born 28 November 1692 [16.pdf #122]
    David, son, born 14 December 1694 [Liber Q Page 24]

Ling, Francis & Mary
    William, son, born 11 March 1669 [16.pdf #120]
    Michaell, son, born 22 January 1671 [16.pdf #120]
    Mary, daughter, born 27 March 1673 [16.pdf #120]
    Francis, son, born 9 October 1676 [16.pdf #120]

VITAL RECORDS

Lomax, Cleborne & Blanch, of ye head of Wiccocomico River
    Railph / Raiph, son, born 31 July 1673 [07.pdf #32] [16.pdf #119]
    Susanna, daughter, born 3 April 1675 [07.pdf #32] [16.pdf #120]
    Katherine, daughter, born 13 May 1677 [08.pdf #41] [16.pdf #120]
    Cleborne, son, born 22 January 1678 [16.pdf #120]
    Thomas, son, born 8 April 1681, baptized 4 July 1681 [16.pdf #120]
    John, son, born 20 November 1683 [16.pdf #120]

Long, Robert
    Jemima, daughter, born 5 January 1667 [03.pdf #299] [16.pdf #119]

Love, William
    Elizabeth, daughter, born 31 May 1668 [Vol. 60:142] [16.pdf #119]

Luckett, Samuell & Elizabeth
    Samuell, son, born 10 October 1685 [16.pdf #120]
    Thomas, son, born 12 August 1688 [16.pdf #121]
    Ignatius, son, born 30 January 1689 [16.pdf #122]

Luckett, Elizabeth, "widdow," married John Hanson Junr., before 12 March 1706 [23.pdf #114] [23.pdf #155]

Lumbrozo, John, son of John Lumbrozo, deceased, born June 1666 [03.pdf #313]

Lyndsey, James
    James, son, born 10 February 1666 [16.pdf #119]

Mackmillion, George, married Grace Carr / Carre, January 1669
    [Vol. 60:221] [16.pdf #119]
    Peter, son, born April 1670 [Vol. 60:221] [16.pdf #119]

Magittee, Patrick & Rose, of ye head of Portobacco Creek
    James, son, born "in ye last week of March" 1695 [Liber Q Page 26]

Maning, John, son of Edmond Maning, born 16 March 1703 [24.pdf #177]

Mankin, Stephen & Mary, of ye head of Portobaccoe Creeke
    Elizabeth, daughter, born 22 June 1682 [16.pdf #120]
    Stephen, son, born 4 July 1685 [16.pdf #120]
    John, son, born 16 January 1686 [16.pdf #120]
    Margarett, daughter, born 20 March 1688 [16.pdf #121]
    Josiah, son, born 18 January 1690 [16.pdf #122]
    Mary, daughter, born 9 February 1692 [16.pdf #123]

VITAL RECORDS

Mankin, Stephen & Mary, of ye head of Wiccocomicoe River [Liber Q Page 24]
    James, son, twin, born 9 January 1694 [Liber Q Page 24]
    Hope, daughter, twin, born 9 January 1694 [Liber Q Page 24]
    Tubbman, son, born 9 April 1696 [Liber Q Page 26]

Manwaring, Mary, daughter of Alice Manwaring, born 1 August 1696 [21.pdf #126]

Maris, Alice, daughter of Alice Maris, born 1 January 1671

Maris, Thomas
    Sarah, daughter, born 11 November 1667 [03.pdf #313]
    Rebeckah, daughter, born January 1669
    Mary, daughter, born 22 October 1673

Marshall, William
    Elizabeth, daughter, born 15 April 1667 [03.pdf #313] [16.pdf #119]

Marshall, William & Elizabeth, of ye head of Wiccocomicoe River
    William, son, born 12 September 1690 [16.pdf #122]
    Barbary, daughter, born 30 October 1692 [16.pdf #122]
    Thomas, son, born 27 January 1695 [Liber Q Page 24]

Martin, James & Elizabeth, of Nanjemy
    Elizabeth, daughter, born 10 April 1683 [Liber Q Page 9]
    Anne, daughter, born 23 April 1686 [Liber Q Page 12]

Martin, John, boatwright, & Damaris, of Wiccocomico
    Penelope, daughter, born 13 November 1690 [16.pdf #122]
    John, son, born 7 December 1693 [Liber Q Page 21]

Martin, John & Mary, of Portobacco
    Katherine, daughter, born 3 December 1681 [16.pdf #120]

Martin, Michaell & Jillian, of Portobaccoe
    John, son, born 15 March 1691 [Liber Q Page 17]

Mason, Philip & Mary, of Piscattaway
    Elizabeth, daughter, born 6 October 1685 [Liber Q Page 11]
    Samuell, son, born 18 April 1687 [Liber Q Page 13]
    Philip, son, born 2 June 1689 [16.pdf #121]
    William, son, born 23 January 1690 [16.pdf #122]
    John, son, born 19 July 1693 [Liber Q Page 21]

Maston, Richard & Mary, of Bakers Creek
    John, son, born 31 December 1693 [Liber Q Page 22]

VITAL RECORDS

Matthews, Victoria, "ye daughter of Thomas & Jane Matthews of Charles County," married William Thompson, "ye son of William & Mary Thompson of St. Maryes County, shee being ye daughter of William Britton of ye said County," 11 April 1681 [Liber Q Page 8]

Maud, John, born 2 May 1680 [21.pdf #93]

Mellor, Sarah, wife of John Mellor and daughter of John Cassock, died before 5 March 1707 [Liber Z Page 267]

Miller, John & Grace, of Nanjamey
    John, son, born 5 November 1673 [16.pdf #121]
    Peter, son, born 7 July 1682 [16.pdf #121]

Milstead, Edward & Susanna
    William, son, born 20 July 1685 [16.pdf #121]

Mingoe, Joseph & Elizabeth, of Nanjemy
    Lewis, son, born 12 March 1682 [Liber Q Page 8]
    Charles, son, born 14 March 1686 [Liber Q Page 11]
    Elizabeth, daughter, born 11 May 1689 [Liber Q Page 15]
    Thomas, son, born 18 October 1691 [Liber Q Page 17]

Moncaster, James & Mary
    Elizabeth, daughter, born 1703 [25.pdf #219]
    Ruth, daughter, born 6 March 1705 [25.pdf #219]
    James, son, born 11 August 1708 [25.pdf #219]
    Benjamin, son, twin, born 18 July 1711 [25.pdf #219]
    Joseph, son, twin, born 18 July 1711 [25.pdf #219]

Moody, William & Jane, of ye head of Wiccocomicoe
    Anne, daughter, born 20 March 1692 [16.pdf #123] [21.pdf #57]
    Elisha, son, born 2 April 1698 [21.pdf #57]

Moore, Henry & Elizabeth [Liber Q Pages 1 2 & 3]
    Elizabeth, daughter, born 30 March 1664 [06.pdf #93] [16.pdf #119]
    Henry, son, born 3 October 1665 [06.pdf #93] [16.pdf #119]
    Thomas, son, born 9 October 1667 [06.pdf #93] [16.pdf #119]
    John, son, born 13 March 1669 [06.pdf #93] [16.pdf #119]

Morrice, Richard
    Morrice, unnamed, son, born 12 September 1667 [03.pdf #297]
    Morrice, unnamed, son, buried 20 September 1667 [03.pdf #297]

VITAL RECORDS

Morris, Richard & Penelope, of Cedarpoint
    Mary, daughter, born 22 December 1680 [16.pdf #123]
    Penelope, daughter, born 13 November 1684 [16.pdf #123]

Morris, Stephen & Anne, of Wiccocomico
    Thomas, son, born 9 November 1693 [Liber Q Page 21]

Mould, John, intention to marry Anna Posey, 12 April 1669 [09.pdf #142]

Murfrey, Dennis, died "at Mr. James Lyndseys," 23 September 1667
    [03.pdf #298] [16.pdf #119]

Murphey, Joseph, parents not named, born 15 November 1707 [23.pdf #390]

Musgrave, Charles, married Susanna Phillpott, daughter of Edward Phillpott, before 12 March 1711 [24.pdf #158]

Musgrave, Dorothy, widow, married Charles Charleson, 14 November 1689 [16.pdf #121]

Neale, Ann, daughter of James Neale Senr., "of Charles County," married Edward Cole Junr., "of St. Marys County," before 10 January 1716 [Liber F Page 85]

Neale, Anthony, son of James Neale, intention to marry Elizabeth Rosewell, daughter of William Rosewell, 13 March 1683 [11.pdf #89]

Newton, Richard & Jane, of Wiccocomico
    Richard, son, baptized 13 May 1693 [16.pdf #123]

Nicholls, John & Bethsheba
    Jonathan, son, born c. 1702 [25.pdf #172]
    William, son, born c. 1706 [25.pdf #144]
    Solomon, son, born August 1710 [25.pdf #144]
    Benjamin, son, born 8 March 1713 [25.pdf #219] [25.pdf #271]

Obryan, Mathias & Elizabeth
    Ellener / Elinor, daughter, born 5 November 1666
        [03.pdf #267] [16.pdf #119]
    Elizabeth, wife, died 6 May 1670 [Vol. 60:221][16.pdf #119]
Obryan, Mathias & Magdalen, of Mattawoman
    William, son, born 6 March 1672 [16.pdf #120]

Obryan, Turlough, servant to Maj. William Dent, consent to marry Frances Hogg, 14 September 1703 [22.pdf #129]

VITAL RECORDS

Ord, Peter & Anne, of Wiccocomicoe
    Mary, daughter, born 24 March 1683 [16.pdf #121]
    Thomas, son, born 19 November 1686 [16.pdf #121]
    James, son, born 21 April 1690 [16.pdf #121]
    Anne, daughter, born 19 September 1694 [Liber Q Page 23]

Paine / Payne, John, married Marie / Mary White, 23 September 1667 [03.pdf #298] [16.pdf #119]

Parry, Susanna, daughter of James Parry, born 1 or 2 September 1674

Pattison, John, parents not stated, born 15 September 1690 [23.pdf #236]

Peale, Henry, servant to Zacharie Wade, died 29 June 1662 [01.pdf #247]

Penn, William & Mary, of ye head of Wiccocomico River
    John, son, born c. 1684 [22.pdf #22]
    Marke, son, born 4 or 24 November 1692 [16.pdf #122] [22.pdf #22]
    Elizabeth, daughter, born 2 June 1696 [22.pdf #22]

Penny, James, parents not named, born 4 February 1698 [25.pdf #33]

Percey / Peircy, Thomas, died 5 November 1666 [03.pdf #297]

Perkins, William, son of John Perkins, born c. July 1708 [23.pdf #321]

Philpot / Phylpot, Edward
    Charles, son, born 19 February 1667 [03.pdf #297] [16.pdf #119]

Philpott, Edward & Susanna, of Wiccocomico
    Edward, son, born 14 January 1687 [16.pdf #122]
    Susanna, daughter, born 9 June 1690 [16.pdf #122]
    John, son, born 13 October 1692 [16.pdf #122]

Phillpott, Susana, daughter of Edward Phillpott, married Charles Musgrave, before 12 March 1711 [24.pdf #158]

Pile, Joseph, son of Capt. Joseph Pile, born 1688 [23.pdf #141]

Posey, Anna, intention to marry John Mould, 12 April 1669 [09.pdf #142]

Posey, Benjamin & Mary, of ye head of Wiccocomico River
    Susanna, daughter, born 1 June 1691 [16.pdf #123]
    Mary, daughter, born 10 September 1693 [Liber Q Page 22]

VITAL RECORDS

Posey, John & Susanna Posey of ye head of Wiccocomico River
    Humphrey, son, born 1 February 1683 [16.pdf #122]
    John, son, born 30 July 1685 [16.pdf #122]

Powell, Robert & _____, of Pyckyawaxon
    Robert, born 17 November 1692, baptized 10 January 1693 [16.pdf #122]

Price, Robert & Anne, of Portobaccoe
    Mary, daughter, born 12 November 1692 [16.pdf #122]

Raines, John & Elizabeth, of Mattawoman
    Elizabeth, daughter, born 26 June 1684 [16.pdf #121]
    Henry, son, born 3 September 1686 [16.pdf #121]
    Lucy, daughter, born 7 December 1688 [16.pdf #121]

Randall, Richard, died 7 September 1667 [03.pdf #298] [16.pdf #119]

Ratclife, John & Batsheba, of Wiccocomicoe
    Richard, son, born 16 December 1692 [16.pdf #122]

Redfern, James & Faith, of Portobaccoe
    Mary, daughter, born 16 December 1694 [Liber Q Page 25]

Reeves, William, son of Mary Reeves, born 7 October 1709 [25.pdf #16]

Regon, James, bricklayer, & Joan, of Nanjemy
    Mary, daughter, born 28 August 1683 [Liber Q Page 9]
    John, son, born 24 March 1685 [Liber Q Page 11]
    Matthew, son, born 24 April 1687 [Liber Q Page 13]
    William, son, born 31 January 1691 [Liber Q Page 16]
    Charles, son, born 20 May 1692 [Liber Q Page 20]
    Margarett, daughter, born 12 February 1695 [Liber Q Page 23]

Right, George
    Ellinore, daughter, born 7 October 1683 [16.pdf #120]

Robinson, John, married Elizabeth Browne, 21 March 1666
    [03.pdf #298] [16.pdf #119]

Robinson, Mary, daughter of _____ Robinson, born 5 December 1688 [14.pdf #111]

Robinson, Richard & Joyce, of ye head of Wiccocomico River
    Susanna, daughter, born 20 October 1677 [16.pdf #121]
    Mary, daughter, born 17 December 1679 [16.pdf #121]

VITAL RECORDS

Rodd, Mary, daughter of Mary Rodd, born 27 September 1701 [23.pdf #79]

Roelants, Robert & Margery, of Wiccomico
    Dinah, daughter, born 2 May 1677 [16.pdf #122]

Rookewood, Edward & Mary, of Chingoemaxon
    Edward, son, born 25 December 1692 [16.pdf #122]

Rosewell, Elizabeth, daughter of William Rosewell, intention to marry Anthony Neale, son of James Neale, 13 March 1683 [11.pdf #89]

Rouse / Rouze, John, servant to John Cage, died 25 January 1666
    [03.pdf #297] [16.pdf #119]

Rozer, Benjamin & Mary
    Notley, son, born 1 July 1673 [06.pdf #142] [16.pdf #119]
    Mary, daughter, born 6 April 1675 [07.pdf #73] [16.pdf #120]

Rue, Elizabeth
    Temperance, daughter, born 14 October 1683 [17.pdf #209]

Russell, Mary, parents not named, born 4 April 1703 [25.pdf #219]

Sapcoate, Abram & Rachell, of ye Riverside
    Elizabeth, daughter, born 12 November 1677 [16.pdf #121]

Saunders, Edward & Jane, of ye west side of Portobaccoe Creeke
    Edward, son, born 6 November 1685 [Liber Q Page 11]
    Thomas, son, born 30 March 1688 [Liber Q Page 14]
    Charles, son, born 18 July 1690 [Liber Q Page 15]

Saunders, John & Sarah, of Portobaccoe
    Mary, daughter, born 19 April 1692 [16.pdf #123]

Scroggin, George & Susanna, of Pyckyawaxon
    Elizabeth, daughter, born 14 May 1686 [16.pdf #122]
    John, son, born 27 December 1687 [16.pdf #122]
    Mary, daughter, born 16 March 1688 [16.pdf #122]
    George, son, born 13 November 1692 [16.pdf #122]
    Susanna, daughter, born 5 February 1695 [Liber Q Page 24]

Semmes. Marmaduke, parents not named, born November 1694 [23.pdf #390]

Sennet, Elizabeth, daughter of Gerrard Sennet, born 31 August 1717 [24.pdf #96]

VITAL RECORDS

Shackerley, John & Francis, of ye head of Wiccocomico River
    Edward, son, born 3 August 1694 [Liber Q Page 23]

Shareman, Elizabeth, parents not named, born 18 October 1705 [25.pdf #171]
Sharman, Bead, parents not named, born 1 November 1708 [25.pdf #171]

Simpson, Andrew, intention to marry Juliana Price, widow, 19 May 1718
    [Liber H Page 173]

Smallwood, James & Esther [Liber Q Pages 2 3 & 4]
    John, son, born January 1666 [06.pdf #154] [16.pdf #119]
    James, son, born October 1668 [06.pdf #154] [16.pdf #119]
    Mary, daughter, born January 1670 [06.pdf #154] [16.pdf #119]
    Matthew, son, born April 1673 [06.pdf #154] [16.pdf #119]

Smith, Anthony, married Martha Baker, orphan of Thomas Baker deceased,
    before 8 November 1692 [17.pdf #277]

Smith, Henry & Margery, of Portobaccoe
    Thomas, son, born 3 March 1692 [Liber Q Page 20]
    Henry, son, born 5 November 1694 [Liber Q Page 24]

Smith / Smyth, John, married Margarett Barker, 14 February 1666/7
    [03.pdf #297] [16.pdf #119]

Smith, John, Junr., son of John Smith Senr., married Ann Hagon, daughter of
    Thomas Hagon, before 3 November 1713 [24.pdf #195]

Smith, Richard & Anne, of Pyckyawaxon
    Richard, son, born 11 July 1688 [Liber Q Page 14]
    Elizabeth, daughter, born 12 September 1690 [Liber Q Page 17]
    Arthur, son, born 23 April 1692 [Liber Q Page 20]
    James, son, born 23 August 1694 [Liber Q Page 25]

Smith, William & Joan, of Wiccocomico
    William, son, born 15 September 1691 [Liber Q Page 17]
    Jane, daughter, born 10 September 1694 [Liber Q Page 23]

Smoote, Edward & Lydia, of Wiccocomico
    John, son, born 22 November 1686 [Liber Q Page 12]
    Edward, born 20 June 1693 [Liber Q Page 21]

Smoote, Grace, wife of William Smoote, died 14 January 1665/6
    [03.pdf #297] [16.pdf #119]

VITAL RECORDS

Smoote, Richard
    Elizabeth, daughter, born 15 December 1666
        [03.pdf #297] [16.pdf #119]
    William, son of Richard Smoote, born June 1671

Steel, George, "a poor motherless bastard boy," born 1 April 1711 [26.pdf #172]

Stigeleer, Jame & Mary, of Portobacco Parrish
    Jane, daughter, born 4 June 1702 [Liber Q Page 26]

Sympson, Andrew, married Elizabeth Green, daughter of Robert Green,
    before 9 November 1702 [Liber Z Page 27]

Synnet / Sinnett, Garret, married Alice Hunt, 21 November 1666
        [03. pdf #298] [16.pdf #119]
    Margarett, daughter, born 24 October 1667 [03.pdf #298] [16.pdf #119]

Taunt, Anne, married Marke Lampton, before 12 March 1706 [23.pdf #114]
    [23.pdf #156]

Tayler, Thomas & Anne, of Pyckyawaxon
    John, son, born 8 January 1692 [16.pdf #122]
    Thomas, son, born 3 March 1695 [Liber Q Page 24]

Theobalds, John & Mary, of Portobaccoe
    John, son, born September 1692 [Liber Q Page 20]

Thirst, Elizabeth, married John Dawson, 16 September 1690 [16.pdf #122]

Thompkins, Giles & Sarah Thompkins of Pyckyawaxon
    Giles, son, born 23 November 1692 [16.pdf #122]

Thompson, John & Mary, of Portobaccoe
    Mary, daughter, born 8 January 1695 [Liber Q Page 25]

Thompson, William, "ye son of William & Mary Thompson of St. Maryes County, shee being ye daughter of William Britton of ye said County," married Victoria Matthews, "ye daughter of Thomas & Jane Matthews of Charles County," 11 April 1681 [Liber Q Page 8]

VITAL RECORDS

Thompson, William & Victoria, of ye head of Wiccocomico River
    Thomas, son, born 12 September 1682 [Liber Q Page 9]
    William, son, born 5 March 1685 [Liber Q Page 10]
    Victoria, daughter, born 30 May 1687 [Liber Q Page 12]
    Jane, daughter, born 13 November 1689 [Liber Q Page 15]
    Cuthbert, son, born 12 September 1692 [Liber Q Page 20]
    Mary, daughter, born 12 February 1695 [Liber Q Page 25]

Toney, John, married Dorothy Charleson, widow, before 9 January 1694
    [18.pdf #140]

Tymothy, William & Mabella, of Pyckyawaxon
    Mabella, daughter, born 12 October 1693 [Liber Q Page 22]

Typpett, Elizabeth, "naturall borne daughter" of Elizabeth Harrison ye wife of
    Benjamin Harrison, born 8 January 1693 [19.pdf #111]

Vassall, Lewis & Elizabeth
    Thomas, son, born 8 September 1680 [16.pdf #120]

Waalwort, Isaac, man servant to William Marshall, buried 31 August 1667
    [03.pdf #297]

Wade, Zachary / Zachery
    Mary, daughter, born 20 April 1661 [01.pdf #146, 247] [16.pdf #119]
    Mary, daughter, died 21 July 1661 [01.pdf #146, 247] [16.pdf #119]
    Sarah / Zarah, daughter, born 7 July 1662 [01.pdf #247] [16.pdf #119]
    Sarah / Zarah, daughter, died 17 August 1662 [01.pdf #247] [16.pdf #119]
    Wade, unnamed, son, born 22 September 1666 [03.pdf #267]
    Wade, unnamed, son, died 1666, "before Baptized" [03.pdf #267]
    Edward, son, born 2 November 1670 [Vol. 60:262] [16.pdf #119]
    Edward, son, died 22 August 1672 [06.pdf #78] [16.pdf #119]
    William, son, died 3 November 1673 [06.pdf #157] [16.pdf #119]

Wakelin, Richard Junior and Catherine
    Richard, son, born 18 August 1687 [17.pdf #113]

Ward, James, "an orphan lad," parents not named, born 27 May 1705 [26.pdf #172]

Ward, John & Damaris [Liber Q Pages 1 & 2]
    Anne, daughter, born 5 February 1663 [03.pdf #297] [16.pdf #119]
    Marie/Mary, daughter, born 5 July 1665 [03.pdf #297] [16.pdf #119]
    Anne, daughter, born 10 April 1667 [03.pdf #297] [16.pdf #119]
    John, son, born 16 March 1671 [06.pdf #154] [16.pdf #119]

VITAL RECORDS

Ward, John, deceased, and Damaris, his wife, alias Damaris Sarjeant, ye naturall mother of James Ward, ref. Deed dated 17 July 1694 [18.pdf #243]

Warren, Humphrey & Elizabeth, of Wikocomico
    Notley, son, born 16 December 1675 [16.pdf #122]

Warren, Humphrey & Margery, of Wiccocomico
    Benjamin, son, born 23 January 1682 [16.pdf #122]
    Charles, son, born 10 November 1684 [16.pdf #122]
    John, son, born 18 June 1687 [16.pdf #122]
    Humphrey, son, born 15 November 1691 [16.pdf #122]

Warren, Thomas & Mary, of Wicccomicoe
    Elinor, daughter, born 7 March 1691 [Liber Q Page 16]

Weavour, Adam
    Adam, son, born 3 January 1701 [23.pdf #254]
    Hannah, daughter, born 31 January 1704 [23.pdf #254]

Wharton, Thomas, parents not named, born March 1697 [23.pdf #390]

Wheeler, Ignatius & Francis, of Portobaccoe
    Luke, son, born 8 February 1694 [Liber Q Page 22]
    Luke, son, died 8 January 1695 [Liber Q Page 24]

Wheeler, John & Mary [Liber Q Pages 1 & 2]
    John, son, born "in the yeare" 1654 [03.pdf #298] [16.pdf #119]
    James, son, born 16 December 1656 [03.pdf #298] [16.pdf #119]
    Marie/Mary, daughter, born 22 March 1658 [03.pdf #298] [16.pdf #119]
    Thomas, son, born 18 March 1660 [03.pdf #298] [16.pdf #119]
    Winnifrett, daughter, born March 1663 [03.pdf #298] [16.pdf #119]
    Ignatius, son, born May 1665 [03.pdf #298] [16.pdf #119]

Whichaley, Jane, "ye wife of Thomas Whichaley of Pyckyawaxon Parish," died 7 November 1693 [Liber Q Page 21]

Whichaley, Thomas, married Elizabeth Ford, widow of Edward Ford deceased, "who was ye daughter of Thomas Allanson of Chingoemuxon deceased," 25 April 1694 [Liber Q Page 23]

White, Marie / Mary, married John Paine / Payne, 23 September 1667 [03.pdf #298] [16.pdf #119]

Whittymore, Christopher & Anne, of Portobaccoe
    Anne, daughter, born 5 September 1690 [Liber Q Page 16]
    Richard, son, born 2 September 1694 [Liber Q Page 25]

VITAL RECORDS

Wilder, John & Ever Elday, of Wiccocomicoe
    Edward, son, born 27 November 1689, baptized 1 December 1689
    [16.pdf #122]
    John, son, born 30 September 1692, baptized 2 October 1692
    [16.pdf #122]

Wilkenson, William, servant to Zachery Wade, died June 1666 [03.pdf #267]

Wilkinson, Lancelott & Mary, of Mattawoman
    Mary, daughter, born 15 October 1687 [Liber Q Page 13]

Williams, John, died February 1661, entered by Joseph Harrisson [01.pdf #224]

Williams, John & Sarah, of ye Riverside
    William, son, born 2 October 1685 [16.pdf #121]
    John, son, born 2 August 1688 [16.pdf #121]

Willson, Ralph, son of Mary Willson, born 25 April 1705 [23.pdf #221]

Withy, Thomas, son of Joan Withy, born 12 or 13 October 1693 [19.pdf #135]

Witter, Thomas & Mary
    Thomas, son, born 9 February 1672 [16.pdf #120] [22.pdf #32]
    Buckeley, son, born 26 July 1675 [16.pdf #120]
    William, son, born 26 September 1678 [16.pdf #120]
    George, son, born 9 October 1683 [16.pdf #122]

Woolcock, Christopher & Mary, of Portobaccoe
    Christian, daughter, born 10 December 1694 [Liber Q Page 24]

Worland, John
    John, son, born 2 January 1685 [13.pdf #19]

Wright, George & Anne
    Elinor, daughter, born 7 October 1683 [Liber Q Page 9]

Wright, Mary, daughter of Elizabeth Wright, born 21 April 1700 [22.pdf #144]

Yates, Robert & Rebeckah, of Pyckyawaxon
    Robert, son, born 10 April 1690 [16.pdf #122]
    Charles, son, born 29 April 1692 [16.pdf #122]

Younge, Lawrance & Sarah, of ye head of Bakers Creeke
    John, son, born 4 December 1673 [16.pdf #120]
    Thomas, son, born 18 May 1678 [16.pdf #120]

WITNESSES WHO STATED THEIR AGES

1658-1732

Adams, Charles	c. 1672	age 60	10 Apr 1732	32.pdf #81
Addams, Charles	c. 1673	age 48	3 May 1721	Liber M:127
Adams, Francis	c. 1644/45	age 25/26	9 Mar 1670	Vol. 60:254
Allanson, Thomas	c. 1638	age 22	17 Apr 1660	01.pdf #93
Allonson, Thomas	c. 1638	age 24	4 Mar 1662	01.pdf #198
Allen, James	c. 1691	age 28	20 Aug 1719	Liber M:50
Allen, John	c. 1663	age 56	12 Aug 1719	Liber M:48
Allen, John, Gent.	c. 1654	age 52	26 Apr 1706	23.pdf #134
Allen, Joseph, Senr.	c. 1665	age 64	7 April 1729	31.pdf #139
Allen, Joseph, Senr.	c. 1665	age 64	7 April 1729	31.pdf #139
Allin, John	c. 1689	age 32	5 Aug 1721	Liber M:146
Allinson, James	c. 1693	age 28	3 May 1721	Liber M:127
Allison, Thomas	c. 1696	age 23	4 Nov 1719	Liber M:67
Allison, Thomas	c. 1697	age 24	20 May 1721	Liber M:122
Annis, Thomas	c. 1687	age 44	2 Mar 1731	31.pdf #240
Annis, Thomas	c. 1687	age 45	10 Apr 1732	32.pdf #81
Ashbrooke, John	c. 1623	age 39	29 Jan 1662	01.pdf #193
Ashbrooke, Rose	c. 1631	age 31	29 Jan 1662	01.pdf #193
Baker, John	c. 1677	age 48	10 Aug 1725	30.pdf #37
Baker, John	c. 1677	age 50	3 Oct 1727	31.pdf #20
Baker, John	c. 1679	age 50	14 Feb 1729	31.pdf #175
Baker, John	c. 1677	age 53	5 May 1730	31.pdf #205
Baker, John	c. 1677	age 53	5 Oct 1730	31.pdf #228
Baker, Mary	c. 1681	age 48	14 Feb 1729	31.pdf #175
Baker, Thomas	c. 1623	age 48	10 Jan 1671	06.pdf #35
Barber, Richard	c. 1677	age 50	14 Mar 1727	30.pdf #211
Barnes, Matthew	c. 1672	age 49	5 Aug 1721	Liber M:146
Batcheler, Francis	c. 1636	age 26	4 Mar 1662	01.pdf #202
Batchelor, Francis	c. 1636	age 26	5 Nov 1662	02.pdf #73
Batchelor, Francis	c. 1636	age 26	5 Nov 1662	02.pdf #73
Bateman, George	c. 1652	age 68	14 Jun 1720	26.pdf #173
Battin, William, Captain	c. 1619	age 43	22 Apr 1662	01.pdf #211
Beck, Lewis	c. 1657	age 13	11 Jan 1670	Vol. 60:235
Beck, Richard	c. 1651	age 19	11 Jan 1670	Vol. 60:234
Bennam, Margaret	c. 1641	age 20	2 Jul 1661	01.pdf #150
Bentley, Nathan	c. 1641	age 30	14 Nov 1671	06.pdf #54
Birch, Oliver	c. 1646	age 80	26 Sep 1726	30.pdf #203
Birch, Thomas	c. 1685	age 41	26 Sep 1726	30.pdf #203
Blakwood, John	c. 1627	age 33	6 Jun 1660	01.pdf #101
Boarman, "Old Major"	c. 1627	age 80	15 Sep 1707	Liber C:158
Bocknell, John	c. 1665	age 66	13 Apr 1731	32.pdf #24
Bonner, Elizabeth	c. 1642	age 63	9 Jun 1705	Liber Z:210
Bonner, Henry	c. 1646	age 28	22 Apr 1674	06.pdf #154

WITNESSES WHO STATED THEIR AGES

Boswell, William	c. 1682	age 38	18 Jul 1720	Liber M:107
Bouls, Margeret	c. 1633	age 30	29 Jul 1663	02.pdf #229
Branson, Anne	c. 1642	age 20	8 Jul 1662	01.pdf #226
Brent, Margaret	c. 1639	age 20	10 Mar 1659	01.pdf #49
Briscoe, John, Capt.	c. 1678	age 47	17 May 1725	30.pdf #21
Brown, Francis	c. 1693	age 39	6 Jun 1732	32.pdf #79
Browne, John	c. 1637	age 26	29 Jul 1663	02.pdf #226
Buckridge, Thomas	c. 1643	age 26	12 Jan 1669	Vol. 60:180
Bull, Thomas	c. 1653	age 21	11 Nov 1674	07.pdf #26
Burch, Jestinian	c. 1682	age 50	14 Jun 1732	32.pdf #80
Burdit, Thomas	c. 1586	age 77	28 Jul 1663	02.pdf #196
Burrell, Joseph	c. 1661	age 47	17 Oct 1708	23.pdf #306
Cable, John	c. 1636	age 24	23 Oct 1660	01.pdf #116
Cadwell, William	c. 1632	age 30	28 Jan 1662	01.pdf #185
Caine, John	c. 1620	age 40	4 Sep 1660	01.pdf #107
Candle, John	c. 1663	age 69	14 Jun 1732	32.pdf #80
Carpender, James	c. 1639	age 23	8 Jul 1662	01.pdf #225
Carr, Peter	c. 1625	age 34	10 Mar 1659	01.pdf #49
Carrington, Timothy	c. 1686	age 40	8 Nov 1726	30.pdf #200
Carter, William	c. 1659	age 60	18 Nov 1719	Liber M:72
Carter, William, Senr.	c. 1661	age 66	28 Feb 1727	30.pdf #213
Castleton, Robert	c. 1661/62	age 19/20	13 Sep 1681	10.pdf #102
Cavenagh, Hugh	c. 1646/47	age 21/22	9 June 1668	03.pdf #316
Chandler, William	c. 1676	age 42	22 Dec 1718	Liber M:41
Chandler, William	c. 1677	age 48	30 Nov 1725	30.pdf #74
Chandler, William	c. 1677	age 49	15 Mar 1726	30.pdf #153
Chapman, Richard	c. 1674	age 52	8 Nov 1726	30.pdf #205
Chapman, Richard	c. 1674	age 54	23 Jul 1728	31.pdf #85
Chapman, Richard	c. 1672	age 59	2 Mar 1731	31.pdf #241
Chapman, Thomas	c. 1642	age 21	10 Feb 1663	02.pdf #134
Charman, Elisabeth	c. 1631	age 32	29 Jul 1663	02.pdf #227
Ching, John	c. 1684	age 36	17 Feb 1720	Liber M:75
Clemens, John	c. 1648	age 78	8 Nov 1726	30.pdf #198
Clemons, John, Junr.	c. 1680	age 40	18 Jul 1720	Liber M:106
Cocks, John	c. 1679	age 52	7 Jun 1731	31,pdf #262
Coleman, Thomas	c. 1664	age 65	13 Sep 1729	31.pdf #174
Conner, Richard	c. 1661	age 45	17 Jul 1706	23.pdf #136
Coombes, Richard	c. 1656	age 63	4 Nov 1719	Liber M:66
Coombes, Richard	c. 1656	age 63	4 Nov 1719	Liber M:67
Coombs, Richard	c. 1654	age 75	29 Apr 1729	31.pdf #140
Cooper, Nicholas	c. 1638	age 67	3 Dec 1705	23.pdf #135
Cornish, John	c. 1695	age 26	21 May 1721	Liber M:123
Cornish, John	c. 1692	age 35	20 Jan 1727	30.pdf #249
Cottington, Edward	c. 1669	age 50	4 Nov 1719	Liber M:66
Cottington, Edward	c. 1671	age 50	2 Jun 1721	Liber M:2

WITNESSES WHO STATED THEIR AGES

Name	Birth	Age	Date	Reference
Cox, James	c. 1643	age 31	11 Nov 1674	07.pdf #29
Craen, John	c. 1674	age 51	17 May 1725	30.pdf #21
Craen, John	c. 1674	age 51	17 May 1725	30.pdf #21
Craen, John	c. 1675	age 51	22 Feb 1726	30.pdf #71
Crakson, Thomas	c. 1639	age 22	24 Sep 1661	01.pdf #163
Crakson, Thomas	c. 1639	age 22	19 Nov 1661	01.pdf #175
Cressey, Samuel	c. 1644	age 27	10 Mar 1671	06.pdf #45
Davies, Walter	c. 1641	age 30	10 Mar 1671	06.pdf #43
Dawson, John	c. 1619	age 80	4 Apr 1699	20.pdf #29
Delahay, Jane	c. 1629	age 30	1 May 1659	01.pdf #64
Delahay, Jane	c. 1629	age 33	22 Apr 1662	01.pdf #212
Delahay, John	c. 1623	age 36	1 May 1659	01.pdf #64
Dent, John, Senr.	c. 1674	age 53	2 May 1727	30.pdf #248
Dent, John	c. 1674	age 53	2 May 1727	30.pdf #248
Dent, Thomas	c. 1686	age 39	12 Nov 1725	30.pdf #72
Dod, Mary	c. 1636	age 26	9 Jul 1662	01.pdf #234
Dod, Richard	c. 1636	age 26	9 Jul 1662	01.pdf #240
Dode, Marie	c. 1638	age 21	26 Jan 1659	01.pdf #43
Dode, Richard	c. 1634	age 25	26 Jan 1659	01.pdf #43
Donaldson, Daniel	c. 1650	age 69	18 Nov 1719	Liber M:72
Dorosall, Joseph	c. 1634	age 36	11 Jan 1670	Vol. 60:234
Dorrosell, Joseph	c. 1623	age 40	12 May 1663	02.pdf #178
Dorrosell, Joseph	c. 1623	age 40	29 July 1663	02.pdf #224
Doughty, Ane	c. 1620	age 42	5 Nov 1662	02.pdf #73
Doughty, Enock	c. 1639	age 22	25 Sep 1661	01.pdf #164
Douglas, John	c. 1636	age 25	19 Nov 1661	01.pdf #176
Dove, Phillip	c. 1675	age 45	18 Jul 1720	Liber M:107
Doyne, Jesse	c. 1677	age 44	2 Aug 1721	Liber M:138
Dyson, Thomas	c. 1679	age 50	7 April 1729	31.pdf #139
Edelen, Richard	c. 1640	age 31	10 Mar 1671	06.pdf #45
Edelen, Richard	c. 1670	age 50	18 Feb 1720	Liber M:77
Edelen, Richard	c. 1670	age 56	8 Nov 1726	30.pdf #202
Edelin, Richard	c. 1671	age 57	12 Aug 1728	31.pdf #86
Edelin, Richard	c. 1671	age 58	14 Feb 1729	31.pdf #175
Edelen, Thomas	c. 1673	age 48	11 Jan 1721	Liber M:109
Ellis, Owen	c. 1678	age 51	13 Sep 1729	31.pdf #174
Empson, William	c. 1630	age 28	23 Nov 1658	01.pdf #36
Etty / Ettye, Arthur	c. 1626	age 67	14 Mar 1693	18.pdf #72
Evans, Peter	c. 1655	age 25	4 Jun 1680	12.pdf #22
Evans, Stephen	c. 1677	age 52	16 May 1729	31.pdf #141
Fearson, Walter	c. 1708	age 24	6 Jun 1732	32.pdf #79
Fendall, John, Capt.	c. 1673	age 46	25 Sep 1719	Liber M:53
Fendall, John, Coll.	c. 1674	age 56	5 May 1730	31.pdf #205
Ferdinando, Peter	c. 1654	age 67	5 Aug 1721	Liber M:145
Ferdinando, Peter	c. 1655	age 71	8 Nov 1726	30.pdf #202

WITNESSES WHO STATED THEIR AGES

Ferneley, Francis	c. 1637	age 30	10 Sep 1667	03.pdf #284
Ford, Thomas	c. 1676	age 51	20 Jan 1727	30.pdf #249
Fowke, Gerard	c. 1662	age 63	12 Nov 1725	30.pdf #72
Fowke, Gerard	c. 1663	age 64	8 Nov 1726	30.pdf #198
Fowke, Gerard	c. 1663	age 64	8 Nov 1726	30.pdf #199
Franklin, John	c. 1672	age 47	20 Aug 1719	Liber M:50
Franklin, John	c. 1672	age 55	20 Jan 1727	30.pdf #250
Franklin, John	c. 1671	age 58	29 Apr 1729	31.pdf #140
French, Daniell	c. 1640	age 60	12 Mar 1700	20.pdf #194
Gabriell, Bartholomew	c. 1631	age 28	1 May 1659	01.pdf #63
Games, John	c. 1691	age 23	5 Dec 1714	Liber F:47
Gartherell, Bartholme	c. 1635	age 27	10 Jul 1662	01.pdf #243
Ges, Ane	c. 1636	age 26	28 Jan 1662	01.pdf #185
Ges, Ane	c. 1636	age 26	4 Mar 1662	01.pdf #202
Gey, Anne	c. 1609	age 50	26 Jan 1659	01.pdf #42
Giles, Peter	c. 1655/56	age 25/26	9 Mar 1681	10.pdf #74
Gilpin, Isaac	c. 1675	age 51	8 Nov 1726	30.pdf #206
Glass, Francis	c. 1674	age 58	4 Mar 1732	32.pdf #45
Glaze, John	c. 1677	age 50	14 Mar 1727	30.pdf #214
Godfrey, William	c. 1678	age 41	22 Dec 1719	Liber M:68
Godfrey, William	c. 1678	age 43	20 May 1721	Liber M:123
Godfrey, William	c. 1679	age 42	24 Jul 1721	Liber M:130
Godfrey, William	c. 1678	age 43	2 Jun 1721	Liber M:2
Goodrick, Francis, Junr.	c. 1670	age 48	22 Dec 1718	Liber M:41
Goodrick, Francis, Senr.	c. 1647	age 79	8 Nov 1726	30.pdf #197
Goodrick, Francis, Senr.	c. 1648	age 78	8 Nov 1726	30.pdf #199
Goodrick, Robert	c. 1635	age 70	7 Dec 1705	Liber Z:226
Gore, Anne	c. 1642	age 60	9 Jun 1702	22.pdf #32
Goudy, William	c. 1668	age 57	19 May 1725	30.pdf #23
Goudy, William	c. 1668	age 57	21 Dec 1725	30.pdf #73
Gourdon, Daniell	c. 1626	age 34	17 Apr 1660	01.pdf #93
Gray, Edward	c. 1685	age 41	15 Mar 1726	30.pdf #153
Green, James	c. 1657	age 69	8 Nov 1726	30.pdf #197
Green, James	c. 1657	age 69	8 Nov 1726	30.pdf #199
Greenfeild, Thomas Trueman, Coll.	c. 1682	age 47	13 Sep 1729	31.pdf #174
Greenfeild, Thomas Trueman, Coll.	c. 1682	age 47	13 Sep 1729	31.pdf #174
Gwinn, John	c. 1673	age 46	6 Feb 1719	Liber H:219
Gwinn, John	c. 1673	age 46	13 Mar 1719	Liber H:219
Haggate, Humpherie	c. 1629	age 33	22 Apr 1662	01.pdf #211
Hamil, John	c. 1692	age 38	5 May 1730	31.pdf #205
Hamil, John	c. 1692	age 38	5 May 1730	31.pdf #205
Hamill, John	c. 1692	age 37	14 Feb 1729	31.pdf #175
Hammill, John	c. 1702	age 29	18 Sep 1731	32.pdf #26

WITNESSES WHO STATED THEIR AGES

Hanson, Robert	c. 1680	age 40	9 Mar 1720	Liber M:87
Hanson, Robert	c. 1680	age 45	10 Aug 1725	30.pdf #36
Hanson, Robert	c. 1680	age 50	5 Oct 1730	31.pdf #228
Hare, James	c. 1628	age 30	27 Oct 1658	01.pdf #32
Harris, Ales	c. 1611	age 48	12 May 1659	01.pdf #59
Harris, George	c. 1633	age 30	29 Jul 1663	02.pdf #228
Harris, Samuell	c. 1619	age 40	12 May 1659	01.pdf #57
Harrise, Samuell	c. 1638	age 24	4 Mar 1662	01.pdf #198
Hatch, John	c. 1614	age 45	26 Jan 1659	01.pdf #40
Hawton, William	c. 1698	age 22	20 Apr 1720	Liber M:83
Hayes, James	c. 1641	age 30	14 Nov 1671	06.pdf #54
Hays, James	c. 1639	age 23	22 Apr 1662	01.pdf #209
Hays, Patrick	c. 1639	age 23	26 Mar 1662	02.pdf #68
Hays, Patrick	c. 1639	age 23	1 Oct 1662	01.pdf #249
Helgar, Thomas	c. 1645	age 26	14 Nov 1671	06.pdf #53
Hennington, Elias	c. 1680	age 40	21 May 1720	Liber M:91
Henson, William	c. 1626	age 35	19 Nov 1661	01.pdf #175
Higdon, John	c. 1650	age 62	11 Mar 1712	24.pdf #34
Hill, Thomas	c. 1676	age 49	12 Mar 1725	30.pdf #22
Hipkis, Peter	c. 1638	age 24	22 Apr 1662	01.pdf #209
Holding, Richard	c. 1688	age 39	20 Jan 1727	30.pdf #250
Hoskins, William	c. 1691	age 28	3 Jul 1719	Liber M:48
Hoskins, William	c. 1690	age 29	17 Nov 1719	Liber M:72
Howard, Edmund	c. 1657	age 46	9 Nov 1703	22.pdf #151
Hulse, Meverell	c. 1631	age 40	10 Jan 1671	06.pdf #36
Hundly, Robert	c. 1617	age 44	19 Nov 1661	01.pdf #176
Hungerford, Barton	c. 1687	age 44	7 Jun 1731	31.pdf #261
Hunkyn, Thomas	c. 1656	age 27	5 Mar 1683	11.pdf #84
Hunt, Thomas	c. 1667	age 53	17 May 1721	Liber M:116
Hussey, Elisabeth	c. 1642	age 20	9 July 1662	01.pdf #234
Hussey, Thomas	c. 1635	age 27	4 Mar 1662	01.pdf #202
Hussey, Thomas	c. 1636	age 26	22 Apr 1662	01.pdf #209
Jenkins, Thomas	c. 1642	age 79	5 Aug 1721	Liber M:146
Johnson, Cornelius	c. 1649	age 29	13 Mar 1678	08.pdf #84
Johnson, Daniell	c. 1636	age 22	26 Oct 1658	01.pdf #29
Johnson, Daniell	c. 1635	age 23	26 Oct 1658	01.pdf #31
Johnson, James	c. 1620	age 45	14 Nov 1665	02.pdf #568
Jones, John	c. 1680	age 51	18 Sep 1731	32.pdf #26
Keene, James	c. 1661	age 66	17 Mar 1727	30.pdf #212
Keene, Mary	c. 1674	age 53	17 Mar 1727	30.pdf #212
Kidd, William	c. 1676	age 57	30 Nov 1732	32.pdf #144
Kimbrow, John	c. 1641	age 29	8 Mar 1670	Vol. 60:248
Kingland, William	c. 1670	age 50	18 Feb 1720	Liber M:77
Kirby, John	c. 1630	age 30	4 Sep 1660	01.pdf #107
Kymborrough, John	c. 1647	age 25	12 Nov 1672	06.pdf #103

WITNESSES WHO STATED THEIR AGES

Lambert, Anne	c. 1640	age 30	11 Jan 1670	Vol. 60:234
Lambert, Edmond	c. 1631	age 39	11 Jan 1670	Vol. 60:234
Landen, Robert	c. 1642	age 20	8 Jul 1662	01.pdf #227
Lane, Anne	c. 1645	age 25	11 Jan 1670	Vol. 60:235
Langhly, Mary	c. 1644	age 26	12 Jan 1670	Vol. 60:242
Lemaistre, Abraham *	c. 1640	age 81	27 Jun 1721	Liber H:415
Lemastre, John	c. 1681	age 39	13 Sep 1720	Liber M:103
Lemastre, Richard	c. 1669	age 51	13 Sep 1720	Liber M:104
Lemastre, Richard	c. 1670	age 58	14 Oct 1728	31.pdf #99
Lamastre, Richard	c. 1670	age 61	13 Apr 1731	32.pdf #24
Lamastre, Richard	c. 1672	age 60	14 Jun 1732	32.pdf #80
Lendsey, Edmond	c. 1607	age 64	14 Nov 1671	06.pdf #53
Lewis, James	c. 1642	age 22	12 Jul 1664	02.pdf #394
Llwellin, John	c. 1654	age 26	10 Nov 1680	10.pdf #36
Lomax, Cleeborn	c. 1678	age 50	12 Aug 1728	31.pdf #86
Lovejoy, Jane	c. 1692	age 37	13 Sep 1729	31.pdf #174
Loyle, John	c. 1650	age 20	11 Jan 1670	Vol. 60:233
Lyndsey, Edmond	c. 1624	age 36	17 Apr 1660	01.pdf #93
Lynsy, Edmond	c. 1614	age 56	12 Jan 1670	Vol. 60:242
Mackune, Lomax	c. 1675	age 46	20 May 1721	Liber M:123
Maddock, Edward	c. 1647/48	age 22/23	8 Mar 1670	Vol. 60:248
Maddock, Edward	c. 1644	age 26	14 Jun 1670	Vol. 60:260
Mankin, Stephen	c. 1684	age 44	12 Aug 1728	31.pdf #86
Manning, John	c. 1679	age 40	3 Nov 1719	Liber M:63
Mansfield, Thomas	c. 1687	age 20	11 Nov 1707	23.pdf #222
Marler, Jonathan	c. 1640	age 26	27 Nov 1666	03.pdf #136
Marler, Jonathan	c. 1642	age 30	13 Aug 1672	06.pdf #74
Marshall, William	c. 1595	age 75	8 Mar 1670	Vol. 60:250
Martin, John	c. 1641	age 40	9 Aug 1681	10.psf #91
Marten, John	c. 1693	age 33	8 Nov 1726	30.pdf #200
Martin, John	c. 1692	age 38	5 Oct 1730	31.pdf #228
Mason, Matthew	c. 1689	age 30	12 Dec 1719	Liber M:68
McKensey, Kennett	c. 1685	age 46	18 Sep 1731	32.pdf #26
Miller, George	c. 1651/52	age 29/30	13 Sep 1681	10.pdf #102
Miller, Mary	c. 1666	age 60	15 Mar 1726	30.pdf #153
Miller, Mary	c. 1664	age 65	14 Feb 1729	31.pdf #175
Miller, Thomas	c. 1645	age 25	9 Mar 1670	Vol. 60:253
Milstead, Edward	c. 1656	age 70	15 Mar 1726	30.pdf #153
Milstead, Thomas	c. 1701	age 24	8 Jun 1725	30.pdf #25
Moore, Hennerie	c. 1636	age 22	26 Oct 1658	01.pdf #30
Moore, Henry	c. 1660	age 59	4 Nov 1719	Liber M:66
Moore, Henry	c. 1661	age 60	2 Jun 1721	Liber M:2
Moore, Henry	c. 1664	age 62	8 Nov 1726	30.pdf #198
Moore, Henry	c. 1664	age 62	8 Nov 1726	30.pdf #199
Moore, Henry	c. 1664	age 63	20 Jan 1727	30.pdf #249

WITNESSES WHO STATED THEIR AGES

Moore, Henry	c. 1663	age 67	15 Jul 1730	31.pdf #199
Moris, John	c. 1632	age 30	8 Jul 1662	01.pdf #225
Moris, Richard	c. 1638	age 24	22 Apr 1662	01.pdf #218
Morrice, Richard	c. 1637	age 24	24 Sep 1661	01.pdf #163
Morris, Elenor	c. 1642	age 20	8 Jul 1662	01.pdf #226
Morris, Richard	c. 1636	age 38	11 Nov 1674	07.pdf #29
Morrise, Richard	c. 1636	age 30	27 Nov 1666	03.pdf #136
Mountagew, Steephen	c. 1634	age 28	4 Mar 1662	01.pdf #198
Mudd, Thomas	c. 1680	age 52	14 Jun 1732	32.pdf #80
Munes, John	c. 1644	age 19	29 Jul 1663	02.pdf #227
Munne, John	c. 1646	age 25	10 Jan 1671	06.pdf #36
Muschamp, John	c. 1650	age 20	9 Mar 1670	Vol. 60:251
Musgrave, Charles	c. 1682	age 44	22 Feb 1726	30.pdf #71
Musgrave, Charles	c. 1680	age 47	31 May 1727	30.pdf #247
Musgrave, Cuthbert	c. 1644	age 22	27 Nov 1666	03.pdf #140
Nailor, George	c. 1655	age 72	28 Feb 1727	30.pdf #213
Nalley, John	c. 1658	age 73	13 Apr 1731	32.pdf #24
Nalley, John	c. 1658	age 74	14 Jun 1732	32.pdf #80
Nash, Susanna	c. 1658	age 19	14 Aug 1677	08.pdf #39
Neale, Raphel	c. 1683	age 49	6 Jun 1732	32.pdf #79
Nellson, Alexander	c. 1684	age 47	2 Mar 1731	31.pdf #241
Nevill, Joan	c. 1627	age 34	2 Jul 1661	01.pdf #149
Nevill, John	c. 1623	age 35	26 Oct 1658	01.pdf #30
Nevill, John	c. 1616	age 44	4 Sep 1660	01.pdf #107
Nevill, John	c. 1620	age 41	2 Jul 1661	01.pdf #149
Nicholls, William	c. 1640	< age 70	14 Nov 1710	24.pdf #32
Noe, John	c. 1700	age 21	9 Mar 1721	Liber H:415
Norman, John	c. 1634	age 28	22 Apr 1662	01.pdf #208
Nutwell, John	c. 1648	age 21	14 Sep 1669	Vol. 60:215
Nutwell, John	c. 1648	age 21	14 Sep 1669	Vol. 60:218
Obrian, Mathias	c. 1628	age 33	12 Feb 1661	01.pdf #128
Obrian, Mathias	c. 1624	age 46	11 Jan 1670	Vol. 60:233
Paget, Benjamin	c. 1695	age 31	4 Nov 1726	30.pdf #204
Paine, John	c. 1636	age 34	9 Mar 1670	Vol. 60:254
Palmer, Samuell	c. 1628	age 33	12 Feb 1661	01.pdf #128
Palmer, Samuell	c. 1630	age 32	28 Jan 1662	01.pdf #191
Parker, Jonas	c. 1661	age 59	30 Aug 1720	Liber M:99
Parker, Samuel	c. 1634	age 24	23 Nov 1658	01.pdf #36
Parrandier, James	c. 1685	age 42	20 Jan 1727	30.pdf #250
Penn, John	c. 1684	age 42	25 May 1726	30.pdf #125
Penn, John	c. 1684	age 48	4 Mar 1732	32.pdf #44
Penn, William	c. 1673	age 46	25 Sep 1719	Liber M:53
Penn, William	c. 1673	age 59	3 Mar 1732	32.pdf #45
Pennock, Obediah	c. 1647	age 33	9 Mar 1670	Vol. 60:253
Philbert, John	c. 1687	age 42	16 May 1729	31.pdf #140

WITNESSES WHO STATED THEIR AGES

Name	Born	Age	Date	Reference
Philips, Hannah	c. 1684	age 42	25 May 1726	30.pdf #125
Philips, Nicolaus	c. 1640	age 21	2 Jul 1661	01.pdf #149
Philips, Robert	c. 1641	age 30	14 Nov 1671	06.pdf #53
Philpot, Edward	c. 1597	age 70	10 Sep 1667	03.pdf #284
Philpott, John	c. 1693	age 34	31 May 1727	30.pdf #247
Philpott, John	c. 1692	age 35	3 Oct 1727	31.pdf #20
Piles, Joseph	c. 1690	age 30	16 Feb 1720	Liber M:75
Piper, John	c. 1628	age 30	26 Oct 1658	01.pdf #31
Piper, John	c. 1628	age 34	9 Jul 1662	01.pdf #239
Plummer, Margret	c. 1687	age 40	9 Jan 1727	30.pdf #214
Pomfret, John Sanders	c. 1671	age 48	3 Jul 1719	Liber M:48
Posey, John	c. 1685	age 34	5 Nov 1719	Liber M:66
Posey, John	c. 1684	age 37	20 May 1721	Liber M:122
Posey, John	c. 1683	age 43	15 Mar 1726	30.pdf #153
Potter, William	c. 1637	age 28	14 Nov 1665	02.pdf #568
Price, John	c. 1642	age 20	4 Mar 1662	01.pdf #198
Price, John	c. 1684	age 36	18 Feb 1720	Liber M:77
Price, Owen	c. 1665	age 55	16 Feb 1720	Liber M:75
Price, Thomas	c. 1645	age 23	9 June 1668	03.pdf #321
Ratclif, Joshua	c. 1701	age 30	25 Oct 1731	32.pdf #25
Reagan, John	c. 1684	age 42	28 Oct 1726	30.pdf #205
Reed, Owen	c. 1670	age 56	17 Oct 1726	30.pdf #206
Reed, Thomas	c. 1662	age 63	25 Sep 1725	30.pdf #51
Reeves, Ubgatt	c. 1669	age 57	8 Nov 1726	30.pdf #201
Robins, Robert	c. 1626	age 55	9 Aug 1681	10.pdf #91
Robinson, William	c. 1631	age 29	4 Sep 1660	01.pdf #107
Roby, John	c. 1686	age 40	8 Nov 1726	30.pdf #200
Routhorne, Joseph	c. 1679	age 48	14 Mar 1727	30.pdf #214
Rozer, John	c. 1637	age 25	2 Oct 1662	01.pdf #255
Russel, Christopher	c. 1614	age 45	26 Jan 1659	01.pdf #40
Sanders, John	c. 1670	age 56	8 Nov 1726	30.pdf #202
Sanders, Matthew	c. 1648	age 71	4 Nov 1719	Liber M:66
Sanders, Matthew	c. 1648	age 71	4 Nov 1719	Liber M:67
Sanders, Matthew	c. 1675	age 50	12 Mar 1725	30.pdf #22
Schuler (?), George	c. 1636	age 25	7 May 1661	01.pdf #137
Scott, John, Junr.	c. 1686	age 34	17 Feb 1720	Liber M:75
Scott, John, Senr.	c. 1660	age 60	16 Feb 1720	Liber M:75
Selbee, John	c. 1642	age 26	9 Jun 1668	03.pdf #321
Semms, James	c. 1670	age 50	9 Mar 1720	Liber M:87
Shaw, John, Senr.	c. 1664	age 67	25 Oct 1731	32.pdf #26
Shelton, Thomas	c. 1633	age 28	2 Jul 1661	01.pdf #147
Simpson, Alexander	c. 1629	age 40	8 Jun 1669	Vol. 60:207
Simpson, Thomas	c. 1662	age 58	16 Feb 1720	Liber M:75
Simpson, Thomas	c. 1663	age 57	16 Aug 1720	Liber M:95
Sly, Robert	c. 1627	age 34	25 Sep 1661	01.pdf #164

WITNESSES WHO STATED THEIR AGES

Smallwood, Ledstone	c. 1682	age 36	22 Dec 1718	Liber M:41
Smallwood, Pryor	c. 1681	age 40	20 May 1721	Liber M:122
Smith, James	c. 1695	age 37	4 Mar 1732	32.pdf #45
Smith, Richard	c. 1638	age 23	2 July 1661	01.pdf #149
Smith, Richard	c. 1687	age 38	25 Sep 1725	30.pdf #51
Smith, Richard	c. 1688	age 43	7 Jun 1731	31,pdf #261
Smith, Samuell	c. 1635	age 24	10 Mar 1659	01.pdf #48
Smith, Thomas	c. 1649	age 31	9 Mar 1680	09.pdf #153
Smith, William	c. 1645	age 17	8 Jul 1662	01.pdf #227
Smith, William	c. 1688	age 42	25 Feb 1730	31.pdf #184
Smith, William	c. 1689	age 42	2 Mar 1731	31.pdf #241
Smith, William	c. 1688	age 43	25 Oct 1731	32.pdf #25
Smith, William	c. 1688	age 44	10 Apr 1732	32.pdf #81
Smoot, Barton, Capt.	c. 1688	age 43	7 Jun 1731	31,pdf #262
Smoot, Barton	c. 1688	age 44	3 Mar 1732	32.pdf #45
Smoote, William	c. 1598	age 63	25 Sep 1661	01.pdf #165
Speake, Bowling	c. 1674	age 52	17 Oct 1726	30.pdf #206
Speak, John	c. 1665	age 54	12 Dec 1719	Liber M:68
Speake, John	c. 1663	age 66	29 Apr 1729	31.pdf #140
Spence, Mary	c. 1680	age 46	13 Jun 1726	30.pdf #124
Stafford, Richard	c. 1681	age 45	4 Nov 1726	30.pdf #204
Stephens, Richard	c. 1680	age 40	31 Aug 1720	Liber M:99
Stigalier, Mary	c. 1661	age 40	24 Sep 1701	21.pdf #159
Stone, Richard	c. 1642	age 18	6 Jun 1660	01.pdf #101
Stone, Thomas, Capt.	c. 1677	age 44	1 Aug 1721	Liber M:137
Stone, William	c. 1667	age 52	3 Jul 1719	Liber M:48
Stone, William	c. 1669	age 50	3 Nov 1719	Liber M:63
Stone, William, Senr.	c. 1666	age 55	2 Aug 1721	Liber M:138
Stone, William, Senr.	c. 1666	age 60	8 Nov 1726	30.pdf #205
Stone, William, Senr.	c. 1667	age 61	23 Jul 1728	31.pdf #86
Stone, William, Junr.	c. 1690	age 37	2 May 1727	30.pdf #248
Stonestreet, Thomas	c. 1683	age 48	22 Jun 1731	32.pdf #5
Story, Mary	c. 1682	age 37	6 Feb 1719	Liber H:219
Story, Walter, Colo.	c. 1667	age 58	21 Dec 1725	30.pdf #73
Stut, William	c. 1619	age 43	8 Jul 1662	01.pdf #226
Swann, Samuel	c. 1676	age 55	22 Jul 1731	32.pdf #5
Symmons, Mary	c. 1687	age 19	13 Jul 1706	23.pdf #138
Sympson, James	c. 1680	age 45	12 Mar 1725	30.pdf #22
Sympson, Thomas	c. 1679	age 42	24 Jul 1721	Liber M:129
Sympson, Thomas	c. 1661	age 64	17 May 1725	30.pdf #21
Sympson, Thomas	c. 1661	age 64	17 May 1725	30.pdf #21
Sympson, Thomas	c. 1661	age 68	14 Feb 1729	31.pdf #175
Tanner, Henry	c. 1649	age 70	20 Aug 1719	Liber M:50
Tanner, Henry	c. 1651	age 68	29 Sep 1719	Liber M:59
Tanner, Henry	c. 1639	age 82	1 Aug 1721	Liber M:137

WITNESSES WHO STATED THEIR AGES

Tanner, Henry	c. 1638	age 87	8 Jun 1725	30.pdf #24
Tarlin, Mary	c. 1639	age 24	11 Feb 1663	02.pdf #153
Tarlin, Richard	c. 1636	age 25	24 Sep 1661	01.pdf #160
Tarline, Richard	c. 1637	age 23	23 Oct 1660	01.pdf #115
Taylor, John	c. 1698	age 30	12 Aug 1728	31.pdf #87
Taylor, Robert	c. 1667	age 53	18 Jul 1720	Liber M:107
Tenneson, John	c. 1667	age 65	14 Jun 1732	32.pdf #80
Thomas, George	c. 1674	age 45	29 Sep 1719	Liber M:58
Thomas, George	c. 1674	age 58	10 Apr 1732	32.pdf #81
Thomas, Hewgh	c. 1638	age 24	1 Oct 1662	01.pdf #254
Thomas, John	c. 1682	age 47	13 Sep 1729	31.pdf #174
Thomas, Susannah	c. 1660	age 59	29 Sep 1719	Liber M:58
Thomas, William	c. 1669	age 50	20 Aug 1719	Liber M:50
Thomas, William	c. 1669	age 50	29 Sep 1719	Liber M:59
Thomas, William	c. 1669	age 52	3 May 1721	Liber M:127
Thomas, William	c. 1671	age 50	29 Jul 1721	Liber M:131
Thomas, William	c. 1673	age 54	8 Mar 1727	30.pdf #246
Thompson, John	c. 1663	age 63	8 Nov 1726	30.pdf #202
Thompson, Thomas	c. 1682	age 48	5 May 1730	31.pdf #205
Thompson, William	c. 1655	age 70	30 Nov 1725	30.pdf #74
Thompson, William	c. 1655	age 73	14 Nov 1728	31.pdf #99
Thompson, William	c. 1659	age 70	14 Feb 1729	31.pdf #175
Thorne, John	c. 1696	age 35	22 Jul 1731	32.pdf #5
Tillotson, James	c. 1649	age 70	4 Nov 1719	Liber M:65
Tillotson, James	c. 1649	age 70	4 Nov 1719	Liber M:66
Towell, David	c. 1645	age 27	10 Sep 1672	06.pdf #86
Trew, Anne	c. 1637	age 26	29 Jul 1663	02.pdf #226
Trew, Richard	c. 1605	age 58	29 Jul 1663	02.pdf #225
Troope, Robert, Capt.	c. 1635	age 28	4 Nov 1663	02.pdf #263
Turner, Arthur	c. 1622	age 40	22 Apr 1662	01.pdf #218
Villett, Peter	c. 1653	age 80	30 Nov 1732	32.pdf #144
Vinyeard, Abraham	c. 1646	age 37	5 Mar 1683	11.pdf #83
Wade, Richard	c. 1665	age 56	3 May 1721	Liber M:127
Waide, Richard	c. 1663	age 62	8 Jun 1725	30.pdf #24
Wade, Richard	c. 1663	age 64	18 Mar 1727	30.pdf #246
Wahope, Archbald	c. 1627	age 33	17 Apr 1660	01.pdf #93
Wales, George	c. 1662	age 58	30 Aug 1720	Liber M:99
Walker, Charles	c. 1665	age 55	17 May 1721	Liber M:116
Walker, James	c. 1619	age 42	24 Sep 1661	01.pdf #162
Walker, James	c. 1619	age 44	10 Feb 1663	02.pdf #137
Waltom, John	c. 1623	age 40	28 Jul 1663	02.pdf #199
Ward, Catherine	c. 1703	age 24	20 Jan 1727	30.pdf #249
Ward, Henry	c. 1677	age 50	20 Jan 1727	30.pdf #249
Ward, John	c. 1669	age 50	3 Nov 1719	Liber M:63
Ware, Francis	c. 1695	age 31	8 Nov 1726	30.pdf #200

WITNESSES WHO STATED THEIR AGES

Waters, Margaret	c. 1686	age 40	13 Jun 1726	30.pdf #124
Wathen, John	c. 1682	age 38	16 Aug 1720	Liber M:95
Wathen, John	c. 1681	age 44	17 May 1725	30.pdf #21
Watson, Andrew	c. 1629	age 30	1 May 1659	01.pdf #63
Weales, Elisabeth	c. 1641	age 22	29 Jul 1663	02.pdf #229
Wheatley, Andrew	c. 1652	age 22	8 Sep 1674	07.pdf #17
Wheeler, John	c. 1633	age 25	26 Oct 1658	01.pdf #30
Wheeler, John, Major	c. 1630	age 61	10 Nov 1691	17.pdf #157
Wheeler, John, Junior	c. 1653	age 22	14 Sep 1675	07.pdf #87
Wheeler, Mary	c. 1630	age 40	9 Mar 1670	Vol. 60:254
Wheeler, Thomas	c. 1661	age 58	22 Dec 1719	Liber M:69
Wheler, Thomas	c. 1661	age 60	20 May 1721	Liber M:122
Wheeler, Thomas	c. 1661	age 65	8 Nov 1726	30.pdf #199
Wicherly, Elizabeth	c. 1673	age 46	5 Nov 1719	Liber M:66
Whicherly, Elizabeth	c. 1675	age 46	20 May 1721	Liber M:122
White, William	c. 1623	age 36	10 Mar 1659	01.pdf #48
Wildman, William	c. 1636	age 32	9 June 1668	03.pdf #321
William, Edward	c. 1626	age 33	26 Jan 1659	01.pdf #41
William, Edward	c. 1627	age 34	19 Nov 1661	01.pdf #176
Williams, William	c. 1640	age 53	24 Apr 1693	18.pdf #77
Williams, William	c. 1686	age 33	29 Sep 1719	Liber M:59
Williams, William	c. 1686	age 44	25 Feb 1730	31.pdf #184
Williams, William	c. 1686	age 45	2 Mar 1731	31.pdf #240
Williams, William	c. 1685	age 46	25 Oct 1731	32.pdf #25
Wilson, Robert	c. 1629	age 30	26 Jan 1659	01.pdf #43
Wine, Francis	c. 1635	age 30	14 Mar 1665	02.pdf #523
Winter, Walter	c. 1681	age 46	20 Jan 1727	30.pdf #249
Winter, Walter	c. 1672	age 60	14 Nov 1732	32.pdf #117
Woodyard, John	c. 1675	age 44	4 Nov 1719	Liber M:67
Woodyard, John	c. 1676	age 43	22 Dec 1719	Liber M:68
Woodyard, John	c. 1677	age 44	21 May 1721	Liber M:123
Woodyard, John	c. 1677	age 48	8 Jun 1725	30.pdf #25
Woodyard, John	c. 1676	age 55	25 Oct 1731	32.pdf #25
Woodyard, Richard	c. 1683	age 43	15 Mar 1726	30.pdf #153
Woolley, Charles	c. 1645	age 25	11 Jan 1670	Vol. 60:233
Wright, Thomas	c. 1681	age 48	16 May 1729	31.pdf #141
Wright, Thomas	c. 1682	age 49	2 Mar 1731	31.pdf #240
Wright, Thomas	c. 1681	age 50	25 Oct 1731	32.pdf #25
Wyeth, Nicholas	c. 1656	age 50	10 Sep 1706	23.pdf #152
Yates, Robert	c. 1690	age 30	20 Apr 1720	Liber M:83
Yates, Robert, Capt.	c. 1685	age 40	19 May 1725	30.pdf #23

* "Abraham Lemaistre the son of John and Sarah Lemaistre aged eighty one years or thereabouts deposeth that he was born in the Old Jersey in the Parish of St. Maries," 27 June 1721 [Liber H Page 415]

GRANTEE INDEX TO DEEDS

1650-1722

Grantee	Grantor	Date	Page/Image
Achilles, Peter	Prouse, Robert	21 Sep 1671	06.pdf #71
Achilles, Peter	Prouse, Robert	9 Jul 1671	06.pdf #71
Achilles, Peter	Hatch, John	9 Mar 1675	07.pdf #65
Achilles, Peter	Warner, Thomas	13 Jun 1693	18.pdf #118
Acton, Henry	Bayne, Walter & Martha	16 Feb 1709	Liber C:126
Addams, Francis	Godfrey, George	13 Nov 1707	Liber C:89
Adams, Francis	Hammon, John	16 Aug 1716	Liber H:17
Adames, Henry & Boareman, William, Major			
	Broade, John & Jane	9 Sep 1678	09.pdf #39
Adams, Mary	Godfrey, George	3 Oct 1704	Liber Z:207
Addisson, John	Hobb, Thomas & Isable	18 Sep 1690	17.pdf #66
Addisson, John	Hutchison, William	9 Apr 1689	17.pdf #296
Addisson, John	Hutchison, William	17 Apr 1689	17.pdf #298
Addison, John	Hutchison, William	11 Apr 1689	18.pdf #52
Addison, John, Capt.	Middleton Robert	24 Dec 1692	18.pdf #89
Addison, John	Conaway, James	14 Feb 1693	18.pdf #108
Allanson, Thomas	Browne, John	4 Apr 1659	01.pdf #218
Allanson, Thomas	Simpson, Thomas	15 Feb 1660	01.pdf #219
Allanson, Thomas	Browne, John	4 Apr 1659	02.pdf #79
Allanson, Thomas	Broune, John	4 Nov 1663	02.pdf #267
Allanson, Thomas	Province of Maryland	19 Jun 1663	02.pdf #301
Allanson, Thomas	Frankam, Henrie	10 Mar 1668	03.pdf #305
Allanson, Thomas	Frankam, Henry & Amie	9 Jun 1668	Vol. 60:154
Allanson, Thomas	Stone, Thomas	8 Jan 1671	06.pdf #17
Allcoks, James	Allanson, Thomas	10 Jan 1664	02.pdf #512
Allcock, Thomas	Rookerd, Edward	8 Jan 1678	08.pdf #61
Alcock, Thomas	Wells, William	10 Aug 1680	10.pdf #17
Allcox, Thomas	Wells, William	4 Jan 1682	10.pdf #132
Allen, James & Allen, John			
	Harrison, Joseph	16 Nov 1717	Liber H:135
Allen, John	Moore, Henry & Elizabeth	11 Mar 1671	06.pdf #41
Allen, John	Coomes, Philip	10 Oct 1670	06.pdf #87
Allen, John, Capt.	Deane, William	6 Mar 1677	08.pdf #25
Allen, John, Capt.	Deane, Wiliam	6 Mar 1677	08.pdf #25
Allen, John	Beade, Nicholas	13 June 1693	18.pdf #81
Allen, John & Ellinor	Lambert, John	10 Jan 1692	24.pdf #176
Allen, John & Allen, James			
	Harrison, Joseph	16 Nov 1717	Liber H:135
Allen, Joseph	Bayne, Ebsworth & Catherine	22 Feb 1716	Liber F:91
Allen, Thomas	Millner, Thomas	1 Apr 1659	02.pdf #175
Allen, Thomas	Miller, Thomas	1 Apr 1659	02.pdf #272

GRANTEE INDEX TO DEEDS

Allen, William; Waed, Zachery; Harrisson, Joseph; & Handson, Randall			
	Hatton, William & Dent, Thomas	9 May 1663	02.pdf #188
Allen, William & Mun, John			
	Boyden, John; Boyden, Wm. & Cooper, Walter	8 Nov 1664	02.pdf #452
Allen, William	Frankam, Henry & Amee	9 Jun 1668	Vol. 60:156
Allinson, Thomas	Toney, Dorothy, widow	8 Sep 1721	Liber H:464
Alword, John & Haydon, Francis			
	Moore, Henry	8 Nov 1669	Vol. 60:219
Alward, John & Heydon, Francis			
	Hussy, Thomas & Joan	13 Jun 1670	04.pdf #56
Alward, John	Heydon, Francis	10 Mar 1674	06.pdf #159
Anderson, Edward	Hanson, Samuel & Elizabeth	23 Sep 1720	Liber H:382
Anderson, John	Farthing, William Maren & Anne	3 Jun 1720	Liber H:354
Ashford, Michael & Rachell			
	Hussy, Thomas & Johannah	13 Nov 1677	08.pdf #50
Ashford, Michaell	Bealle, Ninian	9 Jun 1691	17.pdf #118
Ashman, Richard	Baker, Thomas	2 Jan 1678	08.pdf #57
Ashman, Richard	Dent, John & Mary	1 Jun 1678	09.pdf #17
Askin, George	Smith, John & Anne	20 Oct 1702	Liber Z:92
Aspinall, Henry & Mary			
	Peake, Walter	21 Jan 1668	Vol. 60:151
Aspinall, Henry	Allen, William & Munn, John	9 Jan 1669	Vol. 60:180
Aspenall, Henry	Maddocke, Edward	30 Oct 1674	07.pdf #23
Aspenall, Henry	Holme, John	19 Dec 1674	07.pdf #52
Aspenall, Henry, Capt.	Allen, John, Capt.	20 Feb 1677	08.pdf #48
Aspenall, Henry	Wells, William	4 Jun 1678	08.pdf #93
Athy, George	Hutchison, William	17 Apr 1689	17.pdf #297
Attwicks, Humphrey	Michell, Thomas	3 May 1659	02.pdf #161
Austin, John	Greenfield, Thomas Trueman	13 Sep 1718	Liber H:202
Austin, Thomas	Whichaley, Thomas & Elizabeth	13 Nov 1695	Liber Q:72
Austria, George	Gallant, Alexander	10 Mar 1673	06.pdf #124
Baggott, Samuel	Smith, John & Ann	10 Mar 1714	Liber F:3
Baker, Andrew & Baker, Thomas			
	Hutchison, William & Roeland, Dennis	13 Sep 1692	17.pdf #257
Baker, Thomas	Empson, William	24 Apr 1660	01.pdf #97
Baker, Thomas	Heard, William & Brigit	16 Jul 1664	02.pdf #413
Baker, Thomas	Jarbo, John	3 Sep 1673	06.pdf #138
Baker, Thomas & Baker, Andrew			
	Hutchison, William & Roeland, Dennis	13 Sep 1692	17.pdf #257
Bankes, George	Jones, Humphrey	6 Apr 1668	Vol. 60:160
Bannister, John	Dickison, John	6 May 1709	Liber C:193
Barker, John	Dent, William & Elizabeth	20 May 1685	13.pdf #88
Barker, Sarah	Lambert, John	24 Apr 1676	07.pdf #105
Barnaby, John	Greenfield, Thomas Trueman	25 Dec 1720	Liber H:422
Barns, Henry	Doyne, Jesse	19 Jan 1711	Liber C:226

GRANTEE INDEX TO DEEDS

Grantee	Grantor	Date	Reference
Barnes, Henry	Davis, Thomas	6 Nov 1712	24.pdf #172
Barrett, James	Moore, Thomas	14 Sep 1692	17.pdf #256
Bartlett, Ralph	Boughton, Richard	25 Dec 1684	12.pdf #84
Barton, Nathan	Hawkins, Henry	6 Mar 1668	Vol. 60:145
Barton, Nathan	Mathena, Daniell & Sarah	4 Dec 1682	11.pdf #39
Barton, Sarah, widow	Warren, Thomas	4 Dec 1705	Liber Z:219
Barton, William, Junr.	Smoot, William	28 May 1658	01.pdf #251
Barton, William, Junr.	Johnson, Daniell	12 July 1664	02.pdf #404
Barton, William, Jnr.	Barton, Nathan & Martha	3 Jan 1671	06.pdf #23
Barton, William, Snr.	Fendall, Samuel	9 Jan 1671	06.pdf #26
Batchelor, Francis	Simpson, Thomas & Elizabeth	5 Nov 1660	02.pdf #78
Batchelor, Francis	Simpson, Thomas & Elizabeth	5 Nov 1662	02.pdf #79
Bateman, George	Compton, Matthew & Susannah	21 Oct 1703	Liber C:118
Bateman, George	Neale, Raphael	16 Feb 1715	Liber F:7
Batten, William	Province of Maryland	5 Aug 1658	Liber H:285
Bayly, John	Ashman, Richard & Anne	13 Jan 1680	09.pdf #140
Bayne, Anne	Bayne, John	9 Nov 1691	17.pdf #160
Bayne, Elinor, Widow	Russell, William	8 Jun 1676	07.pdf #128
Bayne, John	Hinson, Randolph & Barbara Wade, Richard & Anne	10 Jul 1691	17.pdf #234
Bayne, John	Hutchison, William	18 Mar 1688	18.pdf #52
Bayne, John	Clarke, Gilbert	29 Oct 1696	24.pdf #199
Beade, Nicholas	Knight, Edward	2 Jan 1671	06.pdf #33
Bead, Nicholas	Knight, Edward	28 Oct 1671	Liber H:179
Beade, Nicholas	Marshall, Richard & Mary	11 Aug 1696	Liber Q:99
Beane, Walter	Doughty, Francis & Anne	9 Feb 1662	02.pdf #237
Beane, Walter	Marshall, William	29 Sep 1660	02.pdf #246
Beane, Walter	Marshall, William	29 Sep 1660	02.pdf #247
Beane, Walter & Marshall, William	Province of Maryland	10 Apr 1660	02.pdf #249
Beck, Richard	Godshall, John	2 Mar 1672	06.pdf #84
Becke, Richard	Rozer, Benjamin	1674	07.pdf #14
Bedford, Henery	Hargesse, William & Thomas	9 Mar 1673	06.pdf #107
Belaine, John	Trew, Richard	4 May 1659	01.pdf #203
Bennett, Thomas	Munn, John	8 Jun 1669	Vol. 60:196
Benson, Robert	Langham, George & Alice	20 Oct 1690	17.pdf #299
Benson, Robert	Hunter, William	8 Mar 1697	Liber Q:118
Benson, William	Warner, Thomas	12 Sep 1704	Liber Z:146
Berry, Benjamin	Evans, Walter & Anne	8 Nov 1694	18.pdf #237
Berry, Samuel, Doctor	Cawood, Stephen & Mary	2 Oct 1704	24.pdf #197
Birth, Richard	Payne, John	13 Mar 1711	Liber C:240
Bladen, William	Ford, Edward & Elizabeth	6 Feb 1711	Liber C:216
Blandford, Thomas	Stoddert, James	19 May 1720	Liber H:367
Blanshett, Francis	Keen, James & Mary	1 Mar 1710	Liber C:176
Blanshett, Henry	Lynes, Philip	14 Jun 1709	Liber C:136

GRANTEE INDEX TO DEEDS

Blanchett, Henry	Keen, James & Mary	14 Mar 1710	23.pdf #372
Blee, John	Bayly, James	1 Jul 1715	Liber F:64
Blee, John	Ashman, John & Anchoram, Richard	29 Jul 1715	Liber F:66
Blee, John	Matthews, William	11 May 1717	Liber H:80
Blizard, Giles	Neale, James Jr. & Elizabeth	11 Mar 1683	11.pdf #237
Blizard, Giles	Caine, John	4 Aug 1684	12.pdf #13
Blizard, Giles	Sanders, Edward & Jane	16 Oct 1684	18.pdf #166
Boarman, Benedict	Boarman, William, Senr. & Mary	13 Nov 1719	Liber H:315
Boarman, Mary	Turner, Thomas	5 Sep 1721	Liber H:457
Borman, William	Province of Maryland	17 May 1658	01.pdf #167
Boareman, William, Major & Adames, Henry			
	Broade, John & Jane	9 Sep 1678	09.pdf #39
Boarman, William, Senr.			
	Green, Robert & Mary, & Green, Thomas	25 Jun 1713	24.pdf #181
Boarman, William, Junr.			
	Hill, John & Anne	6 Oct 1719	Liber H:322
Boswell, John	Harkister, John	10 Nov 1674	07.pdf #21
Boswell, William	Robins, Thomas & Barbara	1 Aug 1712	24.pdf #172
Boughton, Frances	Dent, Thomas	10 Nov 1714	Liber F:45
Boughton, Richard	Thompson, George	30 Nov 1684	12.pdf #38
Boughton, Richard	Gaven, Thomas	25 Dec 1684	12.pdf #84
Boughton, Samuel	Dent, Thomas	23 Apr 1711	Liber C:243
Boy, John	Davis, Thomas & Elizabeth	9 Feb 1705	Liber Z:262
Boyce, John	Moore, Henry	25 Dec 1684	12.pdf #85
Boyden, John; Boyden, William & Cooper, Walter			
	Allen, William & Mun, John	8 Aug 1664	02.pdf #454
Boyden, John	Boyden, William	28 May 1668	Vol. 60:164
Boyden, John	Ashbrooke, Thomas & Lettice	9 Jan 1671	06.pdf #56
Boyden, John	Ashbrooke, Thomas & Lettis	9 Jan 1672	06.pdf #85
Boyden, John	True, Richard & Anne	11 Mar 1673	06.pdf #109
Boyden, Wm.; Boyden, John & Cooper, Walter			
	Allen, William & Mun, John	8 Aug 1664	02.pdf #454
Boyden, William	Boyden, John	10 Jan 1664	02.pdf #542
Boyden, William	Wheeler, John	8 Aug 1665	02.pdf #550
Boyden, William & Cooper, Walter			
	Wheeler, John	8 Aug 1665	02.pdf #553
Boyden, William	Allonson, Thomas	13 Mar 1666	03.pdf #55
Boyden, William	Allanson, Thomas & Mary	8 Jan 1667	03.pdf #159
Boyden, William	Hussey, Thomas	12 Mar 1667	03.pdf #188
Boyden, William & Sanders, Mathew			
	Boyden, John	14 Mar 1671	06.pdf #40
Boyden, William	Mun, John	12 Mar 1672	06.pdf #62
Boyden, William	Munn, John	8 Mar 1672	06.pdf #64
Boyden, William	Boyden, John	11 Mar 1673	06.pdf #118
Bracher, John	Fearnley, John	12 Mar 1689	16.pdf #63

GRANTEE INDEX TO DEEDS

Bradshaw, George	Province of Maryland	26 May 1664	02.pdf #533
Brandt, Marcus	Brandt, Randolph		Liber C:32
Brandt, Randolph	Maycock, Mary	30 Aug 1682	11.pdf #31
Brandt, Randolph	Smith, William	11 Mar 1683	11.pdf #185
Branner, Henry	Pryor, William & Mary	1 Mar 1688	14.pdf #168
Branson, Thomas	Newman, George & Lydia	11 Feb 1663	Liber H:286
Breeden, Gerrard	King, Thomas	7 Apr 1668	Vol. 60:158
Breeden, John	Edelen, Richard, Surveyor	24 Oct 1671	17.pdf #30
Brett, Henry	Woodyard, John & Jane	18 Feb 1713	24.pdf #179
Brett, Henry	Smith, William & Rachael	29 Sep 1719	Liber H:287
Brett, William	Knight, John & Sarah	1 Nov 1713	24.pdf #196
Brett, William	Knight, John & Sarah	5 Nov 1713	24.pdf #196
Briscoe, John	Ellson, Anne	25 Dec 1706	Liber C:79
Briscoe, Philip, Senr.	Davis, Thomas & Mary	4 Nov 1706	Liber C:26
Brown, John	Manning, John	20 Apr 1721	Liber H:454
Browne, Gerrard	Watson, Andrew	10 Nov 1668	Vol. 60:175
Browne, Gerrard	Allanson, Thomas	8 Aug 1672	06.pdf #75
Browne, Gerrard	Allanson, Thomas	8 Aug 1674	06.pdf #166
Brown, Gustavus	Hemsley, Philemon & Mary	2 Nov 1714	Liber F:51
Browne, Gustavus	Dent, Thomas	22 Apr 1718	Liber H:184
Browne, Gustavus	Dent, Thomas	22 Apr 1718	Liber H:187
Browne, Gustavus	Adams, Charles & Elizabeth	18 Aug 1718	Liber H:191
Browne, James	Clements, John	7 Jun 1679	09.pdf #105
Browne, John	Willan, Richard	27 Oct 1658	01.pdf #218
Browne, John	Willan, Richard & Elizabeth	27 Oct 1658	02.pdf #79
Browne, Philip	Corner, Job	9 Nov 1675	07.pdf #91
Bruce, John	Games, John	1 Dec 1714	Liber F:47
Bruce, John	Warren, Judith	21 Jan 1716	Liber F:84
Bryant, Thomas & Saunders, Matthew			
	Sinnett, Garrett	9 Mar 1676	08.pdf #24
Bryon, Daniel	Smallwood, Pryor & Elizabeth	9 Aug 1720	Liber H:377
Bullott, Joseph & Clarke, Samuell			
	Lyndsey, Edmond	6 Nov 1673	06.pdf #142
Bullett, Joseph & Elizabeth			
	Brandt, Randolph & Mary	12 Oct 1685	13.pdf #18
Bullott, Joseph	Dent, William	6 Nov 1693	18.pdf #115
Burch, Jestinian	Burch, Oliver	30 Jan 1714	Liber F:2
Burch, Oliver	Bowling, John & Mary	19 Aug 1703	Liber Z:57
Burch, Thomas	Contee, Alexander	13 Nov 1716	Liber H:21
Burch, Thomas	Bayne, Ebsworth	23 Dec 1717	Liber H:123
Burch, Thomas	Sutre (?), Nathaniel & Elizabeth	11 Mar 1718	Liber H:147
Burford, Thomas	Pope, John	10 Oct 1682	11.pdf #59
Burford, Thomas	Clipsham, Thomas & Susannah	10 Jun 1683	11.pdf #151
Burrowes, Paul	Wakefield, Thomas	30 Nov 1682	11.pdf #33
Butcher, John	Ashford, Michaell & Rachell	10 Aug 1683	11.pdf #144

GRANTEE INDEX TO DEEDS

Byrn, Charles	Coffer, John, Junr.	21 Jan 1717	Liber H:55
Cable, John & Green, Luke			
	Province of Maryland	1 Feb 1672	Liber Z:213
Cadwell, William	Morris, Richard & Ales	9 Oct 1662	02.pdf #81
Cadwell, William	Morrise, Richard & Ales	19 Oct 1662	02.pdf #294
Cage, John	Province of Maryland	20 Mar 1650	02.pdf #247
Cage, John	Clipsham, Susannah	16 Dec 1685	13.pdf #102
Cain, John	Frost, Jheromie	5 Jan 1664	02.pdf #303
Cain, John	Greenhill, John	10 Jun 1663	02.pdf #338
Caine, John	Thompson, George	20 Oct 1665	03.pdf #47
Callihon, Patrick	Sympson, Thomas & Mary	15 Apr 1710	Liber C:181
Cane, Susannah	Cane, John	28 Apr 1684	11.pdf #212
Canole, Jane	Cabshaw, John	9 Jun 1712	24.pdf #164
Carey, Philip	Maddock, Edward	12 Apr 1676	07.pdf #104
Carnell, Christopher	Walker, James	13 Apr 1655	02.pdf #235
Carpenter, Richard	Boyden, John	1673	06.pdf #127
Cartwright, Peter	Slye, John	17 Feb 1720	Liber H:318
Carvell, Thomas	Percy, Thomas	17 Mar 1663	02.pdf #164
Casleton, Robert	Caen, John	8 Sep 1668	Vol. 60:177
Cassock, John	Cassleton, Robert	10 Oct 1673	06.pdf #146
Cassock, John	Lomaire, John	13 Sep 1675	07.pdf #83
Cassocke, John	Lemaire, John & Margaret	9 Mar 1685	12.pdf #83
Cawood, Stephen	Manning, Joseph	31 May 1704	23.pdf #99
Cawood, Stephen	Hutchison, John	30 Sep 1721	Liber H:473
Champ, John	Mackey, James	27 Jan 1710	Liber C:190
Chandler, John	Mellor, John & Sarah	13 Jan 1710	Liber C:186
Chandler, John	Mellor, John & Mary	30 Oct 1719	Liber H:310
Chandler, Richard	Chandler, William, Coll.	29 Nov 1681	10.pdf #110
Chandler, William	Maddock, Edward & Margery	5 Jun 1681	10.pdf #79
Chapman, Edward	Manning, Joseph	4 Dec 1705	23.pdf #135
Chapman, Edward	Lynes, Philip & Anne	13 Nov 1707	Liber Z:223
Chapman, Thomas	Parker, John & Anne	13 Sep 1695	Liber Q:94
Chapman, William	Searson, Francis & Alice; Mahony, Elizabeth & Dennis	4 Aug 1714	Liber F:25
Charles County	Allen, John	11 Nov 1674	07.pdf #31
Chasey, Samuell	Cuttance, Josias	26 Jul 1714	Liber F:33
Cherman, John	Nevill, John	20 Aug 1661	01.pdf #189
Ching, John	Turner, Thomas	11 Mar 1720	Liber H:330
Ching, John	Turner, Thomas	17 Aug 1720	Liber H:370
Chittam, John	Nichulls, Simon & Younge, William	23 Jan 1693	17.pdf #295
Chunn, John, Junr.	Bayne, Ebsworth	23 May 1717	Liber H:62
Chunn, John	Bayne, Ebsworth & Kendrick	16 Sep 1719	Liber H:279
Chunn, John	Compton, William & Mary	28 Feb 1722	Liber H:486
Clarke, Gilbert	Neale, Anthony	31 Oct 1692	17.pdf #277

GRANTEE INDEX TO DEEDS

Clark, John & Clark, Robert			
	Marshall, William	5 Sep 1662	Liber H:284
Clarke, John	Province of Maryland	14 Sep 1663	02.pdf #268
Clarke, John	Jenifer, Daniel & Elizabeth	14 Jul 1721	Liber H:444
Clarke, John & Clarke, Robert			
	Marshall, William	Apr 1676	07.pdf #106
Clark, Robert & Clark, John			
	Marshall, William	5 Sep 1662	Liber H:284
Clarke, Robert & Clarke, John			
	Marshall, William	Apr 1676	07.pdf #106
Clarke, Robert	Clarkson, William & Ruth	4 Jan 1695	18.pdf #231
Clarke, Samuell & Bullott, Joseph			
	Lyndsey, Edmond	6 Nov 1673	06.pdf #142
Clarke, Thomas	Clarke, John	9 Jan 1682	10.pdf #130
Clements, Francis	Green, Francis	7 Nov 1718	Liber H:247
Clements, Jacob	Pye, Walter	10 Nov 1719	Liber H:324
Clements, John & Goodrick, Robert			
	Ward, John & Damaris	9 Aug 1677	08.pdf #38
Clemons, John, Junr. & Clemons, William			
	Thompson, John & Mary	11 Aug 1713	24.pdf #185
Clemons, William & Clemons, John, Junr.			
	Thompson, John & Mary	11 Aug 1713	24.pdf #185
Clements, Joseph	Wheeler, Luke	29 Jul 1717	Liber H:270
Clemont, John	Middleton, Robert & Mary	18 Jul 1692	18.pdf #86
Coates, Ralph	Breeden, Gerrard & Elizabeth	2 Jun 1671	06.pdf #63
Cofer, Francis & Plunkett, Thomas			
	Clement, John & Elizabeth	14 Jan 1696	Liber Q:77
Coffer, John	Sinnett, Garrett	10 Nov 1696	Liber Q:108
Cofer, John	Manning, Joseph	15 Apr 1701	21.pdf #134
Cofer, John	Manning, Joseph	15 Dec 1701	21.pdf #188
Coghill, James & Coghill, William			
	Ratclife, Emannuell	13 Nov 1694	18.pdf #230
Coghill, William & Coghill, James			
	Ratclife, Emannuell	13 Nov 1694	18.pdf #230
Cole, Jeffry	Harrisson, Richard	10 Nov 1691	17.pdf #158
Cole, Jeoffry	Warren, Thomas	13 Jun 1704	Liber Z:150
Cole, John	Turner, Thomas	24 Sep 1721	Liber H:458
Colliar, Giles	Lambert, John & Sarah	22 Feb 1682	10.pdf #149
Collings, Anthony			
	Gardner, Luke & Ann; Godfrey, William & Jannet	12 Nov 1717	Liber H:155
Combs, Robert	Green, Robert & Mary	25 Aug 1703	Liber Z:70
Compton, Matthew	Wakefield, Abell	17 May 1702	Liber C:117
Connell, Mary	Obryan, Ellinor	10 Aug 1703	Liber Z:53
Contee, Alexander	Baker, Thomas	12 May 1719	Liber H:250
Contee, Alexander	Trenn, Henry	10 Nov 1720	Liber H:387

GRANTEE INDEX TO DEEDS

Contee, Alexander	Trenn, Henry	10 Nov 1720	Liber H:388
Contee, John	Baker, John & Mary	13 Nov 1703	Liber Z:64
Contee, John	Rookwood, Edward	12 Jun 1705	Liber Z:192
Contee, John	Chapman, William	12 Mar 1706	Liber Z:231
Contee, John, Coll.	Darnall, Henry, Coll. & Ellinor	1 Jun 1706	Liber C:3
Contee, John	Bayne, Walter & Martha	Mar 1707	Liber C:39
Contee, John	Fanning, Benoni & Hannah	26 Apr 1707	Liber C:53
Contee, John	Simmes, James & Mary	26 Feb 1708	Liber C:91
Contee, John, Esqr.	Manning, Joseph	26 Mar 1708	23.pdf #136
Contee, John	Barton, William & Elizabeth	8 Jun 1708	Liber C:104
Contee, Mary	Lemaster, Richard & Martha	24 Mar 1709	Liber C:161
Contee, Mary	Bayne, Walter & Martha	3 Oct 1709	Liber C:146
Contee, Mary, widdow, & Courts, John, Gent.			
	Rogers, John	1 Feb 1710	23.pdf #408
Coode, William	Marrit, John	11 Mar 1715	Liber F:54
Cooksey, Thomas	Graham, James & Anne	31 Aug 1720	Liber H:390
Coope, Nicholas	Hutchison, William	1 Jun 1689	17.pdf #298
Cooper, Nicholas	Sheerman, John	14 Nov 1693	18.pdf #117
Cooper, Nicholas	Campbell, Martin & Mary	2 Mar 1703	Liber Z:1
Cooper, Walter; Boyden, William & Boyden, John			
	Allen, William & Mun, John	8 Aug 1664	02.pdf #454
Cooper, Walter & Boyden, William			
	Wheeler, John	8 Aug 1665	02.pdf #553
Corker, Thomas	Theobalds, Clement	9 Sep 1673	06.pdf #133
Corker, Thomas	Lyndsey, Edmund	11 Aug 1674	06.pdf #163
Corker, Thomas	Theobald, Clement	8 Jun 1675	07.pdf #67
Cornell, Joseph	Younge, Elizabeth, widow	10 Jul 1685	12.pdf #105
Cornall, Joseph			
	Barrett, James & Elizabeth, & Moore, Henry	7 Dec 1685	14.pdf #117
Corner, Gilber	Swan, Edward & Susannah	11 Aug 1666	03.pdf #95
Corner, Job	Vandrey, John & Elizabeth	8 Aug 1671	06.pdf #56
Corner, Job	Vandrey, John	8 Aug 1671	06.pdf #65
Courts, John	Province of Maryland	23 Oct 1650	Liber H:336
Courts, John	Province of Maryland	18 Aug 1658	Liber H:474
Courte, John, Junior	Courte, John, Senior	13 Mar 1683	11.pdf #87
Courts, John, Gent.	Reeves, William & Anne	18 Feb 1693	18.pdf #76
Courts, John, Gent. & Contee, Mary, widow			
	Rogers, John	1 Feb 1710	23.pdf #408
Cowerd (?), Robert	Godfrey, William & Jannit	12 Nov 1718	Liber H:245
Cox, James	Story, Walter & Mary	3 Jan 1693	18.pdf #44
Crabb, Thomas	Boreman, William	21 Mar 1705	Liber Z:181
Crabb, Thomas	Truman, Thomas	12 Mar 1712	24.pdf #159
Crane, John	Bayne, Walter	9 Nov 1709	Liber C:151
Craine, John	Bayne, Walter & Martha	4 Mar 1717	Liber H:143
Craxon, Thomas	Chapman, Richard	11 Jun 1672	06.pdf #69

GRANTEE INDEX TO DEEDS

Cressey, Samuell	Baker, Thomas	11 Aug 1674	06.pdf #165
Cuttance, Jossias	Gould, James	16 Aug 1710	Liber C:206
Darnall, Henry	Rozer, Notley & Jane	1 Mar 1704	Liber Z:141
Darnall, Henry, Coll.			
	Rozer, Notley & Jane	27 Mar 1706	Liber C:1
Davies, Alexander	King, Thomas	9 Nov 1669	Vol. 60:227
Davies, Walter	Smith, William & Elizabeth	10 Sep 1678	09.pdf #48
Davis, Henry	Davis, Edward	12 Nov 1716	Liber H:23
Davis, John	Bissick, John	Jun 1673	06.pdf #113
Davis, Thomas	Clouder, Richard & Temperance	10 Nov 1696	Liber Q:110
Davis, Thomas	Ashbrooke, James & Elizabeth	9 Feb 1706	Liber Z:230
Deakes, Henry	Green, Thomas	8 Jun 1688	16.pdf #61
Deane, Edward	Lendsey, James & Marie	7 Aug 1660	01.pdf #169
Deane, Edward	Linsey, James & Marie	7 Aug 1660	01.pdf #181
Deane, William	Stannard, William	8 Mar 1676	08.pdf #25
Decregoe, Joane	Coale, Jeoffrey & Sina	27 Feb 1708	Liber C:97
Decregoe, Johanah	Harrison, Thomas & Alice	22 Aug 1713	24.pdf #192
Delahey, John	Province of Maryland	18 Sep 1659	01.pdf #150
Delahey, John	Tomkinson, John	1656	01.pdf #187
Dement, George	Brooks, John	6 Apr 1712	24.pdf #164
Dent, Barbarah & Dent, Rebekah			
	Addison, John & Rebekah	6 Jun 1704	Liber Z:121
Dent, Elizabeth	Newman, William & Mary	13 Nov 1705	Liber Z:217
Dent, George	Baker, Thomas	11 Jul 1719	Liber H:272
Dent, George	Miles, Edward	13 Jun 1721	Liber H:434
Dent, George	Miles, Edward	14 Jun 1721	Liber H:436
Dent, George	Dod, John & Anne	22 Aug 1721	Liber H:456
Dent, Phillip & Dent, William			
	Lynes, Philip	10 Jun 1704	Liber Z:112
Dent, Rebekah & Dent, Barbarah			
	Addison, John & Rebekah	6 Jun 1704	Liber Z:121
Dent, Thomas	Lynes, Philip	9 Oct 1707	Liber C:73
Dent, Thomas	Lynes, Philip	10 Oct 1707	Liber C:75
Dent, William	Barker, John & Joane	10 Apr 1685	12.pdf #109
Dent, William	Warner, Thomas	16 May 1688	16.pdf #28
Dent, William	Smith, Anthony & Martha	25 Sep 1691	17.pdf #159
Dent, William	Addisson, John	14 Jan 1692	17.pdf #191
Dent, William	Baker, Thomas & Elizabeth	14 Sep 1692	17.pdf #257
Dent, William	Hutchison, William	29 May 1689	17.pdf #259
Dent, William	Hutchison, William	29 May 1689	17.pdf #259
Dent, William	Hutchison, William	29 May 1689	17.pdf #259
Dent, William	Lugar, Thomas	16 Dec 1692	18.pdf #26
Dent, William	Makey, James	11 Mar 1695	18.pdf #235
Dent, William	Jenifer, Daniel of St. Thomas	11 Apr 1696	Liber Q:85

GRANTEE INDEX TO DEEDS

Dent, William	Lampton, Marke	9 Mar 1697	Liber Q:120
Dent, William	Matthews, William	20 Jul 1703	Liber Z:49
Dent, William & Dent, Phillip			
	Lynes, Philip	10 Jun 1704	Liber Z:112
Dickeson, Jeromiah	Province of Maryland	29 May 1663	02.pdf #399
Dickeson, Jeromy	Lynsey, James	4 Nov 1664	02.pdf #450
Dickeson, Jeremy	Lyndsey, James	4 Nov 1664	02.pdf #451
Dickeson, Jheromy	Lendsey, James	4 Nov 1664	02.pdf #587
Diceson, Thomas & Wilson, John			
	Bayne, Ebsworth	9 Nov 1716	Liber H:27
Dickinson, Jeremiah	Allen, William & Mary	24 Oct 1666	03.pdf #119
Dickson, William	Wheeler, John	30 Mar 1668	Vol. 60:211
Digges, Charles	Ferson, Percyfull (sic)	23 Aug 1714	Liber F:38
Digges, Edward & Neale, Anthony			
	Rozer, Notley	2 Feb 1703	Liber Z:42
Digges, William	Fendall, Josias & Mary	28 Apr 1683	11.pdf #108
Digges, William	Clarke, Gilbert	16 Jul 1696	Liber Q:101
Dirkeson, Roger	Allen, William	10 Aug 1664	02.pdf #457
Dobson, Samuell	Harmon, Matthew	26 Nov 1674	07.pdf #35
Dod, Richard	Empson, Elenor	1 Apr 1660	01.pdf #152
Dod, Richard	Baker, Thomas	9 Jun 1666	03.pdf #68
Doughty, Francis	Tomkins, Giles	17 Jan 1659	02.pdf #236
Douglas, John	Lyndsy, Edmond	16 Sep 1672	06.pdf #92
Duglas, John	Tyer, James	8 Aug 1676	07.pdf #122
Duglas, John	Bullott, Joseph	8 Jan 1678	08.pdf #58
Douglass, Joseph	Maddox, John & Sarah	19 Apr 1714	Liber F:10
Doyne, Dennis	Doyne, Joshua	17 Jan 1698	Liber C:239
Doyne, Joshua	Clarke, Gilbert	9 Mar 1686	13.pdf #88
Doyne, Joshua	Calvert, Charles & Elizabeth	4 Dec 1684	16.pdf #30
Doyne, Joshua	Wheeler, John & Mary	8 Jan 1689	16.pdf #62
Doyne, Robert	Fendall, Samuell	10 Mar 1676	07.pdf #102
Doyne, Robert	Maston, Richard & Mary	12 Mar 1689	16.pdf #65
Doyne, Robert	Wheeler, John	11 Jun 1689	16.pdf #106
Duke, William	Lynes, Philip	12 Apr 1689	17.pdf #258
Duley, John	Faning, Benoni	10 Mar 1713	24.pdf #178
Dyson, John	Stone, William	11 Aug 1714	Liber F:23
Edelen, Richard	Obrian, Mathias	3 Aug 1673	06.pdf #130
Edelen, Richard	Mun, John	20 Mar 1680	09.pdf #183
Edelin, Richard	Boreman, William & Mary	13 Feb 1700	20.pdf #142
Edelen, Richard	Chiseldyne, Kenelin	28 Sep 1712	24.pdf #170
Edlen, Richard	Sympson, Thomas	9 Jun 1713	24.pdf #193
Edelen, Richard & Willson, Alexander			
	Sympson, Thomas	8 Jun 1714	Liber F:41
Edelen, Richard	Ball, John & Winnifrid	9 Mar 1715	Liber F:56

GRANTEE INDEX TO DEEDS

Grantee	Grantor	Date	Reference
Edelen, Richard	Boarman, John Baptista & Elizabeth	12 Nov 1717	Liber H:117
Edelen, Richard	Dent, Thomas & Ann	2 Dec 1717	Liber H:107
Edelen, Richard	Hill, Giles & Margaret	17 Nov 1718	Liber H:210
Edelen, Richard	Hill, Giles & Margaret	17 Nov 1718	Liber H:216
Edelin, Richard	Hill, John & Anne	20 Dec 1720	Liber H:413
Edgerton, Charles	Calvert, Charles	14 Jan 1690	17.pdf #86
Edmondson, Robert	Ward, John	17 Jul 1694	18.pdf #243
Elgin, George	Delozer, Daniell & Mary	14 Sep 1708	Liber C:111
Elliott, William	Allen, James & Verlinda	16 Dec 1716	Liber H:53
Emanson, Elizabeth	Lendsey, Edmond	13 Jun 1671	06.pdf #48
Emanson, Nicholas	Allanson, Thomas	10 Aug 1668	Vol. 60:171
Emerson, Nicholaus	Lumbrozo, Jacob & Elisabeth	16 Nov 1663	02.pdf #397
Emmett, John	Beall, Ninian & Haddock, Benjamin	31 Jan 1693	17.pdf #295
Empson, William	Marshall, William	18 Jul 1658	01.pdf #94
Empson, William	Baker, Thomas	24 Apr 1660	01.pdf #97
Empson, William	Baker, Thomas	23 Apr 1660	01.pdf #153
Empson, William	Baker, Thomas	23 Apr 1660	02.pdf #412
English, George	Lendsey, Edmond	14 Nov 1665	02.pdf #581
Escridge, George	Gerrard, Jane	20 Dec 1712	24.pdf #168
Escridge, George	Johnson, James	22 Dec 1712	24.pdf #169
Eskridge, George	Bayne, Ebsworth	17 Oct 1713	24.pdf #195
Eskridge, George	Bayne, Ebsworth	22 Sep 1719	Liber H:307
Ette, Nathaniell	Fanning, Benoni & Elizabeth	9 Mar 1703	Liber Z:35
Evans, Charles	Blankensteine, William	17 Jul 1689	17.pdf #135
Evens, Stephen	Waple, Osmond	27 Nov 1717	Liber H:152
Fairfax, John	Philpott, Charles & Elizabeth	7 Oct 1720	Liber H:395
Farrill, Matthew	Waple, Osmond	27 Nov 1716	Liber H:42
Farthing, William Maria	Mudd, John	4 Aug 1715	Liber F:73
Farthing, William Maria	Mudd, Henry	3 Aug 1715	Liber F:75
Farthing, William Maria	Mudd, Thomas & Cassander	9 Aug 1715	Liber F:82
Fearson, Percivall	Thompson, Sarah, widow	2 Jun 1719	Liber H:254
Fendall, John	Bayne, Walter & Martha	23 Sep 1710	Liber C:211
Fendall, John	Clarke, John	11 Jul 1715	Liber F:69
Fendall, John	Spering, John & Barbara	4 Feb 1719	Liber H:234
Fendall, John	Hanson, Samuel	7 Feb 1719	Liber H:239
Fendall, John	Harrison, Richard	18 Feb 1719	Liber H:241
Fendall, John	Marshall, Richard & Mary	30 Jan 1722	Liber H:489
Fendall, Josias	Warren, Humphry	1 Nov 1667	Liber H:431
Fendall, Samuel	Johnson, Daniell	8 Aug 1665	02.pdf #553
Fernandis, Peter	OBryan, William	13 Mar 1694	18.pdf #145
Finley, James	Dickinson, Thomas & Anne	23 Nov 1681	10.pdf #111

GRANTEE INDEX TO DEEDS

Fitz Gerrall, Edward	Games, John	12 Feb 1695	18.pdf #234
Fletcher, Henry	Aspinall, Henry	14 Sep 1669	Vol. 60:216
Fletcher, Henry	Waters, John & Eshter	24 Jan 1676	07.pdf #115
Ford, Edward	Allisson, Charles	14 Feb 1690	17.pdf #42
Ford, Edward	Raines, John	12 Sep 1692	18.pdf #48
Ford, Edward	Worland, John & Stacey	12 Jun 1711	Liber C:251
Ford, Edward	Cage (?), William & Margaret	5 Dec 1719	Liber H:328
Forster, William	Smallwood, James	14 Jan 1696	Liber Q:79
Fowke, Gerrard	Maddocke, Edward & Margery	19 Feb 1685	12.pdf #86
Fowke, Richard	Maddox, Edward	7 Aug 1672	06.pdf #79
Fox, William	Thompson, George	17 Dec 1662	02.pdf #121
Fox, William	Lendsey, Edmond	15 Feb 1662	02.pdf #139
Fox, William	Browne, Mathew	31 Jul 1662	02.pdf #537
Frankome, Hennery & Robinson, Thomas			
	Wheeler, John	11 Sep 1658	01.pdf #116
Francom, Henry	Obrion, Math.	12 May 1663	02.pdf #191
Frasier, John & Anne	Smallwood, James & Mary	26 Jan 1710	Liber C:154
Frawner, Edward	Davis, William	13 Mar 1684	12.pdf #55
Frederick, Thomas; Thompson, John; & Greene, James			
	Hutchison, William	11 Nov 1690	17.pdf #70
French, Hugh	Mountague, Stephen	1 Jul 1670	04.pdf #12
French, Hugh	Morris, John	13 Mar 1677	08.pdf #22
Furnice, Francis	Boyden, William	2 Jun 1673	06.pdf #112
Gambrah, Richard	Thompson, William & Victoria	5 Mar 1695	Liber Q:67
Games, John	Corner, Job	1 Oct 1690	17.pdf #70
Gardner, Thomas	Wade, Zachary	12 Jun 1677	08.pdf #37
Gardener, William	Lyndsey, Edmond	10 Mar 1673	06.pdf #119
Garner, Elizabeth	Brooke, Richard	12 Aug 1718	Liber H:183
Gates, James	Boswell, William & Mary	15 Nov 1721	Liber H:469
Ges, Walter	True, Richard	30 May 1659	Liber H:337
Ges, Walter	True, Richard	30 May 1659	Liber H:475
Gibbon, Philip	Hackister, John	10 Sep 1673	06.pdf #154
Gibson, Thomas	Boyden, William & Elizabeth	30 Jun 1682	10.pdf #178
Gifford, Henry	Gibson, Thomas & Elizabeth	17 Jul 1694	18.pdf #238
Gifford, Henry	Gibson, Thomas & Elizabeth	8 Mar 1695	18.pdf #239
Gilpin, Isaac	Pye, Charles	24 Jul 1706	Liber C:42
Gilpin, Isaac	Rozer, Notley & Jane	1 Nov 1718	Liber H:206
Glass, John	Marston, Constance, widow	28 May 1713	24.pdf #180
Glover, Giles	Linsey, Edmond	19 Aug 1659	01.pdf #140
Glover, Gyles	Harris, Robert	30 Apr 1660	01.pdf #98
Glover, Gyles	Lindsey, Edmond	4 Sep 1660	01.pdf #110
Glover, Giles	Lendsey, Edmond	4 Sep 1660	01.pdf #251
Glover, Gils	Lendsey, Edmond	4 Sep 1660	02.pdf #395
Glover, Gils	Lumbrozo, John	24 May 1664	02.pdf #401
Goady, William	Diamond, George & Mary	21 Apr 1712	24.pdf #165

GRANTEE INDEX TO DEEDS

Godfrey, George			
	Harrison, Joseph & Mountague, Stephen	11 Jun 1672	06.pdf #68
Godfrey, George	Theobald, Clement	8 Mar 1675	07.pdf #53
Godfrey, Mary	Godfrey, William & Jannett	28 Feb 1722	Liber H:484
Godfrey, William	Covert, Robert & Christian	28 Feb 1722	Liber H:485
Godshall, John	Lambert, John & Eleanor	10 Mar 1668	Vol. 60:147
Godshall, John	Cane, John	12 Nov 1683	11.pdf #147
Godson, John	Clarke, Thomas	10 Jan 1682	10.pdf #131
Gooderick, Francis	Gooderick, George	18 Mar 1674	06.pdf #159
Goodrick, Francis	Bladen, William	3 Jul 1716	Liber H:24
Goodrick, Robert & Clements, John			
	Ward, John & Damaris	9 Aug 1677	08.pdf #38
Goodridg, Henry	Smith, Daniell	31 Dec 1690	17.pdf #91
Gover, George	Hagar, Robert & Mary	8 Sep 1685	12.pdf #108
Grant, William	Corner, Jobe	4 Jan 1673	06.pdf #115
Graves, Joshuah	Tickerell, Thomas & Anne	10 Aug 1680	09.pdf #182
Graves, Joshua	Breeden, John	12 Feb 1690	17.pdf #19
Graves, Joshuah	Cornish, John & Martha		
	Smallpage, Robert & Elinor	9 Jun 1691	17.pdf #117
Gray, John	Car, Peter	20 Aug 1677	09.pdf #80
Green, Leonard	Sympson, Thomas & Mary	14 Mar 1711	Liber C:236
Green, Luke & Cable, John			
	Province of Maryland	1 Feb 1672	Liber Z:213
Greene, Luke	Harrison, Joseph	9 Oct 1672	06.pdf #91
Green, Luke	Wharton, Thomas	10 Jun 1673	06.pdf #120
Greene, Francis & Greene, Robert			
	Greene, Leonard	4 Jun 1694	18.pdf #167
Greene, Robert & Greene, Francis			
	Greene, Leonard	4 Jun 1694	18.pdf #167
Greene, James; Thompson, John; & Frederick, Thomas			
	Hutchison, William	11 Nov 1690	17.pdf #70
Greenfield, Thomas, Colo. & Hollyday, Leonard			
	Hill, Clement	18 Sep 1714	Liber F:49
Greenfield, Thomas, Coll. & Hollyday, Leonard			
	Hill, Clement	18 Sep 1714	Liber H:111
Greenehill, John			
	Chandler, Jobe & Oversee, Simon	25 May 1659	02.pdf #336
Greenhill, John	Chandler, Anne	25 May 1659	02.pdf #338
Griffine, William & Phillips, Thomas			
	Cornall, Joseph & Margrett	2 Jun 1687	14.pdf #113
Griffin, William & Phillips, Thomas			
	Cornall, Joseph & Margrett	2 Jun 1688	16.pdf #15
Griffitch, Hugh	Lendsey, James	1 May 1662	01.pdf #220
Griffitch, Hugh	Lendsey, Mary	2 May 1662	01.pdf #220
Grover, William	Fugett, John	10 Nov 1718	Liber H:199

GRANTEE INDEX TO DEEDS

Groves, George	Cole, Philip	7 Jan 1685	12.pdf #41
Guibert, Joshuah	Whichaley, Thomas & Elizabeth	22 Jun 1694	18.pdf #199
Guibert, Joshua & Ann	Boreman, William, Senr.	24 Jul 1712	24.pdf #166
Gwyn, John	Hamilton, John	11 Nov 1679	09.pdf #132
Gwyn, John	Hamilton, John	9 Aug 1680	10.pdf #30
Guinn, John	Compton, John, Junr.	10 Aug 1713	24.pdf #191
Gwinn, John	Cage, William & Margaret	5 Dec 1719	Liber H:342
Hackister, John	Corner, Jobe	1 Aug 1673	06.pdf #153
Haddock, Sarah & Warren, Bazil			
	Barton, William	12 Aug 1712	24.pdf #174
Hagan, Thomas, Junr.			
	Hall, Benjamin & Boarman, William	17 Jan 1709	Liber C:209
Hagan, Thomas	Boarman, William, Senr.	10 Jun 1713	24.pdf #186
Haggar, Robert	Skidmore, Nicholas & Ann	8 Sep 1685	12.pdf #107
Hagar, Robert, Junr.	Hagar, Robert, Senr. & Elizabeth	9 Nov 1708	Liber C:119
Hall, Benjamin	Bowling, John	24 Oct 1706	Liber C:58
Hall, Benjamin	Sympson, Thomas	24 Oct 1707	Liber C:61
Hamilton, Gawen	Attwood, John	9 Dec 1690	17.pdf #84
Hamilton, John	Duglas, John	13 Aug 1678	09.pdf #16
Hamilton, John	Helgar, Thomas & Anne	12 Nov 1678	09.pdf #47
Hamilton, John	Thompson, George	15 Jan 1680	09.pdf #144
Hamond, John	Loveday, William	14 Mar 1676	07.pdf #102
Hamon, John	Loveday, William & Ruth	13 Nov 1677	08.pdf #57
Hanson, John	Corker, Thomas & Mary	11 Jan 1676	07.pdf #97
Hanson, John & Elizabeth			
	Warren, John	19 Nov 1708	Liber C:123
Hanson, John	Wills, William	14 Jul 1721	Liber H:449
Handson, Randall; Waed, Zachery; Harrisson, Joseph; & Allen, William			
	Hatton, William & Dent, Thomas	9 May 1663	02.pdf #188
Hanson, Randolph & Wade, Zachary			
	Brooke, Thomas	12 Nov 1670	06.pdf #95
Hanson, Randolph	Langworth, William & Agatha	20 Feb 1680	09.pdf #167
Hanson, Robert	Lynes, Philip & Anne	19 Sep 1704	Liber Z:167
Hanson, Robert	Luckett, Thomas Hussey	12 Dec 1716	Liber H:34
Hanson, Robert	Lampton, William	1 Mar 1718	Liber H:129
Hanson, Robert	Price, Juliana	28 Apr 1718	Liber H:174
Hanson, Robert	Chandler, William	12 Nov 1720	Liber H:398
Hanson, Samuel	Fendall, John & Elizabeth	4 Feb 1719	Liber H:236
Hanson, Samuel	Green, Thomas & Seele	9 Jun 1719	Liber H:264
Hanson, Samuel	Taylor, Robert	4 May 1720	Liber H:334
Hanson, Samuel	Anderson, Edward & Anne	22 Sep 1720	Liber H:382
Hareister, John	Causine, Ignatius	7 Nov 1670	06.pdf #5
Harris, George	Deane, Edward	16 Dec 1661	01.pdf #181
Harris, George	Balse, Oliver	30 May 1667	03.pdf #230
Harris, Thomas	Smith, Raiph & Sarah	3 Apr 1680	09.pdf #163

GRANTEE INDEX TO DEEDS

Harrison, Francis	Palmer, Samuell	9 Jun 1660	01.pdf #117
Harrison, John	Thomas, Hugh	13 Nov 1684	12.pdf #40
Harrisson, Joseph; Waed, Zachery; Handson, Randall; & Allen, William			
	Hatton, William & Dent, Thomas	9 May 1663	02.pdf #188
Harrison, Joseph	Ming, Mary	26 Jul 1716	Liber H:15
Harrison, Joseph	Allen, John & Katherine	18 Feb 1717	Liber H:43
Harrison, Joseph	Lambert, John & Sarah	14 Nov 1717	Liber H:131
Harrison, Joseph, Junr.	Dent, Thomas	18 Feb 1718	Liber H:127
Harrison, Richard	Troop, Robert, Capt.	14 Jan 1668	03.pdf #297
Harrison, Richard	Hussey, Thomas	10 Aug 1684	12.pdf #103
Harrison, Richard	Delahay, John	27 May 1685	12.pdf #104
Harrison, Richard	Dent, Thomas & Ann	14 Mar 1710	Liber C:182
Hatch, John	Ges, Walter	14 Sep 1659	Liber H:337
Hatch, John	Ges, Walter	14 Sep 1659	Liber H:475
Hatton, William & Wade, Zachary			
	Province of Maryland	26 Apr 1658	Liber H:405
Hatton, William	Boareman, William, Capt.	4 Aug 1674	07.pdf #25
Hatton, William	Dent, Rebekah, widow	20 Nov 1676	Liber Z:116
Hatton, William & Tannyhill, William			
	Athey, George	3 Dec 1694	Liber Q:70
Hawkins, Elizabeth	Wine, Henry	11 Jun 1689	16.pdf #106
Hawkins, Henry	Wine, Francis	25 Apr 1665	02.pdf #539
Hawkins, Henry	Barton, Nathan	14 Jun 1670	04.pdf #61
Hawkins, Henry	Jenkinson, William	8 Nov 1675	07.pdf #89
Hawkins, Henry	Peterson, Jacob	5 Mar 1678	08.pdf #95
Hawkins, Henry	Aspenall, Henry & wife	9 Mar 1680	09.pdf #154
Hawkins, Henry	Fendall, Josias	30 Nov 1681	10.pdf #125
Hawkins, Henrie & Elizabeth			
	Pryor, William & Marie	9 Nov 1686	13.pdf #113
Hawkins, Henry	Moore, Henry	10 Jan 1688	14.pdf #163
Hawkins, Henry	Evans, Charles	11 Aug 1691	17.pdf #139
Hawkins, Henry & Elizabeth			
	Price, Jane, widow	12 Feb 1696	Liber Q:80
Hawkins, Henry	Manning, Joseph	30 Jan 1705	23.pdf #135
Hawkins, Henry, Junr.	Smoot, Barton & Sarah	11 Mar 1713	24.pdf #179
Hawkins, Thomas	Hawkins, John & Elizabeth	6 Jan 1722	Liber H:475
Hawton, William	Hatch, William	17 Sep 1696	Liber Q:103
Haydon, Francis & Alword, John			
	Moore, Henry	8 Nov 1669	Vol. 60:219
Hayes, James & Hoskins, Philip			
	Owen, John	12 Sep 1671	06.pdf #49
Hayes, James & Hoskins, Philip			
	Owen, John	7 Sep 1671	06.pdf #81
Hays, Thomas	Lemaistre, Richard & Martha	13 Aug 1713	Liber F:5

GRANTEE INDEX TO DEEDS

Heydon, Francis & Alward, John			
	Hussy, Thomas & Joan	13 Jun 1670	04.pdf #56
Heard, William	Parker, Samuell	28 Apr 1659	01.pdf #78
Heard, William	Empson, William	12 Feb 1661	01.pdf #154
Heard, William & Morrise, Richard			
	Carnell, Christopher	24 Apr 1656	02.pdf #236
Heard, William	Empson, William	12 Feb 1661	02.pdf #413
Helgar, Thomas & Anne			
	Lee, William	10 May 1677	09.pdf #46
Heline, John	Munn, John	10 Mar 1674	06.pdf #160
Hemsley, Philemon	Smallwood, Samuel & Martha	17 Apr 1712	24.pdf #167
Hemsly, Philemon & Mary			
	Lemaister, Abraham	14 Jun 1713	24.pdf #184
Hemsly, Philemon & Mary			
	Bladen, William & Ann	30 Apr 1713	24.pdf #191
Hensey, William	Robins, Robert	14 Jun 1670	04.pdf #44
Henston, George	Goodricke, Robert	31 Jul 1684	11.pdf #238
Herbert, William	Warren, Thomas	12 Jan 1690	17.pdf #90
Higdon, John	Dent, William	17 Apr 1693	18.pdf #116
Hill, Charles & Prouse, Robert			
	Thompson, George	10 Jan 1665	02.pdf #463
Hill, Charles & Prous, Robert			
	Thompson, George	19 Apr 1666	03.pdf #80
Hobb, Thomas	Proddy, Thomas & Jane	10 Aug 1688	17.pdf #33
Hodgson, Richard	Ashbrooke, James	4 Dec 1682	11.pdf #40
Hodgson, Richard	Doyne, John	11 Jul 1717	Liber H:77
Hollyday, Leonard & Greenfield, Thomas, Colo.			
	Hill, Clement	18 Sep 1714	Liber F:49
Hollyday, Leonard & Greenfield, Thomas, Coll			
	Hill, Clement	18 Sep 1714	Liber H:111
Hollyday, Leonard, Capt.			
Greenfield, Thomas Trueman & Greenfield, James		15 Jun 1720	Liber H:384
Holmes, George	Grubb, John	11 Jun 1672	06.pdf #88
Holmes, George	Grubb, John	11 Jun 1672	06.pdf #89
Horton, Joseph	Bonner, Henery	9 Jun 1673	06.pdf #113
Hoskins, Philip & Hayes, James			
	Owen, John	12 Sep 1671	06.pdf #49
Hoskins, Philip & Hayes, James			
	Owen, John	7 Sep 1671	06.pdf #81
Hoskyns, Philip & Elizabeth			
	Wahob, Archibald	14 Nov 1682	11.pdf #30
Hoskins, Philip	Love, Thomas	26 Apr 1694	18.pdf #160
Hoskins, Philip	Love, Thomas	26 Apr 1694	18.pdf #160
Hoskins, Philip	Sinnett, Garrett & Anne	4 Apr 1705	Liber Z:178
Hoskins, Philip	Meckey, James	10 Apr 1705	Liber Z:176

GRANTEE INDEX TO DEEDS

Hoskins, William	Butts, Richard & Mary	12 Dec 1717	Liber H:120
Hungerford, Thomas	Lucas, Thomas & Anne	22 Nov 1721	Liber H:476
Hungerford, William	Smoote, William	21 Nov 1683	11.pdf #152
Hungerford, William & Margarett			
	Barton, William & Mary	13 Jun 1688	17.pdf #292
Hunter, William	Hutchison, William	18 Apr 1689	18.pdf #85
Hunter, William	Rozer, Notley	20 Nov 1711	Liber C:263
Hunter, William	Rozer, Notley	20 Nov 1711	Liber C:265
Hussey, James	Boyden, William	13 Mar 1666	03.pdf #63
Hussey, James	Boyden, William	13 Mar 1665	03.pdf #154
Hussey, Thomas	Moore, Henery	3 Dec 1659	01.pdf #122
Hussey, Thomas	Wheeler, John	29 Dec 1660	01.pdf #159
Hussey, Thomas	Moore, Henry	28 Jan 1662	01.pdf #187
Hussey, Thomas	Moore, Henry	3 Dec 1659	01.pdf #246
Hussey, Thomas	Moore, Henry	3 Dec 1659	02.pdf #85
Hussey, Thomas & Johannah			
	Nevill, William	13 Aug 1666	03.pdf #98
Hussy, Thomas	Moore, Henry & Elizabeth	17 May 1670	04.pdf #31
Hussy, Thomas	Rookerd, Edward & Mary	8 June 1680	09.pdf #169
Hussy, Thomas	Wharton, Thomas	8 Mar 1681	10.pdf #58
Hussey, Thomas	Rookwood, Edward	7 Dec 1681	10.pdf #167
Hussey, Thomas	Shuttleworth, Thomas	11 Sep 1683	11.pdf #144
Hussey, Thomas	Frawner, Edward	5 Jan 1685	12.pdf #55
Hussey, Thomas	Wade, Richard	14 Sep 1686	13.pdf #103
Hussey, Thomas	Ashford, Michaell & Rachell	10 Jun 1691	17.pdf #118
Hussey, Thomas	Hutchison, William	8 Nov 1687	18.pdf #115
Hussey, Thomas	Hutchison, William	16 Jan 1688	18.pdf #116
Hussey, Thomas	Hutchison, William	17 Mar 1688	18.pdf #116
Hussey, Thomas	Manning, Joseph	18 Sep 1697	19.pdf #167
Hutchinson, John	Jones, Morgan	10 Jun 1667	03.pdf #216
Hutchinson, John	Brown, John & Virlinda	25 Nov 1720	Liber H:415
Hutchinson, Thomas	Hawkins, John & Elizabeth	9 Jun 1696	Liber Q:87
Hutchinson, William	Taylor, Samuell & Verlinda	9 Jan 1703	Liber Z:8
Hutchison, William	Dent, Peter	11 Oct 1688	16.pdf #60
Hutchison, William	Thompson, James	1 Jun 1689	17.pdf #259
Hutchison, William	Thomson, James	3 Jun 1689	17.pdf #259
Hutchison, William	Thomson, James	3 Jun 1689	17.pdf #260
Hutchison, William	West, William	12 Aug 1691	17.pdf #260
Hutchison, William	Clarke, Gilbert	2 Nov 1688	17.pdf #296
Hutchison, William	Province of Maryland	6 Apr 1689	17.pdf #297
Hutchison, William	Thomson, James	22 Jul 1689	18.pdf #52
Hutchison, William	Middleton, Robert	13 Jun 1693 (?)	18.pdf #86
Hutchison, William	Lampton, Marke & Elizabeth	11 Sep 1694	18.pdf #198
Hutcheson, William	Doyne, Mary	17 Apr 1702	Liber Z:19
Hutchison, William	Dawson, Nicholas & Mary	27 Apr 1710	Liber C:200

GRANTEE INDEX TO DEEDS

Iles, Richard & Mason, Phillip			
	Fowkes, Richard	13 Nov 1688	16.pdf #29
Ingelsby, Robert	Thomas, William	18 Feb 1674	06.pdf #152
Jameson, Thomas	Mudd, Thomas	8 Mar 1710	Liber C:164
Jameson, Thomas	Mudd, Thomas	2 Mar 1711	Liber C:227
Jameson, Thomas	Hall, Benjamin	13 Mar 1711	Liber C:231
Jameson, Thomas	Brooke, Clare	30 Jan 1722	Liber H:480
Jameson, Thomas	Clark, Luke	5 Feb 1722	Liber H:481
Jeffers, William	Newton, John	29 Aug 1660	01.pdf #205
Jenkins, Daniell	Smith, Richard	10 May 1688	16.pdf #49
Jenkins, Thomas	Robinson, John & Elizabeth	8 Aug 1671	06.pdf #48
Jenkins, Thomas	Robinson, John	13 Jun 1671	06.pdf #82
Jenkins, Thomas	Shenstone, George & Mary	10 Nov 1674	07.pdf #20
Jenkins, Thomas	Maglockline, Kellam & Elizabeth	13 Nov 1677	08.pdf #76
Jenckins, Thomas	Pye, Charles	9 Aug 1706	Liber C:9
Jenkins, William	Smallwood, James	14 Feb 1671	06.pdf #39
Jervis, Thomas & Oneall, Hugh			
	Philpot, Edward	18 Jan 1657	01.pdf #94
Johnson, Daniell & Morris, Richard			
	Province of Maryland	30 Oct 1661	02.pdf #79
Johnson, Daniell & Maurice, Richard			
	Province of Maryland	1661	02.pdf #90
Johnson, Daniell	Province of Maryland	1661	02.pdf #289
Johnson, Daniell & Morrise, Richard			
	Province of Maryland	20 Oct 1661	02.pdf #292
Johnson, Daniell & Maurise, Richard			
	Province of Maryland	13 Jul 1663	02.pdf #295
Johnson, Daniell	Province of Maryland	9 Jul 1663	02.pdf #298
Johnson, Daniell	Province of Maryland	27 Jun 1663	02.pdf #402
Johnson, Daniell	Fendall, Samuell	10 Feb 1669	Vol. 60:245
Johnson, Samuel	Dent, George & Elizabeth	12 Mar 1721	Liber H:483
Jones, Charles	Caine, Darby	1 Jan 1705	Liber Z:175
Joanes, Humphery & Joanes, Richard			
	Joanes, Owen & Joanne	8 Jan 1666	03.pdf #59
Jones, Humphrey	Jones, Richard	8 Mar 1668	Vol. 60:162
Jones, Lewis	Davis, John	10 Aug 1680	09.pdf #185
Jones, Lewis	Douglas, John	6 Aug 1680	10.pdf #33
Jones, Lewis	Lambert, John	1 Mar 1681	10.pdf #55
Jones, Moses	Hutchison, William	13 Sep 1692	17.pdf #259
Joanes, Moses	Loyd, Morris	18 Feb 1695	Liber Q:76
Jones, Owen	Lyndsey, James & Mary	18 Oct 1664	02.pdf #455
Joanes, Owen	Lendsey, James & Mary	10 Mar 1665	02.pdf #534
Jones, Owen	Province of Maryland	20 Jan 1669	Liber H:177
Joanes, Richard & Joanes, Humphery			
	Joanes, Owen & Joanne	8 Jan 1666	03.pdf #59

GRANTEE INDEX TO DEEDS

Jones, Richard	Adames, Francis	8 Jun 1669	Vol. 60:203
Jones, Richard	Thomas, David	14 Nov 1682	11.pdf #32
Keett, William	Evans, Edward	10 May 1686	14.pdf #21
Kelli, Thomas	Ashbrooke, John	28 Jan 1660	01.pdf #140
Kelli, Thomas	Delahey, John	12 Mar 1660	01.pdf #151
Key, Henry	Cash, William & Rebeckah	1 Jul 1692	17.pdf #240
Key, William	Banister, John	20 May 1710	Liber C:202
Killingsworth, John	Ashman, Richard	25 Jan 1707	Liber C:29
King, John	Walker, William & Mary	14 Mar 1710	Liber C:170
King, Thomas	Stone, Thomas & John	8 Aug 1668	Vol. 60:168
King, Thomas	Browne, Gerard	5 Mar 1669	04.pdf #65
King, Thomas	Wharton, Henry	5 Sep 1713	24.pdf #198
Kingsland, William	Slye, John	13 Mar 1717	Liber H:49
Knight, Edward	Jones, Owen	4 Sep 1669	Vol. 60:217
Knight, Edward	Jones, Owen & Joanna	15 Sep 1670	Liber H:179
Knight, Edward	Midgely, Richard & Wainman, Rice	12 Mar 1672	06.pdf #59
Kylborne, Francis	Mackey, James	12 Mar 1673	06.pdf #132
Lambert, John	Mun, John	7 Dec 1665	03.pdf #153
Lambert, John	True, Richard	8 Jan 1667	03.pdf #159
Lambert, John	Dickenson, Roger	12 Mar 1667	03.pdf #181
Lambert, John	Allanson, Thomas	8 Mar 1673	06.pdf #110
Lambert, John	Theobald, Clement	8 Mar 1675	07.pdf #54
Lambert, John, Junr.	Barefoot, John	24 May 1708	Liber C:107
Lambert, John, Junior	Allen, John & Ellinor	6 Jun 1709	Liber C:138
Lambert, John	Allen, James	14 Jun 1717	Liber H:66
Lambert, William	Jones, Lewis	1 Mar 1681	10.pdf #56
Langham, George	Hutchison, William	25 Jul 1689	17.pdf #298
Lawne, Edward	Higgins, Richard	10 Aug 1715	Liber F:58
Lee, James	Province of Maryland	19 Aug 1658	01.pdf #109
Lee, James	Province of Maryland	19 Aug 1658	01.pdf #166
Lee, Philip	Perrie, Samuel & Sarah	6 Aug 1720	Liber H:406
Lemaire, John	Cassock, John	29 May 1673	06.pdf #110
Lomaire, John & Margaret			
	Price, Jane & Edward	12 Jun 1677	08.pdf #37
Lemaire, Margarett	Waghope, Archibald	1 Feb 1677	08.pdf #24
Lemastre, Isaac	Lemastre, Abraham	9 Sep 1721	Liber H:468
Lentonkis (?), Joseph	Watson, Andrew	20 Jul 1657	01.pdf #187
Lewis, Gilbert	Sympson, Thomas, Senr. & Junr.	17 Feb 1720	Liber H:319
Lewis, Thomas	Mason, Philip & Mary	19 Jul 1692	18.pdf #43
Lewis, Thomas	Stonestreet, Thomas & Christian	9 Mar 1714	24.pdf #202
Lilly, Hennery	Lee, James	22 Jun 1657	01.pdf #110
Linsey, Edmond	Province of Maryland	16 Aug 1653	01.pdf #139
Lendsey, Edmond	Province of Maryland	20 Jul 1662	02.pdf #137
Lyndsey, Edmond	Rozer, Benjamin	13 Mar 1677	08.pdf #25
Linsey, James	Province of Maryland	2 Sep 1659	01.pdf #168

GRANTEE INDEX TO DEEDS

Linsey, James	Province of Maryland	2 Sept 1659	01.pdf #180
Lendsey, James	Province of Maryland	10 Dec 1653	02.pdf #189
Lynsey, James	Province of Maryland	1662	02.pdf #451
Lynsey, James	Province of Maryland	27 Jun 1662	02.pdf #454
Lendsey, James	Allonson, Thomas	12 Jun 1666	03.pdf #79
Lyndsey, James & Macoy, James			
	Montague, Stephen	13 Nov 1667	03.pdf #292
Linzy, Thomas	Lugar, Thomas	25 Feb 1688	16.pdf #47
Littlepage, James & Littlepage, Robert			
	Harris, George	7 Sep 1668	Vol. 60:172
Littlepage, Robert & Littlepage, James			
	Harris, George	7 Sep 1668	Vol. 60:172
Lockar, Thomas, Junr.	Beall, Ninian & Ruth	15 Sep 1694	Liber Q:69
Lomax, Cleborne	Lomax, Thomas	9 Jan 1677	08.pdf #15
Lomax, Ralph & Margarett			
	Contee, Mary, widow	3 Mar 1711	Liber C:245
Lomax, Thomas	Thomas, Hugh	26 Apr 1668	Vol. 60:152
Love, Samuell	Bayne, Ebsworth & Katherine	28 Jan 1716	Liber F:86
Love, Samuell	Bayne, Ebsworth & Kindrick	11 Nov 1718	Liber H:208
Love, William	Markony, Martin	30 Oct 1664	02.pdf #455
Love, William	Davies, Alexander & Susanna	15 Aug 1669	Vol. 60:222
Loveday, William	Jenkins, Thomas & Anne	8 Jun 1675	07.pdf #64
Loyde, Morris & Marbury, Francis			
	Scot, Edward & Mary	28 Nov 1690	17.pdf #83
Loyd, Morris	Boughton, Samuell	29 Dec 1694	18.pdf #233
Luckett, Ignatius	Askin, George	11 Mar 1706	Liber C:45
Lucket, Ignatius	Ashford, Michael	10 Mar 1715	Liber F:61
Luckett, Samuell	Smoote, William	12 Aug 1684	12.pdf #14
Luckett, Samuell	Manning, Joseph	22 May 1706	23.pdf #137
Luckett, Thomas Hussey			
	Price, Juliana, widow	23 Dec 1717	Liber H:140
Luckett, Thomas Hussey			
	Price, Juliana, widow	12 May 1718	Liber H:161
Luckett, Thomas Hussey			
	Price, Juliana, widow	13 May 1718	Liber H:163
Lumbrozo, Jacob alias John			
	Glover, Giles & Elizabeth	1 Oct 1662	01.pdf #262
Lumbrozo, Jacob	Glover, Giles & Elisabeth	2 Oct 1662	02.pdf #396
Lumbrozo, John	Thompson, George	3 May 1664	02.pdf #401
Lurling, Robert	Harrison, John & Martha	14 May 1686	13.pdf #82
Lynes, Philip	Hill, John	9 Jan 1674	06.pdf #146
Lines, Philip	Langham, George	20 Jan 1674	06.pdf #149
Lynes, Philip	Breames, Christopher	Mar 1674	06.pdf #150
Lynes, Philip	Coates, Railph	9 Aug 1674	06.pdf #164
Lynes, Philip	Leah, Jacob	11 Jan 1675	07.pdf #34

GRANTEE INDEX TO DEEDS

Lynes, Philip	Theobald, Clement	11 Jan 1675	07.pdf #35
Lynes, Philip	Pinner, Richard & William	11 Jan 1675	07.pdf #36
Lines, Philip	Furnis, Francis	11 Jan 1675	07.pdf #37
Lines, Philip	Taylor, Edmund	11 Jan 1675	07.pdf #52
Lines, Philip	Boyden, William	8 Jun 1675	07.pdf #64
Lines, Philip	Pinner, Richard	14 Sep 1675	07.pdf #83
Lines, Philip	Goodricke, George	11 Jan 1676	07.pdf #96
Lines, Philip	Maddock, Edward	8 Aug 1676	07.pdf #114
Lines, Philip	Taylor, Edmond	14 Nov 1676	07.pdf #127
Lines, Philip	Athy, George	9 Jan 1677	08.pdf #14
Lines, Philip	Athy, George	9 Jan 1677	08.pdf #15
Lines, Philip	Blumstead, John & Katherin	6 Nov 1676	08.pdf #16
Lines, Philip	Lee, William	15 May 1677	08.pdf #32
Lines, Philip	Sly, Gerrard	8 Jan 1678	09.pdf #61
Lines, Philip	Pinner, William	12 Sep 1679	09.pdf #131
Lynes, Philip	Godshall, John & Sarah	8 Jun 1683	11.pdf #113
Lynes, Phillip	Hamilton, John	15 Jan 1684	11.pdf #161
Lynes, Phillip	French, Hugh	8 Jan 1684	11.pdf #162
Lynes, Phillip	Clark, Robert	12 Sep 1688	16.pdf #28
Lynes, Phillip	Ming, Edward & Jane	8 Jan 1689	16.pdf #47
Lynes, Phillip	Lee, Thomas	8 Jan 1689	16.pdf #48
Lynes, Phillip	Maston, Richard & Mary	12 Mar 1689	16.pdf #61
Lynes, Philip	Middleton, Robert & Mary	13 Mar 1689	16.pdf #64
Lynes, Philip	Hutchison, William	12 Apr 1689	17.pdf #258
Lynes, Philip	Smoote, William	10 Jun 1690	17.pdf #19
Lynes, Philip	Lewgar, Thomas	16 May 1690	17.pdf #32
Lynes, Philip	Nicholls, John & Bathsheba	10 Sep 1706	Liber C:21
Lynes, Philip	Tire, James & Margaret	8 Jan 1707	Liber H:287
Lynes, Phillip	Contee, John, lease	11 Oct 1707	Liber C:78
Macken, Martin	Browne, John	10 Mar 1664	02.pdf #509
Mackey, James	Tompkinson, John	11 Aug 1668	Vol. 60:165
Maconchie, William	Godfrey, George	21 Apr 1713	24.pdf #184
Maconchie, William	Allen, John & Catherine	2 Feb 1719	Liber H:219
Macoy, James & Lyndsey, James			
	Montague, Stephen	13 Nov 1667	03.pdf #292
Maddocke, Cornelius	Butcher, John & Mary	26 Dec 1684	12.pdf #39
Maddock, Edward	Greene, Luke	11 Nov 1673	06.pdf #151
Maddocke, Edward	Aspenall, Henry	29 Oct 1674	07.pdf #24
Maddock, Edward	Athy, George	12 Apr 1676	07.pdf #103
Maddock, Edward	Chandler, Richard	29 Nov 1681	10.pdf #111
Maddocke, James	Shaw, Ralph & Mary	2 May 1718	Liber H:168
Maddocke, James	Shaw, Ralph & Mary	7 Apr 1719	Liber H:225
Maddox, John	Douglass, Joseph	22 Apr 1714	Liber F:19
Maddox, William	Fanning, Benonie & Hannah	5 Sep 1710	Liber C:197
Magrah, John	Story, Walter & Mary	5 Jun 1719	Liber H:268

GRANTEE INDEX TO DEEDS

Manning, Joseph	Shackerly, John & Mary	16 Nov 1716	Liber H:50
Manning, Joseph	Allen, James & Verlinda	16 Nov 1716	Liber H:52
Manning, Joseph	Ellitt, William & Ann	8 Aug 1717	Liber H:114
Marbury, Francis & Loyde, Morris			
	Scot, Edward & Mary	28 Nov 1690	17.pdf #83
Maris, Thomas	Chandler, Job	14 May 1658	01.pdf #80
Maris, Thomas	Langham, George	2 Jan 1671	06.pdf #10
Marlow, William	Acton, Henry & Anne	8 Nov 1715	Liber F:79
Marsh, Gilbert	Turner, Edward	1 Aug 1691	17.pdf #117
Marshall, Richard	Marshall, William & Rebecka	11 Jan 1720	Liber H:308
Marshall, Richard	Fendall, John & Elizabeth	30 Jan 1722	Liber H:487
Marshall, William	Province of Maryland	26 Mar 1650	02.pdf #245
Marshall, William	Province of Maryland	4 Feb 1653	02.pdf #246
Marshall, William	Whit, Thomas	10 Apr 1655	02.pdf #249
Marshall, William & Beane, Walter			
	Province of Maryland	10 Apr 1660	02.pdf #249
Marshall, William	Beane, Walter & Elenor	13 Oct 1663	02.pdf #249
Marston, Constance	Bayley, James	12 Jul 1711	Liber C:255
Martin, Michaell	Austin, Thomas & Susanna	2 Jan 1694	18.pdf #125
Martin, Michael	Luckett, Samuell & Anne	11 Jun 1712	24.pdf #161
Martine, James	Athee, George & Ann	25 May 1683	11.pdf #114
Mason, George, Coll.	Rookwood, Edward	1 May 1702	Liber Z:203
Mason, George	Moss, William	8 Jun 1705	Liber Z:201
Mason, Phillip	Hutchinson, William	Jun 1687	14.pdf #115
Mason, Phillip & Iles, Richard			
	Fowkes, Richard	13 Nov 1688	16.pdf #29
Mason, Susannah, widow			
	Whichaley, Thomas & Elizabeth	14 Jan 1704	Liber Z:76
Maston, Richard	Skidmore, Nicholas	22 May 1684	11.pdf #212
Mathewes, Thomas	Nevill, William & Joane	17 Aug 1666	03.pdf #195
Meeke, Francis	Breams, Christopher	25 Jun 1685	13.pdf #89
Mellor, John	Groves, George, Senr. & Jane	16 Oct 1708	Liber C:113
Mellor, John	Luckett, Thomas Hussey & Elizabeth	30 Oct 1719	Liber H:295
Methenie, Daniell	Wentworth, Thomas	5 Aug 1664	02.pdf #584
Michell, Thomas	Smoot, Richard	8 Jan 1657	02.pdf #161
Middleton, Robert & Mary			
	Wheeler, John	30 Jan 1685	12.pdf #40
Middleton, Robert	Hutchison, William	18 Jun 1690	18.pdf #85
Middleton, Robert	Thomson, James	18 Apr 1690	18.pdf #86
Middleton, Robert	Hutchison, William	19 Apr 1689	18.pdf #89
Midgely, Richard & Wainiman, Rice			
	Greene, Luke	10 Jan 1671	06.pdf #7
Miles, Edward	Baker, Thomas	6 Dec 1719	Liber H:303
Miller, George	Evans, Richard	27 Mar 1691	17.pdf #112
Miller, John	Fairfax, John & Mary	14 Mar 1721	Liber H:420

GRANTEE INDEX TO DEEDS

Milner, Thomas	Province of Maryland	12 Jan 1654	02.pdf #174
Minock, Michaell	Lyndsy, Edmond	8 Nov 1672	06.pdf #93
Mitchell, Thomas	Wakelin, Richard & Mary	13 Mar 1683	11.pdf #88
Mitchell, Thomas	Austrey, George	10 Mar 1689	17.pdf #190
Moncaster, James	Dent, Thomas	3 Feb 1711	Liber C:229
Montague, Stephen	Dickinson, Jeremiah	11 Jun 1667	03.pdf #222
Montague, Stephen	Emanson, Nicholas	29 Jul 1669	Vol. 60:209
Montgomery, Peter	Guibert, Joshua & Ann	1 Dec 1716	Liber H:48
Moore, Hennery	Robisson, William	17 Feb 1658	01.pdf #119
Moore, Henry	Robisson, William	17 Feb 1658	01.pdf #186
Moore, Henry	Clarke, John	20 Feb 1662	01.pdf #197
Moore, Henry	Robisson, William	17 Feb 1658	01.pdf #244
Moore, Henry	Robisson, William	17 Feb 1658	02.pdf #81
Moore, Henry	Allen, William	8 Jun 1669	Vol. 60:225
Moore, Henry	Boyden, William & Anne	2 Mar 1671	06.pdf #40
Moor, Henry	Barrett, James & Elizabeth	7 Dec 1685	13.pdf #29
More, Henry	Manning, Joseph	20 Jul 1705	23.pdf #114
Moore, John	Smith, John & Anne	3 Oct 1715	Liber F:81
Morris, Edward	Breams, Christopher	8 Jun 1672	06.pdf #79
Morris, John	Tomkins, Giles	17 Mar 1660	02.pdf #161
Morris, John & Tomkins, Giles			
	Heard, William & Morris, Richard	27 Jul 1656	02.pdf #236
Morriss, Randolph	Tanney, Jane	7 Oct 1721	Liber H:469
Morris, Richard & Johnson, Daniell			
	Province of Maryland	30 Oct 1661	02.pdf #79
Maurice, Richard & Johnson, Daniell			
	Province of Maryland	1661	02.pdf #90
Maurice, Richard	Johnson, Daniell	16 Dec 1662	02.pdf #92
Morrise, Richard & Heard, William			
	Carnell, Christopher	24 Apr 1656	02.pdf #236
Morris, Richard	Johnson, Daniell	16 Dec 1662	02.pdf #291
Morrise, Richard & Johnson, Daniell			
	Province of Maryland	20 Oct 1661	02.pdf #292
Maurise, Richard & Johnson, Daniell			
	Province of Maryland	13 Jul 1663	02.pdf #295
Morrise, Richard	Johnson, Daniell & Elisabeth	4 Jan 1664	02.pdf #297
Moss, William	Sympson, Thomas	1 Aug 1706	Liber C:16
Mudd, Thomas	Fowke, Gerrard	5 Mar 1686	13.pdf #30
Mudd, Thomas	Clarke, Thomas & Julian	8 Mar 1710	Liber C:166
Mun, John & Allen, William			
	Boyden, John; Boyden, Wm. & Cooper, Walter	8 Nov 1664	02.pdf #452
Mun, John	Stone, Thomas	14 Jun 1665	03.pdf #150
Munn, John	Aspinall, Henry	12 Jan 1669	Vol. 60:182
Mun, John	Price, Edward	12 Mar 1672	06.pdf #62
Munn, John	Prouse, Robert	11 Jun 1672	06.pdf #67

GRANTEE INDEX TO DEEDS

Grantee	Grantor	Date	Reference
Munn, John	Price, Edward	9 Jun 1671	06.pdf #70
Munn, John	Rozer, Benjamin	13 Nov 1672	06.pdf #129
Muns, John	Dickeson, Roger	11 Mar 1683	11.pdf #186
Musgrove, Charles	Cole, John & Elizabeth	25 Apr 1710	Liber C:179
Musgrave, Charles	Davis, William & Priscilla	27 May 1720	Liber H:361
Musgrove, Cuthbert	Wheeler, Robert & Mary	11 Mar 1679	09.pdf #82
Musgrove, Cuthbert	Wheeler, Robert & Mary	8 Mar 1679	09.pdf #142
Musgrave, Cuthbert	Wheeler, Robert & Mary	8 Mar 1682	10.pdf #148
Nailer, James	Stone, John	1 Sep 1713	24.pdf #197
Nailer, James	Brightwell, Richard	21 Sep 1713	24.pdf #198
Nailer, James	Waple, Osmond	14 Mar 1717	Liber H:68
Neale, Anthony & Elizabeth			
	Neale, James, ye Elder & Anne	17 Aug 1682	11.pdf #110
Neale, Anthony	Neale, James, Capt.	5 Jun 1692	18.pdf #43
Neale, Anthony & Digges, Edward			
	Rozer, Notley	2 Feb 1703	Liber Z:42
Neale, Anthony	Robbins, Thomas	8 Nov 1715	Liber H:3
Neale, Anthony	Hemsley, Philemon & Mary	23 Feb 1719	Liber H:223
Neale, Edward & Neale, Henry			
	Chandler, William	8 Nov 1715	Liber H:4
Neale, Henry & Neale, Edward			
	Chandler, William	8 Nov 1715	Liber H:4
Neale, Henry	Neale, James, Senr. & Elizabeth	26 Apr 1716	Liber H:7
Neale, James, Elder	Russell, William	6 Nov 1676	07.pdf #127
Neale, James, Capt.	Harquest, Thomas	17 Dec 1677	08.pdf #75
Neale, James	Harquest, Thomas	23 Mar 1677	08.pdf #75
Neale, James	Hinson, George	10 Jul 1695	Liber Q:92
Neale, James, Junr.	Neale, James, Senr. & Elizabeth	26 Apr 1716	Liber H:11
Neale, John	Hungerford, Barton	18 Nov 1712	24.pdf #174
Neale, Raphael	Callihon, Patrick & Ann	11 Jan 1711	Liber C:234
Neale, Raphaell	Neale, Anthony	13 Nov 1716	Liber H:32
Neale, Raphael	Waters, James & Margarett	19 Oct 1717	Liber H:104
Neale, Raphaell	Waters, James & Margaret	9 Jun 1719	Liber H:255
Nelson, Richard	Hutchison, William	22 Jul 1689	18.pdf #52
Nellson, Richard	Dunnington, Francis & Margarett	4 Apr 1704	Liber Z:96
Nevill, Johannah	Moore, Henry & Elisabeth	24 Jun 1665	03.pdf #38
Nevill, John	Thompson, George	9 Apr 1659	01.pdf #141
Nevill, John	Thompson, George	9 Apr 1659 (?)	01.pdf #189
Nevill, John	Taylor, Robert	15 July 1663	02.pdf #231
Neville, John	Taylor, Robert	4 Nov 1663	02.pdf #271
Nevill, William	Munn, John	8 Jun 1669	Vol. 60:201
Newman, George, Senr.			
	Batten, William	8 Apr 1659	Liber H:286
Newman, George	Branson, Thomas & Nahamie	12 May 1663	Liber H:286
Newman, William	Smoote, William & Anne	5 Aug 1684	14.pdf #115

GRANTEE INDEX TO DEEDS

Newton, John	Thomas, William	9 Dec 1659	01.pdf #205
Newton, John	Woodyard, John & Jean	26 Feb 1717	Liber H:73
Nicholls, John	Lynes, Philip	10 Sep 1706	Liber C:19
Noble, Elizabeth	White, William & Mary	28 Mar 1719	Liber H:228
Noeland, Peirce	Lynsey, Thomas	4 Nov 1692	17.pdf #278
Notley, Thomas	Allen, John	18 Sep 1674	07.pdf #48
Nowland, Stephen Connell, William; Byrn, James & Elizabeth		27 Apr 1714	Liber F:31
Obrion, Math.	Lendsey, James & Mary	12 May 1663	02.pdf #191
Ocaine, Gerrard	Newman, George & Grace	8 Jan 1704	Liber Z:72
Oneall, Hugh & Jervis, Thomas Philpot, Edward		18 Jan 1657	01.pdf #94
Orrell, Thomas	Baker, Thomas & Elizabeth	25 Aug 1694	18.pdf #188
Osborn, Thomas	Sanders, Thomas	14 Mar 1721	Liber H:427
Paggett, Thomas	Mudd, Barbary	13 Jun 1710	Liber C:195
Pain, John	Theoballs, Clement	2 Nov 1663	02.pdf #377
Paine, John	Adames, Francis	1 Mar 1670	06.pdf #29
Palmer, Samuell	Harrison, Joseph	8 Mar 1658	01.pdf #117
Palmer, Samuell	Harrison, Joseph	8 Jun 1660	01.pdf #117
Paris, John	Graves, Joshuah	9 Aug 1681	10.pdf #90
Parnham, John	Pile, Joseph & Gardiner, Luke	9 Mar 1714	Liber F:12
Parrandie, James	Tanner, Henry	22 Dec 1719	Liber H:304
Parrandie, James	Tanner, Henry & Anne	14 Feb 1720	Liber H:418
Parry, Dorothy, widow	Turner, Thomas	12 Nov 1719	Liber H:299
Parry, John	Bayne, Walter & Martha	18 Sep 1710	Liber C:219
Parry, Thomas	Hanson, Robert & Dorothy	27 Mar 1721	Liber H:425
Parry, Thomas	Hanson, Robert & Dorothy	13 Jul 1721	Liber H:442
Peake, Walter	Boyden, William	13 Aug 1667	03.pdf #268
Peake, Walter	Boyden, William	13 Aug 1667	03.pdf #274
Peele, Samuel	Price, Robert	20 Jun 1712	24.pdf #163
Penn, Mark	Chandler, John & Ann	13 Jul 1720	Liber H:380
Penn, William	Bayne, Walter & Martha	22 Sep 1710	Liber C:213
Penn, William	Hubbard, Nathaniel & Eleanor	8 Aug 1717	Liber H:86
Penn, William	Hubbard, Nathaniel & Eleanor	8 Aug 1717	Liber H:88
Penny, John	Perfitt, William & Joan	9 Nov 1680	10.pdf #34
Percie, Thomas	Attwicks, Humphrey & Elisabeth	17 Mar 1663	02.pdf #164
Percy, Thomas	Watson, Richard	4 Jun 1665	02.pdf #564
Perrie, Samuel & Sarah	Barton, William	11 Nov 1713	Liber F:1
Peeterson, Jacob	Moore, Henry & Elisabeth	20 Sep 1665	03.pdf #51
Peterson, Jacob	Moore, Henry & Elizabeth	20 Sep 1665	08.pdf #95
Philbert, John	Harrison, Joseph	5 Nov 1719	Liber H:297
Phillips, Thomas & Griffine, William Cornall, Joseph & Margrett		2 Jun 1687	14.pdf #113
Phillips, Thomas & Griffin, William Cornall, Joseph & Margrett		2 Jun 1687	16.pdf #15

GRANTEE INDEX TO DEEDS

Philpot, Edward	Courts, John & Margeret	11 Aug 1666	03.pdf #91
Phillpott, Edward	Musgrave, Charles	12 Mar 1712	24.pdf #158
Philpott, Edward	Wakefield, Abell	12 May 1714	Liber F:35
Philpott, Edward	Province of Maryland	10 Apr 1715	Liber H:332
Pigeon, John	Smith, John	9 Jun 1713	24.pdf #183
Pidgeon, John	Moore, John & Priscilla	18 Jun 1720	Liber H:357
Pile, Joseph	Turner, Thomas	5 Sep 1721	Liber H:460
Pinnar, Richard & Pinnar, William			
	Pope, Francis	10 Nov 1668	Vol. 60:191
Pinnar, William & Pinnar, Richard			
	Pope, Francis	10 Nov 1668	Vol. 60:191
Pinner, William	Pinner, Richard	14 Sep 1675	07.pdf #82
Pinner, William	Mings, Edward	30 Aug 1683	11.pdf #145
Plater, George	Cottrell, James & Elizabeth	2 Nov 1705	Liber Z:240
Plunkett, Thomas & Cofer, Francis			
	Clement, John & Elizabeth	14 Jan 1696	Liber Q:77
Plunkett, Thomas	Hemsley, Philemon & Mary	10 Aug 1714	Liber F:21
Pope, Francis	Sly, Robert	8 Dec 1661	01.pdf #188
Pope, Francis	Newman, George	4 Aug 1665	02.pdf #582
Pope, Francis	Newman, George & Lydia	29 Sep 1665	Liber H:286
Posey, Benjamin	Davis, William & Priscilla	17 Jun 1720	Liber H:375
Posey, John	Belane, Nicholas	31 Jan 1680	09.pdf #155
Posey, John	Skidmore, Nicholas & Anne	7 Nov 1681	10.pdf #108
Posey, Susanna	Thompson, George	4 Jul 1689	16.pdf #116
Powell, Edward	Baker, Thomas	11 Aug 1668	Vol. 60:166
Powell, Edward	Baker, Thomas	11 Aug 1668	Vol. 60:198
Price, Robert	Rozer, Notley	15 Mar 1710	Liber C:159
Prichard, Thomas	Keech, James	9 Mar 1675	07.pdf #51
Prouse, Robert & Hill, Charles			
	Thompson, George	10 Jan 1665	02.pdf #463
Prous, Robert & Hill, Charles			
	Thompson, George	19 Apr 1666	03.pdf #80
Pryor, William	Mings, Edward	5 Nov 1687	14.pdf #159
Quandoe, Henry	Wheeler, Ignatius	11 Feb 1696	Liber Q:83
Randall, Richard	Bradshaw, George	1 Jun 1665	02.pdf #528
Randall, Richard	Bradshaw, George	10 Mar 1665	02.pdf #534
Randall, Richard	Robinson, John & Elizabeth	8 Jun 1667	03.pdf #243
Raspin, Samuell	Rozer, Benjamin, Coll.	31 Mar 1680	09.pdf #170
Ratchford, Michael	Lynes, Philip	27 Aug 1705	Liber Z:214
Ratcliff, Emanuell	Pennington, Francis	23 Feb 1666	16.pdf #107
Ratcliffe, William	Price, Edward	17 Jan 1673	06.pdf #155
Rea, James	Dent, Thomas	18 May 1718	Liber H:171
Read, Luke	Hutchison, William	14 Mar 1693	18.pdf #47
Read, Thomas	Hall, Benjamin & Mary	8 Jan 1717	Liber H:58

GRANTEE INDEX TO DEEDS

Grantee	Grantor	Date	Reference
Reddick, John	Maddock, Edward & Margery	26 Nov 1678	09.pdf #46
Reddick, John	Maddock, Edward	5 Sep 1678	09.pdf #83
Reeves, Ubgate	Causeen, Williame	11 Feb 1716	Liber F:93
Rigg, Thomas	Noeland, Stephen & Mary	27 Dec 1709	Liber C:203
Rivers, Christopher	Glover, Giles & Elisabeth	26 Sep 1659	01.pdf #140
Rivers, Christopher	Province of Maryland	25 Jun 1663	02.pdf #453
Robbins, Robert	Harris, George	30 Jan 1668	Vol. 60:149
Robinson, Francis	Sanders, Matthew, Senr.	13 Aug 1717	Liber H:76
Robinson, John & Elizabeth	Harris, George	11 Jun 1667	03.pdf #236
Robinson, Richard	Gerrard, Thomas	10 Aug 1680	09.pdf #184
Robinson, Thomas & Frankome, Hennery	Wheeler, John	11 Sep 1658	01.pdf #116
Robinson, William	Nevill, John	26 Mar 1659	01.pdf #95
Robisson, William	Nevill, John	26 Mar 1659	01.pdf #142
Robisson, William	Hussey, Thomas & Elizabeth	6 Sep 1662	01.pdf #246
Robisson, William	Hussey, Thomas & Elisabeth	6 Sep 1662	02.pdf #86
Rockford, Michaell	Lynes, Phillip	27 Aug 1705	Liber C:259
Rookerd, Edward	Allcock, Thomas	8 Jan 1678	08.pdf #61
Rookerd, Edward	Aspenall, Henry	8 Mar 1681	10.pdf #57
Rookwood, Edward	Hussey, Thomas	7 Dec 1681	10.pdf #169
Rookewood, Edward	Jones, Morgan	11 Nov 1690	17.pdf #69
Rookewood, Edward	Joanes, Morgan & Jane	20 Sep 1690	17.pdf #89
Rookewood, Edward	Harrison, Francis & Shuttleworth, Elizabeth	11 May 1704	Liber Z:108
Rossey, John	Allanson, Thomas & Mary	28 May 1673	06.pdf #117
Rozer, Benjamin	Chairman, John	10 Jan 1671	06.pdf #4
Rozer, Benjamin	Gibbon, Philip	2 Mar 1674	06.pdf #154
Rozer, Benjamin	Witter, Thomas	8 Mar 1675	07.pdf #74
Rozer, Benjamin	Lomaire, John	10 Jan 1675	07.pdf #84
Rozer, Benjamin	Witter, Thomas & Mary	7 Sep 1675	07.pdf #84
Rozer, Benjamin	Worland, John	9 Nov 1675	07.pdf #91
Rozer, Benjamin	Becke, Richard	11 Apr 1676	07.pdf #101
Rozer, Benjamin	O'Caine, John	23 Sep 1676	07.pdf #126
Rozer, Benjamin	Lemaire, John, Doctor	10 Apr 1677	08.pdf #25
Rozer, Benjamin	Wyne, Francis	6 Jun 1678	09.pdf #21
Rozer, Benjamin	Hodgshon, Richard	18 Oct 1678	09.pdf #62
Rozer, Benjamin, Coll.	Wells, William	20 May 1679	09.pdf #84
Rozer, Benjamin, Coll.	Thompson, George	9 Sep 1679	09.pdf #113
Rozer, Jane	Rozer, Notley	2 Feb 1703	Liber Z:42
Russell, Walter	Russell, William	8 Mar 1675	07.pdf #50
Salley, Edward	Wakefield, Thomas	10 Mar 1674	06.pdf #151
Sanders, Charles	Doyne, Jesse	1 Jun 1710	Liber C:248
Sanders, Charles	Sanders, Thomas	13 Jun 1721	Liber H:433
Sanders, John & Sarah	Mudd, Thomas	30 Sep 1703	Liber Z:127

GRANTEE INDEX TO DEEDS

Grantee	Grantor	Date	Reference
Saunders, John	Brookes, Thomas	9 Mar 1675	07.pdf #49
Saunders, John	Maddock, Edward	10 Mar 1675	07.pdf #60
Saunders, John	Allen, John	19 Feb 1677	07.pdf #137
Saunders, John	Moore, Henry	4 Oct 1706	23.pdf #167
Sanders, John	More, Henry & Sarah	10 Mar 1708	Liber C:94
Sanders, John	Sanders, Edward	25 Mar 1708	Liber C:99
Sanders, John	Serjant, William	27 Jan 1716	Liber F:89
Sanders, John	Woodyard, John & Jane; Newton, John	7 Mar 1718	Liber H:145
Sanders, John	Marshall, Gerrard	28 May 1720	Liber H:347
Sanders, John	Wichaly, Elizabeth	7 Aug 1721	Liber H:465
Sanders, John	Smoot, John & Postuma	7 Aug 1721	Liber H:466
Sanders, Mathew & Boyden, William	Boyden, John	14 Mar 1671	06.pdf #40
Saunders, Matthew & Bryant, Thomas	Sinnett, Garrett	9 Mar 1676	08.pdf #24
Sanders, Matthew	Lynes, Philip	8 Jun 1683	11.pdf #115
Sanders, Thomas	Pellufus, Joseph & Mary	9 Jun 1710	Liber C:188
Sanders, William	Sanders, Matthew	6 Aug 1713	Liber F:18
Scidmore, Nicholas	Prichard, Thomas	8 Aug 1676	07.pdf #114
Scott, John	Harris, Thomas & Ealice or Alice	10 Aug 1713	24.pdf #188
Searson, Francis, Doctor	Mahauney, Dennis	6 Apr 1705	Liber Z:264
Servise, Thomas	Batchelor, Francis	13 Oct 1663	02.pdf #244
Shakerly, John	Allen, James	10 Jun 1713	24.pdf #181
Shakerly, John	Lambeth, John & Sarah	8 Jun 1714	Liber F:40
Shackerly, John	Manning, Joseph	16 Nov 1716	Liber H:30
Shaw, Ralph	Taylor, George & Elinor	4 Jun 1672	06.pdf #66
Shaw, Ralph, Junr.	Shaw, Ralph, Senr. & Anne	20 Nov 1711	Liber C:268
Sherrell, Samuell	Boyden, John	10 Mar 1674	06.pdf #150
Sherrill, Samuell	Stone, Thomas	15 May 1675	07.pdf #68
Shuttleworth, Lydia	Nevill, William	29 Sep 1682	11.pdf #162
Shuttleworth, Thomas	Athy, George	10 Dec 1686	13.pdf #122
Simmes, James	Chandler, William	7 Apr 1702	Liber Z:162
Simms, James	Rozer, Notley & Jane	10 May 1703	Liber Z:61
Semmes, James	Chandler, William	14 Mar 1710	Liber C:174
Simpson, Alexander	Chandler, Jobe & Overseas, Symon	8 Sep 1659	01.pdf #188
Simpson, Alexander	Chandler, Ann	8 Sep 1659	01.pdf #188
Simpson, Thomas	Allanson, Thomas	15 Feb 1660	01.pdf #219
Simpson, Thomas	Province of Maryland	2 Sep 1658	02.pdf #76
Simpson, Thomas	Allanson, Thomas	15 Feb 1660	02.pdf #79
Sympson, Thomas, Junr.	Sympson, Thomas, Senr.	22 Dec 1718	Liber H:214
Simpson, William	Keett, William	17 Dec 1686	14.pdf #21

GRANTEE INDEX TO DEEDS

Skinner, Thomas	Mellor, John & Mary	17 Dec 1720	Liber H:410
Slingsbie, John & Whit, Thomas			
	Cage, John	18 Dec 1653	02.pdf #249
Smallpage, Robert	Hutchison, William	24 Mar 1687	17.pdf #258
Smallpage, Robert & Elinor			
	Cornish, John & Martha	9 Jun 1691	17.pdf #117
Smallpage, Robert	Moore, Henry	10 Nov 1691	17.pdf #158
Smallwood, Bayne & Smallwood, Pryor			
	Whichaley, Thomas & Elizabeth	11 Aug 1696	Liber Q:97
Smallwood, James	Duglas, John, Coll.	5 Mar 1678	08.pdf #76
Smallwood, James	Lindsey, Edmond	20 Apr 1687	14.pdf #114
Smallwood, James	Maddacke, Cornelious and Mary	27 May 1688	16.pdf #13
Smallwood, James, Major, Senior			
	Griffin, William	10 Aug 1694	18.pdf #196
Smallwood, James	Forster, William & Dorothy	6 Dec 1695	Liber Q:74
Smallwood, John	Hutchison, William	11 Apr 1689	17.pdf #297
Smallwood, John	Smallwood, James	13 Mar 1719	Liber H:231
Smallwood, Ledstone	Smallwood, James	14 Nov 1721	Liber H:471
Smallwood, Pryor & Smallwood, Bayne			
	Whichaley, Thomas & Elizabeth	11 Aug 1696	Liber Q:97
Smallwood, Pryor	Godshall, John & Mary	23 Feb 1710	Liber C:167
Smallwood, Pryor	Godshall, John & Mary	14 Mar 1710	23.pdf #372
Smallwood, Samuell	Hall, Benjamin & Mary	Dec 1707	Liber C:177
Smith, Allexander	Morris, Richard	4 Jan 1663	02.pdf #292
Smith, Alexander	Maurise, Richard	4 Jan 1664	02.pdf #298
Smith, Allexander	Morris, Richard	20 Sep 1672	06.pdf #77
Smith, Alexander	French, Hugh	8 Mar 1681	10.pdf #56
Smith, Daniell	Fowke, Richard	11 Aug 1674	07.pdf #14
Smith, John	Joseph, William	11 Nov 1696	Liber Q:113
Smith, John	Joseph, William	11 Nov 1696	Liber Q:115
Smith, John	Joseph, William	11 Nov 1696	Liber Q:122
Smith, Raiph & Sarah	Harris, Thomas	3 Apr 1680	09.pdf #163
Smith, William	Morris, John & Elinor	17 Jan 1678	09.pdf #41
Smith, William	Hussey, Thomas	19 Nov 1688	16.pdf #62
Smith, William	Brett, Henry & Sarah	29 Sep 1719	Liber H:289
Smoot, Barton	Smoot, William	28 Mar 1719	Liber H:258
Smoot, Edward	Smoot, William	25 Apr 1689	16.pdf #108
Smoot, John Nathan & Smoot, William			
	Bennitt, John & Mary	12 Mar 1706	Liber Z:256
Smoot, Richard	Smoot, William	28 May 1658	02.pdf #161
Smoot, Richard	Smoot, William	28 May 1656	02.pdf #161
Smoot, Thomas	Johnson, Daniell & Elisabeth	4 Jan 1664	02.pdf #301
Smoote, Thomas	Smoote, William	7 May 1683	11.pdf #114
Smoot, William	Province of Maryland	20 May 1658	01.pdf #250
Smoot, William	Province of Maryland	26 May 1658	02.pdf #159

GRANTEE INDEX TO DEEDS

Smoot, William	Province of Maryland	26 Jan 1652	02.pdf #162
Smoote, William			
	Barton, William & Hungerford, William	21 Nov 1683	11.pdf #149
Smoote, William	Hungerford, William	21 Nov 1683	11.pdf #150
Smoot, William & Smoot, John Nathan			
	Bennitt, John & Mary	12 Mar 1706	Liber Z:256
Snell, Jeremiah	Hutchison, William	27 Mar 1695	18.pdf #240
Sothoron, Benjamin	Marshall, William & Rebeckah	29 Mar 1714	Liber F:16
Southeron, John	Marshall, Joshuah	9 Jun 1696	Liber Q:89
Spalding, John	Green, Thomas & Mildred	3 Mar 1714	24.pdf #201
Spalding, John	Greenfeild, Thomas Truman	20 May 1721	Liber H:462
Speake, Bowling	Gardiner, Mary	6 Aug 1718	Liber H:180
Speake, Bowling	Gardiner, Luke & Anne	8 Sep 1718	Liber H:203
Speake, John & Winifred			
	Wheeler, John	11 Aug 1685	12.pdf #105
Speake, John	Wheeler, John	10 Nov 1685	13.pdf #30
Speake, John	Maclane, John	1 Aug 1709	Liber C:138
Speake, John, Junr.	Taylor, Thomas & Barbara	17 Apr 1719	Liber H:243
Speake, John	Clarke, John	30 Oct 1719	Liber H:323
Speake, Richard	Speake, John & Winnifred	28 Nov 1720	Liber H:400
Speake, Thomas	Speake, John & Winnifred	28 Nov 1720	Liber H:403
Standburry, John, Senr.			
	Fanning, Benoni; Eaty, Nathaniell & Elizabeth	26 Apr 1703	Liber Z:188
Standish, Alexander	Barker, John & Joan	13 Mar 1677	08.pdf #23
Stephens, Simon	Brett, George	3 Dec 1678	09.pdf #63
Steward, Daniell	Contee, Mary, widow	6 Feb 1710	Liber C:168
Stoddert, James	Watts, James & Elizabeth	25 Mar 1703	Liber Z:29
Stoddert, James	Dawson, Nicholus & Mary	8 Mar 1715	Liber F:59
Stoddert, James	Brown, John & Virlender	21 Oct 1715	Liber F:76
Stoddart, James	Smith, Adam	28 Jun 1718	Liber H:194
Stoddert, James	Smith, Adam	16 Dec 1719	Liber H:338
Stone, John, et al.	Harrison, Joseph	28 Apr 1694	18.pdf #196
Stone, Richard	Dickenson, Jeremiah	8 Jan 1667	03.pdf #166
Stone, William	Dickison, John	14 Aug 1705	Liber Z:248
Stone, William	Campbell, Martin & Mary	20 Aug 1705	Liber Z:253
Stone, William	Achilles, Peter	15 Nov 1705	Liber Z:250
Stone, William	Manning, Joseph	18 Feb 1706	23.pdf #134
Stone, William	Tyer, James & Margarett	21 Jan 1707	Liber C:50
Stone, William	Davis, William & Priscilla	9 Mar 1709	Liber C:141
Stone, William, Senr.	Dickason, John	14 Aug 1712	24.pdf #166
Stonestreet, Thomas	Stonestreet, Thomas	11 Jun 1706	Liber C:7
Story, Walter	Morris, Richard	26 May 1707	Liber C:66
Story, Walter	Kerricoe, Peter	9 Mar 1708	Liber C:83
Story, Walter	Gore, George	9 Mar 1708	Liber C:84

GRANTEE INDEX TO DEEDS

Swallwell, John	Hutchisson, William	27 May 1691	17.pdf #136
Swallwell, John	Addisson, John & Thomson, James	27 May 1691	17.pdf #136
Swan, Edward	Walker, James	27 Jan 1658	02.pdf #177
Swan, Edward	Walker, James	27 Jan 1659	Vol. 60:193
Swan, Edward	Piper, John & Dobson, Samuel	24 Jan 1663	Vol. 60:194
Swinburne, Elizabeth	Aspinall, Humphrey	1 Mar 1685	Liber Z:196
Swinborne, Elizabeth	Aspinall, Humphery	1 Mar 1685	12.pdf #82
Sympson, Elizabeth	Green, Robert & Mary	9 Nov 1702	Liber Z:27
Tanner, Henry	Wright, Thomas & Mary	4 Mar 1714	Liber F:29
Tannyhill, William & Hatton, William	Athey, George	3 Dec 1694	Liber Q:70
Taylor, Edmund	Diccason, William	14 Sep 1669	Vol. 60:223
Taylor, John & Taylor, Thomas	Bonner, Henry & Elizabeth	1 Sep 1674	07.pdf #15
Taylor, Robert	Thompson, George	14 Nov 1661	01.pdf #178
Taylor, Robert	Linsey, Edmond	7 Oct 1657	01.pdf #178
Taylor, Robert	Linsey, Edmond	22 Nov 1661	01.pdf #179
Taylor, Robert	Wheeler, John	4 Nov 1663	02.pdf #271
Taylor, Thomas & Taylor, John	Bonner, Henry & Elizabeth	1 Sep 1674	07.pdf #15
Taylor, Thomas	Annis, Thomas & Elizabeth	13 May 1720	Liber H:364
Teares, Ellinor & Elizabeth	Teares, Hugh	11 Oct 1705	23.pdf #113
Teares, Elizabeth & Ellinor	Teares, Hugh	11 Oct 1705	23.pdf #113
Theobaldes, Clement	Corker, Thomas	10 Jun 1673	06.pdf #125
Theobalds, Clement	Corker, Thomas	9 Sep 1673	06.pdf #134
Theobalds, Clement	Leah, Jacob	12 Jan 1674	06.pdf #147
Thomas, George	Worland, John & Mary	19 Sep 1709	Liber C:144
Thomas, John	Coleman, Thomas	20 Jun 1721	Liber H:453
Thomas, William	Tomkinson, John	13 Aug 1658	01.pdf #205
Thomas, William	Marchegay, Bennett	11 Jun 1678	09.pdf #18
Thomas, William	Hutchison, William	9 Aug 1692	17.pdf #239
Thompson, George	Watson, Andrew	4 Nov 1659	01.pdf #141
Thompson, George	Taylor, Robert	14 Nov 1661	01.pdf #178
Thompson, George	Watson, Andrew	4 Nov 1659	01.pdf #189
Thompson, George	Province of Maryland	20 Jul 1661	02.pdf #120
Thompson, George	Dickeson, Jheromiah	13 Oct 1663	02.pdf #401
Thompson, George	Boughton, Richard	11 Jun 1690	17.pdf #20
Thompson, John; Greene, James; & Frederick, Thomas	Hutchison, William	11 Nov 1690	17.pdf #70
Thompson, Mary	Green, Robert & Mary	8 Jun 1703	Liber Z:24
Thompson, Victoria, wife of William Thompson	Bread, Jane	10 Jul 1688	16.pdf #20

GRANTEE INDEX TO DEEDS

Thompson, William	Iles, Richard	23 Apr 1689	16.pdf #105
Thompson, William	Skidmore, Ralph	10 Oct 1710	Liber C:208
Thomson, James	Hutchison, William	6 Apr 1690	18.pdf #86
Thorneton, Francis			
	Boyden, William & Sanders, Mathew	10 Jun 1673	06.pdf #107
Tickerell, Thomas	Heydon, Francis & Thomasine	13 Aug 1678	09.pdf #178
Till, Edward	Godshall, John	2 Mar 1688	14.pdf #167
Timothy, Mabell	Lewis, Thomas & Rebecca	26 Feb 1712	24.pdf #165
Tomkins, Giles	Smoot, Richard	22 Nov 1659	02.pdf #161
Tomkins, Giles & Morris, John			
	Heard, William & Morris, Richard	27 Jul 1656	02.pdf #236
Tomkins, Gils	Morrise, John	6 Oct 1659	02.pdf #236
Tomkinson, John & Watson, Andrew			
	Province of Maryland	10 Jan 1654	01.pdf #187
Towell, David	Wheeler, Robert & Mary	6 Jun 1677	08.pdf #33
Trenn (?), Henry	Skidmore, Nicholas & Anne	12 Aug 1690	17.pdf #32
Trew, Richard	Courts, John	25 ___ 1655	Liber H:337
Trew, Richard	Province of Maryland	13 Feb 1658	01.pdf #203
True, Richard	Boarman, William & Sarah	10 Nov 1658	03.pdf #165
Trew, Richard	Courts, John	24 Nov 1658	Liber H:474
Trew, Richard	Borman, William	4 May 1659	01.pdf #168
Trew, Richard	Belayne, John	4 Mar 1661	01.pdf #204
True, Richard	Lambert, John & Ellinor	12 Nov 1666	03.pdf #143
True, Richard	Lambert, John	12 Nov 1666	03.pdf #153
Troope, Robert	Linsey, Edmond	15 Dec 1659	01.pdf #87
Tukerell (?), Thomas	Heydon, Francis	13 Aug 1678	09.pdf #22
Turner, Thomas	Boarman, William, Senr.	8 Dec 1717	Liber H:160
Turner, Thomas	Diggs, William & Elinore	23 Jun 1719	Liber H:275
Turner, Thomas	Boarman, William, Senr. & Mary	6 Oct 1719	Liber H:292
Turner, Thomas	Mattingly, Cesar	12 Nov 1719	Liber H:326
Turvey, Edward	Warren, John, Gent.	17 Oct 1712	24.pdf #167
Twigges, John	Bedford, Henery	10 Jun 1673	06.pdf #121
Tyer, James	Bonner, Henry & Elizabeth	10 May 1681	10.pdf #100
Vandry, John	Causine, Ignatius	27 Dec 1670	06.pdf #14
Veren, Nathaniel	Faning, John & Alice	20 Dec 1679	09.pdf #139
Wade, Zachary & Hatton, William			
	Province of Maryland	26 Apr 1658	Liber H:405
Wade, Zachariah	Hatton, William	24 Mar 1659	Liber H:406
Waed, Zachery; Harrisson, Joseph; Handson, Randall; & Allen, William			
	Hatton, William & Dent, Thomas	9 May 1663	02.pdf #188
Wade, Zachary & Hanson, Randolph			
	Brooke, Thomas	12 Nov 1670	06.pdf #95
Wahope, Archebald	Gourdon, Daniell	27 Apr 1660	01.pdf #118
Wahope, Archebald	Gourdon, Mary	27 Apr 1660	01.pdf #118
Wahop, Archiball	King, Thomas	8 Jun 1669	Vol. 60:200

GRANTEE INDEX TO DEEDS

Wahob, Elizabeth	Wahob, Archibald	15 Mar 1682	10.pdf #151
Wainiman, Rice & Midgely, Richard			
	Greene, Luke	10 Jan 1671	06.pdf #7
Walker, James	Province of Maryland	17 Aug 1658	02.pdf #176
Walker, James	Beane, Walter & Elenor	9 Jun 1666	03.pdf #72
Walker, James	Province of Maryland	17 Aug 1658	Vol. 60:192
Ward, James	Lee, James	23 Sep 1659	01.pdf #110
Ward, John	Lee, James	8 May 1661	01.pdf #167
Ward, John	Woolley, Charles	3 Jun 1673	06.pdf #114
Ward, William	Swan, Edward	9 Mar 1669	Vol. 60:194
Wardner, Thomas	Bennett, Thomas	2 Aug 1669	Vol. 60:207
Ware, Robert	Becke, Richard	8 Nov 1674	07.pdf #22
Waring, Marsham	Boarman, William	14 Mar 1721	Liber H:438
Warner, Thomas	Dent, William & Elizabeth	20 Feb 1691	17.pdf #293
Warner, Thomas	Achilles, Peter	13 Jun 1693	18.pdf #119
Warren, Bazil & Haddock, Sarah			
	Barton, William	12 Aug 1712	24.pdf #174
Warren, Humphrey	Barrett, William	9 Mar 1675	07.pdf #47
Warren, Humphrey	Smoote, William	8 Oct 1683	11.pdf #150
Warren, Humphery	Smoote, Edward	7 Nov 1684	12.pdf #42
Warren, Humphery	Smoot, William & Anne	7 Aug 1686	13.pdf #118
Warren, Humphry	Gooch, John	17 Mar 1688	16.pdf #21
Warren, Humphrey	Smoote, William & Anne	24 Dec 1692	18.pdf #25
Warren, Thomas	Barton, William	13 Jun 1688	16.pdf #16
Warren, Thomas	Fowkes, Richard	17 Jun 1689	16.pdf #115
Waters, James	Neale, Raphael	12 Nov 1717	Liber H:101
Waters, James	Neale, Raphael	9 Jun 1719	Liber H:260
Waters, John	Browne, Gerrard & Lindsy, Edmond	8 Jan 1671	06.pdf #12
Wathen, John	Sympson, Thomas	2 Jun 1707	Liber C:56
Wathen, John	Hall, Benjamin	27 Jan 1717	Liber H:37
Wathen, John	Hall, Benjamin	27 Jan 1717	Liber H:45
Watson, Andrew	Province of Maryland	2 Sep 1659	01.pdf #141
Watson, Andrew & Tomkinson, John			
	Province of Maryland	10 Jan 1654	01.pdf #187
Watson, Andrew	Province of Maryland	2 Sep 1659	01.pdf #189
Watson, Andrew	Trew, Richard	26 Feb 1661	01.pdf #203
Watson, William	Huchison, William	10 Dec 1690	17.pdf #211
Waye, Richard	Sheereman, John	4 Dec 1690	17.pdf #98
Wayman, Rice & Wolph, Joseph			
	Cassock, John & Margarett	12 Oct 1678	09.pdf #64
Wells, William	Godfrey, George	6 June 1677	08.pdf #42
Wells, William	Saunders, John	10 Jun 1678	09.pdf #19
Wells, William	Saunders, John	10 Jun 1678	09.pdf #20
Wells, William	Caine, John	30 Sep 1679	09.pdf #117
Wharton, Thomas	Thorneton, Francis	10 Jun 1673	06.pdf #122

GRANTEE INDEX TO DEEDS

Wheeler, John	Province of Maryland	26 Aug 1651	02.pdf #270
Wheeler, John	Dowin, John & Sarah	9 Nov 1709	Liber C:149
Wheeler, Mary	Hutchison, William & Sarah	29 May 1704	Liber Z:171
Wheeler, Richard	Wheeler, Thomas	19 Apr 1710	Liber C:204
Wheeler, Robert	Aspenall, Henry, Capt.	8 Jun 1678	08.pdf #94
Whit, Thomas & Slingsbie, John			
	Cage, John	18 Dec 1653	02.pdf #249
Whit, Thomas	Slingsby, John	21 Oct 1655	02.pdf #249
White, Alexander	Charman, John	11 Jun 1667	03.pdf #249
White, Allexander	Watson, Andrew	1 Mar 1668	06.pdf #20
White, Cornelius	Charlesworth, Robert & Elinor	7 Apr 1704	Liber Z:234
White, Cornelius	Compton, John	28 Jan 1706	Liber Z:273
White, Cornelius	Morris, Richard	28 Jan 1706	Liber C:70
Wife, Nicholas	Cottrell, James	5 Dec 1690	17.pdf #137
Wilder, John	Smoote, Thomas & Elizabeth	11 Aug 1691	17.pdf #140
Wilder, John	Freeman, Anne, widow	19 Feb 1722	Liber H:478
Wilkinson, William	Craycroft, John & Jane	9 May 1720	Liber H:372
Williams, Edward	Athy, George & Sarah	11 Mar 1689	16.pdf #116
Williams, John	Frankam, Henry	11 Jun 1689	16.pdf #104
Williamson, Ralph	Campbell, Martin & Mary	14 Dec 1703	Liber Z:86
Willin, Richard	Province of Maryland	10 Dec 1653	01.pdf #218
Willan, Richard	Province of Maryland	14 Dec 1653	02.pdf #78
Wills, William	Hanson, John & Elizabeth	13 Jul 1721	Liber H:446
Willson, Alexander & Edelen, Richard			
	Sympson, Thomas	8 Jun 1714	Liber F:41
Willson, Alexander	Sympson, Thomas	8 Jun 1714	Liber F:43
Willson, John	Brassell (?), William & Elizabeth	2 Mar 1703	Liber Z:4
Willson, John	Manning, Joseph	11 May 1703	22.pdf #128
Willson, John	Norris, Henry	28 Oct 1712	24.pdf #173
Wilson, John & Diceson, Thomas			
	Bayne, Ebsworth	9 Nov 1716	Liber H:27
Windsor, Jervis	Smith, John & Elizabeth	11 Nov 1694	18.pdf #230
Wine, Francis	Cadwell, William	12 Jul 1663	02.pdf #183
Wine, Francis	Cadwell, William	12 May 1663	02.pdf #294
Wine, Francis	Johnson, Daniell	5 Jan 1663	02.pdf #295
Wine, Francis	Emanson, Elizabeth	8 Aug 1671	06.pdf #48
Wyne, Francis	Emanson, Elizabeth	16 Jun 1671	06.pdf #83
Wyne, Francis	Robinson, John & Elizabeth	1 Apr 1675	07.pdf #61
Winters, Walter	Chandler, William	11 Mar 1713	24.pdf #177
Winter, Walter	Bayne, Ebsworth & Kindrick	13 Jan 1719	Liber H:248
Winter, Walter	Middleton, William	5 May 1720	Liber H:344
Winter, Walter	Grey, Richard & Johannah	16 Sep 1720	Liber H:393
Witter, Thomas	Theobald, Clement	6 Apr 1674	06.pdf #158
Wolph, Joseph & Wayman, Rice			
	Cassock, John & Margarett	12 Oct 1678	09.pdf #64

GRANTEE INDEX TO DEEDS

Wood, John	Manning, Joseph	15 May 1706	23.pdf #136
Woodyard, John	Posey, John & Lydia	28 Apr 1711	Liber C:253
Worland, John	Walker, Alice	13 Sep 1675	07.pdf #90
Worland, John	Walker, James	18 Jan 1674	16.pdf #116
Worrell, William	Younge, Elizabeth, Widow	9 Jul 1685	12.pdf #107
Wright, John	Lewgar, John & Martha	13 Aug 1666	03.pdf #101
Wright, John	Hill, John	19 Mar 1673	06.pdf #117
Wright, John	Galey, Thomas & Martha	18 Nov 1673	06.pdf #143
Wright, John	Lewgar, Thomas	12 Jun 1688	16.pdf #15
Wyne, Elizabeth	Skidmore, Nicholas	10 Mar 1682	10.pdf #166
Yates, Charles	Penn, William & Fantulenah	4 Jun 1720	Liber H:349
Yates, Robert	Wakefield, Abell & Elizabeth	8 Mar 1703	Liber Z:13
Yates, Robert	Tyer, James & Margarett	5 Aug 1704	Liber Z:134
Yates, Robert	Fanning Benoni & Hannah	4 Oct 1704	Liber Z:153
Yates, Robert	Beamont, James	11 Jun 1712	24.pdf #162
__ ose, Nicholaus	Clarke, John	13 Oct 1663	02.pdf #269

GIFTS OF LIVESTOCK
1661-1733

Allcock, Mary, daughter of Thomas Allcock, 1682 [10.pdf #165]
Allcock, Thomas, son of Thomas Allcock, 1682 [10.pdf #165]
Allen, Ann, daughter of John Allen, 10 March 1711 [Liber C Page 233]
Allen, George, son of John Allen, 10 March 1711 [Liber C Page 233]
Allen, James, son of John Allen, 10 March 1711 [Liber C Page 233]
Allwood, John, son of Susannah Allwood, 10 November 1719 [Liber H Page 312]
Allwood, William, son of Susannah Allwood, 10 November 1719
    [Liber H Page 312]
Anderson, Edward, son of John Anderson, 1694 [18.pdf #187]
Ashforth, Mary, daughter of Michaell & Rachell Ashforth, 21 February 1694
    [18.pdf #142]
Athy, John, son of George Athy, 1691 [17.pdf #187]
Baker, Martha, daughter of Thomas Baker, 1678 [08.pdf #92]
Barker, William, son of Ann Barker, widow, 3 August 1711 [Liber C Page 259]
Barnes, Barbarah, wife of Henry Barnes, 14 June 1709 [Liber C Page 137]
Barnes, Benjamin, son of Henry Barnes, 14 June 1709 [Liber C Page 137]
Barnes, Elizabeth, daughter of Matthew Barnes and Elizabeth Jones, and
    granddaughter of Owen Jones, 18 July 1705 [Liber Z Page 208]
Barnes, Matthew, son of Matthew Barnes, 18 July 1705 [Liber Z Page 208]
Barron, Peter, brother of Martha Barron, 10 June 1707 [Liber Z Page 272]
Barron, Peter, son of John Barron, 10 March 1708 [Liber Z Page 208]
Bartlett, Ralph, son of Ralph Bartlett, 12 March 1684 [11.pdf #194]
Bartlett, Thomas, son of Ralph Bartlett, 12 March 1684 [11.pdf #194]
Barton, William, son of Nathaniell Barton, 1669 [Vol. 60:205]
Bayly, James, son of John Bayly, 1687 [14.pdf #106]
Beade, Mary, daughter of Nicholas Beade, 1680 [09.pdf #144]
Beade, Sarah, daughter of Nicholas Beade, 1680 [09.pdf #144]
Bell, Charles, son of Maj. Ninion Bell, 1688 [14.pdf #173]
Bias, Mary, daughter of Elizabeth Bias, 1 October 1713 [24.pdf #187]
Boswell, John, son of John Boswell, 20 April 1726 [Liber L Page 270]
Boswell, Mathew, son of John Boswell, 1672 [06.pdf #78]; 1678 [08.pdf #92]
Boswell, Martha, daughter of Mary Pounsey, 12 February 1690 [16.pdf #118]
Boswell, Michaell, son of Mary Pounsey, 12 February 1690 [16.pdf #118]
Boswell, William, son of Mary Pounsey, 12 February 1690 [16.pdf #118]
Boughton, Samuell, son of Richard Boughton, 1680 [09.pdf #177]
Boyce, Elizabeth, daughter of John & Elinor Boyce, 1678 [08.pdf #96];
    1682 [10.pdf #190]
Boyce, James, son of John Boyce deceased, 12 June 1686 [13.pdf #61]
Boyce, John, son of John Boyce deceased, 12 June 1686 [13.pdf #61]
Boyce, William, son of John & Elinor Boyce, 1680 [09.pdf #181] [10.pdf #46];
    son of John Boyce deceased, 12 June 1686 [13.pdf #61]
Boyden, Mary, stepdaughter of John Boyce, 1674 [06.pdf #145]; "naturall borne
    daughter of his now wife Elinor, 1678 [08.pdf #96]; 1682 [10.pdf #190]
Boyden, William, son of John Boyden, 12 June 1686 [13.pdf #61]

GIFTS OF LIVESTOCK

Branner, Edward, son of Henry Branner, 14 September 1686 [13.pdf #104]
Brawner, Henry, son of Edward Brawner, 1 August 1726 [Liber L Page 300]
Brawner, Thomas, son of Edward Brawner, 1 August 1726 [Liber L Page 300]
Brawner, William, son of Edward Brawner, 1 August 1726 [Liber L Page 300]
Brayne, Jane, daughter of John Caine, 1680 [09.pdf #164]
Browne, Elizabeth, daughter of William Browne, 1690 [16.pdf #118]
Browne, William, son of William Browne, 1690 [16.pdf #118]
Bruce, Judith, deceased, sister of Mary Hemsley "of Annapolis," 22 April 1722
    [Liber L Page 84]
Burch, Jestinian, son of Oliver Burch, gift of real estate, 30 January 1714
    [Liber F Page 2]
Burford, Elizabeth, daughter of Thomas Burford, 1682 [10.pdf #190]
Burgess, John, son in law of Richard Harris, 1677 [08.pdf #47]
Cable, Mary, daughter of John Cable deceased, 19 July 1690 [16.pdf #118]
Cable, William, son of John Cable deceased, 19 July 1690 [16.pdf #118]
Cassock, Benjamin, son of John Cassock, 1681 [10.pdf #126]; 1687 [14.pdf #111]
Cassock, Sarah, daughter of John Cassock, 1693 [17.pdf #294]
Causin, Jane, daughter of Ignatius Causin, 1695 [18.pdf #244]
Cave, Thomas, son of John & Elizabeth Cave, 7 October 1713 [24.pdf #190]
Chandler, Richard, son of Ann Fowke, 1673 [06.pdf #106]
Chesson, Mary, daughter of Barbary Chesson relict of John Chesson,
    11 November 1678 [09.pdf #46]
Chittam, Isaac, son of Joseph Chattam, 28 October 1731 [Liber M Page 266]
Chittam, Phillis, daughter of Joseph Chattam, 28 October 1731 [Liber M Page 266]
Chittam, Rebeckah, daughter of Joseph Chattam, 28 October 1731
    [Liber M Page 266]
Clarke, Jane, wife of Charles Clarke, 1662 [01.pdf #222]
Clarke, Veteros, daughter of Robert Clarke, 1682 [10.pdf #143]
Clowter, Elizabeth, daughter of John Clowter, 1681 [10.pdf #126]
Clubb, Matthew, son of John Clubb, 3 March 1725 [Liber L Page 204]
Codwell, William, son of William Codwell, Senior, 1661 [01.pdf #144]
Cole, Elizabeth, daughter of Sina Cole, 1714 [Liber F Page 12]
Cole, Mary, daughter of Sina Cole, 1714 [Liber F Page 12]
Cole, William, son of Jeofferey Cole, 20 July 1710 [Liber C Page 185]
Contee, Alexander, nephew of John Contee deceased, 2 February 1712
    [Liber C Page 268]
Coody, William, son of William Coody, 11 February 1726 [Liber L Page 248]
Coomes, Elizabeth, daughter of Philip Coomes, 1682 [10.pdf #190]
Cooper, Mary, daughter of Joseph Cooper, 1668 [Vol. 60:142]
Courts, John, Junior, son of John Courts, Senior, 1664 [02.pdf #319]
Cox, Thomasine, daughter of James Cox, 1681 [10.pdf #103]
Cuttler, Margarett, daughter of Margarett Cutler, 1678 [08.pdf #56]
Darnall, John, son of Edward Darnall, 8 July 1714 [Liber F Page 17]
Darnall, Sarah, daughter of Edward Darnall, 14 December 1726 [Liber L Page 312]
Darnell, Thomas, son of Edward Darnell, 14 December 1726 [Liber L Page 312]
    [Liber H Page 23]

GIFTS OF LIVESTOCK

Davis, Elizabeth, daughter of Griffith Davis, 1694 [18.pdf #191]
Davis, Henry, son of Edward Davis, gift of real estate, 12 November 1716
Dawson, John, servant to Henry Hardy, 24 April 1693 [18.pdf #76]
Delozer, Mary, wife of Daniell Delozer and "the naturall daughter and heir of one
    John Cable of Charles County," sale of real estate, 14 September 1708
    [Liber C Page 111]
Demsey, Allison, daughter of John Demsey, 4 October 1726 [Liber L Page 317]
Denison, John Newton, son of "old" John Newton, 1669 [Vol. 60:186]
Dent, Phillip, infant son of William Dent, deed of real estate, 10 June 1704
    [Liber Z Page 112]
Deverell, Elizabeth, daughter of Thomas & Anne Deverell, 1682 [11.pdf #58]
Dickisson, Mary, daughter of Thomas Dickisson, 1691 [17.pdf #137]
Dike, Mary, wife of Mathew Dike, 25 July 1684 [11.pdf #203].
Dike, Elizabeth, daughter of Matthew & Mary Dike, 11 March 1690 [16.pdf #109]
Dixon, Mary, daughter of Thomas Dixon, 6 February 1719 [Liber H Page 219]
Dode, Marie, daughter of Richard Dod, 1661 [01.pdf #171]
Dodson, Walter, son of John Dodson, 7 April 1727 [Liber L Page 338]
Doyne, Dennis, "eldest son" of Joshua Doyne, gift of real estate, 17 January 1698
    [Liber C Page 239]
Duglas, Benjamin, son of John Duglas, 1691 [17.pdf #153]
Dunnington, Elizabeth, daughter of Margarett Dunnington, granddaughter of
    Elizabeth Brett widow, 10 December 1705 [Liber Z Page 229]
Dunnington, Francis, daughter of Margarett Dunnington, granddaughter of
    Elizabeth Brett widow, 10 December 1705 [Liber Z Page 229]
Dunnington, Rebekah, daughter of Margarett Dunnington, granddaughter of
    Elizabeth Brett widow, 10 December 1705 [Liber Z Page 229]
Eglin, Richard, son of Richard Eglin, 1688 [16.pdf #31]
Ellis, Elizabeth, daughter (?) of Robert Hager Senr., 16 October 1703
    [Liber Z Page 69]
Ensey, Winifrit, daughter of John Ensey, 11 February 1722 [Liber L Page 72]
Faning, Elizabeth, daughter of John Faning, 1 April 1681 [10.pdf #74, 103]
Faning, James, son of John Faning, 1 April 1681 [10.pdf #74, 103]
Faning, Mary, daughter of John Faning, 1 April 1681 [10.pdf #74, 103]
Farnandis, Elizabeth, daughter of Peter Farnandis, 1686 [13.pdf #104]
Fernandos, Wenefrett, daughter of Peter Fernandos, 1682 [10.pdf #165]
Fitzgarrald, Morrice, son of Morrice Fitzgarrald, 17 October 1709
    [Liber C Page 148]
Flower, Elizabeth, daughter of Richard Flower, 16 July 1689 [16.pdf #107]
Fowke, Elizabeth, daughter of Ann Fowke, 1673 [06.pdf #106]
Fowke, Gerrard, son of Ann Fowke, 1673 [06.pdf #106]
Fowke, Mary, daughter of Ann Fowke, 1673 [06.pdf #106]
Frankcum, Amie, widow of Henry Franckum, 22 March 1669 [Vol. 60:185]
Frankcum, Elizabeth, daughter of Amey Franckum, 22 March 1669 [Vol. 60:185]
Frankcum, Henry, son of Amey Franckum, 22 March 1669 [Vol. 60:185]
Frasier, Anne, "the naturall daughter" of Mary Smallwood, gift of real estate,
    26 January 1710 [Liber C Page 154]

GIFTS OF LIVESTOCK

Gardiner, Edward, son of Hugh Gardiner, 1690 [16.pdf #118]
Gardiner / Gardner, John, "a Molatta boy," son of Black Nan," belonging unto
    Mr. Richard Chandler," 1676 [07.pdf #110]; 1681 [10.pdf #103]
Gardner, Bullet (?), son of Edward Gardner, 9 February 1720 [Liber H Page 313]
Gardner, Mary, daughter of Edward Gardner, 9 February 1720 [Liber H Page 313]
Gifford, Douglass, son of Henry Gifford, 22 March 1704 [Liber Z Page 80]
Godfrey, George, son of George Godfrey, 1681 [10.pdf #78]
Godfrey, Mary, daughter of Francis Godfrey, gift of real estate, 28 February 1722
    [Liber H Page 484]
Godfrey, Richard, son of William Godfrey, 1718 [Liber H Page 151]
Godfrey, Thomas, son of George & Mary Godfrey, 1680 [09.pdf #164]
Godfrey, William, son of George Godfrey, 1680 [09.pdf #164]
Goer, George, "naturall borne" son of Anne Goer, relict & administratrix of
    George Goer deceased, 2 August 1690
Goer, Mary, "naturall borne" daughter of Anne Goer, relict & administratrix of
    George Goer deceased, 2 August 1690
Goer, Sarah, "naturall borne" daughter of Anne Goer, relict & administratrix of
    George Goer deceased, 2 August 1690
Graves, Dorothy, orphan daughter of Joshua Graves, granddaughter of Dorothy
    Graves, c. 1709 [25.pdf #19]
Gwinn, Joseph, "eldest son of John Gwinn," gift of real estate, 25 April 1722
    [Liber L Page 11]
Hager, Robert, Junr., son of Robert Hager Senr., 16 October 1703 [Liber Z Page 69]
Hammilton, Elisabeth, daughter of Joseph and Elizabeth Hammilton, granddaughter
    of Richard Harrison, 1 January 1707 [Liber C Page 78]
Hanson, Elizabeth, daughter of Samuel Hanson, 6 September 1709
    [Liber C Page 142]
Hanson, Elizabeth, daughter of John Hanson, 1712 [24.pdf #168]
Hanson, Dorothy, daughter of Robert Hanson, 24 April 1722 [Liber L Page 11]
Hanson, Robert, son of Robert Hanson, 24 April 1722 [Liber L Page 11]
Hanson, William, son of Robert Hanson, 24 April 1722 [Liber L Page 11]
Harguesse, Ann, daughter of William Harguesse, 1690 [16.pdf #117]
Harris, Bethseba, daughter of Thomas Harris, 1684 [12.pdf #14]
Harris, John, son of John Harris, 7 November 1720 [Liber H Page 386]
Harris, Mary, daughter of Thomas Harris, 1684 [12.pdf #14]
Harrison, Benjamin, son of Joseph Harrison deceased, 8 June 1674 [06.pdf #150]
Harrison, Catherine, daughter of Joseph Harrison deceased, 8 June 1674
    [06.pdf #150]
Harrison, Joseph, son of Joseph Harrison deceased, 8 June 1674 [06.pdf #150]
Harrison, Oliver, son of John Harrison, 1689 [16.pdf #46]
Harrison, Richard, brother of Joseph Harrison, 1712 [24.pdf #159]
Hawkins, Elizabeth, wife of Henry Hawkins, 1682 [10.pdf #190]
Hawkins, Henry, son of Henry Hawkins Junior, 1693 [18.pdf #107]
Hawkins, Thomas, brother of John Hawkins, gift of real estate, 6 January 1722
    [Liber H Page 475]

GIFTS OF LIVESTOCK

Hawkins, William, brother of John Hawkins (and Elizabeth his wife), gift of real estate, 14 March 1723 [Liber L Page 81]
Hawling, Mary, daughter of William & Mary Hawling, 11 March 1690 [16.pdf #109]
Herrant, John, son of Peter Herrant, 18 February 1719 [Liber H Page 214]
Hill, Philip, son of Robert Hill deceased, 9 September 1707 [Liber Z Page 260]
Hill, Susannah, daughter of Edith Goffe, "formerly ye widdow & relict of John Wooodard deceased & now wife of Edward Goffe," 8 September 1685 [13.pdf #52]
Hill, William, son of Edith Goffe, "formerly ye widdow & relict of John Wooodard deceased & now wife of Edward Goffe," 8 September 1685 [13.pdf #52]
Hodgson, Richard, son of Johannah Hodgson "widdow," gift of "one East Indian boy," 2 June 1693 [18.pdf #78]
Howard, George, brother of Thomas Howard, 9 May 1709 [Liber C Page 130]
Howard, Margarett, daughter of William & Elizabeth Howard, 24 January 1709 [Liber C: Page 125]
Hulse, Elizabeth, daughter of Meverell (?) Hulse, 1679 [09.pdf #110]
Hulse, James, son of Meverell (?) Hulse, 1682 [10.pdf #190]
Jameson, Henneretta, daughter of Barbarah Jameson, 1705 [Liber Z Page 229]
Jenkins, Anne, sister in law of Moses Jones, 15 March 1692 [17.pdf #294]
Jenkins, Elizabeth, daughter of Thomas Jenkins, 1674 [06.pdf #162]
Jenkins, John, brother in law of Moses Jones, 15 March 1692 [17.pdf #294]
Jenkins, Mary, daughter of Thomas Jenkins, 1674 [06.pdf #162]
Jones, Elizabeth, daughter of Owen Jones, 12 June 1674 [06.pdf #150, 154]
Jones, Joanna, wife of Owen Jones, 1667 [03.pdf #208]
Jones, John, son of Moses Jones, 10 September 1689 [16.pdf #109]
Jones, Owen, Junior, son of Owen Jones, 1674 [06.pdf #154]
King, Catherine, daughter (?) of Thomas King, 26 May 1720 [Liber H Page 346]
King, Elizabeth, daughter of Robert King, 3 August 1721 [Liber H Page 452]
King, Mary, daughter of Robert King, 3 August 1721 [Liber H Page 452]
King, Richard, son (?) of Thomas King, 26 May 1720 [Liber H Page 346]
King, William, son (?) of Thomas King, 26 May 1720 [Liber H Page 346]
Knight, Anne, daughter of John Knight, 1692 [17.pdf #275]
Knight, Elinor, daughter of Edward Knight, 16 July 1689 [16.pdf #107]
Knight, John, son of Edward Knight, 16 July 1689 [16.pdf #107]
Knight, Rebecka, daughter of Edward Knight, 16 July 1689 [16.pdf #107]
Lannum, John, son of John Lannum, 2 August 1690 [16.pdf #117]
Lattimore, Jacob, son (?) of James Lattimore, 30 August 1723 [Liber L Page 96]
Lemastre, Isaac, son of Abraham Lemastre, gift of real estate, 9 September 1721 [Liber H Page 468]
Lewis, Mary, daughter of Thomas Lewis, deposition, 2 May 1723 [Liber L Page 116]
Lindsey, Anne, daughter of Edmond Lindsey, 1666 [03.pdf #110]
Ling, Mary, "naturall borne daughter" of Mary Hall, 1680 [10.pdf #33]
Ling, William, "son in law" of Richard Hall and "ye naturall borne son of Mary his wife," 1680 [09.pdf #164]
Ling, William, son of Francis & Mary Ling, 1681 [10.pdf #78]

GIFTS OF LIVESTOCK

Loften, Priscilla, daughter of Frances Loften widow, 22 June 1721
    [Liber H Page 430]
Lomax, Cleborn, son of Cleborn Lomax, 1721 [Liber H Page 442]
Lomax, John, son of Ralph Lomax, 21 May 1707 [Liber Z Page 267]
Lomax, Thomas, son of Cleborn Lomax, 22 October 1722 [Liber L Page 49]
Lucket, Samuel, son of Thomas Lucket, February 1727 [Liber L Page 335]
Mackormack, Cornelius, son of Cornelius Mackormack, 17 January 1678
    [08.pdf #56]
Mackormack, Margarett, daughter of Cornelius Mackormack, 17 January 1678
    [08.pdf #56]
Mackormack, William, son of Cornelius Mackormack, 17 January 1678
    [08.pdf #56]
Maddocks, Elizabeth, daughter of James Maddocks, 7 July 1711 [Liber C Page 250]
Maglockney, Kellam, son of Kellam Maglockney, 12 June 1686 [13.pdf #61]
Makey, James, son of James Makey, 1683 [11.pdf #77]
Mankin, Elizabeth, daughter of Stephen & Mary Mankin, 14 January 1690
    [16.pdf #109]
Mankin, John, son of Stephen Mankin, 1692 [17.pdf #229]
Mankin, Josiah, son of Stephen & Mary Mankin, 10 January 1693 [17.pdf #292]
Mankin, Josias, brother of John Mankin deceased, 8 May 1705 [Liber Z Page 188]
Mankin, Margarett, daughter of Stephen & Mary Mankin, 10 January 1693
    [17.pdf #292]
Mankin, Stephen, son of Stephen & Mary Mankin, 10 January 1693 [17.pdf #292]
Maris, Sarah, daughter of Thomas Maris, 1668 [03.pdf #313]
Marloe, John, son of William Marloe, 1678 [08.pdf #96]
Marlow, Bur, son (?) of Elizabeth Marlow "widdow," 12 June 1683 [11.pdf #116]
Marlow, Susanna, daughter (?) of Elizabeth Marlow "widdow," 12 June 1683
    [11.pdf #116]
Marsh, John, son of Gilbert Marsh, 1691 [17.pdf #137]
Marsh, Thomas, son of Gilbert Marsh, 1691 [17.pdf #137]
Martin, Ruth, daughter of John Martin "Blacksmith" & Mary Martin,
    1687 [14.pdf #117]; 14 January 1690 [16.pdf #109]
Maston, Elizabeth, daughter (?) of Richard & Mary Maston, 1694 [18.pdf #191]
Maston, Henry, son (?) of Richard & Mary Maston, 1694 [18.pdf #191]
Maston, John, son (?) of Richard & Mary Maston, 1694 [18.pdf #191]
Maston, Mary, daughter of Richard & Mary Maston, 1694 [18.pdf #191]
Maston, Robert, son of Richard Maston, 1680 [09.pdf #181]
Mathena, Elizabeth, daughter of Daniell Mathena, 1680 [09.pdf #164]
Mathena, Mary, daughter of Daniell Mathena, 1676 [07.pdf #116]
Mathena, Sarah, daughter of Daniell Mathena, 1673 [06.pdf #106];
    "now deceased," 1680 [09.pdf #164]
Mee, Elizabeth, daughter of Hugh Mee, 23 October 1722 [Liber L Page 49]
Mellor, Janet, daughter of John Mellor, 3 June 1719 [Liber H Page 254]
Middleton, Smith, son of James Middleton, 20 February 1723 [Liber L Page 75]
Miller, Dinah, daughter of Jacob Miller, 9 June 1718 [Liber H Page 171]

GIFTS OF LIVESTOCK

Miller, Francis, son of John Miller, 1678 [08.pdf #96]
Miller, Jacob, son of Jacob Miller, 9 June 1718 [Liber H Page 171]
Miller, Sophia, daughter of Jacob Miller, 9 June 1718 [Liber H Page 171]
Mires, Jacob, son of William Mires, 1 May 1723 [Liber L Page 85]
Moore, John, son in law of John Smith, gift of real estate, 3 October 1715
    [Liber F Page 81]
Mould, Barbary, daughter of John Mould, 1676 [07.pdf #113]
Mould, Frances, daughter of John Mould, 1676 [07.pdf #113]
Munkaster, James, son of James Munkaster, 1678, [08.pdf #92]
Neale, Margaret, daughter of John Neale, 21 June 1721 [Liber H Page 441]
Neale, Mary, granddaughter of Anna Neale, 20 April 1692 [17.pdf #234]
Neale, Mary, daughter of James Neale, 20 April 1692 [17.pdf #234]
Neale, William, son of John Neale, 21 June 1721 [Liber H Page 441]
Nevill, William, son of John Nevill, 1662 [01.pdf #217]
Newman, Elizabeth, daughter of George Newman, 1693 [18.pdf #110]
Newman, Mary, daughter of George Newman, 1693 [18.pdf #110]
Newman, Sarah, daughter of George Newman, 1693 [18.pdf #110]
Newton, Katherine, daughter of "old" John Newton, 1669 [Vol. 60:186]
Newton, Richard, son of "old" John Newton, 1669 [Vol. 60:186]
Nicholls, Elizabeth, daughter of William Nicholls, 1693 [18.pdf #107]
Nichols, Anne, daughter of William Nichols of Pyckyawaxon, 1691 [17.pdf #137]
OBryan, William, son in law of William Taylor, 1680 [10.pdf #46]
Oden, Elizabeth, wife of Francis Oden, daughter of John & Elizabeth Cave,
Okeley, Giles, son of John Okeley, 1721 [Liber H Page 431]
Oneale, Wenifrett, daughter of Capt. Hugh Oneale, 10 August 1669 [Vol. 60:206]
Orrell, Jane, daughter of Thomas & Isabell Orell, 3 February 1693 [17.pdf #299]
Osborne, Elizabeth, daughter of Thomas Osborne, 16 July 1723 [Liber L Page 96]
Owen, Mary, daughter of William & Sarah Owen, 17 September 1707
    [Liber Z Page 260]
Owen, Jane, "ye second daughter" of William & Sarah Owen, 17 September 1707
    [Liber Z Page 260]
Parker, Elizabeth, daughter of John Parker, 1694 [18.pdf #222]
Parker, William, son of John Parker, 1668 [Vol. 60:145]
Parry, Thomas, son of Dorothy Parry widow, now wife of Robert Hanson,
    gifts of real estate, 27 March 1721 [Liber H Page 425] and 13 July 1721
    [Liber H Page 442]
Payne, John, son in law of George Godfrey, 1674 [06.pdf #148]
Poore, Margarett, daughter of Walter Poore deceased & Margarett Poore,
    21 July 1703 [Liber Z Page 100 & Liber Z Page 103]
Poore, Mary, daughter of Walter Poore deceased & Margarett Poore, 21 July 1703
    [Liber Z Page 100 & Liber Z Page 103]
Poore, Robert, son of Walter Poore deceased & Margarett Poore, 21 July 1703
    [Liber Z Page 100]
Posey, Benjamin, son of Humphrey Posey, 16 August 1717 [Liber H Page 126]
Posey, Benjamin, son of Mary Posey widow, 17 February 1718 [Liber H Page 126]

GIFTS OF LIVESTOCK

Potter, George, son of Robert Potter, 19 July 1690 [16.pdf #118]
Raines, Elizabeth, daughter of John Raines, 1690 [16.pdf #117]
Raines, Lucy, daughter of John Raines, 1690 [16.pdf #117]
Reagon, Matthew, son of John Reagon, 9 April 1726 [Liber L Page 262]
Richison, Joseph, son of William Richison, 5 March 1706 [Liber Z Page 209]
Rigg, Mary, daughter of Thomas Rigg, 1685 [13.pdf #54]
Robbins, James, son of Henry Robbins of Mattawoman, 1704 [Liber Z Page 160]
Robbins, Margarett, daughter of Henry Robbins of Mattawoman, 1704
    [Liber Z Page 161]
Robbins, Thomas, son of Henry Robbins of Mattawoman, 1704 [Liber Z Page 160]
Robins, William, son of Henry Robins, 1691 [17.pdf #187]
Robinson, Susanna, daughter of Richard Robinson, 1678 [08.pdf #96]
Roby, Michael Hinds, son of Sarah Roby, 11 October 1726 [Liber L Page 317]
Roby, Peter, son of John Roby, 15 February 1710 [Liber C Page 157]
Rock, William, son of Charles Rock, 28 November 1718 [Liber H Page 213]
Rought, Anne, daughter of William & Sarah Rought, 1690 [16.pdf #118]
Sanders, Edward, son of John Sanders, 3 January 1724 [Liber L Page 112]
Sanders, Francis, "now Francis Robinson," daughter of Matthew Sanders Senr.,
    gift of real estate, 13 August 1717 [Liber H Page 76]
Sanders, William, son of Matthew Sanders, gift of real estate, 6 August 1713
    [Liber F Page 18]
Saunders, John, son of Matthew Saunders, 1690 [16.pdf #118]
Saunders, Mary, daughter of John Saunders, 1693 [18.pdf #42]
Saunders, Mary, daughter of John & Sarah Saunders, 14 September 1694
    [18.pdf #191]
Scott, William, son of John Scott, 14 September 1703 [Liber Z Page 57]
Semmes, Katherine, daughter of Francis Semmes, 14 August 1733 [29.pdf #46]
Shackerley, Sarah, daughter of John Shackerley, 1694 [18.pdf #162]
Shaw, John, son of John Shaw, 15 October 1709 [Liber C Page 148]
Skinner, Thomas, son of Thomas Skinner, 21 March 1723 [Liber L Page 78]
Smith, Arthur, son of Richard Smith, 1693 [18.pdf #107]
Smith, Elizabeth, daughter of Richard Smith, 1693 [18.pdf #107]
Smith, John, son of Thomas Smith, 8 May 1724 [Liber L Page 139]
Smith, Thomas, son of Henry Smith, 1694 [18.pdf #179]
Smith, William, son of William Smith, 1694 [18.pdf #179]
Smith, William, son of William Smith, 28 February 1724 [Liber L Page 119]
Smoot, Leonard, son in law of John Maud, 14 April 1705
Smoote, Anne, daughter of Thomas & Elizabeth Smoote, 1694 [18.pdf #229]
Smoote, Barton, son of Thomas & Elizabeth Smoote, 1694 [18.pdf #229]
Smoote, Edward, son of Lydia Smoote, 20 January 1697 [19.pdf #109]
Smoote, Elinor, daughter of Lydia Smoote, 20 January 1697 [19.pdf #109]
Smoote, Elizabeth, daughter of Thomas & Elizabeth Smoote, 1694 [18.pdf #229]
Smoote, John, son of Lydia Smoote, 20 January 1697 [19.pdf #109]
Smoote, Rachell, daughter of Thomas & Elizabeth Smoote, 1694 [18.pdf #229]
Speake, James, son of John Speake, 1691 [17.pdf #187]

GIFTS OF LIVESTOCK

Speake, John, son of Thomas Speake, 13 January 1732 [Liber M Page 274]
Speake, Richard, son of John Speake, 8 October 1713 [24.pdf #190]
Speake, Richard, son of John Speake Junr., 8 May 1724 [Liber L Page 138]
Stigeleer, Jane, daughter of James & Mary Stigeleer "of ye head of Wiccocomico," 9 June 1707 [Liber Z Page 272]
Stone, John, son of John Stone cooper, 9 September 1707 [Liber Z Page 260]
Stratton, Mary, daughter of Samuell Dobson's wife, 1662 [01.pdf 217]
Stuart, John, son of Daniel Stuart, 1724 [Liber L Page 119]
Suttel (?), Elizabeth, daughter of John Suttel, 8 February 1710 [Liber C Page 156]
Swann, James, son of Thomas Swann, deposition, 2 May 1723 [Liber L Page 116]
Symons, Elizabeth, daughter in law of John Smith, 1690 [16.pdf #118]
Tanshall, John, son of Edward Tanshall, 1681 [10.pdf #104]
Tanshall, Margarett, daughter of Edward Tanshall, 1679 [09.pdf #110]
Tanshall, Thomas, son of Edward Tanshall, 1681 [10.pdf #104]
Tayler, Magdalen, wife of William Tayler, 14 November 1693 [18.pdf #107]
Taylor, Mary, daughter of William Taylor, 1680 [10.pdf #46]
Teares, Elizabeth, daughter of Hugh Teares, 1694 [18.pdf #191]
Thomas, Anne, daughter of George Thomas, 16 March 1714 [24.pdf #201]
Thomas, George Salisbury, son of William Thomas, 24 June 1725 [Liber L Page 227]
Thomas, John, son of Teresa Ibbetson, gift of real estate, 30 July 1719
  [Liber H Page 298]
Thompson, Anne, mother in law of Robert Thompson, 1681 [10.pdf #78]
Thompson, Anne, daughter of Thomas Thompson, 25 March 1706
  [Liber Z Page 233]
Thompson, Jane, daughter of William & Victoria Thompson, 22 June 1692
  [17.pdf #231]
Tompkinson, Jane, wife of John Tompkinson, 2 October 1672 [06.pdf #106]
Tubman, Elizabeth, daughter of Elinor Tubman, gift of goods, 4 June 1705
  [Liber C Page 129]
Tubman, Richard, son of Elinor Tubman, gift of goods, 4 June 1705
  [Liber C Page 129]
Turling, Rebeckah, daughter of Isable Orrell, 16 February 1694 [18.pdf #142]
Turner, Alexander Smith, son of Edward Turner, 1691 [17.pdf #137]
Turvey, Thomas, son of Edward Turvey, 3 August 1721 [Liber H Page 452]
Wade, Marie, daughter of Zacharie Wade, 1661 [01.pdf #146]
Wade, Zachariah, son of Richard Wade, 15 March 1726 [Liber L Page 253]
Wakefield, Thomas, son of Abell Wakefield, 1694 [18.pdf #179]
Wakefield, Thomas, grandson of Thomas Wakefield, 1694 [18.pdf #179]
Walls, George, Junr., son of George Walls Senr., 13 June 1716 [Liber H Page 14]
Walters, John, son in law of John Barron, 24 February 1719 [Liber H Page 214]
Ward, Benjamin, son of William Ward, deposition, 2 May 1723 [Liber L Page 116]
Ward, John, son in law of Henry Ward, 14 June 1722 [Liber L Page 89]
Ward, Joseph, son of William Ward, deposition, 2 May 1723 [Liber L Page 116]
Ward, Katherine, wife of Henry Ward, 1688 [16.pdf #30]

GIFTS OF LIVESTOCK

Ward, William, and Anne his wife, son of William Ward, gift of real estate, 27 March 1723 [Liber L Page 79]
Warder, William, son of Mary Warder "widdow," 9 January 1713 [24.pdf #177]; 7 October 1713 [24.pdf #189]
Warren, Abraham, son of Humphrey Warren deceased, 1694 [18.pdf #162]
Warren, Elinor, daughter of Thomas Warren, 1694 [18.pdf #162]
Warren, Humphrey, son of Humphrey Warren deceased, 1694 [18.pdf #162]
Wathen, Henry, brother of John Wathen, 29 October 1707 [Liber Z Page 276]
Wathen, Ignatius, brother of John Wathen, 29 October 1707 [Liber Z Page 276]
Waughob, Elizabeth, wife of Archbald Waughob, 7 November 1676 [07.pdf #126]
Wells, Catherine, granddaughter of Mary Wells, 27 March 1719 [Liber H Page 230]
Wharton, Elizabeth, daughter of Thomas Wharton, 1680 [09.pdf #164]
Wharton, Margarett, wife of Thomas Wharton, 1680 [09.pdf #164]
Wheeler, Anne, daughter of Thomas Wheeler, 1694 [18.pdf #143]
Wheeler, Benjamin, son of Thomas Wheeler, 1686 [14.pdf # 11]
Wheeler, Ignatius, son of Thomas Wheeler, 1694 [18.pdf #143]
Wheeler, John, son in law of Dorothy Graves, widow, 3 July 1708 [Liber C Page 109]
Wheeler, Luke, son of Ignatius Wheeler, 1693 [17.pdf #299]
Wheeler, Richard, son of Thomas Wheeler, 1686 [14.pdf # 11]
Wheeler, Thomas, son of Thomas Wheeler, 1686 [14.pdf # 11]
Wheeler, Thomas, son of Thomas Wheeler, 1694 [18.pdf #143]
Whittymore, Anne, daughter of Christopher Whittymore, 1693 [18.pdf #78]
Wilkinson, Mary, daughter of Lancelott & Mary Wilkinson, 14 November 1693 [18.pdf #107]
Wilkinson, Minor, son of Thomas Wilkinson, 29 November 1708 [Liber C Page 12]
Wilkinson, Thomas, son of Thomas Wilkinson, 29 November 1708 [Liber C Page 12]
Wilkinson, William, son of Thomas Wilkinson, 29 November 1708 [Liber C Page 12]
Willard, James, son of John Willard, 25 March 1728 [Liber L Page 467]
Williams, William, son of John Williams, 1693 [18.pdf #52]
Williams, William, son of William Williams, 11 September 1724 [Liber L Page 161]
Willson, Margarett, daughter of Joseph Willson deceased, 25 February 1704 [Liber Z Page 67]
Wolph, Mary, daughter of Joseph Wolph, 1678 [08.pdf #96]; 8 August 1682 [10.pdf #177]
Wood, John, son of John Wood, 1685 [12.pdf #61]
Wood, John, son of John Wood, 1686 [13.pdf #52]
Wood, Mary, daughter of John Wood, 1676 [07.pdf #129]
Woodgard, Richard, son of Henry Woodgard, 1685 [13.pdf #19]
Woodyard, John, son of Richard Woodyard, 24 October 1726 [Liber L Page 318]
Wright, John, grandson of John Booker, 1711 [Liber C Page 250]
Wyne, _____ , daughter of Francis Wyne, 1672 [06.pdf #78]
Yates, Robert, Junr., eldest son of Robert Yates, 9 January 1704 [Liber Z Page 67]
Younge, John, "naturall borne son" of Lawrence Younge, 1681 [10.pdf #55]
Younge, Thomas, son of Lawrence Younge, 11 July 1679 [09.pdf #110]

INDEX TO DEATHS AND ESTATES

1660-1722

Deceased	Heirs, Executors or Administrators	Earliest Date	Page/Image
Abbington, Andrew	Watkins, Samuell & his wife	11 Sep 1694	18.pdf #218
Abbot, Edward	Mitchell, Thomas	12 Jan 1686	13.pdf #48
Addersuch, John	Parker, Anne	14 Nov 1699	20.pdf #130
Agambrah, Domingoe	Iles, Richard & Elizabeth	8 Jan 1689	16.pdf #54
Agambrah, Domindigoe	Agambrah, Richard	12 Aug 1690	Liber Q:12
Agambra, Domindigo	Agambra, Richard	11 Aug 1691	17.pdf #142
Allcock, Thomas		8 Nov 1692	Liber Q:62
Allen, John	Allen, Ellinor	16 Nov 1717	Liber H:135
Allen, William		11 Nov 1674	07.pdf #28
Allwood, John	Allwood, Susannah	10 Nov 1719	Liber H:312
Ambrose, Richard	Worrell, Robert & Margarett	13 Aug 1678	09.pdf #27
Anderson, John	Semmes, James & Mary	13 Aug 1701	21.pdf #141
Arrowsmith, ___	Bruce, John & Thompson, William	14 Aug 1711	24.pdf #135
Arrowsmith, Gerard	Thompson, William	9 Mar 1714	25.pdf #210
Ashcomb, John	Ashcomb, Charles	13 Mar 1722	27.pdf #146
Ashman, Allwood	Ashman, John & Richard	8 Jun 1714	25.pdf #241
Ashman, Richard	Hardy, Henry & Anne	4 Oct 1698	19.pdf #256
Baggley, Ralph	Baggley, Anne	4 Apr 1704	22.pdf #214
Baker, John	Baker, Elizabeth	8 Nov 1687	15.pdf #20
Baker, Thomas		5 Sep 1684	Liber Q:10
Baker, Thomas	Harrison, John & Martha	16 Dec 1686	14.pdf #10
Baker, Thomas	Baker, Martha & Smith, Anthony	8 Nov 1692	17.pdf #277
Baker, Thomas	Baker, Thomas	12 May 1719	Liber H:250
Balye, William	Harrison, Francis	9 Mar 1703	22.pdf #99
Banckes, Richard	Banckes, Sarah	26 Aug 1690	17.pdf #16
Bannister, John	Hodgson, Richard & Elizabeth	10 Aug 1714	25.pdf #246
Barefoot, John	Bartlett, Ralph & Susanna	9 Sep 1685	13.pdf #34
Barker, Barbara	Boye, John	11 Jan 1709	23.pdf #295
Barker, Thomas	Moreland, Jacob	13 Aug 1700	21.pdf #33
Barrett, William	Hall, William, Doctor	9 Jun 1691	Liber Q:31
Barrett, William	Hincks, Daniell	14 Mar 1693	18.pdf #71
Barton, Elizabeth	Hopper, Dave	9 Jun 1719	26.pdf #112
Barton, Nathan	Hamersley, Francis	11 Nov 1690	Liber Q:19
Barton, William, Coll.	Haddock, James & Sarah	10 Nov 1708	23.pdf #280
Barton, William	Barton, William & Warren, Bazil	12 Aug 1712	24.pdf #174
Battin, William, Capt.	Batten, Marjorie	11 Nov 1661	01.pdf #267
Bayly, John	Wilson, Joseph & Mary	13 Jan 1691	17.pdf #92
Bayne, Anne	Bayne, Walter	14 Mar 1704	22.pdf #166
Bayne, John, Capt.	Bayne, Anne	10 Mar 1702	22.pdf #9
Bayne, Walter	Bayne, Ellenor	12 Sep 1671	06.pdf #49

INDEX TO DEATHS AND ESTATES

Name	Related Party	Date	Reference
Beane, Walter	Beane, Elinor, widow	11 Jun 1679	09.pdf #93
Baynes, Christopher	Baynes, Christopher	14 Jun 1698	19.pdf #223
Beade, Nicholas	Beade, John	4 Oct 1698	19.pdf #248
Beaumont, James	Beaumont, Richard	12 Sep 1682	11.pdf #28
Beaumont, Richard	Duglas, Robert & Mary	14 Mar 1693	18.pdf #66
Beck, Richard	Beck, Elizabeth, widow	13 Aug 1678	09.pdf #26
Becke, Richard	Brett, George & Elizabeth	26 Nov 1678	09.pdf #49
Belayne, John	Belayne, Elizabeth	3 Nov 1663	02.pdf #251
Berke, Lewis	Berke, Richard	12 Jun 1677	08.pdf #33
Bickford, Hugh	Bickford, Mary	14 Sep 1697	19.pdf #163
Bird, John	Cacell, Joshua	10 Jun 1707	23.pdf #193
Blackfan, John	Maninge, Joseph & Mary	13 Mar 1678	08.pdf #82
Blackistone, Nehemiah	Rimer, Ralph	3 Dec 1700	21.pdf #62
Blee, John	Lomax, Cleborn	13 Mar 1722	27.pdf #135
Blizard, Giles	Thompson, Robert & Mary	13 Nov 1688	16.pdf #50
Blizard, Giles	Thompson, Robert Junior & Mary	11 Aug 1691	17.pdf #150
Blundell, Richard	Smith, John & Dorothy	11 Mar 1712	25.pdf #66
Boarman, William, Major	Boarman, William, Senr.	25 Jun 1713	24.pdf #181
Bodkin, Dominick	Rozer, Benjamin, Coll.	31 Mar 1680	09.pdf #170
Bodkin, James	Carvill, Robert & Hill, Clement	11 Nov 1684	12.pdf #36
Bouling, Thomas	Bouling, John	11 Jun 1706	23.pdf #129
Bourne, James	Thompson, Richard & Morehouse, Robert	8 Jun 1686	13.pdf #99
Bowder, Roger	Clipsome, Thomas	8 Aug 1676	07.pdf #121
Bowld, John	Bowld, Jane	11 Sep 1694	18.pdf #218
Bowles, John		8 Aug 1676	07.pdf #123
Bowles, John	Tyer, James	14 Mar 1678	08.pdf #89
Bowling, James	Hall, Benjamin & Mary	8 Sep 1696	19.pdf #67
Bowling, John	Bowling (?), Mary	9 Jun 1713	25.pdf #165
Bowling, John	Ruthorne, Joseph & Mary	11 Aug 1719	26.pdf #131
Bowling, Thomas	Bowling, John	13 Aug 1700	21.pdf #35
Bowman, John	Corks, Richard	14 Nov 1693	18.pdf #122
Bowman, John	Cox, Richard	1694	Liber T:90
Box, John		11 Sep 1677	08.pdf #44
Boyce, John	Boyce, Eleanor	12 Jun 1686	13.pdf #61
Boyden, William	Barrett, James & Elizabeth	9 Sep 1685	13.pdf #28
Bradly, William	Price, Robert	12 Nov 1701	21.pdf #169
Brandt, Marcus	Brandt, Randolph, brother	29 Jul 1705	Liber C:34
Brandt, Randolph, Capt.	Brandt, Randolph, son	29 Aug 1700	Liber C:31
Brandt, Randolph	Brandt, Ann, widow	26 Mar 1715	Liber H:6
Brayne, Henry	Sanders, Edward & Jane	16 Oct 1684	18.pdf #166
Breade, John	Breade, Jane	11 Nov 1690	17.pdf #69
Breams, Christopher	Sunley, William	12 Mar 1689	16.pdf #85
Brent, Henry	Marsham, Richard & Anne	10 Aug 1697	19.pdf #141

INDEX TO DEATHS AND ESTATES

Brett, Henry	Brett, Sarah	13 Jun 1721	27.pdf #90
Brett, William	Brett, George	10 Jun 1718	26.pdf #42
Browne, Gerrard	Woodyard, Jean	26 Feb 1717	Liber H:73
Browne, John	Browne, Gerrard	11 Jun 1667	03.pdf #209
Browne, Philip	Wood, John	10 Jan 1678	08.pdf #68
Brayne (sic), Henry	Saunders, Edward & Jane	13 Mar 1683	11.pdf #80
Bryen, Henry	Sanders, Edward & Jean	12 Jun 1683	11.pdf #117
Bryan, William	Connell, Dennis	4 Apr 1699	20.pdf #56
Buckeridge, Thomas	Miller, Francis	12 Nov 1700	21.pdf #56
Bullary, Francis	Martin, Michaell & Wood, John	10 Jan 1699	20.pdf #23
Bullord, Francis	Hatch, John & Rowlands, Robert	10 Mar 1671	06.pdf #38
Burdit, Thomas	Burdit, Verlinda	9 Jun 1668	03.pdf #317
Burford, Samuell	Rozer, Benjamin	9 Jan 1672	06.pdf #55
Burford, Thomas	Burford, Anne	10 Jan 1688	15.pdf #31
Burford, Thomas	Story, Walter	14 Jun 1698	19.pdf #227
Burford, Thomas	Burford, Elizabeth	2 Nov 1705	Liber Z:240
Burford, Thomas	Cottrell, James & Elizabeth	2 Nov 1705	Liber Z:240
Burgess, Samuell	Elie, Arthur	13 Jan 1702	21.pdf #174
Burnham, Samuell	Coe, Richard	12 Mar 1706	23.pdf #115
Burras, John	Lofton, John	12 Nov 1706	23.pdf #159
Burras, Paul	Brooks, John & Jane	8 Jun 1708	23.pdf #263
Butcher, John	Davis, William & Priscilla	11 Nov 1690	17.pdf #79
Byron, Samuell	Cooper, Nicholas	14 Nov 1693	18.pdf #115
Cable, John	Cable, Mary	12 Mar 1689	16.pdf #57
Cage, John	Clipsham, Thomas	14 Jun 1681	10.pdf #89
Cage, John	Clipsham, Thomas & Susanna	15 Mar 1682	10.pdf #152
Cage, John, Senior	Cage, John, Junior	16 Dec 1685	13.pdf #102
Calvert, William, Esq.	Calvert, Elizabeth	8 Jan 1684	11.pdf #170
Calvert, William, Esq.	Calvert, Charles	14 Jan 1690	17.pdf #86
Capshaw, Francis	Diamond, George Junr. & Jemima	12 Jan 1697	19.pdf #101
Carey, Adam	Jones, Charles	14 Mar 1704	22.pdf #168
Carnell, Christopher	Piper, John	25 Nov 1661	01.pdf #264
Carnell, Christopher	Carnell, Elizabeth	25 Nov 1661	01.pdf #264
Carrol, Charles	Carrol, James	9 Mar 1714	25.pdf #199
Cassock, Benjamin	Cassock, Sarah	12 Jun 1705	23.pdf #86
Cassock, Benjamin	Mellor, John & Sarah	10 Sep 1706	23.pdf #147
Catterton, James	Catterton, Mary	13 Jun 1721	27.pdf #88
Chancellor, James	Lee, William	10 Jan 1677	08.pdf #19
Chambers, Christopher	Hawton, William	12 Jan 1703	22.pdf #79
Chandler, Job	Chandler, Nancy, William & Richard	12 Feb 1662	01.pdf #224
Chandler, William, Coll.	Chandler, Mary, Madam	9 Sep 1685	13.pdf #26
Chandler, William, Coll.	Brent, George & Mary	8 Jan 1689	16.pdf #54

INDEX TO DEATHS AND ESTATES

Chapman, Edward	Chapman, Hester	13 Jun 1721	27.pdf #74
Chapman, Richard	Chapman, Barberie	9 Mar 1686	13.pdf #49
Chapman, Richard	Goureley, John & Barbery	8 Jun 1686	13.pdf #79
Chapman, William	Jones, Evan	8 Nov 1709	23.pdf #358
Chapell, Richard	Caine, Darby	8 Aug 1704	23.pdf #20
Chappell, Richard	Jones, Charles	12 Nov 1706	23.pdf #159
Charlett, Richard	Greenfeild, Thomas	19 Apr 1698	19.pdf #211
Chesson, John	Chesson, Barbary	12 Mar 1678	08.pdf #78
Chilman, Richard	Slye, Gerrard	13 Jan 1680	09.pdf #138
Chilman, Richard	Slye, Gerrard, Gent.	13 Jan 1702	21.pdf #184
Ching, John		8 Aug 1721	27.pdf #91
Ching, John	Maccormick, Thomas & Mary	13 Mar 1722	27.pdf #147
Clarke, Andrew	Thompson, James	13 Nov 1688	16.pdf #50
Clark, Benjamin	Clark, Judith, widow	8 Nov 1709	23.pdf #365
Clark, Thomas	Clark, Julian	10 Nov 1713	25.pdf #185
Clarke, Conyers	Wheeler, John	9 Nov 1703	22.pdf #144
Clarke, Gilbert	Clarke, Fantelena	1 April 1701	21.pdf #118
Clark, Robert	Clark, Robert & John	5 Sep 1662	Liber H:284
Clarke, Samuell	Duglas, John, Coll.	15 Nov 1677	08.pdf #55
Clarke, Thomas	Toy, Joseph	13 Jun 1721	27.pdf #89
Clipsham, Thomas	Clipsham, Susannah	12 Aug 1685	12.pdf #98
Coates, Mr.		15 Jan 1679	09.pdf #71
Coates, Thomas	Clarke, John	13 Jun 1682	10.pdf #164
Cole, John	Coomes, Richard	14 Nov 1699	20.pdf #130
Connell, Dennis	Noeland, Stephen & Mary	10 Jun 1707	23.pdf #188
Connell, Dennis	Connell, Elizabeth	5 Feb 1722	Liber L:5
Connell, Dennis	Bowin, Elizabeth	5 Feb 1722	Liber L:5
Conner, John	Waters, James	9 Jun 1719	26.pdf #112
Constable, John		12 Jul 1664	02.pdf #405
Contee, John, Coll.	Contee, Mary	8 Mar 1709	23.pdf #302
Contee, John	Contee, Alexander	2 Feb 1712	Liber C:268
Contee, John, Esq.	Hemsley, Philemon & Mary	11 Mar 1712	25.pdf #50
Coode, John	Hooke, William & Elizabeth	14 Mar 1710	23.pdf #385
Cooksey, Philip		9 Mar 1697	19.pdf #111
Cooksey, Samuell	Lemaster, John & Christian	14 Mar 1710	23.pdf #385
Cooper, Robert	Faning, John	9 Aug 1682	10.pdf #188
Core, Frederick	Robertson, William & Mary	8 Nov 1720	27.pdf #34
Corker, Thomas	Wheeler, James & Elizabeth	11 Sep 1677	08.pdf #45
Cornace, Joseph	Cornace, Margaret	8 Jan 1707	Liber H:287
Cornace, Joseph	Tire, Margaret	8 Jan 1707	Liber H:287
Cornish, John	Cornish, Martha	10 Jan 1699	20.pdf #12
Cotton, Elizabeth	Mackafearson, Elizabeth	9 Nov 1708	23.pdf #279
Cotton, Thomas	Gibson, Thomas	10 Mar 1674	06.pdf #148
Coulson, Anne	Dryden, Isabel	10 Mar 1719	26.pdf #100
Courts, Charity	Courts, John	9 Mar 1714	25.pdf #209

INDEX TO DEATHS AND ESTATES

Courts, John, Esqr.	Courts, Charity, Madam	4 Apr 1704	22.pdf #197
Courts, John, Coll.	Contee, Mary, Maddam	30 Aug 1708	23.pdf #278
Crabb, Thomas	Crabb, Elizabeth	23 Jun 1720	Liber H:360
Craft, Robert	Allen, Thomas	9 Jun 1719	26.pdf #112
Creedwell, George	Ward, William & Mary	14 Mar 1678	08.pdf #89
Cressey, Samuel	Edelen, Richard	8 Aug 1676	07.pdf #121
Crompton, Francis	Beale, John	10 Mar 1719	26.pdf #97
Cugatt, Peter	Mackmillian, Peter	12 Nov 1700	21.pdf #56
Cunny, John	Barker, Martha	11 Jan 1709	23.pdf #295
Dansey, John	Dansey, Robert	10 Mar 1719	26.pdf #103
Davis, Hugh	Warder, William	12 Nov 1706	23.pdf #159
Davis, Thomas	Goer, George & Anne	9 Jan 1683	11.pdf #57
Davis, Thomas	Haggarty, John & Honnour	10 Jun 1707	23.pdf #193
Davis, Walter	Browne, William & Mary	10 Aug 1680	09.pdf #182
Delahay, John	Lee, James	17 Dec 1662	02.pdf #98
Dent, Thomas	Dent, Rebekah	20 Nov 1676	Liber Z:116
Dent, Thomas	Addison, Rebeckah, Mrs.	11 Oct 1688	16.pdf #60
Dent, Thomas	Addison, John & Rebekah	6 Jun 1704	Liber Z:121
Dent, William, Major	Dent, Elizabeth, daughter	13 Nov 1705	Liber Z:217
Dent, William, Coll.	Dent, Thomas	9 Sep 1707	23.pdf #217
Dickinson, Jeremiah	Dent, Thomas & Prodday, Nicholas	15 Nov 1676	07.pdf #130
Digges, Edward	Digges, William	12 Nov 1717	26.pdf #9
Dike, Matthew	Dike, Mary	10 Jan 1699	20.pdf #16
Dine, Thomas	Robinson, Adam & Mary	10 Aug 1680	09.pdf #180
Dixon, Thomas	Dixon, Ann	6 Feb 1719	Liber H:219
Dixon, Thomas	Story, Walter	30 May 1720	Liber H:347
Dixon, Thomas	Story, Walter	13 Jun 1721	27.pdf #89
Dod, Richard	Dod, Mary	11 Sep 1678	09.pdf #111
Dodd, Richard	Miles, Edward	10 Aug 1714	25.pdf #254
Dod, Richard	Dod, John	22 Aug 1721	Liber H:456
Douglas, John, Coll.		6 Sep 1681	10.pdf #100
Downes, Robert	Downes, Margarett	11 Jan 1676	07.pdf #99
Downes, Robert	Warner, Margaret	12 Sep 1676	07.pdf #124
Downes, Robert	Cooper, Nicholas	14 Aug 1694	18.pdf #182
Downes, Robert, Senr.		14 Dec 1703	Liber Z:86
Doy, Jane	Doy, Pidgeon	13 Jun 1721	27.pdf #89
Doyne, Ann		10 Nov 1702	22.pdf #64
Doyne, Dennis		10 Nov 1702	22.pdf #64
Doyne, Joshua	Doyne, Dennis	10 Nov 1702	22.pdf #64
Doyne, Robert	Doyne, Anne	10 Jun 1690	Liber Q:11
Doyne, Robert	Doyne, Joshuah	12 Aug 1690	Liber Q:13
Doyne, Robert	Doyne, Anne	13 Jan 1691	17.pdf #91
Doyne, Robert	Plater, George & Anne	11 Aug 1691	17.pdf #153
Doyne, Robert	Plater, George & Anne	14 June 1692	Liber Q:55

INDEX TO DEATHS AND ESTATES

Doyne, Robert	Dawson, Mary	8 Mar 1715	Liber F:59
Doyne, Robert	Brown, Virlender	21 Oct 1715	Liber F:76
Doyne, Robert	Doyne, Verlinda	25 Nov 1720	Liber H:415
Doyne, Robert	Brown, Verlinda	25 Nov 1720	Liber H:415
Draper, John	Aires, John	29 Nov 1698	19.pdf #262
Dreyden, Henry	Mahony, Timothy	14 Aug 1705	23.pdf #91
Ducket, Francis	Wright, Thomas	11 Nov 1718	26.pdf #73
Duffell, William	Barker, John	11 Mar 1718	26.pdf #22
Dullany, Charity	Dullany, Daniel	10 Mar 1713	25.pdf #142
Dutton, Thomas	Penn, William & Elizabeth	14 Jun 1709	23.pdf #308
Dyzer, Philip	Bayne, Elinor	11 Aug 1691	Liber Q:40
Earle, Thomas	Tawney, Thomas	9 Mar 1697	19.pdf #125
Earle, William	Luckett, Samuell	14 Nov 1704	23.pdf #37
Eaty, Nathaniell	Byas, Moses & Elizabeth	11 Mar 1707	23.pdf #174
Edelen, Richard, Senr.	Edelen, Richard, Junr.	12 Jan 1697	19.pdf #98
Elliot, William	Elliot, Joane	10 Nov 1713	25.pdf #194
Elwes, Thomas	Elwes, George	14 Aug 1688	16.pdf #27
Ellwes, Thomas	Ellwes, George	10 Nov 1691	17.pdf #176
Emanson, Elizabeth	Emanson, Nicholas	14 Nov 1671	06.pdf #52
Emerson, John	Bonner, Henry	11 Nov 1679	09.pdf #129
Emerson, Nicholas & Elizabeth			
	Pryor, William & Marie	9 Nov 1686	13.pdf #113
Ettey, Francis	Rouse, William	12 Nov 1706	23.pdf #152
Eyres, George	Eyres, Ellinor	9 Nov 1703	22.pdf #145
Eyres, George	Charlesworth, Robert & Ellinor	10 Aug 1703	22.pdf #128
Faning, John	Faning, Jane	9 Sep 1685	13.pdf #20
Fanning, John	Whichalley, Thomas & Jane	8 Mar 1687	14.pdf #88
Farthing, William	Farthing, Mary	13 Mar 1722	27.pdf #156
Fautley (?), Christopher	Reeves, Ubgatt	9 Nov 1703	22.pdf #152
Fearneley, Francis	Buckeridge, Thomas	14 Aug 1677	08.pdf #39
Fearneley, Francis	Wyne, Francis	11 Sep 1677	08.pdf #47
Fendall, Josias, Capt.	Fendall, Mary	10 Jun 1690	Liber Q:9
Fishwick, Edward	Fannerwick (?), John	9 Nov 1686	13.pdf #125
Ford, Edward	Ford, Elizabeth	13 Nov 1695	Liber Q:72
Ford, Edward	Whichaley, Thomas & Elizabeth	14 Sep 1697	19.pdf #160
Fowke, Gerrard	Fowke, Anne	11 Jan 1670	Vol. 60:231
Fowke, Richard	Ward, William & Mary	14 Mar 1678	08.pdf #89
Fowkes, Roger	Chandler, William, Coll.	8 Mar 1681	10.pdf #52
Fox, Edward	Waughob, Archibald	10 Jan 1678	08.pdf #70
Francis, John	Benson, Robert	9 Sep 1690	17.pdf #52
Frankcum, Henry	Frankcum, Amey	12 Jan 1669	Vol. 60:185
Franckum, Henry	Franckum, Henry, Jr.	10 Jun 1690	Liber Q:10
Franckum, Henry	Diggs, William, Coll.	9 Jun 1691	Liber Q:31
Frawner, Edward	Bullane, Francis & wife	1694	Liber T:8
Frawner, Edward	Frawner, Elinor	19 Apr 1698	19.pdf #207

INDEX TO DEATHS AND ESTATES

Freeman, Nathaniel	Freeman, Anne	9 Jun 1719	26.pdf #112
Freeman, Nathaniel	Freeman, Anne	19 Feb 1722	Liber H:478
Fry, John	Fry, Constance	4 Apr 1699	20.pdf #57
Gale, Edward	Clarkson, William & Ruth	12 Jun 1688	16.pdf #14
Gambra, Richard	Acton, Henry & Anne	9 Nov 1703	22.pdf #144
Gardiner, William	Taylor, Edmund	13 Jun 1676	07.pdf #110
Gardner, Luke		12 Jun 1677	08.pdf #37
Gardiner, Luke		11 Aug 1719	26.pdf #123
Garforth, Richard	Wharton, Thomas	10 Jun 1690	17.pdf #29
Gary, Lawrence	Gary, Mary, widow	13 Aug 1700	21.pdf #38
Gent, Elizabeth	Wayd, Richard	8 Jun 1686	13.pdf #101
Gent, William	Way, Richard	14 Jun 1687	14.pdf #121
Gerrard, Thomas	Gerrard, Anne	11 Jan 1687	14.pdf #45
Gerrard, Thomas	Bayne, John & Anne	11 Aug 1691	17.pdf #148
Ges, Walter	Ges, Ane	28 Jan 1662	01.pdf #192
Gibbon, Philip		11 Nov 1674	07.pdf #39
Gibson, Thomas	Gooch, John & Newman, George	8 Jun 1686	13.pdf #99
Gifford, Douglass	Holland, Thomas	14 Nov 1721	27.pdf #114
Gilpen, Silvanus	Wharton, Thomas	8 Jun 1680	09.pdf #164
Goaly, Thomas	Buts, John & Maddox, James	13 Jun 1721	27.pdf #89
Godfrey, Francis	Godfrey, Catherine	10 Jun 1718	26.pdf #42
Godfrey, Francis	Godfrey, Mary	28 Feb 1722	Liber H:484
Goer, George	Goer, Anne	10 Jun 1690	Liber Q:10
Goer, George	Goer, Anne	2 Aug 1690	16.pdf #117
Goer, George	Slayde, George & Anne	11 Aug 1691	Liber Q:39
Goosey, Jonathan	Goosey, Martha, widow	10 Mar 1702	22.pdf #8
Gordian, Daniell	Thompson, George	30 Apr 1664	02.pdf #406
Gough, William	Nicholson, Nicholas & Hester	9 Sep 1685	13.pdf #44
Graddock (?), Grace	Newman, George	12 Nov 1706	23.pdf #159
Graves, Joshua	Graves, Dorothy, "widdow"	14 Jan 1701	21.pdf #84
Gray, John	Gray, Thomas & Gray, Richard	12 Nov 1717	26.pdf #7
Gray, John	Gray, Edward	15 Mar 1718	Liber L:14
Grey, John	Grey, Richard & Grey, Thomas	13 Jun 1721	27.pdf #82
Green, Francis	Addames, Henry	12 Jul 1664	02.pdf #408
Greene, Leonard	Evans, Charles & Anne	11 Aug 1691	Liber Q:39
Greene, Leonard	Wheeler, Francis & Winifrid	11 Aug 1691	Liber Q:39
Greene, Leonard	Greene, Robert & Greene, Francis	13 Sep 1692	17.pdf #269
Green, Leonard	Green, Thomas, Winifrid, Mary & Margarett	25 Aug 1703	Liber Z:70
Green, Leonard	Green, Thomas	3 Mar 1714	24.pdf #201
Gregory, Charles	Cage, John	15 Nov 1676	07.pdf #132
Gregory, Charles	Bonner, Henry	10 Jan 1677	08.pdf #18
Gregory, Charles	Clipsham, Thomas	9 Jan 1678	08.pdf #66
Groves, George, Junr.	Gwinn, John	9 Mar 1714	25.pdf #198
Grumball, Thomas	Smith, Bassill	10 Jun 1707	23.pdf #180

INDEX TO DEATHS AND ESTATES

Grunwinn, Thomas	Diggs, Elizabeth	11 Jun 1706	23.pdf #126
Guess, George	Guess, Elizabeth	9 Aug 1687	14.pdf #152
Gwynne, John	Dyson, Thomas & wife	11 Mar 1685	12.pdf #94
Gwinn, John	Dixon, Thomas & Sarah	9 Sep 1685	13.pdf #19
Hagar, Robert	Nowell, Henry & Elizabeth	9 Mar 1714	25.pdf #204
Hagett, John	Hagett, Mary	12 Nov 1717	26.pdf #15
Haggat, Humphrey	Haggat, Anne	3 Nov 1663	02.pdf #252
Hagger, Robert, Junr.	Hagger, Robert, Senr.	8 Aug 1710	23.pdf #420
Haley, Thomas	Haley, Elizabeth	9 Jun 1719	26.pdf #112
Hall, Ambrose	Frost, William	12 Aug 1701	21.pdf #137
Hall, Richard	Hall, Mary	9 Nov 1680	10.pdf #33
Hall, Richard	Martin, John & Mary	12 Sep 1682	11.pdf #24
Hambleton, John	Hambleton, Elizabeth	14 Mar 1710	23.pdf #381
Hamilton, John	Chandler, Richard & Elizabeth	13 Aug 1684	11.pdf #235
Hardy, Henry		8 Jun 1714	25.pdf #241
Hardy, Henry	Hardy, Anne	14 Jun 1715	25.pdf #276
Hardy, Henry	Ashman, Richard	9 Jun 1719	26.pdf #112
Hardy, William	Hardy, Elizabeth	10 Nov 1719	26.pdf #149
Hargis, Thomas	Nalley, John	11 Aug 1719	26.pdf #132
Harris, John	Land, Richard	11 Jan 1687	14.pdf #61
Harris, Richard	Henly, Henry	9 Nov 1680	10.pdf #35
Harris, Richard	Harrison, Joseph	9 Nov 1703	22.pdf #152
Harris, Thomas		5 Dec 1662	01.pdf #264
Harrison, Anne	Barker, John	11 Mar 1718	26.pdf #22
Harrison, Joseph		15 Nov 1676	07.pdf #131
Harrison, Richard			
Harrison, Joseph & Evans, Stephen, his wife		12 Jun 1711	24.pdf #96
Hasteade, Michaell	Hasteade, Elizabeth	11 Aug 1691	Liber Q:40
Hasteade, Michaell	Dillahay, Thomas & Elizabeth	11 Aug 1691	Liber Q:40
Hattrill, Thomas	Hulse, Meverill	13 Aug 1684	11.pdf #221
Hauge (?), Elizabeth	Harrison, Joseph	13 Jun 1721	27.pdf #90
Hawkins, Elizabeth	Hawkins, Henry Holland	11 Mar 1718	26.pdf #27
Hawkins, Henry	Hawkins, Elizabeth	13 Feb 1700	20.pdf #167
Hawkins, John	Leman, Hickford	9 Aug 1709	23.pdf #344
Hawton, William	Yates, Robert	13 Feb 1718	Liber H:150
Heard, Bridget	Dowglas, John	10 Mar 1668	03.pdf #299
Henly, Robert	Court, John	11 Mar 1685	12.pdf #64
Herbert, William	Dent, George`	11 Nov 1718	26.pdf #91
Hide, Thomas	Goffe, Bartholomew & Johanna	4 Apr 1699	20.pdf #30
Higgins, John	Higgins, Eleanor	12 Jun 1705	23.pdf #81
Higgins, John	Wakelin, John & Ellinor	10 Sep 1706	23.pdf #144
Hill, Matthew	Beane, Elinor	13 Jan 1680	09.pdf #137
Hill, Matthew	Bayne, Elinor	9 Mar 1680	09.pdf #150
Hill, Mathew	Hubbard, Eleanor	8 Aug 1717	Liber H:86
Hill, Robert	Hill, Mary	10 Aug 1697	19.pdf #148

INDEX TO DEATHS AND ESTATES

Hill, Robert	Hill, Philip & Hill, Thomas	9 Sep 1707	Liber Z:260
Hingle, Joshuah	Lampton, Marke	10 Mar 1691	17.pdf #108
Hinsey, William	Chapman, Barberie	9 Mar 1686	13.pdf #49
Hinsey, William	Goureley, John & Barbery	12 Jan 1686	13.pdf #69
Hitchinson, John	Allen, John	14 Jun 1670	Vol. 60:256
Hobbart, William	Neale, Anthony; Boreman, William & Hall, Benjamin	14 Nov 1699	20.pdf #123
Holt, James	Holt, Margarett	13 Jan 1702	21.pdf #174
Holt, Margarett	Nicholes, William	10 Sep 1706	23.pdf #141
Hoskins, Lawrence	Tyre, Rebecka	14 Jun 1687	14.pdf #123
Hoskins, Lawrence	Tyre, Lawrence & Rebecka	11 Aug 1691	17.pdf #148
Hoskins, Lawrence	Tyer, James	8 Sep 1691	Liber Q:42
Howard, Edmond	Howard, William & Howard, Thomas	8 Mar 1715	25.pdf #271
Howell, Thomas	Warren, Humphrey	14 Aug 1678	09.pdf #29
Howsine, John	Bigger, James	12 Jan 1697	19.pdf #97
Hungerford, William	Hungerford, Margarett	12 Jun 1705	23.pdf #86
Hunt, John	Hunt, Dorothy, widow	3 Dec 1700	21.pdf #60
Hussey, Thomas	Luckett, Samuel & Elizabeth	12 Nov 1700	21.pdf #55
Hutchison, William		3 Mar 1714	24.pdf #201
Hutchison, William	Stodart, James	10 Nov 1713	25.pdf #189
Hutchison, William	Hutchison, John	30 Sep 1721	Liber H:473
Inglesby, Robert	Hodgson, George	8 Jun 1680	09.pdf #166
Innis, Patrick	Innis, Allexander	8 Nov 1687	15.pdf #21
Jackson, Thomas	Lenion, Thomas & Margret	8 Jan 1689	16.pdf #54
Jackson, Thomas	Yates, Robert	10 Nov 1691	17.pdf #162
Jameson, John	Jameson, Thomas	9 Jun 1719	26.pdf #112
Jartenus, Orlandus Ultra (?)	Jones, George & Johannah	14 Mar 1693	18.pdf #62
Jefferson, James	Wheeler, James	9 Nov 1680	10.pdf #32
Jennett, Daniell	Broomly, Michaell	14 Nov 1710	24.pdf #56
Johnson, Daniell	Johnson, Elizabeth	10 Mar 1671	06.pdf #39
Johnson, Daniell	Kilborne, John & Elizabeth	13 Jun 1671	06.pdf #46
Johnson, Daniell	Wheeler, John	12 Jun 1677	08.pdf #37
Johnson, Elizabeth		12 Jul 1664	02.pdf #405
Jones, Catherine	Jones, Moses	8 Mar 1692	Liber Q:53
Jones, John	Chisledine, Keneline	13 Aug 1678	09.pdf #22
Jones, John	Williams, John & Jones, Elizabeth	9 Jan 1694	18.pdf #140
Jones, Richard	Potts, Robert	11 Jan 1687	14.pdf #49
Jones, Richard	Potts, Robert & Jane	8 Mar 1687	14.pdf #82
Jones, Richard	Booker, John	10 Mar 1702	22.pdf #22
Jones, Richard	Lyndsey, Thomas & Jane	11 Mar 1690	Liber Q:9
Joseph, William	Joseph, Elizabeth	9 Nov 1714	25.pdf #262
Keech, James	Keech, James, Junr.	30 Aug 1708	23.pdf #278
Keech, James	Keech, Elizabeth	11 Mar 1712	25.pdf #45

INDEX TO DEATHS AND ESTATES

Keene, Francis		13 Mar 1678	08.pdf #80
Kelly, Cornelius	Hanson, Robert	11 Nov 1718	26.pdf #87
Kemp, Thomas	Bigger, James	8 Sep 1696	19.pdf #64
Kerr, Robert	Harrison, Joseph	10 Mar 1719	26.pdf #99
Kierstede, Jochem	Kierstede, Margarett	4 Oct 1698	19.pdf #255
King, Thomas	Hodgson, Richard & Johannah	14 Aug 1678	09.pdf #35
Knight, John	Boye, John	1 Feb 1698	19.pdf #187
Knox, James	Moore, Hugh	1 Feb 1698	19.pdf #190
Laftan, Robert	Laftan, Robert	11 Aug 1696	19.pdf #49
Laftan, Robert	Benson, Robert	8 Mar 1698	19.pdf #201
Lambert, Samuell		2 Oct 1662	01.pdf #255
Lamplugh, Edward	Tubman, George	11 Jun 1701	21.pdf #127
Lampton, Marke	Lampton, William	8 Nov 1709	23.pdf #351
Land, Penelope	Storey, Walter	10 Nov 1702	22.pdf #64
Lane, John	Lomax, Blanch	12 Jun 1705	23.pdf #81
Lang, William	Bayne, John	14 Nov 1699	20.pdf #103
Langworth, James	Langworth, William	20 Feb 1680	09.pdf #167
Langworth	Hussey, Thomas	1696	Liber T:351
Langworth, William	Hussey, Thomas	10 Nov 1696	19.pdf #85
Lemaire, John	Lemaire, Margaret	12 Aug 1690	17.pdf #35
Lemar, John	Lemar, Margaret	14 Aug 1688	16.pdf #21
Lemar, Margaret	Hoskins, Phillip & Elizabeth	14 Aug 1688	16.pdf #27
Lemaire, Margaret	Hoskins, Philip & Elizabeth	12 Aug 1690	17.pdf #35
Lenton, Joseph		15 Dec 1660	01.pdf #212
Lewellin, James	Lines, Philip	10 Jun 1674	06.pdf #161
Lewellin, Richard	Lewellin, Jane	13 Mar 1722	27.pdf #155
Lewis, Edward	Higgins, John	10 Mar 1702	22.pdf #4
Lilly, Hennery		12 Feb 1661	01.pdf #131
Ling, Michael	Justice, Henry & Mary	12 Aug 1712	25.pdf #106
Lipscomb, John	Simpson, Elizabeth	9 Nov 1708	23.pdf #276
Littlepage, Robert	Carpenter, Richard & wife	10 Sep 1678	09.pdf #42
Lofton, John	Lofton, Frances	9 Jun 1719	26.pdf #112
Lomax, Cleborne	Lomax, Blanch, widow	12 Mar 1700	20.pdf #185
Lomax, John		13 Nov 1683	11.pdf #130
Lomax, Thomas	Lomax, Cleborne	11 Jan 1682	10.pdf #143
Love, William	Butcher, Adam	8 Mar 1681	10.pdf #52
Love, William	Wahob, Archibald	12 Sep 1682	11.pdf #29
Loveday, John	Collier, Grace	12 Nov 1701	21.pdf #170
Loveday, William	Reddick, John	9 Sep 1679	09.pdf #112
Loveday, William	Mun, John	13 Jan 1680	09.pdf #137
Loyd, Morris	Lynn, Michaell	9 Jun 1696	19.pdf #35
Loyd, Philemon	Loyd, Heneritta Marea	9 Jun 1691	17.pdf #121
Luckett, Ignatius	Hanson, John, Junr.	11 Mar 1706	Liber C:45
Luckett, Samuel	Luckett, Samuel & Elizabeth	14 Aug 1705	23.pdf #97
Luckett, Samuel	Hanson, John & Elizabeth	10 Jun 1707	23.pdf #194

INDEX TO DEATHS AND ESTATES

Lumbrozo, John	Robinson, John	13 Aug 1667	03.pdf #257
Lynes, Ann	Story, Walter & Martin, Michael	11 Nov 1712	25.pdf #111
Lynes, James	Hardy, Henry	10 Mar 1702	22.pdf #11
Lynes, Philip	Story, Walter & Martin, Michael	10 Nov 1713	25.pdf #182
Lynes, Philip	Lynes, Anne	9 Mar 1714	25.pdf #199
Lynn, Michaell	Justice, Henry & Mary	14 Mar 1710	23.pdf #388
Mackartee, Phillis	Daninton (?), Francis	14 Mar 1710	23.pdf #372
Mackdonnald, Grace	Howard, Thomas	14 Jun 1720	26.pdf #173
Macock, Mary	Kirkeley, Christopher	14 Nov 1699	20.pdf #130
Maddocks, Cornelius	Maddocks, James	10 Jun 1707	23.pdf #185
Maddox, David	Wells, William	11 Sep 1677	08.pdf #43
Maggalee, Patrick	Maggalee, Rosamond	11 Aug 1719	26.pdf #124
Maglockney, Kellam	Maglockney, Elizabeth	13 Aug 1684	11.pdf #237
Mahony, Timothy	Mahony, Elizabeth	4 Aug 1714	Liber F:25
Makey, James	Makey, Elizabeth	14 Jun 1681	10.pdf #79
Mankin, Stephen	Howard, Thomas & Mary	4 Apr 1699	20.pdf #54
Marler, John	Marler, Margaret	11 Mar 1718	26.pdf #31
Marloe, Jonathan	Wakefield, Thomas	13 Jan 1674	06.pdf #144
Marshall, Isaack	Edelyn, Richard	19 Nov 1673	06.pdf #142
Marshall, Isaak	Wine, Francis	10 Mar 1674	06.pdf #150
Marshall, Thomas	Harris, John, Captain	6 May 1685	12.pdf #106
Marsham, William	Williamson, Christopher	9 Nov 1698	19.pdf #178
Marston, Robert	Marston, Constance	12 Jul 1711	Liber C:255
Marten, James	Marten, Elizabeth	13 Jun 1721	27.pdf #89
Martiall, William	Henley, Robert	10 Jan 1678	08.pdf #68
Martin, John	Martin, Mary	10 Jan 1699	20.pdf #19
Mason, Robert	Mason, Susannah	12 Jan 1703	22.pdf #86
Matthews, Ignatius	Jameson, Thomas & Mary	13 Feb 1700	20.pdf #161
Matthewes, Thomas	Matthewes, Jane	16 Nov 1676	07.pdf #136
Matthews, Thomas	Matthews, Jane	15 Jan 1678	07.pdf #136
Matthewes, Thomas	Broade, John & Jane	14 Mar 1678	08.pdf #90
Mellor, Sarah	Mellor, John	5 Mar 1707	Liber Z:267
Midgeley, Richard	Hanson, John	13 Mar 1677	08.pdf #23
Miller, Jacob	Courts, John	13 Mar 1722	27.pdf #131
Ming, Edward	Ming, Mary	26 Jul 1716	Liber H:15
Minock, Michaell	Minock, Dorothy	18 Mar 1684	Liber Q:34
Mitchell, Thomas	Mitchell, Mary	11 Jun 1701	21.pdf #127
Moore, Henry	Boyden, William & Elizabeth	16 May 1690	17.pdf #18
Moore, Henry	Moore, Henry	10 Nov 1691	17.pdf #158
Moore, Thomas	Moore, Henry	14 Jan 1701	21.pdf #75
More, Hugh	Knox, James	1696	Liber T:342
Moreland, Patrick	Magrah, John	9 Jun 1719	26.pdf #112
Morris, John	Fearson, Samuell	10 Nov 1702	22.pdf #78
Morris, Richard	Land, Richard & Penelope	11 Nov 1690	17.pdf #79
Morris, Richard	Morris, Richard	28 Jan 1706	Liber C:70

INDEX TO DEATHS AND ESTATES

Morris, Richard	Brown, John & Anderson, Edward	14 Mar 1721	27.pdf #51
Moss, William	Coulson, Robert	14 Sep 1708	23.pdf #275
Mouldin, John	Wilkinson, Lancelot & Margery	8 Mar 1681	10.pdf #53
Mountague, Stephen	Godfrey, George	14 Jan 1673	06.pdf #105
Mudd, Thomas	Hoskins, Phillip & Ann	12 Mar 1700	20.pdf #178
Muncaster, William	King, Thomas & Cooper, John	13 Jun 1721	27.pdf #89
Munroe, Andrew	Munroe, William & Tyler, Charles	9 Aug 1720	27.pdf #19
Murty,	Hill, Clement	12 Mar 1689	16.pdf #59
Murty, Stephen	Hill, Clement, Esqre.	9 Sep 1690	17.pdf #45
Muschamp, George		10 Mar 1713	25.pdf #120
Muschamp, George	Hopewell, Richard & Abinton, John	9 Jun 1713	25.pdf #165
Myers, Christopher	Myers, Mary	11 Aug 1696	19.pdf #53
Neale, James	Neale, Anthony	11 Mar 1685	12.pdf #70
Neale, James, Coll.	Neale, James & Neale, Anthony	15 Aug 1687	17.pdf #236
Nelson, Richard	Nelson, Mary	14 Mar 1710	23.pdf #378
Nevill, John	Lambert, John	23 Jun 1665	03.pdf #42
New, Richard	Dyke, Mathew	13 Sep 1687	15.pdf #15
Newen, Owen	Doyne, Robert	8 Nov 1687	15.pdf #21
Newton, Richard	Newton, John	26 Feb 1717	Liber H:73
Nicholls, John	Sanders, John	9 Jun 1713	25.pdf #144
Notley, Thomas, Esqr.	Rozer, Benjamin, Esqr.	8 Jun 1680	09.pdf #166
Obryan, Matthias	Obryan, Ellinor	10 Aug 1703	Liber Z:53
Oliver, Roger	Oliver, Mary	11 Jun 1679	09.pdf #89
Oneale, Arthur	Oneale, Mary, widow	13 Feb 1700	20.pdf #159
Oneale, Arthur	Glover, William & Mary	10 Jun 1707	23.pdf #188
Oneale, John	Oneale, Mary	9 Jan 1700	20.pdf #137
Osborne, Ann	Parker, Thomas	12 Nov 1700	21.pdf #56
P(?)kter, Daniel	Cooper, Philip	11 Nov 1718	26.pdf #73
Paris, John	Lomax, Cleborne	10 Nov 1691	Liber Q:45
Patrick, Thomas	Garrett, Charles	11 Aug 1691	Liber Q:39
Patrick, Thomas	Garrett, Charles	12 Jan 1692	17.pdf #198
Payne, John	Godfrey, Mary	14 Jun 1681	10.pdf #78
Pearce, Joseph	Rozer, Benjamin	9 Jan 1677	08.pdf #17
Peirce, John	Peirce, John	13 Jan 1680	09.pdf #137
Peirson, Elizabeth	Fawtley (?), Christopher	11 Aug 1702	22.pdf #38
Pembrook, John	Bracher, John	9 Aug 1687	14.pdf #152
Pembrook, John	Pembrook, Jane	9 Aug 1687	14.pdf #153
Pembrooke, John	Bracher, John & Jane	8 Jan 1689	16.pdf #55
Peters, Samuell	Peters, Martha	8 Jun 1708	23.pdf #257
Peters, Martha	Haggett, John	12 Jun 1711	24.pdf #114
Pew, Thomas	Browne, James & Anne	12 Jan 1692	17.pdf #195
Philpott, Edward	Philpott, John & Eleanor	11 Aug 1719	26.pdf #123
Philpott, Edward	Philpott, John	24 Mar 1720	Liber H:332
Pile, Joseph, Capt.	Neale, Anthony	10 Sep 1706	23.pdf #141

INDEX TO DEATHS AND ESTATES

Pile, Joseph	Pile, Joseph	9 Mar 1714	Liber F:12
Piles, Joshuah	Neale, Anthony & Turner, Thomas	12 Jan 1697	19.pdf #99
Pinnar, Richard	Atkins, George	12 Mar 1667	03.pdf #172
Pinner, Richard	Meeke, Francis & Mary	8 Jun 1686	13.pdf #97
Pinner, William	Meekes, Francis & Mary	9 Sep 1685	13.pdf #37
Plater, George	Rousby, John, Esqr. & Anne	13 Mar 1711	24.pdf #77
Poore, Walter	Poore, Margarett	21 Jul 1703	Liber Z:100
Poore, Walter	Witter, William & Margarett	21 Jul 1703	Liber Z:100
Pope, Francis	Pope, Mary	27 Mar 1677	08.pdf #32
Pope, Thomas	Pope, alias Ware, Mary	9 Jan 1678	08.pdf #65
Posey, Humphrey	Rookwood, Thomas	10 Mar 1719	26.pdf #105
Posey, John	Posey, Susanna	4 Jul 1689	16.pdf #116
Posey, John	Posey, Susanna	24 July 1689	Liber Q:6
Posey, John	Austin, Susanna	13 Jan 1691	Liber Q:22
Posey, Francis	Posey, Anne, daughter	12 Apr 1669	09.pdf #142
Potts, Robert	Lindsey, Thomas & Jane	12 Jun 1688	16.pdf #14
Potts, Robert	Lyndsey, Thomas & wife	9 Jun 1691	Liber Q:32
Pouncy, George	Pouncy, Mary	26 Apr 1687	14.pdf #112
Powell, Michel	Hollingsworth, William	12 Mar 1672	06.pdf #58
Pratt, Henry	Raspin, Samuell	8 Jun 1680	09.pdf #176
Price, Edward	Price, Jane	8 Jun 1680	09.pdf #166
Price, John	Garfoot, Richard	12 Jun 1683	11.pdf #118
Probart, John	Wheeler, John	8 Jun 1686	13.pdf #94
Proctor, Robert	Proctor, Rachell	8 Sep 1696	19.pdf #61
Prodday, Nicholas	Addisson, John	8 Jan 1678	08.pdf #59
Proddy, Nicholas	Proddy, Thomas & Jane	10 Aug 1688	17.pdf #33
Purfrey, Peter	Smith, William	12 Aug 1718	26.pdf #62
Pye, Edward, Esqre.	Rozer, Notley	1 Feb 1698	19.pdf #197
Raleigh, Philip	Holiday alias Raleigh, Elizabeth	9 Jun 1719	26.pdf #112
Randall, Richard	Harrison, Joseph & Montague, Stephen	7 Apr 1668	03.pdf #306
Raspin, Samuell	Marshall, Thomas	14 Jun 1681	10.pdf #80
Raynes, John	Tanner, Henry	8 Aug 1710	23.pdf #418
Renialls, John	Renialls, Elizabeth	4 Oct 1698	19.pdf #241
Reynolds, Henry	Hawkins, Henry	10 Mar 1691	Liber Q:24
Rich, John	Neale, James	11 Sep 1694	18.pdf #215
Richardson, William	Bayne, Ebsworth	10 Aug 1714	25.pdf #241
Rigg, John	Rigg, Susanah	11 Mar 1712	25.pdf #35
Rigg, Thomas	Gardiner, John & Constant	9 Sep 1690	17.pdf #47
Rogers, John	Rogers, Elizabeth	10 Jun 1718	26.pdf #43
Rookwood, Edward	Rookwood, Thomas	12 Aug 1718	26.pdf #62
Roswell, William	Roswell, Amia	14 Nov 1699	20.pdf #109
Rought, William	Evans, Benjamin & Sarah	11 Nov 1690	17.pdf #77
Rousby, Christopher	Smith, Richard & Barbery	13 Mar 1688	15.pdf #43
Rousby, John	Smith, Richard & Barbary	13 Mar 1688	16.pdf #43

INDEX TO DEATHS AND ESTATES

Rozer, Benjamin, Coll.	Rozer, Anne, Madam	11 Jan 1682	10.pdf #141
Rozer, Benjamin, Coll.	Pye, Edward & Anne	9 Jan 1683	11.pdf #55
Russell, Christopher, Capt.			
	Fendall, Jonas, Capt. & Hundley, Robert	17 Dec 1662	02.pdf #93
Russell, Walter		17 Dec 1677	08.pdf #75
Russell, William		17 Dec 1677	08.pdf #75
Sample, Joseph	Sample, Mary	9 Sep 1690	17.pdf #56
Sanders, Edward	Sanders, Thomas & Charles	14 Mar 1721	27.pdf #66
Sanders, Robert		10 Mar 1719	26.pdf #103
Sanders, Robert (?)	Sanders, William	13 Jun 1721	27.pdf #90
Sapcoate, Abraham	Fitz Gerrald, Morris & Rachell	10 Nov 1696	19.pdf #77
Scarry, Ann	Beale, John	11 Nov 1712	25.pdf #117
Scarry, Richard	Cooke, John	Nov 1716	Liber G:151
Seaman, John	Carey, John & Bell, Richard	10 Aug 1697	19.pdf #147
Selby, Nicholas	Allin, John	13 Jan 1674	06.pdf #144
Semmes, Anthony	Semmes, Dosebella, widow	14 Mar 1710	23.pdf #376
Shaw, Elizabeth	Bateman, George	9 Nov 1703	22.pdf #143
Shepherd, Charles	Shepherd, Damaris	8 Mar 1692	Liber Q:53
Shepherd, Charles	Sarjeant, William & Damaris	14 Mar 1693	18.pdf #57
Sherrill, Samuel	Kingadon, Thomas	8 Aug 1676	07.pdf #114
Short, Amos	Yeabsley, Thomas	29 Jul 1671	06.pdf #135
Short, Amos	Doniphan, Alexander	1 Oct 1672	06.pdf #135
Short, George	Short, Anne	13 Jun 1721	27.pdf #89
Skidmore, Nicholas	Teares, Hugh	9 Mar 1697	19.pdf #117
Slye, Gerrard	Slye, Gerrard	8 Aug 1704	23.pdf #24
Slye, Robert	Slye, Priscilla	29 Nov 1698	19.pdf #265
Smallwood, John	Smallwood, Thomas	11 Sep 1694	18.pdf #195
Smith, Alexander	Smith alias Hawkins, Sarah	11 Mar 1690	Liber Q:1
Smith, Jane	Yates, Robert	12 Nov 1700	21.pdf #56
Smith, John	Edelin, Richard	10 Sep 1706	23.pdf #141
Smith, John, Senr.	Moore, John	11 Mar 1718	26.pdf #27
Smyth, Richard	Pope, Francis	10 Mar 1668	03.pdf #301
Smith, Richard	Tyer, James & Hardy, Henry	27 Mar 1677	08.pdf #31
Smith, Richard	Smith, Anne	19 Apr 1698	19.pdf #209
Smith, William	Smith, Elizabeth	10 Nov 1696	19.pdf #77
Smith, William	Hoskins, Phillip & Dent, William	10 Sep 1700	21.pdf #43
Smith, William	Smith, Adam	28 Jun 1718	Liber H:194
Smith, William	Spaldin, Priscilla	13 Jun 1721	27.pdf #75
Smoote, Richard	Barton, William	10 Jan 1677	08.pdf #18
Smoote, Richard	Davis, Walter	15 Mar 1683	11.pdf #95
Smoote, Richard	Hatch, William	15 Mar 1683	11.pdf #95
Smoot, Richard	Ocain, Gerrard	12 Jan 1703	22.pdf #82
Smoot, Richard	Hawton, Lydia & William	9 Mar 1703	22.pdf #89
Somerset, Edward	Carroll, Charles	10 Aug 1714	25.pdf #250

INDEX TO DEATHS AND ESTATES

Sothoron, John	Birch, John & Elizabeth	11 Mar 1718	26,pdf #23
Sothoron, Samuel	Seagar, John & Margaret	11 Mar 1718	26.pdf #23
Southeron, Richard	Russell, Brutus	12 Jun 1711	24.pdf #97
Sowerbutt, Richard	West, William	10 Nov 1691	17.pdf #163
Spicer, George	Spicer, Mary	11 Mar 1712	25.pdf #69
Spicer, Hannibal	Jenkings, John, Capt.	4 Sep 1660	01.pdf #108
Spikeman, William	Spikeman, Hesther	14 Aug 1694	18.pdf #182
Spikeman, William	Kirk, James & Esther	8 Mar 1698	19.pdf #202
Standish, Alexander	Herrant, Peter	9 Jun 1719	26.pdf #112
Steward, Daniell	Steward, Elinor	9 Sep 1707	23.pdf #218
Stone, John	Stone, Thomas & Elinor	10 Jan 1699	20.pdf #15
Stone, John	Teares, Eleanor & Stone, Thomas	13 Aug 1700	21.pdf #32
Stone, Matthew	Stone, Margery	9 Jan 1678	08.pdf #64
Stone, Matthew	Maddock, Edward & Margery	26 Nov 1678	09.pdf #54
Stone, Thomas	Maninge, Joseph & Mary	9 Jan 1678	08.pdf #65
Story, Walter	Story, Elizabeth	11 Jun 1673	06.pdf #139
Stowe, Edmond	Stowe, Jane	19 Apr 1698	19.pdf #214
Stowe, Jane	King, John	10 Jan 1699	20.pdf #23
Sutton, George	Willson, Joseph	14 Nov 1699	20.pdf #130
Swinborne, Nicholas	Rookwood, Edward	9 Sep 1685	13.pdf #25
Swinburne, Elizabeth	Moss, William	8 Jun 1705	Liber Z:201
Taney, Michaell	Taney, Thomas	19 Apr 1698	19.pdf #213
Taney, Thomas	Trueman, Thomas	9 Jun 1713	25.pdf #161
Taney, Thomas	Taney, Jane	9 Mar 1714	25.pdf #211
Taylor, William	Taylor, Magdalen	14 Sep 1697	19.pdf #148
Teares, Hugh	Teares, Elizabeth	8 Aug 1704	23.pdf #20
Teares, Hugh	Beale, John & Ellinor	8 Aug 1704	23.pdf #20
Thomas, John	Rookwood, Edward	12 Mar 1700	20.pdf #190
Thomas, William	Thomas, Susannah	15 Jan 1687	Liber Q:44
Thompkins, John	Price, Jane	12 Jun 1677	08.pdf #37
Thompkins, John	Thompkins, Sarah	9 Jun 1719	26.pdf #122
Thompkins, John	Daine, Charles	12 Apr 1720	Liber H:333
Thompkins, Josiah	Goodrick, Robert	11 Sep 1694	18.pdf #207
Thompson, Henry	Thompson, Isabella	8 Aug 1699	20.pdf #85
Thompson, William	Faning, John	26 Nov 1678	09.pdf #49
Thompson, William	Thompson, Mary	8 Jun 1714	25.pdf #227
Tickerell, Thomas	Bright, Thomas & Jane	13 Aug 1684	11.pdf #240
Till, Edward	Till, Sarah	9 Aug 1698	19.pdf #234
Till, John	Plucket, Thomas	14 Nov 1699	20.pdf #130
Till, Sarah	Craxon, Thomas	9 Aug 1698	19.pdf #234
Toale, Robert	Clappam, John	12 Mar 1689	16.pdf #57
Toby (?), Catherine	Woodyard, Richard	8 Nov 1720	27.pdf #29
Towell, David	Rookerd, Edward & Allcock, Thomas	8 Jan 1678	08.pdf #61
Towles, Henry		12 Nov 1700	21.pdf #55

INDEX TO DEATHS AND ESTATES

Tracy, Charles	Small, David	13 Jun 1699	20.pdf #70
Troope, Robert, Capt.			
	Montague, Stephen & Causeen, Ignatius	27 Nov 1666	03.pdf #134
Trover, Patrick	Trover, Mary, "widdow"	13 Mar 1711	24.pdf #71
Trover, Patrick	Ferrill, Patrick & Mary	10 Nov 1713	25.pdf #189
True, Richard	Harrisson, Francis	14 Nov 1699	20.pdf #112
True, Richard	True, Priscilla	9 Mar 1709	Liber C:141
True, Richard	Davis, William & Priscilla	9 Mar 1709	Liber C:141
Trueman, Henry	Taney, Thomas & Jane	10 Mar 1702	22.pdf #7
Tubman, George	Phillpot, Edward & Ellinor	8 Jun 1708	23.pdf #260
Turling, John	Turling, John	14 Mar 1693	18.pdf #65
Turner, Arthur	Beane, Walter	12 Nov 1667	03.pdf #288
Turner, Thomas	Turner, Joshua	10 Mar 1719	26.pdf #109
Tymothy, William		13 Feb 1700	20.pdf #166
Tyer, James	Tyer, Rebecka	11 Jan 1687	14.pdf #45
Tyre, James	Yates, Robert & Rebekah	12 Jun 1688	16.pdf #14
Tyer, James	Tyer, Rebeckah	8 Sep 1691	Liber Q:42
Tyer, James	Yates, Robert & Rebeckah	8 Sep 1691	Liber Q:42
Tyre, James	Conner, John	9 Mar 1714	25.pdf #208
Vanswearingen, Garrett			
	Vanswearingen, Joseph & Mary	14 Jan 1701	21.pdf #73
Venour, Joseph, Docter	Leman, Hickford	13 Mar 1711	24.pdf #58
Venour, Joseph, Docter	Penn, Mark	13 Mar 1711	24.pdf #58
Vering, Nathaniel	Yates, Robert & Rebecca	12 Jun 1688	14.pdf #178
Veron, Nathaniell	Tyre, James	12 Jun 1688	16.pdf #14
Voax, Joseph & wife	Brawner, Mary, widow	19 Apr 1698	19.pdf #207
Wade, Zachary	Hinson, Randolph	15 Jan 1679	09.pdf #77
Wade, Zachary			
	Hatton, William & Hinson, Randolph	9 Sep 1679	09.pdf #111
Walker, James	Walker, Alice	8 Nov 1675	07.pdf #90
Wallis, Michael	Willson, William	11 Aug 1702	22.pdf #47
Waple	Hemsley, Philemon	Aug 1715	Liber G:25
Waple, Thomas	Hemsley, Philemon	12 Nov 1717	26.pdf #12
Warner, Christopher	Wright, John & Pinner, Richard	15 Jan 1679	09.pdf #70
Warner, Thomas	Baker, Thomas & Dod, Richard	14 Nov 1676	08.pdf #32
Warner, Thomas, Sr.	Warner, Thomas, Jr.	16 May 1688	16.pdf #28
Warren, Benjamin	Hanson, Samuell & Elizabeth	19 Nov 1708	Liber C:123
Warren, Humphrey		12 Jun 1694	18.pdf #162
Warren, Humphrey	Warren, Notley	9 Jun 1696	19.pdf #38
Warren, Humphry, Coll.	Bayne, John	12 Mar 1700	20.pdf #179
Warren, John	Warren, Judith	21 Jan 1716	Liber F:84
Warren, Notley	Bayne, John	14 Jan 1701	21.pdf #81
Wathen, John, Senr.	Wathen, John, Junr.	11 Jun 1706	23.pdf #128
Watkins, Samuell	Smith, Thomas	8 Aug 1710	23.pdf #425
Weaver, Adam, Junr.	Weaver, Adam, Senr.	8 Aug 1704	23.pdf #24

INDEX TO DEATHS AND ESTATES

Weireman, John	Jones, George & Honoria	10 Sep 1678	09.pdf #42
Wellman, Michal	White, Thomas & Elizabeth	13 Mar 1722	27.pdf #131
Wentworth, Thomas	Hill, John	10 Mar 1672	06.pdf #117
Wheeler, Ignatius	Wheeler, Thomas	8 Jun 1703	22.pdf #106
Wheeler, James	Jones, Moses & Katherine	9 Sep 1685	13.pdf #20
Wheeler, James	Wheeler, Catherine	8 Mar 1692	Liber Q:53
Wheeler, James	Jones, Catherine	8 Mar 1692	Liber Q:53
White, Cornelius, Gent.			
Perry, John; Barber, Luke; & Norton, Andrew		8 Jun 1714	25.pdf #219
White, Cornelius	Parry, John & Dorothy	11 Nov 1718	26.pdf #75
White, Jonathan	White, Bernard	10 Jun 1718	26.pdf #43
Whiteheart, George	Wilder, John	11 Mar 1690	Liber Q:1
Whiteheart, George	Wilder, John	11 Nov 1690	17.pdf #124
Wight, John	Wight, Anne, widow	9 Sep 1707	23.pdf #214
Wilder, John, Capt.	Wilder, Francis	11 Mar 1707	23.pdf #169
Wilder, Francis	Browne, William	11 Mar 1707	23.pdf #169
Williams, John	Clipsham, Thomas	10 Jan 1677	08.pdf #18
Williams, Rice	Diggs, William, Coll., Esq.	9 Sep 1685	13.pdf #19
Williams, Rice	Diggs, William	9 Sep 1690	Liber Q:18
Williams, Thomas	Throne, William	9 Jun 1719	26.pdf #112
Willson, Jonathan			
	Willson, Catherine & Cecell, Joshua	13 Feb 1700	20.pdf #163
Willson, Joseph		25 Feb 1704	Liber Z:67
Wilson, John	Bayley, Ralph	13 Jun 1721	27.pdf #74
Wincoll, John	Smallwood, James	19 Apr 1698	19.pdf #217
Winstanley, James	Hall, Mary	9 Nov 1698	19.pdf #178
Winston, Richard	Smith, William	11 Jan 1704	22.pdf #161
Witter, Thomas	Witter, William	9 Sep 1707	23.pdf #210
Wolph, Joseph	Waynman, Rice	9 Sep 1685	13.pdf #31
Wolfe, Mary	Waynman, Rice	12 Jan 1686	13.pdf #68
Wolfe, Mary	Waynman, Mary	9 Feb 1686	13.pdf #48
Wood, John	Mankin, Stephen & Margaret	10 Jun 1718	26.pdf #47
Wood, Stephen		13 Oct 1663	02.pdf #244
Woodard, John	Butcher, John	12 Jun 1679	09.pdf #102
Wright, John	Harrison & Wade	1694	Liber T:8
Wright, John	Harrison, Richard & Wade, Richard	10 Nov 1696	19.pdf #78
Wright, Robert	Decregoe, John	13 Mar 1688	16.pdf #43
Wright, William	Thompson, Robert	5 Dec 1682	11.pdf #36
Wright, William	Thompson, Robert, Junior	12 Jun 1683	11.pdf #117
Wyne, Francis	Wyne, Elizabeth	13 Jun 1682	10.pdf #164
Wyne, Francis	Hawkins, Henry & Elizabeth	5 Dec 1682	11.pdf #36
Yates, Ledya	Yates, Robert	13 Feb 1718	Liber H:150
Yates, Robert	Yates, Robert	10 Aug 1714	25.pdf #253
Yeabsley, Thomas	Yeabsley, Thomasine	8 Jun 1675	07.pdf #71
Young, Elizabeth	Boreman, William, Junr.	12 Mar 1700	20.pdf #184

INDEX TO ORPHANS

1667-1722

Acton, Mary, daughter of Mary Acton, "being two years old the second day of May last past," bound to Mary Shinston (?), 13 June 1710 [23.pdf #400]

Allanson, Charles, parents not named, age not stated, bound to George Thompson, 12 November 1684 [12.pdf #24]

Allanson, Elizabeth, parents not named, age not stated, bound to Madame Mary Chandler, 13 January 1685 [12.pdf #50]

Allen, William, "alias Gill a bastard son of Joseph Allen, "being twelve yeares of age the ninth day of July next, bound to ye said Joseph," 12 June 1711 [24.pdf #96]

Allin, Hesther, orphan daughter of Philip Allin deceased, petitioner Murphy Ward states that said "orphan child is now in ye possession of one Joseph Ward of this County, and by ye said Ward & wife is greiveously abused," bound to "ye said Murphy Ward," 4 October 1698 [19.pdf #241]

Ashbrook, James, parents not named, "aged about tenn years last May," bound to Richard Holden "and his wife," 10 August 1714 [25.pdf #254]

Ashbrook, John, parents not named, "aged about thirteen years," bound to Richard Holden "and his wife," 10 August 1714 [25.pdf #254]

Ashbrook, Rose, parents not named, "aged about twelve years," bound to Richard Holden "and his wife," 10 August 1714 [25.pdf #254]

Ashman, Allward Hardy, son of Richard Ashman deceased and Anne his widdow "now wife of Capt. Henry Hardy," (born 12 June 1691), obliges himself "to live with & serve ye said Henry Hardy & Anne his wife & ye survivour of them," 14 September 1703 [22.pdf #129]; see also [25.pdf #241]

Ashman, John, son of Richard Ashman deceased and Anne his widdow "now wife of Capt. Henry Hardy," "nine yeares old ye fourth day of February last," obliges himself "to live with & serve ye said Henry Hardy & Anne his wife & ye survivour of them," 14 September 1703 [22.pdf #129] see also [25.pdf #241]

Ashman, Richard, "ordered that ye said Richard Ashman bee discharged from ye said Capt. Henry Hardyes service," 10 August 1703 [22.pdf #125]; see also [22.pdf #231] [23.pdf #305] [25.pdf #241]

Ashman, Standidge, son of Richard Ashman deceased and Anne his widdow "now wife of Capt. Henry Hardy," (born 1 October 1687), obliges himself "to live with & serve ye said Henry Hardy & Anne his wife & ye survivour of them," 14 September 1703 [22.pdf #129]

Backer, Thomas, son of Thomas Backer and "ye Widdow Backer," master not stated, 10 March 1685 [12.pdf #62]

Baddoe, James, son of Martha Baddoe, "being foure months old," bound to Thomas Coleman," 11 August 1713 [25.pdf #172]

Baker, Andrew, "one of ye orphan children of Thomas & Martha Baker," bound to William Dent, inventory of estate, "three cowes & three calves, one heifer three yeare old, one gelding named Jugler," 11 March 1690 [Liber Q Page 6]; survey of land and division of estate, 9 June 1691 [Liber Q

INDEX TO ORPHANS

Page 28]; inventory of estate, 11 August 1691 [Liber Q Page 36]; see also Deed dated 13 September 1692 [17.pdf #257]; Andrew Baker, "one of ye orphan sons of Thomas Baker deceased, petitioning ye Court here for his freedome," "ye said Andrew Baker is but nineteene yeares of age on ye twenty ninth day of March next comeing," ordered by Court to "returne again to Mr. William Dent his master," 1 February 1698 [19.pdf #186]

Baker, John, son of Thomas Baker deceased, survey of land and division of estate, 9 June 1691 [Liber Q Page 28]

Baker, Martha, "ye orphan daughter" of Thomas Baker deceased, marrying Anthony Smith who petitions for "division of ye said estate," 10 June 1690 [Liber Q Page 10]; see also [Liber Q Page 12] & [Liber Q:23]; survey of land and division of estate, 9 June 1691 [Liber Q Page 28]

Baker, Thomas, son of Thomas Baker deceased, survey of land and division of estate, 9 June 1691 [Liber Q Page 28]

Bannister, Benjamin, parents not named, "a minor orphan under the care & guardianship" of Joseph Harrison Senr., ordered by Court to "receive the rents & profits arising by ye use & occupation of a plantation belonging to Benjamin Bannister," 8 June 1714 [25.pdf #219]; see also [27.pdf #163]

Barefoot, John, son of John Barefoot deceased, age not stated, bound to Richard Boughton, 12 June 1694 [18.pdf #165]

Barker, Samuell, son of Alice Hanby wife of Francis Hanby, "now at ye age of seaven yeares ye second day of Aprill last," bound to Samuel Luckett, 13 November 1695 [18.pdf #243].

Barker, Barbarah, orphan, daughter of William Barker deceased, petition for division of father's estate, 14 March 1704 [22.pdf #163]

Barker, Elizabeth, orphan, daughter of William Barker deceased, petition for division of father's estate, 14 March 1704 [22.pdf #163]

Barker, Sarah, orphan, daughter of William Barker deceased, petition for division of father's estate, 14 March 1704 [22.pdf #163]

Barron, Thomas, son of Anne Barron and "her deceased husband," a minor, age not stated, ordered by Court "that ye said Thomas Barron tarry with his mother in law aforesaid until ye cropp is finisht to wit Christmas next," 11 August 1719 [26.pdf #124]; Thomas Barron, "a minor orphan of about fifteen years of age," bound to John King, he "to learn ye said Thomas ye art and mystery (sic) of a shipwright & to give him six months schooling," 8 March 1720 [26.pdf #161].

Bartlet, Edward, son of Elizabeth Perfrey, "aged about eight years," bound to Richard Holden "and his wife," 10 August 1714 [25.pdf #254]

Bartlet, Winifred, daughter of Elizabeth Perfrey, "aged about six years," bound to Richard Holden "and his wife," 10 August 1714 [25.pdf #254]

Bartlett, Mary, "an orphan child" of Raiph Bartlett deceased, the Grand Jurors "doe present William West planter for educateing & bringing up" said orphan "in ye Roman Catholick religion her parents being Protestants," 9 June 1691 [Liber Q Page 28]; Mary Bartlett ye orphan child of Raiph Bartlett deceased which was in ye possession & tuition of ye aforesaid William

INDEX TO ORPHANS

West," "being nine yeares of age January last past," bound to Moses Jones, 11 August 1691 [Liber Q Page 38]

Bartlett, Thomas, son of Ralph Bartlett deceased, age not stated, bound to Robert Benson, 8 March 1687 [14.pdf #91]

Barton, William, son of Nathan & Martha Barton deceased, petitions "to have ye estate of his two younger brothers & sister," identified as Nathan, Thomas & Martha, "delivered into his custody which said estate is now in ye hands & possession of Mr. Francis Hammersley," 10 June 1690 [Liber Q Page 11]; see also [Liber Q Page 17]; "Nathan Barton who dyed sometime in 1684 or 1685" [Liber Q Page 21]; see also [Liber Q Page 27] & [17.pdf #157]

Bayne, Anne, daughter of Capt. John Bayne deceased, "placed at the house of Mr. William Newman," 8 June 1703 [22.pdf #106]

Bayne, Ebsworth, son of Capt. John Bayne deceased, ordered by Court that Ebsworth Bayne be removed "from the house of Mr. Samuell Luckett & that hee be placed at the house of Mr. William Newman with his sister Anne," 8 June 1703 [22.pdf #106]; Ebsworth Bayne, parents not named, age not stated, "chooses his brother Walter Bayne to be his guardian," 14 August 1705 [23.pdf #89]; Ebsworth Bayne "chooses Coll. James Smallwood and Capt. Thomas Dent for his guardian," 11 January 1709 [23.pdf #293]

Belaine, Grace, daughter of John Belaine deceased, age not stated, "doth choose John Mould & Anne his wife being her Sister in Law to be her Guardian," 8 August 1676 [07.pdf #114]; Grace Belain married Giles Colliar, before 3 February 1679 [09.pdf #142]

Belaine, Nicholas, son of John Belaine deceased, doth "make choice of John Posie "his Brother in Law to be his Guardian," 8 August 1676 [07.pdf #114]; see also [08.pdf #37]; "Nicholas Belaine ye son of John Belaine was at ye full age of twenty one yeares ye tenth day of this instant month November," verified by Robert Henley, 11 November 1679 [09.pdf #132]

Belman, Peter, son of Elizabeth Rue, age not stated, bound to Richard Clowder "with ye mothers consent," 11 June 1684 [11.pdf #204]

Bently, John, son of Hannah Bently, bound to Thomas Osborne, June 1716 [Liber G Page 100]

Betts, Mary, "an orphan," parents not named, "about nine years of age," bound to Samuel King," 9 March 1714 [25.pdf #198]

Bevin, Abraham, "an ophan boy tenn years of age," parents not named, "bound to Anne Brandt widdow," 9 June 1713 [25.pdf #144]

Blanshett, Henry, bound to Elizabeth Blanshett, March 1717 [Liber G Page 173]; Henry Blanshett, parents not named, age not stated, "formerly bound to Elizabeth Blanshett his mother in law who intermarried with William Milstead is now bound to James Parrander, 11 March 1718 [26.pdf #22]

Blizard, Susanna, daughter of Giles Blizard deceased, age not stated, ordered by Court "to remaine in ye custody & tuition of her mother in law Mary Thompson," 13 March 1694 [18.pdf #144]

INDEX TO ORPHANS

Booker, Anne, parents not named, "under age," "makes choice of Henry Brett" for her guardian, 9 June 1713 [25.pdf #144]

Booker, John, parents not named, "a minor," "makes choice" of Thomas Wright for his guardian, 10 March 1713 [25.pdf #120]; John Booker "makes choice of Thomas Price" for his guardian, 9 June 1713 [25.pdf #144]

Boswell, Mathew, orphan of John Boswell deceased and Mary Pouncey, age not stated, bound to Thomas Mitchell, 9 August 1687 [14.pdf #152]; Mathew Bozwell, "eldest son of John Bozwell deceased, petitions that his "younger brother John Bozwell now deceased in his life time was possessed of divers goods & chattles which are now in ye possession of George Pouncey," ordered by Court "that George Pouncey doe deliver unto Matthew Bozwell ye goods & chattls of his brother John Bozwell deceased," "being testifyed here in Court by ye oath of Mary Pouncey ye wife of ye said George Pouncey to be two cowes, two two yeare old heifers, one yearling heifer, one mare & one horse," 10 June 1690 [Liber Q Page 11]

Bowlton, James, son of Mary Bowlton, "being of the age three years the sixth day of September last," bound to John & Mareon Brown, by indenture, 5 January 1714 [Liber F Page 71]

Brafitt, Elizabeth, "infant," parents not named, age not stated, bound to Joyce Robinson, 10 January 1682 [10.pdf #133]

Bramhall, Ann, "six and halfe yeares of age," bound to Mary Haggon and William her son, with the consent of her father, 11 November 1712 [25.pdf #110]

Bramhall, Thomas, "one and halfe yeares of age," bound to Mary Haggon and William her son, with the consent of his father, 11 November 1712 [25.pdf #110]

Bramhall, William, "foure yeares of age the seventh day of December next," "bound by his father Thomas Bramhall unto Richard Estes (?), 11 November 1712 [25.pdf #110]

Branson, Michael, parents not named, age not stated, petitions "to choose Joseph Peters for his guardian which is granted," 11 June 1700 [21.pdf #9]

Breade, John, son of John Breade deceased, age not stated, "made choice of his mother Mrs. Jane Hussey ye wife of Mr. Thomas Hussey and William Matthewes to be his guardians," 9 March 1697 [19.pdf #111]

Bridgets, Elizabeth, parents not named, "now 9 yeares old," bound to "mother Michie," 8 June 1669 [Vol. 60:207]

Browne, not named, two orphans, parents not named, brothers of William Browne, "in the possession of Samuell Fearson," 4 April 1704 [22.pdf #194]

Browne, Elizabeth, parents not named, age not stated, formerly "living with a certain William Barker," by "order made last Court" to "be delivered to Elizabeth Cave," and "now here at this day" "comes the said Elizabeth Cave & brings into Court the said orphan," ordered by Court "that the said Elizabeth Browne do continue with Thomas Butler planter "in consideracion of his having taken care & maintained her hitherto," 8 June 1714 [25.pdf #219]

INDEX TO ORPHANS

Browne, Gerrard, son of Elizabeth Browne, "the said Gerrard being seaven years of age last May," bound to William Dent, 14 June 1687 [14.pdf #141]

Browne, John, orphan, parents not named, ordered by Court "that the said John Browne be free att eighteen yeares of age according to his mothers will, and whereas the orphant complaines that Samuell Fearson hath killed two head of cattle belonging to ye orphant, ordered that the said Samuell Fearson do restore the same to the orphant," 14 June 1709 [23.pdf #305]

Browne, Rebecka, daughter of Elizabeth Browne, "ye said Rebecka tenn years of age last March," bound to William Dent, 14 June 1687 [14.pdf #141]

Brown, William, "an orphan," parents not named, "about eight or nine years of age," bound to Percival Fearson," 9 March 1714 [25.pdf #198]

Bryson, John, son of Agnes Bryson, "about fifteen months old," bound to John Corkain (?), 10 June 1721 [27.pdf #72]

Buckeridge, Thomas, orphan of Thomas Buckeridge deceased, age not stated, ordered "to goe into ye custody" of Stephen Mankin, 14 June 1687 [14.pdf #121]

Burgesse, John, parents not named, "hee now being fifteene yeares of age next March ensueing,"" bound to Obadiah Dunn "of St. Maries County, 14 September 1680 [10.pdf #29]

Cage, William, son of John Cage deceased, age not stated, bound to Coll. Humphrey Warren, 11 March 1690 [16.pdf #114]

Cammell, Elizabeth, bound to William Sanders, petitioned "that she had served her time truely & honestly that the said Sanders was obliged to give her a years schooling which he has failed to doe," "appearing to the Court to be false and groundless was therefore rejected," 14 March 1721 [27.pdf #45]

Campel, Elizabeth, parents not named, "about fifteen years of age," chooses William Sanders for her guardian,"Frances Robertson to whom she was formerly bound being dead," 9 June 1719 [26.pdf #111]; see also [26.pdf #143]

Campbell, Charles, "an orphan boy," parents not named, age not stated, "formerly bound to Robert Sanders deceased, is now bound unto William Sanders, brother & one of ye executors of ye said Robert," 11 March 1718 [26.pdf #22]; see also [26.pdf #143]

Campbell, Elizabeth, "an orphan girl," parents not named, age not stated, "formerly bound to Robert Sanders deceased, is now bound unto Frances Robertson, sister & one of ye executors of ye said Robert," 11 March 1718 [26.pdf #22]

Cane, John, parents not named, age not stated, bound to John Calvin, 11 November 1718 [236.pdf #73]

Capshaw, Francis, "being fourteen yeares of age the thirteenth day of July last past," "bound in Court to his father in law George Diamond," he "to teach him the trade of a cooper," and "at the expiration of his time to give him a good sett of coopers tooles," 9 September 1707 [23.pdf #206]

Capshaw, John, "sonn in law of George Diamond," "being sixteen yeares of age the sixth day of March last past," bound to John Mellor, he "to teach him the trade of a taylor" or "to give him a cow and calfe at the expiration of his time," 9 September 1707 [23.pdf #206]

INDEX TO ORPHANS

Carey, Adam, son of Robert Carey, "aged seaven yeares ye 24th of June next," bound to John Faning, 14 March 1677 [08.pdf #31]

Carey, Robert, son of Robert Carey, "two yeares old July next," bound to John Morris, 14 March 1677 [08.pdf #31]

Carnell, Elizabeth, daughter of Christopher Carnell, deceased, age not stated, bound to John Piper by Last Will and Testament of her father, 25 November 1661 [01.pdf #264]

Carpenter, William, "an orphan lad about eight years old last October," bound to Benjamin Carpenter, he "to put him to school one whole year" and to give him at the expiration of his time "an horse, saddle & bridle," 10 March 1719 [26.pdf #96]

Carrington, Timothy, bound to John Wilkins, March 1717 [Liber G Page 177]

Carver, Ann, parents not named, "nine years old ye twelfth day of May next," bound to Edward Turvey, 14 November 1721 [27.pdf #108]

Carver, John, parents not named, "being eleven years of age ye nineteenth day of September last," "by ye consent of" his father & mother, bound to Richard Barber, he to learn him "ye art of a shipwright," 14 November 1721 [27.pdf #108]

Carver, Richard, parents not named, being "six ye eighth day of May next," "by ye consent of" his father & mother, bound to Richard Barber, he to learn him "ye art of a shipwright," 14 November 1721 [27.pdf #108]

Chapman, Anne, daughter of Robert Chapman deceased and Hester Chapman his relict now intermarryed with Thomas Matthews, bound to William Stone, and Thomas Matthews to "deliver her estate into his hands," 13 June 1721 [27.pdf #74]

Cherrybub, John and William, orphans, twins, (sons of John & Mary Cherrybub of Pyckyawaxon -- ed.) "fourteen years old some time this month," bound to William Harbert, who "promises to bring them up to the trade of shoemakeing," "and at the expiration of their times to give each of them a sett of shoemakers tooles," 13 March 1705 [23.pdf #47]

Chinton, Charity, daughter of Catherine Chinton, "aged four years or thereabouts," bound to Matthew Narrdeena, 11 March 1718 [26.pdf #22]

Clarke, Anne, daughter of Robert Clarke "who is runaway" & Mary Clarke deceased, age not stated, bound to Matthew Stone, 11 January 1676 [07.pdf #96]

Clarke, Anne, orphan daughter of John Clarke deceased, age not stated, ordered by Court, "with ye consent of her mother" to "serve her brother in law William Lambert & her sister his wife," 4 October 1698 [19.pdf #238]; Anne Clarke, orphan, daughter of Conyers Clarke deceased, bound to her brother in law Thomas Perry, 9 November 1703 [22.pdf #144]; see also [22.pdf #130] & [22.pdf #194]

Clarke, Thomas, orphan, son of Conyers Clarke deceased, age not stated, bound to his brother in law Thomas Perry, 9 November 1703 [22.pdf #144]; Thomas Clarke, orphan "of John Clarke and Coniers his wife," [22.pdf #163]; see also [22.pdf #130] & [22.pdf #194]

INDEX TO ORPHANS

Clarke, Beteres, daughter of Robert Clarke "who is runaway" & Mary Clarke deceased, age not stated, bound to Richard Midgeley, 11 January 1676 [07.pdf #96]; ordered by Court "that John Hanson administrator of Richard Midgeley deceased pay unto Rice Wayman ye sume of foure hundred pounds of tobaccoe for ye maintenance of an orphan child of Robert Clarkes," 13 March 1677 [08.pdf #22]; ordered by Court "that Rice Wayman have one thousand pounds of tobaccoe allowed him out of the County Levy this yeare for ye maintenance of Veteres Clarke an orphan child of Robert Clarke," 12 June 1677 [08.pdf #37]; Veteres Clarke, daughter of Robert Clarke deceased, "now adjudged to be five yeares of age," bound to Rice Wayman, 12 March 1678 [08.pdf #73]

Clarke, John, orphan son of John Clarke deceased, age not stated, ordered by Court, "with ye consent of his mother" to serve Ralph Shaw "untill hee arrive to ye age of eighteene yeares," 4 October 1698 [19.pdf #238]; John Clarke, son of Coniers Clarke widdow, "upon ye faire promises of Ralph Shaw to bee in the stead of a father to your petitioners sonne John Clarke and to keep him at schoole your petitioner was consenting to putt her said son to the said Ralph, but soe it is that the said Ralph doth not use him as a son but a servant or rather a white Negro clothing him in such things as Negroes are usually clothed and puting him under an over seer to make tobacco and corne instead of goeing to schoole, therefore she prays that her said son may be returned to her," ordered by Court "that the said Ralph Shaw returne the said John Clarke to his said mother," 2 March 1700 [20.pdf #194]; " order confirmed" at [21.pdf #9] & [23.pdf #305]

Clarke, Mary, daughter of Robert Clarke "who is runaway" & Mary Clarke deceased, age not stated, bound to Henry Hawkins, 11 January 1676 [07.pdf #96]

Clarke, Robert, son of Robert Clarke "who is runaway" & Mary Clarke deceased, age not stated, bound to John Allward, 11 January 1676 [07.pdf #96]

Clarke, Sarah, orphan daughter of John Clarke deceased, age not stated, ordered by Court "with ye consent of her mother" to serve Cleborne Lomax, 4 October 1698 [19.pdf #238]

Clarke, Susanna, daughter of Robert Clarke "who is runaway" & Mary Clarke deceased, age not stated, bound to Robert Thompson, 11 January 1676 [07.pdf #96]

Cockburn, John, parents not named, age not stated, "complaineth against William Barton planter that he hath not complyed with an agreement between them for teaching him the trade of a cooper," 9 November 1708 [23.pdf #279]

Collier, William, orphan, brother to Giles Collier deceased, "he being sixteen yeares of age some time in May last past," bound to Matthew Barnes, he "to teach him the trade of a cooper to give him one whole yeares schooleing," 15 June 1709 [23.pdf #305]; William Collier petitions "that about five years since he was bound to one Mathew Barnes, who was to give him one year's schooling & to learn him the trade of a cooper and deliver him the said William when at age several cattle & one horse all which the said Mathew doth refuse & deny," ordered by Court "that the said William

INDEX TO ORPHANS

Collier take nothing by his petition" "and that the said Mathew recover against ye said William his cost & charges," 8 June 1714 [25.pdf #222]

Cone, Benjamin, son of Elizabeth Cone, "being seaven yeares old the seaventeenth day of September next," bound to William Watts, 8 August 1704 [23.pdf #20]

Connor, Joseph, "now about four years of age," son of John Connor and his wife Margaret formerly the wife of James Yates now "intermarryed with one James Waters," bound to Robert Yates, 12 November 1717 [26.pdf # 17]

Cooksey, Thomas, son of Philip Cooksey deceased, "being nine yeares of age in August next coming," bound to Richard Eastop, "ye desire of his mother on her death bed," 19 April 1698 [19.pdf #207]

Corner, Job, son of Gilbard Corner deceased, "aged eleven yeares June next," bound to John Morris, 14 March 1677 [08.pdf #31]

Cornish, Elizabeth, bound to James Gray, March 1717 [Liber G Page 174]; Elizabeth Cornish, "ordered out of the custody" of James Gray, bound to Thomas Allinson, 14 March 1721 [27.pdf #44]

Cornish, John, bound to James Gray, March 1717 [Liber G Page 174]; John Cornish, "ordered out of the custody" of James Gray, bound to William Stone Junr., 14 March 1721 [27.pdf #44]

Cornish, Richard, bound to James Gray, March 1717 [Liber G Page 174]; Richard Cornish, "ordered out of the custody" of James Gray, bound to Richard Price, 14 March 1721 [27.pdf #44]

Courts, Anne, daughter of Coll. John Courts deceased, "being a minor still and according to the purport of Coll. John Courts's will lately placed with Mr. James Keech deceased and since with James Keech Junr. hath there been verry ill entreated by those her relations being exposed to the drudgery of the house beaten and abused by their daughter, and verry ill provided for not onely by the want of necessary apparrell; butt what is irretrievable not the least care taken of her education," (ref. letter from William Bladen Esqr., Annapolis, 30 August 1708), "upon reading of the letter aforesaid John, Anne and Charity Courts, orphants of Collonell John Courts deceased, cometh into Court and choose Maddam Mary Contee for their guardian," 9 November 1708 [23.pdf #279]

Courts, Charity, daughter of Coll. John Courts deceased, age not stated, makes choice of Maddam Mary Contee for her guardian, 9 November 1708 [23.pdf #279] (see above); identified as Charity Smallwood,. 13 June 1710 [23.pdf #401]

Courts, Charles, age not stated, son of Coll. John Courts deceased, the Grand Jury "presents Mary Hemsley wife of Philemon Hemsley late called Mary Contee widdow for not maintayning Charles Courts nor educateing him according to his Estate," "ordered by Court "that a summons be issued for Philemon Hemsley and Mary his wife" "concerning the waste of the land belonging to ye orphans of Coll. John Courts deceased," 13 November 1711 [25.pdf #15]

INDEX TO ORPHANS

Courts, John, "an hopefull youth about seaventeen years of age," with his three siblings "att Collonell Contees late dwelling house with Maddam Mary Contee his widdow and executrix where they are taken care of and well provided not only for victualls and cloathing, butt allsoe in respect to their education," 9 November 1708 [23.pdf #279]; John Courts, "eldest son of Coll. John Courts deceased," "makes choice of Coll. Phillip Hoskins" as his guardian, 13 November 1711 [25.pdf #15]

Crompton, Francis, parents not named, "petitions the Court for his freedom from Mrs. Elizabeth Hawkins alledgeing that he is full one and twenty yeares of age," 13 August 1706 [23.pdf #139]; "Mrs. Elizabeth Hawkins produceing an Indenture which made mannifest to the Court that the said Francis Crompton is not of full age untill the eighth day of October next," ordered to "returne to Mrs. Hawkins's service," 10 September 1706 [23.pdf #141]

Danson (?), James, "nine years of age the fifteenth instant," son in law of Thomas Bramhall, bound to Richard Estes (?), 11 November 1712 [25,pdf #110]

Darby, William, parents not named, master not stated, "arived to age of one and twenty years," "by the Deposition of Elizabeth Neale and William Compton," ordered by Court "that he be free and discharged from service," 13 November 1711 [25.pdf #16]

Dawson, Anne, daughter of Matthias Dawson deceased, "being four yeares of age ye twenty sixth (?) day of September next ensueing," ordered to serve Samuel Luckett, "with ye consent of John Dawson her grandfather," and "ye said Samuell Lucketts wife to learne ye said Anne Dawson to reade & sowe," 13 June 1699 [20.pdf #69]

Dawson, Jane, orphan, parents not named, "about the age of twelve yeares old," according to petition of George Dymond, "a near relation," she was "by her grandfather John Dawson bound unto John Bowling as an orphant and being troubled with a sore or scald head the said Bowling will neither endeavour to cure nor imploy none that can do it," bound to Thomas Plunckett, who "promises to give her a cow and calfe at the expiration of her time," 12 June 1705 [23.pdf #80]

Dawson, Mary, ye orphan daughter of John & Anne Dawson deceased, ordered by Court to serve James Fox, 4 October 1698 [19.pdf #238]

Dearman, not named, orphan of John Dearman, age not stated, in custody of Mullinax Ratclife, ordered by Court to deliver the orphan child "to ye Vestry of Nanjemy parish in this County, ye said Vestry making him reasonable satisfaction for his care & trouble in looking after ye said orphan child," 14 June 1698 [19.pdf #221]

Dent, Elizabeth, daughter of Major William Dent (deceased -- ed.), "being of lawfull age shee choiceth (sic) for her guardian her brother George Dent," 12 June 1711 [24.pdf #97]

Deveau, James, son of Joane Deveau, "bound by his said mother to Charles (torn) nes of Benedict Leonard Hundred," 10 March 1713 [25.pdf #120]

INDEX TO ORPHANS

Deveau, Margret, daughter to Joane Deveau, "being six years old the fifth day of November next," "by her said mother is bound unto Robert Robinson," 10 March 1713 [25.pdf #120]

Dewell, Thomas, son of John & Mary Dewell, "being two years old the tenth of March next," bound to John Mellor "untill he shall arrive to nineteen yeares of age," 12 November 1706 [23.pdf #152]

Dickason, Jeremiah, parents not named, age not stated, "bound to Capt. Francis Harrison till he arrives to ye age of twenty," he "to learne the trade of a cooper," 12 August 1707 [23.pdf #210]

Dickason, Thomas, son of Jeremy Dickason, age not stated, "doth in Courte choose John Cable to be his Guardian," 13 August 1678 [09.pdf #16]

Discorah, Thomas, son of Martin & Dorothy Discorah, age not stated, bound to Henry Hardy, 14 August 1677 [09.pdf #79]

Doughaley, Robert, "borne at Nanjemy June ye twenty first Anno Domini 1695," son of Grace Mackdonnel, who "acknowledges in Court that she is freely willing to bind her said sonn to Randolph Garland his wife and Elizabeth his now living daughter," and the said Randall promises here in Court to give to the said Robertt at the expiration of his time one good rideing horse upon which termes he is bound," 9 January 1700 [20.pdf #131]

Douglass, Thomas, son of Robert Douglass deceased, petition of John Compton Junr., ordered by Court "to returne into the said John Comptons service," 9 March 1708 [23.pdf #136]; Thomas Douglass, bound to John Chandler with "the consent of Thomas Douglass," he "to learne the trade of a tanner and shoomaker," 10 August 1708 [23.pdf #266]

Dove, Joseph, son of Mary Dove, "about two years old," bound to James Allen son of Catherine Allen, he "to give ye said minor a year's schooling," 8 March 1720 [26.pdf #161].

Dowell, Elizabeth, "an infant," parents not named, bound to John Suttel, "and because being young and freindless he is to be allowed in the Leavey next one thousand pounds of tobacco," 10 November 1713 [25.pdf #181]

Dowell, John, parents not named, "about seven years of age next Christmas," bound to John Miller his Godfather, 11 November 1712 [25.pdf #110]

Downes, ____, "orphans of Robert Downes" deceased, ages not stated, "ordered by ye Courte that Philip Lines take" them "into his custody," 14 August 1678 [09.pdf #39]

Downes, Elizabeth, daughter of Robert Downes deceased, "being ten yeares of age Aprill last past," bound to John Wright, 10 September 1678 [09.pdf #40]

Dowman, Thomas, ye son of Thomas & Anne Dowman deceased, age not stated, ordered to serve Francis Harris, 10 January 1699 [20.pdf #261]

Doy, John, "an orphan," parents not named, age not stated, bound to Mark Penn, he "to learn him the art & mastery of a blacksmith" 8 August 1721 [27.pdf #91]

Doyne, Mary, orphan, daughter of Robert Doyne deceased & Anne Doyne who married George Plater, "being past ye age of fourteene yeares," "doth here

INDEX TO ORPHANS

in Court make choice of William Dent & William Stone to be her guardians," 14 September 1697 [19.pdf #151]

Doyne, Wharton, orphan son of Robert Doyne deceased, ordered that a summons be issued to George Plater & Anne his wife ye executrix of ye last will & testament of Robert Doyne deceased to consider whether Wharton Doyne "be educated & maintained according to" his estate, "and whether ye estate belonging to" ye said orphan "bee in good & sufficient hands," 14 June 1692 [Liber Q Page 55]

Doyne, William, orphan son of Robert Doyne deceased, ordered that a summons be issued to George Plater & Anne his wife ye executrix of ye last will & testament of Robert Doyne deceased to consider whether William Doyne "be educated & maintained according to" his estate, "and whether ye estate belonging to" ye said orphan "bee in good & sufficient hands," 14 June 1692 [Liber Q Page 55]

Duglas, Charles, son of Coll. John Duglas deceased, age not stated, "did choose Major Ninian Beale of Calvert County for his guardian," 13 January 1691 [17.pdf #89]

Dunkin, Nimrod, orphan, son of John Dunkin, "being seaven yeares of age February last past," petition of Elizabeth Collier, "whereas John Dunkin formerly an inhabitant of this County runnaway and left his wife and child destitute of any manner of help or releif, whereupon Giles Collier late of this County deceased being brother to ye distressed woman tooke compassion of the said woman and child which he kept dureing the mothers life and the child surviving the mother," and did "at the time of his death request" his wife "to continue her kindness to the said child," bound to Elizabeth Collier, 14 June 1709 [23.pdf #305]; Nimrod Dunkin, "an orphan child," "he being nine years of age last March," bound to John Sanders, he "to learn the trade of cooper and carpenter," 12 June 1711 [24.pdf #96]

Eaty, not named, orphan of Nathaniell Eaty, age not stated, bound to Elizabeth Eaty, being "a former wife," 10 April 1705 [23.pdf #63]

Edwards, Jane, daughter of Humphrey Edwards, age not stated, bound to Richard Hes (?), with consent of father, 13 March 1688 [14.pdf #176]

Elliot, John, "an orphan child about four years old," parents not named, bound to Pidgeon Boye, 8 August 1721 [27.pdf #91]

Elliot, Teresa, "an orphan girl about fourteen years of age," parents not named, bound to Pidgeon Boye, 8 August 1721 [27.pdf #91]

Elms, John, "bound unto William Card," August 1716 [Liber G Page 140]

Empson, Mary, daughter of William & Mary Empson, age not stated, bound to Thomas Baker, 1 April 1661 [01.pdf #153]

Evans, Margarett, parents not named, "one yeare old," bound to Thomas Wheeler, 12 August 1701 [21.pdf #136]

Evans, William, parents not named, "adjudged to bee five yeares of age," bound to Thomas Wheeler, 12 August 1701 [21.pdf #136]

Fanning, Benoni, orphan son of John Fanning, age not stated, "came here into Court and made choice of Thomas Whichaley for his guardian" 9 June 1696

INDEX TO ORPHANS

[19.pdf #20]; Benoni Fanning, orphan, "proveing himselfe att age by his fathers Will," ordered by Court "that he be discharged from his guardian" Thomas Whichaley, "and his Estate to be delivered to him," 12 March 1700 [20.pdf #177]; see also [21.pdf #10] & [21.pdf #148]

Fanning, John, orphan, parents not named, age not stated, "under the care of John Philips," inventory of "a plantation belonging unto" the said orphan, 21 April 1721 [Liber H Page 442]

Farrell, Joseph, son of Mary Farrell, age not stated, bound to Leonard Wheeler, by indenture, 17 May 1721 [Liber H Page 452]

Fearneley, John, son of Francis Fearneley deceased, age not stated, bound to Francis Wyne, 11 September 1677 [08.pdf #47]

Fish, Elinor, parents not named, "three years of age," bound to Seabright Maycocke, 10 November 1674 [07.pdf #19]

Fitzgerald, James, son of Alice Fitzgerald, age not stated, "formerly bound to Thomas Hussey," ordered that "Alice Fitzgerald hath her sonn delivered to her upon condition that shee pay the Executors of Mr. Luckett five hundred pounds of tobacco for bringing up of her sonn hitherto," 8 June 1708 [23.pdf #254]

Fitzgerrald, Mary, orphan, parents not named, "about three yeares old," bound to Benjamin Burgess, 9 March 1708 [23.pdf #236]

Fitz Gerralds, Elizabeth, ye orphan daughter of Edward & Margarett Fitz Gerralds deceased, "shee being three yeares of age ye last day of Aprill last past," ordered by Court to "serve Thomas Dison & his wife shee being ye said orphans Godmother," 9 August 1698 [19.pdf #231]

Ford, Thomas, son of Christopher Ford, "being tenn years old the 29th of this month," bound to William Stone Senr., he "promiseing to give him one yeares schooling more and to teach him the trade of a tanner and shoemaker," 8 March 1709 [23.pdf #300]

Fountain, Thomas, "a Mollottoe," "he being six yeares old in May next," "formerly bought of William and Mary Vestry by Mrs. Land and given to her daughter Pennellope Douglass is bound to Joseph Douglass," 14 March 1704 [22.pdf #163]

Fowke, Hallilujah, orphan of Richard Fowke deceased, age 15, bound to Henry Hardy, 8 June 1686 [13.pdf #117]

Fowke, Richard, orphan of Richard Fowke deceased, age 18, ordered to "returne to Henry Hardy & remaine with him," 8 June 1686 [13.pdf #117]; Richard Fowke, orphan of Richard Fowke deceased, "is become of ye full age of one & twenty years, ordered that ye said Richard Fowke goe free from ye service of Henry Hardy," 13 March 1688 [14.pdf #175]

Frankham, Henry, son of Henry Frankham deceased, age not stated, guardian not stated, 12 June 1683 [11.pdf #122]

Frankling, John, "an orphan about fifteen years of age next August," bound to Lawrence Moss and wife, 13 March 1722 [27.pdf #125]

Frawner, Edward, orphan son of Edward & Elinor Frawner deceased, "hee being now about twelve yeares of age," ordered to serve Cleborne Lomax, 4 October 1698 [19.pdf #238]; see also [22.pdf #31] [22.pdf #40] & [22.pdf #71]

INDEX TO ORPHANS

Frawner, Elinor, orphan daughter of Edward & Elinor Frawner deceased, "shee being now about ten yeares of age," ordered by Court to serve John Allwood, 4 October 1698 [19.pdf #238]

Frawner, Elizabeth, orphan daughter of Edward & Elinor Frawner deceased, "shee being thirteene yeares of age ye seaventeenth day of this instant October," ordered by Court to serve William Stone, 4 October 1698 [19.pdf #238]

Frawner, Mary, orphan daughter of Edward & Elinor Frawner deceased, "shee being now about seaven yeares of age," ordered by Court to serve Thomas Chapman, 4 October 1698 [19.pdf #238]

Fugett, John, son of Peter Fugett, age not stated, "bound by his father to Edward Philpott deceased, ref. petition dated 11 August 1719 [26.pdf #123]

Furnash, Elizabeth, parents not named, age not stated, bound to Francis Harrison, 13 November 1685 [13.pdf #46]

Gardainer, Edward, orphan, son of Hugh and Mary Gardainer deceased, "leaveing me about seaven or eight yeares of age," and your petitioner is now "about nineteen yeares of age," and hath lived "until this present" with Henry Gifford who "hath neither given your petitioner learning nor trade," asks to "binde himself out to a trade and that he may choose his trade and master," ordered to "returne to the said Henry Giffords service untill he shall arrive to the full age of twenty one years," 30 January 1705 [23.pdf #41]

Garland, Mary, age not stated, daughter of Randolph Garland deceased, who "by his Last Will & Testament in writing did appoint" Thomas Gant, "guardian to his daughter," bound to Thomas Gant, 13 November 1722 [28.pdf #7]

Garrett, Charles, son of Joyce Garrett, age not stated, "acknowledges himselfe bound to John Fendall according to Indenture dated the tenth day of August 1700," 12 November 1700 [21.pdf #52]; see also [22.pdf #104]; "Charles Garrett Senr. petitions ye Court here for his sonne Charles Garrett Junr. whome his wife Joyce Garrett during his absence had bound apprentice to Mr. John Fendall," and "it appearing that ye said Mr. Fendall has no way abused him and promiseing to keep him to his trades" of a carpenter & cooper, ordered to "remaine with ye said Mr. John Fendall ye remainder of his time in ye said Indenture," 14 September 1703 [22.pdf #130]

Garrett, James, son of James Garrett deceased, "hee being now seaven yeares of age," bound to Thomas Clipsham, 8 June 1680 [09.pdf #167]; see also [18.pdf #78]

Gates, John, son of Catherine Ellory, "being six years old next April," bound to William Coody, 8 March 1715 [25.pdf #266]; John Gates, "an orphan formerly bound to William Coody is by the Court here now bound unto James Ellery," 13 March 1722 [27.pdf #125]

Ges, Lewis, son of Ane Ges, widow of Walker Ges, "being about three years old," bound to Henry Addames, 28 January 1662 [01.pdf #192]

Gillroy, Catherine, daughter of Richard Gillroy deceased, age not stated, bound to James Thompson, 8 September 1696 [19.pdf #56]; the Grand Jurors "by ye information of William Thomas & Peter Mackmillian upon their oath doe present James Thompson for not keeping & maintaineing orphan child

INDEX TO ORPHANS

named Catherine Gillroy in his custody but sufferring her to want for lookeing after as she ought to bee," 14 June 1698 [19.pdf #219]; ordered by Court "that ye said James Thompson deliver Catherine Gillroy to Joseph Harrison," "if ye said Joseph Harrison doth like ye said orphan & thinke fitt to take her into his care & custody 4 October 1698 [19.pdf #239]

Glusse, John, son of George Glusse, age not stated, bound to Owen Jones, 8 January 1667 [03.pdf #157]

Godfrey, George, parents not named, age not stated, "makes choice of his brother William Godfrey" as his guardian, 14 August 1722 [27.pdf #177]

Gouldring, William, son of Jane Gouldring alias Woodard, "being four yeares of age some time in July last past," bound to John Godshall, 8 August 1704 [23.pdf #21]

Gray, William, "a minor orphan," parents not named, "he being thirteen years of age," "chooses his brother Richard Gray" as his guardian, who promises "to give his minor brother one years schooling," 12 November 1717 [26.pdf #3]; William Gray, "under the guardianship of Richard Gray," makes choice of Philip Dove" as his guardian, 14 March 1721 [27.pdf #43]

Griggs, not named, orphan children of George Griggs and wife deceased, ordered by Court that Benjamin Hall "take care of the said children and make returne thereof next Court," 11 March 1701 [21.pdf #93]

Griggs, George, son of George Griggs deceased, "being now about nine yeares and a halfe old," bound to Phillip Cropper, "by recommendation of Mr. Benjamin Hall," and "the said Phillip ingages to give the said George one whole yeare and a halfe schooleing and at the expiration to give him the said George one young cow with a calfe by her side," 1 April 1701 [21.pdf #108]

Griggs, John, son of George Griggs deceased, "four yeares old," bound to John Dent Junior, "Mr. Dent promises to learne the boy to read," 1 April 1701 [21.pdf #108]

Griggs, Mary, daughter of George Griggs deceased, "twelve yeares old," bound to John Dent Junior, 1 April 1701 [21.pdf #108]

Groves, Mary, orphan, parents not named, "aged about eleven years," bound to John Gwinn, 9 March 1714 [25.pdf #198]; "John Guinn guardian of the orphan children of George Groves Junr. deceased," 8 June 1714 [25.pdf #220]

Groves, Mathew, orphan, parents not named, aged "about seven years," bound to John Gwinn, 9 March 1714 [25.pdf #198]; "John Guinn guardian of the orphan children of George Groves Junr. deceased," 8 June 1714 [25.pdf #220]

Grumbold, Anne, daughter of Eshter Grumbold, age not stated, bound to William Middleton, "whereas ye said minor girl now has two cows & calves belonging to her which are delivered to ye said William, he thereon obliges himself to redeliver to ye said Anne when she arrives to age so many cattle of like age sexes & value," 11 March 1718 [26.pdf #21]

Gwinn, Ralph, son of Ralph Gwinn planter, "aged six years the last day of May last past," bound by his said father to Ralph Shaw Junr., "to be instructed to write read and cast accompts," 12 June 1711 [24.pdf #96]

INDEX TO ORPHANS

Haden, Grace, "an orphan girl about ten years of age," parents not named, bound to Philip Dove, 8 November 1720 [27.pdf #31]

Haden, John, "an orphan boy about five years of age," parents not named, bound to Stephen Mankin, 8 November 1720 [27.pdf #31]

Haden, Thomas, "an orphan boy about sixteen years of age," parents not named, bound to Richard Chapman, 8 November 1720 [27.pdf #31]

Hagard, John, parents not named, "now fifteen yeares of age," presented by Susannah Greening, bound to Martha Goosey 10 November 1702 [22.pdf #63]

Hague, Jane, orphan, son of John & Elizabeth Hague deceased, age not stated, ordered by Court to remain during his minority with Joseph Harrison & Valinda his wife, 10 November 1719 [26.pdf #141]

Hague, John, orphan, son of John & Elizabeth Hague deceased, age not stated, ordered by Court to remain during his minority with Joseph Harrison & Valinda his wife, 10 November 1719 [26.pdf #141]

Hague, Mary, orphan, daughter of John & Elizabeth Hague deceased, age not stated, ordered by Court to remain during her minority with Joseph Harrison & Valinda his wife, 10 November 1719 [26.pdf #141]

Hall, John, "an orphan," parents not named, age not stated, bound to John Penn, 8 June 1714 [25.pdf #219]

Hall, Susan, bound to John Gray, March 1717 [Liber G Page 174]

Hamilton, John, son of John Hamilton deceased, age not stated, "made choice of Mr. Gerrard Fowke to be his guardian," 14 September 1697 [19.pdf #151]

Hamilton, John, "an orphan child," parents not named, age not stated, ordered by Court "to continue under the care and tuition of ye worshippfull Joseph Harrison and Valinda his wife, 10 November 1719 [26.pdf #141]

Hanby, John, son of Francis Hanby "which he had by Elizabeth Hazleton," "hee ye said John Hanby being one yeare old ye tenth day of February last past," bound to Edward Millsteade, 8 March 1692 [17.pdf #209]

Haream (?), Eleanor, bound to John Glasson, March 1716 [Liber G Page 47]

Haream (?), Thomas, bound to John Glasson, March 1716 [Liber G Page 47]

Harguess, Sarah, daughter of Isabell Harguess, "shee being six yeares old the twelfth day of this November," bound to John Baker, "the said Isabell gives her reasons to the Court for her soe doeing, that shee is not able to maintain her, her father being absconded or runn away," 10 November 1702 [22.pdf #63]

Harguiss, Eleanor, daughter of Mary Nally, age not stated, bound to "John Roby Senr. & Sarah his wife," 14 November 1721 [27.pdf #108]

Harmon, Francis, female, parents not named, "arrived to the age of sixteen years the nine and twentieth day of last January," "but is held as a servant by Mrs. Elizabeth Hawkins who will not lett me goe free butt keep me as a servant and saith by vertue of an Indenture from my deceased mother" "for a longer tyme" than "according to act of assembly," ordered by Court "that shee be free and discharged from the said Elizabeth Hawkins according to petition," 13 March 1711 [24.pdf #60]

INDEX TO ORPHANS

Harris, Susanna, daughter of Richard Harris deceased, age not stated, "doth in open Court choose William Browne & Mary his wife to be her guardians," 10 August 1680 [09.pdf #182]

Harrison, Benjamin, son of Richard Harrison deceased, age not stated, bound to his brother Joseph Harrison, 12 June 1711 [24.pdf #96]; "nothwithstanding which order the said Benjamin is desirous of continueing with his mother who married with Stephen Evans," ordered by Court "that the said Joseph doe deliver the said Benjamin to his mother," 12 June 1711 [24.pdf #97]

Harrison, Martha, orphan, parents not named, age not stated, bound to Joseph Cornell, 10 January 1688 [14.pdf #173]

Harrison, Richard, son of Richard Harrison deceased, "being now tenne yeares of age," bound to Obadiah Dun "of St. Maries County," "hee teaching him ye art & imployment of a carpenter," 11 January 1681 [10.pdf #46]

Harrison, Sarah, daughter of Benjamin Harrison, "shee being now foure yeares old," bound to Michael Martin, 8 June 1703 [22.pdf #105]

Hatch, Sarah, daughter of William Hatch, age not stated, bound to William Hawton with consent of father, 21 December 1686 [14.pdf #12]

Hawton, William, parents not named, "a minor," ordered by Court "that he remaine with the widow Yates," 9 March 1714 [25.pdf #198]

Hayes, not named, orphan, daughter of James Hayes, age not stated, ordered by Court "that Charles Jones doe keep" her "according to the fathers agreement for one whole yeare," 11 January 1709 [23.pdfd #293]

Hayward, John, son of Phillis Hayward, age not stated, bound to William Barton, 12 January 1669 [Vol. 60:180]

Hedges, Ralph, "a minor," "he being foure years old the three and twentieth day of October last," bound to John & Susannah Lovell, to receive "two years schooling," 10 November 1713 [25.pdf #181]

Hedges, Thomas, son of Ralph & Mary Hedges, "aged four years ye nineteenth of December next," bound to Charles Jones, he to "give him a cow & calf" "when he shall arrive to ye age of twenty one," 8 August 1721 [27.pdf #92]

Herrickson, Hans, son of Hans & Judith Herrickson deceased, "being now about four yeares of age," bound to Robert Benson, 8 August 1693 [18.pdf #87]

Heyfeild, Elizabeth, orphan, "seaven years of age this month some tyme," bound to John Willson, and at the expiration of her time to receive "one good cow & calfe," 12 June 1711 [24.pdf #93]

Heyfeild, Phillip Crosser, orphan, "two years of age the fourteenth day of last Febuary (sic)," bound to John Willson, 12 June 1711 [24.pdf #93]; Thomas Burch "by his petition setts forth that he is a near relation to a certain orphan named Philip Crosser Heyfeild," and that "John Wilson and his wife are both lately dead and that the said orphan has since their death been misused," bound to Thomas Burch, 13 June 1721 [27.pdf #74]

Hickson, Edward, orphan of Henry Hickson deceased, age not stated, bound to Richard Harrison" "to be taught or instructed in ye art & mistery (sic) of a boatwright, house carpenter or cooper," 14 November 1693 [18.pdf #114]

INDEX TO ORPHANS

Hickson, James, orphan of Henry Hickson, "now 8 yeares of age," bound to James Hinley, 8 June 1686 [13.pdf #117]

Hickson, Edward and James, orphans of Henry Hickson, ordered by Court "that Capt. Philip Hoskins & Mr. Joseph Manninge two of their majestyes Commissioners of this Court doe see & take care to secure ye estate belonging to ye orphans of Henry Hickson late of this County deceased and now in ye hands & possession of Richard True, before ye same be waisted & imbezzled," 8 August 1693 [18.pdf #88]; "wee doe find that there is due to ye two orphans ye value of four cowes & four calves," report dated 24 August 1693, recorded 14 November 1693 [18.pdf #114]

Higgins, Elizabeth, daughter of John Higgins deceased and Ellinor Higgins, upon motion of Thomas Davis her brother in law, "being eleaven yeares old the twenty seaventh day of this month," bound to Joseph Thomas, 11 January 1704 [22.pdf #153]

Higgins, Margarett, daughter of John Higgins deceased and Ellinor Higgins, upon motion of Thomas Davis her brother in law, "seaven yeares old," bound to Joseph Thomas, 11 January 1704 [22.pdf #153]

Higgins, Mary, daughter of John Higgins deceased and Ellinor Higgins, upon motion of Thomas Davis her brother in law, "neare eight yeares old," bound to Joseph Thomas, 11 January 1704 [22.pdf #153]

Higgins, Richard, son of John Higgins deceased and Ellinor Higgins, upon motion of Thomas Davis his brother in law, "tenn yeares old the twenty eighth day of February next," bound to Joseph Thomas, he "promiseing to give the boy two yeares schooling to lear(n)e him to reade and wright," 11 January 1704 [22.pdf #153]; Richard Higgins, bound to George Elgar or Ellgar, who "promises to give him a three yeares old heiffer and to learne him to read and the trade of a taylor," 12 June 1705 [23.pdf #80]

Hill, _____, orphan child of Thomas Hill deceased, age not stated, "ordered by ye Court that John Hamond have ye sume of eight hundred pounds of tobaccoe" for his maintenance, 13 January 1680 [09.pdf #139]

Hill, Giles, orphan, son of Giles Hill deceased, age not stated, bound to Richard Edelin, he "to teach the boyes the trade of a carpenter," 8 January 1706 [23.pdf #111]; Giles Hill, orphan of Giles Hill deceased, bound to Thomas Williams, he at the expiration of his time to give him "a new suite of clothes and a sett of carpenters tooles," 12 March 1706 [23.pdf #115]; Giles "an orphant," bound to Thomas Williams petitioner, "his age and infirmity has rendered him uncapable to instruct him further in his trade," ordered by Court "the orphan discharged from him to be replaced by one more capable," 10 June 1712 [25.pdf #77]; see also [25.pdf #35]; Giles Hill, "a minor," "is bound unto his brother John Hill," he promiseing "to instruct him in ye mistery (sic) or occupacon of a house carpenter," 12 August 1712 [25.pdf #91]

Hill, Henry, "son of Robert and Mary Hill late of Benedict Hundred deceased," "eight yeares of age the last May," bound to Richard Estip, 12 August 1701 [21.pdf #136]

INDEX TO ORPHANS

Hill, John, orphan, son of Giles Hill deceased, age not stated, bound to Richard Edelin, he "to teach the boyes the trade of a carpenter," 8 January 1706 [23.pdf #111]

Hill, Onsley, parents not named, age not stated, bound to John Hamond, 8 January 1684 [11.pdf #186]; Onsley Hill, "an orphan child" of Thomas Hill deceased," the Grand Jurors "doe present John Hamond planter for beateing & abuseing" said orphan child "bound to him ye said John Hamond by this Court," 9 June 1691 [Liber Q Page 28]; by ye Information of Henry Tanner it appeareing to ye Court that ye said orphan was not abused," ordered that ye said Onsley Hill bee & remaine with ye said John Hammond," 11 August 1691 [Liber Q Page 38]

Hill, Philip, "son of Robert and Mary Hill late of Benedict Hundred deceased," "being eleven yeares of age the next September," bound to Richard Estip, 12 August 1701 [21.pdf #136]

Hill, Susannah, daughter of Judeth Hill "late wife of William Hill," age not stated, "in ye hands of" John Butcher, 12 August 1685 [12.pdf #97]

Hill, Susannah, orphan, daughter of Giles Hill deceased, bound to Richard Edelin, he "to endeavour to have the girle cured of the yawes," 8 January 1706 [23.pdf #111]; Susannah Hill, orphan of Giles Hill deceased, bound to Thomas Williams, he "to gett the girl cured," 12 March 1706 [23.pdf #115]

Hill, William, son of Judeth Hill "late wife of William Hill," age not stated, "in ye hands of" John Butcher, 12 August 1685 [12.pdf #97]

Hodgshon, Richard, son of Johannah Hodgshon deceased, age not stated, "made choice of Thomas Jones for his guardian," 19 April 1698 [19.pdf #207]

Holl, Margaret, orphan, age not stated, daughter (?) of John Blee deceased, bound to John Fendall, inventory of "the plantacon of John Blee," 9 October 1721 [Liber H Page 461]

Horton, Adam, son of Joseph Horton, age not stated, bound to Philip Lines, 8 June 1675 [07.pdf #63]

Howard, George, parents not named, "a minor," "makes choice of his brother Thomas Howard" as his guardian, 9 March 1714 [25.pdf #198]

Howard, John, son of Jeremiah & Phillis Mackmire, age not stated, bound to Robert Littlepage, 10 January 1671 [06.pdf #3]

Howard, Thomas, son of Thomas & Mary Howard, "hee being three yeares old the seaventeenth day of July next," bound to Evan Hughs, "with ye consent of his mother," 10 March 1702 [22.pdf #4]; ordered that James Stigeleer render unto Evan Hughs for the use of Thomas Howard, orphan, "three cowes and three calves one feather bed and furniture and one young mare of three yeares old one iron pott two pewter dishes and three plates which to him they oweth and unjustly detaineth," 10 November 1702 [22.pdf #74]

Hungerford, William, son of William Hungerford deceased, age not stated, bound to Robert Rowland, 18 November 1673 [06.pdf #142]

Hutchison, Thomas, "a minor son of Levina Hutchison about thirteen years of age bound unto Thomas Hint planter," 9 June 1713 [25.pdf #144]

INDEX TO ORPHANS

Hyde, Anne, daughter of Anne & Valentine Hill, "wee doe give our willing consent that our child Anne Hyde being aged seaven yeares doe serve Thomas Dixon untill shee bee eighteene yeares of age or ye day of marryage," 3 January 1690 [16.pdf #112]

Jackson, William, "a minor son of Elizabeth Jackson a single woman," "two years of age the thirteenth day of Aprill last, bound by his said mother unto Daniel Macdonald," and "when he comes of age to give him a cow & calfe," 9 June 1713 [25.pdf #144]

Jackson, or Smith, Abigall, daughter of Elizabeth Jackson, age not stated, "a bastard child begott of her body" by John Smith Junr., he allowed by Court "if he thinks fitt to bind out the said Abigall untill shee comes of age," 9 June 1713 [25.pdf #145]

Jenckins, Mary, parents not named, age not stated, "bound out by this Court about tenn yeares since" to Capt. John Bayne, Mrs. Anne Bayne, and Mr. Walter Bayne, 12 August 1707 [23.pdf #201]

Jenkins, Rice, "being left fatherlesse & motherlesse," parents not named, "being now about six yeares of age," bound to Christopher Williamson his Godfather, 12 January 1697 [19.pdf #92]; see also [23.pdf #305]; Rice Jenkins, "an orphan," petitions that the said Williamson "never taught your pettitioner to read, and sold him twice as a servant where he is still detained as such," ordered by Court "that the said Rice Jenkins be free from William Nicholls to whome he was sold by one Joseph Crisman brother in law to the said Rice to whome the said Christopher Williamson first sold him," "whereupon the said Rice makes choice of James Tyre" as his guardian, 14 August 1711 [24.pdf #122]

Jennians, Charles, "an orphan child about fifteen months old," bound to Edward Philpott, 13 November 1722 [28.pdf #7]

Jennians, Ignatius, "a child about six years of age the twenty ninth day of April next, is by consent of his mother bound unto James Mankin," he "to give him a years schooling," 13 March 1722 [27.pdf #125]

Johnson, Daniell, son of Daniell Johnson deceased, "doth in Court choose Thomas Gerrard to be his guardian," 12 June 1677 [08.pdf #37]

Johnson, Diana, daughter of Mary Acton, "aged five years the 25th day of next month," bound to Benjamin Adams, 13 June 1710 [23.pdf #400]

Johnson, Samuell, son of John Johnson deceased, "he being nine yeares old last November," bound to Edward Davis, 12 January 1703 [22.pdf #80]

Jones, Anne, orphan, daughter of Richard Jones deceased, complaint of Philip Lynes, "that Thomas Lyndsey & Jane his wife ye relict & executor of Richard Jones deceased had embezled & waisted ye cheife part of ye estate belonging to" the said orphan, 11 March 1690 & 10 June 1690 [Liber Q Page 9]; Anne Jones, orphan, daughter of Richard Jones deceased & Jane Lyndsey wife of Thomas Lyndsey, bound to Richard Harrison, 9 June 1691 [Liber Q Page 30]; inventory of estate, 14 March 1693 [Liber Q Page 64]

Jones, James, "an orphan of Alice Fitzgerrald formerly bound to Thomas Hussey," age not stated, 9 March 1708 [23.pdf #237]

INDEX TO ORPHANS

Jones, Richard, orphan, son of Richard Jones deceased, complaint of Philip Lynes, "that Thomas Lyndsey & Jane his wife ye relict & executor of Richard Jones deceased had embezled & waisted ye cheife part of ye estate belonging to" the said orphan, 11 March 1690 & 10 June 1690 [Liber Q Page 9]; Richard Jones, orphan, son of Richard Jones deceased & Jane Lyndsey wife of Thomas Lyndsey, bound to Richard Harrison, he "teaching & instructing him in ye occupation & trade of a boatwright & carpenter," 9 June 1691 [Liber Q Page 30]; The Grand Jurors "doe present Richard Harrisson for not teaching Richard Jones ye orphan son of Richard Jones deceased his trade to witt ye art & mistery (sic) of a boate wright & carpenter but doth turne him to common labor at ye axe & howe instead of learning him his trade," 14 June 1692 [Liber Q Page 55]; and ye said Richard Harrisson alledgeing here in Court that hee was soe young & small that as yett he was not fitt to worke at his trade, and ye same allsoe being here in Court testifyed by severall persons," ordered by Court "that ye said Richard Harrisson be discharged from ye aforesaid presentment & be thereof acquite," 9 August 1692 [Liber Q Page 56]; inventory of estate, 14 March 1693 [Liber Q Page 64]

Jones, William, orphan, parents not named, "he being foure years old next January," "being now in ye possession of Francis Gray Senr.," bound to William Sanders "his godfather," he at the expiracion of his tyme "to give him one cow & calfe" and its increase, 12 June 1711 [24.pdf #97]

Jones, William, son of Elizabeth Dance, bound to John & Sina Vincent, they "to give ye lad a year's schooling," 14 June 1720 [26.pdf #172]

Kate or Katherine, "being now of the age of two yeares," daughter of Elizabeth Edelin spinster, "begotten of my body by a Negro slave in Saint Maryes County," and "being poore and needy" "do on my owne free will and consent" bind her "untill she shall arrive to the full age of thirty yeares and one" to "John Nicholls of Charles County and Batheshebah his wife," by Indenture, 26 February 1708 [23.pdf #236]

Kenneday, Margaret, "sister of ye said William about three years of age," parents not named, bound to Peter Herrant, 9 June 1719 [26.pdf #112]

Kenneday, William, "a poor indigent boy about five years of age," parents not named, bound to Peter Herrant, 9 June 1719 [26.pdf #112]

Kersey, Jane, bound to Mary Newman, March 1716 [Liber G Page 48]

Ketten, Charles, son of Mary Ketten, "aged 2 years the eight and twentieth day of May last," bound to John Wood, 9 August 1709 [23.pdf #323]

Key, Job, orphan son of Henry Key deceased, "foure yeares and three weeks old," bound to Thomas Jenckins, 11 June 1700 [21.pdf #10]

Key, Sarah, parents not named, age not stated, bound to Charles Calvert, 11 November 1701 [21.pdf #159]; Sarah Key, "an orphan formerly bound to Mr. Charles Calvert," 11 March 1707 [23.pdf #169]; "being carryed over to Virginia and being brought over againe the Court thinks fitt to remove her and place her with Mr. Ubgatt Reeves," 10 June 1707 [23.pdf #180]; see also [23.pdf #300] & [23.pdf #321]

INDEX TO ORPHANS

Key, Victoria, orphan daughter of Henry Key deceased, "being now eight yeares & seaven months of age," bound to Derby Caine, 11 June 1700 [21.pdf #10]

Key, William, orphan son of Henry Key deceased, "being twelve yeares and a halfe old," bound to Thomas Jenckins, 11 June 1700 [21.pdf #10]

Killingsworth, Anne, "betweene six and seven years of age," bound by her "grandfathers consent" to Mathew Stone, he obleigeing himselfe not to impose upon her "the makeing or trading any tobacco or corne," 11 August 1713 [25.pdf #172]

Killingsworth, Mary, "about three years of age," bound by her "grandfathers consent" to Mathew Stone, he obleigeing himselfe not to impose upon her "the makeing or trading any tobacco or corne," 11 August 1713 [25.pdf #172]

Kite, Edward, son of Anne Kite, "being two yeares old the twenty fourth day of July last past," bound to John Chandler, he "to learne him the trade of a shoe maker" and "at the expiration of his time to sett him out with a sett of shoe makers tooles," 11 November 1707 [23.pdf #221]

Kite, Elizabeth, daughter of Anne Beaumont, "she being five years of age last October," "formerly bound to Josiah Cullan (?) by an Indenture from her mother," "by the assent of the said Josiah is bound to Barton Hungerford," 8 June 1714 [25.pdf #219]

Kite, John, son of Anne Kite, "being four yeares old," bound to Henry Gifford, 8 January 1706 [23.pdf #111]

Knight, John, son of Edward Knight deceased, the Grand Jurors "doe present Thomas Smith planter for deteineing of ye estate of John Knight," 9 June 1691 [Liber Q Page 28]; ordered by Court "that ye said Thomas Smith after hee hath finished his crop surrender & deliver up ye plantation unto ye said Thomas Smith," 11 August 1691 [Liber Q Page 38]

Knowlwater, John, son of John Knowlwater "late of Charles County but now in ye Colony of Virginia," bound to Capt. Henry Hardy, "and ye said Henry Hardy is willing that in case ye said John Knowlwater shall at any time hereafter come & desire to have his son hee is willing to restore & returne him to him again," 10 August 1697 [19.pdf #135]

Laftan, John, orphan son of Robert Laftan deceased, age not stated, under care of Capt. Philip Hoskins till ye next Court and then to bind him out, 9 November 1697 [19.pdf #169]

Lane, John, son of Florence Lane widow, age not stated, bound to Capt. Henry Aspinall, 12 June 1683 [11.pdf #128]; John Lane, son of John Lane deceased, bound to Henry Aspenall deceased "and now in ye possession of Edward Rookewood who married ye relict of ye said Aspenall," ordered by Court that Edward Rookewood doe returne & deliver ye said John Lane unto his mother Florence Lane," 10 June 1690 [Liber Q Page 8]; see also 12 August 1690 [Liber Q Page 12]; John Lane, son of Florence Lane, "petitioning ye Court here for her son John Lanes freeedome from Mr. Henry Hawkins hee being now twenty one yeares of age, whereupon ye Indentures being produced & read here in Court, and ye time for which he was bound to serve by said Indentures being not yett expired," ordered by

INDEX TO ORPHANS

Court "that ye said John Lane apprentice to Mr. Henry Hawkins returne to his said master," 10 August 1697 [19.pdf #136]

Lange, John, parents not named, "aged tenn years the fifteenth day of November last," bound to Thomas Hunt (?), he obleiging himself that the boy "be instructed to read and in ye trade of a shoemaker " and "to pay John Gates for the clothes the said boy now hath," 10 March 1713 [25.pdf #119]

Lange, Robert, parents not named, "aged eight years next September," bound to John Briscoe, he obleiging himself that the boy "be instructed to read," (much here is damaged or illegible -- ed.), and to pay John Gates "his unkle" for the clothes he now hath, 10 March 1713 [25.pdf #119]

Lange, William, parents not named, "a minor fourteen years of age the one and twentieth day of May next," bound to John Briscoe, he obleiging himself that the boy "be instructed to read," (much here is damaged or illegible -- ed.) and to pay John Gates "his unkle" for the clothes he now hath, 10 March 1713 [25.pdf #119]

Langham, Jane, daughter of George Langham, "shee being seaven yeares old the one and twentieth of this month," bound by her father to William Newman and Mary his wife, engaging "in Court that the said Jane Langham shall not be putt to any laborious worke in the ground but only household worke and sempstering" (sic), 14 August 1705 [23.pdf #88]

Lee, not named, "an orphan girl of Roger & Winifred Lee," age not stated, formerly in custody of Thomas Jameson, bound to Benjamin Burgesse her Godfather, 8 March 1720 [26.pdf #160]

Lee, Elias, a minor orphan child of Roger & Winifred Lee, age not stated, "Laurence Adams by his petition shows to ye Court here" that ye said orphan "is now under Thomas Jameson who is a profest Papist," bound to Laurence Adams her Godfather, 8 March 1720 [26.pdf #160]

Lindsey, Edmond, son of Edmond Lindsey deceased, age not stated, bound to William Chandler, 12 March 1678 [08.pdf #73]

Long, John, son of Anne Tanner, "he being two yeares old last April," bound to Mrs. Elizabeth Hawkins, 11 August 1702 [22.pdf #38]

Lylly, Elizabeth, parents not named, "twelve yeare old or thereabout," bound to Peter Carr who "hath in his keeping and has maintained" her "ever since she hath beene borne," 10 September 1672 [06.pdf #86]

Macdonald, Alice, "a malatto girl aged about thirteen years, daughter of Grace Macdonald now dead or removed out of this County," bound to Thomas & Elizabeth Howard, 14 June 1720 [26.pdf #172]

Macklanan, Elizabeth, "a bastard child" of Margrett Macklanan, servant to John Speake, "two years of age next October," bound to John Speake and wife, 14 August 1711 [24.pdf #121]

McLanan, Dorothy, daughter of Margaret McLanan, bound to John Speake, November 1716 [Liber G Page 151]

Macknemillion, Peter, son of George Macknemillion, age not stated, bound to Peter Carr, 10 June 1673 [06.pdf #137]

INDEX TO ORPHANS

Maddox, Benjamin, "a minor," parents not named, age not stated, ordered to "remain under ye custody & care of his father in law Robert Tailor," 14 June 1720 [26.pdf #173]

Maddox, John, son of Mary Taylor, who "complaines against James Smallwood Junr. that he unlawfully deteins her sonne John Maddox from her," ordered by Court that a summons be issued "for the said James Smallwood and John Maddocks to appeare here next Court to answer ye complaint aforesaid," 10 June 1707 [23.pdf #181]; "ordered that Doctor Samuell Berry or whosoever doth detaine John Maddox doe forthwith returne the said John Maddox to his mother Mrs. Mary Taylor," 12 August 1707 [23.pdf #201]

Magrah, Stephen, "an infant seventeen months old," son of Mary Magrah, bound to George Naylor, 13 November 1722 [28.pdf #7]

Mahall, John, son of Ellinor Mahall, "being four yeares old," bound to Bouling Speake, 2 March 1706 [23.pdf #115]

Mande, Jane, "a poor orphan girl aged about tenn years," bound to Coll. John Fendall, 14 June 1720 [26.pdf #173]

Maning, John, son of Edmond Maning, "a minor being tenn years of age the sixteenth day of March last past," bound to William Middleton, "to serve in any lawfull imployment," and at the expiracion of his time "to give him a cow and calf," 3 April 1713 [24.pdf #177]

Mankin, Hope, child of Stephen Mankin deceased, bound to Mr. George Tubman, by mother, 11 November 1701 [21.pdf #160]

Mankin, James, son of Mary Stigaleer alias Mankin, "seaven yeares old," by agreement with his mother, bound to John Semmes and Susanna his wife, they "to give the said James Mankin schooling whereby to read well," 14 January 1702 [21.pdf #174]; James Mankin, "an orphan formerly bound to John Semmes who at that time was in ye Church of England communion but since professing ye Romish Religeon he is by law rendered incapable to retain the said orphan," bound "to his brother Stephen Mankin," "who obligeth himselfe to learn him ye trades & misteries of a cooper & carpenter," 8 June 1714 [25.pdf #220]

Mankin, Josias, "one of ye the orphans of Stephen Mankin deceased," "he being arrived to lawfull age" (of twenty one years -- ed.), ordered by Court that William Thompson "doe pay unto Josias Mankin" "the one third part of twelve hundred and fifty pounds of tobacco and the other two thirds to be by him retayned until ye other two orphans shall arrive at the same age," 11 March 1712 [25.pdf #34]

Mankin, Tubman, child of Stephen Mankin deceased, bound to Mr. George Tubman, by mother, 11 November 1701 [21.pdf #160]; ordered by Court "that Tubman Mankin stay with his present master namely Edward Philpot according to condicions and that ye ulcer or sore in his leg be cured with conveniente speed by his said master," 9 November 1714 [25.pdf #257]

Mannister, Thomas, son of John Mannister who "late of this County hath absented himselfe," "of ye age of one yeare & a halfe," bound to Philip Cole, 14 June 1681 [10.pdf #79]; Thomas Mainster, son of John Mainster

INDEX TO ORPHANS

deceased, age not stated, bound to John Raines, 8 January 1684
[11.pdf #186]; Thomas Mannister, "an orphan child," son of John
Mannister deceased, the Grand Jurors "doe present John Raines of
Mattawoman planter for selling & disposing of" said orphan child "out of
this Province into ye Collony of Virginia," 9 June 1691 [Liber Q Page 27];
ordered by Court "that ye said John Raines keepe ye said orphan child in
his custody and take care to provide for him, and if any further complaint
be made to this Court then ye said orphan to be removed," 11 August 1691
[Liber Q Page 38]; Thomas Mannister, son of John Mannister deceased,
age not stated, formerly bound to John Raines, "with ye consent of ye Court
assigned to Hugh Teares," 12 January 1692 [17.pdf #190]; Thomas
Mannister, son of John Mannister, age not stated, "formerly bound
to John Raines by this Court, and assigned over to Hugh Teares," ordered
by Court "to serve John Linegar, 9 January 1694 [18.pdf #129]

Manwaring, Mary, daughter of Alice Manwaring alias Fittzgerrald, "desires that
her daughter Mary Manwaring may bee bound to Mr. Samuell Luckett,"
"shee being five yeares of age the first of August next," 10 June 1701
[21.pdf #126]; Mary Manwerring, "bound unto John Speake by her
mother Alice Fitzgarrald" "for the terme of three years not yet expired,
comes and prays that shee be sett free being arrived to ye age of sixteen
years," ordered by Court "that the said Mary be free," and because shee did
not doe & compleat her tyme according to ye Indenture," ordered that the
said John Speake "be discharged and acquitt" "from any thing to pay by
means of any clause in that Indenture," 10 June 1712 [25.pdf #77]

Maris, Avi(?)e, daughter of Avi(?)e Maris, "shee being nine yeares of age ye first day
of this instant moneth January," bound to Thomas Dixon, "by & with ye
consent of her mother," 13 January 1680 [09.pdf #139]

Maris, Elizabeth, daughter of Thomas & Alice (?) Maris, "shee being now about
foure yeares of age," bound to John Hanson, 10 August 1680 [09.pdf #182]

Maris, Mary, daughter of Thomas Maris deceased, "being six yeares of age ye 22d
day of October next," bound to John Lomaire, "by & with ye consent of her
mother," 12 August 1679 [09.pdf #110]

Maris, Rebeckah, daughter of Thomas Maris deceased, "being eleaven yeares of age
sometime in January next," bound to George Godfrey, "by & with ye
consent of her mother," 12 August 1679 [09.pdf #110]

Maris, Sarah, daughter of Thomas & Avi(?)e Maris deceased, age not stated, "shall
serve Johannah Hodgson one yeare," 9 November 1680 [10.pdf #33]

Marshall, not named, orphans of William Marshall, ages not stated, John Fendall
petitions "for leave to fall & saw poplar planck on the land of the orphants
of William Marshall in consideration of the charge that hee is at in
maintaining and schooleing of ye said orphants," ordered by Court "that it
cannot be graunted without committing a waste on the said orphants land,
therefore the petition aforesaid is rejected," 10 March 1702 [22.pdf #4]

Massey, Mary, daughter of John Massey, "about six years old," bound to Catherine
Allen, 10 June 1721 [27.pdf #72]

INDEX TO ORPHANS

Mathews, William, "an orphan," parents not named, age not stated, bound to Henry Gifford, 8 June 1714 [25.pdf #219]

Maud, not named, daughter of Susanna Maud, bound to John Blee, August 1715 [Liber G Page 2]

Maud, Jane, "an orphan girl about five years of age," bound to Thomas Reed, 9 August 1720 [27.pdf #13]

Maud, John, servant to William Herbert, "complaineth against his said master that he deteines him a servant he being arrived to the full age of twenty one yeares, it is the opinion of the Court that he is of age the second day of May next," 11 March 1701 [21.pdf #93]

Milstead, William, "son of Edward Milstead begotten on ye bodie of Susannah Clarke by ye said Edward," age not stated, bound to Thomas Craxton "of Nangemie in Charles Countie," 9 November 1686 [13.pdf #120]

Moncaster, Benjamin, twin, son of James & Mary Moncaster, "born on ye eighteenth day of July seventeen hundred & eleven," bound to Martha Barker, 8 June 1714 [25.pdf #219]; Benjamin Moncaster, "an orphan boy," bound to Henry Brett, 10 June 1718 [26.pdf #38]

Moncaster, Elizabeth, daughter of James & Mary Moncaster, born "seventeen hundred & three," "bound to her uncle William Moncaster," 8 June 1714 [25.pdf #219]

Moncaster, James, son of James & Mary Moncaster, "born on ye eleventh day of August seventeen hundred & eight," bound to Henry Brett, 8 June 1714 [25.pdf #219]; James Muncaster, "an orphan formerly bound to Henry Brett is by order of Court here continued under ye tuition of Francis Meeks who marryed ye relict of said Brett," 14 November 1721 [27.pdf #107]

Moncaster, Joseph, twin, son of James & Mary Moncaster, "born on ye eighteenth day of July seventeen hundred & eleven," "bound to his uncle William Moncaster," 8 June 1714 [25.pdf #219]

Moncaster, Ruth, daughter of James & Mary Moncaster, "born on ye sixth day of March seventeen hundred & five," bound to Thomas Wright, 8 June 1714 [25.pdf #219]

Moody, Anne, daughter of William & Jane Moody, "being nine yeares old the twentieth day of March next ensuing," bound to Thomas Davis "of Newport Hundred," 3 December 1700 [21.pdf #57]

Moody, Elisha, son of William & Jane Moody, "being three yeares old the second day of April next," bound to Thomas Davis "of Newport Hundred," 3 December 1700 [21.pdf #57]

Moore, Semore, "an infant male child whose parents are runaway," age not stated, to Martha Barker, "for keeping and mayntayning Semore Moore for two months already past" and "for the insueing yeare," fourteen hundred pounds of tobacco, 13 November 1711 [25.pdf #15]

Morris, Thomas, "his parents being runnaway," age not stated, bound to Robert Robbison, 12 March 1706 [23.pdf #114]

Moucaler, James, parents not named, age not stated, bound to Richard Way, 11 August 1685 [12.pdf #96]

INDEX TO ORPHANS

Moucaler, William, parents not named, age not stated, bound to Richard Way, 11 August 1685 [12.pdf #96]

Mudd, Thomas, son of Thomas Mudd deceased, age not stated, "made choice of Mr. William Boardman Junr. to be his guardian, 11 January 1698 [19.pdf #180]

Murphey, Daniel, "a minor orphan," parents not named, age not stated, "makes choice of Thomas Dyson" as his guardian, 12 November 1717 [26.pdf #3]

Murphey, Edmond, bound to John Fairfax, November 1716 [Liber G Page 150]

Murphey, James, "a minor orphan about tenn years of age last February," parents not named, bound to James Hagan "untill he arrive to ye age of eighteen yeares," "he promises to learn him ye art & mistery (sic) of a cooper," 11 March 1718 [26.pdf #21]

Murphey, John, "a minor orphan about eight years of age," parents not named, bound to James Hagan "untill he arrive to ye age of eighteen years," "he promises to learn him ye art & mistery (sic) of a cooper," 11 March 1718 [26.pdf #21]

Murphey, Joseph, parents not named, "a child being two years old the 15th day of November last," "bound to Mrs. Elizabeth Hawkins, widdow & her heirs and assignes," 25 April 1710 [23.pdf #390]

Musgrave, Jane, "an orphan girl about two years of age," bound to George Carter, 10 March 1719 [26.pdf #96]

Nettle, Grace, daughter of John & Elizabeth Nettle "both deceased," bound to Samuell Robinson, "according to the request of the mother in her petition expressed," 10 June 1701 [21.pdf #126]

Newman, James, "an orphan about seventeen years of age," parents not named, bound to John Eaton, 13 March 1722 [27.pdfr #125]

Nibbs, son of Edward Nibbs, age not stated, bound to John Beane, 10 March 1685 [12.pdf #62]

Nicholls, Benjamin, son of John & Bethsheba Nicholls deceased, "aged fifteen months," "is put under ye care of Thomas Hill," 8 June 1714 [25.pdf #219]; Benjamin Nicholls "a minor orphan being two years of age ye eighth day of March last past," bound to Thomas Hill, 14 June 1715 [25.pdf #271]

Nichols, Jonathan, "an orphan," "being about eleven years of age," bound to Thomas Harris, "to serve untill he arives at ye age of eighteen," "to be instructed to learne the art & trade of a cordwainer," 11 August 1713 [25.pdf #172]

Nichols, Solomon, "an orphan boy," "being three years of age next August," bound to James Boyce "untill he arives to the age of eighteen years being left so by his fathers Will," 9 June 1713 [25.pdf #144]

Nichols, William, orphan, "being seven years of age," bound to John Leverat, "he being left by his fathers Testament to be of age at eighteen years to the said Leverat," 9 June 1713 [25.pdf #144]; "William Nichols petition against John Leveret for schooling rejected," 13 November 1722 [28.pdf #8]

Ocane, Garrat, orphan, son of Garrat Ocane deceased, age not stated, bound to Matthew Dutton (?), inventory of "the plantation of the said orphan," 13 March 1721 [Liber H Page 429]

INDEX TO ORPHANS

Ocane, Gerrard, son of Gerrard Ocane deceased, "aged eleven years or thereabouts," makes choice of John Smoot planter for his guardian, 8 June 1714 [25.pdf #219]; "Gerard Ocane a minor orphan under the care of John Smoot complains of hard usage from his guardian," ordered "that ye said minor on his own choice & election be put under ye care & guardianship of his brother in law Matthew Dutton," 14 June 1720 [26.pdf #173]

Ocane, Lydia, daughter of Gerrard Ocane deceased, "aged thirteen years or thereabouts," makes choice of John Smoot planter for her guardian, 8 June 1714 [25.pdf #219]

Odouhertee, Robert, son of Grace Mackdonnell, "he being four yeares and a halfe old," bound to Randolph Garland, January 1700 [22.pdf #104]

Olavery, William, son of Patrick & Dorothy Olavery, "being estimated to be now eight yeares of age not haveing a register to prove the certainty," bound to Benoni Thomas, obliging himself "to take what cattell belongs to the said child and allso to deliver them in kind," 14 January 1701 [21.pdf #68]

Oliver, John, orphan, parents not named, "being sixteene yeares old," presented by Charles Guy who "desires that hee may be bound to him," ordered by Court that "some time next spring hee is bound accordingly," 9 November 1703 [22.pdf #143]

Palmer, Elizabeth, daughter of Samuell Palmer deceased, age not stated, "ordered by ye Court that Edward Price looke after ye plantation of Elizabeth Palmer," 11 November 1679 [09.pdf #132]

Pattison, John, "seaventeene yeares of age the 15th day of September last past, who binds himselfe with the Courts consent to Joseph Harrison," he "to give the said Pattison one whole yeares schooling," 9 March 1708 [23.pdf #236]

Parry, Susanna, daughter of James Parry, "shee being five yeares of age ye first or second of September next," bound to John Faning, 12 June 1679 [09.pdf #105]

Payne, John, orphan, parents not named, "being about foure yeares of age," bound to Michaell Bromley, he to "give the said boy two whole years schooleing and att ye expiration" of his time "to give him one heifer," 14 March 1710 [23.pdf #372]

Penn, Elizabeth, daughter of William & Mary Penn, "shee being six yeares of age on the second day of June next comming," "according to the request of her elder brother William Penn," "desires that shee may be bound to" Nicholas Wyeth, 31 March 1702 [22.pdf #22]; see also [22.pdf #4]

Penn, John, son of William & Mary Penn deceased, "he being now eighteen yeares of age," bound to "his elder brother William Penn," he "promiseing to enstruct him in the trades of a carpenter and cooper and to provide him with all necessaryes," 31 March 1702 [22.pdf #22]; see also [22.pdf #4]

Penn, Marke, son of William & Mary Penn, "he being tenn yeares of age the fourth day of November next comeing," "according to the request of his elder brother William Penn," "desires that he may be bound to" John Rowland, 31 March 1702 [22.pdf #22]; see also [22.pdf #4]; Marke Penn, presented by William Penn his brother, who "desires that he may be bound

INDEX TO ORPHANS

to Thomas Osborne, he to "learne the said Marke the trade of a blacksmith" and "at the expiration of his time to assist him in the makeing of such tooles as shall be necessary for that trade," 9 March 1708 [23.pdf #235]; named in Last Will and Testament of Doctor Joseph Venour, presented to Court by Leman Hickford, Trustee for Executrix, 13 March 1711 [24.pdf #58]

Penney, Samuell, son of Anne Penney, "being of the age of two yeares July last past," bound to John Blee, by indenture, 22 December 1703 [Liber C Page 82]

Penny, James, parents not named, "being fourteen years of age the fourth day of February last," bound to William Compton, 11 March 1712 [25.pdf #33]

Perkins, William, age not stated, son of John Perkins "runnaway," petition of William Summers "for a maintenance for a child left in his custody," ordered by Court "that if the said William Summers hath made a foolish bargain, they are no wayes oblidged to stand to itt and therefore the petition is rejected," 14 June 1709 [23.pdf #305]; decision reversed 9 August 1709 [23.pdf #321]; William Perkins, "a child about 13 months old is putt to Joane Pegion to nurse" for one year, "ye said childs mother being dead and his father runaway," 9 August 1709 [23.pdf #321]; William Perkins, "a child," petition of John Piggon, ordered by Court "to keep" the child "the next ensueing yeare," 8 August 1710 [23.pdf #408]; William Perkins, "an orphan child three years of age somtyme about the last month," bound to John Piggeon, and at ye expiracion of his time to receive "one cow and calfe" 14 August 1711 [24.pdf #121]

Perry, Penelope, orphan, daughter of Robert & Elizabeth Perry deceased, age not stated, ordered to serve Susanna Dillahay, 10 January 1699 [20.pdf #4]; Penellope Perry, daughter of Robert & Elizabeth Perry, "shee being now by examination ten yeares of age," ordered to serve Richard Robins, "he promiseing to give her a whole yeares schooleing at Nanjemy Schoole he not to pay for the same," 11 March 1701 [21.pdf #91]

Phipps, John, son of Elizabeth Phipps, "being two yeares old," bound to Mullinaux Ratcliffe, he "to give him a three yeares old heiffer when he is free," 12 June 1705 [23.pdf #80]

Pile, Joseph, son of Capt. Joseph Pile deceased, "now arrived to the age of eighteen yeares the time assigned by the Will of the said deceased for him to possess and enjoy his Estate by the Will bequeathed," petition of Anthony Neale, executor, 10 September 1706 [23.pdf #141]

Pope, John, son of Francis Pope deceased, age not stated, "doth here in Court choose William Hinsey to be his Guardian," 15 November 1676 [07.pdf #130]

Pope, John, son of Thomas Pope deceased, age not stated, "Thomas Harris ye guardian," 14 August 1678 [09.pdf #39]

Posey, Humphrey, and Posey, John, servants to Edward Philpott, 1 February 1698, ordered by Court "that ye said Humphrey Posey & John Posey be acquitt & discharged from any service," and "they return to their mother Susanna Austin again," [19.pdf #187]

Price, Edward, parents not named, age not stated, bound to Domindego Agambra, 11 August 1685 [12.pdf #96]

INDEX TO ORPHANS

Price, John, parents not named, age not stated, bound to Thomas Davis, "by the Vestry of Durham Parrish to learne the trade of a taylor," 13 August 1706 [23.pdf #138]; John Price, formerly bound "in order to learne the trade of a tayler desires to be a planter and to live with the said Thomas Davis," 9 March 1708 [23.pdf #237]

Price, Richard, orphan, parents not named, age not stated, ordered to remain with John Booker untill the next Court, 11 September 1705 [23.pdf #100]; see also [23.pdf #89]; Richard Price, "being eighteen yeares old in February next," bound to John Bannister, who promises "to teach him the trade of a carpenter" and "at the expiration of his time to give him a sett of carpenters tooles," 13 November 1705 [23.pdf #104]

Raleigh, John, son of Elizabeth Halloway, bound to Richard Chapman, August 1715 [Liber G Page 3]

Raleigh, Thomas, son of Elizabeth Halloway, bound to Thomas Craxon, August 1715 [Liber G Page 3]

Raleigh, Anne, daughter of Elizabeth Halloway, bound to John Mellor, August 1715 [Liber G Page 3]

Reede, Anne, daughter of William Reede "runaway," age not stated, bound to William Pen, 13 June 1693 [18.pdf #81]

Reeves, William, son of Mary Reeves, "three years old the seventh day of October ensueing," bound to Brutus Russell, 13 November 1711 [25.pdf #16]

Regon, Charles, orphan, parents not named, age not stated, bound to Edward Williams, he "to learn him the said Charles Regon the trade of a cooper (viz.) to make tobacco hogs heads," "and at the expiration" of his time "to give him a sett of coopers tooles," 8 June 1708 [23.pdf #253]

Richardson, Anne, orphan, parents not named, "about three years old," bound to William Bunsun (?), he to give her "a years schooling," 9 June 1713 [25.pdf #144]

Richardson, Joseph, orphan, parents not named, "nine years of age next August," bound to William Bunsun (?), he to give her "a years schooling," 9 June 1713 [25.pdf #144]

Richardson, Mark, bound to Robert St. Clare, March 1716 [Liber G Page 47]

Roberds, Jane, "orphan of William Roberds (who) departed this Province," age not stated, bound to Phillip Mason, 14 June 1687 [14.pdf #141]

Roberts, Mary, orphan, parents not named, bound to Alexander Standidge, "petitioning ye Court here about her freedome," ordered by Court "that if ye said Mary Roberts be sixteene yeares of age that shee bee free," 19 April 1698 [19.pdf #207]

Robertson, Philip, parents not named, "being about twenty six months old," "formerly bound to John Miller," is "bound to Richard Chapman," 9 November 1714 [25.pdf #257]

Robertson, Robert, orphan of Francis Robertson deceased, ordered by Court to continue under ye care of his grandfather & grandmother Matthew & Eleanor Sanders, 9 June 1719 [26.pdf #113]

INDEX TO ORPHANS

Robertson, William, orphan of Francis Robertson deceased, ordered by Court to continue under ye care of his grandfather & grandmother Matthew & Eleanor Sanders, 9 June 1719 [26.pdf #113]

Rodd, Mary, "naturall" daughter of Mary Rodd "spinster," "three yeares old the twenty seaventh day of September last," bound to Thomas Stonestreet, by the mother, by Indenture, 12 June 1705 [23.pdf #79]

Rose, Elizabeth, daughter of Jane Rose, bound to Oliver Birch, June 1716 [Liber G Page 100]

Rose, Nathan, son of Jane Rose, bound to Justinian Birch, June 1716 [Liber G Page 101]

Rozer, Notley, "the orphan son of Coll. Benjamin Rozer deceased," ordered that a summons be issued to Coll. Edward Pye "who married Anne ye relict & administratrix of Coll. Benjamin Rozer deceased" to consider whether Notley Rozer "be educated & maintained according to his estate, and whether ye estate belonging to ye said Notley Rozer bee in good & sufficient hands," 14 June 1692 [Liber Q Page 55]; see also [Liber Q Page 57] & [Liber Q Page 56]

Rue, Temperance, daughter of Elizabeth Rue, "shee being nine yeares old ye fourteenth day of October next ensueing," bound to James Finley, with "free & voluntary consent" of the mother, 8 March 1692 [17.pdf #209]

Russell, Ann, "an orphan," parents not named, "being under age," "makes choice of John Conner" as her guardian, 10 November 1713 [25.pdf #181]

Russell, Mary, parents not named, age not stated, "an orphan living with Richard Coe," upon complaint "of her being missused," ordered "that Mr. Justice Harbert & Mr. Justice Howard inspect and examine into the same and if soe found to be moved and placed elsewhere," 10 November 1713 [25.pdf #182]; Mary Russell, "eleven years of age the fourth day of April last," bound to Henry Gifford, 8 June 1714 [25.pdf #219]

Ruth, Elizabeth, "aged tenn years last October," parents not named, bound to Capt. John Briscoe, 8 June 1714 [25.pdf #219]

Scarry, Edward, "an orphan foure years of age," bound to Benoni Thomas, "he obligeing himselfe to preserve for him ye following things & deliver them when he shall arrive to age -- in his possession already one cow & calfe, one young heifer, one iron pott, one paile, two old plates & two pair pott hangers & 2 hooks -- those things not in his possession butt will endeavour to gett (viz) 3 killable barrows 9 sholls (?) 8 sows, an old rugg & pestel made of ye barrell of a gunn," 11 November 1712 [25.pdf #110]

Scarry, Elias, son of Richard Scarry deceased, age not stated, "desires to be bound unto" John Hamilton "to learne the trade of a carpenter and boatwright," the said Hamilton at the expiration of his time "to give him a sett of tooles both carpenter and boatwright sufficient to build either a boat or house," 9 November 1708 [23.pdf #280]; Elias Scarry, formerly bound unto John Hammilton, "being now dead," is bound to Thomas Perry under the same obligations as the said Hammilton, the trade of a boat wright only excepted," 11 January 1709 [23.pdf #293]; Elias Scary "desires to be

INDEX TO ORPHANS

bound unto Stephen Evans for the remainder of his time, which by consent of Thomas Perry his former master is done," the said Evans obliging himself to the same as his former master, 13 November 1711 [25.pdf #16]; Elias Scarry, "being arived to ye age of one & twenty yeares," ordered by Court "that the said Elias Scarry be free and discharged," "the said Stephen Evans paying him his just rights and dues," 10 June 1712 [25.pdf #77]

Scarry, Margaret, daughter of Richard Scarry deceased, age not stated, bound to Capt. Bennoni Thomas, 8 March 1709 [23.pdf #300]

Scarry, Richard, son of Richard Scarry deceased, age not stated, bound to Joseph Harrison Junr., he "to teach him the trade of a carpenter, and to find him a good sett of tooles att the expiration of his time of servitude," 11 January 1709 [23.pdf #293]; Mr. Joseph Harrison Junr. "returnes an accompt of what cattle belonging to Richard Scarry ye son of Richard Scarry deceased lately bound to him being two cowes two calves and a two yeares old heifer," 14 June 1709 [23.pdf #305]

Scroggin, not named, "orphants of George Scroggin deceased their mother Susannah being lately deceased also," ages not stated, ordered by Court "that Mr. Robert Yates & Capt. Henry Hardy inspect into the premises for to prevent John Lofton or Loftlee their father in law from squandering away what Estate doth properly belong to the said orphants," 11 June 1700 [21.pdf #10]; and to "demand an account and security from John Lofton their father in law that their Estates bee not by him imbezzelled," 13 August 1700 [21.pdf #19]; see Affidavit and Inventory [21.pdf #189]; see also [22.pdf #31] & [22.pdf #41] & [22.pdf #51]

Scroggin, Elizabeth, orphan, daughter of George Scroggin deceased, age not stated, ordered by Court "that Mr. William Herbert "putt hir to any one that will take care about hir and to make returne next Court shee being represented to be in a languishing condition," 13 August 1700 [21.pdf #19]; ordered by Court "that Mr. William Herbert sell and dispose of the cattle of Elizabeth Scroggin in order to pay for the cure of the said Elizabeth being verry farr gone with the distemper," 10 September 1700 [21.pdf #41]

Scroggin, George, orphan, son of George Scroggin deceased, age not stated, bound to Thomas Plunkett, 13 August 1700 [21.pdf #19]

Scroggin, John, orphan "of George Scroggin and Susannah his wife lately deceased," age not stated, petition of Penelope Land, "that John Loftlee alias Lofton who intermarried with the said Susannah Scroggin takes no due care about the said John Scroggin," ordered by Court that "Penelope Land have the said John Scroggin her Godson," she to "give to the said John Scroggin one whole yeares schooleing and use the best of her skill and endeavour for the cure of the said John Scroggins scald head," 11 June 1700 [21.pdf #10]; "John Scroggen sonne of George Scroggen deceased," "being bound to Mrs. Penelope Land widdow deceased," "your petitioner has a cow and a yearling belonging to him the cow the said Mrs. Land killed the yearling dyed in her possession," asks "that your poor petitioner may be righted he being fatherless and motherless," ordered by Court "that a cow and yearling

INDEX TO ORPHANS

be delivered out of the said Mrs. Lands estate and to be marked for the said John Scroggin" and that he serve Walter Storey the remainder of his time, the said Walter Storey to take care to have his scald head cured & to deliver his cattle to him when free," 10 November 1702 [22.pdf #64]

Scroggin, John, son of Elizabeth Dance, bound to John & Sina Vincent, they "to give ye lad a year's schooling," 14 June 1720 [26.pdf #172]

Scroggin, Margaret, orphan, daughter of George Scroggin deceased, age not stated, "to be referred till next Court," "William Summerton and Margarett his wife who is her Godmother hath refused her," 13 August 1700 [21.pdf #19]

Scroggin, Mary, orphan, daughter of George Scroggin deceased, age not stated, bound to George Bateman, 13 August 1700 [11.pdf #19]

Scroggin, Susannah, orphan, daughter of George Scroggin deceased, age not stated, bound to William Nicholls, 13 August 1700 [11.pdf #19]

Semmes, Marmaduke, "being sixteen years of age next November," "of his owne free and voluntary will here in Court make choice of his mother in law Dosebella Semmes for his gaurdian," she "to give to ye said boy att ye end of (his) tyme one cow and calve and one sow and piggs," 25 April 1710 [23.pdf #390]

Sennet, Elizabeth, daughter of Gerrard Sennet deceased, "being six years of age the last day of August next," bound to William & Mary Newman, they "to instruct her to read and sew and other housewifery," 12 June 1711 [24.pdf #96]

Sharman, Bead, orphan, "five years of age the first of November next," bound to John Cooper, 11 August 1713 [25.pdf #171]

Shareman, Elizabeth, orphan, "eight years of age the eighteenth day of October next," bound to John Cooper, 11 August 1713 [25.pdf #171]

Shoreman, John, parents not named, age not stated, bound to Richard Way, 11 August 1685 [12.pdf #96]

Skeenes, Anne, daughter of Susanna Skeenes, bound to Randoll Brandt, if he "bee willing to keepe the said Ann without impairing her Estate," 11 June 1701 [19.pdf #126]

Skeens, Rachel, parents not named, "shee being eight yeares old sometime in October or November next," bound to Mrs. Lidia Hawton or Hatton, 8 June 1703 [22.pdf #105]

Skidmore, John, son of Nicholas Skidmore deceased, "being eight yeares old ye last September," bound to Doctor John Harrison his Godfather, 13 November 1694 [18.pdf #229]

Skidmore, Nicholas, son of Nicholas Skidmore deceased, age not stated, bound to Hugh Teares, he to teach or instruct ye said Nicholas Skidmore "in ye art & mistery (sic) of a house carpenter," "unlesse to help & assist in makeing a crop of corne yearely," 13 November 1694 [18.pdf #229]

Skidmore, Raiph, youngest son of Nicholas Skidmore deceased, age not stated, bound to Hugh Teares, who doth here in Court to teach or instruct ye said Raiph Skidmore "in ye art & mistery (sic) of a house carpenter," "unlesse

INDEX TO ORPHANS

to help & assist in makeing a crop of corne yearely," 13 November 1694 [18.pdf #229]; Ralph Skidmore, "being now about fifteen yeares of age," "with his own consent" is bound to James Williams, he "to give him one yeares schooling and to teach him the trade of a house carpenter," 8 August 1704 [23.pdf #21]; Ralph Skidmore, "bound to John Beale," he "promiseing in open Court to give him a cow and a calfe at the expiration of his time," 13 August 1706 [23.pdf #139]

Smart, not named, daughter of Edward Smart, age not stated, presented by James Cottrell, who "desires shee may be bound to some one the mother being dead and the father runn away, the Court being credibly informed that Mrs. Anne Brandt the wife of Mr. Randolph Brandt being her God Mother would take her," 8 June 1703 [22.pdf #107]

Smith, Arthur, son of Hannah Willson and "her former husband," age not stated, petition of Hannah Willson, "haveueing provided for and maintained" him from "infancy heitherto," and he "being now able to work and make your peticoner some reperacon for her exterordinary trouble, labour and pay for their suport and maintaynance, through the instigation of some ill neighbours threatens to leave your peticoner," ordered by Court to "be and remaine with the said Hanah Willson," 14 August 1711 [24.pdf #122]

Smith, Elias, "being about sixteene years of age," son of William Smith deceased and Priscilla Smith now the wife of John Spaldin, "makes choice of Mr. Charles Summerset Smith for his guardian," ordered by Court "that the aforesaid John Spalden deliver the estate belonging to the said minor to the guardian aforesaid," 13 June 1721 [27.pdf #75]; "Mr. Charles Somersett Smith who was lately in Court here appointed guardian to Elias Smith a minor in Court now desires to be discharged of his wardship which is granted," 13 March 1722 [27.pdf #125]

Smith, James, son of Hannah Willson and "her former husband," age not stated, petition of Hannah Willson, "haveueing provided for and maintained" him from "infancy heitherto," and he "being now able to work and make your peticoner some reperacon for her exterordinary trouble, labour and pay for their suport and maintaynance, through the instigation of some ill neighbours threatens to leave your peticoner," ordered by Court to "be and remaine with the said Hanah Willson," 14 August 1711 [24.pdf #122]

Smith, Martha, orphan of Thomas Baker, abandoned wife of Anthony Smith, age not stated, bound to Capt. William Barton, 8 November 1692 [17.pdf #277]; bound to Alice Groves, ye wife of George Groves, 10 January 1693 [17.pdf #294]

Smith, Richard, son of Richard Smith deceased, age not stated, "doth here in Court choose William Hinsey to be his Guardian," 15 November 1676 [07.pdf #130]

Smith, William, son of Joane Smith, age not stated, "formerly bound to Mr. Hugh Tears deceased now in the possession of Mr. John Beale," 9 March 1703 [22.pdf #89]; see also [22.pdf #124]; William Smith, son of William Smith, "being fourteen yeares of age some time in September next," bound

INDEX TO ORPHANS

to John Beale, he "at the expiration of his time to give him one cow and calfe not exceeding three yeares old," 10 April 1705 [23.pdf #63]

Smoote, Edward, son of Richard Smoote deceased, age not stated, "in Court chooseth Thomas Taylor for his guardian by ye consent of ye overseers," 9 January 1677 [08.pdf #14]

Smoote, Edward, son of James and Jean Smoote, age not stated, bound to John Elder, he "to give him a yeares schooling and to teach him the trade of a carpenter," 11 November 1701 [21.pdf #160]; "the vestry men of Portobacco Parrish complaines against John Elder for misusing an orphant named Edward Smoot," "ordered that a summons be issued out against ye said John Elder" and "that ye said Edward Smoot remaine with Matthew Barnes untill ye next Court," 10 August 1703 [22.pdf #125]; ordered by Court "that the said Edward Smoot bee & remaine with the said John Elder according to ye time of the Order when hee was first bound unto him," 14 September 1703 [22.pdf #130]; "Wee the Grand Jury doe present John Elder for takeing noe care of Edward Smoote an orphan according to what he was bound to by this Court, 10 June 1707 [23.pdf #180]; itt appeareing to the Court here to be a causeless presentment," ordered by Court "that the said John Elder be acquitted," 12 August 1707 [23.pdf #203]; "Edward Smoot an orphan formerly bound to John Elder is taken from the said John Elder and bound unto Henry Barnes," he "to teach him the trade of a carpender and to pay John Elder four hundred pounds of tobacco for bringing him up hitherto," 8 June 1708 [23.pdf #253]

Smoote, Elizabeth, daughter of Richard Smoote deceased, age not stated, bound to "Elizabeth ye wife of Henry Bonner," 9 January 1677 [08.pdf #14]

Smoote, John, son of James and Jean Smoote, age not stated, bound to John Williams, 11 November 1701 [21.pdf #160]; John Smoote, "an orphant formerly bound to John Williams att Potomack River side the former order of Court confirmed and ye said orphant bound to William Williams son of ye said John Williams," 14 June 1709 [23.pdf #305]; John Smoot his petition aledging that William Williams "will not instruct him in ye trade of a cooper as by the condition that he was bound by this Court," "the said petition was rejected ye former order againe confirmed," 9 August 1709 [23.pdf #321]

Smoote, John, parents not named, age not stated, petitions "that Gerrard Ocaine his father in law refuses to deliver him his land being att age to receive the same," and "the said John Smoot declared the said difference to be agreed," 9 March 1708 [23.pdf #236]

Smoot, Leonard, son of Susana, now wife of John Maud, bound to John Standbury, "to serve in such service & employment as he the said John Standbury & his heirs shall lawfully imploy him, tending of tobacco only excepted," and ye said John Standbury "to learn the aforesaid Leonard Smoote ye art of the cordwainers trade," and at the end of his terme "to find & allow him one sett of tools," 11 June 1712 [24.pdf #162]

INDEX TO ORPHANS

Smoote, Richard, son of Richard Smoote deceased, born August 1660, "in Court chooseth Walter Davies to be his guardian by ye consent of ye overseers, hee being sixteene yeares of age last August," 9 January 1677 [08.pdf #14]

Smoote, Richard, son of Richard Smoote deceased, age not stated, "doth in open Courte choose Richard Morris to be his guardian," 9 March 1680 [09.pdf #153]

Smoote, William, son of Richard Smoote deceased, "hee being nine yeares of age this instant June," bound to William Hatton, 8 June 1680 [09.pdf #167]

Sommers, Jane, "an orphan girl aged about thirteen years of age," parents not stated, "bound to her mother in law May Sommers," she "obliges herself to give her at this time a three year old heifer," 10 June 1718 [26.pdf #38]

Sotherland, Michael Richard, age not stated, son of Mary Russell "widdow," bound to John Rogers, by indenture, 20 May 1714 [Liber F Page 72]

Squires, Elizabeth, daughter of Eleanor Squires, "being about four years old," bound to George Thomas, 8 August 1721 [27.pdf #92]

Squires, John, son of Eleanor Squires, two years old "about the middle of November next," bound to George Thomas, 8 August 1721 [27.pdf #92]

Stanfield, John, "an orphan boy about thirteen years of age," bound to Philip Cooper, he to give him "a year's schooling," 14 June 1720 [26.pdf #172]

Steede, Thomas, parents not named, "being thirteene yeares of age in November next," bound to Richard Waye, 10 September 1678 [09.pdf #40]

Steel, George, "a poor motherless bastard boy aged nine years ye first day of last April," bound to Elizabeth Crabb "in consideration of her having taken care & maintaind him until this time," 14 June 1720 [26.pdf #172]

Stewart, James, orphan, son of John & Ellinor Stewart deceased, "three yeares old," bound to John Bannister, 13 August 1700 [21.pdf #19]

Stewart, John, orphan, son of John & Ellinor Stewart deceased, "being seven years old," bound to John Bannister, he to teach him "the art or trade of a carpenter," 13 August 1700 [21.pdf #19]

Stigaleer, Jane, parents not named, age not stated, bound to Evan Hines (?), he "to instruct her to read, spinn & card," 8 March 1715 [25.pdf #266]

Theobalds, John, son of Clement Theobalds deceased, age not stated, bound to James Wheeler, 14 November 1677 [08.pdf #50]; John Theobalds, son of Clement Theobalds deceased, age not stated, bound to Richard Morris, 8 August 1682 [10.pdf #178]

Thomas, Elizabeth, daughter of Anne Thomas widow, "shee being at this present eight yeare old," bound to Thomas & Mary Mitchell, 10 February 1684 [17.pdf #209]; petition for freedom denied, ordered by Court to serve "till ye tenth day of February next," 8 March 1692 [17.pdf #209]

Thomas, John, bound by his father to John Wathen, August 1716 [Liber G Page 140]

Thomas, Samuell, bound by his father to John Wathen, August 1716 [Liber G Page 140]

Thompson, Thomas, "an orphan," parents not named, age not stated, bound to Timothy Carrington, 13 November 1722 [28.pdf #7]

INDEX TO ORPHANS

Tickerell, John, son of Thomas Tickerell deceased and Jane Tickerell, age not stated, bound to William Hatch, 13 June 1683 [11.pdf #128]

Tomkins, Newman, "five years of age," eldest son of Sarah Tomkins widow, bound to Charles Denny (?), and ye said Sarah Tomkins doth "order and ordain" that he "be free at ye age of eighteen and have his estate fully resigned unto his hands care and management," and ye said Charles Denny doth "in no waye oppose or hinder the aforesaid Newman Tomkins from obtaining his freedom at eighteen years of age," 29 June 1719 [Liber H Page 363]

Tugwell, Elizabeth, daughter of Martha Tugwell, "shee being four yeares old last Christmass," bound to Henry Norriss, by desire of her mother Martha Tugwell as stated in her petition presented to Court by the wife of Henry Norriss, 1 April 1701 [21.pdf #107]

Turner, Anne, daughter of Arthur Turner deceased, age not stated, bound to William Marshall, 12 November 1667 [03.pdf #289]; bound to Joseph Cooper, 8 September 1668 [Vol. 60:142]

Turner, Arthur, eldest son of Arthur Turner deceased, age not stated, bound to Capt. Josias Fendall, 12 November 1667 [03.pdf #289]

Turner, Edward, son of Arthur Turner deceased, age not stated, bound to James Bowling, 12 November 1667 [03.pdf #289]

Turner, James, second son of Arthur Turner deceased, age not stated, bound to Walter Beane, 12 November 1667 [03.pdf #289]

Turner, not named, youngest daughter of Arthur Turner deceased, "about a monthe old," bound to "George Taylor's wife Susannah Taylor," 12 November 1667 [03.pdf #289]

Tyer, Andrew, orphan, parents not named, age not stated, bound to James Waters, inventory of "ye plantations of ye said orphan," 13 January 1718 [Liber H Page 149]

Tyer, Rebeccah, orphan, parents not named, age not stated, bound to James Waters, inventory of "ye plantations of ye said orphan," 13 January 1718 [Liber H Page 149]

Typpett, Elizabeth, "naturall borne daughter" of Ellizabeth Harrison ye wife of Benjamin Harrison, "shee being four yeares of age ye eighth day of January last past," bound to Ralph Shaw "freely & voluntarily" of her mother's own consent, "and in case ye said Ralph Shaw happen to dye before shee arrive to ye age of sixteene yeares then ye said Elizabeth Typpett to be free," 9 March 1697 [19.pdf #111]

Tyre, Anne, parents not named, age not stated, bound to Robert & Charles Yates, 12 November 1717 [26.pdf #112]

Tyre, Rebecca, parents not named, age not stated, bound to Robert & Charles Yates, 12 November 1717 [26.pdf #112]

Vaughan, Elizabeth, bound to John Wilder & John Smoot, November 1716 [Liber G Page 151]

Vaughan, John, bound to John Wilder & John Smoot, November 1716 [Liber G Page 151]

INDEX TO ORPHANS

Vincent, John, son Mary Vincent, "he being two yeares old last November," bound to John Pidgeon, he "at the expiration of his service to finde and allow him three barrells of corne," 13 March 1705 [23.pdf #46]

Vinton, Elizabeth, daughter of Richard Vinton, age not stated, bound to Thomas Dickson, 10 January 1688 [14.pdf #173]

Wakelin, Richard, son of "Catherine Wakelin ye wife of Richard Wakelin Junior," "hee being four yeares of age ye Eighteenth day of August next," bound to John Godshall, 9 June 1691 [17.pdf #113]

Walden, Henry, son of Henry Walden deceased, age not stated, bound to Thomas Wharton, 10 June 1684 [11.pdf #204]

Wallis, John, son of Michael Wallis, "his age at present not being known," bound to William Willson, who "hath received into his custody one cow and calfe and a five yeares old hiefer and a young sow" and "ingages here in Court to look after the said stock and all their feemale increase for the use and benefitt of the said John Wallis," 10 November 1702 [22.pdf #63]

Ward, James, "an orphan lad born ye twenty seventh day of May seventeen hundred and five," parents not named, bound to Edward Milstead, 14 June 1720 [26.pdf #172]

Warner, John, son of Thomas & Isable Warner deceased, age not stated, bound to Richard Dod, 27 March 1677 [08.pdf #32]

Warner, Elizabeth, daughter of Thomas & Isable Warner deceased, age not stated, bound to Richard Dod, 27 March 1677 [08.pdf #32]; see also [09.pdf #172]

Warner, Thomas, son of Thomas & Isable Warner deceased, age not stated, bound to Thomas Baker, 27 March 1677 [08.pdf #32]

Warren, Abraham, son of Mr. Humphrey Warren deceased, age not stated, bound to Coll. Humphrey Warren, 11 March 1690 [16.pdf #114]

Warren, Benjamin, orphan son of Coll. Humphrey Warren, age not stated, "at present" living with John Cage & Richard Morris, ordered by Court to "live with & serve Capt. John Bayne," 29 November 1698 [19.pdf #261]

Warren, Charles, orphan son of Coll. Humphrey Warren, age not stated, "at present" living with John Cage & Richard Morris, ordered by Court to "live with & serve Capt. John Bayne," 29 November 1698 [19.pdf #261]

Warren, Humphrey, son of Mr. Humphrey Warren deceased, age not stated, bound to Coll. Humphrey Warren, 11 March 1690 [16.pdf #114]

Warren, John, son of Coll. Humphrey Warren, age not stated, "now fatherlesse and motherlesse," formerly under the tuition of Notley Warren and afterwards under the tuition of Capt. John Bayne who was Executor of Notley Warren, and is att present under the care of Mrs. Ann Bayne, ordered by Court "that the said orphan and lands bee delivered to John Courts Esqr.," he agreeing to plant "within a twelve month" a hundred trees on the said plantation and "have it carefully looked after as an orchard ought to bee," 11 November 1701 [21.pdf #160]; John Warren "chooses Coll. John Contee for his guardian, who "engages in Court to improve his Estate for the said John Warrens best advantage," 14 April 1705 [23.pdf #88]

INDEX TO ORPHANS

Waters, John, son of Anne Waters, "he being eleven years old on the third day of June now next," bound to John Manning, by indenture, 12 January 1716 [Liber F Page 88]; John Waters, "a lad of sixteen years of age," son of Anne Mackan, bound by his mother with "consent of her husband Peter Mackan" to Hargiss Madding, 14 March 1721 [27.pdf #43]

Weavour, Adam, son of Adam Weavour deceased, "being seaven yeares of age the third day of Jannuary last past," "with the consent of his mother" bound to Charles Musgrove, he "to teach the said Adam Weavour the trade of a carpenter and cooper " and "att the expiration of his time to give him a sett of carpenters tooles," 8 June 1708 [23.pdf #254]

Weavour, Hannah, daughter of Adam Weavour deceased, "she being four yeares old the last day of Jannuary last past," "bound to John Blee and Margarrett his new wife to them onely," "the said John Blee ingages to give her one whole yeares schooleing," 8 June 1708 [23.pdf #254]

Wemmes, Benjamin, bound to Thomas Craxon, March 1716 [Liber G Page 48]

Wemmes, Wrightington, son of Susanah Wemmes, bound to John Wilder, 8 August 1721 [27.pdf #92]

Wharton, Elizabeth, daughter of Thomas Wharton deceased, age not stated, "ordered to live with Martha Barker," she "to instruct her in housewifery," and "ordered that Martha Barker doe pay James Rey foure hundred pounds of tobacco for his the said Rey's maintayninge the said Elizabeth Wharton heitherto," 13 March 1711 [24.pdf #59]

Wharton, Thomas, "an orphan child aged fourteen years next March," bound to Thomas Jenkins, and "the said Jenkins haveing no free hold, and being withall a single person and noe setteled place of abode," ordered that he not "remove himselfe out of the jurisdiccon of this Court into ye Colony of Virginia or else where to prejudice of the said orphan," 25 April 1710 [23.pdf #390]; see also [23.pdf #408] &[24.pdf #32]; the Grand Jury presents Thomas Jenkins joyner for not keeping Thomas Wharton his apprentice to his trade as he was bound to by this Court butt has hired him to James Mancaster to work in the ground this yeare," 12 June 1711 [24.pdf #94]; Thomas Wharton, "an orphan who was by this Court bound unto Thomas Jenkins," complains "that he is neither maintayned nor instructed as he ought, he is taken from the said Jenkins and bound to Joseph Harrison," who "obleiges himselfe to imploy him in such labour as he himselfe works," 11 March 1712 [25.pdf #35]

Wharton, William, son of Thomas Wharton deceased, "being five years of age next March," bound to James Rey who married with Elizabeth the naturall sister of the said orphan, 12 June 1711 [24.pdf #95]; William Wharton, "formerly bound to James Rae (?), ordered to "be removed & putt under ye custody & care of Richard Woodyard untill ye next Court," 11 March 1718 [26.pdf #22]; William Wharton, bound to Richard Woodyard, he "to give ye said orphan two years schooling," 10 June 1718 [26.pdf #38]

Wheeler, Anne, "the choice of her guardian," 1694 [Liber T Page 112]

INDEX TO ORPHANS

Wheeler, not named, "orphants of Ignatius Wheeler," ages not stated, petition of Thomas Wheeler read & continnued until next Court, ordered also a summons for Peter Mills," 8 June 1703 [22.pdf #106]; petition of Thomas Wheeler "concerning waste committed by Peter Mills on ye land belonging to ye orphants of Ignatius Wheeler," 10 August 1703 [22.pdf #125]

Wheeler, James, son of James Wheeler deceased, age not stated, "made choice of his uncle Ignatius Wheeler to be his guardian," 14 June 1698, [19.pdf #219]

Wheeler, John, son of James Wheeler deceased, age not stated, doth "choose his grandfather Major John Wheeler to be his guardian," 10 November 1691 [17.pdf #157]

Whitford, James, son of James and Elizabeth Whitford deceased, "being eight years old in March last past," bound to Mrs. Barbarah Hinson, 11 June 1706 [23.pdf #123]

Whittford, Mary, daughter of James Whittford deceased, "her parents being dead, John Saunders ordered to bring her next Court to be bound," 13 January 1702 [21.pdf #172]; Mary Whittford, daughter of James Whittford & Mary his wife deceased, "adjudged by the Court to be six yeares of age now," "desires shee may be bound to" John Sanders of Chingomuxon, ordered by Court "that the said John Sanders take into his custody a mare running in these woods and another mare at Patuxent when shee can be found which said mares doe both belong to the said Mary Whittford and are to be return'd in kinde when shee shall arrive to sixteene yeares of age," 10 March 1702 [22.pdf #4]

Wilder, Anne, orphan, daughter of Capt. John Wilder deceased, age not stated, bound to Major Walter Storey, ordered by Court that "what estates doth belong to them be delivered into the possession of Major Walter Storey" and that he "doe give to this Court good security," 11 March 1707 [23.pdf #169]

Wilder, John, orphan, son of Capt. John Wilder deceased, age not stated, bound to Major Walter Storey, ordered by Court that "what estates doth belong to them be delivered into the possession of Major Walter Storey" and that he "doe give to this Court good security," 11 March 1707 [23.pdf #169]; "butt since your petitioner was bound by your worshipps, he hath found his mother in laws Will being his owne father dyed without a will and shee thinking her selfe capable to sett your poor pettitioner of age when he arrived at the years of eighteen which your pettitioner is now arrived at and thinks himselfe capable of manageing of what was left him by his mother in law Francis Wilder," asks the Court "to sett him free from the said Walter Story," "said petition is rejected," 14 November 1710 [24.pdf #32]

Wilder, Mary, orphan, daughter of Capt. John and Frances Wilder deceased, age not stated, "complaint being made to the Court against one William Browne administrator for imbezzelling the Estate of the said Capt. John Wilder to the great prejudice of the orphants, the said William Browne appeareing in Court in his propper person itt was by the Court demanded of him to give security for the said Estate which he not being able to performe," bound to Charles Brandt, 11 March 1707 [23.pdf #169]

INDEX TO ORPHANS

Wilder, Sena (?), orphan, daughter of Capt. John and Francis Wilder deceased, age not stated, "complaint being made to the Court against one William Browne administrator for imbezzelling the Estate of the said Capt. John Wilder to the great prejudice of the orphants, the said William Browne appeareing in Court in his propper person itt was by the Court demanded of him to give security for the said Estate which he not being able to performe," bound to Thomas Dixon 11 March 1707 [23.pdf #169]

Wilkinson, Mary, daughter of Lancelott and Mary Wilkinson deceased, age not stated, bound to Francis Miller "by hir owne free consent," 3 December 1700 [21.pdf #57]

Wilkison, Christopher, bound to Elizabeth Hawkins, March 1717 [Liber G Page 176]

Williams, Benjamin, son of Alice (?) Maris, "hee being now about three yeares of age," bound to Haman Norton, 10 August 1680 [09.pdf #182]

Williams, Edward, son of Elizabeth Williams, "hee being three yeares of age and one moneth," bound to Henry Hawkins and Elizabeth his wife, with "very willing" consent of his mother, provided "ye said boy is to learne to reade," 7 November 1694 [18.pdf #229]

Williams, Thomas, "a minor orphan about four years of age," parents not named, "bound unto Samuel Williams & his wife," "they obliging themselves to give ye said Thomas a year's schooling," 12 August 1718 [26.pdf #51]

Williams, William, son of Elizabeth Williams, "hee being ten yeares of age ye last day of October last past," bound to John Hawkins, with "very willing" consent of his mother, provided he "putts him to schoole till hee can reade in ye Bible," 7 November 1694 [18.pdf #229]; petition of William Williams, bound by this Court "about eleaven yeares since to Mr. John Hawkins late of Piscattaway deceased," "and your petitioner hath faithfully served and expired his time which he was bound for with the said Mr. Hawkins and with Mr. Hickford Loman and Mr. Henry Hawkins the administrators of the estate," asks for his freedom clothes and "his learning," ordered that the case "be continued until the next Court," 13 November 1705 [23.pdf #105]; ordered by Court that the said administrator to pay the said William Williams twelve hundred pounds of tobaco in lieu of his schooling aforesaid," 8 January 1706 [23.pdf #111]

Willis, Ann, "a mallato basterd" "brought here into Court" by Kenett Mackenzey, "left at his house," and "for his trouble of lookeing after and mayntaining it being afecnate (affectionate -- ed.) child," bound to Kenett Mackenzey "to serve according to law," 10 November 1713 [25.pdf #182]

Willson, Ralph, son of Mary Willson, "he being three yeares old the twenty fifth day of April next," his mother "desires that her child may be bound" to John Price, 11 November 1707 [23.pdf #221]

Willson, William, Junr., "alias Downes," ordered by Court to "returne to William Willson Senr. untill be arrives at the age of one and twenty yeares," he "promises to give him a cow and a mare," 14 June 1709 [23.pdf #305]

INDEX TO ORPHANS

Wise, Benjamin, "an orphan boy eight years of age," parents not named, bound to Francis Miller, 9 June 1713 [25.pdf #144]; Benjamin Wise, "an orphan about sixteen years of age," bound to Charles Byrne, he "to give him a horse bridle & saddle when free," 14 March 1721 [27.pdf #43]

Wise, Francis, son of Mary Dunaway, "adjudged to be eight years of age," bound to Thomas Austin, 14 November 1710 [24.pdf #32]; ordered by Court "that Francis Wise an orphan be continued in the custody" of Susannah Austin "till the next Court," 10 August 1714 [25.pdf #241]; Francis Wise, bound to John Posey, August 1716 [Liber G Page 140]

Wise, Richard, son of Mary Dunaway, "adjudged to be tenn years old," bound to Edward Cornish, 14 November 1710 [24.pdf #32]

Withy, Mary, daughter of Joan Withy, age not stated, bound to John Barron, 10 August 1697 [19.pdf #135]

Withy, Thomas, son of Joan Withy, age not stated, "hee being four yeares old about ye twelfth or ye thirteenth day of October next, bound to John Godshall, 10 August 1697 [19.pdf #135]; see also [23.pdf #391]

Witter, George, son of Thomas Witter, age not stated, "of his own free will & voluntary consent together with ye consent of his father in law John Duglas cooper," bound to John Martin "as his apprentice servant hee ye said John Martin teaching & instructing him ye said George Witter "ye art & mistery (sic) of a boatwright," 9 January 1694 [18.pdf #128]; George Witter, ye orphan son of Thomas Witter, formerly bound to John Martin boatwright, and "came here into Court his brother Thomas Witter and allsoe ye said John Martin," both consenting & willing "that ye said George Witter serve his said brother Thomas Witter," 10 August 1697 [19.pdf #136]

Witter, William, son of Thomas Witter, age not stated, "doth here in Court choose his father in law John Duglas cooper to be his guardian," "and ye said John Duglas to teach & instruct ye said William Witter in ye art and mistery (sic) of a cooper, 9 January 1694 [18.pdf #129]

Wood, Mary, bound to William Stone Junr., June 1716 [Liber G Page 101]

Worland, John, orphan, "living with" Elizabeth Whichaley wife to Thomas Whichaley, she "petitions the Court about some goods belonging to the Estate of John Worland," 8 August 1704 [23.pdf #20]

Wright, Mary, daughter of Elizabeth Wright, "being foure yeares old ye one & twentieth day of April next," bound to Mrs. Abigail Dent, 9 November 1703 [22.pdf #144]

Yates, Anne, "about seven years of age," daughter of James Yates deceased and his wife Margaret , who "after his decease married John Connor," bound to Robert Yates, 12 November 1717 [26.pdf # 17]

Yates, Rebecca, "now about nine years," daughter of James Yates deceased and his wife Margaret," who "after his decease married John Connor," bound to Robert Yates, 12 November 1717 [26.pdf # 17]

Yopp, Jane, parents not named, age not stated, "makes choice of John Craxon" as her guardian, 13 March 1722 [27.pdf #125]

SURVIVORS FROM ELSEWHERE

ANNE ARUNDEL COUNTY

Ellitt, Matthew, 10 November 1703, age 9, Charles Carroll, thirteen years
Matthew Elliot married Mary Richardson, All Hallows, 30 January 1721

    Son: Thomas Eliot, born 14 January 1722
    Son: John Eliot, born 27 December 1724

Howard, David, 13 June 1704, age 17, John Giles
David Howard married Catherine Barley, Saint James, 22 July 1711

Hutton, Thomas, 13 June 1710, age 16, Nehemiah Burkett

    Mary Hutton, daughter of Thomas & Mary,
    born 1 September 1719, Saint James

CECIL COUNTY

Price, David, 12 November 1700, age 12, John Ryland
David Price married Kathrin Flinn, Saint Stephens, 31 December 1715

    Son: Henry Price, born 29 October 1718

KENT COUNTY

Clark, Samuell, 24 August 1703, age 12, John Davis
Samuell Clark married Mary Clark (?), Saint Pauls, 25 September 1717

    Daughter: Esther Clark, born 27 July 1718
    Son: Samuell Clark, born 3 March 1720

Hopkins, William, 27 March 1677, age 12 "& a halfe," Francis Finch
William Hopkins married Dorthy Willis, Saint Pauls, 31 March 1700

    Daughter: Anne Hopkins, born 22 November 1702,
    Saint Michaels, Talbot County

Jones, Thomas, 25 June 1701, age 20, Charles Lowder
Thomas Jones married Mary Tillard, Shrewsbury, 11 May 1708

    Daughter: Grace Jones, born 29 May 1709
    Married John Stephenson, 1 May 1728

PRINCE GEORGE'S COUNTY

Tinnally, Phillip, 28 November 1705, age 12, Mareen Devall Junior,
    "alledging that he had Indentures"
Phil Tenanly married Grace Thomas, Saint Johns, 2 July 1720

QUEEN ANNE'S COUNTY

Burk, Edward, 24 March 1719, age 10, John Cobreath
Edward Burk married Anne Steward, Saint Luke's, 4 May 1739

Clark, William, 28 June 1729, age 10, Captain William Greenwood
William Clark married Mary Hollingsworth, Saint Luke's, 3 November 1743

SOMERSET COUNTY

Marchment, Samuell, 12 June 1677, age 18-22, Capta. Thomas Jones
Samuell Marchment married Mary Wharton, 2 March 1685

    Daughter: Mary Marchment, born 7 October 1689
    Daughter: Elizabeth Marchment, born 31 October 1691

Marsh, George, 8 June 1675, age 15-18, Daniell Curtis
George Marsh married Elizabeth Davis, 15 August 1681

    Son: George Marsh, born 3 September 1681, died 24 September 1681,
        Annemessex, Somerset
    Son: George Marsh, born 19 January 1682/83

Sawell, Thomas, 4 September 1666, age 17, Randall Revell, seven years
Thomas Seawell married Jeane Boist, 8 October 1677

    Daughter: Mary Sawell, born 7 February 1689, Annemessex, Somerset

TALBOT COUNTY

Browne, Thomas, 18 January 1687, age 13, Samuel Abbott
Thomas Browne married Mary (no surname), Saint Peters, 23 January 1700

Burdin, John, 17 August 1686, age 12, George Robins
John Burden married Rosannah Haines, Saint Peters, 20 June 1703

Crump, Michael, 3 March 1719, age 10, Isaac Dixon
Michael Crump married Susannah Ducksberry, 3 January 1739

TALBOT COUNTY (CONT'D)

Dawson, Richard, 17 June 1679, age 18, John Newman
Richard Dawson married Susannah Foster, Third Haven, 23 August 1698

Dowdell, John, 17 January 1682, age 20, Elizabeth Harris
John Dowdell married Catherine Butler, Saint Peters, 9 May 1697

Goult, George, 21 August 1677, age 17, John Jadwin, seven years
George Goult married Mary Lockwell, 6 March 1691

Hall, Mary, 15 June 1686, age 13, Griffith Jones
Mary Hall married William Thompson, Third Haven, 5 February 1704

Hughs, Catharine, 15 June 1708, age 21, Nathaniell Tougle
Catherine Hues married Samuel Cliff, Saint Peters, 24 November 1715

Joans, William, 17 August 1669, (age 15-18), Joseph Wickes, six years
William Joans married Sarah Hall, Third Haven, 24 December 1679

Libby, John, 20 June 1699, age 14, John Wooters
John Libbey married Emy Elizabeth Cathrop, Saint Peters, 1 January 1712

    Sarah Libby, daughter of John & Emy Elizabeth, born 5 May 1722
    Elizabeth Libbey, daughter of John & Amy, born 18 August 1724

Murphey, John, (torn) 1683, age 16, John Hawkins
John Murphey married Esther (no surname), Saint Peters, 19 January 1700

    Daughter: Mary Murphey, born 10 August 1701
    Married David Sulegar, 15 August 1724

Price, John, 20 November 1682, age 16, Andrew Price
John Price married Elce (no surname), Saint Peters, 6 September 1690

    Elisabeth Price, daughter of John and Alce, born 26 March 1691
    Married Hezekiah Macotter, 1 June 1707

        Daughter: Mary, born 8 November 1708, Saint Peters
        Married William Layhe, 29 January 1729

        Daughter: Priscilla, born 27 September 1713, Saint Peters

        Son: Hezekiah, born 16 April 1716, Saint Peters
        Married Elizabeth Trayman, 10 November 1736 (?)

            James Macotter, Born 4 October 1737

        Daughter: Alce, born 9 July 1718, Saint Peters

TALBOT COUNTY (CONT'D)

>Daughter: Pisislyah, born 7 May 1721, Saint Peters
>Married William Anderson Jr., 31 December 1739
>
>Son: John Price Macotter, born 3 May 1724, Saint Peters
>
>Rebeckah, born 11 October 1726, Saint Peters

John Price, son of John, born 10 August 1701

Shaw, William, 15 September 1702, age 15, Robert Grundy
William Shaw married Jane Cox, Saint Peters, 17 July 1709

>Daughter: Margret Shaw, born 19 October 1712
>Married Silvester Abbott, 22 July 1731
>
>Daughter: Rosanna Shaw, born 2 September 1716

Skinner, William, (torn) November 1684, age 16, William Sharpe
William Skinner married Elizabeth (no surname), Saint Peters,
23 October 1701

>Son: Phillemon Skinner, born 2 December 1701
>
>Son: William Skinner, born 11 July 1703
>
>Daughter: Sarah Skinner, born 1 February 1708
>
>Daughter: Phebe Skinner, born 19 May 1710
>Married Joseph Newnam (sic), 17 January 1723

Steevens, William, 26 February 1684, age 12, Thomas Emerson
William Stevens married Mary Pryor, 6 December 1700

Sullivant, Owen, 21 June 1698, age 17, William Gwin
Owen Sillivane married Mary Dedman, Saint Peters, 24 June 1703

>Daughter: Mary Sullivant, born 12 June 1704

Owen Shulivant married Cathrinne Whaley, Saint Peters, 11 December 1709
Owen Sulivant married Elizabeth Mercer, Saint Peters, 27 June 1713

Sweny, Bryon, 21 June 1698, age 13, David Blany
Bryan Sweney married Sarah Abbott, 1 December 1720

Taylor, Elizabeth, 30 April 1678, age 13, William Parratt, nine years
Elizabeth Taylor married Peter Harwood, Third Haven, 20 July 1690

Thompson, Daniell, 17 June 1701, age 10, John Pope
Daniel Thompson married Eliza Helsby, Saint Peters, 3 December 1719

SURNAME INDEX

Abbington, Abinton 334, 345
Abbott 61, 334, 393, 395
Achilles 289, 318, 321
Acres 61
Acton 195, 251, 289, 310, 340, 351, 369
Adair 190
Adams, Ad(d)am(e)s 2, 31, 61, 62, 65, 69, 70, 71, 73, 75, 78, 79, 80, 202, 205, 240, 278, 289, 293, 307, 313, 340, 363, 369, 372
Addersuch 334
Addis(s)on 21, 89, 93, 203, 289, 297, 319, 338, 346
Agambra(h) 64, 334, 378
Agborough 251
Ailer 61
Aires 339
Aldis 61
Aldon 61
Allanson, Allinson 61, 62, 73, 208, 278, 289, 290, 292, 293, 299, 307, 308, 315, 316, 351, 358
Allcock 289, 315, 324, 334, 348
Allen, Allin 44, 68, 69, 70, 84, 166, 172, 222, 251, 278, 289, 290, 292, 294, 298, 299, 303, 307, 309, 310, 311, 313, 316, 324, 334, 338, 342, 347, 351, 360, 374
Allis(s)on 251, 300
Alward, Allward 85, 251, 290, 357
Allwood 324, 334, 363
Alper 166
Ambros(e) 2, 31, 202, 334
Anderson 61, 166, 174, 232, 251, 290, 302, 324, 334, 345, 395
Andras, Andross 251
Andrews 166, 202
Anglish 61
Annis 191, 278, 319
Archer 166

Archiball, Archibald 33, 34, 35, 61, 161, 202, 203
Armstrong 61, 87, 213
Arnley 61
Arrington 35, 203
Arrowsmith 334
Ashbrook(e) 251, 278, 297, 304, 307, 351
Ashcomb 334
Ashford 177, 218, 290, 293, 305, 308
Ashforth 324
Ashman 10, 11, 12, 251, 290, 291, 292, 307, 334, 341, 351
Askin 290, 308
Aspenall, Aspinall 72, 290, 300, 303, 309, 311, 315, 319, 322, 371
Astere, Austrey 61, 87
Athy, Athey, Athee 290, 303, 309, 310, 316, 322, 324
Atkin, Attkins 61, 185, 346
Atkinson ix, 35, 203
Attchison 61
Atterberry 49, 166
Attwick(s) 61, 72, 290, 313
Attwood 302
Austin 6, 228, 290, 310, 346, 378, 391
Austrey 311
Austria 290
Austrich 61
Avis 61
Babberry 1, 166
Backer 351
Bacon 1, 26, 43, 166
Baddoe 251, 351
Baen, Bayhan 61, 161, 167
Baggley 334
Baggott 290
Bail(e)y, Bayl(e)y, Baylie 61, 62, 88, 167, 252, 291, 292, 310, 324, 334, 350
Baiteman 61
Baker 6, 61, 62, 70, 184, 204, 235, 251, 252, 278, 290, 295, 296, 297, 298, 299, 310, 313, 324, 334, 349, 351, 352, 361, 365, 383, 387

Bald 2, 31, 204
Ball 1, 43, 44, 48, 61, 167, 201, 298
Balse 302
Bankes, Banckes 290, 334
Ban(n)ister 196, 197, 290, 307, 334, 352, 379, 385
Baraclow 61
Barber 174, 192, 247, 278, 350, 356
Barefoot 307, 334, 352
Barker 48, 61, 87, 167, 183, 200, 201, 252, 290, 291, 297, 318, 334, 338, 339, 341, 352, 354, 375, 388
Barley 392
Barlow, Barlowe 61, 167
Barnaby 290
Barnes 31, 62, 182, 204, 235, 252, 278, 290, 324, 357, 358, 384
Baron, Barron 56, 57, 62, 252, 324, 332, 352, 391
Barrett 6, 54, 55, 62, 87, 88, 96, 205, 291, 296, 311, 321, 334, 335
Barrow 62
Bartlett 57, 252, 291, 324, 334, 352, 353
Barton 48, 61, 62, 63, 66, 69, 70, 71, 72, 74, 78, 80, 81, 83, 84, 85, 88, 162, 167, 168, 169, 181, 205, 243, 247, 252, 291, 296, 302, 303, 305, 313, 318, 321, 324, 334, 347, 353, 357, 366, 383
Bass 32, 62, 204
Batchelor 278, 291, 316
Bateman 252, 278, 291, 347, 382
Batten, Battin 278, 291, 312, 334
Battersby 240
Battle 62
Batts 212
Bawdry 55
Bawlding 62

Bayne, Beane 13, 14, 15, 16, 17, 18, 19, 20, 21, 22, 23, 24, 25, 31, 32, 41, 54, 55, 63, 64, 66, 68, 73, 75, 76, 77, 78, 80, 81, 83, 84, 86, 93, 95, 161, 169, 170, 171, 206, 207, 212, 222, 226, 229, 230, 289, 291, 293, 294, 296, 298, 299, 308, 310, 313, 321, 322, 334, 335, 339, 340, 341, 343, 346, 349, 353, 369, 376, 386, 387
Beade 289, 291, 324, 335
Beale, Beall(e) 20, 25, 35, 84, 163, 165, 169, 174, 175, 177, 178, 188, 189, 196, 197, 211, 225, 226, 231, 290, 299, 308, 338, 347, 361, 383, 384
Beard 72, 219
Beaton 62
Beaumont 238, 323, 335
Beck, Becke 65, 68, 81, 244, 253, 278, 291, 315, 321, 335
Bedford 291, 320
Bee 62
Belayne, Belaine, Belane 253, 291, 314, 320, 335, 353
Bell 62, 172, 194, 215, 324, 347
Bellingham 62
Belman 353
Benathon 62
Bene 62, 167, 168
Benjer 29, 168
Benlow 204
Bennam 278
Bennett, Bennitt 2, 8, 28, 31, 62, 88, 89, 168, 204, 205, 291, 317, 318, 321
Benson 31, 54, 57, 58, 60, 62, 65, 89, 90, 205, 291, 339, 343, 353, 366
Bentley, Bently 278, 353
Berry 62, 168, 217, 291, 373
Betts 353
Bevin, Bevins 168, 353
Bias, Byas 324, 339
Bickford 335
Bigger 342, 343
Bigs 62
Binns 62
Birch, Burch 62, 199, 278, 279, 293, 325, 348, 366, 380

Bird 62, 90, 335
Birke, Berke 36, 205, 335
Birth 291
Bishop 63, 90
Bissick 297
Bitton 63
Black 63
Blackbeard 63
Blackfan 335
Blackistone 335
Bladen 7, 291, 301, 304, 358
Blagg 31, 207
Blakwood 278
Blanch 63
Blanchett, Blanshett 291, 292, 353
Blandford 291
Blankensteine 299
Blany 395
Blare 223
Blee 179, 292, 335, 368, 375, 378, 388
Blizard 71, 253, 292, 335, 353
Blumstead 309
Blundell 335
Board 63
Boar(e)man, Bor(e)man, Boardman 39, 61, 62, 65, 68, 69, 80, 85, 168, 193, 278, 292, 296, 298, 299, 302, 303, 320, 321, 335, 342, 350, 376
Bocknell 278
Bodkin 335
Boist 393
Bonard 67, 71
Bone 63
Bonner 32, 63, 70, 74, 110, 161, 168, 216, 239, 278, 304, 319, 320, 339, 340, 384
Booker(s) 59, 60, 63, 94, 162, 178, 333, 342, 354, 379
Booth 63, 90
Boswell 63, 279, 292, 300, 324, 354
Boughton 243, 291, 292, 308, 319, 324, 352
Bould 4, 25
Bouls 279
Bourne 335
Bowder 335
Bowin 337

Bowing 63
Bowld 190, 253, 335
Bowles, Bouls 2, 31, 71, 72, 83, 84, 85, 206, 335
Bowlin, Boulin 62, 63, 81
Bowling, Bouling 69, 79, 80, 83, 293, 302, 335, 386
Bowlton 354
Bowman 25, 33, 56, 63, 90, 125, 160, 202, 216, 217, 233, 236, 239, 335
Box 335
Boy(e) 292, 334, 343, 361
Boyce, Boys, Boice 163, 186, 206, 238, 292, 324, 335, 376
Boyd 63, 168
Boyden 51, 79, 290, 292, 294, 300, 305, 309, 311, 313, 320, 324, 335, 344
Boyne 23
Bracher 292, 345
Bradey 45, 168
Bradly 335
Bradshaw 63, 78, 293, 314
Bradstone 63
Brafitt 354
Bramhall 253, 354, 359
Brandt 45, 67, 80, 167, 168, 183, 293, 335, 353, 382, 383, 389
Branner, Brawner, Braner 53, 55, 63, 90, 205, 253, 293, 325, 349
Branson 279, 293, 312, 354
Brassell 322
Braybanke 63
Brayber 168
Brayne 325, 335
Brayson 63
Bread(e) 210, 319, 335, 354
Bream(e)s 308, 310, 311, 335
Breeden 293, 295, 301
Breeding 63
Brenan, Brennon 63, 161
Brent 279, 335, 336
Brett 69, 162, 189, 293, 317, 318, 335, 336, 354, 375
Bride 63
Bridges 59, 63, 161, 168
Bridgets 354
Bright 63, 91, 348

397

Brightwell 312
Brimins 77
Briscoe 12, 79, 84, 164, 172, 279, 293, 372, 380
Broad, Broade 84, 168, 169, 289, 344
Broadhead 72, 219
Brockwell 168, 169
Bromley 377
Brooke, Brook(e)s 63, 91, 297, 300, 302, 306, 316, 336
Broomly 342
Broonely 63
Brown(e), Broune 25, 60, 63, 64, 66, 91, 92, 93, 167, 169, 183, 191, 193, 201, 206, 240, 243, 253, 279, 289, 293, 300, 305, 307, 309, 318, 321, 325, 336, 338, 339, 345, 350, 354, 355, 366, 389, 390, 393
Bruce 293, 325, 334
Brunon 34, 35, 206
Bryan, Brian, Bryon 17, 22, 23, 24, 29, 64, 93, 94, 169, 206, 240, 241, 293, 336
Bryant 51, 180, 293
Bryson 355
Buckham 64
Buckler 64
Buckner, Bucknam 169
Buck(e)ridge 279, 336, 339, 355
Bull 64, 279
Bullane 339
Bullary 336
Bullett, Bullott 66, 69, 70, 253, 293, 298
Bullord 336
Bunn 1, 43, 169
Bunsun 379
Burchner 2, 31, 207
Burden, Burdin 393
Burdett, Burdit 44, 169, 253, 279, 336
Burford 31, 44, 59, 67, 162, 175, 212, 293, 325, 336
Burges, Burgess(e) 14, 23, 32, 48, 55, 64, 95, 169, 207, 325, 336, 355, 362, 372
Burk, Burke 64, 393
Burkett 392
Burkhaine 64
Burnett 64

Burnham 336
Burras 336
Burrell 279
Burrough(e)s, Burrowes 31, 207, 253, 293
Bushell 25, 169
Butcher 83, 293, 309, 336, 343, 350, 368
Butler 31, 170, 207, 208, 354, 394
Butterfield 35, 44, 170, 208
Buttridge 1, 186
Butts, Buts 305, 340
Byrn, Byrne 64, 186, 294, 313, 391
Byron 336
Cable 279, 294, 325, 326, 336, 360
Cacell 335
Caddington 64
Caddock, Caddick 49, 170
Cadwell 279, 294, 322
Cage 23, 66, 69, 78, 101, 211, 294, 300, 302, 317, 336, 340, 355, 387
Cain(e), Cane, Caen 73, 81, 254, 279, 292, 294, 301, 306, 321, 325, 337, 355, 371
Callihon 294, 312
Calvert 236, 298, 299, 336, 370
Calvin 64, 355
Camell, Cammelle 27, 64, 161, 241, 355
Cameright 19, 22, 23, 64
Cameron 34, 65, 210
Campbell 64, 95, 296, 318, 322, 355
Campin 64
Candle 279
Canland 64
Canole 294
Can(t)ley, Canele 64, 96
Capner 31, 59, 208, 209
Capper, Capard 26, 170
Capshaw, Cabshaw 64, 96, 254, 294, 336, 355
Card 361
Careadale 65
Careless 43, 170
Carey, Carrey 65, 294, 336, 347, 356

Carnegie 65
Carnell 294, 304, 311, 336, 356
Carney 65
Carpenter 65, 96, 232, 279, 294, 343, 356
Carr, Car 5, 27, 63, 64, 69, 70, 73, 76, 77, 84, 241, 254, 279, 301, 372
Carrington 279, 356, 385
Carroll 336, 347, 392
Carter ix, 35, 209, 279, 376
Cartwright 294
Carver 254, 356
Carvill, Carvell 294, 335
Casey, Cusy, Cusack 16, 19, 22, 66, 161, 170, 171
Cash 307
Cassock 52, 294, 307, 321, 322, 325, 336
Castleton 256, 279, 294
Cathew 65
Cathrop 394
Catterton 336
Causeen(e), Causin(e) 25, 61, 62, 72, 78, 81, 82, 83, 85, 194, 241, 254, 302, 315, 320, 325, 349
Cavenaugh 49, 171, 279
Cawood 291, 294
Cave 325, 354
Cayne 65
Cha(i)rman 315, 322
Chambers 336
Champ, Champe 32, 65, 96, 209, 294
Chancellor 336
Chandler, Chantler 25, 56, 57, 61, 65, 67, 68, 73, 75, 77, 78, 79, 97, 197, 198, 212, 227, 232, 241, 254, 279, 294, 301, 302, 309, 310, 312, 313, 316, 322, 325, 327, 336, 339, 341, 351, 360, 371, 372
Chaplin 65
Chapman 64, 65, 69, 161, 183, 191, 254, 279, 294, 296, 337, 342, 356, 363, 365, 379
Chappell, Chapell 337
Charleson 209, 238, 254
Charlesworth 322, 339
Charlett 337
Charman 279

Chasey 294	Cof(f)er 84, 255, 293, 294	Corder 28, 172
Cheatham 48, 171, 201	Coghill 255, 295	Core 337
Cherman 77, 294	Cogwell 255	Corkain 355
Cherrybub 254, 356	Coherin 28, 171	Corker 296, 302, 319, 337
Can(t)ley, Canele 64, 96	Coho 171	Corks 335
Chesson 65, 97, 325, 337	Cole 45, 58, 60, 65, 77, 98, 171, 181, 182, 255, 295, 302, 312, 325, 337, 373	Cornace 337
Chew 65		Cornall, Cornell 52, 82, 296, 301, 366
Childman 65		
Chilman 337	Coleman 166, 171, 173, 199, 279, 319, 351	Corner 62, 255, 293, 296, 300, 301, 302, 358
Ching 279, 294, 337		
Chinton 356	Coleson 171, 241	Cornish 256, 279, 301, 317, 337, 358, 391
Chiseldyne, Chisledine 298, 342	Collard 65	
	Collier, Colliar 255, 295, 343, 353, 357, 358, 361	Cornute 66
Chiston 171		Cornwall 66
Chittam, Chattam 294, 325	Collings 295	Cornwell 200
Chomley 65, 97	Collingwood 65	Corrandell 66
Christoe 65	Collins, Collens 44, 65, 171, 172, 194	Cotterell, Cottrell, Cottwell 6, 59, 60, 66, 74, 99, 100, 256, 314, 322, 336, 383
Chunn 294		
Clampett 27, 171, 241, 242	Colum 172	
Clappam 348	Combs, Coomb(e)s, Coomes 42, 69, 77, 194, 197, 279, 289, 295, 325, 337	Cottington 279
Clark, Clarke, Clerke 17, 27, 56, 57, 65, 69, 72, 78, 79, 80, 82, 83, 189, 193, 195, 255, 291, 294, 295, 298, 299, 301, 305, 306, 309, 311, 318, 323, 325, 337, 356, 357, 375, 392, 393		Cotton 337
		Cottlycott 66
	Comely 65	Couch 173
	Compton 57, 98, 99, 210, 291, 294, 295, 302, 322, 359, 360, 378	Coulson 337, 345
		Court, Court(e)s 20, 21, 33, 35, 61, 63, 66, 69, 70, 71, 73, 74, 77, 78, 79, 83, 85, 93, 125, 161, 162, 182, 186, 221, 256, 296, 314, 320, 325, 337, 338, 341, 344, 358, 359, 387
	Conaway 289	
Clarkson 295, 340	Conders 210	
Clary 65	Cone 255, 358	
Clash, Cloyce 37, 210, 238, 254	Coneper 20	
	Coney 17, 22, 23, 24, 66, 172	Covert 301
Clemens, Clemons 65, 279, 295	Connell 255, 295, 313, 336, 337	Coward 223, 296
		Cowley 173
Clement(s) 175, 198, 293, 295, 314	Connolley 202	Cox 256, 280, 296, 325, 335, 395
	Connor, Conner 172, 279, 337, 349, 358, 380, 391	
Cliff 394		Coyne 173
Clifford 31, 171, 210	Constable 242, 337	Crabb 38, 218, 296, 338, 385
Clipsham, Clipsome 68, 83, 293, 294, 335, 336, 337, 340, 350, 363	Contee 7, 11, 38, 63, 67, 73, 78, 196, 226, 293, 295, 296, 308, 309, 318, 325, 337, 338, 358, 359, 387	Crackingdale 173
		Craft 338
		Crandall 31, 211
Clouder, Clowder, Clowter 194, 255, 297, 325, 353		Crane 280, 296
	Conyers 31, 210, 211, 238	Crawford 66
Clubb 196, 325	Coody, Coode 25, 44, 172, 244, 296, 325, 337, 363	Craxon 76, 173, 280, 296, 348, 388, 391
Coale 297		
Coates 65, 72, 79, 80, 295, 308, 337	Cooke 32, 47, 66, 161, 172, 214, 347	Craxton, Craxstone 56, 77, 189, 375
Cob, Cobb 65, 98	Cooksey 255, 296, 337, 358	Craycroft 322
Cobreath 393	Coope 296	Creedwell 338
Cockburn 357	Cooper 23, 57, 66, 67, 74, 99, 255, 279, 290, 296, 325, 336, 337, 338, 345, 382, 385, 386	Cressey 68, 80, 280, 297, 338
Cocks 171, 279		Crisman 369
Cockshott 228		Crocker 9, 10, 173
Codwell 325	Copp 66	Crommy, Crammy, Crummy 173, 174
Coe 336, 380	Cordea 236	

399

Crompton 256, 338, 359
Cropper 212, 364
Crosman 203
Crottee 66
Crouch 43, 44, 66, 174
Crowson 174
Cruckshanks 174
Crump 393
Cugatt 338
Cullan 371
Cumber 66
Cumberbeech 66
Cumpton 9, 66, 220, 256
Cunningham 66
Cunny 338
Currs 60, 66
Curtis 66, 393
Cuttance 294, 297
Cutler, Cuttler 325
Daine 348
Dallison, Dallyson 47, 66, 174
Damer, Damour 29, 66, 101, 211
Damon 66
Dance 370, 382
Daniellson 18, 22, 66
Daninton 344
Dansey 338
Danson 256, 359
Darby 359
Darnall, Darnell 3, 50, 66, 101, 102, 229, 242, 245, 296, 297, 325
Darnes 180
Daverill, Deverill, Deverell 66, 102, 257, 326
Davie 172
Davies 27, 48, 66, 67, 102, 103, 104, 211, 222, 280, 297, 308, 385
Davis, Davise 1, 34, 35, 43, 67, 104, 167, 174, 191, 197, 211, 256, 257, 291, 292, 293, 297, 300, 306, 312, 314, 318, 326, 336, 347, 349, 367, 369, 375, 379, 392, 393
Davison, Davidson 31, 174, 175, 211
Dawson 9, 257, 280, 305, 318, 326, 339, 359, 394
Day 23

Deakes 297
Deakons 67
Dean(e) 23, 31, 211, 289, 302
Dearman 359
Decregoe, Decreego 83, 297, 350
Dedman 395
Delahay, Delahey 280, 297, 303, 307, 338
Delozer 299, 326
Dement 297
Dempsey, Demsey 242, 326
Denealey 67
Denison 67, 326
Dennis 62, 65, 80
Denny 386
Dent 21, 29, 32, 39, 61, 64, 66, 67, 69, 72, 74, 76, 79, 82, 93, 106, 149, 164, 168, 181, 206, 227, 240, 257, 280, 290, 292, 293, 297, 299, 303, 304, 305, 306, 311, 314, 321, 326, 338, 341, 347, 351, 352, 353, 355, 359, 361, 364, 391
Derritt 67
Devall 393
Deveau 359, 360
Dewell 175, 360
Diamond, Dymond 300, 336, 355, 359
Dickins 175
Dicki(n)son, Dickeson 23, 57, 59, 60, 61, 64, 67, 71, 78, 104, 105, 290, 298, 299, 307, 311, 312, 318, 319, 326, 338, 360, 387
Dicksey 67
Dickson 67, 205, 249, 298
Digginer 175
Diggs, Digges 78, 84, 298, 320, 338, 339, 341, 350
Dike, Dyke 67, 105, 106, 326, 338, 345
Dillahay 341, 378
Dine 338
Dirkeson 298
Discorah 8, 360
Divell 67
Dixon 67, 168, 171, 183, 210, 257, 326, 338, 341, 369, 374, 390, 393
Doane 60, 67

Dobson 73, 298, 319, 332
Dod, Dode, Dods 67, 68, 257, 280, 297, 298, 326, 338, 349, 387
Dodson 166, 326
Dolton 67
Donah 67
Donahan, Donohan 67, 106
Donaldson 166, 280
Doniphan 347
Dorrosell, Dorosall 244, 280
Doughaley 257, 360
Doughty 67, 280, 291, 298
Douglas 1, 25, 40, 56, 57, 63, 64, 66, 67, 68, 76, 80, 81, 175, 178, 181, 257, 280, 298, 302, 306, 309, 317, 326, 335, 337, 338, 341, 360, 361, 362, 391
Doulton 175
Dove 280, 360, 364, 365
Dover 67
Dowdell 394
Dowell 258, 360
Dowen, Dowin 23, 322
Dowman 360
Downes 4, 31, 67, 84, 85, 175, 207, 258, 338, 360
Doy 339, 360
Doyle 67, 106
Doyne 2, 35, 37, 67, 76, 104, 106, 176, 188, 191, 211, 213, 214, 224, 280, 290, 298, 304, 305, 315, 326, 338, 339, 345, 360, 361
Draper 67, 339
Dreyden, Dryden 67, 106, 337, 339
Drishen 67
Drunckore 44, 67, 162, 175, 176
Ducker 176
Ducket 339
Ducksberry 393
Duffell 339
Duke 298
Duley 298
Dullany 141, 219, 339
Dun, Dunn 67, 68, 197, 355, 366
Dunaway 391
Dunkin 258, 361
Dunnavan 178

400

Dunnington 68, 107, 312, 326
Dunstan 176
Duppe 68
Dutton 258, 339, 376, 377
Dyal, Dyall 5, 68, 250
Dyson, Dison 280, 298, 341, 362, 376
Dyzer 339
Eady, Eaty 68, 318, 339, 361
Earle 339
Eason 68
Eastop 358
Eaton 68, 242, 376
Edelen, Edelin, Edelyn 32, 40, 65, 69, 70, 75, 79, 80, 83, 85, 110, 239, 280, 293, 298, 299, 338, 344, 347, 367, 368, 370
Edgar 258
Edge 44, 68, 176
Edgerley 47, 176
Edgerton 299
Edmonds(t)on 202, 299
Edwards 68, 176, 242, 361
Eglin 326
Eingle 212
Elder 384
Elgar, Ellgar 367
Elgin 68, 299
Elie, Etie, Etty, Ettey, Effye 14, 55, 258, 280, 299, 336, 339
Ellery 363
Elliott, Elliot, Eliot 18, 23, 205, 212, 258, 299, 339, 361, 392
Ellis 68, 280, 326
Ellison 26, 49, 68, 176, 293
Ellitt 310, 392
Ellsinge 211
Ellwes 339
Elms 361
Elswood 176, 212
Emanson 25, 243, 244, 299, 311, 322, 339
Emerson 68, 258, 299, 339, 395
Emmett 299
Empson 280, 298, 299, 304, 361
English 299
Eniburson 68
Ennis 68

Ensey 170, 326
Eskridge 299
Estes 354, 359
Estip 367, 368
Ethue 177
Eure 68
Evans, Evens 25, 29, 30, 31, 68, 70, 71, 107, 177, 212, 238, 242, 258, 280, 291, 299, 303, 307, 310, 340, 341, 346, 361, 366, 381
Evers 47, 177
Eyres 339
Fairfax 198, 299, 310, 376
Faning, Fanning 64, 82, 296, 298, 299, 309, 318, 320, 323, 326, 337, 339, 348, 356, 361, 362, 377
Fannerwick 339
Farlowe, Farloe 191, 258
Farmer 68, 212
Farrel(l), Ferril(l), Farrold 49, 68, 108, 162, 177, 178, 299, 349, 362
Farrow 68
Farthing 290, 299, 339
Faulkner 18, 22, 68
Fautley, Fawtley 339, 345
Fearn(e)ley 6, 292, 339, 362
Fe(a)rson 66, 79, 280, 298, 299, 344, 354, 355
Feddiman 68
Feild, Field 68, 108, 212, 213
Fencoke 68
Fendall 35, 71, 72, 73, 74, 76, 81, 82, 84, 85, 86, 227, 247, 280, 291, 298, 299, 302, 303, 306, 310, 339, 347, 363, 368, 373, 374, 386
Fenn 177
Fenner 68
Fentress 47
Fenwick 183
Fernandez, Ferdinando 53, 55, 68, 107, 108, 193, 200, 258, 280, 299, 326
Ferneley 281
Fewtrill, Fowtrell 69, 109, 212
Finch 392
Finley 81, 299, 380
Fish 362
Fisher 68, 242

Fishwick 339
Fitzgerald 29, 31, 35, 68, 108, 213, 238, 242, 243, 258, 300, 326, 347, 362, 369, 374
Flanagen 178
Fleman 68
Fletcher 1, 169, 178, 300
Flinn 392
Flood 68
Flower 326
Forbis 69
Ford, Foard 68, 69, 207, 258, 259, 281, 291, 300, 339, 362
Fordice 60, 69
Forrest 69
Forster, Forester 44, 69, 162, 175, 176, 178, 224, 300, 317
Foster 69, 178, 394
Fountain 1, 25, 40, 178, 201, 362
Fowke(s), Fou(c)ke 9, 19, 63, 64, 66, 70, 75, 77, 79, 81, 82, 106, 169, 182, 191, 213, 214, 216, 226, 238, 259, 281, 300, 306, 310, 311, 317, 321, 325, 326, 339, 362, 365
Fowler 69
Fox 178, 213, 300, 339, 359
Foxton 62
Fraizer 32, 213
Frances, Francis 54, 69, 109, 169, 339
Francisson 69
Franckum, Frank(h)am 69, 289, 290, 300, 322, 326, 339, 362
Franklin 69, 259, 281
Frankling 362
Frasier, Frazier 197, 300, 326
Frawner 35, 213, 214, 300, 305, 339, 362, 363
Frederick 300
Freeman 171, 322, 340
Freete 69
French 32, 62, 69, 88, 89, 204, 214, 249, 281, 300, 309, 317
Frost 6, 294, 341
Fry, Frye 80, 340
Fugett 301, 363
Fuller 41, 163, 178, 221
Furnash 363

401

Furnice, Furnis 300, 309
Furth 69
Gaba, Gaby 178, 179
Gabriell 281
Gains 43, 179
Gale 193, 340
Galey 69, 323
Gallant 86, 290
Gallaway 214
Gallwith 170
Gambra, Gambrah 300, 340
Games 281, 293, 300
Gamon 36, 214
Gandi 69
Ganer 48, 179, 201
Gant 363
Gardner, Gardiner, Gardener 69, 295, 300, 313, 318, 327, 340, 346, 363
Garfoot, Garforth 340, 346
Garland 64, 71, 81, 176, 192, 360, 363, 377
Garner 300
Garnsheer 69
Garrett 170, 259, 345, 363
Gartherell 281
Gary 340
Gaskoyne 69
Gassaway 231
Gateley 69
Gates 183, 259, 300, 363, 372
Gaven 292
Geer 195
Gent 340
German 69
Gerrard 62, 66, 67, 69, 73, 75, 76, 77, 79, 82, 85, 299, 315, 340, 369
Ges 281, 300, 303, 340, 363
Gey 281
Ghost 69
Gibbon, Gibbons 69, 300, 315, 340
Gibbs 69, 109
Gibson 68, 69, 70, 109, 166, 179, 243, 259, 300, 337, 340
Gifford 64, 300, 327, 340, 363, 371, 375, 380
Gilbard 47, 69, 162, 179
Gilbert 69
Giles 281, 392
Gill, Guill 28, 48, 69, 110, 179

Gillcross 69
Gillroy 57, 363, 364
Gilpen, Gilpin 172, 281, 300, 340
Ginney 69
Glass 214, 238, 281, 300
Glasson 57, 69, 110, 365
Glaze 281
Gleeves, Glieve 70, 162, 179
Glew 214, 215
Glover 36, 39, 70, 78, 179, 201, 215, 238, 259, 300, 308, 315, 345
Gluffur 32, 70, 215
Glusse 364
Goady 300
Goaly 340
Goddard, Goddart 49, 70, 179
Godfrey 83, 85, 89, 204, 281, 289, 295, 296, 301, 309, 321, 327, 330, 340, 345, 364, 374
Godshall 84, 165, 197, 291, 301, 309, 317, 320, 364, 387, 391
Godson 73, 301
Goer, Gore 70, 259, 281, 318, 327, 338, 340
Goffe 70, 180, 199, 328, 341
Goles 9, 180
Gooch 64, 321, 340
Good 70
Goodge 81
Goodrick, Goodrich 4, 26, 64, 68, 69, 72, 74, 77, 78, 79, 82, 83, 85, 162, 163, 168, 171, 186, 189, 219, 226, 246, 259, 281, 301, 304, 309, 348
Goodridge 301
Goody 81
Goosey 340, 365
Gordan 215, 216
Gordian 180, 340
Gosh 70
Goudy 281
Gough 340
Gould 297
Gouldring 364
Goult 394
Gourdon 281, 320
Gourel(e)y 118, 183, 244, 259, 337, 342
Gover 301

Gower 168
Graddock 340
Graham 296
Grandsworth 70
Grant 70, 216, 238, 301
Graves 70, 193, 246, 301, 313, 327, 333, 340
Gray, Grey 32, 48, 53, 70, 75, 76, 110, 111, 180, 216, 228, 239, 281, 301, 322, 340, 358, 364, 365, 370
Green, Greene vii, viii, 2, 6, 26, 27, 35, 70, 75, 77, 81, 83, 85, 111, 112, 172, 176, 177, 179, 188, 196, 200, 216, 223, 239, 243, 247, 260, 281, 292, 295, 297, 301, 302, 309, 310, 318, 319, 321, 340
Greenfield 281, 290, 301, 304, 318, 337
Greenhill 294, 301
Greening 365
Greenwood 180, 393
Gregory 180, 197, 340
Grenham 180
Greyden 70
Griffin 52, 243, 301, 317
Griffitch 301
Griggs 364
Grosser 70
Groule 70
Grover 301
Groves 49, 70, 180, 181, 201, 260, 302, 310, 340, 364, 383
Grubb 304
Grumball 340
Grumbold 364
Grundy 395
Grunwinn 341
Gryer 70
Gubbins 181
Guess, Guesse 70, 341
Guibert 302, 311
Guinn, Gwin(n), Gwynn(e) 70, 81, 112, 168, 169, 188, 260, 281, 302, 327, 340, 341, 364, 395
Gulley 181
Gunner 70
Gutridge 70
Guy 260, 377
Hackett 194
Hackister 300, 302

Haddock 167, 299, 302, 334
Haden 365
Hadlowe 260
Hagan 49, 83, 302, 376
Hagar, Hager 42, 68, 70, 112, 185, 301, 302, 326, 327, 341
Hagard 365
Haggarty 338
Haggat(e), Hagett 281, 341, 345
Hagon, Haggon 181, 201, 260, 354
Hague 365
Haines 393
Halerd 70
Haley, Haylee 181, 182, 341
Halfpin 70
Halfway 216
Hall 1, 21, 33, 34, 35, 54, 55, 70, 71, 93, 162, 166, 184, 216, 260, 302, 306, 314, 317, 321, 328, 334, 335, 341, 342, 350, 364, 365, 394
Hallinak 71
Halloway 379
Hambleton 231, 341
Hamilton 72, 76, 181, 217, 302, 309, 327, 341, 365, 380
Ham(m)ersley 334, 353
Hammill 281
Ham(m)ond 31, 52, 56, 57, 71, 112, 113, 114, 217, 218, 231, 239, 289, 302, 367, 368
Hanby, Hambye 56, 57, 71, 112, 260, 352, 365
Handerkin 32, 218
Hanley 199
Hanson, Hansen 36, 39, 63, 75, 77, 81, 83, 172, 178, 179, 188, 200, 210, 215, 221, 239, 260, 261, 282, 290, 299, 302, 313, 322, 327, 330, 343, 344, 349, 357, 374
Hany 196
Harbert 64, 177, 204, 206, 221, 356, 380
Hardy 6, 8, 9, 10, 11, 12, 58, 62, 71, 74, 114, 173, 180, 195, 196, 213, 220, 261, 326, 334, 341, 344, 347, 351, 360, 362, 371, 381
Hare 282
Haream 57, 365

Hareister 302
Hargis, Harguiss, Harg(u)esse 61, 69, 161, 261, 291, 327, 341, 365
Harkister 292
Harmon 261, 298, 365
Harper 71
Harquist 312
Harrard 71
Harris 67, 69, 71, 83, 86, 162, 170, 218, 226, 243, 261, 282, 300, 302, 308, 315, 316, 317, 325, 327, 341, 344, 360, 366, 376, 378, 394
Harrison 30, 45, 47, 61, 63, 65, 67, 71, 72, 77, 79, 84, 86, 110, 161, 162, 181, 182, 204, 208, 218, 223, 235, 239, 261, 262, 289, 295, 297, 299, 301, 303, 308, 313, 315, 318, 327, 334, 341, 343, 346, 349, 350, 352, 360, 363, 364, 365, 366, 369, 370, 377, 381, 382, 386, 388
Harwood 395
Hasell 25, 243, 244
Haslewood 182
Hasteade 341
Hastings 71
Hatch 62, 63, 66, 67, 69, 74, 79, 84, 175, 282, 289, 303, 336, 347, 366, 386
Hatherton 71
Hatton 290, 320, 349, 382, 385
Hattrill 341
Hauge 341
Hawkins 1, 6, 26, 32, 33, 35, 36, 43, 47, 48, 63, 64, 65, 69, 71, 73, 74, 75, 76, 77, 78, 82, 83, 85, 160, 161, 162, 163, 164, 166, 170, 176, 182, 190, 191, 195, 201, 202, 205, 211, 216, 219, 223, 224, 233, 234, 236, 237, 262, 291, 303, 305, 327, 328, 341, 346, 347, 350, 357, 359, 365, 371, 372, 376, 390, 394
Hawling 6, 262, 328
Hawton 21, 23, 65, 67, 282, 303, 336, 341, 347, 366, 382
Hay, Hey 71, 115

Haydon, Heydon 290, 303, 304, 320
Hays, Hayes 38, 71, 115, 218, 219, 282, 303, 366
Hayles 71
Hayward 366
Haywood 71
Hazleton 56
Heard 74, 82, 242, 304, 311, 341
Hedge, Hedges 71, 182, 262, 366
Helgar 282, 302, 304
Heline 304
Helsby 395
Hemsley, Hemsly 98, 293, 304, 312, 314, 325, 337, 349, 358
Hendericks 46
Hendley, Hendly 35, 65, 76, 79, 80, 138, 228
Henley, Henly, Hanly 1, 5, 47, 61, 62, 67, 71, 73, 78, 115, 199, 250, 341, 344, 353
Hennington 282
Henry 71
Hensey 304
Hensley, Hensly 71
Henson 282
Henston 304
Herald 49, 182
Herbert 71, 81, 115, 198, 235, 262, 304, 341, 375, 381
Herman 71
Hernold 71
Herrant 328, 348, 370
Herrickson 57, 366
Hes 361
Heyfeild 366
Hickford 378
Hicks 71, 73
Hickson 366, 367
Hide, Hyde 341, 369
Higdon, Higton 176, 282, 304
Higgins, Higans 177, 210, 262, 307, 341, 343, 367
Hill, Hills 13, 46, 47, 48, 56, 57, 62, 63, 71, 86, 116, 117, 182, 199, 262, 282, 292, 299, 301, 304, 308, 323, 328, 341, 342, 345, 350, 367, 368, 369, 376

Hilton	ix, 35, 219	
Hinch	71	
Hincks	71, 334	
Hinde	72	
Hindle, Hingle	54, 72, 117, 342	
Hine, Hines	182, 385	
Hinley	367	
Hinsey	66, 71, 72, 162, 219, 342, 378, 383, 389	
Hinshaw	80	
Hinsley	72	
Hinson	120, 166, 219, 291, 312, 349	
Hint	368	
Hipkis	282	
Hire	72	
Hitchison	342	
Hobb	289, 304	
Hobbart	342	
Hobkins	72	
Hobson	72	
Hodges	161, 168	
Hodgins	72	
Hodgly	72	
Hodgson, Hodgshon	26, 37, 110, 183, 203, 214, 217, 218, 225, 235, 236, 237, 239, 249, 304, 315, 328, 334, 342, 343, 368, 374	
Hodisson	236	
Hodsworth	182	
Hogdin	72	
Hogg	21, 72, 117, 182, 262	
Hoggin, Hogin	35, 72, 219	
Hoghland	72	
Holberton, Halliburton	71, 162, 181	
Holden	351, 352	
Holding	282	
Holiday, Hollyday	304, 346	
Holl	368	
Holland	340	
Hollingsworth	346, 393	
Hollis	72	
Hollywood, Holliewood	43, 47, 48, 72, 117, 182, 220	
Holme(s)	ix, 35, 48, 72, 118, 183, 220, 244, 290, 304	
Holt, Hoult	20, 72, 118, 188, 263, 342	
Holton	72	
Honnker	72	
Hooke	337	
Hopewell	345	
Hopkins	392	
Hopper	334	
Horton	4, 249, 263, 304, 368	
Hoskins, Hoskings	15, 16, 48, 72, 78, 118, 119, 183, 184, 201, 223, 263, 282, 304, 305, 342, 343, 345, 347, 359, 367, 371	
Houghton	72	
Howard	8, 40, 72, 178, 183, 213, 263, 282, 328, 342, 344, 368, 372, 380, 392	
Howell	66, 72, 219, 342	
Howes	72, 119	
Howsine	342	
Hoyle	72	
Hubbard	313, 341	
Hubberton	72	
Hudson	72	
Hughs, Hues	183, 220, 368, 394	
Hulse	282, 328, 341	
Humble	72	
Humphreys	183	
Hundle, Hundly, Hundley	72, 84, 282, 347	
Hungerford	63, 76, 80, 164, 169, 195, 263, 282, 305, 312, 318, 342, 368, 371	
Hungerlee	72	
Hunkyn	282	
Hunley	81, 82	
Hunt	64, 72, 119, 263, 282, 342, 372	
Hunter	73, 119, 120, 291, 305	
Huntsman	73, 120	
Hus	263	
Huscula	79	
Hussey	66, 67, 68, 70, 73, 74, 75, 80, 81, 85, 163, 168, 169, 170, 184, 204, 282, 290, 292, 303, 305, 315, 317, 342, 343, 354, 362, 369	
Hutchins	73	
Hutchi(n)son	14, 73, 289, 290, 291, 294, 296, 297, 300, 301, 305, 306, 307, 309, 310, 312, 314, 317, 318, 319, 320, 321, 322, 342, 368	
Hutton	392	
Ibbetson	332	
Ide	73	
Iles	306, 320, 334	
Inerehaut	31, 202	
Inglesby	306, 342	
Ingram	25, 244	
Innis	342	
Inscoe	183	
Inskip	220	
Ireland	73	
Ives	73	
Ivory	73	
Jackson	9, 57, 73, 120, 180, 220, 263, 342, 369	
Jadwin	394	
James	67, 73	
Jameson	26, 184, 185, 187, 306, 328, 342, 344, 372	
Jannson	193	
Jartenus	342	
Jeffers	73, 306	
Jefferson	342	
Jeffreyes, Jeffries	73, 183	
Jeffs	73	
Jenifer	68, 295, 297	
Jenkins, Jenckins, Jenkings	17, 22, 23, 26, 64, 66, 169, 173, 213, 263, 282, 306, 308, 328, 348, 369, 370, 371, 388	
Jenkinson	61, 263, 303	
Jennett	342	
Jennians	263, 369	
Jennings	73	
Jervis	306	
Johnson	viii, ix, 61, 66, 73, 74, 80, 83, 111, 170, 183, 184, 239, 244, 264, 282, 291, 299, 306, 311, 317, 322, 342, 369	
Jones, Joans	3, 16, 27, 28, 32, 45, 46, 48, 53, 54, 57, 61, 68, 71, 73, 75, 120, 121, 122, 162, 184, 191, 195, 201, 209, 220, 221, 245, 246, 264, 282, 290, 305, 306, 307, 315, 324, 328, 336, 337, 342, 350, 353, 364, 366, 368, 369, 370, 392, 393, 394	
Jordan	73	
Joseph	317, 342	
Justice	343, 344	
Karnes	264	
Keech	64, 193, 198, 342, 358	

Keelby 73
Keele 167
Keen(e) 282, 291, 292, 343
Keett 307, 316
Kelly, Kelley, Kelli 26, 73, 74, 184, 185, 221, 307, 343
Kemp 343
Kenady, Kenneday 47, 74, 122, 163, 185, 370
Kendall 74
Kenes 60, 74
Kent 74
Kerkley 74
Kerr 343
Kerricoe 318
Kersey 370
Ketten, Ketton 264, 370
Key 307, 370, 371
Kidd 282
Kierstede 343
Kilbo(u)rne, Kylborne vii, viii, ix, 27, 111, 239, 307, 342
Killcart 74
Killingsworth 307, 371
Killpatrick 74, 163, 185
Kimbrow 282
King, Kinge 56, 57, 65, 74, 78, 81, 122, 183, 185, 217, 221, 239, 293, 297, 307, 320, 328, 343, 345, 348, 352, 353
Kingadon 206, 347
Kingersley 264
King(s)land 166, 282, 307
Kingsbury 74
Kingstone 74
Kiniken, Kennekin 74, 122
Kirby 74, 282
Kirk 348
Kirk(e)ley 264, 344
Kirmichael 74
Kirten 74
Kirweather 185
Kite 56, 57, 221, 238, 264, 371
Knelin 185
Knight 264, 291, 293, 307, 328, 343, 371
Knightsmith 35, 74, 163, 221
Knowlwater 9, 371
Knox 343, 344
Kue 74
Kymborrough 282

Lackey, Lacquey, Leckie 49, 74, 163, 186
Laftan 3 43, 371
Lahey, Layhe 394
Lallee, Loller 74, 163
Lamber 74
Lambert 63, 73, 79, 82, 244, 264, 265, 283, 289, 290, 295, 301, 303, 306, 307, 320, 343, 345, 356
Lambeth 316
Lamplugh 343
Lampton 54, 58, 60, 74, 122, 123, 124, 182, 195, 196, 265, 298, 302, 305, 342, 343
Land 34, 40, 173, 195, 200, 206, 265, 341, 343, 344, 381, 382
Landen 283
Landers 223
Lane, Layne 74, 125, 244, 283, 343, 371, 372
Lang, Lange 265, 343, 372
Langham 265, 291, 307, 308, 310, 372
Langhly 283
Langworth 302, 343
Lannum 328
Lattimer, Lattimar, Lattimore 19, 74, 81, 122, 170, 328
Lauler, Lawler 1, 49, 186
Laurence, Lawrence 60, 74
Law 1, 29, 42, 185
Lawne 307
Lawson 74, 125
Leach, Leech 49, 74, 163
Leah 308, 319
Leeds 74
Lee 28, 41, 43, 72, 186, 304, 307, 309, 321, 336, 338, 372
Lees 33, 34, 35, 74, 125, 186, 221
Leete 265
Legg 221, 222, 246
Lemaire, Lomaire, Lemar 294, 307, 315, 343, 374
Leman 6, 47, 186, 341, 349
Lemaster, Lema(i)stre 180, 265, 283, 288, 296, 303, 304, 307, 328, 337
Lematt 187
Lenham, Lennam, Lannam 8, 74, 126

Lenion 342
Lenton 343
Lentonkis 307
Leport 246
Levalley 187
Leverat, Leveret, Liveratt 65, 68, 189, 376
Lew 4, 246
Lewellin, Llewellin 233, 283, 343
Lewis 5, 27, 48, 75, 187, 201, 241, 265, 283, 307, 308, 320, 328, 343
Libby, Libbey 394
Lilly, Lylly 307, 343, 372
Lindsey, Lyndsey, Lendsey 27, 65, 73, 75, 81, 175, 222, 266, 283, 293, 297, 298, 299, 300, 301, 306, 307, 311, 313, 317, 319, 320, 321, 328, 342, 346, 369, 370, 372
Line, Lyne 4, 187, 246
Ling, Linge 75, 126, 265, 328, 343
Linghams 14, 23, 32, 75
Line 248
Linegar 374
Linghams 222
Lipscomb 343
Littlepage 308, 343, 368
Lloyd, Loyd, Loyde 16, 31, 52, 222, 306, 343
Lockar 308
Lockraft, Luccraft 75, 126
Lockwell 394
Loftas 75
Loften, Loftan, Lofton 198, 211, 329, 336
Lofton, Loftee, Loftley 27, 103, 343, 381
Loman 390
Lomax 64, 67, 78, 180, 203, 225, 266, 283, 308, 329, 335, 343, 345, 357, 362
Long 80, 266, 372
Lonsdon 187
Love 83, 165, 167, 266, 304, 308, 343
Loveday 52, 302, 343
Lovejoy 283
Lovell 366
Low, Lowe 48, 75, 126, 127, 187, 222

Lowder 392
Lowry 187
Loyle 283
Lucas, Luces 75, 305
Luckett
 27, 33, 35, 36, 62, 64, 72,
 74, 75, 77, 79, 81, 82, 161,
 163, 164, 172, 173, 178, 186,
 195, 215, 224, 233, 241, 266,
 302, 308, 310, 329, 339, 342,
 343, 352, 353, 359, 362, 374
Lugar, Lewgar
 76, 297, 308, 309, 323
Lumbrozo
 83, 266, 299, 300, 308, 344
Lurling 308
Lurting 208
Lybscome 75
Lyle, Lyall
 2, 31, 75, 127, 222, 223, 228
Lynes, Lines, Linos
 viii, 1, 2, 3, 4, 5, 6, 7,
 25, 26, 27, 28, 30, 31,
 35, 36, 42, 47, 50, 51, 54, 61,
 63, 65, 66, 67, 68, 69, 70, 72,
 73, 74, 76, 77, 79, 80, 83, 84,
 85, 106, 111, 148, 149, 162,
 164, 178, 179, 182, 187, 189,
 190, 192, 193, 196, 197, 202,
 204, 205, 206, 207, 209, 211,
 214, 215, 216, 217, 222, 223,
 227, 229, 230, 234, 235, 239,
 241, 245, 246, 247, 248, 249,
 250, 291, 294, 297, 298, 302,
 308, 309, 313, 314, 315, 316,
 343, 344, 360, 368, 369, 370
Lynn 343, 344
M(?)oat 187
Mackan, Macken, Machen
 75, 309, 388
Mackarles 85
Mackeboy 50, 188
Mackenhine 75
Mackey, Macky, Meckey
 75, 82, 223, 225,
 231, 244, 294, 307, 309
Mackmire 368
Macknew 35
Maclannen, Macklanan
 11, 48, 75, 127, 188, 372
Macock 344
Maconchie 309
Macotter 394, 395

Macrackin 75
Madding 388
Maddock(s), Maddox 27, 75,
 128, 171, 180, 181, 184, 187,
 191, 228, 241, 242, 283, 290,
 294, 298, 300, 309, 315, 316,
 317, 329, 340, 344, 348, 373
Maggalee, Maggelee
 84, 86, 344
Magittee 266
Maglockline 306
Maglockney 329, 344
Magray 75
Mahall 373
Mahon(e)y, Mahawney
 23, 48, 76, 128,
 129, 189, 294, 316, 339, 344
Makey 297, 329, 344
Mancaster 26, 223, 388
Mandam 189
Manhaine 23
Manhew 76
Manithurb 76
Mankin 53, 54, 118, 191,
 210, 220, 224, 238,
 242, 266, 267, 283, 329,
 344, 350, 355, 365, 369, 373
Mannerley 76
Manning, Maning
 30, 41, 65, 69, 70, 71,
 73, 74, 75, 76, 180, 182,
 186, 200, 221, 228, 266, 283,
 293, 294, 295, 296, 303, 305,
 308, 310, 311, 316, 318, 322,
 323, 335, 348, 367, 373, 388
Mannister, Mainster
 373, 374
Mansfield 283
Manwaren, Manwaring
 76, 267, 374
Marbury, Marberry
 52, 76, 129, 310
Marchegay 319
Marchment 393
Marden 76, 189
Maris 267, 310, 329, 374
Markeat 76
Markony 308
Marler 283, 344
Marlow, Marloe
 76, 195, 310, 329, 344
Marr 76
Marrit 296

Marrome 76
Marsh 76, 129, 310, 329, 393
Marshall, Martiall 32, 63,
 65, 67, 68, 70, 76, 79, 84,
 96, 109, 129, 130, 209, 215,
 267, 283, 291, 295, 299, 310,
 316, 318, 344, 346, 374, 386
Marsham 335, 344
Marshegay 85
Marston 300, 310, 344
Martin, Marten
 7, 63, 65, 69, 76, 85,
 163, 166, 171, 185, 189, 199,
 214, 224, 240, 267, 283, 310,
 329, 336, 341, 344, 366, 391
Maslow 70
Mason
 69, 76, 80, 130, 174, 191,
 267, 283, 307, 310, 344, 379
Massey 76, 374
Maston 267, 309, 310, 329
Mathena 291, 329
Matthews 1, 63, 67, 76, 77,
 85, 169, 184, 190, 268, 292,
 298, 310, 344, 354, 356, 375
Mattingly 320
Mattock, Mattox 76, 189
Maud, Maude
 268, 331, 373, 375, 384
Maxfield 76, 130
Maybanck, Maybanke
 76, 164, 189
Maycock(e) 293, 362
McAvoy 189
McCann 75
McCarty 75, 344
McCloud 223
McCollum 34, 75, 223
McCormack. McCormick
 68, 329, 337
McCoy 81, 193, 309
McDaniel
 75, 127, 163, 192, 224
McDonald 40, 57,
 75, 128, 344, 369, 372
McDonnell
 49, 187, 188, 360, 377
McEwen 4, 247, 283
McFail 187
McFe(a)rson
 76, 82, 185, 190, 200, 337
McGough 75

406

McGraw 17, 22, 23, 24, 25, 54, 75, 76, 77, 128, 133, 163, 188, 189, 223, 309, 344, 373
McGregor 76
McIntosh 34, 75, 163, 223, 224, 246, 247
McKenny 188
McKenz(e)y 40, 243, 283, 390
McLaine, McLane 75, 128, 318
McMillian, Mackmillion 26, 35, 223, 247, 266, 338, 363, 372
McNamara 188
McNeil 75
McNew 49, 188, 223, 238
McQueen 188
McWilliam 75
Medcaph 76
Mee 212, 329
Meeke, Meek(e)s 35, 65, 219, 310, 346, 375
Mellor 185, 268, 294, 310, 317, 329, 336, 344, 355, 360
Mercer 169, 395
Methenie 310
Micaney 76
Michell 76, 290, 310
Middleton 61, 173, 210, 289, 295, 305, 309, 310, 322, 329, 364, 373
Midgely, Midgeley 72, 307, 310, 344, 357
Miles 13, 76, 190, 297, 310, 338
Mill, Mills, Milles 17, 22, 23, 31, 76, 77, 164, 192, 235, 389
Millborne 77
Miller 31, 45, 46, 77, 169, 170, 224, 234, 238, 249, 268, 283, 289, 310, 329, 330, 336, 344, 360, 379, 390, 391
Milner, Millner 289, 311
Milshaw 77
Milstead 56, 57, 59, 60, 77, 82, 130, 131, 268, 283, 353, 365, 375, 387
Ming, Mings 70, 164, 182, 189, 303, 309, 314, 344
Mingoe 37, 224, 268

Minock(e), Minoake 62, 175, 211, 213, 311, 344
Mitchell 64, 77, 78, 85, 311, 334, 344, 354, 385
Mohoy 190
Moldoone 190
Mollatto Will 1, 28, 39, 190
Moncaster 268, 311, 375
Mongerrell 77
Monroe, Munroe 31, 77, 191, 225, 345
Montague, Mountague 284, 300, 301, 308, 311, 345, 346, 349
Monteal 77
Montgomery 311
Moody 48, 190, 201, 225, 226, 238, 268, 375
Moones 89
Moore, More 35, 77, 81, 83, 226, 238, 268, 283, 284, 289, 290, 291, 292, 296, 303, 305, 311, 312, 313, 314, 316, 317, 330, 343, 344, 347, 375
Moran 173
Morand, Moreland 16, 22, 24, 54, 77, 93, 132, 334, 344
Morden 190
Morehouse 335
Morgan 190
Morphy 190
Morrell 77, 132
Morris, Morrice, Maurice 48, 60, 61, 62, 74, 77, 79, 133, 190, 191, 194, 219, 240, 268, 269, 284, 294, 300, 311, 317, 318, 320, 322, 344, 345, 356, 358, 375, 385, 387
Moss 68, 171, 310, 311, 345, 362
Moucaler 375, 376
Mould 269, 330, 353
Mouldin 344
Moulton 77
Mounke 77
Mow 77
Mudd 77, 82, 84, 85, 184, 284, 299, 306, 311, 313, 315, 345, 376
Muncaster 330, 345
Munn, Munne, Mun, Muns 81, 82, 84, 284, 291, 292, 298, 304, 307, 311, 312, 343

Murfrey 269
Murphy, Murphey 31, 77, 133, 191, 226, 234, 269, 376, 394
Murraine 77
Murray 208
Murrie 77
Murty 77, 345
Muschamp 284, 345
Musgrave, Musgrove 195, 238, 269, 284, 312, 314, 376
Myers, Mires 77, 131, 132, 330, 345
Nailee, Nalley, Nally 77, 134, 135, 189, 284, 341
Narrdeena 356
Nash 77, 284
Naylor, Nayler, Nailer, Nailor 73, 77, 284, 312, 373
Neagle 234
Neale, Nealle, Neile 31, 61, 64, 68, 69, 70, 73, 77, 78, 81, 162, 168, 171, 176, 179, 180, 182, 190, 192, 207, 208, 226, 239, 269, 284, 291, 292, 294, 312, 321, 330, 342, 345, 346, 359, 378
Neeves 78
Negro Jupiter 38, 226
Neisbut 78
Nelson, Nellson 78, 284, 312, 345
Nelm 226, 227
Nenan 78
Netherton 161, 167
Nettle 376
Nevill, Neville 64, 84, 284, 294, 305, 310, 312, 315, 316, 330, 345
New 345
Newall 78
Newby 46, 47
Newen 65, 345
Newman 31, 61, 66, 69, 74, 78, 84, 135, 161, 193, 227, 237, 239, 293, 297, 312, 313, 314, 330, 340, 353, 370, 372, 376, 382, 394, 395
Newton 26, 53, 74, 78, 161, 164, 172, 191, 269, 306, 313, 316, 326, 330, 345
Nibbs 376

Nichol(e)s, Nicholls, Nicolls
    40, 56, 57, 78,
    135, 136, 137, 227, 269,
    284, 294, 309, 313, 330,
    342, 345, 369, 370, 376, 382
Nicholson   78, 340
Nixon   47
Noble   313
Noe   284
No(e)land, Nolan
            78, 313, 315, 337
Norman   78, 284
Normansell   78
Norris(s)   191, 243, 322, 386
Northon   78
Norton   78, 350, 390
Notley   313, 345
Nowell   341
Nutwell   284
Oakes   78
Oard, Ord   78, 137, 270
Obryan, Obrian, Obrion
            75, 269, 284, 295,
    298, 299, 300, 313, 330, 345
Ocain(e), Ocane
    313, 315, 347, 376, 377, 384
Oden   76, 330
Odouhertee   377
Okeane   62, 66
Okeley   330
Olavery   377
Oliver
    7, 78, 164, 191, 345, 377
Oneale, Oneall
                  313, 330, 345
Orlock   78
Orrell   66, 68,
    167, 192, 313, 330, 332
Orson   78
Orway   23
Osborn, Osborne   78, 80,
    313, 330, 345, 353, 378
Oulson   78
Oversee, Overseas   301, 316
Owen
    23, 35, 227, 303, 304, 330
Oxford   78
P(?)kter   345
Page   78
Paget, Paggett   284, 313
Paine, Payne   61, 63, 74,
    79, 86, 187, 200, 221, 270,
    284, 291, 313, 330, 345, 377
Palmer
    191, 284, 303, 313, 377
Paris   313, 345
Parker
    31, 78, 137, 138, 227, 232,
    284, 294, 304, 330, 334, 345
Parkes   79
Parnham   45, 172, 194, 313
Parrand(i)er
        199, 284, 313, 353
Parratt   395
Parry, Perry, Perrey, Perrie
        35, 68, 79, 164, 171,
    192, 227, 228, 232, 239,
    242, 247, 270, 307, 313, 330,
    350, 356, 377, 378, 380, 381
Partridge   79
Pastorius   46
Patrick   2, 31, 227, 239, 345
Patterson
        32, 79, 164, 227, 228
Pattison   79, 270, 377
Pauding   79
Paul   191
Peacock   79, 138
Peake   290, 313
Peale, Peele
            176, 177, 270, 313
Pears(e), Pearce, Peirce
            192, 204, 345
Pearson, Peirson   79, 345
Peeso   79
Pell   49, 192
Pellufus   316
Pembrook(e)   79, 345
Pen, Penn   82, 180, 210,
    270, 284, 313, 323, 339,
    349, 360, 365, 377, 378, 379
Pennell   208, 214
Pennington   314
Pennock   284
Penny, Penney
    57, 192, 201, 270, 313, 378
Percy, Percey, Percei
        8, 71, 270, 294, 313
Perfect   61, 74, 77
Perfitt   65, 83, 313
Perfrey   352
Perkins   79, 86, 217, 270, 378
Persivall   79
Person   175
Peters   166, 345, 354
Peterson   303, 313
Pew   345
Phegg   79
Phelps   46
Philbert   71, 285, 313
Philips, Phillips, Phyllips
    52, 79, 138, 284, 313, 362
Philpott, Phillpot, Philpot
            63, 67, 77, 85,
    161, 194, 196, 224, 228,
    270, 285, 299, 306, 314,
    345, 349, 363, 369, 373, 378
Phipps   378
Pickard   79
Pickering   35, 79, 138, 228
Pidgeon, Pigeon, Peggeon
                    174, 177,
    188, 197, 314, 378, 387
Pigman   222, 228
Pile, Piles   81, 82, 84, 270,
    285, 313, 314, 345, 346, 378
Pillett   192
Pillion   228
Pinner, Pinnar
        82, 309, 314, 346, 349
Piper   79, 285, 319, 336, 356
Pirks   79
Place   227, 233
Plater   76, 78, 83,
    104, 172, 197, 211, 214,
    240, 314, 338, 346, 360, 361
Player   79
Plummer   285
Plun(c)ket, Plun(c)kett
            74, 85, 177,
    181, 314, 348, 359, 381
Poke   79
Pomfret   285
Poore   79, 192, 330, 346
Pope   62, 70, 82,
    293, 314, 346, 347, 378, 395
Posey, Posie   1, 43,
    66, 83, 85, 167, 228,
    239, 270, 271, 285, 314,
    323, 330, 345, 353, 378, 391
Potter   67, 285, 331
Potts   79, 139, 342, 346
Pouncy, Pounsey
            324, 346, 354
Powcher   79
Powell
    2, 5, 31, 47, 79, 139, 192,
    228, 229, 250, 271, 314, 346

Power 30
Pratt 36, 229, 346
Price 59, 62,
65, 70, 71, 79, 128, 193,
200, 212, 223, 271, 285, 302,
303, 307, 308, 311, 312, 313,
314, 335, 346, 348, 354, 358,
378, 379, 390, 392, 394, 395
Prichard 314, 316
Prince 79
Probart 346
Proctor, Procter 193, 346
Prodday, Proddy
66, 304, 338, 346
Proser 79
Prouse, Prouce
62, 289, 311, 314
Pryor
293, 303, 314, 339, 395
Purfrey 346
Purnie 79
Puttuck 193
Pye 37, 210,
211, 218, 222, 228, 246,
295, 300, 306, 346, 347, 380
Quandoe 314
Raines, Raynes 205, 271,
300, 331, 346, 373, 374
Raleigh 346, 379
Randall 66, 271, 314, 346
Ranford 79
Raspin
109, 110, 212, 239, 314, 346
Raston 236
Ratchford 314
Ratcliffe 14, 71, 271,
285, 295, 314, 359, 378
Rawfeild 79
Rawlins
17, 18, 23, 31, 229, 230
Rawson 80
Ray, Raye, Rey, Rea
80, 180, 314, 388
Read, Reed, Reede
80, 193, 285, 314, 375, 379
Reader 187
Red(d)ick, Redich
72, 76, 236, 315, 343
Redfern 271
Redman 80, 139
Reeding 80

Reeves 7, 78, 80, 141,
164, 181, 217, 231, 271,
285, 296, 315, 339, 370, 379
Regon, Reagon, Reagan
56, 57, 271, 285, 331, 379
Renes 80
Renisson 80
Rennicke, Rhennick 80, 139
Revell 393
Reynolds 172, 194, 230, 346
Rhyne 80
Riardine 230
Rich 346
Richardson 57, 62, 74,
80, 140, 193, 346, 379, 392
Richison 331
Rigby 193
Rigg 315, 331, 346
Right 271
Rilson 80
Rimer 335
Ring 80
Riscorla 31, 231
Rivers 315
Roads 163
Robert 63
Roberts, Roberds 48, 80,
81, 140, 193, 201, 379
Robertson 57, 80,
164, 337, 355, 379, 380
Robins, Robbins
65, 71, 80, 140, 285, 292,
304, 312, 315, 331, 378, 393
Robinson 1, 80, 140,
164, 193, 194, 271,
285, 306, 314, 315, 322,
331, 338, 344, 354, 360, 376
Robisson, Robbison
74, 80, 311, 315, 375
Roby 285, 331, 365
Rochforth 16
Rock, Roch 200, 331
Rockford 218, 315
Rodd 272, 380
Roder 194
Roeland, Roelants 272, 290
Rogers
68, 80, 247, 296, 346, 385
Rookard, Rookerd
86, 289, 305, 315, 348

Rook(e)wood, Rockwood
18, 31, 63,
175, 230, 272, 296,
305, 310, 315, 346, 348, 371
Rose 23, 80, 380
Rosewell 272
Ross, Rosse ix, 18, 22, 31,
35, 42, 80, 141, 194, 231
Rossey 315
Roswell 346
Rought 331, 346
Rousby 346
Rouse, Rouze
49, 80, 194, 272, 339
Routhorne 285
Rowaine 194
Rowland(s), Rowlants
71, 78, 79,
80, 86, 177, 368, 377
Roy 81
Rozer, Rozier
viii, 31, 36, 56, 65,
69, 70, 71, 72, 73, 75, 76, 79,
80, 84, 85, 86, 111, 210, 217,
218, 225, 227, 232, 239, 250,
272, 285, 291, 297, 298, 300,
305, 307, 312, 314, 315, 316,
335, 336, 345, 346, 347, 380
Ruby ix, 35, 232
Rue 194, 201, 272, 353, 380
Russell 13, 36, 45, 46, 172,
194, 232, 272, 285, 291, 312,
315, 347, 348, 379, 380, 385
Ruth 48, 194, 201, 380
Ruthorne 335
Rye 19, 22, 23, 81
Ryland 392
Ryley, Reyley, Rayley
80, 139, 167
St. Clare 379
Sall 195
Salley 315
Salt 81, 141
Sample 347
Sanders, Saunders
51, 57, 59, 60, 66, 81,
141, 142, 193, 208, 209, 272,
285, 292, 313, 315, 316, 320,
321, 331, 335, 336, 345, 347,
355, 361, 370, 379, 380, 389
Sapcoate 272, 347

Sarjeant, Serjeant
   196, 242, 243, 316, 347
Savage   81
Scarry   347, 380, 381
Scarryott   81
Schuler   285
Scot, Scott   52, 81, 195, 222, 227, 285, 308, 316, 331
Scoutch   81
Scroggin   27, 272, 381, 382
Seagar   348
Seaman   347
Searson   89, 294, 316
Seawell, Sawell   81, 393
Sedgely, Sigley   81, 143
Seer   81
Selby, Selbee   285, 347
Semms, Semmes
   73, 78, 232, 272, 285, 316, 331, 334, 347, 373, 382
Seney   81
Sennet   272, 382
Serson   70
Service   316
Settle   202
Seymour   6, 7
Shackerl(e)y
   273, 310, 316, 331
Shalter   4, 247
Shanhikin   81
Sharman   57, 273, 382
Sharp, Sharpe   199, 395
Shaw   27, 31, 61, 62, 79, 81, 143, 168, 179, 223, 285, 309, 316, 331, 347, 357, 364, 386, 395
Shellson   236
Shelton   81, 285
Shenstone   306
Shepherd   178, 347
Sher(e)man   296, 321
Sherrell, Sherrill
   206, 316, 347
Shihorr   81
Shiner   81
Shinston   351
Shoreman   382
Short   81, 143, 144, 347
Shott   81
Shuttleworth   305, 315, 316
Sidney   195
Simm(e)s, Symm(e)s
   81, 83, 144, 183, 296, 316

Simmons, Symmons
   11, 12, 81, 144, 196, 286
Simpson, Sympson, Simson
   61, 65, 76, 77, 81, 83, 144, 145, 212, 213, 273, 274, 285, 286, 289, 291, 294, 298, 301, 302, 307, 311, 316, 319, 321, 322, 343
Singleton   81
Sinnett, Synnett   51, 65, 70, 274, 293, 295, 304
Skeen(e)s   382
Skidmore   302, 310, 314, 316, 320, 323, 347, 382, 383
Skinner
   81, 145, 164, 317, 331, 395
Slater   81
Slayde   340
Slingsby, Slingsbie   317, 322
Sly, Slye   285, 294, 307, 309, 314, 337, 347
Small   81, 202, 349
Smallpage   31, 182, 187, 220, 232, 233, 239, 301, 317
Smallwood
   1, 3, 21, 28, 42, 63, 65, 68, 69, 71, 72, 83, 84, 93, 163, 165, 168, 171, 173, 179, 180, 185, 195, 198, 199, 200, 204, 227, 230, 240, 242, 245, 273, 286, 293, 300, 304, 306, 317, 326, 347, 350, 353, 358, 373
Smart   383
Smith, Smyth   5, 28, 33, 34, 35, 36, 39, 47, 50, 60, 61, 62, 63, 64, 66, 68, 69, 71, 72, 73, 74, 79, 80, 81, 82, 83, 85, 103, 118, 145, 161, 164, 171, 174, 177, 178, 181, 182, 183, 188, 195, 206, 208, 212, 214, 215, 218, 222, 232, 233, 238, 250, 273, 286, 290, 293, 297, 301, 302, 306, 311, 314, 317, 318, 322, 330, 331, 332, 335, 340, 346, 347, 349, 350, 352, 369, 371, 383, 384
Smoot, Smoote   57, 63, 65, 68, 70, 72, 74, 76, 77, 84, 163, 199, 273, 274, 286, 291, 303, 305, 308, 309, 310, 312, 316, 317, 318, 320, 321, 322, 331, 347, 377, 384, 385, 386
Snell   82, 318

Sneton   82
Snoggen   40, 178
Snosell   82
Snowden   82, 145
Somerset   347
Sommers   385
Soot   82
Southerland   82, 385
Southerly   26, 195
So(u)theron
   36, 66, 229, 318, 348
Sowerbutt   348
Spalden, Spaldin   347, 383
Spalding   318
Speake, Speeke
   11, 61, 62, 68, 71, 75, 77, 81, 162, 177, 181, 188, 230, 286, 318, 331, 332, 372, 373, 374
Spence   286
Spering   299
Spicer   348
Spikeman   348
Spurling
   33, 34, 35, 82, 164, 233
Squires   385
Stafford   286
Standbury   318, 384
Standidge   379
Standish   192, 318, 348
Standly   82
Stanfield   385
Stannard   297
Steede   385
Steel, Steele   195, 274, 385
Stephens, Stevens   82, 183, 195, 233, 286, 318, 395
Stephenson   392
Steward   82, 318, 348, 393
Stewart, Stuart   34, 82, 145, 146, 233, 332, 385
Stidman   82
Stigaleer, Stigalier   54, 220, 274, 286, 332, 368, 373, 385
Still   82
Stoddert, Stodart
   291, 318, 342
Stone   19, 20, 37, 61, 67, 70, 73, 75, 77, 78, 79, 82, 83, 84, 86, 103, 148, 165, 180, 187, 195, 217, 224, 226, 286, 289, 298, 307, 311, 312, 316, 318, 332, 348, 356, 358, 361, 362, 363, 371, 391

Stonehouse 82
Stonestreet
  82, 190, 286, 307, 318, 380
Storker 82
Story, Storey 7, 12, 28,
  31, 41, 80, 164, 186, 193,
  211, 286, 296, 309, 318, 336,
  338, 343, 344, 348, 382, 389
Stowe 348
Stratton 82, 332
Stringer 82, 146
Stut 286
Sudburie 82
Sulegar 394
Sullivant 395
Sumerton 47, 195, 196, 382
Summer(s) 82, 378
Sunley 233, 335
Sutorne 234
Sutre 293
Suttel 332, 360
Sutton 196, 348
Swaine 82
Swallwell 319
Swan, Swann, Swanne
  72, 73, 85,
  286, 296, 319, 321, 332
Sweenehee 82
Sweny, Sweney 395
Swillavan 82
Swinborne, Swinburne
  319, 348
Symons 174, 332
Taney, Tanney 311, 348, 349
Tanner 196, 200, 286,
  287, 313, 319, 346, 368, 372
Tannyhill 319
Tanshall 332
Tarlin, Tarline 287
Taunt 274
Tawney 339
Taylor, Tayler 1, 16,
  53, 72, 74, 80, 83, 85,
  154, 163, 169, 189, 196,
  237, 274, 287, 302, 305, 309,
  312, 316, 318, 319, 330, 332,
  340, 348, 373, 384, 386, 395
Teares, Tears 67, 68, 75,
  76, 163, 175, 179, 188, 319,
  332, 347, 348, 374, 382, 383
Tenanly, Tinnally 393
Tench 180
Tenneson, Tennison
  163, 185, 287
Thatcher 83, 218
Theobald(s) 70, 81, 84, 188,
  227, 233, 235, 274, 296, 301,
  307, 309, 313, 319, 322, 385
Thirst 274
Thomas 1, 28, 39,
  75, 81, 83, 188, 190,
  220, 221, 287, 303, 306, 307,
  308, 313, 319, 332, 348, 363,
  367, 377, 380, 381, 385, 393
Thompkins 274, 348
Thompson, Thomson
  1, 3, 6, 16, 28, 32,
  35, 43, 45, 47, 48, 53, 54,
  57, 62, 67, 70, 71, 72, 82, 83,
  146, 147, 148, 167, 181, 195,
  196, 201, 203, 204, 209, 221,
  222, 245, 246, 274, 275, 287,
  292, 294, 295, 299, 300, 302,
  304, 305, 308, 310, 312, 314,
  315, 319, 320, 334, 335, 337,
  340, 348, 350, 351, 353, 357,
  363, 364, 373, 385, 394, 395
Thorett 83
Thorne 287
Thornebrooke, Thornborrow
  2, 3, 34, 35, 83,
  148, 149, 234, 245, 247
Thorneton 320, 321
Thornley, Thornely
  31, 196, 234
Thorrowgood 234
Throne 350
Tibbitt 83
Tickerell 301, 320, 348, 386
Tidror 83
Till 320, 348
Tillard 392
Tillee 83
Tillotson 287
Tillzey 83
Tipton, Typton, Thypton
  34, 35, 83, 149, 227, 234
Toale 348
Toby 83, 348
Tod, Todd
  25, 43, 49, 83, 165, 196, 197
Tolson 101
Tomkins
  83, 298, 311, 320, 386
Tom(p)kinson
  297, 309, 319, 320, 332
Tomson 83
Toney 275, 290
Tougle 394
Towell, Towles
  83, 287, 320, 348
Townley 7
Toy
  48, 83, 149, 150, 197, 337
Tracy 349
Trayman 394
Treemairne 83
Trenn 295, 296, 320
Trewne 61
Troop(e) 287, 303, 320, 349
Trover 349
True, Trew 287, 291,
  300, 307, 320, 321, 349, 367
Tru(e)man 296, 349
Tubb 83
Tubman 74, 75,
  163, 332, 343, 349, 373
Tuborne 83
Tugwell 386
Tukerell 320
Turlayes, Turley
  1, 4, 42, 49, 197, 248
Turling 332, 349
Turner
  28, 61, 66, 76, 84, 197,
  248, 287, 292, 294, 295, 310,
  313, 314, 320, 332, 349, 386
Turvey 332, 356
Tusan 84
Twifer 84
Twigges 320
Tyer, Tyre, Tire
  61, 67, 74, 83, 161, 168,
  298, 309, 318, 320, 323, 335,
  337, 342, 347, 349, 369, 386
Tyler 81, 345
Tymothy, Tymothie
  57, 59, 60, 74, 77, 84, 150,
  151, 161, 168, 275, 320, 349
Typpett 275, 386
Tytchett 197
up de(n) Graef(f) 46
Underwood 197
Uppenbridge 84
Vaine 84
Vandr(e)y
  65, 70, 82, 161, 296, 320
Van Swearingen 234, 349
Vassall 275

Vaughan 84, 386
Vaux, Voux 55, 84, 151, 349
Yearly 197
Venour 349, 378
Veren, Veron 320, 349
Vering 349
Verritt 84
Villett 78, 287
Villson 63
Vincent 370, 382, 387
Vinton 59, 387
Vinyeard 287
Violett 84
Waalwort 84, 275
Wade
 32, 62, 65, 66, 68, 71, 73,
 76, 83, 84, 120, 165, 197,
 198, 207, 221, 275, 287, 291,
 300, 305, 320, 332, 349, 350
Waedman, Wayman,
Waynman, Wainman
 52, 53, 54, 57, 84,
 151, 152, 307, 321, 350, 357
Wager 84
Wahob, Waughob 63, 76, 81,
 84, 304, 321, 333, 339, 343
Wahop, Wahope, Waughope
 287, 307, 320
Wales, Weales 287, 288
Wakefield 64, 293, 295,
 314, 315, 323, 332, 344
Wakelin 275, 311, 341, 387
Walden 223, 387
Walker 63, 64, 84,
 184, 197, 234, 235, 287,
 294, 307, 319, 321, 323, 349
Walkup 72, 82
Wallen 84
Wallis, Wollis
 85, 235, 349, 387
Walls 332
Walsh 31, 84, 235
Walters 332
Waltom 84, 287
Waple 299, 312, 349
Ward, Warde
 1, 28, 57, 59, 67, 68, 69,
 77, 84, 152, 167, 248, 249,
 275, 276, 287, 295, 299, 321,
 332, 333, 338, 339, 351, 387

Warder 333, 338
Wardner 321
Ware 44, 49, 84,
 165, 197, 198, 287, 321
Waring 321
Warner
 31, 84, 152, 235, 239, 289,
 291, 297, 321, 338, 349, 387
Warren 4, 18, 20, 21,
 22, 23, 29, 62, 64, 65, 67,
 68, 71, 74, 76, 78, 80, 81, 82,
 83, 84, 85, 101, 149, 198, 226,
 234, 235, 245, 249, 276, 291,
 293, 295, 299, 302, 304, 320,
 321, 333, 342, 349, 355, 387
Waters 48, 84, 152,
 153, 198, 288, 300,
 312, 321, 337, 358, 386, 388
Waterworth 13, 14, 23, 84
Wathen 29, 168, 187,
 288, 321, 333, 349, 385
Watkins 198, 334, 349
Watson 8, 30, 288, 293,
 307, 313, 319, 321, 322
Watts 318, 358
Way, Waye 223, 321,
 340, 375, 376, 382, 385
Weatherburne 84
Weaver, Weavour
 72, 276, 349, 388
Webb 84, 180, 198, 227, 233
Webster
 26, 84, 235, 236, 249
Weekes 64
Weireman 350
Welch, Welsh 28, 48,
 84, 153, 198, 236, 240
Wellman 350
Wells 76, 289,
 290, 315, 321, 333, 344
Wemmes 388
Wentworth 310, 350
West 305, 348, 352, 353
Westbrooke 84
Whaland 85
Whaley 395
Wharton, Whorton 26, 85,
 249, 276, 301, 305, 307,
 321, 333, 340, 387, 388, 393
Wheatley 167, 288

Wheeler
 16, 29, 62, 64, 67, 69, 71, 75,
 85, 169, 176, 177, 187, 190,
 242, 246, 247, 249, 276, 288,
 292, 295, 298, 300, 305, 310,
 312, 314, 315, 318, 319, 320,
 322, 333, 337, 340, 342, 346,
 350, 361, 362, 385, 388, 389
Whichal(l)ey, Wichal(e)y
 14, 17, 18, 19, 20, 21, 23, 55,
 170, 276, 288, 290, 302, 310,
 316, 317, 339, 361, 362, 391
Whilden 85
Whit, Whitt 85, 310, 322
White
 50, 63, 64, 85, 164, 187, 192,
 200, 276, 288, 313, 322, 350
Whitehead 85, 198
Whiteheart 350
Whitehorne 85
Whitford, Whittford 389
Whitter 29, 177, 213
Whittimore, Whittymore
 32, 33, 34, 35,
 85, 153, 236, 237, 276, 333
Whitworth 236, 237
Wickes 394
Wight 350
Wife 322
Wiggs 85
Wiggsby 198
Wild 43, 199
Wilder 25, 57, 64, 73, 75,
 77, 85, 154, 175, 277,
 322, 350, 386, 388, 389, 390
Wildman 288
Wilfray 85
Wilkins 356
Wilkinson 15, 34, 35, 53,
 63, 82, 85, 154, 155, 174,
 185, 198, 226, 227, 236, 237,
 249, 277, 322, 333, 345, 390
Wilkison 65, 85, 390
Willan 293
Willard 333
Willbee 85
William 37, 237, 288

Williams 1, 8, 33, 47, 56, 57, 59, 60, 69, 70, 71, 83, 85, 125, 156, 157, 158, 160, 189, 191, 199, 203, 215, 216, 233, 236, 238, 246, 277, 288, 322, 333, 342, 350, 367, 368, 379, 383, 384, 390
Williamson 199, 322, 344, 369
Willin, Willan 322
Willis 40, 390
Willman 85
Wills 302, 322
Wilson, Willson 1, 29, 42, 76, 85, 158, 183, 185, 200, 240, 241, 288, 322, 333, 334, 348, 349, 350, 366, 383, 387, 390
Wincoll, Wincell 197, 350
Windsor 322
Wine, Wyne 61, 66, 76, 288, 303, 315, 322, 323, 333, 339, 344, 350, 362
Winslow 47
Winstanley 350
Winston 350
Winter, Winters 65, 82, 85, 159, 188, 288, 322
Wise 391
Withy 277, 391
Witter 193, 277, 315, 322, 346, 350, 391
Wolfe, Woolf(e), Wolph 52, 53, 54, 86, 159, 322, 333, 350
Wood 48, 55, 63, 76, 79, 85, 159, 164, 200, 249, 323, 333, 336, 350, 370, 391
Woodard 350, 364
Wooden 229
Woodgard 333
Woodkeepe 85
Woodyard 288, 293, 313, 316, 323, 333, 336, 348, 388
Woolcock 277
Woolley 288, 321
Wooters 394
Worland 277, 300, 315, 319, 323, 391
Wormely 43, 86, 200
Wornell 86
Worrell 71, 86, 323, 334
Worthington 86, 160
Wright 68, 73, 74, 79, 85, 86, 160, 200, 277, 288, 319, 323, 333, 339, 349, 350, 354, 360, 375, 391
Wyeth 288, 377
Wyott 86
Yappe, Yopp 33, 34, 35, 86, 160, 237, 391
Yates 56, 70, 217, 239, 277, 288, 323, 333, 341, 342, 347, 349, 350, 358, 366, 381, 386, 391
Yeabsley 347, 350
Young, Younge 63, 71, 86, 231, 277, 294, 296, 323, 333, 350
Youngsen 200
Yount 47

www.ingramcontent.com/pod-product-compliance
Lightning Source LLC
Chambersburg PA
CBHW071235300426
44116CB00008B/1049